BOSWELL'S LIFE OF JOHNSON

Edited by G. B. HILL

Revised by L. F. POWELL

SAMUEL JOHNSON
from the painting by SIR JOSHUA REYNOLDS, 1769
in the National Gallery

BOSWELL'S
LIFE OF JOHNSON

TOGETHER WITH BOSWELL'S JOURNAL OF A TOUR TO THE HEBRIDES

AND JOHNSON'S DIARY OF A JOURNEY INTO NORTH WALES

EDITED BY

GEORGE BIRKBECK HILL, D.C.L.

REVISED AND ENLARGED EDITION BY

L. F. POWELL

IN SIX VOLUMES

VOLUME II.   THE LIFE (1766–1776)

OXFORD
AT THE CLARENDON PRESS
MCMXXXIV

OXFORD
UNIVERSITY PRESS
AMEN HOUSE, E.C. 4
London Edinburgh Glasgow
Leipzig New York Toronto
Melbourne Capetown Bombay
Calcutta Madras Shanghai
HUMPHREY MILFORD
PUBLISHER TO THE
UNIVERSITY

PRINTED IN GREAT BRITAIN AT THE UNIVERSITY PRESS, OXFORD
BY JOHN JOHNSON, PRINTER TO THE UNIVERSITY

CONTENTS

VOLUME I

VOLUME II

VOLUME III

Contents

VOLUME IV

VOLUME V

VOLUME VI

ILLUSTRATIONS

THE LIFE OF
SAMUEL JOHNSON, LL.D.

IN 1764 and 1765 it should seem that Dr. Johnson was so busily employed with his edition of Shakspeare, as to have had little leisure for any other literary exertion, or, indeed, even for private correspondence [1]. He did not favour me with a single letter for more than two years, for which it will appear that he afterwards apologised.

He was, however, at all times ready to give assistance to his friends, and others, in revising their works, and in writing for them, or greatly improving their Dedications. In that courtly species of composition no man excelled Dr. Johnson. Though the loftiness of his mind prevented him from ever dedicating in his own person [2], he wrote a very great number of Dedications

[1] Had he been ' busily employed ' he would, no doubt, have finished the edition in a few months. He himself had recorded at Easter, 1765 : ' My time has been unprofitably spent, and seems as a dream that has left nothing behind.' *Pr. and Med.* ¶ 54.

[2] Dedications had been commonly used as a means of getting money by flattery. I. D'Israeli in his *Calamities of Authors*, i. 64, says :—' Fuller's *Church History* is disgraced by . . . twelve . . . particular dedications. . . . It was an expedient to procure dedication fees ; for publishing books by subscription was an art not yet discovered.' The price of the dedication of a play was, he adds, in the time of George I, twenty guineas. So much then, at least, Johnson lost by not dedicating *Irene*. However, when he addressed the *Plan* of his Dictionary to Lord Chesterfield (*ante*, i. 183), he certainly came very near a dedication. Boswell, in the *Hypo-chondriack*, No. lxi, writes :—' For my own part, I own I am proud enough. But I do not relish the stateliness of not dedicating at all. I prefer pleasure to pride, and it appears to me that there is much pleasure in honestly expressing one's admiration, esteem, or affection, in a publick manner, and in thus contributing to the happiness of another by making him better pleased with himself.' *London Mag.*, 1782, p. 454. His dedications were dedications of friendship, not of flattery or servility. He dedicated his *Account of Corsica* to Paoli, his *Tour to the Hebrides* to Malone, and his *Life of Johnson* to Sir Joshua Reynolds. Goldsmith, in like manner, distrest though he so often was, dedicated his *Traveller* to his brother, the *Deserted Village* to Sir Joshua, and *She Stoops to Conquer* to Johnson. ⟨See Wheatley, *The Dedication of Books* and A. S. Collins, *Authorship in the Days of Johnson*, pp. 180 ff.⟩

B

for others. Some of these, the persons who were favoured with them are unwilling should be mentioned, from a too anxious apprehension, as I think, that they might be suspected of having received larger assistance [1] ; and some, after all the diligence I have bestowed, have escaped my enquiries. He told me, a great many years ago, ' he believed he had dedicated to all the Royal Family round [2] ; ' and it was indifferent to him what was the subject of the work dedicated, provided it were innocent. He once dedicated some Musick for the German Flute to Edward, Duke of York. In writing Dedications for others, he considered himself as by no means speaking his own sentiments.

Notwithstanding his long silence, I never omitted to write to him when I had any thing worthy of communicating. I generally kept copies of my letters to him, that I might have a full view of our correspondence, and never be at a loss to understand any reference in his letters [3]. He kept the greater part of mine very carefully ; and a short time before his death was attentive enough to seal them up in bundles, and order them to be delivered to me, which was accordingly done. Amongst them I found one, of which I had not made a copy, and which I own I read with pleasure at the distance of almost twenty years. It is dated November, 1765, at the palace of Pascal Paoli, in Corte,

---

[1] A passage in Boswell's letter to Malone of Jan. 29, 1791 (Boswell's *Letters*, No. 292, ii. 417), shows that it is Reynolds of whom he is writing. ' I am,' he writes, ' to cancel a leaf of the first volume, having found that though Sir Joshua certainly assured me he had no objection to my mentioning that Johnson wrote a dedication for him, he now thinks otherwise.' It was no doubt Reynolds's Dedication of his *Discourses* to the King in the year 1778 that Johnson wrote. The first sentence is in a high degree Johnsonian: ' The regular progress of cultivated life is from necessaries to accommodations, from accommodations to ornaments.' ⟨See *post*, iii. 369. The other dedication referred to in the text is that to the first edition of Percy's *Reliques* (1765). Boswell forgot to delete the reference to this in the Index of the first edition. See *ante*, i. 554, *post*, iv. App. K, and R. W. Chapman in *Johnson and Boswell Revised*, 1928, pp. 45 ff.⟩

[2] ' That is to say,' he added, ' to the last generation of the Royal Family.' See *post*, ii. 225. We may hope that the Royal Family were not all like the Duke of Gloucester, who, when Gibbon brought him the second volume of the *Decline and Fall*, ' received him with much good nature and affability, saying to him, as he laid the quarto on the table, " Another d–mn'd thick, square book ! Always scribble, scribble, scribble ! Eh ! Mr. Gibbon ? " ' Best's *Memorials*, p. 68.

[3] Such care was needless. Boswell complained (*post*, ii. 279), that Johnson did not *answer* his letters, but only sent him *returns*.

the capital of Corsica, and is full of generous enthusiasm [1]. After giving a sketch of what I had seen and heard in that island, it proceeded thus : ' I dare to call this a spirited tour. I dare to challenge your approbation.'

This letter produced the following answer, which I found on my arrival at Paris.

A Mr. Mr. BOSWELL, *chez Mr.* WATERS, *Banquier, à Paris.*

' DEAR SIR,

' APOLOGIES are seldom of any use. We will delay till your arrival the reasons, good or bad, which have made me such a sparing and ungrateful correspondent. Be assured, for the present, that nothing has lessened either the esteem or love with which I dismissed you at Harwich. Both have been increased by all that I have been told of you by yourself or others ; and [2] when you return, you will return to an unaltered, and, I hope, unalterable friend.

' All that you have to fear from me is the vexation of disappointing me. No man loves to frustrate expectations which have been formed in his favour ; and the pleasure which I promise myself from your

[1] ' On one of the days that my ague disturbed me least, I walked from the convent to Corte, purposely to write a letter to Mr. Samuel Johnson. I told my revered friend, that from a kind of superstition agreeable in a certain degree to him, as well as to myself, I had, during my travels, written to him from LOCA SOLENNIA, places in some measure sacred. That, as I had written to him, from the Tomb of Melancthon (*post*, iii. 118, 122, note 1), sacred to learning and piety, I now wrote to him from the palace of Pascal Paoli, sacred to wisdom and liberty.' Boswell's *Corsica*, p. 359. How delighted would Boswell have been had he lived to see the way in which he is spoken of by the biographer of Paoli : ' En traversant la Méditerranée sur de frêles navires pour venir s'asseoir au foyer de la nationalité corse, *des hommes graves* tels que Boswel et Volney, obéissaient sans doute à un sentiment bien plus élevé, qu' au besoin vulgaire d'une puérile curiosité.' *Histoire de Pascal Paoli*,

par A. Arrighi, i. 231. By every Corsican of any education the name of Boswell is known and honoured. One of them told me that it was in Boswell's pages that Paoli still lived for them. He informed me also of a family which still preserved by tradition the remembrance of Boswell's visit to their ancestral home.

[2] The twelve following lines of this letter were published by Boswell in his *Corsica* (p. 360) without Johnson's leave. (See *post*, ii. 46, 58.) Temple, to whom the book had been shewn before publication, had, it should seem, advised Boswell to omit this extract. Boswell replied :—' Your remarks are of great service to me. . . : But I must have my great preceptour Mr. Johnson introduced.' *Letters*, No. 76, i. 137. In writing to excuse himself to Johnson (*post*, ii. 58), he says, ' Surely you have no reason to complain of my publishing a single paragraph of one of your letters; the temptation to it was so strong.'

journals and remarks is so great, that perhaps no degree of attention or discernment will be sufficient to afford it.

' Come home, however, and take your chance. I long to see you, and to hear you ; and hope that we shall not be so long separated again. Come home, and expect such a welcome as is due to him, whom a wise and noble curiosity has led, where perhaps no native of this country ever was before [1].

' I have no news to tell you that can deserve your notice ; nor would I willingly lessen the pleasure that any novelty may give you at your return. I am afraid we shall find it difficult to keep among us a mind which has been so long feasted with variety. But let us try what esteem and kindness can effect.

' As your father's liberality has indulged you with so long a ramble, I doubt not but you will think his sickness, or even his desire to see you, a sufficient reason for hastening your return. The longer we live, and the more we think, the higher value we learn to put on the friendship and tenderness of parents and of friends. Parents we can have but once ; and he promises himself too much, who enters life with the expectation of finding many friends. Upon some motive, I hope, that you will be here soon ; and am willing to think that it will be an inducement to your return, that it is sincerely desired by, dear Sir,

' Your affectionate humble servant,

' SAM. JOHNSON.'

' Johnson's-court, Fleet-street,
　　　January 14, 1766.'

I returned to London in February, and found Dr. Johnson in

---

[1] ' Tell them [the court],' said Paoli to Boswell, ' what you have seen here. They will be curious to ask you. A man come from Corsica will be like a man come from the Antipodes.' Boswell's *Corsica*, p. 322. He was not indeed the first ' native of this country ' to go there. He found in Bastia ' an English woman of Penrith in Cumberland. When the Highlanders marched through that country in the year 1745, she had married a soldier of the French picquets in the very midst of all the confusion and danger, and when she could hardly understand one word he said.' *Ib.*, p. 370. Boswell nowhere quotes Mrs. Barbauld's fine

lines on Corsica. Yet he must have been pleased when he read :—

' Such were the working thoughts
　　which swell'd the breast
Of generous Boswel ; when with
　　nobler aim
And views beyond the narrow
　　beaten track
By trivial fancy trod, he turn'd his
　　course
From polish'd Gallia's soft delicious
　　vales,' &c.

　　　Mrs. Barbauld's *Poems* (1773), 2.
⟨These lines are quoted in the biographical memoir, published in the *European Magazine* (1791, xix. 325), which is now accepted as Boswell's.⟩

a good house in Johnson's-court, Fleet-street [1], in which he had accommodated Miss Williams with an apartment on the ground floor, while Mr. Levett occupied his post in the garret : his faithful Francis was still attending upon him. He received me with much kindness. The fragments of our first conversation, which I have preserved, are these : I told him that Voltaire, in a conversation with me, had distinguished Pope and Dryden thus :—' Pope drives a handsome chariot, with a couple of neat trim nags ; Dryden a coach, and six stately horses.' JOHNSON. ' Why, Sir, the truth is, they both drive coaches and six ; but Dryden's horses are either galloping or stumbling : Pope's go at a steady even trot [2].' He said of Goldsmith's ' Traveller ', which had been published in my absence, ' There has not been so fine a poem since Pope's time [3].'

And here it is proper to settle, with authentick precision, what has long floated in publick report, as to Johnson's being himself the authour of a considerable part of that poem. Much, no doubt,

[1] Murphy, in the *Monthly Review*, lxxvi. 376, thus describes Johnson's life in Johnson's Court after he had received his pension. ' His friend Levett, his physician in ordinary, paid his daily visits with assiduity ; attended at all hours, made tea all the morning, talked what he had to say, and did not expect an answer ; or if occasion required it, was mute, officious, and ever complying. . . . There Johnson sat every morning, receiving visits, hearing the topics of the day, and indolently trifling away the time. Chemistry afforded some amusement.' Hawkins (*Life*, p. 452) says :—' An upper room, which had the advantages of a good light and free air, he fitted up for a study. . . . A silver standish, and some useful plate, which he had been prevailed on to accept as pledges of kindness from some who most esteemed him, together with furniture that would not have disgraced a better dwelling, banished those appearances of squalid indigence, which, in his less happy days, disgusted those who came to see him.' Some of the

plate Johnson had bought. See *post*, iv. 92. ⟨Johnson's residence in Johnson's Court dates at least from 26 September 1765. *Letters*, No. 174·1.⟩

[2] It is remarkable, that Mr. Gray has employed somewhat the same image to characterise Dryden. He, indeed, furnishes his car with but two horses, but they are of ' ethereal race ' :
' Behold where Dryden's less presumptuous car,
Wide o'er the fields of glory bear
Two coursers of ethereal race,
With necks in thunder cloath'd, and long resounding pace.'
Ode on the Progress of Poesy. BOSWELL.

In the *Life of Pope*, 309, Johnson says :—' The style of Dryden is capricious and varied, that of Pope is cautious and uniform ; Dryden obeys the motions of his own mind, Pope constrains his mind to his own rules of composition. Dryden is sometimes vehement and rapid ; Pope is always smooth, uniform, and gentle.'

[3] ⟨See App. B, p. 478.⟩

both of the sentiments and expression, were derived from conversation with him ; and it was certainly submitted to his friendly revision : but in the year 1783, he, at my request, marked with a pencil the lines which he had furnished, which are only line 420th,

'To stop too fearful, and too faint to go ; '

and the concluding ten lines, except the last couplet but one, which I distinguish by the Italick character :

'How small of all that human hearts endure,
That part which kings or laws [1] can cause or cure.
Still to ourselves in every place consign'd,
Our own felicity we make or find [2] ;
With secret course, which no loud storms annoy,
Glides the smooth current of domestick joy.[a]
The lifted axe, the agonizing wheel,
Luke's iron crown, and Damien's bed of steel,
To men remote from power, but rarely known,
Leave reason, faith, and conscience, all our own.'

He added, 'These are all of which I can be sure [3].' They bear a small proportion to the whole, which consists of four hundred and thirty-eight verses. Goldsmith, in the couplet which he inserted, mentions *Luke* as a person well known, and superficial readers have passed it over quite smoothly ; while those of more

[a] joy. 1, 2 : joy : 3.

[1] In the original *laws or kings*.

[2] 'The mind is its own place, and in itself
Can make a Heaven of Hell, a Hell of Heaven.'
Paradise Lost, i. 254.
'Caelum, non animum, mutant qui trans mare currunt.'
Horace, *Epis*. i. 11. 27.
See also *ante*, i. 381, note 2.

[3] 'I once inadvertently put him,' wrote Reynolds, 'in a situation from which none but a man of perfect integrity could extricate himself. I pointed at some lines in the *Traveller* which I told him I was sure he wrote. He hesitated a little ; during this hesitation I recollected myself, that as I knew he would not lye I put him in a cleft stick, and should have had but my due if he had given me a rough answer ; but he only said, " Sir, I did not write them, but that you may not imagine that I have wrote more than I really have, the utmost I have wrote in that poem, to the best of my recollection, is not more than eighteen lines." It must be observed there was then an opinion about town that Dr. Johnson wrote the whole poem for his friend, who was then in a manner an unknown writer.' Leslie and Taylor's *Reynolds*, ii. 458. See also *post*, iii. 252. For each line of *The Traveller* Goldsmith was paid 11¼d. (*ante*, i. 193, note). Johnson's present, therefore, of nine lines was, if reckoned in money, worth 8/5¼. ⟨See also App. B, p. 478 and *John. Misc*. ii. 7.⟩

attention have been as much perplexed by *Luke*, as by *Lydiat* [1],
in 'The Vanity of Human Wishes.' The truth is, that Goldsmith himself was in a mistake. In the ' *Respublica Hungarica* ' [2],
there is an account of a desperate rebellion in the year 1514,
headed by two brothers, of the name of *Zeck*, George and Luke.
When it was quelled, *George*, not *Luke*, was punished by his
head being encircled with a red hot iron crown : ' *coronâ candes-
cente ferreâ coronatur* [3].' The same severity of torture was
exercised on the Earl of Athol, one of the murderers of King
James I. of Scotland.

Dr. Johnson at the same time favoured me by marking the
lines which he furnished to Goldsmith's ' Deserted Village,' which
are only the last four :

> ' That trade's proud empire hastes to swift decay,
> As ocean sweeps the labour'd mole away :
> While self-dependent power can time defy,
> As rocks resist the billows and the sky.'

Talking of education, ' People have now a-days, (said he,) got
a strange opinion that every thing should be taught by lectures.
Now, I cannot see that lectures can do so much good as reading
the books from which the lectures are taken. I know nothing
that can be best taught by lectures [4], except where experiments

---

[1] See *ante*, i. 194, note 2.

[2] *Respublica et Status Regni Hun-
gariae. Ex Officina Elzeviriana*, 1634,
p. 136. This work belongs to the
series of *Republics* mentioned by Johnson, *post*, iii. 52.

[3] ' " Luke " had been taken simply
for the euphony of the line. He was
one of two brothers Dosa. . . . The
origin of the mistake [of Zeck for
Dosa] is curious. . . . The two brothers
belonged to one of the native races
of Transylvania called Szeklers or
Zecklers, which descriptive addition
follows their names in the German
biographical authorities ; and this,
through abridgment and misappre-
hension, in subsequent books came
at last to be substituted for the family
name.' Forster's *Goldsmith*, i. 370.
The iron crown was not the worst of

the tortures inflicted. ⟨' Son nom
[Dosza] est resté populaire dans le
peuple hongrois.' Leger, *Hist. de
l'Autriche-Hongrie*, p. 239.⟩

[4] See *post*, iv. 92. In the Preface to
the *Preceptor*, 1748, Johnson had
written (*Works*, v. 231) : ' At a time
when so many schemes of education
have been projected, . . . so many
schools opened for general knowledge,
and so many lectures in particular
sciences attended.' Goldsmith, in his
Life of Nash (published in 1762),
describes the lectures at Bath ' on
the arts and sciences, which are frequently taught there in a pretty superficial manner, so as not to teaze the
understanding, while they afford
the imagination some amusement.'
Goldsmith's *Works*, ed. Cunningham,
iv. 59.

are to be shewn. You may teach chymistry by lectures.—You might teach making of shoes by lectures ¹ ! '

At night I supped with him at the Mitre tavern, that we might renew our social intimacy at the original place of meeting. But there was now a considerable difference in his way of living. Having had an illness, in which he was advised to leave off wine, he had, from that period, continued to abstain from it, and drank only water, or lemonade ².

I told him that a foreign friend of his ³, whom I had met with abroad, was so wretchedly perverted to infidelity, that he treated the hopes of immortality with brutal levity ; and said, ' As man dies like a dog, let him lie like a dog.' JOHNSON. ' *If* he dies like a dog, *let* him lie like a dog.' I added, that this man said to me, ' I hate mankind, for I think myself one of the best of them, and I know how bad I am.' JOHNSON. ' Sir, he must be very singular in his opinion, if he thinks himself one of the best of men ; for none of his friends think him so.'—He said, no honest man could be a Deist ; for no man could be so after a fair examination of the proofs of Christianity.' I named Hume ⁴. JOHNSON.

¹ Perhaps Gibbon had read this passage at the time when he wrote in his *Memoirs* (1900), p. 54 :—' It has indeed been observed, nor is the observation absurd, that excepting in experimental sciences, which demand a costly apparatus and a dexterous hand, the many valuable treatises, that have been published on every subject of learning, may now supersede the ancient mode of oral instruction.' ⟨Gibbon's passage was written in 1792–3. See J. Murray's edit., p. 72.⟩ See *post*, ii. 448, note 2.

² See *ante*, i. 103.

³ Probably Baretti. CROKER. He was in Italy at the same time as Boswell. That they met seems to be shewn by a passage in Boswell's letter (*post*, ii. 24). Malone wrote of him :—' He appears to be an Infidel.' Prior's *Malone*, p. 399.

⁴ Lord Charlemont records (*Life*, i. 235) that Mrs. Mallet, meeting Hume at an assembly, ' boldly accosted him in these words : " Mr. Hume, give me leave to introduce myself to you ; we deists ought to know each other." " Madame," replied he, " I am no deist. I do not style myself so, neither do I desire to be known by that appellation." ' Hume, in 1763 or 1764, wrote to Dr. Blair about the men of letters at Paris :—' It would give you . . . and Robertson great satisfaction to find that there is not a single deist among them.' J. H. Burton's *Hume*, ii. 181. There was no deist, I suppose, because they were all atheists. Romilly (*Life*, i. 179) records the following anecdote, which he had from Diderot in 1781 :—' Hume dîna avec une grande compagnie chez le Baron d'Holbach. Il était assis à côté du Baron ; on parla de la religion naturelle. " Pour les Athées," disait Hume, " je ne crois pas qu'il en existe ; je n'en ai jamais vu." " Vous avez été un peu malheureux," répondit l'autre, " vous voici à table avec dix-sept pour la première fois." ' It was on the same day that Diderot

' No, Sir; Hume owned to a clergyman in the bishoprick of Durham, that he had never read the New Testament with attention.' I mentioned Hume's notion [1], that all who are happy are equally happy ; a little miss with a new gown at a dancing-school ball, a general at the head of a victorious army, and an orator, after having made an eloquent speech in a great assembly. JOHNSON. ' Sir, that all who are happy, are equally happy, is not true. A peasant and a philosopher may be equally *satisfied*, but not equally *happy*. Happiness consists in the multiplicity of agreeable consciousness. A peasant has not capacity for having equal happiness with a philosopher.' I remember this very question very happily illustrated in opposition to Hume, by the Reverend Mr. Robert Brown [2], at Utrecht. ' A small drinking-glass and a large one, (said he,) may be equally full ; but the large one holds more than the small.'

Dr. Johnson was very kind this evening, and said to me, ' You have now lived five-and-twenty years, and you have employed them well.' ' Alas, Sir, (said I,) I fear not. Do I know history ? Do I know mathematicks ? Do I know law ? ' JOHNSON. ' Why, Sir, though you may know no science so well as to be able to teach it, and no profession so well as to be able to follow it, your general mass of knowledge of books and men renders you very capable to make yourself master of any science, or fit yourself for any profession.' I mentioned that a gay friend [3] had

related this that he said to Romilly, ' Il faut *sabrer* la théologie.'

[1] ' The inference upon the whole is, that it is not from the value or worth of the object, which any person pursues, that we can determine his enjoyment ; but merely from the passion with which he pursues it, and the success which he meets with in his pursuit. Objects have absolutely no worth or value in themselves. They derive their worth merely from the passion. If that be strong, and steady, and successful, the person is happy. It cannot reasonably be doubted, but a little miss, dressed in a new gown for a dancing-school ball, receives as compleat enjoyment as the greatest orator, who triumphs in the splendor of his eloquence, while he governs the passions and resolutions of a numerous assembly.' Hume's *Essays*, i. 179 (*The Sceptic*). Pope had written in the *Essay on Man* (iv. 57) :
' Condition, circumstance, is not the thing ;
Bliss is the same in subject or in king.'
See also *post*, iii. 288.

[2] ⟨The Rev. Robert Brown was, like his brother, William Brown (*Boswelliana*, p. 220), and his nephew, William Laurence Brown (*D.N.B.*), minister of the Scottish Church at Utrecht. He died in 1777. D. Irving's *Lives of Scotish Writers*, ii. 328.⟩

[3] ⟨Perhaps Wilkes, who is described *post*, ii. 11 as Boswell's ' gay friend '.⟩

advised me against being a lawyer, because I should be excelled by plodding block-heads. JOHNSON. ' Why, Sir, in the formulary and statutory part of law, a plodding block-head may excel ; but in the ingenious and rational part of it a plodding block-head can never excel.'

I talked of the mode adopted by some to rise in the world, by courting great men, and asked him whether he had ever submitted to it. JOHNSON. ' Why, Sir, I never was near enough to great men to court them. You may be prudently attached to great men, and yet independent. You are not to do what you think wrong ; and, Sir, you are to calculate, and not pay too dear for what you get. You must not give a shilling's worth of court for six-pence worth of good. But if you can get a shilling's worth of good for six-pence worth of court, you are a fool if you do not pay court [1].'

He said, ' If convents should be allowed at all, they should only be retreats for persons unable to serve the publick, or who have served it. It is our first duty to serve society, and, after we have done that, we may attend wholly to the salvation of our own souls. A youthful passion for abstracted devotion should not be encouraged [2].'

I introduced the subject of second sight, and other mysterious manifestations ; the fulfilment of which, I suggested, might happen by chance. JOHNSON. ' Yes, Sir ; but they have happened so often, that mankind have agreed to think them not fortuitous [3].'

[1] We may compare with this what he says in *The Rambler*, No. 21, about the ' cowardice, which always encroaches fast upon such as spend their lives in the company of persons higher than themselves.' In No. 104 he writes :—' It is dangerous for mean minds to venture themselves within the sphere of greatness.' In the court that Boswell many years later paid to Lord Lonsdale, he suffered all the humiliations that the brutality of this petty greatness can inflict. Boswell's *Letters*, No. 277, ii. 396–7. See also *ante*, i. 131 and *post*, iii. 189.

[2] See *post*, v. 62.

[3] Johnson (*Journey to Western Isl.*, 1924, p. 100) thus sums up his examination of second-sight :—' There is, against it, the seeming analogy of things confusedly seen, and little understood ; and for it, the indistinct cry of national persuasion, which may be perhaps resolved at last into prejudice and tradition. I never could advance my curiosity to conviction ; but came away at last only willing to believe.' See also *post*, ii. 318. Hume said of the evidence in favour of second-sight :—' As finite added to finite never approaches a hair's breadth nearer to infinite ; so a fact incredible in itself, acquires not the smallest accession of probability by

I talked to him a great deal of what I had seen in Corsica, and of my intention to publish an account of it. He encouraged me by saying, ' You cannot go to the bottom of the subject ; but all that you tell us will be new to us. Give us as many anecdotes as you can [1].'

Our next meeting at the Mitre was on Saturday the 15th of February, when I presented to him my old and most intimate friend, the Reverend Mr. Temple [2], then of Cambridge. I having mentioned that I had passed some time with Rousseau in his wild retreat [3], and having quoted some remark made by Mr. Wilkes, with whom I had spent many pleasant hours in Italy, Johnson said, (sarcastically,) ' It seems, Sir, you have kept very good company abroad, Rousseau and Wilkes ! ' Thinking it enough to defend one at a time, I said nothing as to my gay friend, but answered with a smile, ' My dear Sir, you don't call Rousseau bad company. Do you really think *him* a bad man ? ' JOHNSON. ' Sir, if you are talking jestingly of this, I don't talk with you. If you mean to be serious, I think him one of the worst of men ; a rascal, who ought to be hunted out of society, as he has been. Three or four nations have expelled him ; and it is a shame that he is protected in this country [4].' BOSWELL. ' I don't deny, Sir, but that his novel [5] may, perhaps, do harm ;

the accumulation of testimony.' J. H. Burton's *Hume*, i. 480.

[1] ' I love anecdotes,' said Johnson (*post*, v. 39). Boswell wrote, ' It [the *Life*] will . . . be . . . full of literary and characteristical anecdotes (which word . . . Johnson always condemned as used in the sense that the French, and we from them, use it, as signifying *particulars*).' *Letters*, No. 269, ii. 382. In his *Dictionary*, he defined *Anecdote*, ' Something yet unpublished ; secret history.' In the fourth edition, 1773, he added : ' It is now used, after the French, for a biographical incident; a minute passage of private life.'

[2] See *ante*, i. 436.

[3] Boswell, writing to Wilkes in 1776, said :—' Though we differ widely in religion and politicks, *il y a des points où nos âmes sont unies*, as Rousseau said to me in his wild retreat.' *Letters*,

No. 159, i. 248. ⟨For Boswell's visits to Rousseau, see *Boswell Papers*, iv.⟩

[4] ⟨Rousseau fled from France, 9 June 1762, to Yverdun : ten days later his arrest was ordered at Geneva if he ventured in the town. He was expelled from Yverdun, 9 July, and went to Motiers Travers, Neuchâtel, where he remained until 8 September, 1765, when he again took flight to escape from the anger of the mob. He was finally banished from Bernese territory, in the following October. He then went to Strasbourg and Paris, where he met Hume, who accompanied him to England. He landed at Dover on 11 January 1766, and reached London on the 13th. See *La Grande Encyclopédie*, xxviii. 1067, and *Annales J. J. Rousseau* xv. pp. 129, 133, 175 ff.⟩

[5] Rousseau had by this time published his *Nouvelle Héloïse* and *Émile*.

but I cannot think his intention was bad.' JOHNSON. ' Sir,
that will not do. We cannot prove any man's intention to be
bad. You may shoot a man through the head, and say you
intended to miss him ; but the Judge will order you to be
hanged. An alledged want of intention, when evil is committed,
will not be allowed in a court of justice. Rousseau, Sir, is a
very bad man. I would sooner sign a sentence for his transport-
ation, than that of any felon who has gone from the Old
Bailey these many years. Yes, I should like to have him work
in the plantations [1].' BOSWELL. ' Sir, do you think him as bad
a man as Voltaire ? ' JOHNSON. ' Why, Sir, it is difficult to
settle the proportion of iniquity between them [2].'

This violence seemed very strange to me, who had read many
of Rousseau's animated writings with great pleasure, and even
edification ; had been much pleased with his society [3], and was
just come from the Continent, where he was very generally
admired. Nor can I yet allow that he deserves the very severe
censure which Johnson pronounced upon him. His absurd
preference of savage to civilised life [4], and other singularities,
are proofs rather of a defect in his understanding, than of any
depravity in his heart. And notwithstanding the unfavourable
opinion which many worthy men have expressed of his ' *Profession de Foi du Vicaire Savoyard*,' I cannot help admiring it as
the performance of a man full of sincere reverential submission

---

[1] Less than three months after the
date of this conversation Rousseau
wrote to General Conway, one of the
Secretaries of State, thanking him for
the pension which George III proposed secretly to confer on him.
Hume's *Private Corres.*, p. 165. Miss
Burney, in her Preface to *Evelina*, a
novel which was her introduction to
Johnson's strong affection, mentioning Rousseau and Johnson, adds
in a footnote :—' However superior
the capacities in which these great
writers deserve to be considered,
they must pardon me that, for the
dignity of my subject, I here rank
the authors of *Rasselas* and *Eloïse*
as Novelists.'

[2] Rousseau thus wrote of himself:
—' Dieu est juste ; il veut que je
souffre ; et il sait que je suis innocent. Voilà le motif de ma confiance,
mon cœur et ma raison me crient
qu'elle ne me trompera pas. Lais-
sons donc faire les hommes et la
destinée ; apprenons à souffrir sans
murmure ; tout doit à la fin rentrer
dans l'ordre, et mon tour viendra tôt
ou tard.' Rousseau's *Œuvres*, xx. 223.

[3] ' He entertained me very courteously,' wrote Boswell in his *Corsica*,
p. 262.

[4] In this preference Boswell pretended at times to share. See *post*,
ii. 73.

to Divine Mystery, though beset with perplexing doubts ; a state
of mind to be viewed with pity rather than with anger.

On his favourite subject of subordination, Johnson said, ' So
far is it from being true that men are naturally equal [1], that no
two people can be half an hour together, but one shall acquire
an evident superiority over the other.'

I mentioned the advice given us by philosophers, to console
ourselves, when distressed or embarrassed, by thinking of those
who are in a worse situation than ourselves. This, I observed,
could not apply to all, for there must be some who have nobody
worse than they are. JOHNSON. ' Why, to be sure, Sir, there
are ; but they don't know it. There is no being so poor and
so contemptible, who does not think there is somebody still
poorer, and still more contemptible.'

As my stay in London at this time was very short, I had not
many opportunities of being with Dr. Johnson ; but I felt my
veneration for him in no degree lessened, by my having seen
multorum hominum mores et urbes [2]. On the contrary, by
having it in my power to compare him with many of the most
celebrated persons of other countries [3], my admiration of his
extraordinary mind was increased and confirmed.

The roughness, indeed, which sometimes appeared in his
manners, was more striking to me now, from my having been
accustomed to the studied smooth complying habits of the
Continent ; and I clearly recognised in him, not without respect
for his honest conscientious zeal, the same indignant and

---

[1] Johnson seems once to have held
this view to some extent ; for, writing
of Savage's poem *On Public Spirit*, he
says (*L. P., Savage*, 210) :—' He has
asserted the natural equality of mankind, and endeavoured to suppress
that pride which inclines men to
imagine that right is the consequence
of power.' See also *post*, iii. 202,
where he asserts :—' It is impossible
not to conceive that men in their
original state were equal.' For the
opposite opinion, see *ante*, i. 408, 442,
and *post*, ii. 219, &c.

[2] ' Qui mores hominum multorum
vidit et urbes.' ' Manners and towns
of various nations viewed.' FRANCIS.
Horace, *Ars Poetica*, l. 142.

[3] By the time Boswell was twenty-
six years old he could boast that he
had made the acquaintance of Voltaire,
Rousseau, and Paoli among foreigners
and of Adam Smith, Robertson, Hume,
Johnson, Goldsmith, Garrick, Horace
Walpole, Wilkes, ⟨Churchill⟩, and perhaps Reynolds, among Englishmen.
He had twice at least received a letter
from the Earl of Chatham.

sarcastical mode of treating every attempt to unhinge or weaken good principles.

One evening, when a young gentleman ¹ teized him with an account of the infidelity of his servant, who, he said, would not believe the scriptures, because he could not read them in the original tongues, and be sure that they were not invented. ' Why, foolish fellow, (said Johnson,) has he any better authority for almost every thing that he believes ? '—Boswell. ' Then the vulgar, Sir, never can know they are right, but must submit themselves to the learned.'—Johnson. ' To be sure, Sir. The vulgar are the children of the State, and must be taught like children ².'—Boswell. ' Then, Sir, a poor Turk must be a Mahometan, just as a poor Englishman must be a Christian ³ ? '— Johnson. ' Why, yes, Sir ; and what then ? This now is such stuff as I used to talk to my mother, when I first began to think myself a clever fellow ; and she ought to have whipt me for it.'

Another evening Dr. Goldsmith and I called on him, with the hope of prevailing on him to sup with us at the Mitre. We found him indisposed, and resolved not to go abroad. ' Come then, (said Goldsmith,) we will not go to the Mitre to-night, since we cannot have the big man ⁴ with us.' Johnson then called for a bottle of port, of which Goldsmith and I partook, while our friend, now a water-drinker, sat by us. Goldsmith. ' I think, Mr. Johnson, you don't go near the theatres now. You give yourself no more concern about a new play, than if you had never had any thing to do with the stage.' Johnson. ' Why, Sir, our tastes greatly alter. The lad does not care for the child's rattle, and the old man does not care for the young man's whore.' Goldsmith. ' Nay, Sir ; but your Muse was not a whore.' Johnson. ' Sir, I do not think she was. But as we advance in the journey of life, we drop some of the things which have pleased us ; whether it be that we are fatigued and

---

¹ In such passages as this we may generally assume that the gentleman, whose name is not given, is Boswell himself. See *post*, ii. 84, note 3, and 193, note 1.

² See *post*, iv. 12, where this assertion is called ' his usual remark,' and iv. 216.

³ See *post*, iii. 299.

⁴ These two little words may be observed as marks of Mr. Boswell's accuracy in reporting the expressions of his personages. It is a jocular Irish phrase, which, of all Johnson's acquaintances, no one, probably, but Goldsmith, *could* have used.—Croker.

don't choose to carry so many things any farther, or that we find other things which we like better.' BOSWELL. ' But, Sir, why don't you give us something in some other way ? ' GOLD-SMITH. ' Ay, Sir, we have a claim upon you [1].' JOHNSON. ' No, Sir, I am not obliged to do any more. No man is obliged to do as much as he can do. A man is to have part of his life to himself. If a soldier has fought a good many campaigns, he is not to be blamed if he retires to ease and tranquillity. A physician, who has practised long in a great city, may be excused if he retires to a small town, and takes less practice. Now, Sir, the good I can do by my conversation bears the same proportion to the good I can do by my writings, that the practice of a physician, retired to a small town, does to his practice in a great city [2].' BOSWELL. ' But I wonder, Sir, you have not more pleasure in writing than in not writing.' JOHN-SON. ' Sir, you *may* wonder.'

He talked of making verses, and observed, ' The great difficulty is to know when you have made good ones. When composing, I have generally had them in my mind, perhaps fifty at a time, walking up and down in my room ; and then I have written [a] them down, and often, from laziness, have written only half lines. I have written a hundred lines in a day. I remember I wrote a hundred lines of " The Vanity of Human Wishes " in a day [3]. Doctor, (turning to Goldsmith,) I am not quite idle ; I made one line t'other day ; but I made no more.' GOLDSMITH. ' Let us hear it ; we'll put a bad one to it.' JOHN-SON. ' No, Sir ; I have forgot it [4].'

[a] wrote 1 : written 2, 3.

[1] See *ante*, i. 398 ; *post*, ii. 40, 441.
[2] Johnson's best justification for the apparent indolence of the latter part of his life may be found in his own words : ' Every man of genius has some arts of fixing the attention peculiar to himself, by which, honestly exerted, he may benefit mankind. . . . To the position of Tully, that if Virtue could be seen, she must be loved, may be added, that if Truth could be heard, she must be obeyed.' *The Rambler*, No. 87. He fixed the attention best by his talk. For ' the position of Tully,' see *post*, ii. 443.

[3] See *ante*, i. 192, and *post*, iv. 219. Goldsmith wrote *The Traveller* and *Deserted Village* on a very different plan. ' To save himself the trouble of transcription, he wrote the lines in his first copy very wide, and would so fill up the intermediate space with reiterated corrections, that scarcely a word of his first effusions was left unaltered.' *Percy Memoir* in Gold-smith's *Misc. Works*, i. 113.
[4] Mrs. Thrale, in a letter to Dr. Johnson, said :—' Don't sit making verses that never will be written.'

Such specimens of the easy and playful conversation of the great Dr. Samuel Johnson are, I think, to be prized ; as exhibiting the little varieties of a mind so enlarged and so powerful when objects of consequence required its exertions, and as giving us a minute knowledge of his character and modes of thinking.

' To BENNET LANGTON, ESQ. AT LANGTON, NEAR SPILSBY, LINCOLNSHIRE.

' DEAR SIR,

' WHAT your friends have done, that from your departure till now nothing has been heard of you, none of us are able to inform the rest ; but as we are all neglected alike, no one thinks himself entitled to the privilege of complaint.

' I should have known nothing of you or of Langton, from the time that dear Miss Langton † left us, had not I met Mr. Simpson §, of Lincoln, one day in the street, by whom I was informed that Mr. Langton, your Mamma, and yourself, had been all ill, but that you were all recovered.

' That sickness should suspend your correspondence, I did not wonder ; but hoped that it would be renewed at your recovery.

' Since you will not inform us where you are, or how you live, I know not whether you desire to know any thing of us. However, I will tell you that THE CLUB subsists ; but we have the loss of Burke's company since he has been engaged in publick business ¹, in which he has gained more reputation than perhaps any man at his [first] appearance ever gained before. He made two speeches in the House for repealing the Stamp-act, which were publickly commended by Mr. Pitt, and have filled the town with wonder ².

' Burke is a great man by nature, and is expected soon to attain civil

---

Piozzi Letters, ii. 183. Baretti noted opposite this in the margin of his copy: ' Johnson was always making Latin or English verses in his mind, but never would write them down.'

† ⟨Langton's eldest sister. CROKER.⟩

§ ⟨See *post*, iii. 359.⟩

¹ Burke entered Parliament as member for Wendover borough on Dec. 23, 1765. William Burke, writing to Barry the artist on the following March 23, says :—' Ned's success has exceeded our most sanguine hopes, all at once he has darted into fame. He is full of real business, intent upon

doing real good to his country, as much as if he was to receive twenty per cent. from the commerce of the whole empire, which he labours to improve and extend.' Barry's *Works*, i. 42.

² It was of these speeches that Macaulay wrote :—' The House of Commons heard Pitt for the last time, and Burke for the first time, and was in doubt to which of them the palm of eloquence should be assigned. It was indeed a splendid sunset and a splendid dawn.' Macaulay's *Hist. Essays, Earl of Chatham*, (1923), 771.

greatness [1]. I am grown greater too, for I have maintained the news-papers these many weeks [2] ; and what is greater still, I have risen every morning since New-year's day, at about eight ; when I was up, I have indeed done but little ; yet it is no slight advancement to obtain for so many hours more, the consciousness of being.

' I wish you were in my new study [3] ; I am now writing the first letter in it. I think it looks very pretty about me.

' Dyer [4] is constant at THE CLUB ; Hawkins is remiss ; I am not over diligent. Dr. Nugent, Dr. Goldsmith, and Mr. Reynolds, are very constant. Mr. Lye is printing his Saxon and Gothick Dictionary [5] ; all THE CLUB subscribes.

' You will pay my respects to all my Lincolnshire friends. I am, dear Sir,

' Most affectionately yours,[a]
' SAM. JOHNSON.'

' March 9, 1766.
Johnson's-court, Fleet-street [6].'

' To BENNET LANGTON, ESQ. AT LANGTON, NEAR SPILSBY, LINCOLNSHIRE.

' DEAR SIR,

' IN supposing that I should be more than commonly affected by the death of Peregrine Langton [7], you were not mistaken ; he was one of those whom I loved at once by instinct and by reason. I have seldom indulged more hope of any thing than of being able to improve our ac-quaintance to friendship. Many a time have I placed myself again at Langton, and imagined the pleasure with which I should walk to Part-ney [8] in a summer morning ; but this is no longer possible. We must now endeavour to preserve what is left us,—his example of piety and œconomy. I hope you make what enquiries you can, and write down what is told you. The little things which distinguish domestick characters are soon forgotten : if you delay to enquire, you will have no information ; if you neglect to write, information will be vain [9].

[a] yours 2 : your's 3.

[1] See *post*, ii. 450.

[2] Boswell has already stated (*ante*, i. 497) that Johnson's *Shakespeare* was ' virulently attacked ' by Kenrick. No doubt there were other attacks and rejoinders too. ⟨See Courtney, *Biblio-graphy*, p. 104.⟩

[3] Two days earlier he had drawn up a prayer on entering *Novum Museum*. *Pr. and Med.* ¶ 61.

[4] See *post*, iv. 11.

[5] *Dictionarium Saxonico et Gothico-Latinum*. Lond., 1772. Lye died in 1767. O. Manning completed the work. ⟨See App. B, p. 478.⟩

[6] ⟨See *ante*, ii. 5, note 1.⟩

[7] Mr. Langton's uncle. BOS-WELL.

[8] The place of residence of Mr. Peregrine Langton. BOSWELL.

[9] Mr. Langton did not disregard this counsel, but wrote the following

' His art of life certainly deserves to be known and studied. He lived in plenty and elegance upon an income which, to many would

account, which he has been pleased to communicate to me :

' The circumstances of Mr. Peregrine Langton were these. He had an annuity for life of two hundred pounds *per annum*. He resided in a village in Lincolnshire ; the rent of his house, with two or three small fields, was twenty-eight pounds ; the county he lived in was not more than moderately cheap ; his family consisted of a sister, who paid him eighteen pounds annually for her board, and a niece. The servants were two maids, and two men in livery. His common way of living, at his table, was three or four dishes ; the appurtenances to his table were neat and handsome ; he frequently entertained company at dinner, and then his table was well served with as many dishes as were usual at the tables of the other gentlemen in the neighbourhood. His own appearance, as to clothes, was genteelly neat and plain. He had always a post-chaise, and kept three horses.

' Such, with the resources I have mentioned, was his way of living, which he did not suffer to employ his whole income : for he had always a sum of money lying by him for any extraordinary expences that might arise. Some money he put into the stocks ; at his death, the sum he had there amounted to one hundred and fifty pounds. He purchased out of his income his household-furniture and linen, of which latter he had a very ample store ; and, as I am assured by those that had very good means of knowing, not less than the tenth part of his income was set apart for charity : at the time of his death, the sum of twenty-five pounds was found, with a direction to be employed in such uses.

' He had laid down a plan of living proportioned to his income, and did not practise any extraordinary degree of parsimony, but endeavoured that in his family there should be plenty without waste ; as an instance that this was his endeavour, it may be worth while to mention a method he took in regulating a proper allowance of malt liquor to be drunk in his family, that there might not be a deficiency, or any intemperate profusion : On a complaint made that his allowance of a hogshead in a month, was not enough for his own family, he ordered the quantity of a hogshead to be put into bottles, had it locked up from the servants, and distributed out, every day, eight quarts, which is the quantity each day at one hogshead in a month ; and told his servants, that if that did not suffice, he would allow them more ; but, by this method, it appeared at once that the allowance was much more than sufficient for his small family ; and this proved a clear conviction, that could not be answered, and saved all future dispute. He was, in general, very diligently and punctually attended and obeyed by his servants ; he was very considerate as to the injunctions he gave, and explained them distinctly ; and, at their first coming to his service, steadily exacted a close compliance with them, without any remission ; and the servants finding this to be the case, soon grew habitually accustomed to the practice of their business, and then very little further attention was necessary. On extraordinary instances of good behaviour, or diligent service, he was not wanting in particular encouragements and presents above their wages ; it is remarkable that he would permit their relations to visit them, and stay at his house two or three days at a time.

appear indigent, and to most, scanty. How he lived, therefore, every man has an interest in knowing. His death, I hope, was peaceful ; it was surely happy.

' I wish I had written sooner, lest, writing now, I should renew your grief ; but I would not forbear saying what I have now said.

' This loss is, I hope, the only misfortune of a family to whom no misfortune at all should happen, if my wishes could avert it. Let me know how you all go on. Has Mr. Langton got him the little horse that I recommended ? It would do him good to ride about his estate in fine weather.

' Be pleased to make my compliments to Mrs. Langton, and to dear Miss Langton, and Miss Di, and Miss Juliet, and to every body else.

' The wonder, with most that hear an account of his œconomy, will be, how he was able, with such an income, to do so much, especially when it is considered that he paid for every thing he had ; he had no land, except the two or three small fields which I have said he rented ; and, instead of gaining any thing by their produce, I have reason to think he lost by them ; however, they furnished him with no further assistance towards his housekeeping, than grass for his horses, (not hay, for that I know he bought,) and for two cows. Every Monday morning he settled his family accounts, and so kept up a constant attention to the confining his expences within his income ; and to do it more exactly, compared those expences with a computation he had made, how much that income would afford him every week and day of the year. One of his œconomical practices was, as soon as any repair was wanting in or about his house, to have it immediately performed. When he had money to spare, he chose to lay in a provision of linen or clothes, or any other necessaries ; as then, he said, he could afford it, which he might not be so well able to do when the actual want came ; in consequence of which method, he had a considerable supply of necessary articles lying by him, beside what was in use.

' But the main particular that seems to have enabled him to do so much with his income, was, that he paid for every thing as soon as he had it, except, alone, what were current accounts, such as rent for his house and servants' wages ; and these he paid at the stated times with the utmost exactness. He gave notice to the tradesmen of the neighbouring market-towns that they should no longer have his custom, if they let any of his servants have any thing without their paying for it. Thus he put it out of his power to commit those imprudences to which those are liable that defer their payments by using their money some other way than where it ought to go. And whatever money he had by him, he knew that it was not demanded elsewhere, but that he might safely employ it as he pleased.

' His example was confined, by the sequestered place of his abode, to the observation of few, though his prudence and virtue would have made it valuable to all who could have known it.—These few particulars, which I knew myself, or have obtained from those who lived with him, may afford instruction, and be an incentive to that wise art of living, which he so successfully practised.' BOS-WELL.

' THE CLUB holds very well together. Monday is my night [1]. I continue to rise tolerably well, and read more than I did. I hope something will yet come on it [2]. I am, Sir,

'Your most affectionate servant,

' SAM. JOHNSON.'

' May 10, 1766,
Johnson's-court, Fleet-street.'

After I had been some time in Scotland, I mentioned to him in a letter that ' On my first return to my native country, after some years of absence, I was told of a vast number of my acquaintance who were all gone to the land of forgetfulness, and I found myself like a man stalking over a field of battle, who every moment perceives some one lying dead.' I complained of irresolution, and mentioned my having made a vow as a security for good conduct. I wrote to him again, without being able to move his indolence ; nor did I hear from him till he had received a copy of my inaugural Exercise, or Thesis in Civil Law, which I published at my admission as an Advocate, as is the custom in Scotland. He then wrote to me as follows :

' To JAMES BOSWELL, ESQ.

' DEAR SIR,

' THE reception of your Thesis put me in mind of my debt to you. Why did you * * * * * * * * * * * * *3. I will punish you for it, by telling you that your Latin wants correction [4]. In the beginning, *Spei alteræ*, not to urge that it should be *primæ*, is not grammatical : *alteræ* should be *alteri*. In the next line you seem to use *genus* absolutely,

---

[1] Of his being in the chair of THE LITERARY CLUB, which at this time met once a week in the evening. BOSWELL. See *ante*, i. 478, note 3.

[2] See *post*, ii. 35, where he told the King that ' he . . . must now read to acquire more knowledge.'

[3] The passage omitted alluded to a private transaction. BOSWELL.

[4] This censure of my Latin relates to the Dedication, which was as follows :

VIRO NOBILISSIMO, ORNATISSIMO,
JOANNI,
VICECOMITI MOUNTSTUART,
ATAVIS EDITO REGIBUS
EXCELSÆ FAMILIÆ DE BUTE SPEI ALTERÆ ;
LABENTE SECULO,
QUUM HOMINES NULLIUS ORIGINIS
GENUS ÆQUARE OPIBUS AGGREDIUNTUR,
SANGUINIS ANTIQUI ET ILLUSTRIS
SEMPER MEMORI,
NATALIUM SPLENDOREM VIRTUTIBUS AUGENTI :

for what we call *family*, that is, for *illustrious extraction*, I doubt without authority. *Homines nullius originis*, for *Nullis orti majoribus*, or, *Nullo loco nati*, is, I am afraid, barbarous.—Ruddiman is dead [1].

' I have now vexed you enough, and will try to please you. Your resolution to obey your father I sincerely approve ; but do not accustom yourself to enchain your volatility by vows : they will sometime leave a thorn in your mind, which you will, perhaps, never be able to extract or eject. Take this warning, it is of great importance [2].

' The study of the law is what you very justly term it, copious and generous [3] ; and in adding your name to its professors, you have done exactly what I always wished, when I wished you best. I hope that you will continue to pursue it vigorously and constantly [4]. You gain, at least, what is no small advantage, security from those troublesome and wearisome discontents, which are always obtruding themselves upon a mind vacant, unemployed, and undetermined.

AD PUBLICA POPULI COMITIA

JAM LEGATO ;

IN OPTIMATIUM VERO MAGNÆ BRITANNIÆ SENATU,

JURE HÆREDITARIO,

OLIM CONSESSURO :

VIM INSITAM VARIA DOCTRINA PROMOVENTE,

NEC TAMEN SE VENDITANTE,

PRÆDITO :

PRISCA FIDE, ANIMO LIBERRIMO,

ET MORUM ELEGANTIA

INSIGNI :

IN ITALIÆ VISITANDÆ ITINERE,

SOCIO SUO HONORATISSIMO,

HASCE JURISPRUDENTIÆ PRIMITIAS

DEVINCTISSIMÆ AMICITIÆ ET OBSERVANTIÆ

MONUMENTUM,

D. D. C Q.[a]

JACOBUS BOSWELL.   BOSWELL.

[1] See *ante*, i. 211.

[2] See *post*, iii. 357, ⟨and *John. Misc.* i. 299⟩.

[3] This alludes to the first sentence of the *Procemium* of my Thesis. 'JURISPRUDENTIÆ *studio nullum uberius, nullum generosius : in legibus enim agitandis, populorum mores, variasque fortunæ vices ex quibus leges oriuntur, contemplari simul solemus.*' BOSWELL.

[4] ' Mr. Boswell,' says Malone, ' professed the Scotch and the English law, but had never taken very great

pains on the subject. His father, Lord Auchinleck, told him one day, that it would cost him more trouble to hide his ignorance, in those professions, than to shew his knowledge. This Mr. B. owned he had found to be true.' *European Magazine*, 1798, p. 376. Boswell wrote to Temple, 18 March, 1775 :—' You are very kind to encourage me by saying that I may overtake you in learning. Believe me, though, I have a kind of impotency of study.' *Letters*, No. 136, i. 214.

[a] (Dat dedicat consecratque)

' You ought to think it no small inducement to diligence and perseverance, that they will please your father. We all live upon the hope of pleasing somebody ; and the pleasure of pleasing ought to be greatest, and at last always will be greatest, when our endeavours are exerted in consequence of our duty.

' Life is not long, and too much of it must not pass in idle deliberation how it shall be spent ; deliberation, which those who begin it by prudence, and continue it with subtilty, must, after long expence of thought, conclude by chance [1]. To prefer one future mode of life to another, upon just reasons, requires faculties which it has not pleased our Creator to give us.

' If, therefore, the profession you have chosen has some unexpected inconveniencies, console yourself by reflecting that no profession is without them ; and that all the importunities and perplexities of business are softness and luxury, compared with the incessant cravings of vacancy, and the unsatisfactory expedients of idleness.

" *Hæc sunt quæ nostrâ potui te voce monere* [2] ;
   Vade, age."

' As to your History of Corsica, you have no materials which others have not, or may not have. You have, somehow [a] or other, warmed your imagination. I wish there were some cure, like the lover's leap, for all heads of which some single idea has obtained an unreasonable and irregular possession. Mind your own affairs, and leave the Corsicans to theirs †. I am, dear Sir,

' Your most humble servant,
                                                              ' SAM. JOHNSON.'
' London, Aug. 21, 1766.'

' To DR. SAMUEL JOHNSON.

                                             ' Auchinleck, Nov. 6, 1766.

' MUCH ESTEEMED AND DEAR SIR,

   ' I PLEAD not guilty to [3] *
* * * * * * * * *.

---

a somehow 1 : somehow, 2, 3.

[1] This is a truth that Johnson often enforced. ' Very few, said the poet, live by choice. Every man is placed in his present condition by causes which acted without his foresight, and with which he did not always willingly co-operate.' *Rasselas*, chap. 16. ' To him that lives well, answered the hermit, every form of life is good ; nor can I give any other rule for choice,

than to remove from all apparent evil.' *Ib.* chap. 21. ' Young man, said Omar, it is of little use to form plans of life.' *The Idler*, No. 101.

[2] ' Hæc sunt quæ nostra *liceat* te voce moneri.' *Æneid*, iii. 461.

[3] The passage omitted explained the transaction to which the preceding letter had alluded. BOSWELL.

† ⟨See *post*, ii. 58–59.⟩

' Having thus, I hope, cleared myself of the charge brought against me, I presume you will not be displeased if I escape the punishment which you have decreed for me unheard. If you have discharged the arrows of criticism against an innocent man, you must rejoice to find they have missed him, or have not been pointed so as to wound him.

' To talk no longer in allegory, I am, with all deference, going to offer a few observations in defence of my Latin, which you have found fault with.

' You think I should have used *spei primæ*, instead of *spei alteræ*. *Spes* is, indeed, often used to express something on which we have a future dependence, as in Virg. Eclog. i. l. 14,

> "———— *modo namque gemellos*
> Spem *gregis ah silice in nudâ connixa reliquit.*"

and in Georg. iii. l. 473,

> " Spemque *gregemque simul,*"

for the lambs and the sheep. Yet it is also used to express any thing on which we have a present dependence, and is well applied to a man of distinguished influence, our support, our refuge, our *præsidium*, as Horace calls Mæcenas. So, Æneid xii. l. 57, Queen Amata addresses her son-in-law Turnus :—" Spes *tu nunc una* : " and he was then no future hope, for she adds,

> " —— *decus imperiumque Latini*
> Te *penes* ; "

which might have been said of my Lord Bute some years ago. Now I consider the present Earl of Bute to be " *Excelsæ familiæ de Bute* spes prima ; " and my Lord Mountstuart, as his eldest son, to be " *spes altera.*" So in Æneid xii. l. 168, after having mentioned Pater Æneas, who was the *present* spes, the *reigning* spes, as my German friends would say, the *spes prima*, the poet adds,

> " *Et juxta Ascanius, magnæ* spes altera *Romæ.*"

' You think *alteræ* ungrammatical, and you tell me it should have been *alteri*. You must recollect, that in old times *alter* was declined regularly ; and when the ancient fragments preserved in the *Juris Civilis Fontes* were written, it was certainly declined in the way that I use it. This, I should think, may protect a lawyer who writes *alteræ* in a dissertation upon part of his own science. But as I could hardly venture to quote fragments of old law to so classical a man as Mr. Johnson, I have not made an accurate search into these remains, to find examples

of what I am able to produce in poetical composition. We find in
Plaut. Rudens, act iii. scene 4,

"*Nam huic* alteræ *patria quæ sit profecto nescio.*"

Plautus is, to be sure, an old comick writer ; but in the days of Scipio
and Lelius, we find, Terent. Heautontim. act ii. scene 3,

"————— *hoc ipsa in itinere* alteræ
Dum narrat, forte audivi."

' You doubt my having authority for using *genus* absolutely, for what
we call *family*, that is, for *illustrious extraction*. Now I take *genus* in
Latin, to have much the same signification with *birth* in English ; both
in their primary meaning expressing simply descent, but both made to
stand κατ᾽ ἐξοχήν, for noble descent. *Genus* is thus used in Hor. lib. ii.
Sat. v. l. 8,

"*Et* genus *et virtus, nisi cum re, vilior alga est.*"

And in lib. i. Epist. vi. l. 37,

"*Et* genus *et formam Regina pecunia donat.*"

And in the celebrated contest between Ajax and Ulysses, Ovid's
Metamorph. lib. xiii. l. 140,

"*Nam* genus *et proavos, et quæ non fecimus ipsi,*
Vix ea nostra voco."

' *Homines nullius originis*, for *nullis orti majoribus*, or *nullo loco nati*,
is, you are " afraid, barbarous."

' *Origo* is used to signify extraction, as in Virg. Æneid i. l. 286,

"*Nascetur pulchrâ Trojanus origine Cæsar.*"

And in Æneid x. l. 618,

"*Ille tamen nostrâ deducit* origine *nomen.*"

And as *nullus* is used for obscure, is it not in the genius of the Latin
language to write *nullius originis*, for obscure extraction ?

' I have defended myself as well as I could.

' Might I venture to differ from you with regard to the utility of vows?
I am sensible that it would be very dangerous to make vows rashly,
and without a due consideration. But I cannot help thinking that they
may often be of great advantage to one of a variable judgement and
irregular inclinations. I always remember a passage in one of your
letters to our Italian friend Baretti ; where talking of the monastick life,
you say you do not wonder that serious men should put themselves under
the protection of a religious order, when they have found how unable

they are to take care of themselves [1]. For my own part, without affecting to be a Socrates, I am sure I have a more than ordinary struggle to
maintain with *the Evil Principle ;* and all the methods I can devise are
little enough to keep me tolerably steady in the paths of rectitude.

*   *   *   *   *   *   *

' I am ever, with the highest veneration,
                ' Your affectionate humble servant,
                                ' JAMES BOSWELL.'

It appears from Johnson's diary, that he was this year at Mr.
Thrale's, from before Midsummer till after Michaelmas, and that
he afterwards passed a month at Oxford§. He had then contracted a great intimacy with Mr. Chambers of that University,
afterwards Sir Robert Chambers, one of the Judges in India [2].

He published nothing this year in his own name ; but the noble
dedication [3] * to the King, of Gwyn's ' London and Westminster
Improved,' was written by him ; and he furnished the Preface,†
and several of the pieces, which compose a volume of Miscellanies by Mrs. Anna Williams, the blind lady who had an
asylum in his house. Of these, there are his ' Epitaph on Philips [4] ;' *
' Translation of a Latin Epitaph on Sir Thomas Hanmer [5] ;' †
' Friendship, an Ode [6] ;' * and, ' The Ant,' * a paraphrase from the
Proverbs, of which I have a copy in his own hand-writing ; and,
from internal evidence, I ascribe to him, ' To Miss —— on her
giving the Authour a gold and silk net-work Purse of her own
weaving [7] ; ' † and, ' The happy Life [8].' †—Most of the pieces in

[1] See *ante*, i. 365.

[2] Mr. Croker says :—' It was by
visiting Chambers, when a fellow of
University College, that Johnson became acquainted with Lord Stowell
[at that time William Scott] ; and
when Chambers went to India, Lord
Stowell, as he expressed it to me,
seemed to succeed to his place in
Johnson's friendship.' Croker's *Boswell*, p. 90, note. John Scott (Earl
of Eldon), Sir William Jones and
Mr. Windham, were also members
of University College. An engraving
of Johnson is in the Common Room.
   § 〈He returned to London, Sat.
8 Nov. *Letters*, No. 187.〉

[3] It is not easy to discover any-
thing noble or even felicitous in this
Dedication. *Works*, v. 444. 〈See
App. B, p. 479.〉

[4] See *ante*, i. 148.

[5] See *ante*, i. 177, note 2.

[6] See *ante*, i. 158 and 534.

[7] See *ante*, i. 178, note 2.

[8] This poem is scarcely Johnson's,
though all the lines but the third in
the following couplets may be his.
' Whose life not sunk in sloth is free
       from care,
Nor tost by change, nor stagnant in
       despair ; . . .
Who with wise authors pass the in-
       structive day,

this volume have evidently received additions from his superiour pen, particularly ' Verses to Mr. Richardson, on his Sir Charles Grandison ; ' ' The Excursion ; ' ' Reflections on a Grave digging in Westminster Abbey ¹.' There is in this collection a poem ' On the Death of Stephen Grey, the Electrician ; ' * which, on reading it, appeared to me to be undoubtedly Johnson's. I asked Mrs. Williams whether it was not his. ' Sir, (said she, with some warmth,) I wrote that poem before I had the honour of Dr. Johnson's acquaintance.' I, however, was so much impressed with my first notion, that I mentioned it to Johnson, repeating, at the same time, what Mrs. Williams had said. His answer was, ' It is true, Sir, that she wrote it before she was acquainted with me ; but she has not told you that I wrote it all over again, except two lines ².' ' The Fountains,' † a beautiful little Fairy tale in prose, written with exquisite simplicity, is one of Johnson's productions ; and I cannot with-hold from Mrs. Thrale the praise of being the authour of that admirable poem, ' The Three Warnings.'

He wrote this year a letter, not intended for publication, which has, perhaps, as strong marks of his sentiment and style, as any of his compositions. The original is in my possession. It is addressed to the late Mr. William Drummond, bookseller in Edinburgh, a gentleman of good family, but small estate, who took arms for the house of Stuart in 1745 ; and during his

---

And wonder how the moments stole
    away ; . . .
Who not retir'd beyond the sight of
    life,
Behold its weary cares, its noisy
    strife.'—p. 18.
¹ Johnson's additions to these three poems are not at all evident.
² In a note to the poem it is stated that Miss Williams, when, before her blindness ' she was assisting Mr. Grey in his experiments, was the first that observed and notified the emission of the electrical spark from a human body.' The best lines are the following :—
Now, hoary Sage, pursue thy happy
    flight,

With swifter motion haste to purer
    light,
Where Bacon waits with Newton and
    with Boyle
To hail thy genius, and applaud thy
    toil ;
Where intuition breaks through time
    and space,
And mocks experiment's successive
    race ;
Sees tardy Science toil at Nature's
    laws,
And wonders how th' effect obscures
    the cause.
Yet not to deep research or happy
    guess
Is ow'd the life of hope, the death of
    peace.' p.42. ⟨See App. B, p. 480.⟩

concealment in London till the act of general pardon came out, obtained the acquaintance of Dr. Johnson, who justly esteemed him as a very worthy man. It seems, some of the members of the society in Scotland for propagating Christian knowledge, had opposed the scheme of translating the holy scriptures into the Erse or Gaelick language, from political considerations of the disadvantage of keeping up the distinction between the High- landers and the other inhabitants of North-Britain. Dr. Johnson being informed of this, I suppose by Mr. Drummond, wrote with a generous indignation as follows :

'To Mr. William Drummond.

' Sir,
' I did not expect to hear that it could be, in an assembly convened for the propagation of Christian knowledge, a question whether any nation uninstructed in religion should receive instruction ; or whether that instruction should be imparted to them by a translation of the holy books into their own language. If obedience to the will of God be necessary to happiness, and knowledge of his will be necessary to obedience, I know not how he that with-holds this knowledge, or delays it, can be said to love his neighbour as himself. He that voluntarily continues ignorance, is guilty of all the crimes which ignorance pro- duces ; as to him that should extinguish the tapers of a light-house, might justly be imputed the calamities of shipwrecks. Christianity is the highest perfection of humanity ; and as no man is good but as he wishes the good of others, no man can be good in the highest degree, who wishes not to others the largest measures of the greatest good. To omit for a year, or for a day, the most efficacious method of advancing Christianity, in compliance with any purposes that terminate on this side of the grave, is a crime of which I know not that the world has yet had an example, except in the practice of the planters of America [1], a race of mortals whom, I suppose, no other man wishes to resemble [2].

' The Papists have, indeed, denied to the laity the use of the bible ; but this prohibition, in few places now very rigorously enforced, is

[1] A gentleman, writing from Vir- ginia to John Wesley, in 1755, about the need of educating the negro slaves in religion, says :—' Their masters generally neglect them, as though immortality was not the privilege of their souls in common with their own.' Wesley's *Journal*, 27 July, iv. 125. But much nearer home Johnson might have found this criminal enforcement of ignorance. Burke, writing in 1779, about the Irish, accuses the legislature of ' condemning a million and a half of people to ignorance, according to act of parliament.' Burke's *Corres*. ii. 294.

[2] See *post*, ii. 312 and App. A.

defended by arguments, which have for their foundation the care of souls. To obscure, upon motives merely political, the light of revelation, is a practice reserved for the reformed ; and, surely, the blackest midnight of popery is meridian sunshine to such a reformation. I am not very willing that any language should be totally extinguished. The similitude and derivation of languages afford the most indubitable proof of the traduction of nations, and the genealogy of mankind [1]. They add often physical certainty to historical evidence ; and often supply the only evidence of ancient migrations, and of the revolutions of ages which left no written monuments behind them.

' Every man's opinions, at least his desires, are a little influenced by his favourite studies. My zeal for languages may seem, perhaps, rather over-heated, even to those by whom I desire to be well-esteemed. To those who have nothing in their thoughts but trade or policy, present power, or present money, I should not think it necessary to defend my opinions ; but with men of letters I would not unwillingly compound, by wishing the continuance of every language, however narrow in its extent, or however incommodious for common purposes, till it is re- posited in some version of a known book, that it may be always hereafter examined and compared with other languages, and then permitting its disuse. For this purpose, the translation of the bible is most to be desired. It is not certain that the same method will not preserve the Highland language, for the purposes of learning, and abolish it from daily use. When the Highlanders read the Bible, they will naturally wish to have its obscurities cleared, and to know the history, collateral or appendant. Knowledge always desires increase : it is like fire, which must first be kindled by some external agent, but which will afterwards propagate itself. When they once desire to learn, they will naturally have recourse to the nearest language by which that desire can be grati- fied ; and one will tell another that if he would attain knowledge, he must learn English.

' This speculation may, perhaps, be thought more subtle than the grossness of real life will easily admit. Let it, however, be remembered, that the efficacy of ignorance has been long tried, and has not produced the consequence expected. Let knowledge, therefore, take its turn ; and let the patrons of privation stand awhile aside, and admit the operation of positive principles.

' You will be pleased, Sir, to assure the worthy man who is employed in the new translation [2], that he has my wishes for his success ; and if

---

[1] Johnson said very finely :—' Lan- guages are the pedigree of nations.' *Post*, v. 225.

[2] The Rev. Mr. John Campbell, Minister of the Parish of Kippen, near Stirling, who has lately favoured me with a long, intelligent, and very obliging letter upon this work, makes

here or at Oxford I can be of any use, that I shall think it more than honour to promote his undertaking.

' I am sorry that I delayed so long to write.

' I am, Sir,

' Your most humble servant,

' SAM. JOHNSON.'

' Johnson's-court, Fleet-street,
    Aug. 13, 1766.'

The opponents of this pious scheme being made ashamed of their conduct, the benevolent undertaking was allowed to go on [1].

The following letters, though not written till the year after, being chiefly upon the same subject, are here inserted.

' To MR. WILLIAM DRUMMOND.

' DEAR SIR,

' THAT my letter should have had such effects as you mention, gives me great pleasure. I hope you do not flatter me by imputing to me more good than I have really done. Those whom my arguments have persuaded to change their opinion, show such modesty and candour as deserve great praise.

' I hope the worthy translator goes diligently forward. He has a higher reward in prospect than any honours which this world can bestow. I wish I could be useful to him.

' The publication of my letter, if it could be of use in a cause to which all other causes are nothing, I should not prohibit. But first, I would have you consider whether the publication will really do any

the following remark. ' Dr. Johnson has alluded to the worthy man employed in the translation of the New Testament. Might not this have afforded you an opportunity of paying a proper tribute of respect to the memory of the Rev. Mr. James Stuart, late Minister of Killin, distinguished by his eminent Piety, Learning and Taste ? The amiable simplicity of his life, his warm benevolence, his indefatigable and successful exertions for civilizing and improving the Parish of which he was Minister for upwards of fifty years, entitle him to the gratitude of his country, and the veneration of all good men. It certainly would be a pity, if such a character should be permitted to sink into oblivion.' BOSWELL.

⟨Stuart died in 1789, aged 89. For his translation, see *post*, App. B, p. 508.⟩

[1] Seven years later Johnson received from the Society the New Testament and other works in Erse. See *post*, ii. 279. Yet in his *Journey to the Western Islands* (1924, p. 94), he had to record of the parochial schools in those islands that ' by the rule of their institution, they teach only *English*, so that the natives read a language which they may never use or understand.'

good ; next, whether by printing and distributing a very small number, you may not attain all that you propose ; and, what perhaps I should have said first, whether the letter, which I do not now perfectly remember, be fit to be printed.

' If you can consult Dr. Robertson, to whom I am a little known, I shall be satisfied about the propriety of whatever he shall direct. If he thinks that it should be printed, I entreat him to revise it ; there may, perhaps, be some negligent lines written, and whatever is amiss, he knows very well how to rectify ¹.

' Be pleased to let me know, from time to time, how this excellent design goes forward.

' Make my compliments to young Mr. Drummond, whom I hope you will live to see such as you desire him.

' I have not lately seen Mr. Elphinston ², but believe him to be prosperous. I shall be glad to hear the same of you, for I am, Sir,

' Your affectionate humble servant,

' SAM. JOHNSON.'

' Johnson's-court, Fleet-street,
April 21, 1767.'

' TO THE SAME.

' SIR,

' I RETURNED this week from the country, after an absence of near six months, and found your letter with many others, which I should have answered sooner, if I had sooner seen them.

' Dr. Robertson's opinion was surely right. Men should not be told of the faults which they have mended. I am glad the old language is taught, and honour the translator as a man whom GOD has distinguished by the high office of propagating his word.

' I must take the liberty of engaging you in an office of charity. Mrs. Heely ³, the wife of Mr. Heely, who had lately some office in your theatre, is my near relation, and now in great distress. They wrote me word of their situation some time ago, to which I returned them an answer which raised hopes of more than it is proper for me to give them. Their representation of their affairs I have discovered to be such as cannot be trusted ; and at this distance, though their case requires haste, I know not how to act. She, or her daughters, may be heard of at Canongate Head. I must beg, Sir, that you will enquire after them, and let me know what is to be done. I am willing to go to ten pounds,

---

¹ This paragraph shews Johnson's real estimation of the character and abilities of the celebrated Scottish Historian, however lightly, in a mo- ment of caprice, he may have spoken of his works. BOSWELL.

² See *ante*, i. 210.

³ ⟨See *post*, App. B, p. 480.⟩

and will transmit you such a sum, if upon examination you find it likely
to be of use. If they are in immediate want, advance them what you
think proper. What I could do, I would do for the women, having no
great reason to pay much regard to Heely himself [1].

' I believe you may receive some intelligence from Mrs. Baker, of the
theatre, whose letter I received at the same time with yours ; and to
whom, if you see her, you will make my excuse for the seeming neglect
of answering her.

' Whatever you advance within ten pounds shall be immediately returned to you, or paid as you shall order. I trust wholly to your judgement.

' I am, Sir, &c.
' SAM. JOHNSON.'

' London, Johnson's-court, Fleet-street,
  Oct. 24, 1767.'

Mr. Cuthbert Shaw [2], alike distinguished by his genius, misfortunes, and misconduct, published this year a poem, called ' The
Race, by Mercurius Spur, Esq. [3] ' in which he whimsically made
the living poets of England contend for pre-eminence of fame by
running :

 ' Prove by their heels the prowess of the head.'

In this poem there was the following portrait of Johnson :

 ' Here Johnson comes,—unblest with outward grace,
 His rigid morals stamp'd upon his face.
 While strong conceptions struggle in his brain ;
 (For even Wit is brought to-bed with pain :)
 To view him, porters with their loads would rest,

[1] This is the person concerning whom Sir John Hawkins has thrown out very unwarrantable reflections both against Dr. Johnson and Mr. Francis Barber. BOSWELL. See *post*, iv. 370–1. In 1775, Heely applied through Johnson for the post that was soon to be vacant of ' master of the tap ' at Ranelagh House. ' He seems,' wrote Johnson, ' to have a genius for an alehouse.' *Letters*, No. 370. 〈He obtained the post, but resigned it. Hawkins's *Life*, 601.〉

[2] See an account of him in the European Magazine, Jan. 1786. BOSWELL.

There we learn that he was in his time a grammar-school usher, actor, poet, the puffing partner in a quack medicine, and tutor to a youthful Earl. He was suspected of levying blackmail by threats of satiric publica-tions, and he suffered from a disease which rendered him an object almost offensive to sight. He was born in 1739, and died in 1771. 〈See *D.N.B.*〉

[3] 〈It was published in 1765, a second and enlarged edition appearing in 1766. For Johnson's comment on the ' portrait ' see *post*, App. B, p. 480.〉

And babes cling frighted to the nurse's breast.
With looks convuls'd, he roars in pompous strain,
And, like an angry lion, shakes his mane.
The Nine, with terror struck, who ne'er had seen,
Aught human with so horrible a mien,
Debating whether they should stay or run,
Virtue steps forth, and claims him for her son.
With gentle speech she warns him now to yield,
Nor stain his glories in the doubtful field ;
But wrapt in conscious worth, content sit down,
Since Fame, resolv'd his various pleas to crown,
Though forc'd his present claim to disavow,
Had long reserv'd a chaplet for his brow.
He bows, obeys ; for Time shall first expire,
Ere Johnson stay, when Virtue bids retire.'

The Honourable Thomas Hervey [1] and his lady having unhappily disagreed, and being about to separate, Johnson interfered
as their friend, and wrote him a letter of expostulation, which I
have not been able to find ; but the substance of it is ascertained
by a letter to Johnson,[a] in answer to it, which Mr. Hervey printed.
The occasion of this correspondence between Dr. Johnson and
Mr. Hervey, was thus related to me by Mr. Beauclerk [2]. ' Tom
Hervey had a great liking for Johnson, and in his will had left
him a legacy of fifty pounds. One day he said to me, " Johnson
may want this money now, more than afterwards. I have a
mind to give it him directly. Will you be so good as to carry a
fifty pound note from me to him ? " This I positively refused to
do, as he might, perhaps, have knocked me down for insulting
him, and have afterwards put the note in his pocket. But I said,
if Hervey would write him a letter, and enclose a fifty pound
note, I should take care to deliver it. He accordingly did write
him a letter, mentioning that he was only paying a legacy a little
sooner. To his letter he added, " *P.S. I am going to part with my
wife.*" Johnson then wrote to him, saying nothing of the note,
but remonstrating with him against parting with his wife.'

a Johnson, 1, 2 : Johnson 3.

[1] The Hon. Thomas Hervey, whose
Letter to Sir Thomas Hanmer in 1742
was much read at that time. He was the
second son of John, first Earl of Bristol,
and one of the brothers of Johnson's
early friend, Henry Hervey. He died

Jan. 20, 1775. MALONE. See *post*, ii. 341.
[2] See *post*, iii. 194–5, for another
story told at the same time by Beauclerk against Johnson of Henry Hervey. ⟨See also Boswell's *Note Book*,
1925, p. 15 ; and *post*, App. B, p. 480.⟩

When I mentioned † to Johnson this story, in as delicate terms as I could, he told me that the fifty pound note was given to him by Mr. Hervey in consideration of his having written for him a pamphlet against Sir Charles Hanbury Williams, who, Mr. Hervey imagined, was the authour of an attack upon him ; but that it was afterwards discovered to be the work of a garreteer who wrote ' The Fool ' [1] : the pamphlet therefore against Sir Charles was not printed [2].

In February, 1767, there happened one of the most remarkable incidents of Johnson's life, which gratified his monarchical enthusiasm, and which he loved to relate with all its circumstances, when requested by his friends. This was his being honoured by a private conversation with his Majesty, in the library at the Queen's house [3]. He had frequently visited those splendid rooms and noble collection of books [4], which he used to say was more numerous and curious than he supposed any person could have made in the time which the King had employed. Mr. Barnard, the librarian, took care that he should have every accommodation

---

[1] ⟨Essays published in 1746–7 in the *Daily Gazetteer* and in 1748 collected into two vols. According to a note in Alex. Chalmers's copy they were by William Horsley. See *Hope Catalogue*, p. 73, and Croker's *Boswell*.⟩

[2] Mr. Croker regrets that Johnson employed his pen for hire in Hervey's ' disgusting squabbles,' and in a long note describes Hervey's letter to Sir Thomas Hanmer with whose wife he had eloped. But the attack to which Johnson was hired to reply was not made by Hanmer, but, as was supposed, by Sir C. H. Williams. Because a man has wronged another, he is not therefore to submit to the attacks of a third. Williams, moreover, it must be remembered, was himself a man of licentious character.

[3] Buckingham House, bought in 1761, by George III, and settled on Queen Charlotte. The present Buckingham Palace occupies the site. P. CUNNINGHAM. Here, according to Hawkins (*Life*, p. 470), Johnson met the Prince of Wales (George IV) when a child, ' and enquired as to

his knowledge of the Scriptures : the prince, in his answers, gave him great satisfaction.' Horace Walpole, writing of the Prince at the age of nineteen, says (*Journal of the Reign of George III*, ii. 503) :—' Nothing was coarser than his conversation and phrases ; and it made men smile to find that in the palace of piety and pride his Royal Highness had learnt nothing but the dialect of footmen and grooms.'

[4] Dr. Johnson had the honour of contributing his assistance towards the formation of this library ; for I have read a long letter from him to Mr. Barnard, giving the most masterly instructions on the subject. I wished much to have gratified my readers with the perusal of this letter, and have reason to think that his Majesty would have been graciously pleased to permit its publication ; but Mr. Barnard, to whom I applied, declined it ' on his own account.' BOSWELL.

⟨It is No. 206 of Dr. Hill's edition.⟩

† ⟨Sept. 1777. Boswell's *Note Book*, p. 15.⟩

that could contribute to his ease and convenience, while indulging his literary taste in that place ; so that he had here a very agreeable resource at leisure hours.

His Majesty having been informed of his occasional visits, was pleased to signify a desire that he should be told when Dr. Johnson came next to the library. Accordingly, the next time that Johnson did come, as soon as he was fairly engaged with a book, on which, while he sat by the fire, he seemed quite intent, Mr. Barnard stole round to the apartment where the King was, and, in obedience to his Majesty's commands, mentioned that Dr. Johnson was then in the library. His Majesty said he was at leisure, and would go to him ; upon which Mr. Barnard took one of the candles that stood on the King's table, and lighted his Majesty through a suite of rooms, till they came to a private door into the library, of which his Majesty had the key. Being entered, Mr. Barnard stepped forward hastily to Dr. Johnson, who was still in a profound study, and whispered him, ' Sir, here is the King.' Johnson started up, and stood still. His Majesty approached him, and at once was courteously easy [1].

[1] The particulars of this conversation I have been at great pains to collect with the utmost authenticity, from Dr. Johnson's own detail to myself ; from Mr. Langton, who was present when he gave an account of it to Dr. Joseph Warton, and several other friends, at Sir Joshua Reynolds's ; from Mr. Barnard ; from the copy of a letter written by the late Mr. Strahan the printer, to Bishop Warburton ; and from a minute, the original of which is among the papers of the late Sir James Caldwell, and a copy of which was most obligingly obtained for me from his son Sir John Caldwell, by Sir Francis Lumm. To all these gentlemen I beg leave to make my grateful acknowledgements, and particularly to Sir Francis Lumm, who was pleased to take a great deal of trouble, and even had the minute laid before the King by Lord Caermarthen, now Duke of Leeds, then one of his Majesty's Principal Secretaries of State, who announced to Sir Francis the Royal pleasure concerning it by a letter, in these words : ' I have the King's commands to assure you, Sir, how sensible his Majesty is of your attention in communicating the minute of the conversation previous to its publication. As there appears no objection to your complying with Mr. Boswell's wishes on the subject, you are at full liberty to deliver it to that gentleman, to make such use of in his Life of Dr. Johnson, as he may think proper.' BOSWELL.

In 1790, Boswell published in a quarto sheet of eight pages *A Conversation between His Most Sacred Majesty George III. and Samuel Johnson, LLD. Illustrated with Observations. By James Boswell, Esq. London. Printed by Henry Baldwin, for Charles Dilly, in the Poultry. MDCCXC. Price Half a Guinea. Entered in the Hall-Book of the Company of Stationers*. It is of the same impression as the first edition of the *Life*. ⟨See App. B, p. 480.⟩

His Majesty began by observing, that he understood he came sometimes to the library ; and then mentioning his having heard that the Doctor had been lately at Oxford [1], asked him if he was not fond of going thither. To which Johnson answered, that he was indeed fond of going to Oxford sometimes, but was likewise glad to come back again. The King then asked him what they were doing at Oxford. Johnson answered, he could not much commend their diligence, but that in some respects they were mended, for they had put their press under better regulations, and were at that time printing Polybius. He was then asked whether there were better libraries at Oxford or Cambridge. He answered, he believed the Bodleian was larger than any they had at Cambridge ; at the same time adding, ' I hope, whether we have more books or not than they have at Cambridge, we shall make as good use of them as they do.' Being asked whether All-Souls or Christ-Church library [2] was the largest, he answered, ' All-Souls library is the largest we have, except the Bodleian.' ' Aye, (said the King,) that is the publick library.'

His Majesty enquired if he was then writing any thing. He answered, he was not, for he had pretty well told the world what he knew, and must now read to acquire more knowledge [3]. The King, as it should seem with a view to urge him to rely on his own stores as an original writer, and to continue his labours [4], then said,[a] ' I do not think you borrow much from any body.' Johnson said, he thought he had already done his part as a writer. ' I should have thought so too, (said the King,) if you had not written so well.'—Johnson observed to me, upon this, that ' No man could have paid a handsomer compliment ; and it was fit for a King to pay. It was decisive.' When asked by another friend, at Sir Joshua Reynolds's, whether he made any reply to this high compliment, he answered, ' No, Sir. When the King had said it, it was to be so. It was not for me to bandy civilities with my Sovereign [5].' Perhaps no man who had spent his whole

a said, 1 : said 2, 3.

[1] After Michaelmas, 1766. See *ante*, ii. 25.

[2] See *post*, ii. 67, note 2.

[3] Writing to Langton, on May 10, of the year before, he had said, ' I . . . read more than I did. I hope something will yet come on it.' *Ante*, ii. 20.

[4] Boswell and Goldsmith had in like manner urged him ' to continue his labours.' See *ante*, i. 398, ii. 15, and *post*, ii. 441.

[5] Johnson had written to Lord

life in courts could have shewn a more nice and dignified sense of true politeness, than Johnson did in this instance.

His Majesty having observed to him that he supposed he must have read a great deal ; Johnson answered, that he thought more than he read [1] ; that he had read a great deal in the early part of his life, but having fallen into ill health, he had not been able to read much, compared with others : for instance, he said he had not read much, compared with Dr. Warburton [2]. Upon which the King said, that he heard Dr. Warburton was a man of such general knowledge, that you could scarce talk with him on any subject on which he was not qualified to speak ; and that his

Chesterfield in the *Plan of his Dictionary* (*Works*, v. 19), ' Ausonius thought that modesty forbad him to plead inability for a task to which Cæsar had judged him equal : *Cur me posse negem posse quod ille putat ?*' We may compare also a passage in Mme. D'Arblay's *Diary* (ii. 377) :— ' THE KING. " I believe there is no constraint to be put upon real genius ; nothing but inclination can set it to work. Miss Burney, however, knows best." And then, hastily returning to me, he cried, " What ? what ? " " No, sir, I—I—believe not, certainly," quoth I, very awkwardly, for I seemed taking a violent compliment only as my due ; but I knew not how to put him off as I would another person.'

[1] In one part of the character of Pope (*Life of Pope*, 291), Johnson seems to be describing himself :—' He certainly was in his early life a man of great literary curiosity, and when he wrote his *Essay on Criticism* had, for his age, a very wide acquaintance with books. When he entered into the living world, it seems to have happened to him as to many others, that he was less attentive to dead masters ; he studied in the academy of Paracelsus, and made the universe his favourite volume. . . . His frequent references to history, his allusions to various kinds of knowledge, and his

images selected from art and nature, with his observations on the operations of the mind and the modes of life, shew an intelligence perpetually on the wing, excursive, vigorous, and diligent, eager to pursue knowledge, and attentive to retain it.' See *ante*, i. 57.

[2] Johnson thus describes Warburton (*Pope*, 184) :—' About this time [1732] Warburton began to make his appearance in the first ranks of learning. He was a man of vigorous faculties, a mind fervid and vehement, supplied by incessant and unlimited enquiry, with wonderful extent and variety of knowledge.' Cradock (*Memoirs*, i. 188) says that ' Mr. [= Bp.] Hurd always wondered where it was possible for Warburton to meet with certain anecdotes, with which not only his conversation, but likewise his writings frequently abounded. " I could have readily informed him," replied Mrs. Warburton, " for, when we passed our winters in London, he would often, after his long and severe studies, send out for a whole basketfull of books from the circulating libraries ; and at times I have gone into his study, and found him laughing, though alone." ' Lord Macaulay was, in this respect, the Warburton of our age. ⟨See *Johnsonian Miscellanies*, ii. 15.⟩

learning resembled Garrick's acting, in its universality [1]. His
Majesty then talked of the controversy between Warburton and
Lowth, which he seemed to have read, and asked Johnson what
he thought of it. Johnson answered, ' Warburton has most
general, most scholastick learning ; Lowth is the more correct
scholar. I do not know which of them calls names best.' The
King was pleased to say he was of the same opinion ; adding,
' You do not think then, Dr. Johnson, that there was much argument in the case.' Johnson said, he did not think there was [2].
' Why truly, (said the King,) when once it comes to calling names,
argument is pretty well at an end.'

His Majesty then asked him what he thought of Lord Lyttel-

---

[1] The Reverend Mr. Strahan clearly
recollects having been told by Johnson, that the King observed that Pope
made Warburton a Bishop. ' True,
Sir, (said Johnson,) but Warburton
did more for Pope ; he made him
a Christian : ' alluding, no doubt, to
his ingenious Comments on the ' Essay
on Man.' BOSWELL.

The statements both of the King
and Johnson are supported by two
passages in Johnson's *Life of Pope*
(190, 194). He says of Warburton's
Comments :—' Pope, who probably
began to doubt the tendency of his
own work, was glad that the positions,
of which he perceived himself not to
know the full meaning, could by any
mode of interpretation be made to
mean well. . . . From this time Pope
lived in the closest intimacy with his
commentator, and amply rewarded his
kindness and his zeal ; for he introduced him to Mr. Murray, by whose
interest he became preacher at Lincoln's Inn, and to Mr. Allen, who
gave him his niece and his estate, and
by consequence a bishoprick.' See
also the account given by Johnson, in
Boswell's *Hebrides, post*, v. 80. Bishop
Law in his Revised Preface to Archbishop King's *Origin of Evil* (1781),
p. xvii, writes :—' I had now the satis-

faction of seeing that those very
principles which had been maintained
by Archb. King were adopted by Mr.
Pope in his Essay on Man ; this I
used to recollect, and sometimes
relate, with pleasure, conceiving that
such an account did no less honour
to the poet than to our philosopher ;
but was soon made to understand
that anything of that kind was taken
highly amiss by one [Warburton] who
had once held the doctrine of that
same Essay to be rank *Atheism*, but
afterwards turned a warm advocate
for it, and thought proper to deny the
account above-mentioned, with heavy
menaces against those who presumed
to insinuate that Pope borrowed any
thing from any man whatsoever.' See
post, iii. 402.

[2] In Gibbon's *Memoirs* (p. 49), a
fine passage is quoted from Lowth's
Defence of the University of Oxford,
against Warburton's reproaches. ' I
transcribe with pleasure this eloquent
passage,' writes Gibbon, ' without inquiring, whether in this angry controversy the spirit of Lowth himself
is purified from the intolerant zeal,
which Warburton had ascribed to the
genius of the place.' See *post*, v.
125.

ton's history, which was then just published [1]. Johnson said, he thought his style pretty good, but that he had blamed Henry the Second rather too much. ' Why, (said the King), they seldom do these things by halves.' ' No, Sir, (answered Johnson), not to Kings.' But fearing to be misunderstood, he proceeded to explain himself ; and immediately subjoined, ' That for those who spoke worse of Kings than they deserved, he could find no excuse ; but that he could more easily conceive how some might speak better of them than they deserved, without any ill intention ; for, as Kings had much in their power to give, those who were favoured by them would frequently, from gratitude, exaggerate their praises ; and as this proceeded from a good motive, it was certainly excuseable, as far as errour could be excuseable.'

The King then asked him what he thought of Dr. Hill [2]. Johnson answered, that he was an ingenious man, but had no veracity ; and immediately mentioned, as an instance of it, an assertion of that writer, that he had seen objects magnified to a much greater degree by using three or four microscopes at a time, than by using one. ' Now, (added Johnson,) every one

---

[1] See *post*, ii. 221, where Johnson says that Lyttelton ' is obliged in his History to write the most vulgar Whiggism,' and iii. 32. ⟨See also Johnson's *Lyttelton*, 19.⟩ Gibbon, who had reviewed it this year, says in his *Memoirs* (p. 173) : ' The public has ratified my judgment of that voluminous work, in which sense and learning are not illuminated by a ray of genius.'

[2] Hawkins says of him (*Life*, p. 211) :—' He obtained, from one of those universities which would scarce refuse a degree to an apothecary's horse, a diploma for that of doctor of physic.' He became a great compiler and in one year earned £1500. In the end he turned quack-doctor. He was knighted by the King of Sweden ' in return for a present to that monarch of his " Vegetable System " ' (*Ib.* 213). He at least thrice attacked Garrick (Murphy's *Garrick*, pp. 136, 189, 212), who replied with three epigrams, of which the last is well-known :—

' For *Farces* and *Physic*, his equal there scarce is ;
His *Farces* are *Physic*, his *Physic* a *Farce* is.'

Walpole (*Letters*, v. 15), writing on Jan. 3, 1761, said :—' Would you believe, what I know is fact, that Dr. Hill earned fifteen guineas a week by working for wholesale dealers ? he was at once employed on six voluminous works of botany, husbandry, &c., published weekly.' Churchill in the *Rosciad* (lines 111–114) thus writes of him :—

' Who could so nobly grace the motley list,
Actor, Inspector, Doctor, Botanist ?
Knows any one so well—sure no one knows,—
At once to play, prescribe, compound, compose ? '

In the *Gent. Mag.* xxii. 568, it is stated that he had acted pantomime, tragedy and comedy, and had been damned in all.

acquainted with microscopes knows, that the more of them he looks through, the less the object will appear.' ' Why, (replied the King,) this is not only telling an untruth, but telling it clumsily; for, if that be the case, every one who can look through a microscope will be able to detect him [1].'

' I now, (said Johnson to his friends, when relating what had passed,) began to consider that I was depreciating this man in the estimation of his Sovereign, and thought it was time for me to say something that might be more favourable.' He added, therefore, that Dr. Hill was, notwithstanding, a very curious observer ; and if he would have been contented to tell the world no more than he knew, he might have been a very considerable man, and needed not to have recourse to such mean expedients to raise his reputation [2].

The King then talked of literary journals, mentioned particularly the *Journal des Savans*, and asked Johnson if it was well done. Johnson said, it was formerly very well done, and gave some account of the persons who began it, and carried it on for some years ; enlarging, at the same time, on the nature and use of such works. The King asked him if it was well done now. Johnson answered, he had no reason to think that it was [3]. The King then asked him if there were any other literary journals published in this kingdom, except the Monthly and Critical Reviews [4] ; and on being answered there were no other, his

---

[1] Mr. Croker quotes Bishop Elrington, who says, ' Dr. Johnson was unjust to Hill, and showed that *he* did not understand the subject.' Croker's *Boswell*, p. 186.

[2] D'Israeli (*Curiosities of Literature*, ed. 1834, i. 201) says that ' Hill, once when he fell sick, owned to a friend that he had over fatigued himself with writing seven works at once ! one of which was on architecture, and another on cookery.' D'Israeli adds that Hill contracted to translate a Dutch work on insects for fifty guineas. As he was ignorant of the language, he bargained with another translator for twenty-five guineas. This man, who was equally ignorant,

rebargained with a third, who perfectly understood his original, for twelve guineas.

[3] Gibbon (*Misc. Works*, v. 442), writing on Dec. 20, 1763, of the *Journal des Savans*, says :—' I can hardly express how much I am delighted with this Journal ; its characteristics are erudition, precision, and taste. . . . This Journal, the father of all the rest, is still their superior. . . . There is nothing to be wished for in this Journal but a little more boldness and philosophy ; but it is published under the Chancellor's eye.'

[4] Goldsmith, in his *Present State of Polite Learning* (ch. xi.), published in 1759, says :—' We have two literary

Majesty asked which of them was the best : Johnson answered,
that the Monthly Review was done with most care, the Critical
upon the best principles ; adding that the authours of the Monthly
Review were enemies to the Church [1]. This the King said he
was sorry to hear.

The conversation next turned on the Philosophical Transactions, when Johnson observed, that they had now a better
method of arranging their materials than formerly. ' Aye, (said
the King,) they are obliged to Dr. Johnson for that ; ' for his
Majesty had heard and remembered the circumstance, which
Johnson himself had forgot [2].

His Majesty expressed a desire to have the literary biography
of this country ably executed, and proposed to Dr. Johnson to
undertake it. Johnson signified his readiness to comply with his
Majesty's wishes.

During the whole of this interview, Johnson talked to his
Majesty with profound respect, but still in his firm manly
manner, with a sonorous voice, and never in that subdued tone
which is commonly used at the levee and in the drawing-room [3].
After the King withdrew, Johnson shewed himself highly pleased
with his Majesty's conversation [a] and gracious behaviour. He
said to Mr. Barnard, ' Sir, they may talk of the King as they will ;
but he is the finest gentleman I have ever seen [4].' And he after-

[a] conversation 1, 2 : conversation, 3.

reviews in London, with critical news-
papers and magazines without number. The compilers of these resemble
the commoners of Rome ; they are
all for levelling property, not by en-
creasing their own, but by diminish-
ing that of others. . . . The most
diminutive son of fame, or of famine,
has his *we* and his *us*, his *firstlys*
and his *secondlys* as methodical, as if
bound in cow-hide and closed with
clasps of brass. Were these Monthly
Reviews and Magazines frothy, pert,
or absurd, they might find some pardon ; but to be dull and dronish, is an
encroachment on the prerogative of
a folio.' ⟨Goldsmith had contributed
to both reviews.⟩

[1] See *post*, iii. 32.

[2] Mr. White, the Librarian of the

Royal Society, has, at my request,
kindly examined the records of the
Royal Society, but has not been able to
discover what the ' circumstance ' was.
Neither is any light thrown on it by
Johnson's reviews of Birch's *History
of the Royal Society* and *Philosophical
Transactions*, vol. xlix. (*ante*, i. 309),
which I have examined.

[3] ' Were you to converse with a
King, you ought to be as easy, and
unembarrassed as with your own
valet de chambre : but yet every
look, word, and action, should imply
the utmost respect. What would be
proper and well-bred with others,
much your superiors, would be absurd
and ill-bred with one so very much so.'
Chesterfield, *Letters*, ii. 164.

[4] Imlac thus described to Rasselas

wards observed to Mr. Langton, ' Sir, his manners are those of as
fine a gentleman as we may suppose Lewis the Fourteenth or
Charles the Second.'

At Sir Joshua Reynolds's, where a circle of Johnson's friends
was collected round him to hear his account of this memorable
conversation, Dr. Joseph Warton, in his frank and lively manner [1],
was very active in pressing him to mention the particulars.

his interview with the Great Mogul :
—' The emperour asked me many
questions concerning my country and
my travels ; and though I cannot now
recollect any thing that he uttered
above the power of a common man,
he dismissed me astonished at his
wisdom, and enamoured of his goodness.' *Rasselas*, chap. ix. Wraxall
(*Memoirs*, edit. of 1884, i. 283) says
that Johnson was no judge of a fine
gentleman. ' George III,' he adds,
' was altogether destitute of these
ornamental and adventitious endow-
ments.' He mentions ' the oscilla-
tions of his body, the precipitation of
his questions, none of which, it was
said, would wait for an answer, and
the hurry of his articulation.' John
Adams, the first Envoy from the
United States to Great Britain, in
1785 said ' The King, I really think,
is the most accomplished courtier in
his dominions.' *Works* (1856), viii.
350.

[1] ' Dr. Warton made me a most
obsequious bow. . . . He is what Dr.
Johnson calls a rapturist, and I saw
plainly he meant to pour forth much
civility into my ears. . . . He is a very
communicative, gay, and pleasant con-
verser, and enlivened the whole day
by his readiness upon all subjects.'
Mme. D'Arblay's *Diary*, ii. 236. It
is very likely that he is ' an ingenious
writer ' mentioned *post*, iv. 33, of
whom Johnson said, ' Sir, he is an
enthusiast by rule.' Mr. Windham
records that Johnson, speaking of
Warton's admiration of fine passages,
said :—' His taste is amazement.'

Croker's *Boswell*, 1848, p. 838, and
Johnson's *Letters* (ed. Hill), ii. 441.
In her *Memoirs of Dr. Burney* (ii. 82),
Mme. D'Arblay says that Johnson ' at
times, when in gay spirits, . . . would
take off Dr. Warton with the strongest
humour ; describing, almost convul-
sively, the ecstasy with which he would
seize upon the person nearest to him,
to hug in his arms, lest his grasp should
be eluded, while he displayed some
picture, or some prospect.' In that
humourous piece, *Probationary Odes
for the Laureateship* (p. xlv), Dr. Joseph
is made to hug his brother in his arms,
when he sees him descend safely
from the balloon in which he had
composed his *Ode*. Thomas Warton
is described in the same piece (p.
116) as ' a little, thick, squat, red-
faced man.' There was for some time
a coolness between Johnson and Dr.
Warton. Warton, writing on Jan.
22, 1766, says :—' I only dined with
Johnson, who seemed cold and indifferent, and scarce said any thing to
me ; perhaps he has heard what I
said of his *Shakespear*, or rather was
offended at what I wrote to him—
as he pleases.' Wooll's *Warton*, p.
312. Wooll says that a dispute took
place between the two men at Reynolds's house. ' One of the company
overheard the following conclusion of
the dispute. JOHNSON. " Sir, I am
not used to be contradicted." WAR-
TON. " Better for yourself and friends,
Sir, if you were ; our admiration
could not be encreased, but our love
might." ' *Ib*. p. 98.

' Come now, Sir, this is an interesting matter ; do favour us with it.' Johnson, with great good humour, complied.

He told them, ' I found his Majesty wished I should talk, and I made it my business to talk. I find it does a man good to be talked to by his Sovereign. In the first place, a man cannot be in a passion—.' Here some question interrupted him, which is to be regretted, as he certainly would have pointed out and illustrated many circumstances of advantage, from being in a situation, where the powers of the mind are at once excited to vigorous exertion, and tempered by reverential awe.

During all the time in which Dr. Johnson was employed in relating to the circle at Sir Joshua Reynolds's the particulars of what passed between the King and him, Dr. Goldsmith remained unmoved upon a sopha at some distance, affecting not to join in the least in the eager curiosity of the company. He assigned as a reason for his gloom and seeming inattention, that he apprehended Johnson had relinquished his purpose of furnishing him with a Prologue to his play [1], with the hopes of which he had been flattered ; but it was strongly suspected that he was fretting with chagrin and envy at the singular honour Dr. Johnson had lately enjoyed. At length, the frankness and simplicity of his natural character prevailed. He sprung from the sopha, advanced to Johnson, and in a kind of flutter, from imagining himself in the situation which he had just been hearing described, exclaimed, ' Well, you acquitted yourself in this conversation better than I should have done ; for I should have bowed and stammered through the whole of it [2].'

---

[1] *The Good-Natured Man, post*, ii. 45. ⟨See *post*, ii. 260 for Goldsmith's envy.⟩

[2] ' It has been said, that the King only sought one interview with Dr. Johnson. . . . There was nothing to complain of : it was a compliment paid by rank to letters, and once was enough. The King was more afraid of this interview than Dr. Johnson was ; and went to it as a schoolboy to his task. But he did not want to have this trial repeated every day, nor was it necessary. The very jealousy of his self-love marked his respect :

and if he had thought less of Dr. Johnson, he would have been more willing to risk the encounter.' Hazlitt's *Conversations of Northcote*, p. 45. It should seem that Johnson had a second interview with the King thirteen years later. In 1780, Hannah More records (*Memoirs*, i. 174) :— ' Johnson told me he had been with the king that morning, who enjoined him to add Spenser to his Lives of the Poets.' It is strange that, so far as I know, this interview is not mentioned by any one else. It is perhaps alluded to, *post*, iv. 410, when Mr.

I received no letter from Johnson this year ; nor have I discovered any of the correspondence [1] he had, except the two
letters to Mr. Drummond, which have been inserted, for the sake
of connection with that to the same gentleman in 1766. His
diary affords no light as to his employment at this time. He
passed three months at Lichfield [2] ; and I cannot omit an affecting and solemn scene there, as related by himself [3] :

' Sunday, Oct. 18, 1767. Yesterday, Oct. 17, at about ten in the
morning, I took my leave for ever of my dear old friend, Catherine
Chambers, who came to live with my mother about 1724, and has been
but little parted from us since. She buried my father, my brother, and
my mother. She is now fifty-eight years old.

' I desired all to withdraw, then told her that we were to part for
ever ; that as Christians, we should part with prayer ; and that I would,
if she was willing, say a short prayer beside her. She expressed great
desire to hear me ; and held [a] up her poor hands, as she lay in bed, with
great fervour, while I prayed, kneeling by her, nearly in the following
words :

' Almighty and most merciful Father, whose loving kindness is
over all thy works, behold, visit, and relieve this thy servant, who is
grieved with sickness. Grant that the sense of her weakness may add
strength to her faith, and seriousness to her repentance. And grant
that by the help of thy Holy Spirit, after the pains and labours of this
short life, we may all obtain everlasting happiness, through JESUS
CHRIST our Lord ; for whose sake hear our prayers. Amen. Our
Father, &c. [b]

' I then kissed her. She told me, that to part was the greatest pain
that she had ever felt, and that she hoped we should meet again in a
better place. I expressed, with swelled eyes, and great emotion of

---

[a] me, held *Pr. and Med.*   [b] &c. *added by Boswell.*

Nichols told Johnson that he wished
' he would favour the world, and gratify
his sovereign, by a Life of Spenser.'

[1] It is proper here to mention, that
when I speak of his correspondence,
I consider it independent of the voluminous collection of letters which,
in the course of many years, he
wrote to Mrs. Thrale, which forms
a separate part of his works ; and
as a proof of the high estimation
set on any thing which came from
his pen, was sold by that lady for
the sum of five hundred pounds.

BOSWELL. ⟨See Boswell's *Letters,*
No. 247, ii. 340. See also *ante,* i.
546–7.⟩

[2] He was away from London ' near
six months.' See *ante,* ii. 30 ⟨and
post, iii. App. B⟩.

[3] On August 17 he recorded :—' I
have communicated with Kitty, and
kissed her. I was for some time distracted but at last more composed.
I commended my friends and Kitty.
Lucy and I were much affected. Kitty
is, I think, going to heaven.' *Pr. and
Med.* ¶ 70. ⟨See App. B, p. 481.⟩

tenderness, the same hopes. We kissed, and parted. I humbly hope
to meet again, and to part no more ¹.'

By those who have been taught to look upon Johnson as a man
of a harsh and stern character, let this tender and affectionate
scene be candidly read ; and let them then judge whether more
warmth of heart, and grateful kindness, is often found in human
nature.

We have the following notice in his devotional record :

'August 2, 1767. I have been disturbed and unsettled for a long
time, and have been without resolution to apply to study or to business,
being hindered by sudden snatches ².'

He, however, furnished Mr. Adams with a Dedication * to the
King of that ingenious gentleman's ' Treatise on the Globes,' conceived and expressed in such a manner as could not fail to be
very grateful to a Monarch, distinguished for his love of the
sciences.

This year was published a ridicule of his style, under the title
of ' Lexiphanes.' Sir John Hawkins ascribes it to Dr. Kenrick ³ ;
but its authour was one Campbell, a Scotch purser in the navy.
The ridicule consisted in applying Johnson's ' words of large
meaning ⁴ ' to insignificant matters, as if one should put the armour
of Goliath upon a dwarf. The contrast might be laughable ; but
the dignity of the armour must remain the same in all considerate
minds. This malicious drollery, therefore, it may easily be supposed, could do no harm to its illustrious object ⁵.

¹ Prayers and Meditations, pp. 77
and 78. [¶ 71.] BOSWELL.

² *Ibid.* p. 73. [¶ 68.] BOSWELL.
On Aug. 17, he recorded :—' By abstinence from wine and suppers I
obtained sudden and great relief, and
had freedom of mind restored to me,
which I have wanted for all this year,
without being able to find any means
of obtaining it.' *Ib.* p. 74. [¶ 69.]

³ Hawkins, in his second edition
(p. 347), assigns it to Campbell, ' who,'
he says, ' as well for the malignancy
of his heart as his terrific countenance,
was called horrible Campbell.' 〈He
was the son of the Rev. Archibald

Campbell (*ante*, i. 359). ' His morals
were as bad as his principles.' Ramsay's *Scotl. and Scotsmen*, i. 268. See
also *Philol. Quarterly*, iii. 302.〉

⁴ See *ante*, i. 218.

⁵ The book is as dull as it is in-
decent. The ' drollery ' is of the following kind. Johnson is represented
as saying :—' Without dubiety you
misapprehend this dazzling scintilla-
tion of conceit in totality, and had you
had that constant recurrence to my
oraculous dictionary, which was in-
cumbent upon you from the vehemence of my monitory injunctions,'
&c. p. 2.

' To Bennet Langton, Esq. at Mr. Rothwell's, Perfumer, in
New Bond-Street, London.

' Dear Sir,

' That you have been all summer in London, is one more
reason for which I regret my long stay in the country. I hope that
you will not leave the town before my return. We have here only the
chance of vacancies in the passing carriages, and I have bespoken one
that may, if it happens, bring me to town on the fourteenth of this
month ; but this is not certain.

' It will be a favour if you communicate this to Mrs. Williams : I
long to see all my friends.

                              ' I am, dear Sir,
                                   ' Your most humble servant,
                                        ' Sam. Johnson.'
' Lichfield, Oct. 10, 1767.'

1768 : Ætat. 59.]—It appears from his notes of the state of his
mind [1], that he suffered great perturbation and distraction in 1768.
Nothing of his writing was given to the publick this year, except
the Prologue * to his friend Goldsmith's comedy of ' The Good-
natured Man [2].' The first lines of this Prologue are strongly
characteristical of the dismal gloom of his mind ; which in his case,
as in the case of all who are distressed with the same malady of
imagination, transfers to others its own feelings. Who could
suppose it was to introduce a comedy, when Mr. Bensley solemnly
began,

> ' Press'd with [3] the load of life, the weary mind
> Surveys the general toil of human kind.'

[1] Pr. and Med. p. 81. [¶ 80.] Boswell. ' This day,' he wrote on his
birthday, ' has been past in great perturbation, I was distracted at church in an
uncommon degree, and my distress
has had very little intermission. . . .
This day it came into my mind to
write the history of my melancholy.
On this I purpose to deliberate. I
know not whether it may not too
much disturb me.' Pr. and Med. ¶ 76.
See post, iii. 421.

[2] It is strange that Boswell nowhere
quotes the lines in The Good-Natured
Man, in which Paoli is mentioned.

' That 's from Paoli of Corsica,' said
Lofty. Act v. sc. 1.

[3] In the original, ' Prest by.' Boswell, in thus changing the preposition,
forgot what Johnson says in his Plan
of an English Dictionary (Works, v.
12) :—' We say, according to the
present modes of speech, The soldier
died of his wounds, and the sailor
perished with hunger ; and every man
acquainted with our language would
be offended with a change of these
particles, which yet seem originally
assigned by chance.'

But this dark ground might make Goldsmith's humour shine the more.

In the spring of this year, having published my ' Account of Corsica, with the Journal of a Tour to that Island ',[1] I returned to London [2], very desirous to see Dr. Johnson, and hear him upon the subject. I found he was at Oxford, with his friend Mr. Chambers [3], who was now Vinerian Professor, and lived in New Inn Hall. Having had no letter from him since that in which he criticised the Latinity of my Thesis, and having been told by somebody that he was offended at my having put into my book

---

[1] Boswell, writing to Temple on March 24, says :—' My Book has amazing celebrity. Lord Lyttelton, Mr. Walpole, Mrs. Macaulay, Mr. Garrick have all written me noble letters about it.' *Letters*, No. 82, i. 148. ⟨The first edition was entered in the Stationers' Register on 15 Feb., and was sold out in six weeks. 3,500 copies of the first and second editions were printed. F. A. Pottle, *Bibliography*, No. 24. The third edition was advertised for 1 May, 1769. *Lond. Chron.* xxv. 395.⟩ Dilly must have done very well by it, as he purchased the copyright for one hundred guineas. Boswell's *Letters*, No. 62, i. 118. 'Pray read the new *Account of Corsica*,' wrote Walpole to Gray on Feb. 18, 1768 (*Letters*, vii. 164). ' The author, Boswell, is a strange being, and . . . has a rage of knowing anybody that ever was talked of. He forced himself upon me at Paris in spite of my teeth and my doors.' To this Gray (*Works*, ed. 1835, iv. 112) replied :—' Mr. Boswell's book . . . has pleased and moved me strangely, all (I mean) that relates to Paoli. He is a man born two thousand years after his time ! The pamphlet proves what I have always maintained, that any fool may write a most valuable book by chance, if he will only tell us what he heard and saw with veracity.' In Boswell's *Letters* (No. 76, i. 137) there is the following under date of Nov. 9, 1767 :

—' I am always for fixing some period for my perfection as far as possible. Let it be when my *Account of Corsica* is published. I shall then have a character which I must support.'

[2] Boswell used to put notices of his movements in the newspapers, such as—' James Boswell, Esq ; is expected in Town.' *Public Advertiser*, Feb. 29, 1768. ' Yesterday James Boswell, Esq ; arrived from Scotland, at his Lodgings in Half-moon street, Piccadilly.' *Ib.* March 24, 1768.

[3] Johnson was very ill during this visit. Mrs. Thrale had at the same time given birth to a daughter, and had been nursed by her mother. His thoughts, therefore, were turned on illness. Writing to Mrs. Thrale, 28 April, 1768, he says :—' To roll the weak eye of helpless anguish, and see nothing on any side but cold indifference, will, I hope, happen to none whom I love or value ; it may tend to withdraw the mind from life, but has no tendency to kindle those affections which fit us for a purer and a nobler state. . . . These reflections do not grow out of any discontent at C—'s behaviour : he has been neither negligent nor troublesome ; nor do I love him less for having been ill in his house. This is no small degree of praise.' *Letters*, No. 204. ⟨Chambers was Principal of New Inn Hall at the time. See *ante*, ii. 25 and, for the duration of Johnson's visit, *post*, ii. 58.⟩

an extract of his letter to me at Paris [1], I was impatient to be
with him, and therefore followed him to Oxford, where I was entertained by Mr. Chambers, with a civility which I shall ever
gratefully remember. I found that Dr. Johnson had sent a letter
to me to Scotland, and that I had nothing to complain of but his
being more indifferent to my anxiety than I wished him to be.
Instead of giving, with the circumstances of time and place, such
fragments of his conversation as I preserved during this visit to
Oxford, I shall throw them together in continuation [2].

I asked him whether, as a moralist, he did not think that the
practice of the law, in some degree, hurt the nice feeling of
honesty. JOHNSON. ' Why no, Sir, if you act properly. You
are not to deceive your clients with false representations of
your opinion : you are not to tell lies to a judge.' BOSWELL.
' But what do you think of supporting a cause which you know
to be bad ? ' JOHNSON. ' Sir, you do not know it to be good or
bad till the Judge determines it. I have said that you are to
state facts fairly ; so that your thinking, or what you call knowing, a cause to be bad, must be from reasoning, must be from
your supposing your arguments to be weak and inconclusive.
But, Sir, that is not enough. An argument which does not
convince yourself, may convince the Judge to whom you urge
it : and if it does convince him, why, then, Sir, you are wrong,
and he is right. It is his business to judge ; and you are not to
be confident in your own opinion that a cause is bad, but to say
all you can for your client, and then hear the Judge's opinion.'
BOSWELL. ' But, Sir, does not affecting a warmth when you have
no warmth, and appearing to be clearly of one opinion when you
are in reality of another opinion, does not such dissimulation
impair one's honesty ? Is there not some danger that a lawyer
may put on the same mask in common life, in the intercourse
with his friends ? ' JOHNSON. ' Why no, Sir. Every body knows
you are paid for affecting warmth for your client ; and it is,
therefore, properly no dissimulation : the moment you come from
the bar you resume your usual behaviour. Sir, a man will no

---

[1] See *ante*, ii. 3, note 2.
[2] The editor of the *Letters of Boswell*, 1857, justly says (p. 149) :—' The
detail in the *Life of Johnson* is rather
scanty about this period ; dissipation,
the *History of Corsica*, wife-hunting,
. . . interfered perhaps at this time
with his pursuit of Dr. Johnson.'

more carry the artifice of the bar into the common intercourse of society, than a man who is paid for tumbling upon his hands will continue to tumble upon his hands when he should walk on his feet [1].'

Talking of some of the modern plays, he said ' False Delicacy ' was totally void of character [2]. He praised Goldsmith's ' Good-natured Man ; ' said, it was the best comedy that had appeared since ' The Provoked Husband[3], ' and that there had not been of late any such character exhibited on the stage as that of Croaker. I observed it was the Suspirius of his Rambler. He said, Goldsmith had owned he had borrowed it from thence [4]. ' Sir, (continued he,) there is all the difference in the world between characters of nature and characters of manners ; and *there* is the difference between the characters of Fielding and those of

---

[1] See Boswell's *Hebrides*, Aug. 15, *post*, v. 26, for a discussion of the same question. Lord Eldon has recorded (Twiss's *Life*, i. 106), that when he first went the Northern Circuit (about 1776–1780), he asked Jack Lee (*post*, iii. 224), who was not scrupulous in his advocacy, whether his method could be justified. ' Oh, yes,' he said, ' undoubtedly. Dr. Johnson had said that counsel were at liberty to state, as the parties themselves would state, what it was most for their interest to state.' After some interval, and when he had had his evening bowl of milk punch and two or three pipes of tobacco, he suddenly said, ' Come, Master Scott, let us go to bed. I have been thinking upon the questions that you asked me, and I am not quite so sure that the conduct you represented will bring a man peace at the last.' Lord Eldon, after stating pretty nearly what Johnson had said, continues :—' But it may be questioned whether even this can be supported.'

[2] Garrick brought out Hugh Kelly's *False Delicacy* at Drury Lane six days before Goldsmith's *Good-Natured Man* was brought out at Covent Garden. ' It was the town talk,' says Mr.

Forster (*Goldsmith*, ii. 93), ' some weeks before either performance took place, that the two comedies . . . were to be pitted against each other.' *False Delicacy* had a great success. Ten thousand copies of it were sold before the season closed. (*Ib.* p. 96.) According to Murphy (*Life of Garrick*, p. 287), Garrick's prologue to *False Delicacy*, ' promised a moral and senti-mental comedy, and with an air of pleasantry, called it a sermon in five acts. The critics considered it in the same light, but the general voice was in favour of the play, during a run of near twenty nights. Foote, at last, by a little piece, called, *Piety in Pattens*, brought that species of composition into disrepute.' It is recorded in Johnson's *Works* (1787), xi. 201, that when some one asked Johnson, whether they should introduce Hugh Kelly to him ; ' No, Sir,' says he, ' I never desire to converse with a man who has written more than he has read.' See *post*, iii. 113 ; iv. 407, note 4, col. 2.

[3] *The Provoked Husband, or A Journey to London*, by Vanbrugh and Colley Cibber. It was brought out on 10 Jan. 1728. See *post*, iv. 284.

[4] See *ante*, i. 213.

Richardson. Characters of manners are very entertaining ; but they are to be understood, by a more superficial observer, than characters of nature, where a man must dive into the recesses of the human heart.'

It always appeared to me that he estimated the compositions of Richardson too highly, and that he had an unreasonable prejudice against Fielding [1]. In comparing those two writers, he used this expression ; ' that there was as great a difference between them as between a man who knew how a watch was made, and a man who could tell the hour by looking on the dial-plate [2].' This was a short and figurative state of his distinction between drawing characters of nature and characters only of manners. But I cannot help being of opinion, that the neat watches of Fielding are as well constructed as the large clocks of Richardson, and that his dial-plates are brighter. Fielding's characters, though they do not expand themselves so widely in dissertation, are as just pictures of human nature, and I will venture to say, have more striking features, and nicer touches of the pencil ; and though Johnson used to quote with approbation a saying of Richardson's, ' that the virtues of Fielding's heroes were the vices of a truly good man,' I will venture to add, that the moral tendency of Fielding's writings, though it does not encourage a strained and rarely possible virtue, is ever favourable to honour and honesty, and cherishes the benevolent and generous affections. He who is as good as Fielding would make him, is an amiable member of society, and may be led on by more regulated instructors, to a higher state of ethical perfection.

[1] See *post*, ii. 173–5 and iii. 43. 〈Mrs. Piozzi reports Johnson as saying :—' Richardson had picked the kernel of life, while Fielding was contented with the husk.' *Anec.,* p. 198 : John. Misc. i. 282.〉

[2] Richardson, writing on Dec. 7, 1756, to Miss Fielding, about her Familiar Letters, says :—' What a knowledge of the human heart ! Well might a critical judge of writing say, as he did to me, that your late brother's knowledge of it was not (fine writer as he was) comparable to your's. His was but as the knowledge of the out-side of a clock-work machine, while your's was that of all the finer springs and movements of the inside.' *Corres.* ii. 104. Mrs. Calderwood, writing of her visit to the Low Countries in 1756, says :—' All Richison's books are translated, and much admired abroad ; but for Feilding's, the forreigners have no notion of them, and do not understand them, as the manners are so intirely English.' *Letters, &c.,* p.208. 〈*Joseph Andrews* was translated into French in 1743, *Tom Jones* in 1750, *Amelia* in 1762, and *Jonathan Wild* in 1763.〉

Johnson proceeded : 'Even Sir Francis Wronghead is a character of manners, though drawn with great humour.' He then repeated, very happily, all Sir Francis's credulous account to Manly of his being with 'the great man,' and securing a place [1]. I asked him, if 'The Suspicious Husband' [2] did not furnish a well-drawn character, that of Ranger. JOHNSON. 'No, Sir ; Ranger is just a rake, a mere rake [3], and a lively young fellow, but no *character*.'

The great Douglas Cause [4] was at this time a very general subject of discussion. I found he had not studied it with much attention, but had only heard parts of it occasionally. He, however, talked of it, and said, 'I am of opinion that positive proof of fraud should not be required of the plaintiff, but that the Judges should decide according as probability shall appear to preponderate, granting to the defendant the presumption of filiation to be strong in his favour. And I think too, that a good deal of weight should be allowed to the dying declarations, because they were spontaneous. There is a great difference between what is said without our being urged to it, and what is

---

[1] *TheProvoked Husband*, act iv. sc. 1.

[2] By Dr. Hoadly, brought out in Feb. 1747. ⟨See Genest, iv. 216.⟩ 'This was the first good comedy from the time of the *Provoked Husband* in 1727[8].' Murphy's *Garrick*, p. 78.

[3] Madame Riccoboni, writing to Garrick from Paris on Sept. 7, 1768, says :—' On ne supporteroit point ici l'indécence de Ranger. Les très-indécens François deviennent délicats sur leur théâtre à mesure qu'ils le sont moins dans leur conduite.' *Garrick's Corres.* ii. 548.

[4] 'The question in dispute was as to the heirship of Mr. Archibald Douglas. If he were really the son of Lady Jane Douglas, he would inherit large family estates ; but if he were supposititious, then they would descend to the Duke of Hamilton. . . . The Judges of the Court of Session . . . had been divided in opinion, eight against seven, the Lord-President Dundas giving the casting vote in favour of the Duke of Hamilton ; and, in consequence of it, he and several

other of the Judges had, on the reversal by the Lords, their houses attacked by a mob.' *Letters of Boswell* (1857), p. 86. See *post*, ii. 230, iii. 8, and v. 353–9. J. H. Burton, in his *Life of Hume* (ii. 150), says :—' Men about to meet each other in company, used to lay an injunction on themselves not to open their lips on the subject, so fruitful was it in debates and brawls.' Boswell was the author of *Dorando, A Spanish Tale*. London, 1767. In this tale the Douglas cause is narrated under the thinnest disguise. ⟨See Boswell's *Letters*, Nos. 67, 70, 71, ed. 1924, i. 124, 128, 130. Boswell also published in 1767 *The Douglas Cause*, a ballad, and *The Essence of the Douglas Cause*, (*post*, ii. 230, note 1) ; he was one of the editors of the *Letters of Lady Jane Douglas* and 'took care to keep the newspapers and other publications incessantly warm with various writings' on the subject. See Mr. F. A. Pottle's *Lit. Career of Boswell*, pp. xxxv, 26 ff., 216 ff., etc.⟩

said from a kind of compulsion. If I praise a man's book
without being asked my opinion of it, that is honest praise, to
which one may trust. But if an authour asks me if I like his
book, and I give him something like praise, it must not be taken
as my real opinion.'

'I have not been troubled for a long time with authours
desiring my opinion of their works [1]. I used once to be sadly
plagued with a man who wrote verses, but who literally had no
other notion of a verse, but that it consisted of ten syllables.
Lay your knife and your fork, across your plate, was to him
a verse :

Lay yōur knife ānd your fōrk, acrōss your plāte.

As he wrote a great number of verses, he sometimes by chance
made good ones, though he did not know it.'

He renewed his promise of coming to Scotland, and going
with me to the Hebrides, but said he would now content himself with seeing one or two of the most curious of them. He
said, ' Macaulay [2], who writes the account of St. Kilda, set out
with a prejudice against prejudices, and wanted to be a smart
modern thinker ; and yet he affirms for a truth, that when a ship
arrives there all the inhabitants are seized with a cold [3].'

Dr. John Campbell [4], the celebrated writer, took a great deal
of pains to ascertain this fact, and attempted to account for it on
physical principles, from the effect of effluvia from human
bodies. Johnson, at another time [5], praised Macaulay for his
' *magnanimity*,' in asserting this wonderful story, because it was

---

[1] See *post*, ii. 195, iii. 373, and iv.
121, 175.

[2] Revd. Kenneth Macaulay (1723–
79). See *post*, v. 118–21. He was
the great-uncle of Lord Macaulay.

[3] Martin, in his *St. Kilda* (p. 39),
had stated that the people of St.
Kilda ' are seldom troubled with a
Cough, except at the Steward's Landing. . . . I told them plainly,' he continues, ' that I thought all this Notion
of Infection was but a meer Fancy, at
which they seemed offended, saying,
that never any, before the Minister

and my self, was heard to doubt of
the Truth of it ; which is plainly
demonstrated upon the landing of
every Boat.' The usual ' infected
cough ' came, he says, upon his visit.
Macaulay (*History of St. Kilda*, p. 204)
says that he had gone to the island a
disbeliever, but that by eight days
after his arrival all the inhabitants
were infected with this disease. See
also *post*, ii. 150, v. 278, ⟨and App. B
to this vol., p. 482⟩.

[4] See *ante*, i. 417.

[5] *Post*, ii. 150.

well attested. A Lady of Norfolk, by a letter to my friend Dr. Burney, has favoured me with the following solution : ' Now for the explication of this seeming mystery, which is so very obvious as, for that reason, to have escaped the penetration of Dr. Johnson and his friend, as well as that of the authour. Reading the book with my ingenious friend, the late Reverend Mr. Christian of Docking—after ruminating a little, " The cause, (says he,) is a natural one. The situation of St. Kilda renders a North-East Wind indispensably necessary before a stranger can land [1]. The wind, not the stranger, occasions an epidemic cold." If I am not mistaken, Mr. Macaulay is dead ; if living, this solution might please him, as I hope it will Mr. Boswell, in return for the many agreeable hours his works have afforded us.'

Johnson expatiated on the advantages of Oxford for learning [2]. ' There is here, Sir, (said he,) such a progressive emulation. The students are anxious to appear well to their tutors ; the tutors are anxious to have their pupils appear well in the college ; the colleges are anxious to have their students appear well in the University ; and there are excellent rules of discipline in every college. That the rules are sometimes ill observed, may be true ; but is nothing against the system. The members of an University may, for a season, be unmindful of their duty. I am arguing for the excellency of the institution [3].'

Of Guthrie [4], he said, ' Sir, he is a man of parts. He has no great regular fund of knowledge ; but by reading so long, and writing so long, he no doubt has picked up a good deal.'

He said he had lately been a long while at Lichfield, but had grown very weary before he left it [5]. BOSWELL. ' I wonder at that, Sir ; it is your native place.' JOHNSON. ' Why, so is Scotland *your* native place.'

---

[1] This is not the case. Martin (p. 12) says that the only landing place is inaccessible except under favour of a neap tide, a north-east or west wind, or with a perfect calm. He himself was rowed to St. Kilda, ' the Inhabitants . . . admiring to see us get thither contrary to Wind and Tide ' (p. 9).

[2] That for one kind of learning Oxford has no advantages, he shows in a letter that he wrote there on Aug. 4, 1777. ' I shall enquire about

the harvest when I come into a region where any thing necessary to life is understood.' *Letters*, No. 533. At Lichfield he reached that region. Aug. 7. ' My barber, a man not unintelligent, speaks magnificently of the harvest.' No. 535. ⟨See *post*, ii. 425. ' Our scholastick ignorance of mankind.'⟩

[3] See *post*, iii. 138.

[4] See *ante*, i. 116 ; *post*, iv. 30.

[5] ⟨See *ante*, ii. 30 ; *Letters*, Nos. 190, 191.⟩

His prejudice against Scotland appeared remarkably strong at this time. When I talked of our advancement in literature [1], ' Sir, (said he,) you have learnt a little from us, and you think yourselves very great men. Hume would never have written History, had not Voltaire written it before him [2]. He is an echo of Voltaire.' BOSWELL. ' But, Sir, we have Lord Kames [3].' JOHNSON. ' You *have* Lord Kames. Keep him ; ha, ha, ha ! We don't envy you him. Do you ever see Dr. Robertson ? ' BOSWELL. ' Yes, Sir.' JOHNSON. ' Does the dog talk of me ? ' BOSWELL. ' Indeed, Sir, he does, and loves you.' Thinking that I now had him in a corner, and being solicitous for the literary fame of my country, I pressed him for his opinion on the merit of Dr. Robertson's History of Scotland. But, to my surprize, he escaped.—' Sir, I love Robertson, and I won't talk of his book [4].'

It is but justice both to him and Dr. Robertson to add, that though he indulged himself in this sally of wit, he had too good taste not to be fully sensible of the merits of that admirable work.

An essay, written by Mr. Deane, a divine of the Church of

---

[1] The advancement had been very rapid. ' When Dr. Robertson's career commenced,' writes Dugald Stewart in his *Life* of that historian (p. 157), ' the trade of authorship was unknown in Scotland.' Smollett, in *Humphry Clinker*, published three years after this conversation, makes Mr. Bramble write (Letter of Aug. 8) : —' Edinburgh is a hot-bed of genius. I have had the good fortune to be made acquainted with many authors of the first distinction ; such as the two Humes [David Hume and John Home, whose names had the same pronunciation], Robertson, Smith, Wallace, Blair, Ferguson, Wilkie, &c.' To these might be added Smollett himself, Boswell, Reid, Beattie, Kames, Monboddo. Henry Mackenzie and Dr. Henry began to publish in 1771. Gibbon, writing to Robertson in 1779, says :—' I have often considered, with some sort of envy, the valuable society which you possess in so narrow a com-

pass.' Stewart's *Robertson*, p. 363.

[2] See *post*, ii. 236, where Johnson owned that he had not read Hume. Burton (*Life of Hume*, ii. 129), after stating that ' Hume was the first to add to a mere narrative of events, an inquiry into the progress of the people, &c.,' says :—' There seems to be no room for the supposition [that he had borrowed the idea from Voltaire's *Essai sur les Mœurs*]. Hume's own *Political Discourses* are as close an approach to this method of inquiry as the work of Voltaire ; and if we look for such productions of other writers as may have led him into this train of thought, it would be more just to name Bacon and Montesquieu.' ⟨Johnson is reported to have said :—' Hume has taken his style from Voltaire.' *John. Misc.* ii. 10. Hume denied Voltaire's influence. *Englische Studien*, lxiii. 353, 383.⟩

[3] See *post*, iii. 340, 351.

[4] See *post*, ii. 236–7 ; iii. 331–2, 404.

England, maintaining the future life of brutes, by an explication
of certain parts of the scriptures [1], was mentioned, and the
doctrine insisted on by a gentleman who seemed fond of curious
speculation. Johnson, who did not like to hear of any thing
concerning a future state which was not authorised by the regular canons of orthodoxy, discouraged this talk ; and being
offended at its continuation, he watched an opportunity to
give the gentleman a blow of reprehension. So, when the poor
speculatist, with a serious metaphysical pensive face, addressed
him, ' But really, Sir, when we see a very sensible dog, we don't
know what to think of him.' Johnson, rolling with joy at the
thought which beamed in his eye, turned quickly round, and
replied, ' True, Sir : and when we see a very foolish *fellow*, we
don't know what to think of *him*.' He then rose up, strided to
the fire, and stood for some time laughing and exulting.

I told him that I had several times, when in Italy, seen the
experiment of placing a scorpion within a circle of burning
coals ; that it ran round and round in extreme pain ; and finding
no way to escape, retired to the centre, and like a true Stoick
philosopher, darted its sting into its head, and thus at once
freed itself from its woes. ' *This must end 'em* [2].' I said, this
was a curious fact, as it shewed deliberate suicide in a reptile.
Johnson would not admit the fact. He said, Maupertuis [3] was

---

[1] *An Essay on the Future Life of
Brutes*. By Richard Dean, Curate
of Middleton, Manchester, 1767. The
' part of the Scriptures ' on which the
author chiefly relies is the *Epistle to
the Romans*, viii. 19–23. He also
finds support for his belief in ' those
passages in *Isaiah* where the Prophet speaks of new Heavens, and
a new Earth, of the Lion as eating straw like the Ox, &c.' Vol. ii.
pp. x, 4.

[2] The words that Addison's Cato
uses as he lays his hand on his sword.
Act v. sc. 1.

[3] I should think it impossible not
to wonder at the variety of Johnson's
reading, however desultory it may
have been. Who could have imagined
that the High Church of England-

man would be so prompt in quoting
Maupertuis, who, I am sorry to think,
stands in the list of those unfortunate
mistaken men, who call themselves
esprits forts. I have, however, a high
respect for that Philosopher whom the
Great Frederick of Prussia loved and
honoured, and addressed pathetically
in one of his Poems,
' *Maupertuis cher Maupertuis,
Que notre vie est peu de chose.*'
There was in Maupertuis a vigour
and yet a tenderness of sentiment,
united with strong intellectual powers,
and uncommon ardour of soul. Would
he had been a Christian ! I cannot
help earnestly venturing to hope that
he is one now. BOSWELL. Voltaire
writing to D'Alembert on Aug. 25,
1759, says :—' Que dites-vous de Mau-

of opinion that it does not kill itself, but dies of the heat ; that it gets to the centre of the circle, as the coolest place ; that its turning its tail in upon its head is merely a convulsion, and that it does not sting itself. He said he would be satisfied if the great anatomist Morgagni, after dissecting a scorpion on which the experiment had been tried, should certify that its sting had penetrated into its head.

He seemed pleased to talk of natural philosophy. ' That woodcocks, (said he,) fly over to the northern countries, is proved, because they have been observed at sea. Swallows certainly sleep all the winter. A number of them conglobulate together [1], by flying round and round, and then all in a heap throw themselves under water, and lye in the bed of a river [2].' He told us, one of his first essays was a Latin poem upon the glow-worm. I am sorry I did not ask where it was to be found.

Talking of the Russians and the Chinese, he advised me to read Bell's travels [3]. I asked him whether I should read Du Halde's account of China [4]. ' Why yes, (said he) as one reads such a book ; that is to say, consult it.'

He talked of the heinousness of the crime of adultery, by which the peace of families was destroyed. He said, ' Confusion

pertuis, mort entre deux capucins ? ' Voltaire's *Œuvres,* xl. 157. The stanza from which Boswell quotes is as follows :—
' O Maupertuis, cher Maupertuis,
Que notre vie est peu de chose !
Cette fleur qui brille aujourd'hui,
Demain se fane à eine éclose !
Tout périt, tout est emporté
Par la dure fatalité
Des arrêts de la Destinée ;
Votre Vertu, vos grands talens
Ne pourront obtenir du temps
Le seul délai d'une journée.'
    La vie est un songe. Œuvres de Frédéric II (édit. 1789), iv. 37.
[1] Johnson does not give *Conglobulate* in his *Dictionary* ; only *conglobe* ⟨and *conglobate*⟩. If he used the word it is not likely that he said ' conglobulate *together.*'
[2] Gilbert White, writing on Nov. 4,

1767, after mentioning that he had seen swallows roosting in osier-beds by the river, says :—' This . . . seems to give some countenance to the northern opinion (strange as it is) of their retiring under water.' White's *Selborne,* Letter xii. See also *post,* ii. 248 ⟨and Daines Barrington's *Miscellanies* (1781), 228 foll.⟩.
[3] *Travels from St. Petersburgh in Russia, to divers parts of Asia.* By John Bell, Glasgow, 1763 : two vols., quarto.
[4] I. D'Israeli (*Curiosities of Literature,* ed. 1834, i. 194) ranks this book among Literary Impostures. ' Du Halde . . . never travelled ten leagues from Paris in his life ; though he appears, by his writings, to be familiar with Chinese scenery.' See *ante,* i. 136, ⟨157 ; *post,* iv. 30, and App. B to this vol., p. 483⟩.

of progeny constitutes the essence of the crime ; and therefore a woman who breaks her marriage vows is much more
criminal than a man who does it [1]. A man, to be sure, is
criminal in the sight of GOD : but he does not do his wife a
very material injury, if he does not insult her ; if, for instance,
from mere wantonness of appetite, he steals privately to her
chambermaid. Sir, a wife ought not greatly to resent this. I
would not receive home a daughter who had run away from her
husband on that account. A wife should study to reclaim her
husband by more attention to please him. Sir, a man will not,
once in a hundred instances, leave his wife and go to a harlot, if
his wife has not been negligent of pleasing.'

Here he discovered that acute discrimination, that solid judgement, and that knowledge of human nature, for which he was
upon all occasions remarkable. Taking care to keep in view the
moral and religious duty, as understood in our nation, he shewed
clearly from reason and good sense, the greater degree of culpa-
bility in the one sex deviating from it than the other ; and, at
the same time, inculcated a very useful lesson as to *the way to
keep him* §.

I asked him if it was not hard that one deviation from chastity
should so absolutely ruin a young woman. JOHNSON. ' Why
no, Sir ; it is the great principle which she is taught. When she
has given up that principle, she has given up every notion of
female honour and virtue, which are all included in chastity.'

A gentleman [2] talked to him of a lady whom he greatly
admired and wished to marry, but was afraid of her superiority
of talents. ' Sir, (said he,) you need not be afraid ; marry her.
Before a year goes about, you'll find that reason much weaker,

---

[1] See *post*, iii. 406.

[2] Boswell, in his correspondence
with Temple in 1767 and 1768, passes
in review the various ladies whom he
proposes to marry. The lady described in this paragraph—for the
' gentleman ' is clearly Boswell—is
' the fair and lively Zelide,' a Dutch-
woman. She was translating his
Corsica into French. On March 24,
1768, he wrote, ' I must have her.'
On April 26, he asked his father's
permission to go over to Holland to
see her. But on May 14 he forwarded
to Temple one of her letters. ' Could,'
he said, ' any actress, at any of the
theatres, attack me with a keener (what
is the word ? not *fury*, something
softer)—The lightening that flashes
with so much brilliance may scorch.
And does not her *esprit* do so ? ' *Letters*, Nos. 82, 87, 92. ⟨See App. B.⟩

§ ⟨*The way to keep him* is the title of
Murphy's comedy, produced in 1760.⟩

and that wit not so bright.' Yet the gentleman may be justified
in his apprehension by one of Dr. Johnson's admirable sentences
in his life of Waller : ' He doubtless praised many [1] whom he
would have been afraid to marry ; and, perhaps, married one
whom he would have been ashamed to praise. Many qualities
contribute to domestick happiness, upon which poetry has no
colours to bestow ; and many airs and sallies may delight
imagination, which he who flatters them never can approve.'

He praised Signor Baretti. ' His account of Italy is a very
entertaining book [2] ; and, Sir, I know no man who carries his
head higher in conversation than Baretti [3]. There are strong
powers in his mind. He has not, indeed, many hooks ; but with
what hooks he has, he grapples very forcibly.'

At this time I observed upon the dial-plate of his watch [4] a
short Greek inscription, taken from the New Testament, Νυξ
γαρ ερχεται [5], being the first words of our SAVIOUR's solemn
admonition to the improvement of that time which is allowed us
to prepare for eternity : ' the night cometh, when no man can
work.' He some time afterwards laid aside this dial-plate ; and
when I asked him the reason, he said, ' It might do very well
upon a clock which a man keeps in his closet ; but to have it
upon his watch which he carries about with him, and which is
often looked at by others, might be censured as ostentatious.'

[1] ⟨The first and second editions of
The Lives of the Poets read *many*, the
third *some*. *Life of Waller*, 16.⟩

[2] *An Account of the Manners and
Customs of Italy*, by Joseph Baretti,
London, 1768. The book would be
still more entertaining were it not
written as a reply to Samuel Sharp's
Letters from Italy. *Post*, iii. 55. ⟨See
App. B.⟩

[3] Mrs. Piozzi wrote of him : ' His
character is easily seen, and his soul
above disguise, haughty and insolent,
and breathing defiance against all
mankind ; while his powers of mind
exceed most people's, and his powers
of purse are so slight that they leave
him dependent on all. Baretti is for
ever in the state of a stream dammed
up : if he could once get loose, he
would bear down all before him.'
Hayward's *Piozzi*, ed. 2, i. 103.

[4] According to Hawkins (*Life*, p.
460), the watch was new this year,
and was, he believed, the first Johnson ever had.

[5] *St. John*, ix. 4. In *Pr. and Med.*
¶ 182, is the following :—' Ejaculation. *Imploring Diligence.* O God,
make me to remember *that the night
cometh when no man can work.*' Porson,
in his witty attack on Sir John Hawkins,
originally published in the *Gent. Mag.*
for 1787, quotes the inscription as a
proof of Hawkins's Greek. ' Νυξ γαρ
ερχεται. The meaning is (says Sir
John) *For the night cometh.* And so
it is, Mr. Urban.' Porson's *Tracts*,
p. 337. ⟨Dr. Hill points out, *John.
Misc.* i. 123, n. 4, that Scott put the
same Greek inscription on the dial at
Abbotsford. See Lockhart's *Scott*,
1838, vii. 297.⟩

Mr. Steevens is now possessed of the dial-plate inscribed as above.

He remained at Oxford a considerable time [1]; I was obliged to go to London, where I received his letter, which had been returned from Scotland.

' To James Boswell, Esq.

' My dear Boswell,

' I have omitted a long time to write to you, without knowing very well why. I could now tell why I should not write ; for who would write to men who publish the letters of their friends, without their leave [2] ? Yet I write to you in spite of my caution, to tell you that I shall be glad to see you, and that I wish you would empty your head of Corsica, which I think has filled it rather too long. But, at all events, I shall be glad, very glad to see you.

' I am, Sir,
' Yours affectionately,
' Sam. Johnson.'

' Oxford, March 23, 1768.'

I answered thus :

' To Mr. Samuel Johnson.

' London, 26th April, 1768 [3].

' My dear Sir,

' I have received your last letter, which, though very short, and by no means complimentary, yet gave me real pleasure, because it contains these words, " I shall be glad, very glad to see you."—Surely you have no reason to complain of my publishing a single paragraph of one of your letters [4] ; the temptation to it was so strong. An irrevocable grant of your friendship, and your dignifying my desire of visiting

---

[1] He thus wrote of himself from Oxford to Mrs. Thrale, 14 Mar. 1768 : —' This little dog does nothing, but I hope he will mend ; he is now reading Jack the Giant-killer. Perhaps so noble a narrative may rouse in him the soul of enterprise.' *Letters*, No. 197. ⟨He was at Oxford from 29 Feb. (at least) to 30 April. *Letters*, Nos. 194·1, 195, and 204.⟩

[2] See *ante*, ii. 3, n. 2 ; *post*, iv. 102.

[3] Under the same date, Boswell thus begins a letter to Temple :—

' Your moral lecture came to me yesterday, in very good time, while I lay suffering severely for immorality. If there is any firmness at all in me, be assured that I shall never again behave in a manner so unworthy the friend of Paoli. My warm imagination looks forward with great complacency on the sobriety, the healthfulness, and the worth of my future life.' *Letters*, No. 87, i. 153.

[4] ⟨See *ante*, ii. 46.⟩

Corsica with the epithet of " a wise and noble curiosity," are to me
more valuable than many of the grants of kings.

' But how can you bid me " empty my head of Corsica ¹ ? " My
noble-minded friend, do you not feel for an oppressed nation bravely
struggling to be free ? Consider fairly what is the case. The Corsicans
never received any kindness from the Genoese ². They never agreed
to be subject to them. They owe them nothing ; and when reduced
to an abject state of slavery, by force, shall they not rise in the great
cause of liberty, and break the galling yoke ? And shall not every
liberal soul be warm for them ? Empty my head of Corsica ! Empty it
of honour, empty it of humanity, empty it of friendship, empty it of
piety. No ! while I live, Corsica and the cause of the brave islanders
shall ever employ much of my attention, shall ever interest me in the
sincerest manner.

*   *   *   *   *   *   *

' I am, &c.
' JAMES BOSWELL.'

Upon his arrival in London in May, he surprized me one
morning with a visit at my lodgings in Half-Moon-street ³, was

¹ Johnson so early as Aug. 21,
1766, had given him the same advice (*ante*, ii. 22). How little Boswell
followed it is shewn by his letter to
the Earl of Chatham, on April 8, 1767,
in which he informed him of his
intention to publish his *Corsica*, and
concluded :—' Could your Lordship
find time to honour me now and
then with a letter ? I have been told
how favourably your Lordship has
spoken of me. To correspond with
a Paoli and with a Chatham is enough
to keep a young man ever ardent in
the pursuit of virtuous fame.' Boswell's *Letters*, No. 57. On the same
day on which he wrote to Johnson,
he said in a letter to Temple, ' Old
General Oglethorpe (who has come
to see me and is with me often, just on
account of my book) bids me not marry
till I have first put the Corsicans in a
proper situation. " You may make a
fortune in the doing of it," said he ; " or,
if you do not, you will have acquired
such a character as will entitle you to

any fortune." ' *Ibid*. No. 87, i. 154.
On 24 Aug. 1768, Boswell wrote :—
' By private subscription in Scotland,
I am this week sending £700 worth
of ordinance [to Corsica].. . . It is
really a tollerable train of artillery.'
Ib. No. 93, i. 164. In 1769 he brought
out a small volume entitled *British
Essays in Favour of the Brave Corsicans :
by Several Hands. Collected and Published by James Boswell, Esq.* ⟨See
Mr. F. A. Pottle's *Bibliography*, No. 44.⟩
² From about the beginning of the
fourteenth century, Corsica had belonged to the Republic of Genoa. In
the great rising under Paoli, the Corsicans would have achieved their independence, had not Genoa ceded the
island to the crown of France.
³ Boswell, writing to Temple on
May 14, says :—' I am really the
Great Man now. I have had David
Hume in the forenoon and Mr. Johnson in the afternoon of the same day
visiting me. Sir John Pringle, Dr.
Franklin, and some more company

quite satisfied with my explanation, and was in the kindest and most agreeable frame of mind. As he had objected to a part of one of his letters being published, I thought it right to take this opportunity of asking him explicitly whether it would be improper to publish his letters after his death. His answer was, ' Nay, Sir, when I am dead, you may do as you will [1].'

He talked in his usual style with a rough contempt of popular liberty [2]. ' They make a rout about *universal* liberty, without considering that all that is to be valued, or indeed can be enjoyed by individuals, is *private* liberty. Political liberty is good only so far as it produces private liberty. Now, Sir, there is the liberty of the press, which you know is a constant topick [3]. Suppose you and I and two hundred more were restrained from printing our thoughts : what then ? What proportion would that restraint upon us bear to the private happiness of the nation [4] ? '

dined with me today ; and Mr. Johnson and General Oglethorpe one day, Mr. Garrick alone another, and David Hume and some more literati another, dine with me next week. I give admirable dinners and good claret and the moment I go abroad again, which will be in a day or two, I set up my chariot. This is enjoying the fruit of my labours, and appearing like the friend of Paoli.' *Letters*, No. 92.

[1] See *post*, iii. 276 and iv. 102.

[2] The talk arose no doubt from the general election that had just been held amid all the excitement about Wilkes. Dr. Franklin (*Writings*, v. 122), in a letter dated April 16, 1768, describes the riots in London. He had seen ' the mob . . . requiring gentlemen and ladies of all ranks, as they passed in their carriages, to shout for Wilkes and liberty, marking the same words on all their coaches with chalk, and No. 45 on every door . . . I went last week to Winchester, and observed, that for fifteen miles out of town there was scarce a door or window shutter next the road unmarked ; and this continued, here and there, quite to Winchester.'

[3] In his *Vindication of the Licensers*

of the Stage, he thus writes :—' If I might presume to advise them [the Ministers] upon this great affair, I should dissuade them from any direct attempt upon the liberty of the press, which is the darling of the common people, and, therefore, cannot be attacked without immediate danger.' *Works*, v. 344. In his Introd. to the *Harleian Miscellany* (*Ib.* v. 191), he shows some of the benefits that arise in England from ' the boundless liberty with which every man may write his own thoughts.' See also in his *Life of Milton*, 58, the passage about *Areopagitica.* The liberty of the press was likely to be ' a constant topick.' Walpole (*Memoirs of the Reign of George III*, ii. 15), writing of the summer of 1764, says :—' Two hundred informations were filed against printers : a larger number than had been prosecuted in the whole thirty-three years of the last reign.'

[4] ' The sun has risen, and the corn has grown, and, whatever talk has been of the danger of property, yet he that ploughed the field commonly reaped it ; and he that built a house was master of the door ; the vexation excited by injustice suffered,

This mode of representing the inconveniencies of restraint as light and insignificant, was a kind of sophistry in which he delighted to indulge himself, in opposition to the extreme laxity for which it has been fashionable for too many to argue, when it is evident, upon reflection, that the very essence of government is restraint ; and certain it is, that as government produces rational happiness, too much restraint is better than too little. But when restraint is unnecessary, and so close as to gall those who are subject to it, the people may and ought to remonstrate ; and, if relief is not granted, to resist. Of this manly and spirited principle, no man was more convinced than Johnson himself [1].

About this time Dr. Kenrick [2] attacked him, through my sides, in a pamphlet, entitled ' An Epistle to James Boswell, Esq. occasioned by his having transmitted the moral Writings of Dr. Samuel Johnson to Pascal Paoli, General of the Corsicans.[3] ' I was at first inclined to answer this pamphlet ; but Johnson, who knew that my doing so would only gratify Kenrick, by keeping alive what would soon die away of itself, would not suffer me to take any notice of it [4].

or supposed to be suffered, by any private man, or single community, was local and temporary, it neither spread far, nor lasted long.' Johnson's *False Alarm, Works*, vi. 170. See also *post*, ii. 170. Dr. Franklin (*Writings*, ix. 578) wrote to the Abbé Morellet, on April 22, 1787 :—' Nothing can be better expressed than your sentiments are on this point, where you prefer liberty of trading, cultivating, manufacturing, &c., even to civil liberty, this being affected but rarely, the other every hour.'

[1] See *ante*, i. 424.

[2] See *ante*, i. 497.

[3] ' I was diverted with Paoli's English library. It consisted of some broken volumes of the *Spectatour* and *Tatler* : Pope's *Essay on Man* : *Gulliver's Travels* : A *History of France*, in old English : and Barclay's *Apology for the Quakers*. I promised to send him some English books. . . . I have sent him . . . some of our best books

of morality and entertainment, in particular the Works of Mr. Samuel Johnson.' Boswell's *Corsica*, p. 297.

[4] Johnson, as Boswell believed, only once ' in the whole course of his life . . . condescended to oppose any thing that was written against him.' (See *ante*, i. 314.) In this he followed the rule of Bentley and of Boerhaave. ' It was said to old Bentley, upon the attacks against him, " Why, they'll write you down." " No, sir, he replied ; depend upon it, no man was ever written down but by himself." ' *Post*, v. 274. Bentley shewed prudence in his silence. ' He was right,' Johnson said, ' not to answer ; for, in his hazardous method of writing, he could not but be often enough wrong.' *Post*, v. 174. In the life of *Boerhaave* Johnson says : ' He was never soured by calumny and detraction, nor ever thought it necessary to confute them : " for they are sparks," said he, " which, if you do not blow them, will go out

His sincere regard for Francis Barber, his faithful negro servant, made him so desirous of his further improvement, that he now placed him at a school at Bishop Stortford, in Hertfordshire.[1] This humane attention does Johnson's heart much honour. Out of many letters which Mr. Barber received from his master, he has preserved three, which he kindly gave me, and which I shall insert according to their dates.

'To Mr. Francis Barber.

'Dear Francis,

'I have been very much out of order. I am glad to hear that

---

of themselves." ' *Works*, vi. 288. Swift, in his lines *On Censure* which begin,—
'Ye wise, instruct me to endure
An evil, which admits no cure.'
ends by saying :—
'The most effectual way to baulk
Their malice, is—to let them talk.'
Swift's *Works*, 1824, xiv. 208. Young, in his *Second Epistle to Pope*, had written :—
'Arm'd with this truth, all criticks I defy ;
For if I fall, by my *own* pen I die.'
Hume, in his *Auto.* (p. ix.) says :—
'I had a fixed resolution, which I inflexibly maintained, never to reply to any body.' This is not quite true. See J. H. Burton's *Life of Hume*, ii. 252, for an instance of a violent reply. The following passages in Johnson's writings are to the same effect :—' I . . . am inclined to believe that few attacks either of ridicule or invective make much noise, but by the help of those that they provoke.' *Letters*, No. 863. 'It is very rarely that an author is hurt by his criticks. The blaze of reputation cannot be blown out, but it often dies in the socket.' *Ib.* No. 663. 'The writer who thinks his works formed for duration mistakes his interest when he mentions his enemies. He degrades his own dignity by shewing that he was affected by their censures, and gives

lasting importance to names, which, left to themselves, would vanish from remembrance.' *Life of Dryden*, 173. 'If . . . it had been possible for those who were attacked to conceal their pain and their resentment, *The Dunciad* might have made its way very slowly in the world.' *Life of Pope*, 146. Hawkins (*Life of Johnson*, p. 348) says that, 'against personal abuse Johnson was ever armed, by a reflection, that I have heard him utter : "Alas ! reputation would be of little worth, were it in the power of every concealed enemy to deprive us of it." ' In his *Parl. Debates* (*Works*, x. 359), Johnson makes Mr. Lyttelton say :—
'No man can fall into contempt but those who deserve it.' Addison in *The Freeholder*, No. 40, says, that 'there is not a more melancholy Object in the Learned World, than a Man who has written himself down.' See also *post*, v. 400, ⟨and *John. Misc.* i. 271 note, where Dr. Hill gives other instances of authors who refused to reply to criticism⟩.

[1] ⟨Hawkins (*Life*, p. 328) says that Johnson kept Frank at school for five years, and, on the authority of Miss Williams, that he 'expended three hundred pounds in an endeavour to have him taught Latin and Greek '. He had left the school in March, 1772 (*post*, ii. 146). See also A. L. Reade, *Gleanings*, ii. 18.⟩

you are well, and design to come soon to see you. I would have you stay at Mrs. Clapp's for the present, till I can determine what we shall do. Be a good boy.

'My compliments to Mrs. Clapp [1] and to Mr. Fowler [1]. I am,

'Yours affectionately,

'SAM. JOHNSON.'

'May 28, 1768.'

Soon afterwards, he supped at the Crown and Anchor tavern, in the Strand, with a company whom I collected to meet him. They were Dr. Percy, now Bishop of Dromore, Dr. Douglas, now Bishop of Salisbury, Mr. Langton, Dr. Robertson the Historian [2], Dr. Hugh Blair, and Mr. Thomas Davies, who wished much to be introduced to these eminent Scotch literati; but on the present occasion he had very little opportunity of hearing them talk, for with an excess of prudence, for which Johnson afterwards found fault with them, they hardly opened their lips, and that only to say something which they were certain would not expose them to the sword of Goliath; such was their anxiety for their fame when in the presence of Johnson [3]. He was this evening in remarkable vigour of mind, and eager to exert himself in conversation, which he did with great readiness and fluency; but I am sorry to find that I have preserved but a small part of what passed.

He allowed high praise to Thomson as a poet [4]; but when one of the company said he was also a very good man, our moralist contested this with great warmth, accusing him of gross sensuality and licentiousness of manners. I was very much afraid that in writing Thomson's life, Dr. Johnson would have treated his private character with a stern severity, but I was agreeably disappointed; and I may claim a little merit in it, from my

---

[1] ⟨Mrs. Clapp was the widow of the Rev. J. Clapp, head master of the school from 25 May 1764 till his death in Nov. 1767. The Rev. R. Fowler succeeded on 1 Dec. 1767: he resigned two years later, to be followed, 1 Jan. 1770, by the Rev. W. Ellis (see *post*, ii. 116). Reade, *Gleanings*, ii. 17–19.⟩

[2] ⟨Boswell in an undated letter to Blair writes: 'Dr. Robertson and I and one or two more friends are to sup with Mr. Johnson on Tuesday night. . . . Mr. Johnson says, "I wish to see Blair."' *Letters*, No. 90, i. 156. See also *post*, ii. 66, for another supper with Robertson.⟩

[3] In like manner the professors at Aberdeen and Glasgow seemed afraid to speak in his presence. See *post*, v. 92, 371. See also *post*, iii. 332.

[4] See *ante*, i. 453.

having been at pains to send him authentick accounts of the affectionate and generous conduct of that poet to his sisters, one of whom, the wife of Mr. Thomson, schoolmaster at Lanark, I knew, and was presented by her with three of his letters, one of which Dr. Johnson has inserted in his life [1].

He was vehement against old Dr. Mounsey, of Chelsea College [2], as ' a fellow who swore and talked bawdy.' ' I have been often in his company, (said Dr. Percy,) and never heard him swear or talk bawdy.' Mr. Davies, who sat next to Dr. Percy, having after this had some conversation aside with him, made a discovery which, in his zeal to pay court to Dr. Johnson, he eagerly proclaimed aloud from the foot of the table : ' O, Sir, I have found out a very good reason why Dr. Percy never heard Mounsey swear or talk bawdy ; for he tells me, he never saw him but at the Duke of Northumberland's table.' ' And so, Sir, (said Johnson loudly, to Dr. Percy,) you would shield this man from the charge of swearing and talking bawdy, because he did not do so at the Duke of Northumberland's table. Sir, you might as well tell us that you had seen him hold up his hand at the Old Bailey, and he neither swore nor talked bawdy ; or that you had seen him in the cart at Tyburn, and he neither swore nor talked bawdy. And is it thus, Sir, that you presume to controvert what I have related ? ' Dr. Johnson's animadversion was uttered in such a manner, that Dr. Percy seemed to be displeased, and soon afterwards left the company, of which Johnson did not at that time take any notice.

[1] Johnson, in inserting this letter, says (*Life of Thomson*, 39) :—' I communicate [it] with much pleasure, as it gives me at once an opportunity of recording the fraternal kindness of Thomson, and reflecting on the friendly assistance of Mr. Boswell, from whom I received it.' See *post*, iii. 116, 360.

[2] ⟨Messenger Monsey, physician to Chelsea Hospital.⟩ Murphy, in his *Life of Garrick*, p. 183, says that Garrick once brought Dr. Munsey— so he writes the name—to call on him. ' Garrick entered the dining room, and turning suddenly round, ran to the door, and called out, " Dr. Munsey, where are you going ? " " Up stairs to see the author," said Munsey. " Pho ! pho ! come down, the author is here." Dr. Munsey came, and, as he entered the room, said, in his free way, " You scoundrel ! I was going up to the garret : who could think of finding an author on the first floor ? " ' Mrs. Montagu wrote to Lord Lyttelton from Tunbridge in 1760 :—' The great Monsey came hither on Friday . . . He is great in the coffee-house, great in the rooms, and great on the pantiles.' *Montagu Letters*, iv. 291. In Rogers's *Table-Talk*, p. 211, there is a curious account of him. ⟨See also R. Blunt's *Mrs. Montagu*, 1923.⟩

Swift having been mentioned, Johnson, as usual, treated him with little respect as an authour [1]. Some of us endeavoured to support the Dean of St. Patrick's by various arguments. One in particular praised his ' Conduct of the Allies.' JOHNSON. ' Sir, his " Conduct of the Allies " is a performance of very little ability.' ' Surely, Sir, (said Dr. Douglas,) you must allow it has strong facts [2].' JOHNSON. ' Why yes, Sir ; but what is that to the merit of the composition ? In the Sessions-paper of the Old Bailey there are strong facts. Housebreaking is a strong fact ; robbery is a strong fact ; and murder is a *mighty* strong fact : but is great praise due to the historian of those strong facts ? No, Sir. Swift has told what he had to tell distinctly enough, but that is all. He had to count ten, and he has counted it right [3].'—Then recollecting that Mr. Davies, by acting as an *informer*, had been the occasion of his talking somewhat too harshly to his friend [4] Dr. Percy, for which, probably, when the first ebullition was over, he felt some compunction, he took an opportunity to give him a hit ; so added, with a preparatory laugh, ' Why, Sir, Tom Davies might have written " the Conduct of the Allies ".' Poor Tom being thus suddenly dragged into ludicrous notice in presence of the Scottish Doctors, to whom he was ambitious of appearing to advantage, was grievously mortified. Nor did his punishment rest here ; for upon subsequent occasions, whenever he, ' statesman all

---

[1] See *ante*, i. 452; *post*, ii. 318; iv. 61; v. 44.

[2] My respectable friend, upon reading this passage, observed, that he probably must have said not simply, ' strong facts,' but ' strong facts well arranged.' His Lordship, however, knows too well the value of written documents to insist on setting his recollection against my notes taken at the time. He does not attempt to *traverse the record.* The fact, perhaps, may have been, either that the additional words escaped me in the noise of a numerous company, or that Dr. Johnson, from his impetuosity, and eagerness to seize an opportunity to make a lively retort, did not allow Dr. Douglas to finish his sentence. BOSWELL. ⟨This note was added in the second edition.⟩

[3] ' It is boasted that between November [1712] and January, eleven thousand [of *The Conduct of the Allies*] were sold. . . . Yet, surely, whoever surveys this wonder-working pamphlet with cool perusal will confess that its efficacy was supplied by the passions of its readers ; that it operates by the mere weight of facts, with very little assistance from the hand that produced them.' *Life of Swift*, 47, 48. ⟨In the *Life of Prior*, 21, Johnson glances at it as ' unreasonable '.⟩

[4] ' Every great man, of whatever kind be his greatness, has among his friends those who officiously, or insidiously, quicken his attention to offences, heighten his disgust, and stimulate his resentment.' Johnson's *Life of Pope*, 105.

over [1],' assumed a strutting importance, I used to hail him—
' *the Authour of the Conduct of the Allies.*'

When I called upon Dr. Johnson next morning, I found him
highly satisfied with his colloquial prowess the preceding evening.
' Well, (said he,) we had good talk [2].' BOSWELL. ' Yes, Sir ;
you tossed and gored several persons [3].'

The late Alexander, Earl of Eglintoune [4], who loved wit more
than wine, and men of genius more than sycophants, had a
great admiration of Johnson ; but from the remarkable elegance of his own manners, was, perhaps, too delicately sensible
of the roughness which sometimes appeared in Johnson's behaviour. One evening about this time, when his Lordship did
me the honour to sup at my lodgings with Dr. Robertson and
several other men of literary distinction, he regretted that Johnson had not been educated with more refinement, and lived
more in polished society. ' No, no, my Lord, (said Signor
Baretti,) do with him what you would, he would always have
been a bear.' ' True, (answered the Earl, with a smile,) but
he would have been a *dancing* bear.'

To obviate all the reflections which have gone round the
world to Johnson's prejudice, by applying to him the epithet
of a *bear* [5], let me impress upon my readers a just and happy
saying of my friend Goldsmith, who knew him well : ' Johnson,
to be sure, has a roughness in his manner ; but no man alive
has a more tender heart. *He has nothing of the bear but his
skin.*'

1769 : ÆTAT. 60.]—IN 1769, so far as I can discover, the
publick was favoured with nothing of Johnson's composition,
either for himself or any of his friends [6]. His ' Meditations ' [7] too
strongly prove that he suffered much both in body and mind ;

---

[1] See the hard drawing of him in
Churchill's ROSCIAD. BOSWELL. See
ante, i. 391, note 2.

[2] For *talk*, see *post*, iv. 186.

[3] See *post*, ii. 80, and iii. 338, where
Johnson tosses Boswell.

[4] See *post*, iii. 188, and v. 374.

[5] See *post*, ii. 269, note 1 ; ii. 347 ;

iv. 113, note 2 ; v. 384.

[6] He wrote the character of Mr.
Mudge. See *post*, iv. 76–7.

[7] ' Sept. 18, 1769. This day com-
pletes the sixtieth year of my age. . . .
The last year has been wholly spent
in a slow progress of recovery.' *Pr.
and Med.* ¶ 79.

yet was he perpetually striving against *evil*, and nobly endeavouring to advance his intellectual and devotional improvement. Every generous and grateful heart must feel for the distresses of so eminent a benefactor to mankind ; and now that his unhappiness is certainly known, must respect that dignity of character which prevented him from complaining.

His Majesty having the preceding year instituted the Royal Academy of Arts in London, Johnson had now the honour of being appointed Professor in Ancient Literature [1]. In the course of the year he wrote some letters to Mrs. Thrale, passed some part of the summer at Oxford † and at Lichfield, and when at Oxford wrote the following letter :

' To the Reverend Mr. Thomas Warton.

' Dear Sir,

' Many years ago, when I used to read in the library of your College, I promised to recompence the College for that permission, by adding to their books a Baskerville's Virgil. I have now sent it, and desire you to reposit it on the shelves in my name [2].

[1] In which place he has been succeeded by Bennet Langton, Esq. When that truly religious gentleman was elected to this honorary Professorship, at the same time that Edward Gibbon, Esq. noted for introducing a kind of sneering infidelity into his Historical Writings, was elected Professor in Ancient History, in the room of Dr. Goldsmith, I observed that it brought to my mind, ' Wicked Will Whiston and good Mr. Ditton.'—I am now also of that admirable institution as Secretary for Foreign Correspondence, by the favour of the Academicians, and the approbation of the Sovereign. Boswell. Goldsmith, writing to his brother in Jan., 1770, said :—' The King has been lately pleased to make me Professor of ancient history in a Royal Accademy of Painting which he has just establishd, but there is no sallary anex'd and I took it rather as a compliment to the institution than any benefit to myself. Honours to one in my situation, are something like ruffles to a man that wants a shirt.' *Letters*, ed. Balderston, p. 84. ' Wicked Will Whiston,' &c.,

comes from Swift's *Ode for Music, On the Longitude* (Swift's *Works*, ed. 1824, xiii. 336), which begins,—

' The longitude miss'd on
By wicked Will Whiston ;
And not better hit on
By good Master Ditton.'

It goes on so grossly and so offensively as regards one and the other, that Boswell's comparison was a great insult to Langton as well as to Gibbon. ⟨It was at the suggestion of Reynolds that the honorary professorships were established. Leslie and Taylor, *Life of Reynolds*, i. 310.⟩

† ⟨Johnson's visit to Oxford lasted from late in May to 7 July, when he returned to London. On 10 Aug. he set out for Lichfield and was at Brighton on 26 Aug. *Letters*, Nos. 215–221. This was the second visit this year, see *ante*, i. App. G, p. 546.⟩

[2] It has this inscription in a blank leaf : ' *Hunc librum D. D. Samuel Johnson, eo quod hic loci studiis interdum vacaret.*' Of this library, which is an old Gothick room, he was very fond. On my observing to him that some of the *modern* libraries of the

' If you will be pleased to let me know when you have an hour of
leisure, I will drink tea with you. I am engaged for the afternoon,
to-morrow and on Friday : all my mornings are my own [1].

'   ' I am, &c.,

'   ' SAM. JOHNSON.'
' May 31, 1769.'

I came to London in the autumn, and having informed him
that I was going to be married in a few months, I wished to
have as much of his conversation as I could before engaging in a
state of life which would probably keep me more in Scotland,
and prevent my [a] seeing him so often as when I was a single
man ; but I found he was at Brighthelmstone with Mr. and Mrs.
Thrale. I was very sorry that I had not his company with me
at the Jubilee, in honour of Shakspeare, at Stratford-upon-
Avon, the great poet's native town [2]. Johnson's connection both

[a] my 1 : me 2, 3.

University were more commodious
and pleasant for study, as being more
spacious and airy, he replied, ' Sir, if
a man has a mind to *prance*, he must
study at Christ-Church and All-
Souls.' BOSWELL. ⟨See App. B,
p. 485.⟩

[1] During this visit he seldom or
never dined out. He appeared to be
deeply engaged in some literary work.
Miss Williams was now with him at
Oxford. BOSWELL.

It was more likely the state of his
health which kept him at home.
Writing from Oxford on June 27 of
this year to Mrs. Thrale, who had
been ill, he says :—' I will not encrease
your uneasiness with mine. I hope
I grow better. I am very cautious,
and very timorous.' *Letters*, No. 216.

[2] Boswell wrote a letter, signed
with his own name, to the *London
Magazine* for 1769 (p. 451) describing
the Jubilee. It is followed by a print
of himself ' in the dress of an armed
Corsican chief,' and by an account,
no doubt written by himself. It says :
—' Of the most remarkable masks
upon this occasion was James Boswell,
Esq., in the dress of an armed Corsican

chief. He entered the amphitheatre
about twelve o'clock. . . On the front
of his cap was embroidered in gold
letters, VIVA LA LIBERTA ; and on one
side of it was a handsome blue feather
and cockade, so that it had an elegant,
as well as a warlike appearance. . . He
wore no mask ; saying, that it was not
proper for a gallant Corsican. So soon
as he came into the room he drew universal attention.' Cradock (*Memoirs*,
i. 217) gives a melancholy account of
the festival. The preparations were
all behind-hand and the weather was
stormy. ' There was a masquerade in
the evening, and all zealous friends endeavoured to keep up the spirit of it
as long as they could ; till they were
at last informed, that the Avon was
rising so very fast, that no delay could
be admitted. The ladies of our party
were conveyed by planks from the
building to . . . the coach ; and we
found that the wheels had been two
feet deep in water.' Garrick in 1771
was asked by the Stratford committee
to join them in celebrating a Jubilee
every year, as ' the most likely method
to promote the interest and reputation
of their town.' Boswell caught at the

with Shakspeare and Garrick founded a double claim to his presence ; and it would have been highly gratifying to Mr. Garrick. Upon this occasion I particularly lamented that he had not that warmth of friendship for his brilliant pupil, which we may suppose would have had a benignant effect on both [1]. When almost every man of eminence in the literary world was happy to partake in this festival of genius, the absence of Johnson could not but be wondered at and regretted. The only trace of him there, was in the whimsical advertisement of a haberdasher, who sold *Shaksperian ribbands* of various dyes ; and, by way of illustrating their appropriation to the bard, introduced a line from the celebrated Prologue [2] at the opening of Drury-lane theatre :

> ' Each change of *many-colour'd* life he drew.'

From Brighthelmstone Dr. Johnson wrote me the following letter, which they who may think that I ought to have suppressed, must have less ardent feelings than I have always avowed [3].

proposal eagerly, and writing to Garrick said :—' I please myself with the prospect of attending you at several more Jubilees at Stratford upon Avon.' *Garrick Corres.* i. 414, 435. ⟨See also *post*, App. B, p. 485.⟩

[1] Garrick's correspondents not seldom spoke disrespectfully of Johnson. Thus, Mr. Sharp, writing to him in 1769, talks of ' risking the sneer of one of Dr. Johnson's ghastly smiles.' *Ib.* i. 334. Dr. J. Hoadly, in a letter dated July 25, 1775, says :—' Mr. Goodenough has written a kind of parody of Puffy Pensioner's *Taxation no Tyranny*, under the noble title of *Resistance no Rebellion*.' *Ib.* ii. 68.

[2] See *ante*, i. 181.

[3] In the Preface to my Account of Corsica, published in 1768, I thus express myself :

' He who publishes a book affecting not to be an authour, and professing an indifference for literary fame, may possibly impose upon many people such an idea of his consequence as he wishes may be received. For my part, I should be proud to be known as an authour, and I have an ardent ambition for literary fame ; for, of all possessions, I should imagine literary fame to be the most valuable. A man who has been able to furnish a book, which has been approved by the world, has established himself as a respectable character in distant society, without any danger of having that character lessened by the observation of his weaknesses. To preserve an uniform dignity among those who see us every day, is hardly possible ; and to aim at it, must put us under the fetters of perpetual restraint. The authour of an approved book may allow his natural disposition an easy play, and yet indulge the pride of superior genius, when he considers that by those who know him only as an authour, he never ceases to be respected. Such an authour, when in his hours of gloom and discontent, may have the consolation to think, that his writings are, at that very time, giving pleasure to numbers ;

' To James Boswell, Esq.

' Dear Sir,

' Why do you charge me with unkindness ? I have omitted nothing that could do you good, or give you pleasure, unless it be that I have forborne to tell you my opinion of your " Account of Corsica." I believe my opinion, if you think well of my judgement, might have given you pleasure ; but when it is considered how much vanity is excited by praise, I am not sure that it would have done you good. Your History is like other histories, but your Journal is in a very high degree curious and delightful. There is between the history and the journal that difference which there will always be found between notions borrowed from without, and notions generated within. Your history was copied from books ; your journal rose out of your own experience and observation. You express images which operated strongly upon yourself, and you have impressed them with great force upon your readers. I know not whether I could name any narrative by which curiosity is better excited, or better gratified.

' I am glad that you are going to be married ; and as I wish you well in things of less importance, wish you well with proportionate ardour in this crisis of your life. What I can contribute to your happiness, I should be very unwilling to with-hold ; for I have always loved and valued you, and shall love you and value you still more, as you become more regular and useful : effects which a happy marriage will hardly fail to produce.

' I do not find that I am likely to come back very soon from this place. I shall, perhaps, stay a fortnight longer ; and a fortnight is a long time to a lover absent from his mistress. Would a fortnight ever have an end ?

' I am, dear Sir,
' Your most affectionate humble servant,

' Sam. Johnson.'

' Brighthelmstone,
Sept. 9, 1769.'

and such an authour may cherish the hope of being remembered after death, which has been a great object to the noblest minds in all ages.' Boswell.

His preface to the third edition thus ends :—' When I first ventured to send this book into the world, I fairly owned an ardent desire for literary fame. I have obtained my desire : and whatever clouds may overcast my days, I can now walk here among the rocks and woods of my ancestors, with an agreeable consciousness that I have done something worthy.' The dedication of the first edition and the preface of the third are both dated Oct. 29— one 1767, and the other 1768. Oct. 29 was his birthday. ⟨Boswell's book was translated into German in 1768, French ᴤwice), Dutch, and Italian in 1769.⟩

After his return to town, we met frequently, and I continued the practice of making notes of his conversation, though not with so much assiduity as I wish I had done. At this time, indeed, I had a sufficient excuse for not being able to appropriate so much time to my journal ; for General Paoli [1], after Corsica had been overpowered by the monarchy of France, was now no longer at the head of his brave countrymen, but having with difficulty escaped from his native island, had sought an asylum in Great-Britain ; and it was my duty, as well as my pleasure, to attend much upon him [2]. Such particulars of Johnson's conversation at this period as I have committed to writing, I shall here introduce,

[1] Paoli's father had been one of the leaders of the Corsicans in their revolt against Genoa in 1734. Paoli himself was chosen by them as their General-in-chief in 1755. In 1769 the island was conquered by the French. He escaped in an English ship, and settled in England. Here he stayed till 1789, when Mirabeau moved in the National Assembly the recall of all the Corsican patriots. Paoli was thereupon appointed by Louis XVI. Lieutenant-general and military commandant in Corsica. He resisted the violence of the Convention, and was, in consequence, summoned before it. Refusing to obey, an expedition was sent to arrest him. Napoleon Buonaparte fought in the French army, but Paoli's party proved the stronger. The islanders sought the aid of Great Britain, and offered the crown of Corsica to George III. The offer was accepted, but by an act of incredible folly, not Paoli, but Sir Gilbert Elliot, was made Viceroy. Paoli returned to England, where he died in 1807, at the age of eighty-two. In 1796 Corsica was abandoned by the English. By the Revolution it ceased to be a conquered province, having been formally declared an integral part of France. At the present day the Corsicans are proud of being citizens of that great country ; no less proud, however, are they of Pascal Paoli, and of the gallant struggle for independence of their forefathers.

[2] ⟨According to the *Lond. Chron.* 23 Sept. (xxvi. 290), Paoli arrived in London on Sept. 20. Boswell on 3 Oct. says : ' The arrival of General Paoli has been the occasion of my being very much taken up. . . . Our illustrious chief has been received here with the greatest honour. The King desired to see him privately at the Queen's palace, where he went accordingly, and was a long time alone with his Majesty.' *Letters*, No. 100, i. 174. On 12 Oct. the *Lond. Chron.* (xxvi. 360) announces that the General ' will set out in a few days, accompanied by Mr. Boswell . . . to view the Dock-yards, etc. at Portsmouth.'⟩ In the *Public Advertiser* for Oct. 4 there is the following entry, inserted no doubt by Boswell :—' On Sunday last, General Paoli, accompanied by James Boswell, Esq., took an airing in Hyde Park in his coach.' Prior's *Goldsmith*, i. 450. Walpole writes :—' Paoli's character had been so advantageously exaggerated by Mr. Boswell's enthusiastic and entertaining account of him, that the Opposition were ready to . . . incorporate him in the list of popular tribunes. The Court artfully intercepted the project ; and deeming patriots of all nations equally corruptible, bestowed a pension of *l.*1000 a-year on the unheroic fugitive.' *Memoirs of the Reign of George III*, iii. 387.

without any strict attention to methodical arrangement. Sometimes short notes of different days shall be blended together, and sometimes a day may seem important enough to be separately distinguished.

He said, he would not have Sunday kept with rigid severity and gloom, but with a gravity and simplicity of behaviour [1].

I told him that David Hume had made a short collection of Scotticisms [2]. ' I wonder, (said Johnson,) that *he* should find them.'

He would not admit the importance of the question concerning the legality of general warrants [3]. ' Such a power (he observed,) must be vested in every government, to answer particular cases of necessity ; and there can be no just complaint but when it is abused, for which those who administer government must be

---

[1] Johnson, writes Mrs. Piozzi (*Anec.* p. 228 : John. Misc. i. 301), ridiculed a friend ' who, looking out on Streatham Common from our windows . . ., lamented the enormous wickedness of the times, because some bird-catchers were busy there one fine Sunday morning. " While half the Christian world is permitted (said he) to dance and sing, and celebrate Sunday as a day of festivity, how comes your puritanical spirit so offended with frivolous and empty deviations from exactness ? Whoever loads life with unnecessary scruples, Sir (continued he), provokes the attention of others on his conduct, and incurs the censure of singularity without reaping the reward of superior virtue." ' See *post*, ii. 376, v. 69, and *John. Misc.* i. 17, ii. 413.

[2] The first edition of Hume's *History of England* was full of Scotticisms, many of which he corrected in subsequent editions. MALONE.

According to Burton (*Life of Hume*, ii. 79), ' He appears to have earnestly solicited the aid of Lyttelton, Mallet, and others, whose experience of English composition might enable them to detect Scotticisms.' Mr. Burton gives instances of alterations made in the second edition. He says also that ' in none of his historical or

philosophical writings does any expression used by him, unless in those cases where a Scoticism has escaped his vigilance, betray either the district or the country of his origin.' *Ib.* i. 9. Hume was shown in manuscript Reid's *Inquiry into the Human Mind*. Though it was an attack on his own philosophy, yet in reading it ' I kept,' he says, ' a watchful eye all along over your style,' so that he might point out any Scotticisms. *Ib.* ii. 154. Nevertheless, as Dugald Stewart says in his *Life of Robertson* (p. 214), ' Hume fails frequently both in purity and grammatical correctness.' ⟨Asking Wilkes to correct his *History* Hume says, 16 Oct. 1754, ' Notwithstanding all the pains which I have taken in the study of the English Language, I am still jealous of my Pen.' *Englische Studien*, lxiii. 363. See also Dr. Hill's *Letters of Hume*, i. 7–9.⟩

[3] In 1763 Wilkes, as author of *The North Briton*, No. 45, had been arrested on ' a general warrant directed to four messengers to take up any persons without naming or describing them with any certainty, and to bring them, together with their papers.' Such a warrant as this Chief Justice Pratt (Lord Camden) declared to be ' unconstitutional, illegal, and absolutely void.' *Ann. Reg.* vi. 145.

answerable. It is a matter of such indifference, a matter about which the people care so very little, that were a man to be sent over Britain to offer them an exemption from it at a halfpenny a piece, very few would purchase it.' This was a specimen of that laxity of talking, which I have heard him fairly acknowledge [1]; for, surely, while the power of granting general warrants was supposed to be legal, and the apprehension of them hung over our heads, we did not possess that security of freedom, congenial to our happy constitution, and which, by the intrepid exertions of Mr. Wilkes, has been happily established.

He said, ' The duration of Parliament, whether for seven years or for [a] the life of the King, appears to me so immaterial, that I would not give half a crown to turn the scale the [b] one way or the other [2]. The *habeas corpus* is the single advantage which our government has over that of other countries.'

On the 30th of September we dined together at the Mitre. I attempted to argue for the superior happiness of the savage life, upon the usual fanciful topics. JOHNSON. ' Sir, there can be nothing more false. The savages have no bodily advantages beyond those of civilised men. They have not better health ; and as to care or mental uneasiness, they are not above it, but below it, like bears. No, Sir ; you are not to talk such paradox [3] : let

---

[a] for *omitted* 2, 3.   [b] the *omitted* 2, 3.

[1] See *ante*, i. 476 ; *post*, v. 352.

[2] In the Spring of this year, at a meeting of the electors of Southwark, ' instructions ' had been presented to Mr. Thrale and his brother-member, Sir Joseph Mawbey, of which the twelfth was :—' That you promote a bill for shortning the duration of parliaments.' *Gent. Mag.* xxxix. 162.

[3] This paradox Johnson had exposed twenty-nine years earlier, in his *Life of Sir Francis Drake, Works*, vi. 366. In *Rasselas*, chap. xi, he considers also the same question. Imlac is ' inclined to conclude, that, if nothing counteracts the natural consequence of learning, we grow more happy as our minds take a wider range.' He then enumerates the advantages which civilisation con-

fers on the Europeans. ' They are surely happy, said the prince, who have all these conveniencies.' . . . ' The Europeans, answered Imlac, are less unhappy than we, but they are not happy. Human life is every where a state in which much is to be endured, and little to be enjoyed.' Writing to Mrs. Thrale from Sky, Johnson said :—' The traveller wanders through a naked desert, gratified sometimes, but rarely, with the sight of cows, and now and then finds a heap of loose stones and turf in a cavity between rocks, where a being born with all those powers which education expands, and all those sensations which culture refines, is condemned to shelter itself from the wind and rain. Philosophers there are who me have no more on't. It cannot entertain, far less can it instruct. Lord Monboddo [1], one of your Scotch Judges, talked a great deal of such nonsense. I suffered *him* ; but I will not suffer *you*.'— BOSWELL. ' But, Sir, does not Rousseau talk such nonsense ? ' JOHNSON. ' True, Sir ;[a] but Rousseau *knows* he is talking nonsense, and laughs at the world for staring at him.' BOSWELL. ' How so, Sir ? ' JOHNSON. ' Why, Sir, a man who talks nonsense so well, must know that he is talking nonsense. But I am *afraid*, (chuckling and laughing,) Monboddo does *not* know that he is talking nonsense [2].' BOSWELL. ' Is it wrong then, Sir, to affect singularity, in order to make people stare ? ' JOHNSON. ' Yes, if you do it by propagating errour : and, indeed, it is wrong in any way. There is in human nature a general inclination to make people stare ; and every wise man has himself to cure of it, and does cure himself [3]. If you wish to make people stare by doing

[a] Sir ; 1, 2 ; Sir, 3.

try to make themselves believe that this life is happy ; but they believe it only while they are saying it, and never yet produced conviction in a single mind.' *Letters*, No. 329. See *post*, ii. 228, 248 ; iii. 49 ; iv. 309.

[1] James Burnet, a Scotch Lord of Session, by the title of Lord Monboddo. ' He was a devout believer in the virtues of the heroic ages, and the deterioration of civilized mankind ; a great contemner of luxuries, insomuch that he never used a wheel-carriage.' WALTER SCOTT, quoted in Croker's *Boswell*, i. 138. There is some account of him in Chambers's *Traditions of Edinburgh*, ii. 175. In his *Origin of Language*, to which Boswell refers in his next note, after praising Henry Stephen for his *Greek Dictionary*, he continues :—' But to compile a dictionary of a barbarous language, such as all the modern are, compared with the learned, is a work which . . . a man of real genius, rather than undertake, would choose to die of hunger, the most cruel, it is said, of all deaths. I should, however, have

praised this labour of the Doctor's more, though of the meanest kind,' &c. Monboddo's *Origin of Language*, v. 274. On p. 271, he says :—' Dr. Johnson was the most invidious and malignant man I have ever known.' See *post*, ii. 147, 259, and v. 77.

[2] His Lordship having frequently spoken in an abusive manner of Dr. Johnson, in my company, I on one occasion during the life-time of my illustrious friend could not refrain from retaliation, and repeated to him this saying. He has since published I don't know how many pages in one of his curious books, attempting, in much anger, but with pitiful effect, to persuade mankind that my illustrious friend was not the great and good man which they esteemed and ever will esteem him to be. BOSWELL.

[3] Mrs. Piozzi (*Anec.* p. 108 : *John. Misc.* i. 221) says :—' Mr. Johnson was indeed unjustly supposed to be a lover of singularity. Few people had a more settled reverence for the world than he, or was less captivated by new modes of behaviour introduced, or innovations on the long-received

better than others, why, make them stare till they stare their
eyes out. But consider how easy it is to make people stare,
by being absurd. I may do it by going into a drawing-room
without my shoes. You remember the gentleman in " The Spectator," who had a commission of lunacy taken out against him for
his extreme singularity, such as never wearing a wig, but a
night-cap. Now, Sir, abstractedly, the night-cap was best ; but,
relatively, the advantage was overbalanced by his making the
boys run after him [1].'

Talking of a London life, he said, ' The happiness of London
is not to be conceived but by those who have been in it. I will
venture to say, there is more learning and science within the cir-
cumference of ten miles from where we now sit, than in all the
rest of the kingdom.' BOSWELL. ' The only disadvantage is the
great distance at which people live from one another.' JOHNSON.
' Yes, Sir ; but that is occasioned by the largeness of it, which is
the cause of all the other advantages.' BOSWELL. ' Sometimes I
have been in the humour of wishing to retire to a desart.' JOHN-
SON. ' Sir, you have desart enough in Scotland.'

customs of common life.' In writing
to Dr. Taylor, 3 Sept. 1763, to urge
him to take a certain course, he says :
—' This I would have you do, not
in compliance with solicitation or
advice, but as a justification of yourself to the world ; the world has
always a right to be regarded.' *Letters*,
No. 159. In *The Adventurer*, No.
131, he has a paper on ' Singularities.'
After quoting Fontenelle's observation on Newton that ' he was not distinguished from other men, by any
singularity either natural or affected,'
he goes on, ¶ 11 :—' Some . . may
be found, who, supported by the
consciousness of great abilities, and
elevated by a long course of reputation and applause, voluntarily consign
themselves to singularity, affect to
cross the roads of life because they
know that they shall not be justled,
and indulge a boundless gratification
of will, because they perceive that
they shall be quietly obeyed.' And,
¶ 13, ' Singularity is, I think, in its

own nature, universally and invariably
displeasing.' Writing of Swift (*Life of
Swift*, 128), he says :—' Whatever he
did, he seemed willing to do in a manner
peculiar to himself, without sufficiently
considering that singularity, as it implies a contempt of the general practice, is a kind of defiance which justly
provokes the hostility of ridicule ; he
therefore who indulges peculiar habits
is worse than others, if he be not
better.' See *ante*, i. 500, for the
record in ' one of his journals ' :—' To
avoid all singularity.'

[1] ' He had many other particularities, for which he gave sound and
philosophical reasons. As this humour still grew upon him, he chose to
wear a turban instead of a periwig ;
concluding very justly, that a bandage
of clean linnen about his head was
much more wholesome, as well as
cleanly, than the caul of a wig, which
is soiled with frequent perspirations.'
Spectator, No. 576.

Although I had promised myself a great deal of instructive conversation with him on the conduct of the married state, of which I had then a near prospect, he did not say much upon that topick. Mr. Seward [1] heard him once say, that ' a man has a very bad chance for happiness in that state, unless he marries a woman of very strong and fixed principles of religion.' He maintained to me, contrary to the common notion, that a woman would not be the worse wife for being learned [2] ; in which, from all that I have observed of *Artemisias* [3], I humbly differed from him. That a woman should be sensible and well informed, I allow to be a great advantage ; and think that Sir Thomas Overbury [4], in his rude versification, has very judiciously pointed out that degree of intelligence which is to be desired in a female companion :

> ' Give me, next *good*, an *understanding wife*,
>   By Nature *wise*, not *learned* by much art ;
> Some *knowledge* on her side will all my life
>   More scope of conversation impart ;
> Besides, her inborne virtue fortifie ;
> They are most firmly good, who [5] best know why.'

When I censured a gentleman of my acquaintance for marrying a second time, as it shewed a disregard of his first wife, he said, ' Not at all, Sir. On the contrary, were he not to marry again, it might be concluded that his first wife had given him a disgust to marriage ; but by taking a second wife he pays the highest compliment to the first, by shewing that she made him so happy as a married man, that he wishes to be so a second time [6].'

---

[1] See *post*, iii. 123, note 1. ⟨See App. B, p. 485.⟩

[2] ' Depend upon it,' he said, ' no woman is the worse for sense and knowledge.' *Post*, v. 226. See, however, *post*, iv. 32, where he says :—' Supposing . . . a wife to be of a studious or argumentative turn, it would be very troublesome.'

[3] ' Tho' Artemisia talks, by fits,
  Of councils, classics, fathers, wits ;
   Reads Malbranche, Boyle, and Locke :
  Yet in some things methinks she fails ;

'Twere well if she would pare her nails,
   And wear a cleaner smock.'
POPE. *Imitations of English Poets, Dorset.*

[4] ' A Wife,' a poem, 1614. BOSWELL.
[5] In the original *that*.
[6] What a succession of compliments was paid by Johnson's old school-fellow, whom he met a year or two later in Lichfield, who ' has had, as he phrased it, *a matter of four wives*, for which,' added Johnson to Mrs. Thrale, ' neither you nor I like him much the better.' *Letters*, No. 256. ⟨See App. B, p. 486.⟩

So ingenious a turn did he give to this delicate question. And yet, on another occasion, he owned that he once had almost asked a promise of Mrs. Johnson that she would not marry again, but had checked himself. Indeed, I cannot help thinking, that in his case the request would have been unreasonable ; for if Mrs. Johnson forgot, or thought it no injury to the memory of her first love,—the husband of her youth and the father of her children,— to make a second marriage, why should she be precluded from a third, should she be so inclined ? In Johnson's persevering fond appropriation of his *Tetty*, even after her decease, he seems totally to have overlooked the prior claim of the honest Birmingham trader. I presume that her having been married before had, at times, given him some uneasiness ; for I remember his observing upon the marriage of one of our common friends, ' He has done a very foolish thing, Sir ; he has married a widow, when he might have had a maid [1].'

We drank tea with Mrs. Williams. I had last year the pleasure of seeing Mrs. Thrale at Dr. Johnson's one morning, and had conversation enough with her to admire her talents, and to shew her that I was as Johnsonian as herself. Dr. Johnson had probably been kind enough to speak well of me, for this evening he delivered me a very polite card from Mr. Thrale and her, inviting me to Streatham.

On the 6th of October I complied with this obliging invitation, and found, at an elegant villa, six miles from town, every circumstance that can make society pleasing. Johnson, though quite at home, was yet looked up to with an awe, tempered by affection, and seemed to be equally the care of his host and hostess. I rejoiced at seeing him so happy.

He played off his wit against Scotland with a good humoured pleasantry, which gave me, though no bigot to national prejudices, an opportunity for a little contest with him. I having said that England was obliged to us for gardeners, almost all their good gardeners being Scotchmen ;—JOHNSON. ' Why, Sir, that is because gardening is much more necessary amongst you than with us, which makes so many of your people learn it. It is *all* gardening with you. Things which grow wild here, must

---

[1] Mr. Langton married, 24 May, 1770, the widow of the ninth Earl of Rothes ; *post*, ii. 136, note 3.

be cultivated with great care in Scotland. Pray now, (throwing himself back in his chair, and laughing,) are you ever able to bring the *sloe* to perfection ? '

I boasted that we had the honour of being the first to abolish the unhospitable, troublesome, and ungracious custom of giving vails to servants [1]. JOHNSON. ' Sir, you abolished vails, because you were too poor to be able to give them.'

Mrs. Thrale disputed with him on the merit of Prior. He attacked him powerfully ; said he wrote of love like a man who had never felt it : his love verses were college verses : and he repeated the song ' Alexis shunn'd his fellow swains [2],' &c. in so ludicrous a manner, as to make us all wonder how any one could have been pleased with such fantastical stuff. Mrs. Thrale stood to her gun with great courage, in defence of amorous ditties, which Johnson despised, till he at last silenced her by saying, ' My dear Lady, talk no more of this. Nonsense can be defended but by nonsense [3].'

Mrs. Thrale then praised Garrick's talent for light gay poetry ; and, as a specimen, repeated his song in ' Florizel and Perdita,' and dwelt with peculiar pleasure on this line :

' I'd smile with the simple, and feed with the poor [4].'

[1] Walpole, writing of 1764, says :—
' As one of my objects was to raise the characters and popularity of our party, I had inserted a paragraph in the newspapers observing that the abolition of vails to servants had been set on foot by the Duke of Bedford, and had been opposed by the Duke of Devonshire. . . . Soon after a riot happened at Ranelagh, in which the footmen mobbed and ill-treated some gentlemen who had been active in that reformation.' *Memoirs of the Reign of George III*, ii. 3.

[2] ' Alexis shunn'd his fellow swains,
Their rural sports, and jocund strains,
(Heav'n guard us all from Cupid's bow !)
He lost his crook, he left his flocks ;

And wand'ring through the lonely rocks,
He nourish'd endless woe.'
The Despairing Shepherd.

[3] ' In his Amorous Effusions he [Prior] is less happy ; for they are not dictated by nature or by passion, and have neither gallantry nor tenderness. They have the coldness of Cowley without his wit ; the dull exercises of a skilful versifier resolved at all adventures to write something about Chloe, and trying to be amorous by dint of study. . . . In his private relaxation he revived the tavern, and in his amorous pedantry he exhibited the college.' Johnson's *Life of Prior*, 56, 79.

[4] *Florizel and Perdita* is Garrick's version of *The Winter's Tale*. He cut down the five acts to three. The

JOHNSON. ' Nay, my dear Lady, this will never do. Poor David ! Smile with the simple ! [a] What folly is that ! [b] And who would feed with the poor that can help it ? No, no ; let me smile with the wise, and feed with the rich.' I repeated this sally to Garrick, and wondered to find his sensibility as a writer not a little irritated by it. To sooth him, I observed, that Johnson spared none of us ; and I quoted the passage in Horace [1], in which he compares one who attacks his friends for the sake of a laugh, to a pushing ox [2], that is marked by a bunch of hay put upon his horns : ' *fœnum habet in cornu.*' ' Ay, (said Garrick, vehemently,) he has a whole *mow* of it.'

Talking of history, Johnson said, ' We may know historical facts to be true, as we may know facts in common life to be true. Motives are generally unknown. We cannot trust to the characters we find in history, unless when they are drawn by those who knew the persons ; as those, for instance, by Sallust and by Lord Clarendon [3].'

He would not allow much merit to Whitefield's oratory. ' His popularity, Sir, (said he,) is chiefly owing to the peculiarity of his manner. He would be followed by crowds were he to wear a night-cap in the pulpit, or were he to preach from a tree [4].'

[a] simple ! 1 : simple ? 2 : simple ;— 3.   [b] that ! 1 : that. 2 : that ? 3.

line, which is misquoted, is in one of Perdita's songs :—

  ' That giant ambition we never can dread ;
  Our roofs are too low for so lofty a head ;
  Content and sweet chearfulness open our door,
  They smile with the simple, and feed with the poor.'
              Act ii. sc. 1.

[1] Horace. *Sat.* i. 4. 34.

[2] See *ante*, ii. 66.

[3] Walpole told Malone that ' he was about twenty-two [twenty-four] years old when his father retired ; and that he remembered his offering one day to read to Lord Orford, finding that time hung heavy on his hands. '' What,'' said Lord Orford, '' will you read, child ? '' Mr. Walpole, considering that his father had been long engaged in publick business, proposed to read some history. '' No,'' said Lord Orford, '' don't read history to me ; that can't be true.'' ' Prior's *Malone*, p. 387. See also *post*, ii. 237 ; iii. 404.

[4] See *ante*, i. 75, *post*, iii. 409, and v. 35. Boswell himself had met Whitefield ; for mentioning him in his *Letter to the People of Scotland* (1785, p. 25), he adds :—' Of whose pious and animated society I had some share.' Southey thus describes Whitefield in his *Life of Wesley* (i. 104) :—
' His voice excelled both in melody and compass, and its fine modulations were happily accompanied by that grace of action which he possessed in an eminent degree, and which has been said to be the chief requisite of an orator. An ignorant man described his eloquence oddly but strikingly,

I know not from what spirit of contradiction he burst out into a violent declamation against the Corsicans, of whose heroism I talked in high terms. ' Sir, (said he,) what is all this rout about the Corsicans ? They have been at war with the Genoese for upwards of twenty years, and have never yet taken their fortified towns. They might have battered down their walls, and reduced them to powder in twenty years. They might have pulled the walls in pieces, and cracked the stones with their teeth in twenty years.' It was in vain to argue with him upon the want of artillery : he was not to be resisted for the moment.

On the evening of October 10, I presented Dr. Johnson to General Paoli. I had greatly wished that two men, for whom I had the highest esteem, should meet [1]. They met with a manly ease, mutually conscious of their own abilities, and of the abilities of each other. The General spoke Italian, and Dr. Johnson English, and understood one another very well, with a little aid of interpretation from me, in which I compared myself to an isthmus which joins two great continents. Upon Johnson's approach, the General said, ' From what I have read of your works, Sir, and from what Mr. Boswell has told me of you, I have long held you in great veneration.' The General talked of languages being formed on the particular notions and manners of a people, without knowing which, we cannot know the language. We may know the direct signification of single words ; but by these no beauty of expression, no sally of genius, no

when he said that Mr. Whitefield preached like a lion. So strange a comparison conveyed no unapt a notion of the force and vehemence and passion of that oratory which awed the hearers, and made them tremble like Felix before the apostle.' Benjamin Franklin writes (*Writings*, i. 356) :—' Mr. Whitefield's eloquence had a wonderful power over the hearts and purses of his hearers, of which I myself was an instance.' He happened to be present at a sermon which, he perceived, was to finish with a collection for an object which had not his approbation. ' I silently resolved he should get nothing from me. I had in my pocket a handful of copper money, three or four silver dollars, and five pistoles in gold. As he proceeded I began to soften, and concluded to give the coppers. Another stroke of his oratory made me asham'd of that, and determin'd me to give the silver ; and he finish'd so admirably, that I empty'd my pocket wholly into the collector's dish, gold and all.'

[1] ' What an idea may we not form of an interview between such a scholar and philosopher as Mr. Johnson, and such a legislatour and general as Paoli ! ' Boswell's *Corsica*, p. 334.

wit is conveyed to the mind. All this must be by allusion to other ideas. ' Sir, (said Johnson,) you talk of language, as if you had never done any thing else but study it, instead of governing a nation.' The General said, ' *Questo e un troppo gran complimento* ; ' this is too great a compliment. Johnson answered. ' I should have thought so, Sir, if I had not heard you talk.' The General asked him, what he thought of the spirit of infidelity which was so prevalent [1]. JOHNSON. ' Sir, this gloom of infidelity, I hope, is only a transient cloud passing through the hemisphere [2], which will soon be dissipated, and the sun break forth with his usual splendour.' ' You think then, (said the General,) that they will change their principles like their clothes.' JOHNSON. ' Why, Sir, if they bestow no more thought on principles than on dress, it must be so.' The General said, that ' a great part of the fashionable infidelity was owing to a desire of shewing courage. Men who have no opportunities of shewing it as to things in this life, take death and futurity as objects on which to display it.' JOHNSON. ' That is mighty foolish affectation. Fear is one of the passions of human nature, of which it is impossible to divest it. You remember that the Emperour Charles V, when he read upon the tomb-stone of a Spanish nobleman, " Here lies one who never knew fear," wittily said, " Then he never snuffed a candle with his fingers." '

He talked a few words of French [3] to the General ; but

[1] John Stewart, who in 1768 was sent on a secret mission to Paoli, in his interesting report says :—' Religion seems to sit easy upon Paoli, and notwithstanding what his historian Boswell relates, I take him to be very free in his notions that way. This I suspect both from the strain of his conversation, and from what I have learnt of his conduct towards the clergy and monks.' Fitzmaurice's *Shelburne*, i. 384. See *post*, ii. 359, where Johnson said :—' Sir, there is a great cry about infidelity ; but there are, in reality, very few infidels.' Yet not long before he had complained of an ' inundation of impiety.' *Post*, v. 271.

[2] I suppose Johnson said atmo-

sphere. CROKER. In *Humphry Clinker*, in the letter of June 2, there is, however, a somewhat similar use of the word. Lord Bute is described as ' the Caledonian luminary, that lately blazed so bright in our hemisphere ! Methinks, at present, it glimmers through a fog.' A star, however, unlike a cloud, may pass from one hemisphere to the other. ⟨Johnson was probably thinking of the early sense of hemisphere, ' the sky above us ': see *O.E.D.*, s.v. *Hemisphere* sense 2.⟩

[3] See *post*, ii. 404-5. Hannah More, writing in 1782 (*Memoirs*, i. 242), says :—' Paoli . . . will not talk in English, and his French is mixed with Italian. He speaks no language with purity.'

finding he did not do it with facility, he asked for pen, ink, and paper, and wrote the following note :

' *J'ai lu dans la geographie de Lucas de Linda un Pater-noster écrit dans une langue tout à-fait differente de l'Italienne, et de toutes autres lesquelles se derivent du Latin.* L'auteur l'appelle linguam Corsicæ rusticam ; *elle a peut-etre passé, peu à peu ; mais elle a certainement pre-value autrefois dans les montagnes et dans la campagne. Le même auteur dit la même chose en parlant de Sardaigne ; qu'il y a deux langues dans l'Isle, une des villes, l'autre de la campagne.'*

The General immediately informed him that the *lingua rustica* was only in Sardinia.

Dr. Johnson went home with me, and drank tea till late in the night. He said, ' General Paoli had the loftiest port of any man he had ever seen [1].' He denied that military men were always the best bred men. ' Perfect good breeding, he observed, consists in having no particular mark of any profession, but a general elegance of manners ; whereas, in a military man, you can commonly distinguish the *brand* of a soldier, *l'homme d'épée* †.'

Dr. Johnson shunned to-night any discussion of the perplexed question of fate and free will, which I attempted to agitate: ' Sir, (said he,) we *know* our will is free, and *there's* an end on't [2].'

He honoured me with his company at dinner on the 16th of October, at my lodgings in Old Bond-street, with Sir Joshua Reynolds, Mr. Garrick, Dr. Goldsmith, Mr. Murphy, Mr. Bickerstaff [3], and Mr. Thomas Davies. Garrick played round him with

---

[1] Walpole writes :—' Paoli was a man of decent deportment, . . . with as much ease as suited a prudence that seemed the utmost effort of a wary understanding, and so void of anything remarkable in his aspect, that being asked if I knew who it was, I judged him a Scottish officer (for he was sandy-complexioned and in regimentals) who was cautiously awaiting the moment of promotion.' *Memoirs of the Reign of George III*, iii. 387. ⟨See App. B, p. 486.⟩

† ⟨See App. B, p. 486.⟩

[2] Boswell introduced this subject

often. See *post*, ii. 104 ; iii. 290–1 ; iv. 71, 329; v. 117. Like Milton's fallen angels, he ' found no end, in wand'ring mazes lost.' *Paradise Lost*, ii. 561.

[3] ' To this wretched being, himself by his own misconduct lashed out of human society, the stage was indebted for several very pure and pleasing entertainments ; among them, *Love in a Village*, *The Maid of the Mill*.' Forster's *Goldsmith*, ii. 136, *n*. 'When,' says Mrs. Piozzi (*Anec.* p. 168 : *John. Misc.* i. 262), ' Mr. Bickerstaff's flight confirmed the report of his guilt, and

a fond vivacity, taking hold of the breasts of his coat, and, looking up in his face with a lively archness, complimented him on the good health which he seemed then to enjoy ; while the sage, shaking his head, beheld him with a gentle complacency. One of the company not being come at the appointed hour, I proposed, as usual upon such occasions, to order dinner to be served ; adding, ' Ought six people to be kept waiting for one ? ' ' Why, yes, (answered Johnson, with a delicate humanity,) if the one will suffer more by your sitting down, than the six will do by waiting.' Goldsmith, to divert the tedious minutes, strutted about, bragging of his dress, and I believe was seriously vain of it, for his mind was wonderfully prone to such impressions [1]. ' Come, come, (said Garrick,) talk no more of that. You are, perhaps, the worst—eh, eh ! '—Goldsmith was eagerly attempting to interrupt him, when Garrick went on, laughing ironically, ' Nay, you will always *look* like a gentleman [2] ; but I am talking of being well or ill[a] *drest*.' ' Well, let me tell you, (said Goldsmith,) when my tailor brought home my bloom-coloured coat, he said, " Sir, I have a favour to beg of you. When any body asks you who made your clothes, be pleased to mention John Filby, at the Harrow, in Water-lane." ' JOHNSON. ' Why, Sir, that was because he knew the strange colour would attract crouds to gaze at it, and thus they might hear of him, and see how well he could make a coat even of so absurd a colour [3].'

a ill 1, 2 : *ill* 3.

my husband said in answer to Johnson's astonishment, that he had long been a suspected man : " By those who look close to the ground, dirt will be seen, Sir (was the lofty reply) : I hope I see things from a greater distance." ' In the *Garrick Corres.* (i. 473) is a piteous letter in bad French, written from St. Malo, by Bickerstaff to Garrick, endorsed by Garrick, ' From that poor wretch Bickerstaff. I could not answer it.'

[1] Boswell, only a couple of years before he published *The Life of Johnson*, in fact while he was writing it, had written to Temple :—' I was the *great man* (as we used to say) at the late drawing room in a suit of imperial blue lined with rosecoloured silk, and ornamented with rich gold-wrought buttons.' *Letters*, No. 261 ii. 367.

[2] Miss Reynolds, in her *Recollections* (*John. Misc.* ii. 269), says, ' One Day at Sir Joshua Reynolds's . . . he [Goldsmith] was relating how he had been insulted by some gentleman he had accidently met. . . " The fellow," he said, " took me for a tailor ! " on which all the Party either laugh'd aloud or shew'd they suppress'd a laugh.'

[3] In Prior's *Goldsmith*, ii. 232, is given Filby's bill for a suit of clothes

After dinner our conversation first turned upon Pope. Johnson said, his characters of men were admirably drawn, those of women not so well [1]. He repeated to us, in his forcible melodious manner, the concluding lines of the Dunciad [2]. While he was talking loudly in praise of those lines, one of the company [3] ventured to say, ' Too fine for such a poem :—a poem on what ? ' JOHNSON, (with a disdainful look,) ' Why, on *dunces*. It was worth while being a dunce then. Ah, Sir, hadst *thou* lived in those days ! It is not worth while being a dunce now, when there are no wits [4].' Bickerstaff observed, as a peculiar circumstance, that Pope's fame was higher when he was alive than it was then [5]. Johnson said, his Pastorals were poor things, though the versification was fine [6]. He told us, with high satisfaction,

sent to Goldsmith this very day :—
Oct. 16.—   £   s.   d.
To making a half-dress
  suit of ratteen, lined
  with satin - - - 12 12 0
To a pair of silk stocking
  breeches - - - -   2   5   0
To a pair of bloom-
  coloured ditto - -   1   4   6
Nothing is said in this bill of the colour of the coat ; it is the breeches that are bloom-coloured. The tailor's name was William, not John, Filby ; *ib.* i. 378. Goldsmith in his *Life of Nash* had said :—' Dress has a mechanical influence upon the mind, and we naturally are awed into respect and esteem at the elegance of those whom even our reason would teach us to contemn. He seemed early sensible of human weakness in this respect ; he brought a person genteelly dressed to every assembly.' Goldsmith's *Works*, ed. Cunningham, iv. 46.

[1] ' The *Characters of Men and Women* are the product of diligent speculation upon human life ; much labour has been bestowed upon them, and Pope very seldom laboured in vain. . . . The *Characters of Men*, however, are written with more, if not with deeper, thought, and exhibit many passages exquisitely beautiful.

. . . In the women's part are some defects.' Johnson's *Life of Pope*, 368.

[2] Mr. Langton informed me that he once related to Johnson (on the authority of Spence) that Pope himself admired those lines so much, that when he repeated them, his voice faltered : ' and well it might, Sir, (said Johnson) for they are noble lines.' J. BOSWELL, JUN.

[3] We have here an instance of that reserve which Boswell, in his Dedication to Sir Joshua Reynolds (*ante*, i. 4), says that he has practised. In one particular he had ' found the world to be a great fool,' and, ' I have, therefore,' as he writes, ' in this Work been more reserved ; ' yet the reserve is slight enough. Everyone guesses that ' one of the company ' was Boswell. ⟨See App. B, p. 486.⟩

[4] Yet Johnson, in his *Life of Pope* (146), seems to be much of Boswell's opinion ; for in writing of *The Dunciad*, he says :—' The subject itself had nothing generally interesting ; for whom did it concern to know that one or another scribbler was a dunce ? '

[5] ⟨Johnson differed from this opinion in 1778 : see *post*, iii. 332.⟩

[6] ' It is surely sufficient for an author of sixteen . . . to have obtained sufficient power of language and skill

the anecdote of Pope's inquiring who was the authour of his
'London,' and saying, he will be soon *déterré* [1]. He observed,
that in Dryden's poetry there were passages drawn from a
profundity which Pope could never reach [2]. He repeated some
fine lines on love, by the former, (which I have now forgotten [3],)
and gave great applause to the character of Zimri [4]. Goldsmith
said, that Pope's character of Addison [5] shewed a deep knowledge
of the human heart. Johnson said, that the description of the
temple, in 'The Mourning Bride [6],' was the finest poetical passage
he had ever read ; he recollected none in Shakspeare equal to
it.—' But, (said Garrick, all alarmed for " the god [a] of his idolatry [7],") we know not the extent and variety of his powers.

a god 1 : God 2, 3.

in metre to exhibit a series of versification, which had in English poetry
no precedent, nor has since had an
imitation.' Johnson's *Pope*, 314.

[1] See *ante*, i. 129.

[2] ' If the flights of Dryden . . . are
higher, Pope continues longer on the
wing . . . Dryden is read with frequent
astonishment, and Pope with perpetual delight.' Johnson's *Pope*, 310.

[3] ⟨Croker happily conjectured that
the lines Boswell had forgotten were
those from *Tyrannic Love* quoted by
Johnson in the *Life of Dryden*, 323.
Boswell's revise read : ' He repeated
his lines on love (Gentle, tempestuous,
&c.).'⟩

[4] The Duke of Buckingham in
Dryden's *Absalom and Achitophel.*

[5] *Epistle to Arbuthnot*, l. 193.

[6] *Almeria.*—' It was a fancy'd
Noise ; for all is hush'd.
Leonora.—It bore the Accent of a
Humane Voice.
Almeria.—It was thy Fear ; or else
some transient Wind
Whistling thro' Hollows of this vaulted
Isle
We'll listen—
Leonora.—Hark !
Almeria.—No, all is hush'd, and still
as Death—'Tis dreadful !
How rev'rend is the Face of this tall
Pile,

Whose antient Pillars rear their
Marble Heads,
To bear aloft its arch'd and pond'rous
Roof,
By its own Weight, made stedfast and
immoveable,
Looking Tranquility. It strikes an
Awe
And Terror on my aking Sight ; the
Tombs
And Monumental Caves of Death look
cold,
And shoot a Chilness to my trembling
Heart.
Give me thy Hand, and speak to me,
nay, speak,
And let me hear thy Voice ;
My own affrights me with its Echo's.
Act ii. sc. 1 (1697), p. 16.

[7] ' Swear by thy gracious self,
Which is the god of my idolatry.'
Romeo and Juliet, act ii. sc. 2.

He was a god with whom he ventured
to take great liberties. Thus on
Jan. 10, 1776, he wrote :—' I have
ventured to produce *Hamlet*, with
alterations. It was the most imprudent thing I ever did in all my
life ; but I had sworn I would not
leave the stage till I had rescued that
noble play from all the rubbish of
the fifth act. I have brought it forth
without the Grave-digger's trick and
the fencing-match. The alteration

We are to suppose there are such passages in his works. Shak-speare must not suffer from the badness of our memories.' Johnson, diverted by this enthusiastick jealousy, went on with greater ardour : ' No, Sir ; Congreve has *nature* ; ' (smiling on the tragick eagerness of Garrick ;) but composing himself, he added, ' Sir, this is not comparing Congreve on the whole, with Shak-speare on the whole ; but only maintaining that Congreve has one finer passage than any that can be found in Shakspeare. Sir, a man may have no more than ten guineas in the world, but he may have those ten guineas in one piece ; and so may have a finer piece than a man who has ten thousand pounds : but then he has only one ten-guinea piece.—What I mean is, that you can shew me no passage where there is simply a description of material objects, without any intermixture of moral notions, which produces such an effect [1].' Mr. Murphy mentioned Shakspeare's

was received with general approbation, beyond my most warm expectations.' *Garrick Corres.* ii. 126. See *ante*, ii. 78, note 4.

[1] This comparison between Shake-speare and Congreve is mentioned perhaps oftener than any passage in Boswell. Almost as often as it is mentioned, it may be seen that John-son's real opinion is misrepresented or misunderstood. A few passages from his writings will shew how he regarded the two men. In the *Life of Congreve*, 34, he repeats what he says here :—' If I were required to select from the whole mass of English poetry the most poetical para-graph, I know not what I could prefer to an exclamation in *The Mourn-ing Bride*.' Yet in writing of the same play, he says :—' In this play . . . there is more bustle than senti-ment ; the plot is busy and intricate and the events take hold on the attention, but, except a very few passages, we are rather amused with noise and perplexed with stratagem than entertained with any true de-lineation of natural characters.' *Ib.* 16. In the preface to his *Shake-speare*, published four years before

this conversation, he almost answered Garrick by anticipation. ' It was said of Euripides, that every verse was a precept ; and it may be said of Shakespeare, that from his works may be collected a system of civil and economical prudence. Yet his real power is not shown in the splen-dour of particular passages, but by the progress of his fable and the tenour of his dialogue ; and he that tries to recommend him by select quotations, will succeed like the pedant in Hierocles, who, when he offered his house to sale, carried a brick in his pocket as a specimen.' *Works*, v. 106. Ignorant, indeed, is he who thinks that Johnson was insen-sible to Shakespeare's ' transcendent and unbounded genius,' to use the words that he himself applied to him. *The Rambler*, No. 156. ' It may be doubted,' he writes, ' whether from all his successors more maxims of theoretical knowledge, or more rules of practical prudence, can be col-lected, than he alone has given to his country.' *Pref. Shaks., Works*, v. 131. ' He that has read Shakespeare, with attention, will, perhaps, find little new in the crowded world.' *Dedic. Mrs.*

description of the night before the battle of Agincourt [1] ; but
it was observed, it had *men* in it. Mr. Davies suggested the
speech of Juliet, in which she figures herself awaking in the tomb
of her ancestors [2]. Some one mentioned the description of Dover
Cliff [3]. JOHNSON. ' No, Sir ; it should be all precipice,—all
vacuum. The crows impede your fall. The diminished appearance of the boats, and other circumstances, are all very good
description ; but do not impress the mind at once with the horrible idea of immense height. The impression is divided ; you
pass on by computation, from one stage of the tremendous
space to another. Had the girl in " The Mourning Bride "
said, she could not cast her shoe to the top of one of the
pillars in the temple, it would not have aided the idea, but
weakened it.'

Talking of a Barrister who had a bad utterance, some one, (to
rouse Johnson,) wickedly said, that he was unfortunate in not
having been taught oratory by Sheridan [4]. JOHNSON. ' Nay, Sir,
if he had been taught by Sheridan, he would have cleared the
room.' GARRICK. ' Sheridan has too much vanity to be a good
man.' We shall now see Johnson's mode of *defending* a man ;
taking him into his own hands, and discriminating. JOHNSON.
' No, Sir. There is, to be sure, in Sheridan, something to repre-
hend, and every thing to laugh at ; but, Sir, he is not a bad man.
No, Sir ; were mankind to be divided into good and bad, he
would stand considerably within the ranks of good. And,

Lennox's Shaks. Illustr., ib. p. 434.
' Let him, that is yet unacquainted
with the powers of Shakespeare, and
who desires to feel the highest pleasure
that the drama can give, read every
play, from the first scene to the last,
with utter negligence of all his commentators. When his fancy is once
on the wing, let it not stoop at correction or explanation.' *Pref. Shaks.,
ib.* p. 152. And lastly he quotes
Dryden's words [from Dryden's
Essay of Dramatick Poesie, edit. of
1701, i. 19], ' that Shakespeare was
the man, who, of all modern and,
perhaps, ancient poets, had the
largest and most comprehensive soul.'

Ib. p. 153. Mrs. Piozzi records
(*Anec.* p. 58 : John. Misc. i. 186),
that she ' forced him one day, . . . to
prefer Young's description of Night
to the so much admired ones of
Dryden and Shakespeare.' He ended
however by saying :—' Young froths,
and foams, and bubbles sometimes
very vigorously ; but we must not
compare the noise made by your tea-
kettle here with the roaring of the
ocean.' See also *post*, ii. 96.
[1] *Henry V*, act iv, Prologue
[2] *Romeo and Juliet*, act iv, sc. 3.
[3] *King Lear*, act iv, sc. 6.
[4] See *ante*, i. 453.

Sir, it must be allowed that Sheridan excels in plain declamation, though he can exhibit no character.'

I should, perhaps, have suppressed this disquisition concerning a person of whose merit and worth I think with respect, had he not attacked Johnson so outrageously in his Life of Swift, and, at the same time, treated us his admirers as a set of pigmies [1]. He who has provoked the lash of wit, cannot complain that he smarts from it.

Mrs. Montagu, a lady distinguished for having written an Essay on Shakspeare, being mentioned;—REYNOLDS. 'I think that essay does her honour.' JOHNSON. 'Yes, Sir ; it does *her* honour, but it would do nobody else honour. I have, indeed, not read it all. But when I take up the end of a web, and find it packthread, I do not expect, by looking further, to find embroidery. Sir, I will venture to say, there is not one sentence of true criticism in her book.' GARRICK. 'But, Sir, surely it shews how much Voltaire has mistaken Shakspeare, which nobody else has done [2].' JOHNSON. 'Sir, nobody else has thought it worth while. And what merit is there in that ? You may as well praise a schoolmaster for whipping a boy who has construed ill. No, Sir, there is no real criticism in it : none shewing the beauty of thought, as formed on the workings of the human heart.'

The admirers of this Essay [3] may be offended at the slighting

---

[1] See *ante*, i. 388.

[2] In spite of the gross nonsense that Voltaire has written about Shakespeare, yet it was with justice that in a letter to Walpole (dated July 15, 1768,) he said :—' Je suis le premier qui ait fait connaître Shakespeare aux Français. . . . Je peux vous assurer qu'avant moi personne en France ne connaissait la poésie anglaise.' Voltaire's *Œuvres*, xlvi. 78.

[3] Of whom I acknowledge myself to be one, considering it as a piece of the secondary or comparative species of criticism ; and not of that profound species which alone Dr. Johnson would allow to be ' real criticism.' It is, besides, clearly and elegantly expressed, and has done effectually what it professed to do, namely, vin-

dicated Shakspeare from the misrepresentations of Voltaire ; and considering how many young people were misled by his witty, though false observations, Mrs. Montagu's Essay was of service to Shakspeare with a certain class of readers, and is, therefore, entitled to praise. Johnson, I am assured, allowed the merit which I have stated, saying, (with reference to Voltaire,) ' it is conclusive *ad hominem*.' BOSWELL.

That this dull essay, which would not do credit to a clever school-girl of seventeen, should have had a fame, of which the echoes have not yet quite died out, can only be fully explained by Mrs. Montagu's great wealth and position in society. Contemptible as was her essay, yet a saying of hers

manner in which Johnson spoke of it ; but let it be remembered,
that he gave his honest opinion, unbiassed by any prejudice, or
any proud jealousy of a woman intruding herself into the chair of
criticism ; for Sir Joshua Reynolds has told me, that when the
Essay first came out, and it was not known who had written it,
Johnson wondered how Sir Joshua could like it [1]. At this time
Sir Joshua himself had received no information concerning the
authour, except being assured by one of our most eminent literati,
that it was clear its authour did not know the Greek tragedies in
the original. One day at Sir Joshua's table, when it was related
that Mrs. Montagu, in an excess of compliment to the authour of
a modern tragedy, had exclaimed, ' I tremble for Shakspeare ; '
Johnson said, ' When Shakspeare has got —— † for his rival, and
Mrs. Montagu for his defender, he is in a poor state indeed.'

Johnson proceeded : ' The Scotchman [2] has taken the right
method in his " Elements of Criticism." I do not mean that he

about Voltaire was clever. ' He sent
to the Academy an invective [against
Shakespeare] that bears all the marks
of passionate dotage. Mrs. Montagu
happened to be present when it was
read. Suard, one of their writers,
said to her, " Je crois, Madame, que
vous êtes un peu fâchée de ce que
vous venez d'entendre." She replied,
" Moi, Monsieur ! point du tout ! Je
ne suis pas amie de M. Voltaire."
Walpole's *Letters*, No. 445. Her own
Letters are very pompous and very
poor, and her wit would not seem to
have flashed often ; for Miss Burney
wrote of her :—' She reasons well,
and harangues well, but wit she
has none.' Mme. D'Arblay's *Diary*,
i. 335. Yet in this same *Diary* (i.
112) we find evidence of the absurdly
high estimate that was commonly
formed of her. ' Mrs. Thrale asked
me if I did not want to see Mrs.
Montagu ? I truly said, I should be
the most insensible of all animals, not
to like to see our sex's glory.' That
she was a very extraordinary woman
we have Johnson's word for it. (See
post, iv. 275). It is impossible, how-

ever, to discover anything that rises
above commonplace in anything that
she wrote, and, so far as I know, that
she said, with the exception of her
one saying about Voltaire. Johnson
himself, in one of his letters to Mrs.
Thrale, has a laugh at her. He had
mentioned Shakespeare, nature and
friendship, and continues :—' Now, of
whom shall I proceed to speak ? Of
whom but Mrs. Montague ? Having
mentioned Shakespeare and Nature,
does not the name of Montague force
itself upon me ? ' *Letters*, No. 657. See
post, iii. 244. ⟨Dr. Hill had seen
only those of Mrs. Montagu's letters
published by Lord Rokeby ; perhaps
he would have revised his opinion of
her wit and learning if he had read
the collection printed by Mr. Blunt
in his *Mrs. Montagu, Queen of the
Blues*, 1923.⟩

[1] ' Reynolds is fond of her book,
and I wonder at it ; for neither I, nor
Beauclerk, nor Mrs. Thrale, could
get through it.' *Post*, v. 245.

[2] Lord Kames is ' the Scotchman.'
See *ante*, i. 393.

† ⟨Robert Jephson. See App. B.⟩

has taught us any thing ; but he has told us old things in a new way.' MURPHY. 'He seems to have read a great deal of French criticism, and wants to make it his own ; as if he had been for years anatomising the heart of man, and peeping into every cranny of it.' GOLDSMITH. 'It is easier to write that book, than to read it ¹.' JOHNSON. 'We have an example of true. criticism in Burke's " Essay on the Sublime and Beautiful ; " and, if I recollect, there is also Du Bos ² ; and Bouhours ³, who shews all beauty to depend on truth. There is no great merit in telling how many plays have ghosts in them, and how this ghost is better than that. You must shew how terrour is impressed on the human heart.—In the description of night in Macbeth ⁴, the beetle and the bat detract from the general idea of darkness,— inspissated gloom.'

Politicks being mentioned, he said, ' This petitioning is a new mode of distressing government, and a mighty easy one. I will undertake to get petitions either against quarter-guineas or half-guineas, with the help of a little hot wine. There must be no yielding to encourage this. The object is not important enough. We are not to blow up half a dozen palaces, because one cottage is burning ⁵.'

¹ ' When Charles Townshend read some of Lord Kames's *Elements of Criticism*, he said, " This is the work of a dull man grown whimsical " —a most characteristical account of Lord Kames as a writer.' *Boswelliana*, p. 278. Hume wrote of it : —' Some parts of the work are ingenious and curious ; but it is too abstruse and crabbed ever to take with the public.' J. H. Burton's *Hume*, ii. 131. ' Kames,' he says, ' had much provoked Voltaire, who never forgives, and never thinks any enemy below his notice.' *Ib.* p. 195. Voltaire (*Œuvres*, xxv. 459) thus ridicules his book :—' Il nous prouve d'abord que nous avons cinq sens, et que nous sentons moins l'impression douce faite sur nos yeux et sur nos oreilles par les couleurs et par les sons que nous ne sentons un grand coup sur la jambe ou sur la tête.'

² L'Abbé Dubos, 1670–1742. ' Tous les artistes lisent avec fruit ses *Réflexions sur la poésie, la peinture et la musique.* C'est le livre le plus utile qu'on ait jamais écrit sur ces matières chez aucune des nations de l'Europe.' Voltaire's *Siècle de Louis XIV, Œuvres*, xiv. 66.

³ Dominique Bouhours, 1628–1702. Voltaire, writing of Bouhours' *Manière de bien penser sur les ouvrages d'esprit*, says that he teaches young people ' à éviter l'enflure, l'obscurité, le recherché, et le faux.' *Ib.* p. 44. Johnson, perhaps, knew him through *The Spectator*, No. 62, where it is said that he ' has taken pains to shew that it is impossible for any thought to be beautiful which is not just, . . . that the basis of all wit is truth.' ⟨Cf. Johnson's *Pref. to Preceptor, Works*, v. 240.⟩

⁴ *Macbeth*, act iii. sc. 2.

⁵ In *The False Alarm*, that was published less than three months after this

The conversation then took another turn.   JOHNSON. ' It is amazing what ignorance of certain points one sometimes finds in men of eminence.   A wit about town, who wrote Latin bawdy verses, asked me, how it happened that England and Scotland, which were once two kingdoms, were now one :—and Sir Fletcher Norton [1] did not seem to know that there were such publications as the Reviews.'

' The ballad of Hardyknute [2] has no great merit, if it be really ancient.   People talk of nature.   But mere obvious nature may be exhibited with very little power of mind.'

On Thursday, October 19, I passed the evening with him at his house.   He advised me to complete a Dictionary of words peculiar to Scotland, of which I shewed him a specimen.   ' Sir, (said he,) Ray has made a collection of north-country words [3].

conversation, Johnson describes how petitions were got. ' The progress of a petition is well known.   An ejected placeman goes down to his county or his borough, tells his friends of his inability to serve them, and his constituents of the corruption of the government.   His friends readily understand that he who can get nothing, will have nothing to give.   They agree to proclaim a meeting ; meat and drink are plentifully provided ; a crowd is easily brought together, and those who think that they know the reason of their meeting, undertake to tell those who know it not ; ale and clamour unite their powers. . . . The petition is read, and universally approved.   Those who are sober enough to write, add their names, and the rest would sign it, if they could.' *Works*, vi. 172.   Yet, when the petitions for Dr. Dodd's life were rejected, Johnson said :—' Surely the voice of the publick, when it calls so loudly, and calls only for mercy, ought to be heard.' *Post*, iii. 120. Walpole, writing of the numerous petitions presented to the King this year (1769), blames ' an example so inconsistent with the principles of liberty, as appealing to the Crown against the House of Commons.'

Some of them prayed for a dissolution of Parliament. *Memoirs of the Reign of George III*, iii. 382, 390. Two years earlier Lord Shelburne, when Secretary of State, had found among the subscribers to a petition for his impeachment, a friend of his, a London alderman. ' Oh, aye,' said the alderman when asked for an explanation, ' I did sign a petition at the Royal Exchange, which they told me was for the impeachment of a minister ; I always sign a petition to impeach a minister, and I recollect that as soon as I had subscribed it, twenty more put their names to it.' *Parl. Hist.* xxxv. 167.

[1] See *post*, ii. 472.

[2] ⟨Percy writes : ' This fine morsel of heroic poetry hath generally past for ancient,' but adds : ' There is more than reason to suspect, that most of its beauties are of modern date ; and that these at least (if not its whole existence) have flowed from the pen of a lady, within this present century.' *Reliques* (1765), ii. 87.   The lady was Elizabeth Halket, Lady Wardlaw, who died in 1727.   The ballad was first printed in 1719.⟩

[3] John Ray published, in 1674, *A Collection of English Words Not Generally used . . . in two Alphabetical Catalogues.*

By collecting those of your country, you will do a useful thing towards the history of the language.' He bade me also go on with collections which I was making upon the antiquities of Scotland. ' Make a large book ; a folio.' BOSWELL. ' But of what use will it be, Sir ? ' JOHNSON. ' Never mind the use ; do it.'

I complained that he had not mentioned Garrick in his Preface to Shakspeare [1] ; and asked him if he did not admire him. JOHNSON. ' Yes, as " a poor player, who frets and struts his hour upon the stage ; "—as a shadow [2].' BOSWELL. ' But has he not brought Shakspeare into notice [3] ? ' JOHNSON. ' Sir, to allow that, would be to lampoon the age. Many of Shakspeare's plays are the worse for being acted : Macbeth, for instance [4].' BOSWELL. ' What, Sir, is nothing gained by decoration and action ? Indeed, I do wish that you had mentioned Garrick.' JOHNSON. ' My dear Sir, had I mentioned him, I must have mentioned many more : Mrs. Pritchard, Mrs. Cibber, —nay, and Mr. Cibber too ; he too altered Shakspeare.' BOSWELL. ' You have read his apology, Sir ? ' JOHNSON. ' Yes, it is very entertaining. But as for Cibber himself, taking from his conversation all that he ought not to have said [5], he was a poor creature. I remember when he brought me one of his Odes to

The one of such as are proper to the Northern, the other to the Southern Counties. The running title of the first part is ' North Countrey Words '.

[1] See *post*, v. 244; ⟨and App. B to this vol., p. 488.⟩

[2] ' Life 's but a walking shadow, a poor player That struts and frets his hour upon the stage.' *Macbeth*, act v. sc. 5.

[3] In the *Garrick Corres.* i. 385, there is a letter from Mrs. Montagu to Garrick, which shows the ridiculous way in which Shakespeare was often patronised last century, and ' brought into notice.' She says :— ' Mrs. Montagu is a little jealous for poor Shakspeare ; for if Mr. Garrick often acts Kitely, Ben Jonson will eclipse his fame.'

[4] ' Familiar comedy is often more powerful on the theatre, than in the page ; imperial tragedy is always less.' Johnson's *Preface to Shakespeare, Works*, v. 122. See also *post*, v. 38, where Johnson 'displayed another of his heterodox opinions,—a contempt of tragick acting.' Murphy (*Life*, p. 145) thus writes of Johnson's slighting Garrick and the stage :—' The fact was, Johnson could not see the passions as they rose and chased one another in the varied features of that expressive face ; and by his own manner of reciting verses, which was wonderfully impressive, he plainly shewed that he thought there was too much of artificial tone and measured cadence in the declamation of the theatre.' Reynolds said of Johnson's recitation, that it ' had no more tone than it should have.' *Post*, v. 116. See *post*, ii. 211, and *John. Misc.* i. 347, ii. 393.

[5] See *post*, ii. 340, where Johnson,

have my opinion of it [1], I could not bear such nonsense, and would not let him read it to the end ; so little respect had I for *that great man !* (laughing.) Yet I remember Richardson wondering that I could treat him with familiarity [2].'

I mentioned to him that I had seen the execution of several convicts at Tyburn [3], two days before, and that none of them seemed to be under any concern. JOHNSON. ' Most of them, Sir, have never thought at all.' BOSWELL. ' But is not the fear of death natural to man ? ' JOHNSON. ' So much so, Sir, that the whole of life is but keeping away the thoughts of it [4].' He then, in a low and earnest tone, talked of his meditating upon the aweful hour of his own dissolution, and in what manner he should conduct himself upon that occasion : ' I know not (said he,) whether I should wish to have a friend by me, or have it all between GOD and myself.'

speaking of Cibber's ' talents of conversation,' said :—' He had but half to furnish ; for one half of what he said was oaths.'

[1] See *ante*, i. 401–2.

[2] See *post*, iii. 183–4.

[3] On Oct. 18, one day, not two days before, four men were hanged at Tyburn for robbery on the highway, one for stealing money and linen, and one for forgery. *Gent. Mag.* xxxix. 508. Boswell, in *The Hypochondriack*, No. 68 (*London Mag.* for 1783, p. 203), republishes a letter which he had written on April 26, 1768, to the *Public Advertiser*, after he had witnessed the execution of an attorney named Gibbon, and a youthful highwayman. He says :—' I must confess that I myself am never absent from a public execution. . . . When I first attended them, I was shocked to the greatest degree. I was in a manner convulsed with pity and terror, and for several days, but especially nights after, I was in a very dismal situation. Still, however, I persisted in attending them, and by degrees my sensibility abated ; so that I can now see one with great composure. . . . I can account for this curiosity in a philosophical manner,

when I consider that death is the most aweful object before every man, whoever directs his thoughts seriously towards futurity. . . . Therefore it is that I feel an irresistible impulse to be present at every execution, as I there behold the various effects of the near approach of death.' He maintains ' that the curiosity which impels people to be present at such affecting scenes, is certainly a proof of sensibility, not of callousness. For it is observed, that the greatest proportion of the spectators is composed of women.' See *post*, iv. 328. ⟨Boswell induced Sir Joshua Reynolds to attend the execution of an old servant of Mrs. Thrale. Leslie and Taylor,*Reynolds*, ii. 588.⟩

[4] Of Johnson, perhaps, might almost be said what he said of Swift (*Life of Swift*, 66) :—' The thoughts of death rushed upon him, at this time, with such incessant importunity, that they took possession of his mind, when he first waked, for many years together.' Writing to Mrs. Thrale from Lichfield on Oct. 27, 1781, he says :—' All here is gloomy ; a faint struggle with the tediousness of time ; a doleful confession of present misery, and the approach seen and felt of

Talking of our feeling for the distresses of others ;—JOHNSON. ' Why, Sir, there is much noise made about it, but it is greatly exaggerated. No, Sir, we have a certain degree of feeling to prompt us to do good : more than that, Providence does not intend. It would be misery to no purpose [1].' BOSWELL. ' But suppose now, Sir, that one of your intimate friends were apprehended for an offence for which he might be hanged.' JOHNSON. ' I should do what I could to bail him, and give him any other assistance ; but if he were once fairly hanged, I should not suffer.' BOSWELL. ' Would you eat your dinner that day, Sir ? ' JOHNSON. ' Yes, Sir ; and eat it as if he were eating it with me. Why, there's Baretti, who is to be tried for his life to-morrow, friends have risen up for him on every side ; yet if he should be hanged, none of them will eat a slice of plumb-pudding the less. Sir, that sympathetick feeling goes a very little way in depressing the mind [2].'

I told him that I had dined lately at Foote's, who shewed me a letter which he had received from Tom Davies, telling him that he had not been able to sleep from the concern which he felt on account of ' *This sad affair of Baretti* [3],' begging of him to try if he could suggest any thing that might be of service ; and, at the same time, recommending to him an industrious young man who kept a pickle-shop. JOHNSON. ' Ay, Sir, here you have a specimen of human sympathy ; a friend hanged, and a cucumber pickled. We know not whether Baretti or the pickle-man has kept Davies from sleep ; nor does he know himself. And as to his not sleeping, Sir ; Tom Davies is

what is most dreaded and most shunned. But such is the lot of man.' *Letters*, No. 744.

[1] Johnson, during a serious illness, thus wrote to Mrs. Thrale :—' When any man finds himself disposed to complain with how little care he is regarded, let him reflect how little he contributes to the happiness of others, and how little, for the most part, he suffers from their pains. It is perhaps not to be lamented, that those solicitudes are not long nor frequent, which must commonly be vain ; nor can we wonder that, in a

state in which all have so much to feel of their own evils, very few have leisure for those of another.' *Letters* No. 204. See *post*, iii. 136.

[2] ' I was shocked to find a letter from Dr. Holland, to the effect that poor Harry Hallam is dying at Sienna. What a trial for my dear old friend ! I feel for the lad himself, too. Much distressed. I dined, however. We dine, unless the blow comes very, very, near the heart indeed.' Macaulay in Trevelyan's *Life*, ii. 287. See also *ante*, i. 355.

[3] See *post*, ii. 205, for ' a furious quarrel ' between Davies and Baretti.

a very great man ; Tom has been upon the stage, and knows
how to do those things : I have not been upon the stage, and
cannot do those things.' BOSWELL. ' I have often blamed
myself, Sir, for not feeling for others as sensibly as many say
they do.' JOHNSON. ' Sir, don't be duped by them any more.
You will find these very feeling people are not very ready to do
you good. They *pay* you by *feeling.*'

BOSWELL. ' Foote has a great deal of humour ? ' JOHNSON.
' Yes, Sir.'   BOSWELL. ' He has a singular talent of exhibiting
character.' JOHNSON. ' Sir, it is not a talent ; it is a vice ; it is
what others abstain from. It is not comedy, which exhibits the
character of a species, as that of a miser gathered from many
misers : it is farce, which exhibits individuals.' BOSWELL. ' Did
not he think of exhibiting you, Sir ? ' JOHNSON. ' Sir, fear
restrained him ; he knew I would have broken his bones. I
would have saved him the trouble of cutting off a leg ; I would
not have left him a leg to cut off [1].' BOSWELL. ' Pray, Sir, is
not Foote an infidel ? ' JOHNSON. ' I do not know, Sir, that
the fellow is an infidel ; but if he be an infidel, he is an infidel
as a dog is an infidel ; that is to say, he has never thought
upon the subject [2].' BOSWELL. ' I suppose, Sir, he has thought

---

[1] ⟨In 1766 Foote lost a leg through
a fall from a spirited horse on which
he had been mounted as a practical
joke. See *D.N.B.*⟩ See *post*, ii. 299.

[2] When Mr. Foote was at Edinburgh, he thought fit to entertain a
numerous Scotch company, with a
great deal of coarse jocularity, at the
expence of Dr. Johnson, imagining it
would be acceptable. I felt this as
not civil to me ; but sat very patiently
till he had exhausted his merriment
on that subject ; and then observed,
that surely Johnson must be allowed
to have some sterling wit, and that
I had heard him say a very good
thing of Mr. Foote himself. ' Ah,
my old friend Sam, (cried Foote,) no
man says better things ; do let us
have it.' Upon which I told the
above story, which produced a very
loud laugh from the company. But
I never saw Foote so disconcerted.

He looked grave and angry, and
entered into a serious refutation of
the justice of the remark. ' What,
Sir, (said he,) talk thus of a man of
liberal education ;—a man who for
years was at the University of Oxford ;
—a man who has added sixteen new
characters to the English drama of
his country ! ' BOSWELL.

Foote was at Worcester College, but
he left without taking his degree. He
was constantly in scrapes. When the
Provost, Dr. Gower, who was a
pedant, sent for him to reprimand
him, ' Foote would present himself . . .
with great apparent gravity and submission, but with a large dictionary
under his arm ; when, on the Doctor
beginning in his usual pompous manner with a surprisingly long word, he
would immediately interrupt him,
and, after begging pardon with great
formality, would produce his dic-

superficially, and seized the first notions which occurred to his mind.' JOHNSON. ' Why then, Sir, still he is like a dog, that snatches the piece next him. Did you never observe that dogs have not the power of comparing ? A dog will take a small bit of meat as readily as a large, when both are before him.'

' Buchanan (he observed,) has fewer *centos* [1] than any modern Latin poet. He not only had great knowledge of the Latin language, but was a great poetical genius. Both the Scaligers praise him.'

He again talked of the passage in Congreve † with high commendation, and said, ' Shakspeare never has six lines together without a fault. Perhaps you may find seven: but this does not refute my general assertion. If I come to an orchard, and say there 's no fruit here, and then comes a poring man, who finds two apples and three pears, and tells me, " Sir, you are mistaken, I have found both apples and pears," I should laugh at him : what would that be to the purpose ? '

BOSWELL. ' What do you think of Dr. Young's " Night Thoughts," Sir ? ' JOHNSON. ' Why, Sir, there are very fine things in them [2].' BOSWELL. ' Is there not less religion in the nation now, Sir, than there was formerly ? ' JOHNSON. ' I don't know, Sir, that there is.' BOSWELL. ' For instance, there used to be a chaplain in every great family [3], which we do not find now.' JOHNSON. ' Neither do you find many [a] of the state servants which great families used formerly to have. There is a change of modes in the whole department of life.'

Next day, October 20, he appeared, for the only time I suppose in his life, as a witness in a Court of Justice, being called to give evidence to the character of Mr. Baretti, who having stabbed

[a] many 1: any 2, 3.

tionary, and pretending to find the meaning of the word, would say, " Very well, sir ; now please to go on." ' Forster's *Essays*, ii. 307. Dr. Gower is mentioned by Dr. W. King (*Anec.* p. 174) as one of the three persons he had known ' who spoke English with that elegance and propriety, that if all they said had been immediately committed to writing, any judge of the English language would have pronounced it an excellent and very beautiful style.' The other two were Bp. Atterbury and Dr. Johnson.

[1] ' *Cento.* A composition formed by joining scrapes from other authours.' Johnson's *Dictionary*.

[2] See *post*, v. 270.

[3] For the position of these chaplains see *The Tatler*, No. 255, and *The Guardian*, No. 163.

† ⟨See *ante*, ii. 85.⟩

a man in the street, was arraigned at the Old Bailey for murder [1]. Never did such a constellation of genius enlighten the

[1] 'He had been assailed in the grossest manner possible by a woman of the town, and, driving her off with a blow, was set upon by three bullies. He thereupon ran away in great fear, for he was a timid man, and being pursued, had stabbed two of the men with a small knife he carried in his pocket.' Garrick and Beauclerk testified that every one abroad carried such a knife, for in foreign inns only forks were provided. ' When you travel abroad do you carry such knives as this ? ' Garrick was asked. ' Yes,' he answered, ' or we should have no victuals.' *Dr. Johnson : His Friends and His Critics*, p. 288. I have extracted from the *Sessional Reports* for 1769, p. 431, the following evidence as to Baretti's character :—' SIR JOSHUA REYNOLDS. I have known Mr. Baretti fifteen or sixteen years. He is a man of great humanity, and very active in endeavouring to help his friends. He is a gentleman of a good temper ; I never knew him quarrelsome in my life ; he is of a sober disposition. . . . This affair was on a club night of the Royal Academicians. We expected him there, and were inquiring about him before we heard of this accident. He is secretary for foreign correspondence.' ' DR. JOHNSON. I believe I began to be acquainted with Mr. Baretti about the year '53 or '54. I have been intimate with him. He is a man of literature, a very studious man, a man of great diligence. He gets his living by study. I have no reason to think he was ever disordered with liquor in his life. A man that I never knew to be otherwise than peaceable, and a man that I take to be rather timorous.' Qu. ' Was he addicted to pick up women in the street ? ' ' Dr. J. I never knew that he was.' Qu. ' How is he as to his eye-sight ? ' ' Dr. J. He does not see me now, nor I do not [*sic*] see him. I do not believe he could be capable of assaulting anybody in the street without great provocation.' ' EDMUND BURKE, ESQ. I have known him between three and four years ; he is an ingenious man, a man of remarkable humanity—a thorough good-natured man.' ' DAVID GARRICK, ESQ. I never knew a man of a more active benevolence. . . . He is a man of great probity and morals.' ' DR. GOLDSMITH. I have had the honour of Mr. Baretti's company at my chambers in the Temple. He is a most humane, benevolent, peaceable man. . . . He is a man of as great humanity as any in the world.' Mr. Fitzherbert and Dr. Hallifax also gave evidence. ' There were divers other gentlemen in court to speak for his character, but the Court thought it needless to call them.' It is curious that Boswell passes over Reynolds and Goldsmith among the witnesses. Baretti's bail before Lord Mansfield were Burke, Garrick, Reynolds, and Fitzherbert. Mrs. Piozzi tells the following anecdotes of Baretti :—' When Johnson and Burke went to see Baretti in Newgate, they had small comfort to give him, and bid him not hope too strongly. " Why what can *he* fear," says Baretti, placing himself between 'em, " that holds two such hands as I do ? " An Italian came one day to Baretti, when he was in Newgate for murder, to desire a letter of recommendation for the teaching of his scholars, when he (Baretti) should be hanged. " You rascal," replies Baretti, in a rage, " if I were not *in my own apartment*, I would kick you down stairs directly." ' Hayward's *Piozzi* (ed. 2), i. 97. Dr. T. Campbell, in his *Diary* (*John. Misc.* ii. 44), wrote on April 1, 1775 :—' Boswell and Baretti,

aweful Sessions-House, emphatically called JUSTICE HALL ;
Mr. Burke, Mr. Garrick, Mr. Beauclerk, and Dr. Johnson : and
undoubtedly their favourable testimony had due weight with the
Court and Jury. Johnson gave his evidence in a slow, deliberate,
and distinct manner, which was uncommonly impressive. It is
well known that Mr. Baretti was acquitted.

On the 26th of October, we dined together at the Mitre
tavern. I found fault with Foote for indulging his talent of
ridicule at the expence of his visitors, which I colloquially
termed making fools of his company. JOHNSON. ' Why, Sir,
when you go to see Foote, you do not go to see a saint : you go
to see a man who will be entertained at your house, and then
bring you on a publick stage ; who will entertain you at his
house, for the very purpose of bringing you on a publick stage.
Sir, he does not make fools of his company ; they whom he
exposes are fools already : he only brings them into action.'

Talking of trade, he observed, ' It is a mistaken notion that a
vast deal of money is brought into a nation by trade. It is not
so. Commodities come from commodities ; but trade produces
no capital accession of wealth. However, though there should be
little profit in money, there is a considerable profit in pleasure,
as it gives to one nation the productions of another ; as we
have wines and fruits, and many other foreign articles, brought
to us.' BOSWELL. ' Yes, Sir, and there is a profit in pleasure,
by its furnishing occupation to such numbers of mankind.'
JOHNSON. ' Why, Sir, you cannot call that pleasure to which all
are averse, and which none begin but with the hope of leaving
off ; a thing which men dislike before they have tried it, and
when they have tried it.' BOSWELL. ' But, Sir, the mind must
be employed, and we grow weary when idle.' JOHNSON. ' That
is, Sir, because, others being busy, we want company ; but if we
were all idle, there would be no growing weary ; we should all
entertain one another. There is, indeed, this in trade :—it gives
men an opportunity of improving their situation. If there were
no trade, many who are poor would always remain poor. But

. . . as I learned . . . are mortal foes, so
much so that Murphy and Mrs. Thrale
agreed that Boswell expressed a desire
that Baretti should be hanged upon
that unfortunate affair of his killing,
&c.' ⟨For other evidence of their
mutual dislike see *ante*, ii. 8 ; *post*, iii.
135, note 2 ; v. 121.⟩

no man loves labour for itself.' BOSWELL. ' Yes, Sir, I know a
person who does. He is a very laborious Judge, and he loves
the labour [1].' JOHNSON. ' Sir, that is because he loves respect
and distinction. Could he have them without labour, he would
like it less.' BOSWELL. ' He tells me he likes it for itself.'—
' Why, Sir, he fancies so, because he is not accustomed to
abstract.'

We went home to his house to tea. Mrs. Williams made it
with sufficient dexterity, notwithstanding her blindness, though
her manner of satisfying herself that the cups were full enough
appeared to me a little aukward ; for I fancied she put her
finger down a certain way, till she felt the tea touch it [2]. In my
first elation at being allowed the privilege of attending Dr.
Johnson at his late visits to this lady, which was like being
é secretioribus consiliis [3], I willingly drank cup after cup, as if it
had been the Heliconian spring. But as the charm of novelty
went off, I grew more fastidious ; and besides, I discovered
that she was of a peevish temper [4].

There was a pretty large circle this evening. Dr. Johnson was
in very good humour, lively, and ready to talk upon all subjects.
Mr. Fergusson, the self-taught philosopher, told him of a new-
invented machine which went without horses : a man who sat in
it turned a handle, which worked a spring that drove it forward.
' Then, Sir, (said Johnson,) what is gained is, the man has his
choice whether he will move himself alone, or himself and the
machine too.' Dominicetti [5] being mentioned, he would not
allow him any merit. ' There is nothing in all this boasted
system. No, Sir ; medicated baths can be no better than warm

---

[1] Lord Auchinleck, we may assume.
Johnson said of Pope (*Life*, 298),
that ' he was one of those few
whose labour is their pleasure.' ⟨See
App. B, p. 489.⟩

[2] I have since had reason to think
that I was mistaken ; for I have been
informed by a lady, who was long intimate with her, and likely to be a
more accurate observer of such matters, that she had acquired such a
niceness of touch, as to know, by the
feeling on the outside of the cup, how
near it was to being full. BOSWELL.

Baretti, in a MS. note on *Piozzi
Letters*, ii. 84 ⟨Hill, No. 645⟩, says
that he dined with Johnson as seldom
as he could, ' though often scolded
for it ; but I hated to see the victuals paw'd by poor Mrs. Williams,
that would often carve, though stone
blind.' ⟨Mrs. Piozzi commenting on
Boswell's note writes in the 1816
edition of the *Life* : ' Not She poor
Soul ; the 1st Story is the truest.'⟩

[3] See *ante*, i. 421 and 463.

[4] See *ante*, i. 232, note 1.

[5] ⟨See App. B, p. 489.⟩

H 2

water : their only effect can be that of tepid moisture.' One of the company took the other side, maintaining that medicines of various sorts, and some too of most powerful effect, are introduced into the human frame by the medium of the pores ; and, therefore, when warm water is impregnated with salutiferous substances, it may produce great effects as a bath. This appeared to me very satisfactory. Johnson did not answer it ; but talking for victory, and determined to be master of the field, he had recourse to the device which Goldsmith imputed to him in the witty words of one of Cibber's comedies : ' There is no arguing with Johnson ; for when his pistol misses fire, he knocks you down with the butt end of it [1].' He turned to the gentleman [2], ' Well, Sir, go to Dominicetti, and get thyself fumigated ; but be sure that the steam be directed to thy *head*, for *that* is the *peccant part*.' This produced a triumphant roar of laughter from the motley assembly of philosophers, printers, and dependents, male and female.

I know not how so whimsical a thought came into my mind, but I asked, ' If, Sir, you were shut up in a castle, and a new-born child with you, what would you do ? ' JOHNSON. ' Why, Sir, I should not much like my company.' BOSWELL. ' But would you take the trouble of rearing it ? ' He seemed, as may well be supposed, unwilling to pursue the subject : but upon my persevering in my question, replied, ' Why yes, Sir, I would ; but I must have all conveniencies. If I had no garden, I would

---

[1] The same saying is recorded *post*, iv. 274, and v. 292. W. Cook reports another saying of Goldsmith's to the same effect :—' There 's no chance in *arguing* with such a man [Johnson] ; for, like the Tartar horse, if he does not conquer you in front, his kick from behind is sure to be fatal.' *Monthly Mag.* 1793, xxiv. 261. ' In arguing,' wrote Reynolds, ' he did not trouble himself with much circumlocution, but opposed, directly and abruptly, his antagonist. He fought with all sorts of weapons ; with ludicrous comparisons and similies ; and if all failed, with rudeness and overbearing. He thought it necessary never to be worsted in argument.

He had one virtue which I hold one of the most difficult to practise. After the heat of contest was over, if he had been informed that his antagonist resented his rudeness, he was the first to seek after a reconciliation. . . . That he was not thus strenuous for victory with his intimates in tête-à-tête conversations when there were no witnesses, may be easily believed. Indeed, had his conduct been to them the same as he exhibited to the public, his friends could never have entertained that love and affection for him which they all feel and profess for his memory.' Leslie and Taylor's *Reynolds*, ii. 457, 462.

[2] ⟨' Bozzy himself.' MRS. PIOZZI.⟩

make a shed on the roof, and take it there for fresh air. I should feed it, and wash it much, and with warm water to please it, not with cold water to give it pain.' BOSWELL. ' But, Sir, does not heat relax ? ' JOHNSON. ' Sir, you are not to imagine the water is to be very hot. I would not *coddle* the child. No, Sir, the hardy method of treating children does no good. I'll take you five children from London, who shall cuff five Highland children. Sir, a man bred in London will carry a burthen, or run, or wrestle, as well as a man brought up in the hardiest manner in the country.' BOSWELL. ' Good living, I suppose, makes the Londoners strong.' JOHNSON. ' Why, Sir, I don't know that it does. Our chairmen from Ireland, who are as strong men as any, have been brought up upon potatoes. Quantity makes up for quality.' BOSWELL. ' Would you teach this child that I have furnished you with, any thing ? ' JOHNSON. ' No, I should not be apt to teach it.' BOSWELL. ' Would not you have a pleasure in teaching it ? ' JOHNSON. ' No, Sir, I should *not* have a pleasure in teaching it.' BOSWELL. ' Have you not a pleasure in teaching men ?—*There* I have you. You have the same pleasure in teaching men, that I should have in teaching children.' JOHNSON. ' Why, something about that.'

BOSWELL. ' Do you think, Sir, that what is called natural affection is born with us ? It seems to me to be the effect of habit, or of gratitude for kindness. No child has it for a parent whom it has not seen.' JOHNSON. ' Why, Sir, I think there is an instinctive natural affection in parents towards their children.'

Russia being mentioned as likely to become a great empire, by the rapid increase of population :—JOHNSON. ' Why, Sir, I see no prospect of their propagating more. They can have no more children than they can get. I know of no way to make them breed more than they do. It is not from reason and prudence that people marry, but from inclination. A man is poor ; he thinks, " I cannot be worse, and so I'll e'en take Peggy." ' BOSWELL. ' But have not nations been more populous at one period than another ? ' JOHNSON. ' Yes, Sir ; but that has been owing to the people being less thinned at one period than another, whether by emigrations, war, or pestilence, not by their being more or less prolifick. Births at all times bear the same proportion to the same number of people.' BOSWELL. ' But, to consider the state of our own country ;—does not throwing a number of farms into one hand hurt population ? ' JOHNSON. ' Why no, Sir ; the same quantity of food being produced, will be consumed by the same number of mouths, though the people may be disposed of in different ways. We see, if corn be dear, and butchers' meat cheap, the farmers all apply themselves to the raising of corn, till it becomes plentiful and cheap, and then butchers' meat becomes dear ; so that an equality is always preserved. No, Sir, let fanciful men do as they will, depend upon it, it is difficult to disturb the system of life.' BOSWELL. ' But, Sir, is it not a very bad thing for landlords to oppress their tenants, by raising their rents ? ' JOHNSON. ' Very bad. But, Sir, it never can have any general influence ; it may distress some individuals. For, consider this : landlords cannot do without tenants. Now tenants will not give more for land, than land is worth. If they can make more of their money by keeping a shop, or any other way, they'll do it, and so oblige landlords to let land come back to a reasonable rent, in order that they may get tenants. Land, in England, is an article of commerce. A tenant who pays his landlord his rent, thinks himself no more obliged to him than you think yourself obliged to a man in whose shop you buy a piece of goods. He knows the landlord does not let him have his land for less than he can get from others, in the same manner as the shopkeeper sells his goods. No shopkeeper sells a yard of ribband for sixpence when seven-pence is the current price.' BOSWELL. ' But, Sir, is it not better that tenants should be dependent on landlords ? ' JOHNSON. ' Why, Sir, as there are many more tenants than landlords, perhaps, strictly speaking, we should wish not. But if you please you may let your lands cheap, and so get the value, part in money and part in homage. I should agree with you in that.' BOSWELL. ' So, Sir, you laugh at schemes of political improvement.' JOHNSON. ' Why, Sir, most schemes of political improvement are very laughable things.'

He observed, ' Providence has wisely ordered that the more numerous men are, the more difficult it is for them to agree in any thing, and so they are governed. There is no doubt, that if the poor should reason, " We'll be the poor no longer, we'll make the rich take their turn," they could easily do it, were it not that they can't agree. So the common soldiers, though so much more numerous than their officers, are governed by them for the same reason.'

He said, ' Mankind have a strong attachment to the habitations to which they have been accustomed. You see the inhabitants of Norway do not with one consent quit it, and go to some part of America, where there is a mild climate, and where they may have the same produce from land, with the tenth part of the labour. No, Sir ; their affection for their old dwellings, and the terrour of a general change, keep them at home. Thus, we see many of the finest spots in the world thinly inhabited, and many rugged spots well inhabited.'

' The London Chronicle [1],' which was the only news-paper he constantly took in, being brought, the office of reading it aloud was assigned to me. I was diverted by his impatience. He made me pass over so many parts of it, that my task was very easy. He would not suffer one of the petitions to the King about the Middlesex election to be read [2].

I had hired a Bohemian as my servant [3] while I remained in London, and being much pleased with him, I asked Dr. Johnson whether his being a Roman Catholick should prevent my taking him with me to Scotland. JOHNSON. ' Why no, Sir. If *he* has no objection, you can have none.' BOSWELL. ' So, Sir, you are no great enemy to the Roman Catholick religion.' JOHNSON. ' No more, Sir, than to the Presbyterian religion.' BOSWELL. ' You are joking.' JOHNSON. ' No, Sir, I really think so. Nay, Sir, of the two, I prefer the Popish [4].' BOSWELL. ' How so, Sir ? ' JOHNSON. ' Why, Sir, the Presbyterians have no church, no apostolical ordination.' BOSWELL. ' And do you think that absolutely essential, Sir ? ' JOHNSON. ' Why, Sir, as it was an apostolical institution, I think it is dangerous to be without it. And, Sir, the

[1] He had written the *Preliminary Discourse* to it. *Ante*, i. 317. ⟨For other contributions see *ante*, i. 553 and *post*, iv. 77. See also *post*, ii. 209.⟩

[2] See *post*, ii. 111–12.

[3] He accompanied Boswell on his tour to the Hebrides. *Post*, v. 53. ⟨See also *post*, ii. 411, note 2.⟩

[4] While he was in Scotland he never entered one of the churches. ' I will not give a sanction,' he said, ' by my presence, to a Presbyterian assembly.' *Post*, v. 121. When he was in France he went to a Roman Catholic service ; *post*, ii. 398. ⟨See also *post*, iii. 336 ; v. 384.⟩

Presbyterians have no publick worship : they have no form of
prayer in which they know they are to join. They go to hear a
man pray, and are to judge whether they will join with him.'
BOSWELL. ' But, Sir, their doctrine is the same with that of the
Church of England. Their confession of faith, and the thirty-
nine articles, contain the same points, even the doctrine of
predestination.' JOHNSON. ' Why yes, Sir ; predestination was a
part of the clamour of the times, so it is mentioned in our articles,
but with as little positiveness as could be.' BOSWELL. ' Is it
necessary, Sir, to believe all the thirty-nine articles ? ' JOHNSON.
' Why, Sir, that is a question which has been much agitated.
Some have thought it necessary that they should all be believed ;
others have considered them to be only articles of peace, that is
to say, you are not to preach against them [1].' BOSWELL. ' It
appears to me, Sir, that predestination, or what is equivalent to
it, cannot be avoided, if we hold an universal prescience in the
Deity.' JOHNSON. ' Why, Sir, does not GOD every day see
things going on without preventing them ? ' BOSWELL. ' True,
Sir ; but if a thing be *certainly* foreseen, it must be fixed, and
cannot happen otherwise ; and if we apply this consideration to
the human mind, there is no free will, nor do I see how prayer
can be of any avail.' He mentioned Dr. Clarke, and Bishop
Bramhall on Liberty and Necessity, and bid me read South's
Sermons on Prayer ; but avoided the question which has excru-
ciated philosophers and divines, beyond any other. I did not
press it further, when I perceived that he was displeased [2], and
shrunk from any abridgement of an attribute usually ascribed to
the Divinity, however irreconcileable in its full extent with the
grand system of moral government. His supposed orthodoxy
here cramped the vigorous powers of his understanding. He was
confined by a chain which early imagination and long habit
made him think massy and strong, but which, had he ventured to
try, he could at once have snapt asunder.

I proceeded : ' What do you think, Sir, of Purgatory [3], as
believed by the Roman Catholicks ? ' JOHNSON. ' Why, Sir, it is
a very harmless doctrine. They are of opinion that the generality
of mankind are neither so obstinately wicked as to deserve ever-

---

[1] See *post*, ii. 150. ⟨See also App. B, p. 489.⟩   [2] See *ante*, ii. 82.
[3] See *post*, ii. 163.

lasting punishment, nor so good as to merit being admitted into the society of blessed spirits ; and therefore that GOD is graciously pleased to allow of a middle state, where they may be purified by certain degrees of suffering. You see, Sir, there is nothing unreasonable in this.' BOSWELL. ' But then, Sir, their masses for the dead ? ' JOHNSON. ' Why, Sir, if it be once established that there are souls in purgatory, it is as proper to pray for *them*, as for our brethren of mankind who are yet in this life.' BOSWELL. ' The idolatry of the Mass ? '—JOHNSON. ' Sir, there is no idolatry in the Mass. They believe GOD to be there, and they adore him.' BOSWELL. ' The worship of Saints ? '—JOHNSON. ' Sir, they do not worship saints ; they invoke them ; they only ask their prayers [1]. I am talking all this time of the *doctrines* of the Church of Rome. I grant you that in *practice*, Purgatory is made a lucrative imposition, and that the people do become idolatrous as they recommend themselves to the tutelary protection of particular saints. I think their giving the sacrament only in one kind is criminal, because it is contrary to the express institution of CHRIST, and I wonder how the Council of Trent admitted it.' BOSWELL. ' Confession ? '—JOHNSON. ' Why, I don't know but that is a good thing. The scripture says, " Confess your faults one to another [2] ; " and the priests confess as well as the laity. Then it must be considered that their absolution is only upon repentance, and often upon penance also. You think your sins may be forgiven without penance, upon repentance alone.'

I thus ventured to mention all the common objections against the Roman Catholick Church, that I might hear so great a man upon them. What he said is here accurately recorded. But it is not improbable that if one had taken the other side, he might have reasoned differently.

I must however mention, that he had a respect for ' *the old religion*,' as the mild Melancthon [3] called that of the Roman Catholick Church, even while he was exerting himself for its reformation in some particulars. Sir William Scott informs me, that he heard Johnson say, ' A man who is converted from Protestantism to Popery, may be sincere : he parts with nothing : he is only superadding to what he already had. But a convert from

---

[1] See *post*, ii. 163, 255 ; iii. 407 ; iv. 289.

[2] *St. James*, v. 16.

[3] See *post*, iii. 122, note 2.

Popery to Protestantism, gives up so much of what he has held
as sacred as any thing that he retains ; there is so much *laceration
of mind* [1] in such a conversion, that it can hardly be sincere and
lasting [2].' The truth of this reflection may be confirmed by many
and eminent instances, some of which will occur to most of my
readers.

When we were alone, I introduced the subject of death, and
endeavoured to maintain that the fear of it might be got over. I
told him that David Hume said to me, he was no more uneasy
to think he should *not be* after this life, than that he *had not been*
before he began to exist. JOHNSON. ' Sir, if he really thinks so,
his perceptions are disturbed ; he is mad : if he does not think so,
he lies. He may tell you, he holds his finger in the flame of a
candle, without feeling pain ; would you believe him ? When he
dies, he at least gives up all he has.' BOSWELL. ' Foote, Sir,
told me, that when he was very ill he was not afraid to die.'
JOHNSON. ' It is not true, Sir [3]. Hold a pistol to Foote's breast,
or to Hume's breast, and threaten to kill them, and you'll see
how they behave.' BOSWELL. ' But may we not fortify our
minds for the approach of death ? '—Here I am sensible I was in
the wrong, to bring before his view what he ever looked upon
with horrour ; for although when in a celestial frame, in his
' Vanity of human Wishes,' he has supposed death to be ' kind
Nature's signal for retreat,' from this state of being to ' a happier
seat [4],' his thoughts upon this aweful change were in general full
of dismal apprehensions. His mind resembled the vast amphitheatre, the Colisæum at Rome. In the centre stood his judgement, which, like a mighty gladiator, combated those apprehensions that, like the wild beasts of the *Arena*, were all around in
cells, ready to be let out upon him. After a conflict, he drove [a]
them back into their dens ; but not killing them, they were still
assailing him. To my question, whether we might not fortify our
minds for the approach of death, he answered, in a passion, ' No,
Sir, let it alone. It matters not how a man dies, but how he

[a] *For* drives *read* drove, *Errata* 1, *but it remained unchanged.*

[1] ⟨For Johnson's use of *laceration*
and *lacerate* see *post*, App. B, p. 489 ;
iii. 419 ; Johnson's *Letters*, Nos. 302,
466, and 580.⟩   [2] See *post*, iii. 298.
[3] See *post*, iii. 154 and v. 179.

[4] He bids us pray
' For Faith, that panting for a happier
      Seat,
Counts Death kind Nature's Signal
      of Retreat.'

lives. The act of dying is not of importance, it lasts so short a time [1].' He added, (with an earnest look,) ' A man knows it must be so, and submits. It will do him no good to whine.'

I attempted to continue the conversation. He was so provoked, that he said, ' Give us no more of this ; ' and was thrown into such a state of agitation, that he expressed himself in a way that alarmed and distressed me ; shewed an impatience that I should leave him, and when I was going away, called to me sternly, ' Don't let us meet to-morrow.'

I went home exceedingly uneasy. All the harsh observations which I had ever heard made upon his character, crowded into my mind ; and I seemed to myself like the man who had put his head into the lion's mouth a great many times with perfect safety, but at last had it bit off.

Next morning I sent him a note, stating, that I might have been in the wrong, but it was not intentionally ; he was therefore, I could not help thinking, too severe upon me. That notwithstanding our agreement not to meet that day, I would call on him in my way to the city, and stay five minutes by my watch. ' You are, (said I,) in my mind, since last night, surrounded with cloud and storm. Let me have a glimpse of sunshine, and go about my affairs in serenity and chearfulness.'

Upon entering his study, I was glad that he was not alone, which would have made our meeting more awkward. There were with him, Mr. Steevens [2] and Mr. Tyers [3], both of whom I now saw for the first time. My note had, on his own reflection, softened him, for he received me very complacently ; so that I unexpectedly found myself at ease, and joined in the conversation.

He said, the criticks had done too much honour to Sir Richard Blackmore, by writing so much against him [4]. That in his

[1] ' To die, is landing on some silent shore,
  Where billows never beat, nor tempests roar :
  Ere well we feel the friendly stroke, 'tis o'er.'
GARTH. ⟨*Dispensary*, iii. 225–7.⟩
Quoted in Johnson's *Works*, vi. 61.
Bacon, if he was the author of *An Essay on Death*, says, ' I do not believe

that any man fears to be dead, but only the stroke of death.' Spedding's *Bacon*, vi. 600. Cicero (*Tuscul. Quæst.* i. 8) quotes Epicharmus's saying :—' Emori nolo, sed me esse mortuum nihil æstimo.'

[2] See *post*, ii. 204 ; iii. 281, note 3.
[3] See *post*, iii. 308.
[4] Johnson says of Blackmore (1) that he ' is one of those men whose

' Creation ' he had been helped by various wits, a line by Philips and a line by Tickell ; so that by their aid, and that of others, the poem had been made out [1].

I defended Blackmore's supposed lines, which have been ridiculed as absolute nonsense :

> ' A painted vest Prince Voltiger had on,
> Which from a naked Pict his grandsire won [2].'

I maintained it to be a poetical conceit. A Pict being painted, if he is slain in battle, and a vest is made of his skin, it is a painted vest won from him, though he was naked [3].

... lot it has been to be much oftener mentioned by enemies than by friends.'

[1] This account Johnson says he had from an eminent bookseller, who had it from Ambrose Philips the poet. He adds : ' The relation of Philips, I suppose, was true, but when all reasonable, all credible allowance is made for this friendly revision the author will still retain an ample dividend of praise. . . . Correction seldom effects more than the suppression of faults : a happy line or a single elegance may perhaps be added ; but of a large work the general character must always remain.' *Blackmore*, 24.

[2] An acute correspondent of the European Magazine, April 1792, has completely exposed a mistake which has been unaccountably frequent in ascribing these lines to Blackmore, notwithstanding that Sir Richard Steele, in that very popular work, ' The Spectator,' mentions them as written by the Authour of ' The British Princes,' the Honourable Edward Howard. The correspondent above mentioned, shews this mistake to be so inveterate, that not only *I* defended the lines as Blackmore's, in the presence of Dr. Johnson, without any contradiction or doubt of their authenticity, but that the Reverend Mr. Whitaker has asserted in print, that he understands they were *suppressed* in the late edition or editions of Blackmore. ' After all (says this in-

telligent writer) it is not unworthy of particular observation, that these lines so often quoted do not exist either in Blackmore or Howard.' In ' The British Princes,' 8vo. 1669, now before me, p. 96, they stand thus :
' A vest as admir'd Voltiger had on,
Which, from this Island's foes, his
grandsire won,
Whose artful colour pass'd the
Tyrian dye,
Oblig'd to triumph in this legacy.'
It is probable, I think, that some wag, in order to make Howard still more ridiculous than he really was, has formed the couplet as it now circulates. BOSWELL.

⟨The preceding note and ' supposed ' of the text were added to ed. 2.⟩ Swift in his *Poetry : A Rhapsody*, thus joins Howard and Blackmore together :—
' Remains a difficulty still,
To purchase fame by writing ill.
From Flecknoe down to Howard's
time
How few have reached the low
sublime !
For when our high-born Howard
died,
Blackmore alone his place supplied.'
Swift's *Works* (1824), xiv. 328.

[3] Boswell seems to have borrowed the notion from *The Spectator*, No. 43, where Steele, after saying that the poet blundered because he was ' vivacious as well as stupid,' con-

Johnson spoke unfavourably of a certain pretty voluminous authour, saying, ' He used to write anonymous books, and then other books commending those books, in which there was something of rascality.'

I whispered him, ' Well, Sir, you are now in good humour.' JOHNSON. ' Yes, Sir.' I was going to leave him, and had got as far as the staircase. He stopped me, and smiling, said, ' Get you gone *in* [a] ; ' † a curious mode of inviting me to stay, which I accordingly did for some time longer.

This little incidental quarrel and reconciliation, which, perhaps, I may be thought to have detailed too minutely, must be esteemed as one of many proofs which his friends had, that though he might be charged with *bad humour* at times, he was always a *good-natured* man ; and I have heard Sir Joshua Reynolds [1], a nice and delicate observer of manners, particularly remark, that when upon any occasion Johnson had been rough to any person in company, he took the first opportunity of reconciliation, by drinking to him, or addressing his discourse to him [2] ; but if he found his dignified indirect overtures sullenly neglected, he was quite indifferent, and considered himself as having done all that he ought to do, and the other as now in the wrong.

Being to set out for Scotland on the 10th of November, I

---

a ' Get you gone,' in 1 : ' Get you gone *in* ' 2, 3.

tinues :—' A fool of a colder constitution would have staid to have flayed the Pict, and made buff of his skin, for the wearing of the conqueror.'

† ⟨' For, " get you gone," she doth not mean, " away ! " ' *Two Gent.* III. i. 101.⟩

[1] See *ante*, ii. 100, note 1.

[2] Mrs. Piozzi (*Anec.* p. 97 : John. Misc. i. 213) tells how one day at Streatham ' when he was musing over the fire . . ., a young gentleman called to him suddenly, and I suppose he thought disrespectfully, in these words: Mr. Johnson, Would you advise me to marry ? " I would advise no man to marry, Sir (returns for answer in a very angry tone Dr. Johnson), who is not likely to propagate understanding;" and so left the room. Our companion looked confounded, and I believe had

scarce recovered the consciousness of his own existence, when Johnson came back, and drawing his chair among us, with altered looks and a softened voice, joined in the general chat, insensibly led the conversation to the subject of marriage, where he laid himself out in a dissertation so useful, so elegant, so founded on the true knowledge of human life, and so adorned with beauty of sentiment, that no one ever recollected the offence, except to rejoice in its consequences.' This ' young gentleman,' according to Mr. Hayward (Mrs. Piozzi's *Auto.* ed. 2, i. 78), was Sir John Lade, the hero of the ballad which Johnson recited on his death-bed (*post*, iv. 413). For other instances of Johnson's seeking a reconciliation, see *post*, ii. 256 ; iii. 273, 338.

wrote to him at Streatham, begging that he would meet me in town on the 9th ; but if this should be very inconvenient to him, I would go thither. His answer was as follows :

'To James Boswell, Esq.

'Dear Sir,

'Upon balancing the inconveniencies of both parties, I find it will less incommode you to spend your night here, than me to come to town. I wish to see you, and am ordered by the lady of this house to invite you hither. Whether you can come or not, I shall not have any occasion of writing to you again before your marriage, and therefore tell you now, that with great sincerity I wish you happiness.

'I am, dear Sir,

'Your most affectionate humble servant,

'Sam. Johnson.'

'Nov. 9, 1769.'

I was detained in town till it was too late on the ninth, so went to him early in the morning of the tenth of November. 'Now (said he,) that you are going to marry, do not expect more from life, than life will afford. You may often find yourself out of humour, and you may often think your wife not studious enough to please you ; and yet you may have reason to consider yourself as upon the whole very happily married.'

Talking of marriage in general, he observed, 'Our marriage service is too refined. It is calculated only for the best kind of marriages ; whereas, we should have a form for matches of convenience, of which there are many.' He agreed with me that there was no absolute necessity for having the marriage ceremony performed by a regular clergyman, for this was not commanded in scripture.

I was volatile enough to repeat to him a little epigrammatick song [1] of mine, on matrimony, which Mr. Garrick had a few days before procured to be set to musick by the very ingenious Mr. Dibden.

A Matrimonial Thought.

'In the blithe days of honey-moon,
    With Kate's allurements smitten,
I lov'd her late, I lov'd her soon,
    And call'd her dearest kitten.

[1] ⟨See App. B, p. 489.⟩

> But now my kitten's grown a cat,
>   And cross like other wives,
> O ! by my soul, my honest Mat,
>   I fear she has nine lives.'

My illustrious friend said, ' It is very well, Sir ; but you should not swear.' Upon which I altered ' O ! by my soul,' to ' alas, alas ! '

He was so good as to accompany me to London, and see me into the post-chaise which was to carry me on my road to Scotland. And sure I am, that, however inconsiderable many of the particulars recorded at this time may appear to some, they will be esteemed by the best part of my readers as genuine traits of his character, contributing together to give a full, fair, and distinct view of it.

1770 : ÆTAT. 61.]—IN 1770 he published a political pamphlet, entitled ' The False Alarm [1],' intended to justify the conduct of ministry and their majority in the House of Commons, for having virtually assumed it as an axiom, that the expulsion of a Member of Parliament was equivalent to exclusion, and thus having declared Colonel Lutterel to be duly elected for the county of Middlesex, notwithstanding Mr. Wilkes had a great majority of votes [2]. This being justly considered as a gross violation of the right of election, an alarm for the constitution extended itself all over the kingdom. To prove this alarm to be false, was the purpose of Johnson's pamphlet ; but even his vast powers were

---

[1] ' The False Alarm, his first and favourite pamphlet, was written at our house between eight o'clock on Wednesday night and twelve o'clock on Thursday night ; we read it to Mr. Thrale when he came very late home from the House of Commons.' Piozzi's *Anec.* p. 41 : John. Misc. i. 173. See also *post,* ii. 288, where Johnson says that ' " The Patriot " was called for by my political friends on Friday, was written on Saturday.'

[2] Wilkes was first elected member for Middlesex at the General Election of March, 1768. He did not take his seat, having been thrown into prison before Parliament met. On Feb. 3, 1769, he was declared incapable of being elected, and a new writ was ordered. On Feb. 16 he was again elected, and without opposition. His election was again declared void. On March 16 he was a third time elected, and without opposition. His election was again declared void. On April 13 he was a fourth time elected by 1143 votes against 296 given for Colonel Luttrell. On the 14th the poll taken for him was declared null and void, and on the 15th, Colonel Luttrell was declared duly elected. *Parl. Hist.* xvi. 437, and Almon's *Wilkes,* iv. 4. See *post,* iii. 408 ⟨and iv. 104⟩.

inadequate to cope with constitutional truth and reason, and his argument failed of effect ; and the House of Commons have since expunged the offensive resolution from their Journals [1]. That the House of Commons might have expelled Mr. Wilkes repeatedly, and as often as he should be re-chosen, was not denied ; but incapacitation cannot be but by an act of the whole legislature. It was wonderful to see how a prejudice in favour of government in general, and an aversion to popular clamour, could blind and contract such an understanding as Johnson's, in this particular case ; yet the wit, the sarcasm, the eloquent vivacity which this pamphlet displayed, made it be read with great avidity at the time, and it will ever be read with pleasure, for the sake of its composition. That it endeavoured to infuse a narcotick indifference, as to publick concerns, into the minds of the people, and that it broke out sometimes into an extreme coarseness of contemptuous abuse, is but too evident.

It must not, however, be omitted, that when the storm of his violence subsides, he takes a fair opportunity to pay a grateful compliment to the King, who had rewarded his merit : ' These low-born railers [2] have endeavoured, surely without effect, to alienate the affections of the people from the only King who for almost a century has much appeared to desire, or much endeavoured to deserve them.' And, ' Every honest man must lament, that the faction has been regarded with frigid neutrality by the Tories, who being long accustomed to signalise their principles by opposition to the Court, do not yet consider, that they have at last a King who knows not the name of party, and who wishes to be the common father of all his people.'

To this pamphlet, which was at once discovered to be Johnson's, several answers § came out, in which, care was taken to remind the publick of his former attacks upon government, and of his now being a pensioner, without allowing for the honourable terms upon which Johnson's pension was granted and accepted, or the change of system which the British court had undergone upon the accession of his present Majesty [3]. He was, however,

---

[1] The resolution of expulsion was carried on Feb. 3, 1769. *Parl. Hist.* xvi. 545. It was expunged on May 3, 1782. *Ib.* xxii. 1407.

[2] Misprinted *rulers* in 1, 2, 3. See *False Alarm*, p. 50.

§ ⟨See Courtney, *Bibliography*, p. 114, and *post*, iv. 30.⟩

[3] How slight the change of system was is shown by a passage in For-

soothed ¹ in the highest strain of panegyrick, in a poem called
'The Remonstrance,' by the Rev. Mr. Stockdale ², to whom he was,
upon many occasions, a kind protector.

The following admirable minute made by him, describes so well
his own state, and that of numbers to whom self-examination is
habitual, that I cannot omit it :

'June 1, 1770. Every man naturally persuades himself that he can
keep his resolutions, nor is he convinced of his imbecility but by
length of time and frequency of experiment ³. This opinion of our

ster's *Goldsmith*, ii. 388. Mr. Forster
mentions a 'memorial in favour of
the most worthless of hack-partisans,
Shebbeare, .. which absolutely availed
to obtain for him his pension of 200 *l.*
a year. It is signed by fifteen members of the House of Commons, and it
asks for a pension "that he may be
enabled to pursue that laudable *inclination which he has* of manifesting
his zeal for the service of his Majesty
and his Government" ; in other
words, that a rascal shall be bribed to
support a corrupt administration.'
Walpole, in 1757 (*Letters,* iv. 26),
described Shebbeare as one 'who
made a pious resolution of writing
himself into a place or the pillory,
but ' who ' miscarried in both views.'
He added in a note, ' he did write
himself into a pillory before the conclusion of that reign, and into a pension at the beginning of the next, for
one and the same kind of merit,
writing against King William and
the Revolution.' See also *post,* iv.
113.

¹ Johnson could scarcely be soothed
by lines such as the following :—
'Never wilt thou retain the hoarded
    store,
In virtue affluent, but in metal
    poor ;

. . . .

Great is thy prose ; great thy
    poetic strain ;
Yet to dull coxcombs are they
    great in vain.' pp. 16, 17.

² Stockdale, who was born in 1736
and died in 1811, wrote *Memoirs of
his Life*—a long, dull book, but containing a few interesting anecdotes of
Johnson. He thought himself, and
the world also, much ill-used by the
publishers, when they passed him
over and chose Johnson to edit the
Lives of the Poets. He lodged both
in Johnson's Court and in Bolt
Court, but preserved little good-will
for his neighbour. Johnson, in the
Life of Waller (61), quoting from
Stockdale's *Life* of that poet, calls
him 'his last ingenious biographer.'
I. D'Israeli says that ' the bookseller
Flexney complained, that whenever
this poet came to town, it cost him
£20. Flexney had been the publisher
of Churchill's works ; and, never
forgetting the time when he published
The Rosciad, . . . he was still speculat-
ing all his life for another Churchill,
and another quarto poem. Stockdale
usually brought him what he wanted
—and Flexney found the workman,
but never the work.' *Calamities of
Authors,* ed. 1812, ii. 314.

³ ' I believe most men may review
all the lives that have passed within
their observation, without remember-
ing one efficacious resolution, or
being able to tell a single instance
of a course of practice suddenly
changed in consequence of a change
of opinion, or an establishment of
determination.' *Idler,* No. 27. ' These
sorrowful meditations fastened upon

own constancy is so prevalent, that we always despise him who suffers his general and settled purpose to be overpowered by an occasional desire. They, therefore, whom frequent failures have made desperate, cease to form resolutions ; and they who are become cunning, do not tell them. Those who do not make them are very few, but of their effect little is perceived ; for scarcely any man persists in a course of life planned by choice, but as he is restrained from deviation by some external power. He who may live as he will, seldom lives long in the observation of his own rules ¹.'

Of this year I have obtained the following letters :

'To THE REVEREND DR. FARMER ², CAMBRIDGE.

'Sir,

'As no man ought to keep wholly to himself any possession that may be useful to the publick, I hope you will not think me unreasonably intrusive, if I have recourse to you for such information as you are more able to give me than any other man.

'In support of an opinion ³ which you have already placed above the need of any more support, Mr. Steevens, a very ingenious gentleman, lately of King's College, has collected an account of all the translations which Shakspeare might have seen and used. He wishes his catalogue to be perfect, and therefore intreats that you will favour him by the insertion of such additions as the accuracy of your inquiries has enabled you to make. To this request, I take the liberty of adding my own solicitation.

'We have no immediate use for this catalogue, and therefore do not desire that it should interrupt or hinder your more important employments. But it will be kind to let us know that you receive it.

'I am, Sir, &c.

'SAM. JOHNSON.'

'Johnson's-court, Fleet-street,
    March 21, 1770.'

'To THE REVEREND MR. THOMAS WARTON.

'DEAR SIR,

'THE readiness with which you were pleased to promise me some notes on Shakspeare, was a new instance of your friendship.

---

his [Rasselas's] mind ; he past four months in resolving to lose no more time in idle resolves.' *Rasselas*, ch. iv.
    ¹ Prayers and Meditations, p. 95. [¶ 89.] BOSWELL.
    ² See *ante*, i. 368 ; *post*, iii. 38.
    ³ ⟨Farmer published in 1767 his

Essay on the Learning of Shakespeare, in which he sought to prove that Shakespeare's knowledge of the Classics was for the most part obtained through translations. See App. B, p. 489 ; iii. 38 ; iv. 18.⟩

I shall not hurry you ; but am desired by Mr. Steevens, who helps me in this edition, to let you know, that we shall print the tragedies first, and shall therefore want first the notes which belong to them. We think not to incommode the readers with a supplement ; and therefore, what we cannot put into its proper place, will do us no good. We shall not begin to print before the end of six weeks, perhaps not so soon.

'I am, &c.

'London, June 23, 1770.' 'SAM. JOHNSON.'

'TO THE REV. DR. JOSEPH WARTON.

'DEAR SIR,

'I AM revising my edition of Shakspeare, and remember that I formerly misrepresented your opinion of Lear. Be pleased to write the paragraph as you would have it, and send it [1]. If you have any remarks of your own upon that or any other play, I shall gladly receive them.

'Make my compliments to Mrs. Warton. I sometimes think of wandering for a few days to Winchester, but am apt to delay. I am, Sir,

'Your most humble servant,

'Sept. 27, 1770.' 'SAM. JOHNSON.'

'TO MR. FRANCIS BARBER, AT MRS. CLAPP'S, BISHOP-STORTFORD, HERTFORDSHIRE.

'DEAR FRANCIS,

'I AM at last sat down to write to you, and should very much blame myself for having neglected you so long, if I did not impute that and many other failings to want of health [2]. I hope not to be so long silent again. I am very well satisfied with your progress, if you can

---

[1] ⟨The edition referred to is the first Johnson-Steevens, 1773. The passage was not revised.⟩

[2] Johnson had suffered greatly from rheumatism this year, as well as from other disorders. He mentions, 14 April, ' spasms in my stomach which disturbed me for many years, and for two past harassed me almost to distraction.' These, however, by means of strong remedies, had at Easter nearly ceased. ' The pain,' he adds, ' harasses me much, yet many have the disease perhaps in a much higher degree, with want of food, fire, and covering, which I find thus grievous, with all the succours that riches and kindness can buy and give.' (He was staying at Mr. Thrale's.) *Pr. and Med.* ¶ 85. ' Shall I ever,' he asks on Easter Day, ' receive the Sacrament with tranquillity ? Surely the time will come.' *Ib.* ¶ 87.

I 2

really perform the exercises which you are set ; and I hope Mr. Ellis does not suffer you to impose on him, or on yourself.

'Make my compliments to Mr. Ellis, and to Mrs. Clapp, and Mr. Smith.

'Let me know what English books you read for your entertainment. You can never be wise unless you love reading.

'Do not imagine that I shall forget or forsake you ; for if, when I examine you, I find that you have not lost your time, you shall want no encouragement from

'Yours affectionately,

'London, Sept. 25, 1770.'   'SAM. JOHNSON.'

TO THE SAME.

'DEAR FRANCIS,

'I HOPE you mind your business. I design you shall stay with Mrs. Clapp these holidays. If you are invited out you may go, if Mr. Ellis gives leave. I have ordered you some clothes, which you will receive, I believe, next week. My compliments to Mrs. Clapp and to Mr. Ellis, and Mr. Smith, &c.

'I am

'Your affectionate,

'December 7, 1770.'   'SAM. JOHNSON.'

During this year there was a total cessation of all correspondence between Dr. Johnson and me, without any coldness on either side, but merely from procrastination, continued from day to day ; and as I was not in London, I had no opportunity of enjoying his company and recording his conversation. To supply this blank, I shall present my readers with some *Collectanea*, obligingly furnished to me by the Rev. Dr. Maxwell, of Falkland, in Ireland, some time assistant preacher at the Temple, and for many years the social friend of Johnson, who spoke of him with a very kind regard.

'MY acquaintance with that great and venerable character commenced in the year 1754. I was introduced to him by Mr. Grierson [1], his Majesty's printer at Dublin, a gentleman of uncommon learning, and great wit and vivacity. Mr. Grierson died in Germany, at the age

[1] Son of the learned Mrs. Grierson, who was patronised by the late Lord Granville, and was the editor of several of the classicks. BOSWELL.
⟨For Grierson see Piozzi, *Anec.*

117 : John. Misc. i. 226. In 1766 Johnson had 'a very tender remembrance of his learning and his humour.' See Miss Gaussen's *Percy*, p. 221 n.⟩

of twenty-seven. Dr. Johnson highly respected his abilities, and often observed, that he possessed more extensive knowledge than any man of his years he had ever known. His industry was equal to his talents ; and he particularly excelled in every species of philological learning, and was, perhaps, the best critick of the age he lived in.

' I must always remember with gratitude my obligation to Mr. Grierson, for the honour and happiness of Dr. Johnson's acquaintance and friendship, which continued uninterrupted and undiminished to his death : a connection, that was at once the pride and happiness of my life.

' What pity it is, that so much wit and good sense as he continually exhibited in conversation, should perish unrecorded ! Few persons quitted his company without perceiving themselves wiser and better than they were before. On serious subjects he flashed the most interesting conviction upon his auditors ; and upon lighter topicks, you might have supposed—*Albano musas de monte locutas* [1].

' Though I can hope to add but little to the celebrity of so exalted a character, by any communications I can furnish, yet out of pure respect to his memory, I will venture to transmit to you some anecdotes concerning him, which fell under my own observation. The very *minutiæ* of such a character must be interesting, and may be compared to the filings of diamonds.

' In politicks he was deemed a Tory, but certainly was not so in the obnoxious or party sense of the term ; for while he asserted the legal and salutary prerogatives of the crown, he no less respected the constitutional liberties of the people. Whiggism, at the time of the Revolution, he said, was accompanied with certain principles ; but latterly, as a mere party distinction under Walpole [2] and the Pelhams,[a] was no better than the politicks of stock-jobbers, and the religion of infidels.

' He detested the idea of governing by parliamentary corruption, and asserted most strenuously, that a prince steadily and conspicuously pursuing the interests of his people, could not fail of parliamentary concurrence. A prince of ability, he contended, might and should be the directing soul and spirit of his own administration ; in short, his own minister, and not the mere head of a party : and then, and not till then, would the royal dignity be sincerely respected.

a Pelhams, 1, 2 : Pelhams 3.

[1] ' Pontificum libros, annosa volumina vatum,
    Dictitet Albano Musas in monte locutas.'
' Then swear, transported, that the sacred Nine

Pronounc'd on Alba's top each hallow'd line.'
FRANCIS. Horace, *Epis.* II. i. 26.
    [2] See *ante*, i. 131, where Boswell says ' Johnson . . . afterwards honestly acknowledged the merit of Walpole.'

' Johnson seemed to think, that a certain degree of crown influence over the Houses of Parliament, (not meaning a corrupt and shameful dependence,) was very salutary, nay, even necessary, in our mixed government [1]. " For, (said he,) if the members were under no crown influence, and disqualified from receiving any gratification from Court, and resembled, as they possibly might, Pym and Haslerig, and other stubborn and sturdy members of the long Parliament, the wheels of government would be totally obstructed. Such men would oppose, merely to shew their power, from envy, jealousy, and perversity of disposition ; and not gaining themselves, would hate and oppose all who did : not loving the person of the prince, and conceiving they owed him little gratitude, from the mere spirit of insolence and contradiction, they would oppose and thwart him upon all occasions."

' The inseparable imperfection annexed to all human governments, consisted, he said, in not being able to create a sufficient fund of virtue and principle to carry the laws into due and effectual execution. Wisdom might plan, but virtue alone could execute. And where could sufficient virtue be found ? A variety of delegated, and often discretionary, powers must be entrusted somewhere ; which, if not governed by integrity and conscience, would necessarily be abused, till at last the constable would sell his for a shilling.

' This excellent person was sometimes charged with abetting slavish and arbitrary principles of government. Nothing in my opinion could be a grosser calumny and misrepresentation ; for how can it be rationally supposed, that he should adopt such pernicious and absurd opinions, who supported his philosophical character with so much dignity, was extremely jealous of his personal liberty and independence, and could not brook the smallest appearance of neglect or insult, even from the highest personages ?

' But let us view him in some instances of more familiar life.

' His general mode of life, during my acquaintance, seemed to be pretty uniform. About twelve o'clock I commonly visited him, and frequently found him in bed, or declaiming over his tea, which he drank very plentifully. He generally had a levee of morning visitors, chiefly men of letters [2] ; Hawkesworth, Goldsmith, Murphy, Langton, Steevens, Beauclerk, &c. &c. and sometimes learned ladies, particularly I remember a French lady [3] of wit and fashion doing him the honour of a visit. He seemed to me to be considered as a kind of publick

[1] See *post*, iv. 220.

[2] ' His acquaintance was sought by persons of the first eminence in literature ; and his house, in respect of the conversations there, be- came an academy.' Hawkins's *Johnson*, p. 329. See *ante*, i. 247, 350, note 3.

[3] Madame de Boufflers. MRS. PIOZZI. See *post*, ii. 405.

oracle, whom every body thought they had a right to visit and consult [1] ; and doubtless they were well rewarded. I never could discover how he found time for his compositions [2]. He declaimed all the morning, then went to dinner at a tavern, where he commonly staid late, and then drank his tea at some friend's house, over which he loitered a great while, but seldom took supper. I fancy he must have read and wrote chiefly in the night, for I can scarcely recollect that he ever refused going with me to a tavern, and he often went to Ranelagh [3], which he deemed a place of innocent recreation.

' He frequently gave all the silver in his pocket to the poor, who watched him, between his house and the tavern where he dined [4]. He walked the streets at all hours, and said he was never robbed [5], for the rogues knew he had little money, nor had the appearance of having much.

' Though the most accessible and communicative man alive,[a] yet

a alive, 1 2 : alive ; 3.

[1] ' To talk in publick, to think in solitude, to read and to hear, to inquire, and answer inquiries, is the business of a scholar.' *Rasselas*, ch. viii. Miss Burney mentions an amusing instance of a consultation by letter. The letter ' was dated from the Orkneys, costing Dr. Johnson 1s. 6d.' The writer, a clergyman, says he ' labours under a most peculiar misfortune, for which he can give no account ; and which is,—that, though he very often writes letters to his friends and others, he never gets any answers ; he entreats, therefore, that Dr. Johnson will take this into consideration, and explain to him to what so strange a thing may be attributed.' Mme. D'Arblay's *Diary*, ii. 96.

[2] ' How he [Swift] spent the rest of his time, and how he employed his hours of study, has been enquired with hopeless curiosity. For who can give an account of another's studies ? Swift was not likely to admit any to his privacies, or to impart a minute account of his business or his leisure.' Johnson's *Life of Swift*, 69.

[3] See *post*, ii. 168.

[4] ' He loved the poor,' says Mrs. Piozzi (*Anec.* p. 84 : *John. Misc.* i. 204), ' as I never yet saw any one else do, with an earnest desire to make them happy.—What signifies, says some one, giving halfpence to common beggars ? they only lay it out in gin or tobacco. "And why should they be denied such sweeteners of their existence (says Johnson) ? "' The harm done by this indiscriminate charity had been pointed out by Fielding in his *Covent Garden Journal* for June 2, 1752. He took as the motto for the paper :
' O bone, ne te
Frustrere, insanis et tu ' ;
which he translates,
' My good Friend, do not deceive thyself ; for with all thy Charity, thou also art a silly Fellow.' ' The giving our Money to Common Beggars ', he describes as a ' kind of Bounty ' that ' is a Crime against the Public.' Johnson once allowed (*post*, iv. 3) that ' one might give away five hundred pounds in a year to those that importune in the streets, and not do any good.' See also *post*, iii. 56 and 401.

[5] He was once attacked, though whether by robbers is not made clear. See *post*, ii. 299.

when he suspected he was invited to be exhibited, he constantly spurned the invitation.

'Two young women from Staffordshire visited him when I was present, to consult him on the subject of Methodism, to which they were inclined. "Come, (said he,) you pretty fools, dine with Maxwell and me at the Mitre, and we will talk over that subject;" which they did, and after dinner he took one of them upon his knee, and fondled her for half an hour together.

'Upon a visit to me at a country lodging near Twickenham, he asked what sort of society I had there. I told him, but indifferent; as they chiefly consisted of opulent traders, retired from business. He said, he never much liked that class of people; "For, Sir, (said he,) they have lost the civility of tradesmen, without acquiring the manners of gentlemen[1]."

'Johnson was much attached to London: he observed, that a man stored his mind better there, than any where else; and that in remote situations a man's body might be feasted, but his mind was starved, and his faculties apt to degenerate, from want of exercise and competition. No place, (he said,) cured a man's vanity or arrogance so well as London; for as no man was either great or good *per se*, but as compared with others not so good or great, he was sure to find in the metropolis many his equals, and some his superiors. He observed, that a man in London was in less danger of falling in love indiscreetly, than any where else; for there the difficulty of deciding between the conflicting pretensions of a vast variety of objects, kept him safe. He told me, that he had frequently been offered country preferment, if he would consent to take orders[2]; but he could not leave the improved society of the capital, or consent to exchange the exhilarating joys and splendid decorations of publick life, for the obscurity, insipidity, and uniformity of remote situations.

'Speaking of Mr. Harte[3], Canon of Windsor, and writer of "The History of Gustavus Adolphus," he much commended him as a scholar, and a man of the most companionable talents he had ever known. He said, the defects in his history proceeded not from imbecility, but from foppery.

'He loved, he said, the old black letter books; they were rich in matter, though their style was inelegant; wonderfully so, considering how conversant the writers were with the best models of antiquity.

---

[1] Perhaps it was this class of people which is described in the following passage:—'It was never against people of coarse life that his contempt was expressed, while poverty of sentiment in men who considered themselves to be company for the *parlour*, as he called it, was what he would not bear.' Piozzi's *Anec.*, p. 215: *John. Misc.* i. 293.

[2] See *ante*, i. 320, for one such offer.

[3] See *ante*, i. 163, note 1, and *post*, iv. 78, 333.

' Burton's " Anatomy of Melancholy," he said, was the only book that ever took him out of bed two hours sooner than he wished to rise.

' He frequently exhorted me to set about writing a History of Ireland, and archly remarked, there had been some good Irish writers, and that one Irishman might at least aspire to be equal to another. He had great compassion for the miseries and distresses of the Irish nation, particularly the Papists ; and severely reprobated the barbarous debili-tating policy of the British government, which, he said, was the most detestable mode of persecution. To a gentleman, who hinted such policy might be necessary to support the authority of the English government, he replied by saying, " Let the authority of the English government perish, rather than be maintained by iniquity. Better would it be to restrain the turbulence of the natives by the authority of the sword, and to make them amenable to law and justice by an effectual and vigorous police, than to grind them to powder by all manner of disabilities and incapacities. Better (said he,) to hang or drown people at once, than by an unrelenting persecution to beggar and starve them [1]." The moderation and humanity of the present times have, in some measure, justified the wisdom of his observations.

' Dr. Johnson was often accused of prejudices, nay, antipathy, with regard to the natives of Scotland. Surely, so illiberal a prejudice never entered his mind : and it is well known, many natives of that respectable country possessed a large share in his esteem ; nor were any of them ever excluded from his good offices, as far as opportunity permitted. True it is, he considered the Scotch, nationally, as a crafty, designing people, eagerly attentive to their own interest, and too apt to overlook the claims and pretentions of other people. " While they confine their

---

[1] Dr. T. Campbell, in his *Survey of the South of Ireland*, ed. 1777 (*post*, ii. 339), says :—' By one law of the penal code, if a papist have a horse worth fifty, or five hundred pounds, a protestant proprietor may become the purchaser upon paying him down five. By another of the same code, a son may say to his father, " Sir, if you don't give me what money I want, I'll turn *discoverer*, and in spite of you and my elder brother too, on whom at marriage you settled your estate, I shall become heir," ' p. 251. Father O'Leary, in his *Remarks on Wesley's Letter*, published in 1780 (*post*, v. 35, note 3), says (p. 41):— ' He has . . . seen the venerable matron, after twenty-four years mar-riage, banished from the perjured husband's house, though it was proved in open court, that for six months before his marriage, he went to mass. But the law requires that he should be a year and a day of the same religion.' Burke wrote in 1792 : ' The Castle considers the outlawry (or what at least I look on as such) of the great mass of the people as an unalterable maxim in the government of Ireland.' *Burke's Corres.* iii. 378. See *post*, ii. 130, 255, and iii. 410.

benevolence, in a manner, exclusively to those of their own country, they expect to share in the good offices of other people. Now (said Johnson,) this principle is either right or wrong; if right, we should do well to imitate such conduct ; if wrong, we cannot too much detest it [1]."

' Being solicited to compose a funeral sermon for the daughter of a tradesman, he naturally enquired into the character of the deceased; and being told she was remarkable for her humility and condescension to inferiours, he observed, that those were very laudable qualities, but it might not be so easy to discover who the lady's inferiours were.

' Of a certain player [2] he remarked, that his conversation usually threatened and announced more than it performed ; that he fed you with a continual renovation of hope, to end in a constant succession of disappointment.

' When exasperated by contradiction, he was apt to treat his opponents with too much acrimony : as, " Sir, you don't see your way through that question : "—" Sir, you talk the language of ignorance." On my observing to him that a certain gentleman had remained silent the whole evening, in the midst of a very brilliant and learned society, " Sir, (said he,) the conversation overflowed, and drowned him."

' His philosophy, though austere and solemn, was by no means morose and cynical, and never blunted the laudable sensibilities of his character, or exempted him from the influence of the tender passions. Want of tenderness, he always alledged, was want of parts, and was no less a proof of stupidity than depravity.

' Speaking of Mr. Hanway, who published " An Eight Days' Journey from London to Portsmouth," " Jonas, (said he,) acquired some reputation by travelling abroad [3], but lost it all by travelling at home [4]."

' Of the passion of love he remarked, that its violence and ill effects were much exaggerated ; for who knows any real sufferings on that head, more than from the exorbitancy of any other passion ?

' He much commended " Law's Serious Call," which he said was the finest piece of hortatory theology in any language [5]. " Law, (said he,) fell latterly into the reveries of Jacob Behmen [6], whom Law alledged

[1] See post, ii. 306–7.

[2] ' Of Sheridan's writings on Elocution, Johnson said, they were a continual renovation of hope, and an unvaried succession of disappointments.' Johnson's Works (1787), xi. 197. See post, iv. 222.

[3] In 1753, Jonas Hanway published An Historical Account of the British Trade over the Caspian Sea : with a Journal of Travels from London through Russia into Persia. 4 vols.

[4] ⟨He published in 1756 A Journal of Eight Days Journey from Portsmouth to Kingston upon Thames ; with Miscellaneous Thoughts, etc. To which is added An Essay on Tea, etc. 4to. A second ed. in two vols. octavo was published in 1757.⟩ See ante, i. 313.

[5] See ante, i. 68, and post, iv. 286, note 3, where he varies the epithet, calling it ' the best piece of Parenetick Divinity.'

[6] ' " I taught myself," Law tells us,

to have been somewhat in the same state with St. Paul, and to have seen *unutterable things*[1]. Were it even so, (said Johnson,) Jacob would have resembled St. Paul still more, by not attempting to utter them."

'He observed, that the established clergy in general did not preach plain enough ; and that polished periods and glittering sentences flew over the heads of the common people, without any impression upon their hearts. Something might be necessary, he observed, to excite the affections of the common people, who were sunk in languor and lethargy, and therefore he supposed that the new concomitants of methodism might probably produce so desirable an effect[2]. The mind, like the body, he observed, delighted in change and novelty, and even in religion itself, courted new appearances and modifications. Whatever might be thought of some methodist teachers, he said, he could scarcely doubt the sincerity of that man, who travelled nine hundred miles in a month, and preached twelve times a week ; for no adequate reward, merely temporal, could be given for such indefatigable labour[3].

" the High Dutch language, on purpose to know the original words of the blessed Jacob." ' Overton's *Life of Law*, p. 181. Behmen, or Böhme, the mystic shoemaker of Görlitz, was born in 1575, and died in 1624. ' His books may not hold at all honourable places in libraries ; his name may be ridiculous. But he *was* a generative thinker. What he knew he knew for himself. It was not transmitted to him, but fought for.' J. F. D. Maurice's *Moral and Meta. Phil.*, 1862, 325. Of Hudibras's squire, Ralph, it was said :

'He Anthroposophus, and Floud,
And Jacob Behmen, understood.'
                        Hudibras, i. i. 542.
Wesley (*Journal*, iii. 17) writes of Behmen's *Mysterium Magnum*, ' I can and must say thus much (and that with as full evidence as I can say two and two make four), it is most sublime nonsense, inimitable bombast, fustian not to be paralleled ! '

[1] ' He heard unspeakable words, which it is not lawful for a man to utter,' 2 *Corinthians*, xii. 4.
[2] See *ante*, i. 458. In *Humphry Clinker*, in the letter of June 11, the turnkey of Clerkenwell Prison thus speaks of a Methodist :—' I don't care if the devil had him ; . . . here has been nothing but canting and praying since the fellow entered the place.—Rabbit him ! the tap will be ruined—we han't sold a cask of beer, nor a dozen of wine, since he paid his garnish—the gentlemen get drunk with nothing but your damned religion.'

[3] ' Wesley probably paid more for turnpikes than any other man in England, for no other person travelled so much.' Southey's *Wesley*, i. 340, note. On 14 May, 1765 he writes in his *Journal* : ' I preach about eight hundred sermons in a year.' In one of his *Appeals to Men of Reason and Religion*, he asks :—' Can you bear the summer sun to beat upon your naked head ? Can you suffer the wintry rain or wind, from whatever quarter it blows ? Are you able to stand in the open air, without any covering or defence, when God casteth abroad his snow like wool, or scattereth his hoar frost like ashes ? And yet these are some of the smallest inconveniences which accompany field-preaching. For beyond all these, are the contradiction of sinners, the scoffs both of the great vulgar and the

' Of Dr. Priestley's theological works, he remarked, that they tended to unsettle every thing, and yet settled nothing.

' He was much affected by the death of his mother, and wrote to me to come and assist him to compose his mind, which indeed I found extremely agitated. He lamented that all serious and religious conversation was banished from the society of men, and yet great advantages might be derived from it. All acknowledged, he said, what hardly any body practised, the obligation we were under of making the concerns of eternity the governing principles of our lives. Every man, he observed, at last wishes for retreat : he sees his expectations frustrated in the world, and begins to wean himself from it, and to prepare for everlasting separation.

' He observed, that the influence of London now extended every where, and that from all manner of communication being opened, there shortly would be no remains of the ancient simplicity, or places of cheap retreat to be found.

' He was no admirer of blank-verse, and said it always failed, unless sustained by the dignity of the subject. In blank-verse, he said, the language suffered more distortion, to keep it out of prose, than any inconvenience or limitation to be apprehended from the shackles and circumscription [a] of rhyme [1].

' He reproved me once for saying grace without mention of the name of our Lord Jesus Christ, and hoped in future I would be more mindful of the apostolical injunction [2].

' He refused to go out of a room before me at Mr. Langton's house, saying, he hoped he knew his rank better than to presume to take place of a Doctor in Divinity. I mention such little anecdotes, merely to shew the peculiar turn and habit of his mind.

' He used frequently to observe, that there was more to be endured than enjoyed, in the general condition of human life ; and frequently quoted those lines of Dryden :

[a] circumscription 1 : circumspection 2, 3.

small ; contempt and reproach of every kind—often more than verbal affronts —stupid, brutal violence, sometimes to the hazard of health, or limbs, or life. Brethren, do you envy us this honour ? What, I pray you, would buy you to be a field-preacher ? Or what, think you, could induce any man of common sense to continue therein one year, unless he had a full conviction in himself that it was the will of God concerning him ? ' Southey's *Wesley*, i. 339.

[1] Stockdale reported to Johnson, that Pope had told Lyttelton that the reason why he had not translated Homer into blank verse was ' that he could translate it more easily into rhyme. Johnson replied, " Sir, when Pope said that, he knew that he lied." ' Stockdale's *Memoirs*, ii. 44. In the *Life of Somervile* (8) Johnson says :—' If blank verse be not tumid and gorgeous, it is crippled prose.' See *post*, iv. 20, 42.

[2] *Ephesians*, v. 20.

"Strange cozenage! none would live past years again,
Yet all hope pleasure from what still remain [1]."

For his part, he said, he never passed that week in his life which he would wish to repeat, were an angel to make the proposal to him.

' He was of opinion, that the English nation cultivated both their soil and their reason better than any other people ; but admitted that the French, though not the highest, perhaps, in any department of literature, yet in every department were very high [2]. Intellectual pre-eminence, he observed, was the highest superiority ; and that every nation derived their highest reputation from the splendour and dignity of their writers [3]. Voltaire, he said, was a good narrator, and that his principal merit consisted in a happy selection and arrangement of circumstances.

' Speaking of the French novels, compared with Richardson's, he said, they might be pretty baubles, but a wren was not an eagle.

' In a Latin conversation with the Pere Boscovitch, at the house of Mrs. Cholmondeley, I heard him maintain the superiority of Sir Isaac Newton over all foreign philosophers [4], with a dignity and eloquence that surprized that learned foreigner [5]. It being observed to him, that

[1] In the original—
'Yet all hope pleasure in what yet remain.'
See post, iv. 303.

[2] See post, iii. 254, iv. 237, and v. 310.

[3] ' The chief glory of every people arises from its authors.' Johnson's Pref. to Dictionary (Works, v. 49).

[4] In a Discourse by Sir William Jones, addressed to the Asiatick Society [in Calcutta], Feb. 24, 1785, is the following passage :
' One of the most sagacious men in this age who continues, I hope, to improve and adorn it, Samuel Johnson, remarked in my hearing, that if Newton had flourished in ancient Greece, he would have been worshipped as a Divinity.' MALONE.

Johnson, in An Account of an Attempt to ascertain the Longitude (Works, v. 299), makes the supposed author say :—' I have lived till I am able to produce, in my favour, the testimony of time, the inflexible enemy of false hypotheses ; the only testimony which it becomes human understanding to oppose to the authority of Newton.'

[5] Murphy (Life, p. 91) places the scene of such a conversation in the house of the Bishop of Salisbury. ' Boscovich,' he writes, ' had a ready current flow of that flimsy phraseology with which a priest may travel through Italy, Spain, and Germany. Johnson scorned what he called colloquial barbarisms. It was his pride to speak his best. He went on, after a little practice, with as much facility as if it was his native tongue. One sentence this writer well remembers. Observing that Fontinelle at first opposed the Newtonian philosophy, and embraced it afterwards, his words were : Fontinellus, ni fallor, in extremâ senectute, fuit transfuga ad castra Newtoniana." ' See post, ii. 406. Boscovitch, the Jesuit astronomer, was a professor in the University of Pavia. When Dr. Burney visited him, ' he complained very much of the silence of the English astronomers who answer none of his letters.' Burney's Pres. State of Music in France & Italy, p. 89.

a rage for every thing English prevailed much in France after Lord
Chatham's glorious war, he said, he did not wonder at it, for that we
had drubbed those fellows into a proper reverence for us, and that their
national petulance required periodical chastisement.

'Lord Lyttelton's Dialogues, he deemed a nugatory performance.
" That man, (said he,) sat down to write a book, to tell the world what
the world had all his life been telling him [1]."

'Somebody observing that the Scotch Highlanders, in the year 1745,
had made surprising efforts, considering their numerous wants and disadvantages : " Yes, Sir, (said he,) their wants were numerous ; but you
have not mentioned the greatest of them all,—the want of law."

'Speaking of the *inward light*, to which some methodists pretended,
he said, it was a principle utterly incompatible with social or civil
security. " If a man (said he,) pretends to a principle of action of which
I can know nothing, nay, not so much as that he has it, but only that
he pretends to it ; how can I tell what that person may be prompted to
do ? When a person professes to be governed by a written ascertained
law, I can then know where to find him."

'The poem of Fingal [2], he said, was a mere unconnected rhapsody ,
a tiresome repetition of the same images. " In vain shall we look for
the *lucidus ordo* [3], where there is neither end or object, design or moral,
nec certa recurrit imago."

'Being asked by a young nobleman, what was become of the gallantry
and military spirit of the old English nobility, he replied, " Why, my
Lord, I'll tell you what is become of it ; it is gone into the city to look
for a fortune."

'Speaking of a dull tiresome fellow, whom he chanced to meet, he
said, " That fellow seems to me to possess but one idea, and that is a
wrong one."

'Much enquiry having been made concerning a gentleman, who had
quitted a company where Johnson was, and no information being obtained ; at last Johnson observed, that " he did not care to speak ill of any
man behind his back, but he believed the gentleman was an *attorney* [4]."

---

[1] See *post*, iv. 57–8.

[2] The first of Macpherson's for-
geries was *Fragments of Ancient
Poetry collected in the Highlands*.
Edinburgh, 1760. In 1762, he published in London, *Fingal, an Ancient
Epic Poem, in Six Books ; together
with several other Poems, composed by
Ossian the Son of Fingal*. See *post*,
ii. 292, 298.

[3] Horace, *Ars Poetica*, l. 41.

[4] Perhaps Johnson had some ill-
will towards attorneys, such as he
had towards excisemen (*ante*, i. 36,
note 5, and 294). In *London*, which
was published in May, 1738, he
couples them with street robbers :
'There ambush here relentless ruf-
    fians lay,
And here the fell attorney prowls
    for prey.'
Works, i. 1. In a paper in the *Gent*.

' He spoke with much contempt of the notice taken of Woodhouse, the poetical shoemaker [1]. He said, it was all vanity and childishness : and that such objects were, to those who patronised them, mere mirrours of their own superiority. " They had better (said he,) furnish the man with good implements for his trade, than raise subscriptions for his poems. He may make an excellent shoemaker, but can never make a good poet. A school-boy's exercise may be a pretty thing for a school-boy ; but is [a] no treat for a man."

' Speaking of Boetius, who was the favourite writer of the middle ages [2], he said it was very surprizing, that upon such a subject, and in such a situation, he should be *magis philosophus quàm Christianus*.

' Speaking of Arthur Murphy, whom he very much loved, " I don't know (said he,) that Arthur can be classed with the very first dramatick writers ; yet at present I doubt much whether we have any thing superiour to Arthur [3]."

' Speaking of the national debt, he said, it was an idle dream to suppose that the country could sink under it. Let the publick creditors be ever so clamorous, the interest of millions must ever prevail over that of thousands [4].

[a] is no treat 1 : it is no treat 2, 3.

Mag. for the following June (p. 287), written, I have little doubt, by him, the profession is thus savagely attacked :—' Our Ancestors, in ancient times, had some Regard to the moral character of the Person sent to represent them in their national Assemblies, and would have shewn some Degree of Resentment or Indignation, had their Votes been asked for a Murderer, an Adulterer, a known Oppressor, an hireling Evidence, an Attorney, a Gamester, or a Pimp.' In the *Life of Blackmore* (2), he has a sly hit at the profession. ' He was the son of Robert Blackmore . . ., styled by Wood *Gentleman*, and supposed to have been an attorney.' We may compare Goldsmith's lines in *Retaliation* :—

' Then what was his failing ? come tell it, and burn ye.
He was—could he help it ?—a special attorney.'

See also *post*, iv. 313.
[1] See *ante*, i. Appendix F, p. 520.
[2] Dr. Maxwell is perhaps here

quoting *Idler*, No. 69, where Johnson, speaking of *Boethius on the Comforts of Philosophy*, calls it ' the book which seems to have been the favourite of the middle ages.' ⟨See App. B, p. 491.⟩
[3] Yet it is of Murphy's tragedy of *Zenobia* that Mrs. Piozzi writes (*Anec.* p. 280 : *John. Misc.* i. 332) :—' A gentleman carried him his tragedy, which, because he loved the author, Johnson took, and it lay about our rooms some time. " What answer did you give your friend, Sir ? " said I, after the book had been called for. " I told him (replied he) that there was too much *Tig* and *Tirry* in it." Seeing me laugh most violently, " Why, what would'st have, Child ? " (said he). " I looked at nothing but the dramatis, and there was *Tig*ranes and *Tiri*dates, or Teribazus, or such stuff. A man can tell but what he knows, and I never got any further than the first page." ' In *Zenobia* two of the characters are Teribazus and Tigranes.
[4] Hume was one who had this idle dream. Shortly before his death one

' Of Dr. Kennicott's Collations, he observed, that though the text should not be much mended thereby, yet it was no small advantage to know, that we had as good a text as the most consummate industry and diligence could procure [1].

' Johnson observed, that so many objections might be made to every thing, that nothing could overcome them but the necessity of doing something. No man would be of any profession, as simply opposed to not being of it : but every one must do something.

' He remarked, that a London parish was a very comfortless thing ; for the clergyman seldom knew the face of one out of ten of his parishioners.

' Of the late Mr. Mallet he spoke with no great respect : said, he was ready for any dirty job : that he had written [a] against Byng at the instigation of the ministry [2], and was equally ready to write for him, provided he found his account in it.

' A gentleman who had been very unhappy in marriage, married immediately after his wife died : Johnson said, it was the triumph of hope over experience.

' He observed, that a man of sense and education should meet a suitable companion in a wife [3]. It was a miserable thing when the conversation could only be such as, whether the mutton should be boiled or roasted, and probably a dispute about that.

' He did not approve of late marriages, observing,[b] that more was lost in point of time, than compensated for by any possible advantages [4]. Even ill assorted marriages were preferable to cheerless celibacy.

' Of old Sheridan he remarked, that he neither wanted parts nor literature ; but that his vanity and Quixotism obscured his merits.

' He said, foppery was never cured ; it was the bad stamina of the

---

a wrote 1, 2, 3 : written *Corrections & Addit.* (*1793*).   b *no comma* 3.

of his friends wrote :—' He still maintains, that the national debt must be the ruin of Britain ; and laments that the two most civilized nations, the English and French, should be on the decline ; and the barbarians, the Goths and Vandals of Germany and Russia, should be rising in power and renown.' J. H. Burton's *Hume*, ii. 497.

[1] Hannah More was with Dr. Kennicott at his death. ' Thus closed a life,' she wrote (*Memoirs*, i. 289), ' the last thirty years of which were honourably spent in collating the Hebrew Scriptures.' See also *post*, v. 42.

[2] Johnson says that Mallet (*Life*, 21), in return for what he wrote against Byng, ' had a considerable pension bestowed upon him, which he retained to his death.' See *ante*, i. 268.

[3] See *ante*, ii. 76.

[4] ' It is dangerous for a man and woman to suspend their fate upon each other, at a time when opinions are fixed, and habits are established ; when friendships have been contracted on both sides, when life has been planned into method, and the mind has long enjoyed the contemplation of its own prospects.' *Rasselas*, ch. xxviii.

mind, which, like those of the body, were never rectified : once a cox-comb, and always a coxcomb.

' Being told that Gilbert Cowper called him the Caliban of literature ; " Well, (said he,) I must dub him the Punchinello [1]."

' Speaking of the old Earl of Corke and Orrery, he said, " that man spent his life in catching at an object, [literary eminence,] which he had not power to grasp [2]."

' To find a substitution for violated morality, he said, was the leading feature in all perversions of religion.

' He often used to quote, with great pathos, those fine lines of Virgil :

> " *Optima quæque dies miseris mortalibus ævi*
> *Prima fugit [3] ; subeunt morbi, tristisque senectus,*
> *Et labor, et duræ rapit inclementia mortis [4]."*

' Speaking of Homer, whom he venerated as the prince of poets, Johnson remarked that the advice given to Diomed [5] by his father, when he sent him to the Trojan war, was the noblest exhortation that could be instanced in any heathen writer, and comprised in a single line :

> Αἰὲν ἀριστεύειν, καὶ ὑπείροχον ἔμμεναι ἄλλων·

which, if I recollect well, is translated by Dr. Clarke thus : *semper appetere præstantissima, et omnibus aliis antecellere.*

' He observed, " it was a most mortifying reflexion for any man to consider, *what he had done*, compared with what *he might have done.*"

[1] Malone records that ' Cooper was round and fat. He was . . . well acquainted with the English poets, and a good classical scholar ; but an insufferable coxcomb. Dr. Warton one day, when dining with Johnson, urged these circumstances in his favour : " He was at least very well-informed, and a good scholar." " Yes," said Johnson, " it cannot be denied that he has good materials for playing the fool ; and he makes abundant use of them." ' Prior's *Malone*, p. 428. See *post*, iii. 149, note 2.

[2] See *post*, iii. 183, and v. 238.

[3] But see *ante*, i. 299, where Johnson owned that his happier days had come last.

[4] ' In youth alone, unhappy mortals live ;

But, ah ! the mighty bliss is fugitive ;
Discolour'd sickness, anxious labours come,
And age, and death's inexorable doom.'
DRYDEN. Virgil, *Georgics*, iii. 66. In the first edition Dr. Maxwell's *Collectanea* ended here. What follows to p. 133 was given in the second edition in *Additions . . . received after the second edition was printed*, i. p. v.

[5] To Glaucus. Clarke's translation is :—' Ut semper fortissime rem gererem, et superior virtute essem aliis.' *Iliad*, vi. 208. Cowper's version is :—
' That I should outstrip always all mankind
In worth and valour.'

' He said few people had intellectual resources sufficient to forego the pleasures of wine. They could not otherwise contrive how to fill the interval between dinner and supper.

' He went with me, one Sunday, to hear my old Master, Gregory Sharpe [1], preach at the Temple.—In the prefatory prayer, Sharpe ranted about *Liberty*, as a blessing most fervently to be implored, and its continuance prayed for. Johnson observed, that our *liberty* was in no sort of danger :—he would have done much better, to pray against our *licentiousness*.

' One evening at Mrs. Montagu's, where a splendid company was assembled, consisting of the most eminent literary characters, I thought he seemed highly pleased with the respect and attention that were shewn him, and asked him on our return home if he was not highly *gratified* by his visit : " No, Sir, (said he) not highly *gratified* ; yet I do not recollect to have passed many evenings *with fewer objections*."

' Though of no high extraction himself, he had much respect for birth and family, especially among ladies. He said, " adventitious accomplishments may be possessed by all ranks ; but one may easily distinguish the *born gentlewoman*."

' He said, " the poor in England [2] were better provided for, than in any other country of the same extent : he did not mean little Cantons, or petty Republicks. Where a great proportion of the people (said he,) are suffered to languish in helpless misery, that country must be ill policed, and wretchedly governed : a decent provision for the poor, is the true test of civilization.—Gentlemen of education, he observed, were pretty much the same in all countries ; the condition of the lower orders, the poor especially, was the true mark of national discrimination."

' When the corn laws were in agitation in Ireland, by which that country has been enabled not only to feed itself, but to export corn to a large amount [3] ; Sir Thomas Robinson [4] observed, that those laws might be prejudicial to the corn-trade of England. " Sir Thomas, (said he,) you

---

[1] Maxwell calls him his old master, because Sharpe was Master of the Temple when Maxwell was assistant preacher ⟨really Reader⟩. CROKER.

[2] Dr. T. Campbell, in his *Survey of the South of Ireland*, p. 185, writes :—' In England, . . . the meanest cottager is better fed, better lodged, and better dressed, than the most opulent farmers here.' See *post*, iii. 401.

[3] In the vice-royalty of the Duke of Bedford, which began in Dec. 1756, ' in order to encourage tillage a law was passed granting bounties on the land carriage of corn and flour to the metropolis.' Lecky's *Hist. of Eng.* ii. ch. vii. 435. In 1773-4 a law was passed granting bounties upon the export of Irish corn to foreign countries. *Ib.* iv. ch. xvi. 415.

[4] See *ante*, i. 434.

talk the language of a savage : what, Sir ? would you prevent any people from feeding themselves, if by any honest means they can do it [1]."

' It being mentioned, that Garrick assisted Dr. Brown, the authour of the " Estimate [2]," in some dramatick composition, " No, Sir ; (said Johnson,) he would no more suffer Garrick to write a line in his play, than he would suffer him to mount his pulpit."

' Speaking of Burke, he said, " It was commonly observed, he spoke too often in parliament ; but nobody could say he did not speak well, though too frequently and too familiarly [3]."

' Speaking of economy, he remarked, it was hardly worth while to save anxiously twenty pounds a year. If a man could save to that degree, so as to enable him to assume a different rank in society, then indeed, it might answer some purpose.

' He observed, a principal source of erroneous judgement was, viewing things partially and only on *one side :* as for instance, *fortune-hunters,* when they contemplated the fortunes *singly* and *separately,* it was a dazzling and tempting object ; but when they came to possess the wives

---

[1] See *ante,* ii. 121. Lord Kames, in his *Sketches of the History of Man,* published in 1774, says :—' In Ireland to this day, goods exported are loaded with a high duty, without even distinguishing made work from raw materials ; corn, for example, fish, butter, horned cattle, leather, &c. And that nothing may escape, all goods exported that are not contained in the book of rates, pay five *per cent. ad valorem.*' i. 490. These export duties were selfishly levied in what was supposed to be the interest of England.

[2] *An Estimate of the Manners and Principles of the Times,* 1757. ' At this time [1756] appeared Brown's *Estimate,* a book now remembered only by the allusions in Cowper's *Table Talk* [lines 384–5] and in Burke's *Letters on a Regicide Peace* [Payne's *Burke,* p. 9]. It was universally read, admired, and believed. The author fully convinced his readers that they were a race of cowards and scoundrels ; that nothing could save them ; that they were on the point of being enslaved by their enemies, and that they richly deserved their

fate.' Macaulay's *Hist. Essays, Pitt* (1923), 258. Dr. J. H. Burton says : —' Dr. Brown's book is said to have . . . run to a seventh edition in a few months. It is rather singular that the edition marked as the seventh has precisely the same matter in each page, and the same number of pages as the first.' *Life of Hume,* ii. 23. Brown wrote two tragedies, *Barbarossa* and *Athelstan,* both of which Garrick brought out at Drury Lane. In *Barbarossa* Johnson observed ' that there were two improprieties ; in the first place, the use of a bell is unknown to the Mahometans ; and secondly, Otway had tolled a bell before Dr. Browne, and we are not to be made April fools twice by the same trick.' Murphy's *Garrick,* p. 173. Brown's vanity is shown in a letter to Garrick (*Garrick Corres.* i. 220), written on Jan. 19, 1766, in which he talks of going to St. Petersburg, and drawing up a System of Legislation for the Russian Empire. In the following September, in a fit of madness, he made away with himself.

[3] See *post,* iv. 104 and note 1.

and their fortunes *together*, they began to suspect they had not made quite so good a bargain.

' Speaking of the late Duke of Northumberland living very magnificently when Lord Lieutenant of Ireland, somebody remarked, it would be difficult to find a suitable successor to him : then exclaimed Johnson, *he is only fit to succeed himself* [1].

' He advised me, if possible, to have a good orchard. He knew, he said, a clergyman of small income, who brought up a family very reputably, which he chiefly fed with apple dumplins.

' He said, he had known several good scholars among the Irish gentlemen ; but scarcely any of them correct in *quantity*. He extended the same observation to Scotland.

' Speaking of a certain Prelate, who exerted himself very laudably in building churches and parsonage-houses ; " however, said he, I do not find that he is esteemed a man of much professional learning, or a liberal patron of it ;—yet, it is well, where a man possesses any strong positive excellence.—Few have all kinds of merit belonging to their character. We must not examine matters too deeply—No, Sir, a *fallible being will fail some-where*."

' Talking of the Irish clergy, he said, Swift was a man of great parts, and the instrument of much good to his country [2].—Berkeley was a profound scholar, as well as a man of fine imagination ; but Usher, he said, was the great luminary of the Irish church ; and a greater, he added, no church could boast of ; at least in modern times.

' We dined *tête à tête* at the Mitre, as I was preparing to return to

---

[1] Walpole, writing in May, 1764, says :—' The Earl of Northumberland returned from Ireland, where his profusion and ostentation had been so great, that it seemed to lay a dangerous precedent for succeeding governors.' *Memoirs of the Reign of George III*, i. 417. He was created Duke in 1766. For some pleasant anecdotes about this nobleman and Goldsmith, see Goldsmith's *Misc. Works*, i. 66, and Forster's *Goldsmith*, i. 379, and ii. 227.

[2] Johnson thus writes of him (*Swift*, 64) :—' The Archbishop of Dublin gave him at first some disturbance in the exercise of his jurisdiction ; but it was soon discovered, that between prudence and integrity he was seldom in the wrong ; and that, when he was

right, his spirit did not easily yield to opposition.' And : ' He delivered Ireland from plunder and oppression, and shewed that wit, confederated with truth, had such force as authority was unable to resist. He said truly of himself that Ireland " was his debtor." It was from the time when he first began to patronize the Irish, that they may date their riches and prosperity.' *Ib.* 110. Pope, in his *Imitations of Horace*, II. i. 221, says :—
' Let Ireland tell, how Wit upheld her cause,
Her Trade supported, and supplied her Laws ;
And leave on SWIFT this grateful verse engrav'd,
" The Rights a Court attack'd, a Poet sav'd." '

Ireland, after an absence of many years. I regretted much leaving London, where I had formed many agreeable connexions : " Sir, (said he,) I don't wonder at it ; no man, fond of letters, leaves London without regret. But remember, Sir, you have seen and enjoyed a great deal ;—you have seen life in its highest decorations, and the world has nothing new to exhibit.—No man is so well qualifyed to leave publick life as he who has long tried it and known it well. We are always hankering after untried situations, and imagining greater felicity from them than they can afford. No, Sir, knowledge and virtue may be acquired in all countries, and your local consequence will make you some amends for the intellectual gratifications you relinquish." Then he quoted the following lines with great pathos :

> " He who has early known the pomps of state,
>   (For things unknown, 'tis ignorance to condemn ;)
> And after having viewed the gaudy bait,
> Can boldly say, the trifle I contemn ;
> With such a one contented could I live,
> Contented could I die [1] ; "—

' He then took a most affecting leave of me ; said, he knew, it was a point of *duty* that called me away.—" We shall all be sorry to lose you," said he : " *laudo tamen* [2]." '

---

[1] These lines have been discovered by the author's second son in the *London Magazine* for July, 1732, where they form part of a poem on *Retirement*, copied, with some slight variations, from one of Walsh's smaller poems, entitled *The Retirement*. They exhibit another proof that Johnson retained in his memory fragments of obscure or neglected poetry. In quoting verses of that description, he appears by a slight variation to have sometimes given them a moral turn, and to have dexterously adapted them to his own sentiments, where the original had a very different tendency. In 1782, when he was at Brighthelmstone, he repeated to Mr. Metcalfe, some verses, as very characteristick of a celebrated historian, since deceased. They are found among some anonymous poems appended to the second volume of a collection frequently printed by Lintot, under the title of ' Pope's Miscellanies ' :—

' See how the wand'ring Danube flows,
   Realms and religions parting ;
A friend to all true christian foes,
   To Peter, Jack, and Martin.
Now Protestant, and Papist now,
   Not constant long to either,
At length an infidel does grow,
   And ends his journey neither.
Thus many a youth I've known set out,
   Half Protestant, half Papist,
And rambling long the world about,
   Turn infidel or atheist.'
MALONE (1811). For similar instances of Johnson's retentive memory, see *post*, iv. 14 ; v. 117, 368. ⟨See App. B, p. 491.⟩

[2] Juvenal, *Sat.* iii. l. 2.
' Yet still my calmer thoughts his choice commend.'
                    Johnson's *London*, l. 3.
⟨Maxwell obtained the rectory of Mount Temple, Westmeath, in 1775.⟩

1771 : ÆTAT. 62.]—IN 1771 he published another political pamphlet, entitled ' Thoughts on the late Transactions respecting Falkland's Islands [1],' in which, upon materials furnished to him by ministry, and upon general topicks expanded in his richest style, he successfully endeavoured to persuade the nation that it was wise and laudable to suffer the question of right to remain undecided, rather than involve our country in another war. It has been suggested by some, with what truth I shall not take upon me to decide, that he rated the consequence of those islands to Great-Britain too low [2]. But however this may be, every humane mind must surely applaud the earnestness with which he averted the calamity of war ; a calamity so dreadful, that it is astonishing how civilised, nay, Christian nations, can deliberately continue to renew it. His description of its miseries in this pamphlet, is one of the finest pieces of eloquence in the English language [3]. Upon this occasion, too, we find Johnson lashing the party in opposition with unbounded severity, and making the fullest use of what he ever reckoned a most effectual argumentative instrument,—contempt [4]. His character of their

[1] It was published without the author's name.

[2] ' What have we acquired ? What, but a bleak and gloomy solitude, an island thrown aside from human use ; . . . an island, which not the southern savages have dignified with habitation.' *Works*, vi. 198.

[3] ' It is wonderful with what coolness and indifference the greater part of mankind see war commenced. Those that hear of it at a distance, or read of it in books, but have never presented its evils to their minds, consider it as little more than a splendid game, a proclamation, an army, a battle, and a triumph. Some, indeed, must perish in the most successful field, but they die upon the bed of honour, " resign their lives, amidst the joys of conquest, and, filled with England's glory, smile in death " ⟨Addison's *Campaign*, 313–14⟩. The life of a modern soldier is ill represented by heroick fiction. War has means of destruction more formidable

than the cannon and the sword. Of the thousands and ten thousands, that perished in our late contests with France and Spain, a very small part ever felt the stroke of an enemy ; the rest languished in tents and ships, amidst damps and putrefaction ; pale, torpid, spiritless, and helpless ; gasping and groaning, unpitied among men made obdurate by long continuance of hopeless misery ; and were, at last, whelmed in pits, or heaved into the ocean, without notice and without remembrance. By incommodious encampments and unwholesome stations, where courage is useless, and enterprise impracticable, fleets are silently dispeopled, and armies sluggishly melted away.' *Works*, vi. 199.

[4] Johnson wrote of the Earl of Chatham :—' This, surely, is a sufficient answer to the feudal gabble of a man, who is every day lessening that splendour of character which once illuminated the kingdom, then dazzled,

very able mysterious champion, JUNIUS, is executed with all the force of his genius, and finished with the highest care. He seems to have exulted in sallying forth to single combat against the boasted and formidable hero, who bade defiance to ' principalities and powers, and the rulers of this world [1].'

This pamphlet, it is observable, was softened in one particular, after the first edition [2]; for the conclusion of Mr. George Grenville's character stood thus : ' Let him not, however, be depreciated in his grave. He had powers not universally possessed : could he have enforced payment of the Manilla ransom, *he could have counted it* [3].' Which, instead of retaining its sly sharp point, was reduced to a mere flat unmeaning expression, or, if I may use the word,—*truism :* ' He had powers not universally possessed : and if he sometimes erred, he was likewise sometimes right.'

' TO BENNET LANGTON, ESQ.

' DEAR SIR,

' AFTER much lingering of my own, and much of the ministry, I have at length got out my paper [4]. But delay is not yet at an end :

and afterwards inflamed it ; and for whom it will be happy if the nation shall, at last, dismiss him to nameless obscurity, with that equipoise of blame and praise which Corneille allows to Richelieu.' *Works*, vi. 197.

[1] *Ephesians*, vi. 12. Johnson (*Works*, vi. 198) calls Junius ' one of the few writers of his despicable faction, whose name does not disgrace the page of an opponent.' But he thus ends his attack:—' What, says Pope, must be the priest, where a monkey is the god ? What must be the drudge of a party, of which the heads are Wilkes and Crosby, Sawbridge and Townsend ? ' *Ib.* p. 206.

[2] This softening was made in the later copies of the *first* edition. A second change seems to have been made. In the text, as given in Hawkins's edition (1787, x. 75), the last line of the passage stands :—' If he was sometimes wrong, he was often right.' Walpole describes Gren-

ville's ' plodding, methodic genius, ⟨which⟩ made him take the spirit of detail for ability.' *Memoirs of the Reign of George III*, i. 36. For the fine character that Burke drew of him, see Payne's *Burke*, i. 122. There is, I think, a hit at Lord Bute's Chancellor of the Exchequer, Sir F. Dashwood (Lord Le Despencer), who was described as ' a man to whom a sum of five figures was an impenetrable secret.' Walpole's *Memoirs of the Reign of George III*, i. 172, note. He himself said, ' People will point at me, and cry, " there goes the worst Chancellor of the Exchequer that ever appeared." ' *Ib.* p. 250.

[3] Boswell, I suspect, quoted this passage from hearsay, for originally it stood :—' If he could have got the money, he could have counted it ' (p. 68). In the British Museum there are copies of the first edition both *softened* and *unsoftened*.

[4] ' Thoughts on the late Trans-

Not many had been dispersed, before Lord North ordered the sale to stop. His reasons I do not distinctly know. You may try to find them in the perusal ¹. Before his order, a sufficient number were dispersed to do all the mischief, though, perhaps, not to make all the sport that might be expected from it.

' Soon after your departure, I had the pleasure of finding all the danger past with which your navigation ² was threatened. I hope nothing happens at home to abate your satisfaction ; but that Lady Rothes ³, and Mrs. Langton, and the young ladies, are all well.

' I was last night at THE CLUB. Dr. Percy has written a long ballad ⁴ in many *fits* ; it is pretty enough. He has printed, and will soon publish it. Goldsmith is at Bath, with Lord Clare ⁵. At Mr. Thrale's, where I am now writing, all are well. I am, dear Sir,

' Your most humble servant,

' SAM. JOHNSON.'

' March 20, 1771.'

Mr. Strahan ⁶, the printer, who had been long in intimacy with Johnson, in the course of his literary labours, who was at

actions respecting Falkland's Islands.' BOSWELL.

¹ By comparing the first with the subsequent editions, this curious circumstance of ministerial authourship may be discovered. BOSWELL.

² *Navigation* was the common term for canals, which at that time were getting rapidly made. ⟨Frank Barber's annuity of £70 was secured on Langton's profits from the *navigation* of the River Wey in Surrey. See Reade, *Gleanings*, ii. 58, and *post*, iv. 401. See also iii. 362.⟩

³ It was, Mr. Chalmers told me, a saying about that time, ' Married a Countess Dowager of Rothes ! Why, every body marries a Countess Dowager of Rothes !' And there were, in fact, about 1772, three ladies of that name married to second husbands. CROKER. Mr. Langton married one of these ladies ⟨see *ante*, ii. 77, note 1⟩.

⁴ *The Hermit of Warkworth : A Northumberland Ballad. In three fits or cantos.* T. Davis and S. Leacroft, 1771, 4to. 2s. 6d. Cradock

(*Memoirs*, i. 207) quotes Johnson's parody on a stanza in *The Hermit :*
' I put my hat upon my head,
    And walk'd into the Strand,
And there I met another man
    With his hat in his hand.'
' Mr. Garrick,' he continues, ' asked me, Whether I had seen Johnson's criticism on the *Hermit* ; " it is already," said he, " over half the town." ' ⟨For another parody, see *post*, ii. 212, n. 4.⟩

⁵ ' " I am told," says a letter-writer of the day, " that Dr. Goldsmith now generally lives with his countryman, Lord Clare, who has lost his only son, Colonel Nugent." ' Forster's *Goldsmith*, ii. 228. ' *The Haunch of Venison* was written this year (1771), and appears to have been written for Lord Clare alone ; nor was it until two years after the writer's death that it obtained a wider audience than his immediate circle of friends.' *Ib.* p. 230. See *post*, iii. 311.

⁶ Gibbon (*Memoirs*, p. 194) mentions Mr. Strahan :—' I agreed, upon easy terms, with Mr. Thomas Cadell, a

once his friendly agent in receiving his pension for him [1], and his banker in supplying him with money when he wanted it ; who was himself now a Member of Parliament, and who loved much to be employed in political negociation [2] ; thought he should do eminent service, both to government and Johnson, if he could be the means of his getting a seat in the House of Commons [3]. With this view, he wrote a letter to one of the Secretaries of the Treasury, of which he gave me a copy in his own hand-writing, which is as follows :

' SIR,

' YOU will easily recollect, when I had the honour of waiting upon you some time ago, I took the liberty to observe to you, that Dr. Johnson would make an excellent figure in the House of Commons, and heartily wished he had a seat there. My reasons are briefly these :

' I know his perfect good affection to his Majesty, and his government, which I am certain he wishes to support by every means in his power.

' He possesses a great share of manly, nervous, and ready eloquence ;

respectable bookseller, and Mr. William Strahan, an eminent printer ; and they undertook the care and risk of the publication [of the *Decline and Fall*], which derived more credit from the name of the shop than from that of the author. . . . So moderate were our hopes, that the original impression had been stinted to five hundred, till the number was doubled, by the prophetic taste of Mr. Strahan.' Hume, by his will, left to Strahan's care all his manuscripts, ' trusting,' he says, ' to the friendship that has long subsisted between us, for his careful and faithful execution of my intentions.' J. H. Burton's *Hume*, ii. 494. See *ib*. p. 512, for a letter written to Hume on his death-bed by Strahan.

[1] Dr. Franklin, writing of the year 1773, says (*Memoirs*, 1818, i. 398) :— ' An acquaintance [*editor's note* Mr. Strahan, M.P.] calling on me, after having just been at the treasury, showed me what he styled *a pretty thing*, for a friend of his ; it was an order for 150*l*., payable to Dr. Samuel Johnson, said to be one half of his yearly pension.' ⟨Strahan was not elected M.P. until 1774, when he was returned for Malmesbury.⟩

[2] See *post*, iii. 364.

[3] Hawkins (*Life*, p. 513) says that Mr. Thrale made the same attempt. He ' had two meetings with the minister, who, at first, seemed inclined to find him ⟨Johnson⟩ a seat.' ' Lord Stowell told me,' says Mr. Croker, ' that it was understood amongst Johnson's friends that " Lord North was afraid that Johnson's *help* (as he himself said of Lord Chesterfield's) might have been sometimes *embarrassing*." " He perhaps thought, and not unreasonably," added Lord Stowell, " that, like the elephant in the battle, he was quite as likely to trample down his friends as his foes." ' Lord Stowell referred to Johnson's letter to Chesterfield (*ante*, i. 262), in which he describes a patron as ' one who encumbers a man with help.'

is quick in discerning the strength and weakness of an argument ; can express himself with clearness and precision, and fears the face of no man alive.

' His known character, as a man of extraordinary sense and unimpeached virtue, would secure him the attention of the House, and could not fail to give him a proper weight there.

' He is capable of the greatest application, and can undergo any degree of labour, where he sees it necessary, and where his heart and affections are strongly engaged. His Majesty's ministers might therefore securely depend on his doing, upon every proper occasion, the utmost that could be expected from him. They would find him ready to vindicate such measures as tended to promote the stability of government, and resolute and steady in carrying them into execution. Nor is any thing to be apprehended from the supposed impetuosity of his temper. To the friends of the King you will find him a lamb, to his enemies a lion.

' For these reasons, I humbly apprehend that he would be a very able and useful member. And I will venture to say, the employment would not be disagreeable to him ; and knowing, as I do, his strong affection to the King, his ability to serve him in that capacity, and the extreme ardour with which I am convinced he would engage in that service, I must repeat, that I wish most heartily to see him in the House.

' If you think this worthy of attention, you will be pleased to take a convenient opportunity of mentioning it to Lord North. If his Lordship should happily approve of it, I shall have the satisfaction of having been, in some degree, the humble instrument of doing my country, in my opinion, a very essential service. I know your good-nature, and your zeal for the publick welfare, will plead my excuse for giving you this trouble. I am, with the greatest respect, Sir,

' Your most obedient and humble servant,

' New-street,   ' WILLIAM STRAHAN.'
March 30, 1771.'

This recommendation, we know, was not effectual ; but how, or for what reason, can only be conjectured. It is not to be believed that Mr. Strahan would have applied, unless Johnson had approved of it [1]. I never heard him mention the subject ; but at a later period of his life, when Sir Joshua Reynolds told him that Mr. Edmund Burke had said, that if he had come early into parliament, he certainly would have been the greatest speaker

---

[1] ⟨Mrs. Piozzi exclaims in a marginal note to her copy of the 1816 edition : ' Yes, Yes ; he would have *approved* it.'⟩

that ever was there, Johnson exclaimed, ' I should like to try my hand now.'

It has been much agitated among his friends and others, whether he would have been a powerful speaker in Parliament, had he been brought in when advanced in life. I am inclined to think, that his extensive knowledge, his quickness and force of mind, his vivacity and richness of expression, his wit and humour, and above all his poignancy of sarcasm, would have had great effect in a popular assembly ; and that the magnitude of his figure, and striking peculiarity of his manner, would have aided the effect. But I remember it was observed by Mr. Flood, that Johnson, having been long used to sententious brevity and the short flights of conversation, might have failed in that continued and expanded kind of argument, which is requisite in stating complicated matters in publick speaking ; and as a proof of this he mentioned the supposed speeches in Parliament written by him for the magazine, none of which, in his opinion, were at all like real debates. The opinion of one who was himself so eminent an orator, must be allowed to have great weight. It was confirmed by Sir William Scott, who mentioned that Johnson had told him, that he had several times tried to speak in the Society of Arts and Sciences, but ' had found he could not get on [1].' From Mr. William Gerrard Hamilton I have heard, that Johnson, when observing to him that it was prudent for a man who had not been accustomed to speak in publick, to begin his speech in as simple a manner as possible, acknowledged that he rose in that society to deliver a speech which he had prepared ; ' but (said he,) all my flowers of oratory forsook me.' I however cannot help wishing, that he *had* ' tried his hand ' in Parliament ; and I wonder that ministry did not make the experiment.

I at length renewed a correspondence which had been too long discontinued :

' To Dr. Johnson.

' My Dear Sir,   ' Edinburgh, April 18, 1771.

' I can now fully understand those intervals of silence in your correspondence with me, which have often given me anxiety and uneasiness ; for although I am conscious that my veneration and love

---

[1] ⟨Dr. Kippis (*Biogr. Britan.*, iv. 266) says, ' I once heard Dr. Johnson   speak in the Society of Arts and Manufactures, upon a subject relative to

for Mr. Johnson have never in the least abated, yet I have deferred for almost a year and a half to write to him.'

In the subsequent part of this letter, I gave him an account of my comfortable life as a married man [1], and a lawyer in practice at the Scotch bar; invited him to Scotland, and promised to attend him to the Highlands, and Hebrides.

'To JAMES BOSWELL, ESQ.

'DEAR SIR,

'IF you are now able to comprehend that I might neglect to write without diminution of affection, you have taught me, likewise, how that neglect may be uneasily felt without resentment. I wished for your letter a long time, and when it came, it amply recompensed the delay. I never was so much pleased as now with your account of yourself; and sincerely hope, that between publick business, improving studies, and domestick pleasures, neither melancholy nor caprice will find any place for entrance. Whatever philosophy may determine of material nature, it is certainly true of intellectual nature, that it *abhors a vacuum :* our minds cannot be empty; and evil will break in upon them, if they are not pre-occupied by good. My dear Sir, mind your studies, mind your business, make your lady happy, and be a good Christian. After this,

> "——————— *tristitiam et metus*
> *Trades protervis in mare Creticum*
> *Portare ventis* [2]."

'If we perform our duty, we shall be safe and steady, " *Sive per* [3]," &c. whether we climb the Highlands, or are tost among the Hebrides; and I hope the time will come when we may try our powers both with cliffs and water. I see but little of Lord Elibank [4], I know not why;

mechanics, with a propriety, perspicuity, and energy, which excited general admiration.'⟩

[1] Boswell married his cousin Margaret Montgomerie on Nov. 25, 1769. On the same day his father married for the second time. *Scots Mag.* for 1769, p. 615. Boswell, in his *Letter to the People of Scotland* (1785, p. 55), describes his wife as 'a true *Montgomerie*, whom I esteem, whom I love, after fifteen years, as on the day when she gave me her hand.' See *post*, v. 24, and Boswell's *Letters*, Nos. 105, 148, 193.

[2] ' Musis amicus, tristitiam et metus
Tradam, &c.
While in the Muse's friendship blest,
Nor fear, nor grief, shall break my rest;
Bear them, ye vagrant winds, away,
And drown them in the Cretan Sea.'
    FRANCIS. Horace, *Odes*, i. 26. 1.
[3] Horace. *Odes*, i. 22. 5.
[4] Lord Elibank wrote to Boswell two years later :—' Old as I am, I shall be glad to go five hundred miles to enjoy a day of his [Johnson's] company.' *Post*, v. 181. See *ib.*, p. 387 and *post*, iii. 24.

perhaps by my own fault. I am this day going into Staffordshire and
Derbyshire for six weeks [1].

> ' I am, dear Sir,
> > ' Your most affectionate [a]
> > > ' And most humble servant,
> > > > ' SAM. JOHNSON.'

' London, June 20, 1771.'

' To SIR JOSHUA REYNOLDS, IN LEICESTER-FIELDS.

' DEAR SIR,

' WHEN I came to Lichfield, I found that my portrait [2] had been
much visited, and much admired. Every man has a lurking wish to
appear considerable in his native place ; and I was pleased with the
dignity conferred by such a testimony of your regard.

' Be pleased, therefore, to accept the thanks of, Sir,

> ' Your most obliged
> > ' And most humble servant,
> > > ' SAM. JOHNSON.'

' Ashbourn in Derbyshire,
        July 17, 1771.'

' Compliments to Miss Reynolds.'

' To DR. JOHNSON.

' Edinburgh, July 27, 1771.

' MY DEAR SIR,

' THE bearer of this, Mr. Beattie [3], Professor of Moral Philosophy
at Aberdeen, is desirous of being introduced to your acquaintance.

---

a affectionate 1 : affectionate, 2, 3.

[1] Goldsmith wrote to Langton on
Sept. 7, 1771 :—' Johnson has been
down upon a visit to a country parson, Doctor Taylor's, and is returned
to his old haunts at Mrs. Thrale's.'
Goldsmith's *Letters*, 1928, 104.

[2] ⟨This was the ' Knole ' portrait
painted by Sir Joshua Reynolds and
exhibited in 1770. There were three
versions, all by Sir Joshua ; a study,
also by him, is in the National Portrait
Gallery. See *post*, iv. 421, note 2.⟩

[3] ' Johnson,' wrote Beattie on
Sept. 8 of this year, ' has been
greatly misrepresented. I have passed
several entire days with him, and
found him extremely agreeable.' Sir

W. Forbes's *Life*, ed. 1806, i. 213.
⟨For Boswell's letter of instruction to
Beattie, see his *Letters*, No. 107.
Beattie wrote on 28 Aug. : ' I waited
on Dr. Samuel Johnson as soon as he
came to town, and gave him Mr.
Boswell's letter. He received me
with the utmost kindness and affection, and desired me to be with him
as much as possible. We dined together at a tavern on Saturday last,
where we sat by ourselves from two
o'clock till it was dark. . . . Had I been
his brother he could not have treated
me with more attention and kindness.'
Margaret Forbes, *Beattie and his
Friends*, 1904, 60–1. See *post*, ii. 203.⟩

His genius and learning, and labours in the service of virtue and religion, render him very worthy of it ; and as he has a high esteem of your character, I hope you will give him a favourable reception. I ever am, &c.

'JAMES BOSWELL.'

'TO BENNET LANGTON, ESQ. AT LANGTON, NEAR SPILSBY, LINCOLNSHIRE.

'DEAR SIR,

'I AM lately returned from Staffordshire and Derbyshire. The last letter mentions two others which you have written to me since you received my pamphlet. Of these two I never had but one, in which you mentioned a design of visiting Scotland, and, by consequence, put my journey to Langton out of my thoughts. My summer wanderings are now over, and I am engaging in a very great work, the revision of my Dictionary [1] ; from which I know not, at present, how to get loose.

'If you have observed, or been told, any errours or omissions, you will do me a great favour by letting me know them.

'Lady Rothes, I find, has disappointed you and herself. Ladies will have these tricks. The Queen and Mrs. Thrale, both ladies of experience, yet both missed their reckoning this summer. I hope, a few months will recompence your uneasiness.

'Please to tell Lady Rothes how highly I value the honour of her invitation, which it is my purpose to obey as soon as I have disengaged myself. In the mean time I shall hope to hear often of her Ladyship, and every day better news and better, till I hear that you have both the happiness, which to both is very sincerely wished, by, Sir,

'Your most affectionate, and

'Most humble servant,

'SAM. JOHNSON.'

'August 29, 1771.'

In October I again wrote to him, thanking him for his last letter, and his obliging reception of Mr. Beattie ; informing him that I had been at Alnwick lately, and had good accounts of him from Dr. Percy.

In his religious record of this year, we observe that he was better than usual, both in body and mind, and better satisfied with the regularity of his conduct [2]. But he is still 'trying his

---

[1] He was preparing the fourth edition. See *post*, ii. 155.

[2] '1771, Sept. 18, 9 at night. I am now come to my sixty third year. For

ways [1] ' too rigorously. He charges himself with not rising early enough ; yet he mentions what was surely a sufficient excuse for this, supposing it to be a duty seriously required, as he all his life appears to have thought it. ' One great hindrance is want of rest ; my nocturnal complaints grow less troublesome towards morning ; and I am tempted to repair the deficiencies of the night [2].' Alas ! how hard would it be if this indulgence were to be imputed to a sick man as a crime. In his retrospect on the following Easter-eve, he says, ' When I review the last year, I am able to recollect so little done, that shame and sorrow, though perhaps too weakly, come upon me.' Had he been judging of any one else in the same circumstances, how clear would he have been on the favourable side. How very difficult, and in my opinion almost constitutionally impossible it was for him to be raised early, even by the strongest resolutions, appears from a note in one of his little paper-books, (containing words arranged for his Dictionary,) written, I suppose, about 1753 : ' I do not remember that since I left Oxford I ever rose early by mere choice, but once or twice at Edial, and two or three times for the Rambler.' I think he had fair ground enough to have quieted his mind on this subject, by concluding that he was physically incapable of what is at best but a commodious regulation.

In 1772 he was altogether quiescent as an authour [3] ; but it will be found from the various evidences which I shall bring together, that his mind was acute, lively, and vigorous.

---

the last year I have been slowly recovering both from the violence of my last illness, and, I think, from the general disease of my life : . . . Some advances I hope have been made towards regularity. I have missed Church since Easter only two Sundays. . . . But Indolence and Indifference has been neither conquered nor opposed.' *Pr. and Med.* ¶ 91.

[1] ' Let us search and try our ways.' *Lamentations* iii. 40.

[2] Prayers and Meditations, p. 101 [105 : ¶ 91]. BOSWELL.

[3] ⟨Boswell means that Johnson published nothing in this year. He was of course ' engaged in a very great work ', the revision of his *Dictionary* for the fourth edition (see previous page). On 6 Oct. 1772, Johnson writes to Dr. Taylor :—' I am now within a few hours of being able to send the whole dictionary to the press.' It was published in 1773.⟩ In *Pr. and Med.* ¶ 100, at Easter, 1773, as he ' reviews the last year,' he records :—' Of the Spring and Summer, I remember that I was able in those seasons to examine and improve my dictionary, and was seldom witheld from the work, but by my own unwillingness.'

' To Sir Joshua Reynolds.

' Dear Sir,

' Be pleased to send to Mr. Banks, whose place of residence I do not know, this note, which I have sent open, that, if you please, you may read it.

' When you send it, do not use your own seal.

'   I am, Sir,

'   Your most humble servant,

' Feb. 27, 1772.'   ' Sam. Johnson.'

' To Joseph Banks, Esq.

" *Perpetua ambitâ bis terrâ præmia lactis*
Hæc habet altrici Capra secunda Jovis [1]."

' Sir,

' I return thanks to you and to Dr. Solander for the pleasure which I received in yesterday's conversation. I could not recollect a motto for your Goat, but have given her one. You, Sir, may perhaps have an epick poem from some happier pen than, Sir,

'   Your most humble servant,

' Johnson's-court, Fleet-street,   ' Sam. Johnson.'
    February 27, 1772.'

' To Dr. Johnson.†

' My Dear Sir,   ' Edinburgh, March 3, 1772 [a].

' It is hard that I cannot prevail on you to write to me oftener. But I am convinced that it is in vain to expect from you a private correspondence with any regularity. I must, therefore, look upon you as a fountain of wisdom, from whence few rills are communicated to a distance, and which must be approached at its source, to partake fully of its virtues.   *   *   *   *   *   *

' I am coming to London soon, and am to appear in an appeal from the Court of Session in the House of Lords. A schoolmaster in Scotland was, by a court of inferiour jurisdiction, deprived of his office, for being somewhat severe in the chastisement of his scholars [2]. The

[a] *The address and date omitted* 2, 3.

[1] Thus translated by a friend.
' In fame scarce second to the nurse
    of Jove,
This Goat, who twice the world
    had traversed round,
Deserving both her master's care
    and love,

Ease and perpetual pasture now has
    found.' Boswell. ⟨See App. B.⟩
    † ⟨Boswell edited this letter : see
Prof. Tinker's print of the original.
Boswell's Letters, No. 111.⟩
    [2] Cockburn (*Life of Jeffrey*, i. 4)
says that the High School of Edin-

Court of Session, considering it to be dangerous to the interest of learning and education, to lessen the dignity of teachers, and make them afraid of too indulgent parents, instigated by the complaints of their children, restored him. His enemies have appealed to the House of Lords, though the salary is only twenty pounds a year. I was Counsel for him here. I hope there will be little fear of a reversal ; but I must beg to have your aid in my plan of supporting the decree. It is a general question, and not a point of particular law.

*　　*　　*　　*　　*　　*

'I am, &c.

'JAMES BOSWELL.'

'To JAMES BOSWELL, ESQ.

'DEAR SIR,

'THAT you are coming so soon to town I am very glad ; and still more glad that you are coming as an advocate. I think nothing more likely to make your life pass happily away, than that consciousness of your own value, which eminence in your profession will certainly confer. If I can give you any collateral help, I hope you do not suspect that it will be wanting. My kindness for you has neither the merit of singular virtue, nor the reproach of singular prejudice. Whether to love you be right or wrong, I have many on my side : Mrs. Thrale loves you, and Mrs. Williams loves you, and what would have inclined me to love you, if I had been neutral before, you are a great favourite of Dr. Beattie.

'Of Dr. Beattie I should have thought much, but that his lady puts him out of my head : she is a very lovely woman.

'The ejection which you come hither to oppose, appears very cruel, unreasonable, and oppressive. I should think there could not be much doubt of your success.

'My health grows better, yet I am not fully recovered. I believe it is held, that men do not recover very fast after threescore. I hope yet to see Beattie's College : and have not given up the western voyage. But however all this may be or not, let us try to make each other happy when we meet, and not refer our pleasure to distant times or distant places.

'How comes it that you tell me nothing of your lady ? I hope to see her some time, and till then shall be glad to hear of her.

'I am, dear Sir, &c.

'March 15, 1772.'　　　　'SAM. JOHNSON.'

burgh, in 1781, 'was cursed by two under masters, whose atrocities young men cannot be made to believe, but old men cannot forget, and the criminal law would not now endure.' ⟨See also *post*, ii. 183, 202.⟩

' To BENNET LANGTON, ESQ. NEAR SPILSBY, LINCOLNSHIRE.

' DEAR SIR,
    ' I CONGRATULATE you and Lady Rothes [1] on your little man, and hope you will all be many years happy together.
    ' Poor Miss Langton can have little part in the joy of her family. She this day called her aunt Langton to receive the sacrament with her ; and made me talk yesterday on such subjects as suit her condition. It will probably be her *viaticum*. I surely need not mention again that she wishes to see her mother. I am, Sir,
                ' Your most humble servant,
                      ' SAM. JOHNSON.'
' March 14, 1772.'

    On the 21st of March, I was happy to find myself again in my friend's study, and was glad to see my old acquaintance, Mr. Francis Barber, who was now returned home [2]. Dr. Johnson received me with a hearty welcome ; saying, ' I am glad you are come, and glad you are come upon such an errand : ' (alluding to the cause of the schoolmaster.) BOSWELL. ' I hope, Sir, he will be in no danger. It is a very delicate matter to interfere between a master and his scholars : nor do I see how you can fix the degree of severity that a master may use.' JOHNSON. ' Why, Sir, till you can fix the degree of obstinacy and negligence of the scholars, you cannot fix the degree of severity of the master. Severity must be continued until obstinacy be subdued, and negligence be cured.' He mentioned the severity of Hunter, his own master [3]. ' Sir, (said I,) Hunter is a Scotch name : so it should seem this schoolmaster who beat you so severely was a Scotchman. I can now account for your prejudice against the Scotch.' JOHNSON. ' Sir, he was not Scotch ; and abating his brutality, he was a very good master [4].'

---

[1] Mr. Langton married the Countess Dowager of Rothes. BOSWELL.
[2] From school. See *ante*, ii. 62.
[3] See *ante*, i. 44 ⟨and 526⟩.
[4] ' Johnson used to say that schoolmasters were worse than the Egyptian task-masters of old. No boy, says he, is sure any day he goes to school to escape a whipping : how can the schoolmaster tell what the boy has really forgotten, and what he has neglected to learn ? ' Johnson's *Works* (1787), xi. 209. ' I rejoice,' writes J. S. Mill (*Auto.* p. 53), ' in the decline of the old, brutal and tyrannical system of teaching, which, however, did succeed in enforcing habits of application ; but the new, as it seems

We talked of his two political pamphlets, ' The False Alarm,' and ' Thoughts concerning Falkland's Islands.' JOHNSON. ' Well, Sir, which of them did you think the best ? ' BOSWELL. ' I liked the second best.' JOHNSON. ' Why, Sir, I liked the first best ; and Beattie liked the first best. Sir, there is a subtlety of disquisition in the first, that is worth all the fire of the second.' BOSWELL. ' Pray, Sir, is it true that Lord North paid you a visit, and that you got two hundred a year in addition to your pension ? ' JOHNSON. ' No, Sir. Except what I had from the bookseller, I did not get a farthing by them [1]. And, between you and me, I believe Lord North is no friend to me.' BOSWELL. ' How so, Sir ? ' JOHNSON. ' Why, Sir, you cannot account for the fancies of men.—Well, how does Lord Elibank ? and how does Lord Monboddo ? ' BOSWELL. ' Very well, Sir. Lord Monboddo still maintains the superiority of the savage life [2].' JOHNSON. ' What strange narrowness of mind now is that, to think the things we have not known, are better than the things which we have known.' BOSWELL. ' Why, Sir, that is a common prejudice.' JOHNSON. ' Yes, Sir;[a] but a common prejudice should not be found in one whose trade it is to rectify errour.'

A gentleman having come in who was to go as a Mate in the ship along with Mr. Banks and Dr. Solander, Dr. Johnson asked what were the names of the ships destined for the expedition. The gentleman answered, they were once to be called the Drake and the Raleigh, but now they were to be called the Resolution and the Adventure [3]. JOHNSON. ' Much better ; for had the Raleigh [4] returned without going round the world, it would have been ridiculous. To give them the names of the Drake and the Raleigh was laying a trap for satire.' BOSWELL. ' Had not you

[a] Sir; 1, 2: Sir, 3.

to me, is training up a race of men who will be incapable of doing anything which is disagreeable to them.'

[1] See *ante*, i. 373.

[2] See *ante*, ii. 74.

[3] The ship in which Mr. Banks and Dr. Solander were to have sailed was the Endeavour. It was, they said, unfit for the voyage. The Admiralty altered it in such a way as to render it top-heavy. It was nearly overset on going down the river.

Then it was rendered safe by restoring it to its former condition. When the explorers raised their former objections, they were told to take it or none. *Ann. Reg.* xv. 108. See also *post*, v. 328.

[4] I suspect that *Raleigh* is here an error of Mr. Boswell's pen, for *Drake* : Johnson knew very well that it was Drake, and not Raleigh, that went round the world. CROKER. He had, of course, written Drake's *Life*.

some desire to go upon this expedition, Sir ? ' JOHNSON. ' Why yes, but I soon laid it aside. Sir, there is very little of intellectual, in the course. Besides, I see but at a small distance. So it was not worth my while to go to see birds fly, which I should not have seen fly ; and fishes swim, which I should not have seen swim.'

The gentleman being gone, and Dr. Johnson having left the room for some time, a debate arose between the Reverend Mr. Stockdale and Mrs. Desmoulins, whether Mr. Banks and Dr. Solander were entitled to any share of glory from their expedition. When Dr. Johnson returned to us, I told him the subject of their dispute. JOHNSON. ' Why, Sir, it was properly for botany that they went out : I believe they thought only of culling of simples ¹.'

I thanked him for showing civilities to Beattie. ' Sir, (said he,) I should thank *you*. We all love Beattie. Mrs. Thrale says, if ever she has another husband, she'll have Beattie. He sunk upon us ² that he was married ; else we should have shewn his

---

¹ *Romeo and Juliet*, act v. sc. i.

² ' TO JAMES BOSWELL, ESQ.

' *Edinburgh, May* 3, 1792.

' MY DEAR SIR,

' As I suppose your great work will soon be reprinted, I beg leave to trouble you with a remark on a passage of it, in which I am a little misrepresented. Be not alarmed ; the misrepresentation is not imputable to you. Not having the book at hand, I cannot specify the page, but I suppose you will easily find it. Dr. Johnson says, speaking of Mrs. Thrale's family, " Dr. Beattie *sunk upon us* that he was married, or words to that purpose." I am not sure that I understand *sunk upon us*, which is a very uncommon phrase : but it seems to me to imply, (and others, I find, have understood it in the same sense,) *studiously concealed from us his being married*. Now, Sir, this was by no means the case. I could have no motive to

conceal a circumstance, of which I never was nor can be ashamed ; and of which Dr. Johnson seemed to think, when he afterwards became acquainted with Mrs. Beattie, that I had, as was true, reason to be proud. So far was I from concealing her, that my wife had at that time almost as numerous an acquaintance in London as I had myself ; and was, not very long after, kindly invited and elegantly entertained at Streatham by Mr. and Mrs. Thrale.

' My request, therefore, is, that you would rectify this matter in your new edition. You are at liberty to make what use you please of this letter.

' My best wishes ever attend you and your family. Believe me to be, with the utmost regard and esteem, dear Sir,

' Your obliged and affectionate humble servant, J. BEATTIE.'

I have, from my respect for my friend Dr. Beattie, and regard to his extreme sensibility, inserted the fore-

lady more civilities. She is a very fine woman. But how can
you shew civilities to a non-entity ? I did not think he had been
married. Nay, I did not think about it one way or other ; but
he did not tell us of his lady till late.'

He then spoke of St. Kilda [1], the most remote of the Hebrides.
I told him, I thought of buying it. JOHNSON. 'Pray do, Sir.
We will [a] go and pass a winter amid the blasts there. We shall
have fine fish, and we will [a] take some dried tongues with us, and
some books. We will [a] have a strong built vessel, and some
Orkney men to navigate her. We must build a tolerable house :
but we may carry with us a wooden house ready made, and requiring nothing but to be put up. Consider, Sir, by buying St.
Kilda, you may keep the people from falling into worse hands.
We must give them a clergyman, and he shall be one of Beattie's
choosing. He shall be educated at Marischal College. I'll be
your Lord Chancellor, or what you please.' BOSWELL. 'Are
you serious, Sir, in advising me to buy St. Kilda ? for if you
should advise me to go to Japan, I believe I should do it.'
JOHNSON. 'Why yes, Sir, I am serious.' BOSWELL. 'Why then,
I'll see what can be done.'

I gave him an account of the two parties in the church of
Scotland, those for supporting the rights of patrons, independent
of the people, and those against it. JOHNSON. 'It should be
settled one way or other. I cannot wish well to a popular
election of the clergy, when I consider that it occasions such
animosities, such unworthy courting of the people, such
slanders between the contending parties, and other disadvantages.
It is enough to allow the people to remonstrate against the
nomination of a minister for solid reasons.' (I suppose he meant
heresy or immorality.)

[a] shall 1, 2: will 3.

going letter, though I cannot but
wonder at his considering as any imputation a phrase commonly used
among the best friends. BOSWELL.
Mr. Croker says 'there was a cause
for this " extreme sensibility." Dr.
Beattie was conscious that there was
something that might give a colour
to such an imputation. It became
known, shortly after the date of this
letter, that the mind of poor Mrs.

Beattie had become deranged.' ⟨Since
1781 Beattie and his wife had lived
apart. See Margaret Forbes, *Beattie*,
pp. 175 foll. Johnson in his *Dictionary* gives ' to suppress ; to conceal ' as one meaning of *sink* ; but
the construction *sink upon* was uncommon and no earlier instance of it
has been found. See the *Oxford
Dictionary*, s.v. SINK, *v.* 25 b.⟩

[1] See *ante*, i. 450.

He was engaged to dine abroad, and asked me to return to him in the evening, at nine, which I accordingly did.

We drank tea with Mrs. Williams, who told us a story of second sight [1], which happened in Wales where she was born.— He listened to it very attentively, and said he should be glad to have some instances of that faculty well authenticated. His elevated wish for more and more evidence for spirit [2], in opposition to the groveling belief of materialism, led him to a love of such mysterious disquisitions. He again [3] justly observed, that we could have no certainty of the truth of supernatural appearances, unless something was told us which we could not know by ordinary means, or something done which could not be done but by supernatural power ; that Pharaoh in reason and justice required such evidence from Moses ; nay, that our Saviour said, ' If I had not done among them the works which none other man did, they had not had sin [4].' He had said in the morning, that ' Macaulay's History of St. Kilda,' was very well written, except some foppery about liberty and slavery. I mentioned to him that Macaulay told me, he was advised to leave out of his book the wonderful story that upon the approach of a stranger all the inhabitants catch cold [5] ; but that it had been so well authenticated, he determined to retain it. JOHNSON, ' Sir, to leave things out of a book, merely because people tell you they will not be believed, is meanness. Macaulay acted with more magnanimity.'

We talked of the Roman Catholick religion, and how little difference there was in essential matters between ours and it. JOHNSON. ' True, Sir ; all denominations of Christians have really little difference in point of doctrine, though they may differ widely in external forms. There is a prodigious difference between the external form of one of your Presbyterian churches in Scotland, and a church in Italy ; yet the doctrine taught is essentially the same [6].'

I mentioned the petition to Parliament for removing the subscription to the Thirty-nine Articles [7]. JOHNSON. ' It was soon

---

[1] See *ante*, ii. 10.
[2] See *post*, iii. 298, note 1, and iv. 299.
[3] See *ante*, i. 405.
[4] *St. John*, xv. 24.

[5] See *ante*, p. 51 of this volume. BOSWELL. ⟨See also *post*, v. 278.⟩
[6] See *ante*, ii. 105.
[7] The petition was presented on Feb. 6 of this year. By a majority

thrown out. Sir, they talk of not making boys at the University subscribe to what they do not understand [1]; but they ought to consider, that our Universities were founded to bring up members for the Church of England, and we must not supply our enemies with arms from our arsenal. No, Sir, the meaning of subscribing is, not that they fully understand all the articles, but that they will adhere to the Church of England [2]. Now take it in this way, and suppose that they should only subscribe their adherence to the Church of England, there would be still the same difficulty; for still the young men would be subscribing to what they do not understand. For if you should ask them, what do you mean by the Church of England? Do you know in what it differs from the Presbyterian Church? from the Romish Church? from the Greek Church? from the Coptick Church? they could not tell you. So, Sir, it comes to the same thing.' BOSWELL. 'But, Sir [a], would it not be sufficient to subscribe the Bible [3]?' JOHNSON. 'Why no, Sir; for all sects will subscribe the Bible; nay, the Mahometans will subscribe the Bible; for the Mahometans acknowledge JESUS CHRIST, as well as Moses, but maintain that GOD sent Mahomet as a still greater prophet than either.'

I mentioned the motion which had been made in the House

a Sir, *omitted* 2, 3.

of 217 to 71 leave was refused for it to be brought up. *Parl. Hist.* xvii. 245–97. Gibbon, in a letter dated Feb. 8, 1772 (*Misc. Works*, ii. 74), congratulates Mr. Holroyd 'on the late victory of our dear mamma, the Church of England. She had, last Thursday, 71 rebellious sons, who pretended to set aside her will on account of insanity: but 217 worthy champions, headed by Lord North, Burke, and Charles Fox, &c., though they allowed the thirty-nine clauses of her testament were absurd and unreasonable, supported the validity of it with infinite humour. By the bye, Charles Fox prepared himself for that holy war, by passing twenty-two hours in the pious exercise of hazard; his devotion cost him only about 500*l.* *per* hour—in all, 11,000*l.*' See *post*, v. 64.

[1] 'Lord George Germayne,' writes Walpole, 'wondered the House did not take some steps on this subject with regard to the Universities, where boys were made to subscribe the Articles without reading them—a scandalous abuse.' *Journal of the Reign of George III*, i. 11.

[2] See *ante*, ii. 104.

[3] Burke had thus answered Boswell's proposal:—'What is that Scripture, to which they are content to subscribe? . . . The Bible is a vast collection of different treatises: a man, who holds the divine authority of one, may consider the other as merely human. . . . Therefore to ascertain Scripture you must have one Article more; and you must define what that Scripture is, which you mean to teach.' *Parl. Hist.* xvii. 284.

of Commons, to abolish the fast of the 30th of January [1].
JOHNSON. ' Why, Sir, I could have wished that it had been
a temporary act, perhaps, to have expired with the century. I
am against abolishing it ; because that would be declaring it
was [a] wrong to establish it ; but I should have no objection to make
an act, continuing it for another century, and then letting it
expire.'

He disapproved of the Royal Marriage Bill ; ' Because (said
he,) I would not have the people think that the validity of marriage depends on the will of man, or that the right of a King
depends on the will of man. I should not have been against
making the marriage of any of the royal family,[b] without the
approbation of King and Parliament, highly criminal [2].'

a was *omitted* 2, 3.   b family, 1 : family 2, 3.

[1] Dr. Nowell (*post*, iv. 295) had
this year preached the fast sermon
before the House of Commons on
Jan. 30, the anniversary of the execution of Charles I, and received the
usual vote of thanks. *Parl. Hist.* xvii.
245. On Feb. 25 the entry of the
vote was, without a division, ordered
to be expunged. On the publication
of the sermon it had been seen that
Nowell had asserted that George III
was endued with the same virtues as
Charles I, and that the members of
the House were the descendants of
those who had opposed that King.
Ib. p. 313, and *Ann. Reg.* xv. 79. On
March 2, Mr. Montague moved for
leave to bring in a bill to abolish the
fast, but it was refused by 125 to 97.
Parl. Hist. xvii. 319. The fast was
abolished in 1859—thirteen years
within the century that Johnson was
ready to allow it. ' It is remarkable,'
writes Walpole, ' that the present King
had never from the beginning of his
reign gone to church on the 30th of
January, whereas George II always
did.' *Journal of the Reign of George
III*, i. 41.

[2] This passage puzzled Mr. Croker
and Mr. Lockhart. The following
extract from the *Gent. Mag.* for Feb.
1772, p. 92, throws light on Johnson's

meaning :—' This, say the opposers
of the Bill, is putting it in the King's
power to change the Order of Succession, as he may for ever prevent, if
he is so minded, the elder branches
of his family from marrying, and
therefore may establish the succession in the younger. Be this as it
may, is it not, in fact, converting the
holy institution of Marriage into a
mere state contract ? ' See also the
Protest of fourteen of the peers in
Parl. Hist. xvii. 391, and *post*, ii. 224,
note 1. Walpole ends his account
of the Marriage Bill by saying :—
' Thus within three weeks were the
Thirty-nine Articles affirmed, and
the New Testament deserted.' *Journal of the Reign of George III*, i. 37.
How carelessly this Act was drawn
was shown by Lord Eldon, when
Attorney-General, in the case of the
marriage of the Duke of Sussex to
Lady Augusta Murray. ' Lord Thurlow said to me angrily [at the Privy
Council,] " Sir, why have you not
prosecuted, under the Act of Parliament, all the parties concerned in
this abominable marriage ? " To
which I answered, " That it was a
very difficult business to prosecute—
that the Act . . . had been drawn by
Lord Mansfield, and *Mr. Attorney*

In the morning we had talked of old families, and the respect due to them. JOHNSON. ' Sir, you have a right to that kind of respect, and are arguing for yourself. I am for supporting the principle, and am disinterested in doing it, as I have no such right [1].' BOSWELL. ' Why, Sir, it is one more incitement to a man to do well.' JOHNSON. ' Yes, Sir, and it is a matter of opinion, very necessary to keep society together. What is it but opinion, by which we have a respect for authority, that prevents us, who are the rabble, from rising up and pulling down you who are gentlemen from your places, and saying " We will be gentlemen in our turn " ? Now, Sir, that respect for authority is much more easily granted to a man whose father has had it, than to an upstart [2], and so Society is more easily supported.' BOSWELL. ' Perhaps, Sir, it might be done by the respect belonging to office, as among the Romans, where the dress, the *toga*, inspired reverence.' JOHNSON. ' Why, Sir [a], we know very little about the Romans. But, surely, it is much easier to respect a man who has always had respect, than to respect a man who we know was last year no better than ourselves, and will be no better next year. In republicks there is not a respect for authority, but a fear of power.' BOSWELL. ' At present, Sir, I think riches seem to gain most respect.' JOHNSON. ' No, Sir, riches do not gain hearty respect ; they only procure external attention. A very rich man, from low beginnings, may buy his election in a borough ; but, *cæteris paribus*, a man of family will be preferred. People will prefer a man for whose father their fathers have voted, though they should get no more money, or even less. That shows that the respect for family is not merely fanciful, but has an actual operation. If gentlemen of family would allow the rich upstarts to spend their money profusely, which they are ready enough to do, and not vie with them in expence, the upstarts would soon

a Sir, *omitted* 2, 3.

General Thurlow, and Mr. Solicitor General Wedderburne, and unluckily they had made all parties present at the marriage guilty of felony ; and as nobody could prove the marriage except a person who had been present at it, there could be no prosecution, because nobody present could be compelled to be a witness." This put

an end to the matter.' Twiss's *Eldon*, i. 236.

1 See *post*, ii. 261 ; iii. 353.
2 See Boswell's *Hebrides*, Aug. 25, *post*, v. 106, where Johnson, discussing the same question, says :—' There is generally a *scoundrelism* about a low man.'

be at an end, and the gentlemen would remain : but if the
gentlemen will vie in expence with the upstarts, which is very
foolish, they must be ruined.'

I gave him an account of the excellent mimickry of a friend
of mine in Scotland [1] ; observing, at the same time, that some
people thought it a very mean thing. JOHNSON. ' Why, Sir, it
is making a very mean use of a man's powers. But to be a good
mimick, requires great powers,[a] great acuteness of observation,
great retention of what is observed, and great pliancy of organs,
to represent what is observed. I remember a lady of quality in
this town, Lady —————————, who was a wonderful mimick, and
used to make me laugh immoderately. I have heard she is now
gone mad.' BOSWELL. ' It is amazing how a mimick can not
only give you the gestures and voice of a person whom he
represents ; but even what a person would say on any particular
subject.' JOHNSON. ' Why, Sir, you are to consider that the
manner and some particular phrases of a person do much to impress you with an idea of him, and you are not sure that he
would say what the mimick says in his character.' BOSWELL.
' I don't think Foote [2] a good mimick, Sir.' JOHNSON. ' No, Sir ;
his imitations are not like. He gives you something different
from himself, but not the character which he means to assume.
He goes out of himself, without going into other people. He
cannot take off any person unless he is very strongly marked, such as
George Faulkner [3]. He is like a painter, who can draw the portrait
of a man who has a wen upon his face, and who, therefore, is
easily known. If a man hops upon one leg, Foote can hop

[1] Mackintosh told Croker that this
friend was Robert Cullen, afterwards a judge by the name of Lord
Cullen. In *Boswelliana* (pp. 250–2),
Boswell mentions him thrice, and
always as ' Cullen the mimick.' His
manner, he says, was wretched, and
his physiognomy worse than Wilkes's.
Dr. A. Carlyle (*Auto*. p. 268) says that
' Cullen . . . in his youth possessed
the talent of mimicry beyond all mankind ; for his was not merely an exact
imitation of voice and manner of
speaking, but a perfect exhibition of
every man's manner of thinking on

every subject.' Carlyle mentions some
striking instances of this. ⟨See *D.N.B.*⟩
[2] See *post*, iii. 69.
[3] ' The prince of Dublin printers,'
as Swift called him. Swift's *Works*
(1824), xviii. 83. He was taken off
by Foote under the name of Peter
Paragraph, in *The Orators*, the piece
in which he had meant to take off
Johnson (*ante*, ii. 95). ' Faulkner consoled himself (pending his prosecution of the libeller) by pirating the
libel and selling it most extensively.'
Forster's *Goldsmith*, i. 287. See *post*,
v. 130.

upon one leg [1]. But he has not that nice discrimination which your friend seems to possess. Foote is, however, very entertaining, with a kind of conversation between wit and buffoonery [2].'

On Monday, March 23, I found him busy, preparing a fourth edition of his folio Dictionary. Mr. Peyton, one of his original amanuenses, was writing for him. I put him in mind of a meaning of the word *side*, which he had omitted, viz. relationship ; as father's side, mother's side. He inserted it. I asked him if *humiliating* was a good word. He said, he had seen it frequently used, but he did not know it to be legitimate English. He would not admit *civilization*, but only *civility* [3]. With great deference to him, I thought *civilization*, from *to civilize*, better in the sense opposed to *barbarity*, than *civility* ; as it is better to have a distinct word for each sense, than one word with two senses, which *civility* is, in his way of using it.

He seemed also to be intent on some sort of chymical operation. I was entertained by observing how he contrived to send Mr. Peyton on an errand, without seeming to degrade him. ' Mr. Peyton,—Mr. Peyton, will you be so good as to take a walk to Temple-Bar ? You will there see a chymist's shop ; at which you will be pleased to buy for me an ounce of oil of vitriol ; not spirit of vitriol, but oil of vitriol. It will cost three half-pence.'

[1] Faulkner had lost one of his legs. ' When Foote had his accident (*ante*, ii. 95), "Now I shall take off old Faulkner indeed to the life ! " was the first remark he made when what he had to suffer was announced to him.' Forster's *Essays*, ii. 400.

[2] A writer in the *Monthly Review*, lxxvi. 374 (no doubt Murphy), says :— ' A large number of friends, such as Johnson, Mr. Burke, Mr. Murphy, and others dined at Garrick's, at Christmas, 1760. Foote was then in Dublin. It was said at table, that he had been horse-whipped by an apothecary for taking him off upon the stage. . . . " But I wonder," said Garrick, " that any man would shew so much resentment to Foote : . . . nobody ever thought it *worth his while* to quarrel with him in London."

" And I am glad," said Johnson, " to find that the man is *rising* in the world." The anecdote was, afterwards, told to Foote, who, in return, gave out that he would in a short time produce the Caliban of literature on the stage. Being informed of this design, Johnson sent word to Foote, that, the theatre being intended for the reformation of vice, he would go from the boxes on the stage, and correct him before the audience. Foote abandoned the design. No ill-will ensued.' ⟨See also *ante*, ii. 95, *post*, ii. 299, iii. 69, and Mrs. Piozzi's *Anec.* p. 173 : *John. Misc.* i. 265.⟩

[3] See *post*, iii. 77, where Johnson says :—' I turned Boswell loose at Lichfield, my native city, that he might see for once real civility.'

Peyton immediately went, and returned with it, and told him it cost but a penny.

I then reminded him of the schoolmaster's cause, and proposed to read to him the printed papers concerning it. ' No, Sir, (said he,) I can read quicker than I can hear.' So he read them to himself.

After he had read for some time, we were interrupted by the entrance of Mr. Kristrom, a Swede, who was tutor to some young gentlemen in the city. He told me, that there was a very good History of Sweden, by Daline [1]. Having at that time an intention of writing the history of that country, I asked Dr. Johnson whether one might write a history of Sweden, without going thither. ' Yes, Sir, (said he,) one for common use.'

We talked of languages. Johnson observed, that Leibnitz had made some progress in a work, tracing all languages up to the Hebrew. ' Why, Sir, (said he,) you would not imagine that the French *jour*, day, is derived from the Latin *dies*, and yet nothing is more certain ; and the intermediate steps are very clear. From *dies*, comes *diurnus*. *Diu* is, by inaccurate ears, or inaccurate pronunciation, easily confounded with *giu* ; then the Italians form a substantive of the ablative of an adjective, and thence *giurno*, or, as they make it, *giorno* ; which is readily contracted into *giour*, or *jour*.' He observed, that the Bohemian language was true Sclavonick. The Swede said, it had some similarity with the German. JOHNSON. ' Why, Sir, to be sure, such parts of Sclavonia as confine with Germany, will borrow German words ; and such parts as confine with Tartary, will borrow Tartar words.'

He said, he never had it properly ascertained that the Scotch Highlanders and the Irish understood each other [2]. I told him that my cousin Colonel Graham, of the Royal Highlanders, whom I met at Drogheda [3], told me they did. JOHNSON. ' Sir, the Highlanders understood Irish, why translate the New Testament into Erse, as was done lately at Edinburgh, when there is an Irish translation ? ' BOSWELL. ' Although the Erse and Irish are both dialects of the same language, there may be a good

---

[1] ⟨Olof von Dalin, 1708–63, one of the fathers of modern Swedish literature. His history, *Svea rikes historia*, was first published in 1747–60.⟩

[2] See *post*, ii. 347.

[3] Boswell visited Ireland in May, 1769. *Letters*, No. 97, i. 170.

deal of diversity between them, as between the different dialects in Italy.'—The Swede went away, and Mr. Johnson continued his reading of the papers. I said, ' I am afraid, Sir, it is troublesome to you ª.' ' Why, Sir, (said he,) I do not take much delight in it ; but I'll go through it.'

We went to the Mitre, and dined in the room where he and I first supped together. He gave me great hopes of my cause. ' Sir, (said he,) the government of a schoolmaster is somewhat of the nature of military government ; that is to say, it must be arbitrary, it must be exercised by the will of one man, according to particular circumstances. You must shew some learning upon this occasion. You must shew, that a schoolmaster has a prescriptive right to beat ; and that an action of assault and battery cannot be admitted against him, unless there is some great excess, some barbarity. This man has maimed none of his boys. They are all left with the full exercise of their corporeal faculties. In our schools in England, many boys have been maimed ; yet I never heard of an action against a schoolmaster on that account. Puffendorf, I think, maintains the right of a schoolmaster to beat his scholars ¹.'

On Saturday, March 27 ᵇ, I introduced to him Sir Alexander Macdonald ², with whom he had expressed a wish to be acquainted. He received him very courteously.

Sir Alexander observed, that the Chancellors in England are chosen from views much inferiour to the office, being chosen from temporary political views. JOHNSON. ' Why, Sir, in such a government as ours, no man is appointed to an office because he is the fittest for it, nor hardly in any other government ; because there are so many connections and dependencies to be studied ³. A despotick prince may choose a man to an office,

---

ª to you *om.* 2, 3.　　　　ᵇ *Saturday was the 28th.*

¹ Puffendorf states that ' tutors and schoolmasters have a right to the moderate use of gentle discipline over their pupils '—viii. 3–10 ; adding, rather superfluously, Grotius's caveat, that ' it shall not extend to a power of *death*.' CROKER.

² The brother of Sir J. Macdonald, mentioned *ante*, i. 449. ⟨For Johnson's visit to him in the Isle of Skye

and its consequences, see *post*, v. 148, and Mr. Chapman's edition of Johnson's *Journey* and Boswell's *Journal*, 1924, p. 482.⟩

³ Lord Campbell (*Lives of the Chancellors*, v. 449) points out that this conversation followed close on the appointment of ' the incompetent Bathurst ' as Chancellor. ' Such a conversation,' he adds, ' would not have

merely because he is the fittest for it. The King of Prussia may do it.' SIR A. ' I think, Sir, almost all great lawyers, such at least as have written upon law, have known only law, and nothing else.' JOHNSON. ' Why no, Sir ; Judge Hale was a great lawyer, and wrote upon law ; and yet he knew a great many other things, and has written upon other things. Selden too.' SIR A. ' Very true, Sir ; and Lord Bacon. But was not Lord Coke a mere lawyer ? ' JOHNSON. ' Why, I am afraid he was ; but he would have taken it very ill if you had told him so. He would have prosecuted you for scandal.' BOSWELL. ' Lord Mansfield is not a mere lawyer.' JOHNSON. ' No, Sir. I never was in Lord Mansfield's company ; but,[a] Lord Mansfield was distinguished at the University. Lord Mansfield, when he first came to town, " drank champagne with the wits," as Prior says [1]. He was the friend of Pope [2].' SIR A. ' Barristers, I believe, are not so abusive now as they were formerly. I fancy they had less law long ago, and so were obliged to take to abuse, to fill up the time. Now they have such a number of precedents, they have no occasion for abuse.' JOHNSON. ' Nay, Sir, they had more law long ago than they have now. As to precedents, to be sure they will increase in course of time ; but the more precedents there are, the less occasion is there for law ; that is to say, the less occasion is there for investigating principles.' SIR A. ' I have been correcting several Scotch accents [3] in my friend Boswell. I doubt, Sir, if any Scotchman ever attains to a perfect English pronunciation.' JOHNSON. ' Why, Sir, few of them do, because they do not persevere after acquiring a certain degree of it. But, Sir, there can be no doubt that they may attain to a perfect English pronunciation, if they will. We find how near they come to it ; and certainly, a man who conquers nineteen parts of the Scottish accent, may conquer the twentieth. But, Sir, when a man has got the better of nine tenths,[b] he grows weary, he relaxes his diligence, he finds he has corrected his accent so

---

a but, Lord Mansfield 1, 2: but Lord Mansfield, 3.   b *comma omitted* 3.

occurred during the Chancellorship of Lord Hardwicke or Lord Somers.'
[1] ' But if, at first, he minds his hits, And drinks champagne among the wits,' &c.
Prior's *Chameleon*, l. 39.

[2] ' Plain truth, dear MURRAY, needs no flow'rs of speech.' Pope thus addresses him in Epistle vi. Book i. of his *Imitations of Horace*, which he dedicated to him.
[3] See *ante*, i. 386.

far as not to be disagreeable, and he no longer desires his friends
to tell him when he is wrong ; nor does he choose to be told.
Sir, when people watch me narrowly, and I do not watch myself,
they will find me out to be of a particular county [1]. In the same
manner, Dunning [2] may be found out to be a Devonshire man. So
most Scotchmen may be found out. But, Sir, little aberrations
are of no disadvantage. I never catched Mallet in a Scotch
accent [3] ; and yet Mallet, I suppose, was past five-and-twenty
before he came to London.'

Upon another occasion I talked to him on this subject, having
myself taken some pains to improve my pronunciation, by the
aid of the late Mr. Love [4], of Drury-lane theatre, when he was a
player at Edinburgh, and also of old Mr. Sheridan. Johnson
said to me, ' Sir, your pronunciation is not offensive.' With this
concession I was pretty well satisfied ; and let me give my countrymen of North-Britain an advice not to aim at absolute perfection
in this respect ; not to speak *High English*, as we are apt to
call what is far removed from the *Scotch*, but which is by no
means *good English*, and makes ' the fools who use it [5],' truly
ridiculous [6]. Good English is plain, easy, and smooth in the

---

[1] See *post*, ii. 463–4.

[2] Afterwards Lord Ashburton.
Described by Johnson (*post*, iii. 128),
as ' Mr. Dunning, the great lawyer.'

[3] ' Having cleared his tongue from
his native pronunciation so as to be
no longer distinguished as a Scot, he
seems inclined to disencumber himself from all adherences of his original,
and took upon him to change his
name from Scotch *Malloch* to English
Mallet, without any imaginable reason
of preference which the eye or ear can
discover. What other proofs he gave
of disrespect to his native country I
know not ; but it was remarked of
him, that he was the only Scot whom
Scotchmen did not commend.' Johnson's *Life of Mallet*, 9. See *ante*, i.
268, and *post*, iv. 217.

[4] ⟨James Dance, alias Love, 1722–
74, actor, playwright, and poetaster.⟩
He was, so far as is known, the first
who advised Boswell to keep a journal.

When Boswell was but eighteen,
writing of a journey he had taken, he
says :—' I kept an exact journal, at
the particular desire of my friend
Mr. Love, and sent it to him, in sheets,
every post.' *Letters*, No. 2, i. p. 6.

[5] ' That's villainous, and shows a
most pitiful ambition in the fool that
uses it.' *Hamlet*, act iii, scene 2.

[6] Jeffrey wrote from Oxford, where
he spent nine months in 1791–2 :—
' The only part of a Scotchman I mean
to abandon is the language ; and
language is all I expect to learn in
England.' (Cockburn's *Jeffrey*, i. 46).
His biographer says :—' He certainly
succeeded in the abandonment of his
habitual Scotch. . . . The change . . .
was so sudden and so complete, that
it excited the surprise of his friends,
and furnished others with ridicule for
many years. . . . The result, on the
whole, was exactly as described by
Lord Holland, who said that though

mouth of an unaffected English Gentleman. A studied and factitious pronunciation, which requires perpetual attention, and imposes perpetual constraint, is exceedingly disgusting. A small intermixture of provincial peculiarities may, perhaps, have an agreeable effect, as the notes of different birds concur in the harmony of the grove, and please more than if they were all exactly alike. I could name some gentlemen of Ireland, to whom a slight proportion of the accent and recitative of that country is an advantage. The same observation will apply to the gentlemen of Scotland. I do not mean that we should speak as broad as a certain prosperous member of Parliament from that country [1]; though it has been well observed, that ' it has been of no small use to him ; as it rouses the attention of the House by its uncommonness ; and is equal to tropes and figures in a good English speaker.' I would give as an instance of what I mean to recommend to my countrymen, the pronunciation of the late Sir Gilbert Elliot [2]; and may I presume to add that of the present Earl of Marchmont [3], who told me, with great good humour, that the master of a shop in London, where he was not known, said to him, ' I suppose, Sir, you are an American.' ' Why so, Sir ? ' (said his Lordship.) ' Because, Sir, (replied the shopkeeper,) you speak neither English nor Scotch, but something different from both, which I conclude is the language of America.'

Jeffrey " had lost the broad Scotch at Oxford, he had only gained the narrow English." ' Cockburn, in forgetfulness of Mallet's case, says that ' the acquisition of a pure English accent by a full-grown Scotchman . . . is fortunately impossible.'

[1] Henry Dundas, afterwards Viscount Melville. See *post*, iii. 213. Boswell wrote to Temple on May 22, 1775 :—' Harry Dundas is going to be made King's Advocate—Lord Advocate at thirty three ! I cannot help being angry and somewhat fretful at this. He has, to be sure, strong parts. But he is a coarse, unlettered, unfanciful dog.' *Letters*, No. 142, i. p. 225. Walpole describes him as ' the rankest

of all Scotchmen, and odious for that bloody speech that had fixed on him the nick-name of *Starvation.' Journal of the Reign of George III*, ii. 479. On p. 637 he adds :—' The happily coined word " starvation " delivered a whole continent from the Northern harpies that meant to devour it.' The speech in which Dundas introduced *starvation* was made in 1775. Walpole's *Letters*, ed. Cunningham, viii. 30. See *Parl. Hist.* xviii. 387. His character is drawn with great force by Cockburn. *Life of Jeffrey*, i. 77.

[2] The correspondent of Hume. See J. H. Burton's *Hume*, i. 320.

[3] See *post*, iii. 342-4.

BOSWELL. ' It may be of use, Sir, to have a Dictionary to ascertain the pronunciation.' JOHNSON. ' Why, Sir, my Dictionary shows you the accents of words, if you can but remember them.' BOSWELL. ' But, Sir, we want marks to ascertain the pronunciation of the vowels. Sheridan, I believe, has finished such a work.' JOHNSON. ' Why, Sir, consider how much easier it is to learn a language by the ear, than by any marks. Sheridan's Dictionary may do very well ; but you cannot always carry it about with you : and, when you want the word, you have not the Dictionary. It is like a man who has a sword that will not draw. It is an admirable sword, to be sure : but while your enemy is cutting your throat, you are unable to use it. Besides, Sir, what entitles Sheridan to fix the pronunciation of English ? He has, in the first place, the disadvantage of being an Irishman : and if he says he will fix it after the example of the best company, why they differ among themselves. I remember an instance : when I published the Plan for my Dictionary, Lord Chesterfield told me that the word *great* should be pronounced so as to rhyme to *state* ; and Sir William Yonge sent me word that it should be pronounced so as to rhyme to *seat*, and that none but an Irishman would pronounce it *grait* [1]. Now here were two men of the highest rank, the one, the best speaker in the House of Lords, the other, the best speaker in the House of Commons, differing entirely.'

I again visited him at night. Finding him in a very good humour, I ventured to lead him to the subject of our situation in a future state, having much curiosity to know his notions on that

---

[1] In the *Plan* (*Works*, v. 9), Johnson noticed the difference of the pronunciation of *great*. ' Some words have two sounds, which may be equally admitted, as being equally defensible by authority. Thus *great* is differently used :
' For Swift and him despised the farce of state,
The sober follies of the wise and great.—POPE.
As if misfortune made the throne her seat,
And none could be unhappy but the great.—ROWE.'

In the *Preface to the Dictionary* (*Works*, v. 25), Johnson says that ' the vowels . . . are so capriciously pronounced, and so differently modified, by accident or affectation, not only in every province, but in every mouth, that [etc.].' Swift gives both rhymes within ten lines :—
' My lord and he are grown so great—
Always together, *tête-à-tête*.'

. . . .

' You, Mr. Dean, frequent the great,
Inform us, will the emperor treat ? '
Swift's *Works* (1824), xii. 320.

point. JOHNSON. ' Why, Sir, the happiness of an unembodied
spirit will consist in a consciousness of the favour of GOD, in the
contemplation of truth, and in the possession of felicitating
ideas.' BOSWELL. ' But, Sir, is there any harm in our forming
to ourselves conjectures as to the particulars of our happiness,
though the scripture has said but very little on the subject ?
" We know not what we shall be." ' JOHNSON. ' Sir, there is
no harm. What philosophy suggests to us on this topick is
probable : what scripture tells us is certain. Dr. Henry More ¹
has carried it as far as philosophy can. You may buy both his
theological and philosophical works in two volumes folio, for
about eight shillings.' BOSWELL. ' One of the most pleasing
thoughts is, that we shall see our friends again.' JOHNSON.
' Yes, Sir ; but you must consider, that when we are become
purely rational, many of our friendships will be cut off. Many
friendships are formed by a community of sensual pleasures : all
these will be cut off. We form many friendships with bad men,
because they have agrecable qualities, and they can be useful to
us ; but, after death, they can no longer be of use to us. We
form many friendships by mistake, imagining people to be
different from what they really are. After death, we shall see
every one in a true light. Then, Sir, they talk of our meeting
our relations : but then all relationship is dissolved ; and we shall
have no regard for one person more than another, but for their
real value. However, we shall either have the satisfaction of
meeting our friends, or be satisfied without meeting them ².'
BOSWELL. ' Yet, Sir, we see in scripture, that Dives still
retained an anxious concern about his brethren.' JOHNSON.
' Why, Sir, we must either suppose that passage to be meta-
phorical, or hold with many divines, and all the Purgatorians,
that departed souls do not all at once arrive at the utmost
perfection of which they are capable.' BOSWELL. ' I think,
Sir, that it is a very rational supposition.' JOHNSON. ' Why
yes, Sir ; but we do not know it is a true one. There is

¹ ' Dr. Henry More, of Cambridge,
Johnson did not much affect : he was
a Platonist, and, in Johnson's opinion,
a visionary. He would frequently
cite from him, and laugh at, a passage to this effect :—" At the consummation of all things, it shall
come to pass, that eternity shall shake
hands with opacity." ' Hawkins's
Johnson, p. 543.

² See *post*, iii. 312 ; iv. 280.

no harm in believing it : but you must not compel others
to make it an article of faith ; for it is not revealed.' BOSWELL.
' Do you think, Sir, it is wrong in a man who holds the doctrine
of purgatory, to pray for the souls of his deceased friends ? '
JOHNSON. ' Why no, Sir [1].' BOSWELL. ' I have been told, that
in the liturgy of the Episcopal Church of Scotland, there was a
form of prayer for the dead.' JOHNSON. ' Sir, it is not in the
liturgy which Laud framed for the Episcopal Church of Scotland :
if there is a liturgy older than that, I should be glad to see it.'
BOSWELL. ' As to our employment in a future state, the sacred
writings say little. The Revelation, however, of St. John gives
us many ideas, and particularly mentions musick [2].' JOHNSON.
' Why, Sir, ideas must be given you by means of something which
you know [3] : and as to musick,[a] there are some philosophers and
divines who have maintained that we shall not be spiritualized to
such a degree, but that something of matter, very much refined,
will remain. In that case, musick may make a part of our future
felicity.'

BOSWELL. ' I do not know whether there are any well-attested
stories of the appearance of ghosts. You know there is a famous
story of the appearance of Mrs. Veal, prefixed to " Drelincourt on
Death ".' JOHNSON. ' I believe, Sir, that is given up. I believe
the woman declared upon her death-bed that it was a lie [4].'
BOSWELL. ' This objection is made against the truth of ghosts
appearing : that if they are in a state of happiness, it would be a
punishment to them to return to this world ; and if they are in
a state of misery, it would be giving them a respite.' JOHNSON.
' Why, Sir, as the happiness or misery of unembodied [b] spirits does
not depend upon place, but is intellectual, we cannot say that
they are less happy or less miserable by appearing upon earth.'

[a] *comma omitted* 3.   [b] unembodied 1 : embodied 2, 3.

[1] See *ante*, i. 240, and ii. 105.
[2] *Revelation*, xiv. 2.
[3] Johnson, in *The Rambler*, No.
78, describes man's death as ' a
change not only of the place, but the
manner of his being ; an entrance
into a state not simply which he
knows not, but which perhaps he has
not faculties to know.'
[4] This fiction is known to have been
invented by Daniel Defoe, and was
added to Drelincourt's book, to make
it sell. The first edition had it not.
MALONE. ' More than fifty editions
have not exhausted its popularity.
The hundreds of thousands who have
bought the silly treatise of Drelincourt
have borne unconscious testimony to
the genius of De Foe.' Forster's
Essays, ii. 70. ⟨See App. B, p. 493.⟩

We went down between twelve and one to Mrs. Williams's room, and drank tea. I mentioned that we were to have the remains of Mr. Gray, in prose and verse, published by Mr. Mason [1]. JOHNSON. ' I think we have had enough of Gray. I see they have published a splendid edition of Akenside's works. One bad ode may be suffered ; but a number of them together makes one sick [2].' BOSWELL. ' Akenside's distinguished poem is his "Pleasures of Imagination": but,[a] for my part, I never could admire it so much as most people do.' JOHNSON. ' Sir, I could not read it through.' BOSWELL. ' I have read it through ; but I did not find any great power in it.'

I mentioned Elwal, the heretick, whose trial Sir John Pringle [3] had given me to read. JOHNSON. ' Sir, Mr. Elwal was, I think, an ironmonger at Wolverhampton ; and he had a mind to make himself famous, by being the founder of a new sect, which he wished much should be called *Elwallians*. He held, that every thing in the Old Testament that was not typical, was to be of perpetual observance ; and so he wore a ribband in the plaits of his coat, and he also wore a beard. I remember I had the honour of dining in company with Mr. Elwal. There was one Barter, a miller, who wrote against him ; and so [b] you had the controversy between Mr. ELWAL and Mr. BARTER. To try to make himself distinguished, he wrote a letter to King George the Second, challenging him to dispute with him, in which he said, " George, if you be afraid to come by yourself, to dispute with a poor old man, you may bring a thousand of your *black*-guards with you ; and if you should still be afraid, you may bring a thousand of your *red*-guards." The letter had something of the impudence of Junius to our present King. But the men of Wolverhampton were not so inflammable as the Common-Council of London [4] ; so Mr. Elwal failed in his scheme of making himself a man of great consequence [5].'

---

[a] *comma omitted* 2, 3.
[b] so *omitted* 2, 3.

[1] See *ante*, i. 29 ⟨; and App. B, p. 494⟩.

[2] In his *Life of Akenside* (23, 24) he says :—' Of his odes nothing favourable can be said. . . . To examine such compositions singly cannot be required ; they have doubtless brighter and darker parts : but when they are once found to be generally dull, all further labour may be spared ; for to what use can the work be criticised that will not be read ? ' See *post*, iii. 32.

[3] See *post*, iii. 65.

[4] See *post*, iii. 201.

[5] The account of his trial is entitled :—' *The Grand Question in*

On Tuesday, March 31, he and I dined at General Paoli's. A question was started, whether the state of marriage was natural to man. JOHNSON. ' Sir, it is so far from being natural for a man and woman to live in a state of marriage, that we find all the motives which they have for remaining in that connection, and the restraints which civilized society imposes to prevent separation, are hardly sufficient to keep them together.' The General said, that in a state of nature a man and woman uniting together [a] would form a strong and constant affection, by the mutual pleasure each would receive ; and that the same causes of dissention would not arise between them, as occur between husband and wife in a civilized state. JOHNSON. ' Sir, they would have dissentions enough, though of another kind. One would choose to go a hunting in this wood, the other in that ; one would choose to go a fishing in this lake, the other in that ; or, perhaps, one would choose to go a hunting, when the other would choose to go a fishing ; and so they would part. Besides, Sir, a savage man and a savage woman meet by chance ; and when the man sees another woman that pleases him better, he will leave the first.'

[a] together 1 : together, 2, 3.

Religion Consider'd. Whether we shall obey God, or Man ; Christ, or the Pope ; the Prophets and Apostles, or Prelates and Priests. Humbly offered to the King and Parliament of Great Britain. By E. Elwall. With an Account of the Author's Tryal or Prosecution at Stafford-Assizes before Judge Denton. London.' No date. Elwall seems to have been a Unitarian Quaker. He was prosecuted for publishing a book against the doctrines of the Trinity, but was discharged, being, he writes, treated by the Judge with great humanity. In his pamphlet he says (p. 49) :—' You see what I have already done in my former Book ; I have challeng'd the greatest Potentates on earth ; yea, even the King of Great Britain, whose true and faithful Subject I am, in all temporal things, and whom I love and honour : Also, his noble and valiant Friend, John Argyle, and his great Friends Robert Walpole, Charles Wager, and Arthur Onslow ; all these can speak well, and who is like them ; and yet, behold, none of all these car'd to engage with their Friend Elwall.' See *post*, ii. 251. Dr. Priestley had received an account of the trial from a gentleman who was present, who described Elwall as ' a tall man, with white hair, a large beard and flowing garments, who struck everybody with respect. He spake about an hour with great gravity, fluency, and presence of mind.' The trial took place, he said, in 1726. ' It is impossible,' adds Priestley (*Works*, ed. 1831, ii. 417), ' for an unprejudiced person to read Elwall's account of his trial, without feeling the greatest veneration for the writer.' In truth, Elwall spoke with all the simple power of the best of the early Quakers. ⟨Elwall never joined the Society of Friends, but appears to have been a Seventh-day Baptist. He was by trade a mercer and grocer. See *D.N.B.*⟩

We then fell into a disquisition whether there is any beauty independent of utility. The General maintained there was not. Dr. Johnson maintained that there was ; and he instanced a coffee-cup which he held in his hand, the painting of which was of no real use, as the cup would hold the coffee equally well if plain ; yet the painting was beautiful.

We talked of the strange custom of swearing in conversation [1]. The General said, that all barbarous nations swore from a certain violence of temper, that could not be confined to earth, but was always reaching at the powers above. He said, too, that there was greater variety of swearing, in proportion as there was a greater variety of religious ceremonies.

Dr. Johnson went home with me to my lodgings in Conduit-street and drank tea, previous to our going to the Pantheon, which neither of us had seen before.

He said, ' Goldsmith's Life of Parnell [2] is poor ; not that it is poorly written, but that he had poor materials ; for nobody can write the life of a man, but those who have eat and drunk and lived in social intercourse with him.'

I said, that if it was not troublesome and presuming too much, I would request him to tell me all the little circumstances of his life ; what schools he attended, when he came to Oxford, when he came to London, &c. &c. He did not disapprove of my curiosity as to these particulars ; but said, ' They'll come out by degrees as we talk together [3].'

He censured Ruffhead's Life of Pope [4] ; and said, ' he knew

[1] Boswell, in the *Hypochondriack*, No. 69 (*London Mag.* 1783, p. 290), writing on swearing, says :—' I have the comfort to think that my practice has been blameless in that respect.' He continues (p. 293) :—' To do the present age justice, there is much less swearing among genteel people than in the last age.'

[2] ' The Life of Dr. Parnell is a task which I should very willingly decline, since it has been lately written by Goldsmith, a man of such variety of powers, and such felicity of performance, that he always seemed to do best that which he was doing. . . .

What such an author has told, who would tell again ? I have made an abstract from his larger narrative ; and have this gratification from my attempt, that it gives me an opportunity of paying due tribute to the memory of Goldsmith. Tὸ γὰρ γέρας ἔστι θανόντων.' Johnson's *Life of Parnell* (1, 2).

[3] See *ante*, i. 26 ; *post*, ii. 217 ; and v. 312.

[4] ' Mr. Ruffhead says of fine passages, that they are fine, and of feeble passages, that they are feeble ; but recommending poetical beauty, is like remarking the splendor of sunshine ; to those who can see, it is unnecessary,

nothing of Pope, and nothing of poetry.' He praised Dr. Joseph
Warton's Essay on Pope [1]; but said, he supposed we should have
no more of it, as the authour had not been able to persuade the
world to think of Pope as he did. BOSWELL. ' Why, Sir, should
that prevent him from continuing his work ? He is an ingenious
Counsel, who has made the most of his cause : he is not obliged
to gain it.' JOHNSON. ' But, Sir, there is a difference when the
cause is of a man's own making.'

We talked of the proper use of riches. JOHNSON. ' If I were
a man of a great estate, I would drive all the rascals whom I did
not like out of the county at an election [2].'

I asked him how far he thought wealth should be employed in
hospitality. JOHNSON. ' You are to consider that ancient hospitality, of which we hear so much, was in an uncommercial
country, when men being idle, were glad to be entertained at rich
men's tables. But in a commercial country, a busy country, time
becomes precious, and therefore hospitality is not so much
valued. No doubt there is still room for a certain degree of it ;
and a man has a satisfaction in seeing his friends eating and
drinking around him. But promiscuous hospitality is not the
way to gain real influence. You must help some people at table
before others ; you must ask some people how they like their
wine oftener than others. You therefore offend more people than
you please. You are like the French statesman, who said, when
he granted a favour, " *J'ai fait dix mécontents et un ingrat* [3]."
Besides, Sir, being entertained ever so well at a man's table, im-
presses no lasting regard or esteem. No, Sir, the way to make
sure of power and influence is, by lending money confidentially
to your neighbours at a small interest, or, perhaps, at no interest
at all, and having their bonds in your possession [4].' BOSWELL.
' May not a man, Sir, employ his riches to advantage in educating
young men of merit ? ' JOHNSON. ' Yes, Sir, if they fall in your

and to those who are blind, absurd.'
Gent. Mag. May, 1769, p. 255. The
review in which this passage occurs
is, perhaps, in part Johnson's.

[1] See *ante*, i. 448.
[2] See *post*, ii. 340.
[3] It was Lewis XIV who said it
' Toutes les fois que je donne une

place vacante, je fais cent mécontents
et un ingrat.' Voltaire, *Siècle de
Louis XIV*, ch. 26. ' When I give
away a place,' said Lewis XIV, ' I
make an hundred discontented, and
one ungrateful.' Johnson's *Life of
Swift*, 51. ⟨Cf. *Rasselas*, ch. xxvii.⟩
[4] See *post*, iv. 222.

way; but if it is ^a understood that you patronize young men of merit, you will be harassed with solicitations. You will have numbers forced upon you who have no merit; some will force them upon you from mistaken partiality; and some from downright interested motives, without scruple; and you will be disgraced.'

' Were I a rich man, I would propagate all kinds of trees that will grow in the open air. A green-house is childish. I would introduce foreign animals into the country; for instance, the rein-deer ¹.'

The conversation now turned on critical subjects. JOHNSON. 'Bayes, in "The Rehearsal," is a mighty silly character. If it was intended to be like a particular man, it could only be diverting while that man was remembered. But I question whether it was meant for Dryden, as has been reported; for we know some of the passages said to be ridiculed, were written since the Rehearsal; at least a passage mentioned in the Preface ² is of a later date.' I maintained that it had merit as a general satire on the self-importance of dramatick authours. But even in this light he held it very cheap.

We then walked to the Pantheon. The first view of it did not strike us so much as Ranelagh, of which he said, the ' *coup d'œil* was the finest thing he had ever seen.' The truth is, Ranelagh is of a more beautiful form; more of it, or rather indeed the whole *rotunda*, appears at once, and it is better lighted. However, as Johnson observed, we saw the Pantheon in time of mourning, when there was a dull uniformity; whereas we had seen Ranelagh

_a *is* 1 : be 2, 3.

¹ This project has since been realized. Sir Henry Liddel, who made a spirited tour into Lapland, brought two rein-deer to his estate in Northumberland, where they bred; but the race has unfortunately perished. BOSWELL.

² There is no Preface to ' The Rehearsal,' as originally published. Dr. Johnson seems to have meant the Address to the Reader with a KEY subjoined to it; which have been prefixed to the modern editions of that play. He did not know it appears, that several *additions* were made to

' The Rehearsal ' after the first edition. MALONE. In his *Life of Dryden* (94, 97, 98) Johnson writes :—' Buckingham characterised Dryden in 1671 by the name of Bayes in *The Rehearsal*. . . . It is said that this farce was originally intended against Davenant, who in the first draught was characterised by the name of Bilboa. . . . It is said, likewise, that Sir Robert Howard was once meant. The design was probably to ridicule the reigning poet, whoever he might be. Much of the personal satire, to which it might owe its first reception, is now lost or obscured.'

when the view was enlivened with a gay profusion of colours [1].
Mrs. Bosville [2], of Gunthwait, in Yorkshire, joined us, and entered
into conversation with us. Johnson said to me afterwards, ' Sir,
this is a mighty intelligent lady.'

I said there was not half a guinea's worth of pleasure in seeing
this place. JOHNSON. ' But, Sir, there is half a guinea's worth
of inferiority to other people in not having seen it.' BOSWELL.
' I doubt, Sir, whether there are many happy people here.'
JOHNSON. ' Yes, Sir, there are many happy people here. There
are many people here who are watching hundreds, and who think
hundreds are watching them [3].'

Happening to meet Sir Adam Fergusson [4], I presented him to
Dr. Johnson. Sir Adam expressed some apprehension that the
Pantheon would encourage luxury. ' Sir, (said Johnson,) I am a
great friend to publick amusements ; for they keep people from

[1] ' The Pantheon,' wrote Walpole
(*Letters*, viii. 313), July 9, 1773, ' is
still the most beautiful edifice in England.' Gibbon, two months before
Johnson's visit to the Pantheon,
wrote :—' The Pantheon, in point of
ennui and magnificence, is the wonder
of the eighteenth century and of the
British empire.' Gibbon's *Misc.
Works*, ii. 74. Evelina, in Miss
Burney's novel (i. xxiii.) contrasts the
Pantheon and Ranelagh :—' I was
extremely struck with the beauty of
the building, which greatly surpassed
whatever I could have expected or
imagined. Yet it has more the appearance of a chapel than of a place
of diversion ; and, though I was quite
charmed with the magnificence of
the room, I felt that I could not be as
gay and thoughtless there as at Ranc-
lagh ; for there is something in it which
rather inspires awe and solemnity, than
mirth and pleasure.' Ranelagh was at
Chelsea, the Pantheon was in Oxford-
street. ⟨The Pantheon was opened in
January of this year. See *Public Advert*.
13 Jan. 1772.⟩ See *ante*, ii. 119, and
post, iii. 199.

[2] Her husband, Squire Godfrey
Bosville, Boswell (*post*, iii. 439), calls
' my Yorkshire Chief.' Their daughter was one of the young ladies whom
he passes in review in his letters
to Temple. ' What say you to my
marrying ? I intend, next autumn,
to visit Miss Bosville in Yorkshire.
But I fear, my lot being cast in
Scotland, that beauty would not be
content. She is, however, grave. I
shall see.' *Letters*, No. 56, i. 108. She
married Sir A. Macdonald, Johnson's
inhospitable host in Skye (*ante*, ii.
157 ; *post*, v. 147).

[3] In *The Adventurer*, No. 120,
Johnson, after describing ' a gay assembly,' continues :—' The world, in
its best state, is nothing more than a
larger assembly of beings, combining
to counterfeit happiness which they
do not feel.' *Works*, iv. 120.

[4] ⟨M.P. for Ayrshire from 1774
to 1792. Boswell, who wrongly
described him as ' the great-grandson
of a messenger,' said that he became
member ' by a strange coincidence of
chances.' *Boswelliana*, p. 283. For Sir
Adam's ' odious coalition ' with Lord
Eglintoune for the representation of
the county, for which Boswell was a
candidate, see Boswell's *Letters*, Nos.
256, 263, 283 b ; ii. 355, 370, 526.⟩

vice. You now (addressing himself to me,) would have been with a wench, had you not been here.—O ! I forgot you were married.'

Sir Adam suggested, that luxury corrupts a people, and destroys the spirit of liberty. JOHNSON. ' Sir, that is all visionary. I would not give half a guinea to live under one form of government rather than another. It is of no moment to the happiness of an individual [1]. Sir, the danger of the abuse of power is nothing to a private man. What Frenchman is prevented from passing his life as he pleases ? ' SIR ADAM. ' But, Sir, in the British constitution it is surely of importance to keep up a spirit in the people, so as to preserve a balance against the crown.' JOHNSON. ' Sir, I perceive you are a vile Whig.—Why all this childish jealousy of the power of the crown ? The crown has not power enough. When I say that all governments are alike, I consider that in no government power can be abused long. Mankind will not bear it. If a sovereign oppresses his people to a great degree, they will rise and cut off his head. There is a remedy in human nature against tyranny, that will keep us safe under every form of government [2]. Had not the people of France thought themselves honoured as sharing in the brilliant actions of Lewis XIV, they would not have endured him ; and we may say the same of the King of Prussia's people.' Sir Adam introduced the ancient Greeks and Romans. JOHNSON. ' Sir, the mass of both of them were barbarians. The mass of every people must be barbarous where there is no printing, and consequently knowledge is not generally diffused. Knowledge is diffused among our people by the news-papers [3].' Sir Adam mentioned the orators, poets, and artists of Greece. JOHNSON.

---

[1] See *ante*, ii. 60.

[2] See *ante*, i. 424. Hume wrote of the judgement of Charles I. (*Hist. of Eng.* vii. 148) :—' If ever, on any occasion, it were laudable to conceal truth from the populace, it must be confessed, that the doctrine of resistance affords such an example ; and that all speculative reasoners ought to observe, with regard to this principle, the same cautious silence, which the laws in every species of government have ever prescribed to themselves.'

[3] ' All foreigners remark, that the knowledge of the common people of England is greater than that of any other vulgar. This superiority we undoubtedly owe to the rivulets of intelligence [i.e. the newspapers] which are continually trickling among us, which every one may catch, and of which every one partakes.' *Idler*, No. 7. In number 30, he speaks very

' Sir, I am talking of the mass of the people. We see even what the boasted Athenians were. The little effect which Demosthenes's orations had upon them, shews that they were barbarians ¹.'

Sir Adam was unlucky in his topicks ; for he suggested a doubt of the propriety of Bishops having seats in the House of Lords. JOHNSON. ' How so, Sir ? Who is more proper for having the dignity of a peer, than a Bishop, provided a Bishop be what he ought to be ; and if improper Bishops be made, that is not the fault of the Bishops, but of those who make them.'

On Sunday, April 5, after attending divine service at St. Paul's church, I found him alone. Of a schoolmaster ² of his acquaintance, a native of Scotland, he said, ' He has a great deal of good about him ; but he is also very defective in some respects. His inner part is good, but his outer part is mighty aukward. You in Scotland do not attain that nice critical skill in languages, which we get in our schools in England. I would not put a boy to him, whom I intended for a man of learning. But for the sons of citizens, who are to learn a little, get good morals, and then go to trade, he may do very well.'

I mentioned a cause in which I had appeared as counsel at the bar of the General Assembly of the Church of Scotland, where a *Probationer* ³, (as one licensed to preach, but not yet ordained, is called,) was opposed in his application to be inducted, because it was alledged that he had been guilty of fornication five years before. JOHNSON. ' Why, Sir, if he has repented, it is not a sufficient objection. A man who is good enough to go to heaven,

---

contemptuously of news-writers. ' In Sir Henry Wotton's jocular definition, *An ambassador* is said to be *a man of virtue sent abroad to tell lies for the advantage of his country*. A newswriter is *a man without virtue, who writes lies at home for his own profit.*'

¹ See *post*, ii. 211.

² Mr. Elphinston. CROKER. See *ante*, i. 210; *post*, ii. 226 ; iii. 379. Dr. Carlyle (*Auto.*, 1910, p. 518) wrote of a friend :—' He had overcome many disadvantages of his education, for he had been sent to a Jacobite seminary

of one Elphinston at Kensington, where his body was starved, and his mind also. He returned to Edinburgh to college. He had hardly a word of Latin, and was obliged to work hard with a private tutor.' ⟨See App. B.⟩

³ ⟨The ' Act anent Probationers,' Apr. 11, 1694, ' expressly provided and declared that the . . . probationers are not to be esteemed . . . to preach by virtue of any pastoral office, but only to make way for their being called to a pastoral charge.' *Acts Gen. Assembly Church Scotl.* c. 10.⟩

is good enough to be a clergyman.' This was a humane and
liberal sentiment. But the character of a clergyman is more sacred
than that of an ordinary Christian. As he is to instruct with
authority, he should be regarded with reverence, as one upon
whom divine truth has had the effect to set him above such
transgressions, as men less exalted by spiritual habits, and yet
upon the whole not to be excluded from heaven, have been betrayed into by the predominance of passion. That clergymen
may be considered as sinners in general, as all men are, cannot
be denied ; but this reflection will not counteract their good precepts so much, as the absolute knowledge of their having been
guilty of certain specifick immoral acts. I told him, that by the
rules of the Church of Scotland, in their ' Book of Discipline,' if a
scandal, as it is called, is not prosecuted for five years, it cannot
afterwards be proceeded upon, ' unless it be *of a heinous nature*,
or again become flagrant ; ' and that hence a question arose,
whether fornication was a sin of a heinous nature ; and that I
had maintained, that it did not deserve that epithet, in as much
as it was not one of those sins which argue very great depravity
of heart : in short, was not, in the general acceptation of mankind, a heinous sin. JOHNSON. ' No, Sir, it is not a heinous sin.
A heinous sin is that for which a man is punished with death or
banishment [1].' BOSWELL. ' But, Sir, after I had argued that it
was not a heinous sin, an old clergyman rose up, and repeating
the text of scripture denouncing judgement against whore-
mongers [2], asked, whether, considering this, there could be any
doubt of fornication being a heinous sin. JOHNSON. ' Why, Sir,
observe the word *whoremonger*. Every sin, if persisted in, will
become heinous. Whoremonger is a dealer in whores [3], as ironmonger is a dealer in iron. But as you don't call a man an ironmonger for buying and selling a pen-knife ; so you don't call a
man a whoremonger for getting one wench with child [4].'

I spoke of the inequality of the livings of the clergy in

---

[1] In his *Dictionary* he defines
heinous as *atrocious ; wicked in a high
degree*.

[2] *Ephesians*, v. 5.

[3] His second definition of *whoremonger* is *one who converses with a
fornicatress*.

[4] It must not be presumed that
Dr. Johnson meant to give any
countenance to licentiousness, though
in the character of an Advocate he
made a just and subtle distinction
between occasional and habitual trans-
gression. BOSWELL.

England, and the scanty provisions of some of the Curates. JOHNSON. ' Why yes, Sir ; but it cannot be helped. You must consider, that the revenues of the clergy are not at the disposal of the state, like the pay of the army. Different men have founded different churches ; and some are better endowed, some worse. The State cannot interfere and make an equal division of what has been particularly appropriated. Now when a clergyman has but a small living, or even two small livings, he can afford very little to a Curate.'

He said, he went more frequently to church when there were prayers only, than when there was also a sermon, as the people required more an example for the one than the other ; it being much easier for them to hear a sermon, than to fix their minds on prayer.

On Monday, April 6, I dined with him at Sir Alexander Macdonald's, where was a young officer in the regimentals of the Scots Royal, who talked with a vivacity, fluency, and precision so uncommon, that he attracted particular attention. He proved to be the Honourable Thomas Erskine, youngest brother to the Earl of Buchan, who has since risen into such brilliant reputation at the bar in Westminster-hall [1].

Fielding being mentioned, Johnson exclaimed, ' he was a blockhead [2] ; ' and upon my expressing my astonishment at so strange an assertion, he said, ' What I mean by his being a blockhead is

[1] Erskine was born in 1750, entered the navy in 1764, the army in 1768, he matriculated at Trinity College, Cambridge, in 1776, was called to the Bar in 1778, was made a King's counsel in 1783, and Lord Chancellor in 1806. He died in 1823. Campbell's *Chancellors*, vi. 368–674.

[2] Johnson had called Churchill ' a blockhead.' *Ante*, i. 419. ' I have remarked,' said Miss Reynolds, ' that his dislike of any one seldom prompted him to say much more than that the fellow is a *blockhead*.' Croker's *Boswell*, v. 394 : *John. Misc.* ii. 270, n. 6. In like manner Goldsmith called Sterne a blockhead ; for Mr. Forster (*Life of Goldsmith*, i. 260) is, no doubt,

right in saying that the author of *Tristram Shandy* is aimed at in the following passage in *The Citizen of the World* (Letter 75) :—' In England, if a bawdy blockhead thus breaks in on the community, he sets his whole fraternity in a roar ; nor can he escape, even though he should fly to nobility for shelter.' That Johnson did not think so lowly of Fielding's powers is shown by a compliment that he paid Miss Burney, on one of the characters in *Evelina*. ' " Oh, Mr. Smith, Mr. Smith is the man ! " cried he, laughing violently. " Harry Fielding never drew so good a character ! " ' Mme. D'Arblay's *Diary*, i. 78. ⟨See App. B, p. 494.⟩

that he was a barren rascal.' BOSWELL. ' Will you not allow, Sir, that he draws very natural pictures of human life ? ' JOHNSON. ' Why, Sir, it is of very low life. Richardson used to say, that had he not known who Fielding was, he should have believed he was an ostler [1]. Sir, there is more knowledge of the heart in one letter of Richardson's, than in all " Tom Jones " [2]. I, indeed, never read " Joseph Andrews " '[3]. ERSKINE. ' Surely, Sir, Richard-

---

[1] Richardson wrote of Fielding (*Corres.* vi. 154) :—' Poor Fielding ! I could not help telling his sister, that I was equally surprised at and concerned for his continued lowness. Had your brother, said I, been born in a stable, or been a runner at a sponging-house, we should have thought him a genius, and wished he had had the advantage of a liberal education, and of being admitted into good company.' Other passages show Richardson's dislike or jealousy of Fielding. Thus he wrote :—' You guess that I have not read *Amelia*. Indeed I have read but the first volume. I had intended to go through with it ; but I found the characters and situations so wretchedly low and dirty, that I imagined I could not be interested for any one of them.' *Ib.* iv. 60. ' So long as the world will receive, Mr. Fielding will write.' *Ib.* p. 285.

[2] Hannah More wrote in 1780 (*Memoirs*, i. 168), ' I never saw Johnson really angry with me but once. I alluded . . . to some witty passage in *Tom Jones* ; he replied, " I am shocked to hear you quote from so vicious a book. I am sorry to hear you have read it : a confession which no modest lady should ever make. I scarcely know a more corrupt work." . . . He went so far as to refuse to Fielding the great talents which are ascribed to him, and broke out into a noble panegyric on his competitor, Richardson ; who, he said, was as superior to him in talents as in virtue ; and whom he pronounced to be the greatest genius

that had shed its lustre on this path of literature.' Yet Miss Burney in her Preface to *Evelina* describes herself as ' exhilarated by the wit of Fielding, and humour of Smollett.' It is strange that while Johnson thus condemned Fielding, he should ' with an ardent and liberal earnestness ' have revised Smollett's epitaph. Boswell's *Hebrides*, *post*, v. 367. Macaulay in his *Speech on Copyright* (*Speeches*, 1854, p. 241) said of Richardson's novels :—' No writings have done more to raise the fame of English genius in foreign countries. No writings are more deeply pathetic. No writings, those of Shakespeare excepted, show more profound knowledge of the human heart.' Walpole (*Letters*, vi. 163), on the other hand, spoke of Richardson as one ' who wrote those deplorably tedious lamentations, *Clarissa* and *Sir Charles Grandison*, which are pictures of high life as conceived by a bookseller, and romances as they would be spiritualized by a Methodist teacher.' Lord Chesterfield says of *Sir Charles Grandison*, that ' it is too long, and there is too much mere talk in it. Whenever he goes *Ultra crepidam*, into high life, he grossly mistakes the modes ; but, to do him justice, he never mistakes nature, and he has surely great knowledge and skill both in painting and in interesting the heart.' *Ib.* ed. Cunningham, iv. 305, note. See *ante*, ii. 48–9. ⟨See App. B, p. 495.⟩

[3] *Amelia* he read through without stopping. *Post*, iii. 43. Shenstone (*Works*, iii. 80) writes of ' the tedious

son is very tedious.' JOHNSON. ' Why, Sir, if you were to read Richardson for the story, your impatience would be so much fretted that you would hang yourself [1]. But you must read him for the sentiment, and consider the story as only giving occasion to the sentiment.'—I have already given my opinion of Fielding ; but I cannot refrain from repeating here my wonder at Johnson's excessive and unaccountable depreciation of one of the best writers that England has produced. ' Tom Jones ' has stood the test of publick opinion with such success, as to have established its great merit, both for the story, the sentiments, and the manners, and also the varieties of diction, so as to leave no doubt of its having an animated truth of execution throughout [2].

A book of travels, lately published under the title of *Coriat Junior*, and written by Mr. Paterson [3], was mentioned. Johnson said, this book was an imitation of Sterne [4], and not of Coriat, whose name Paterson had chosen as a whimsical one. ' Tom Coriat, (said he,) was a humourist about the court of James the First. He had a mixture of learning, of wit, and of buffoonery.

character of Parson Adams,' and calls the book ' a very mean performance ; ' of which ' the greater part is *unnatural* and *unhumourous*.'

[1] Johnson wrote, 9 Mar. 1751, to Richardson of *Clarissa*, ' though the story is long, every letter is short.' He begged him to add an *index rerum*, ' for Clarissa is not a performance to be read with eagerness, and laid aside for ever ; but will be occasionally consulted by the busy, the aged, and the studious.' *Letters*, No. 31.

[2] Gibbon describes *Tom Jones* as ' that exquisite picture of human manners.' *Memoirs*, p. 5. Richardson, five years after *Tom Jones* was published, wrote (*Corres.* v. 275) :—' Its run is over, even with us. Is it true, that France had virtue enough to refuse a licence for such a profligate performance ? '

[3] Mr. Samuel Paterson, eminent for his knowledge of books. BOSWELL. In the first two editions this note does not appear, but Mr. Paterson is described as ' the auctioneer.'

See *post*, iii. 90. ⟨His book of travels was entitled *Another Traveller ! or Cursory Remarks and Tritical Observations made upon a Journey through Part of the Netherlands in the latter End of the Year 1766.* 3 parts in 2 vols. 1767–9. Nichols wrote of him :—' Few men of this country had so much bibliographical knowledge ; and perhaps we never had a Bookseller who knew so much of the contents of books generally.' *Lit. Anecd.* iii. 439. See also *Ib.* pp. 733–6. ' Paterson was really a walking library.' J. T. Smith's *Book for a Rainy Day*, ed. Whitten, p. 110. Johnson was godfather to one of his sons, *post*, iv. 227, 269. For the unlucky accident which deprived us of a *Bibliotheca Johnsoniana* from his hand, see *post*, iv. App. F.⟩

[4] Mr. Paterson, in a pamphlet, produced some evidence to show that his work was written before Sterne's ' Sentimental Journey ' appeared. BOSWELL.

He first travelled through Europe, and published his travels [1]. He afterwards travelled on foot through Asia, and had made many remarks ; but he died at Mandoa, and his remarks were lost.'

We talked of gaming, and animadverted on it with severity. JOHNSON. ' Nay, gentlemen, let us not aggravate the matter. It is not roguery to play with a man who is ignorant of the game, while you are master of it, and so win his money ; for he thinks he can play better than you, as you think you can play better than he ; and the superiour skill carries it.' ERSKINE. ' He is a fool, but you are not a rogue.' JOHNSON. ' That's much about the truth, Sir. It must be considered, that a man who only does what every one of the society to which he belongs would do, is not a dishonest man. In the republick of Sparta, it was agreed, that stealing was not dishonourable, if not discovered. I do not commend a society where there is an agreement that what would not otherwise be fair, shall be fair ; but I maintain, that an individual of any society, who practises what is allowed, is not a dishonest man.' BOSWELL. ' So then, Sir, you do not think ill of a man who wins perhaps forty thousand pounds in a winter ? ' JOHNSON. ' Sir, I do not call a gamester a dishonest man ; but I call him an unsocial man, an unprofitable man. Gaming is a mode of transferring property without producing any intermediate good. Trade gives employment to numbers, and so produces intermediate good.'

Mr. Erskine told us, that when he was in the island of Minorca, he not only read prayers, but preached two sermons to the regiment [2]. He seemed to object to the passage in scripture where we are told that the angel of the Lord smote in one night forty thousand Assyrians [3]. ' Sir, (said Johnson,) you should recollect that there was a supernatural interposition ; they were destroyed by pestilence. You are not to suppose that the angel of the LORD went about and stabbed each of them with a dagger, or knocked them on the head, man by man.'

---

[1] *Coryats Crudities hastily gobled vp in five Moneths Trauells in France, Sauoy, Italy,* [etc.]. *London,* 1611. ⟨Coryat died at Surat. See *D.N.B.*⟩

[2] Lord Erskine was fond of this anecdote. He told it to me the first time that I had the honour of being in his company, and often repeated it, boasting that he had been a sailor, a soldier, a lawyer, and a parson. CROKER.

[3] 185,000. 2 *Kings,* xix. 35, etc. MALONE.

After Mr. Erskine was gone, a discussion took place, whether the present Earl of Buchan, when Lord Cardross, did right to refuse to go Secretary of the Embassy to Spain, when Sir James Gray, a man of inferiour rank, went Ambassadour [1]. Dr. Johnson said, that perhaps in point of interest he did wrong ; but in point of dignity he did well. Sir Alexander insisted that he was wrong ; and said that Mr. Pitt intended it as an advantageous thing for him. ' Why, Sir, (said Johnson,) Mr. Pitt might think it an advantageous thing for him to make him a vintner, and get him all the Portugal trade ; but he would have demeaned himself strangely had he accepted of such a situation. Sir, had he gone Secretary while his inferiour was Ambassadour, he would have been a traitor to his rank and family.'

I talked of the little attachment which subsisted between near relations in London. ' Sir, (said Johnson,) in a country so commercial as ours, where every man can do for himself, there is not so much occasion for that attachment. No man is thought the worse of here, whose brother was hanged. In uncommercial countries, many of the branches of a family must depend on the stock ; so, in order to make the head of the family take care of them, they are represented as connected with his reputation, that, self-love being interested, he may exert himself to promote their interest. You have first large circles, or clans ; as commerce increases, the connection is confined to families. By degrees, that too goes off, as having become unnecessary, and there being few opportunities of intercourse. One brother is a merchant in the city, and another is an officer in the guards. How little intercourse can these two have ! '

I argued warmly for the old feudal system [2]. Sir Alexander opposed it, and talked of the pleasure of seeing all men free and

---

[1] Lord Chatham writes on Oct. 12, 1766, to Lord Shelburne that he ' has extremely at heart to obtain this post for Lord Cardross, . . . a young nobleman of great talents, learning, and accomplishments, and son of the Earl of Buchan, an intimate friend of Lord Chatham, from the time they were students together at Utrecht.' *Chatham Corres.* iii. 106. Horace Walpole wrote on Oct. 26, ' Sir James Gray goes to Madrid. The embassy has been sadly hawked about ; not a peer that would take it.' Walpole's *Letters*, vii. 58. ' Sir James Gray's father was first a box-keeper, and then footman to James II.' *Ib.* iii. 205.

[2] See *ante*, ii. 134, for Johnson's attack on Lord Chatham's ' feudal gabble.'

independent. JOHNSON. ' I agree with Mr. Boswell that there must be a high satisfaction in being a feudal Lord ; but we are to consider, that we ought not to wish to have a number of men unhappy for the satisfaction of one ¹.'—I maintained that numbers, namely, the vassals or followers, were not unhappy ; for that there was a reciprocal satisfaction between the Lord and them : he being kind in his authority over them ; they being respectful and faithful to him.

On Thursday, April 9, I called on him to beg he would go and dine with me at the Mitre tavern. He had resolved not to dine at all this day, I know not for what reason ; and I was so unwilling to be deprived of his company, that I was content to submit to suffer a want, which was at first somewhat painful, but he soon made me forget it ; and a man is always pleased with himself when he finds his intellectual inclinations predominate.

He observed, that to reason too ᵃ philosophically on the nature of prayer, was very unprofitable.

Talking of ghosts ², he said, he knew one friend, who was an honest man and a sensible man, who told him he had seen a ghost, old Mr. Edward Cave, the printer at St. John's Gate. He said, Mr. Cave did not like to talk of it, and seemed to be in great horrour whenever it was mentioned. BOSWELL. ' Pray, Sir, what did he say was the appearance ? ' JOHNSON. ' Why, Sir, something of a shadowy being.'

I mentioned witches, and asked him what they properly meant. JOHNSON. ' Why, Sir, they properly mean those who make use of the aid of evil spirits.' BOSWELL. ' There is no doubt, Sir, a general report and belief of their having existed ³.' JOHNSON. ' Sir,ᵇ you have not only the general report and belief, but you have many voluntary solemn confessions.' He did not affirm any thing positively upon a subject which it is the fashion of the times to

---

ᵃ too *omitted* 2, 3.   ᵇ Sir, you 1 : You 2, 3.

¹ In Boswell's *Hebrides, post,* v. 106, Johnson makes much the same answer to a like statement by Boswell. See *post,* iv. 164.

² See *ante,* i. 343, 405 ; *post,* ii. 182.

³ ' I cannot,' wrote John Wesley (*Journal,* 23 May, 1776), ' give up to all the Deists in Great Britain the existence of witchcraft, till I give up the credit of all history, sacred and profane. And at the present time I have not only as strong, but stronger proofs of this, from eye and ear witnesses, than I have of murder ; so that I cannot rationally doubt of one any more than the other.'

laugh at as a matter of absurd credulity. He only seemed willing, as a candid enquirer after truth, however strange and inexplicable, to shew that he understood what might be urged for it [1].

On Friday, April 10, I dined with him at General Oglethorpe's, where we found Dr. Goldsmith.

Armorial bearings having been mentioned, Johnson said,[a] they were as ancient as the siege of Thebes, which he proved by a passage in one of the tragedies of Euripides [2].

I started the question whether duelling was consistent with moral duty. The brave old General fired at this, and said, with a lofty air, ' Undoubtedly a man has a right to defend his honour.' GOLDSMITH, (turning to me.) ' I ask you first, Sir, what would you do if you were affronted ? ' I answered I should think it necessary to fight [3]. ' Why then, (replied Goldsmith,) that solves the question.' JOHNSON. ' No, Sir, it does not solve the question. It does not follow that what a man would do is therefore right.' I said, I wished to have it settled, whether duelling was contrary to the laws of Christianity. Johnson immediately entered on the subject, and treated it in a masterly manner ; and so far as I have been able to recollect, his thoughts were these : ' Sir, as men become in a high degree refined, various causes of offence arise ;

[a] *comma omitted* 3.

[1] See this curious question treated by him with most acute ability, ' Journal of a Tour to the Hebrides,' 3d edit. p. 33. [*Post*, v. 45.] BOSWELL. Johnson, in his *Observations on Macbeth* (*Works*, v. 55–7), shews his utter disbelief in witchcraft. ' These phantoms,' he writes, ' have indeed appeared more frequently, in proportion as the darkness of ignorance has been more gross ; but it cannot be shown, that the brightest gleams of knowledge have at any time been sufficient to drive them out of the world.' He describes the spread of the belief in them in the middle ages, and adds :—' The reformation did not immediately arrive at its meridian, and though day was gradually increasing upon us, the goblins of witchcraft still continued to hover in the twilight.' See *post*, iii. 382 ; iv. 17.

[2] The passage to which Johnson alluded is to be found (as I conjecture) in the *Phœnissæ*, l. 1120. J. BOSWELL, JUN.

[3] Boswell (*Letters*, No. 277, ii. 397), on June 21, 1790, described to Temple the insults of that ' brutal fellow,' Lord Lonsdale, and continued :—' In my fretfulness I used such expressions as irritated him almost to fury, so that he used such expressions towards me, that I should have, according to the irrational laws of honour, sanctioned by the world, been under the necessity of risking my life, had not an explanation taken place.' ⟨In November 1785 Boswell was prepared to risk his life in a duel with Sir Alexander (then Lord) Macdonald on account of some derogatory remarks which the latter had made in connexion with the exceptionable passages in *The Tour to the Hebrides* (*post*, v. 148). See Mr. Pottle's *Lit. Career of Boswell*, p. 118.⟩ Boswell's eldest son, Sir Alexander Boswell, lost his life in a duel.

which are considered to be of such importance, that life must be
staked to atone for them, though in reality they are not so. A
body that has received a very fine polish may be easily hurt.
Before men arrive at this artificial refinement, if one tells his
neighbour he lies, his neighbour tells him he lies ; if one gives his
neighbour a blow, his neighbour gives him a blow : but in a state
of highly polished society, an affront is held to be a serious injury.
It must,[a] therefore, be resented, or rather a duel must be fought
upon it ; as men have agreed to banish from their society one
who puts up with an affront without fighting a duel. Now, Sir,
it is never unlawful to fight in self-defence. He, then, who fights
a duel, does not fight from passion against his antagonist, but out
of self-defence ; to avert the stigma of the world, and to prevent
himself from being driven out of society. I could wish there
was not that superfluity of refinement ; but while such notions
prevail, no doubt a man may lawfully fight a duel [1].'

Let it be remembered, that this justification is applicable only
to the person who *receives* an affront. All mankind must condemn the aggressor.

The General told us, that when he was a very young man, I
think only fifteen [2], serving under Prince Eugene of Savoy, he
was sitting in a company at table with a Prince of Wirtemberg.
The Prince took up a glass of wine, and, by a fillip, made some
of it fly in Oglethorpe's face. Here was a nice dilemma. To
have challenged him instantly, might have fixed a quarrelsome
character upon the young soldier : to have taken no notice of it
might have been considered as cowardice. Oglethorpe, therefore,
keeping his eye upon the Prince, and smiling all the time, as if

[a] *comma omitted* 3.

[1] Johnson might have quoted the
lieutenant in *Tom Jones*, book vii.
chap. 13. ' My dear boy, be a good
Christian as long as you live : but be
a man of honour too, and never put
up an affront ; not all the books, nor
all the parsons in the world, shall ever
persuade me to that. I love my religion very well, but I love my honour
more. There must be some mistake
in the wording of the text, or in the
translation, or in the understanding

it, or somewhere or other. But however that be, a man must run the
risque, for he must preserve his
honour.' See *post*, ii. 226 ; iv. 211 ;
and v. 230.

[2] Oglethorpe was born in 1696. In
1710 he entered the army. Prince
Eugene's campaigns against the Turks
in which Oglethorpe served were
in 1716-17. *Dict. Nat. Biography*.
He was not therefore quite so young
as Boswell thought.

he took what his Highness had done in jest, said ' *Mon Prince,—*'
(I forget the French words he used, the purport however was,)
' That's a good joke ; but we do it much better in England ; '
and threw a whole glass of wine in the Prince's face. An old
General who sat by, said, ' *Il a bien fait, mon Prince, vous l'avez
commencé* : ' and thus all ended in good humour.

Dr. Johnson said, ' Pray, General, give us an account of the
siege of Belgrade [1].' Upon which the General, pouring a little
wine upon the table, described every thing with a wet finger :
' Here we were, here were the Turks,' &c. &c. Johnson listened
with the closest attention.

A question was started, how far people who disagree in any [a]
capital point can live in friendship together. Johnson said they
might. Goldsmith said they could not, as they had not the *idem
velle atque idem nolle* [2]—the same likings and the same aversions.
JOHNSON. ' Why, Sir, you must shun the subject as to which you
disagree. For instance, I can live very well with Burke : I love
his knowledge, his genius, his diffusion, and affluence of conversation ; but I would not talk to him of the Rockingham party.'
GOLDSMITH. ' But, Sir, when people live together who have something as to which they disagree, and which they want to shun,
they will be in the situation mentioned in the story of Bluebeard :
" You may look into all the chambers but one." But we should
have the greatest inclination to look into that chamber, to talk of
that subject.' JOHNSON. (with a loud voice.) ' Sir, I am not
saying that *you* could live in friendship with a man from whom
you differ as to some point : I am only saying that *I* could do it.
You put me in mind of Sappho in Ovid [3].'

Goldsmith told us, that he was now busy in writing a natural

[a] any 1   [a] 2, 3.

[1] In the first two editions *Bender*.
Belgrade was taken by Eugene in
1717.
[2] ' Idem velle atque idem nolle, ea
demum firma amicitia est.' Sallust,
Catilina, xx. 4.
[3] More than one conjecture has
been hazarded as to the passage to
which Johnson referred. I believe
that he was thinking of the lines—
' Et variis albae iunguntur saepe
    columbae,

Et niger a viridi turtur amatur ave.'
        Sappho to Phaon, line 37.
' Turtles and doves of diff'ring hues
    unite,
And glossy jet is pair'd with shining
    white.' (POPE.)
Goldsmith had said that people to
live in friendship together must have
the same likings and aversions. Johnson thereupon calls to mind Sappho,
who had shown that there could be
love where there was little likeness.

history [1], and, that he might have full leisure for it, he had taken lodgings, at a farmer's house, near to the six mile-stone, on the Edgeware-road, and had carried down his books in two returned post-chaises. He said, he believed the farmer's family thought him an odd character, similar to that in which the *Spectator* appeared to his landlady and her children : he was *The Gentleman* [2]. Mr. Mickle, the translator of ' The Lusiad [3],' and I, went to visit him at this place a few days afterwards. He was not at home ; but having a curiosity to see his apartment, we went in and found curious scraps of descriptions of animals, scrawled upon the walls [a] with a black lead pencil [4].

The subject of ghosts being introduced, Johnson repeated what he had told me of a friend of his, an honest man [b] and a man of sense, having asserted to him, that he had seen an apparition [5]. Goldsmith told us, he was assured by his brother, the Reverend Mr. Goldsmith, that he also had seen one. General Oglethorpe told us, that Prendergast, an officer in the Duke of Marlborough's army, had mentioned to many of his friends, that he should die on a particular day. That upon that day a battle took place with the French ; that after it was over, and Prendergast was still alive, his brother officers, while they were yet in the field, jestingly asked him, where was his prophecy now. Prendergast gravely answered. ' I shall die, notwithstanding what you see.' Soon afterwards, there came a shot from a French battery, to

---

[a] walls 1 : wall 2, 3.

[b] man 1 : man, 2, 3.

[1] 〈*A History of the Earth, and Animated Nature.* 8 vols. ' On February 29, 1769, Goldsmith signed an agreement to write this work at one hundred guineas per volume. . . . He managed to get paid the whole amount by June 27, 1772, when he had only completed a third of the work, which he did not finish till March, 1774.' It was published on June 30. I. A. Williams, *18th-C. Bibliographies*, p. 166.〉

[2] ' Upon my opening the Door the young Women broke off their Discourse, but my Land-lady's Daughters telling them that it was no Body but the Gentleman (for that is the Name which I go by in the Neighbourhood as well as in the Family) they went on without minding me.' *Spectator*, No. 12.

[3] Bishop Horne says that ' Mickle inserted in the *Lusiad* an angry note against Garrick, who, as he thought, had used him ill, by rejecting a tragedy of his.' Shortly afterwards, he saw Garrick act for the first time. The play was *Lear*. ' During the first three acts, he said not a word. In a fine passage of the fourth, he fetched a deep sigh, and, turning to his friend, " I wish," said he, " the *note* was out of my book ! " ' *Essays*, ed. 1808, p. 38. See *post*, ii. 495, iv. 250 and v. 349.

[4] The farmer's son told Mr. Prior that ' he felt much reluctance in erasing during the repairs rendered necessary some years afterward, these memorials of an eminent man.' Prior's *Goldsmith*, ii. 335.

[5] See *ante*, ii. 178.

which the orders for a cessation of arms had not yet reached, and he was killed upon the spot. Colonel Cecil, who took possession of his effects, found in his pocket-book the following solemn entry :

[Here the date.] 'Dreamt—or ———— [1] Sir John Friend meets me : ' (here the very day on which he was killed was mentioned.) Prendergast had been connected with Sir John Friend, who was executed for high treason. General Oglethorpe said, he was in company with [a] Colonel Cecil when Pope came and enquired into the truth of this story, which made a great noise at the time, and was then confirmed by the Colonel.

On Saturday, April 11, he appointed me to come to him in the evening, when he should be at leisure to give me some assistance for the defence of Hastie, the schoolmaster of Campbelltown, for whom I was to appear in the House of Lords. When I came, I found him unwilling to exert himself. I pressed him to write down his thoughts upon the subject. He said, 'There's no occasion for my writing. I'll talk to you.' He was, however, at last prevailed on to dictate to me, while I wrote as follows :

'The charge is, that he has used immoderate and cruel correction. Correction, in itself, is not cruel ; children, being not reasonable, can be governed only by fear. To impress this fear, is therefore one of the first duties of those who have the care of children. It is the duty of a parent ; and has never been thought inconsistent with parental tenderness. It is the duty of a master, who is in his highest exaltation

[a] in company with 1 ; with 2, 3.

[1] Here was a blank, which may be filled up thus :—' *was told by an apparition ;* '—the writer being probably uncertain whether he was asleep or awake, when his mind was impressed with the solemn presentiment with which the fact afterwards happened so wonderfully to correspond. BOSWELL.
'Lord Hardinge, when Secretary at War,' writes Mr. Croker, ' informed me, that it appears that Colonel Sir Thomas Prendergast, of the twenty-second foot, was killed at Malplaquet, Aug. 31, 1709 ; but no trace can be found of any *Colonel* Cecil in the army at that period. The well-known Jacobite, Colonel William Cecil, who was sent to the Tower in 1744, could hardly have been, in 1709, of the age, rank, and station which Oglethorpe's anecdote seems to imply.' Prendergast, or Pendergrass, in the year 1696, informed the government of the plot to assassinate William III, in which Friend was one of the leaders. Macaulay (*Hist. of Eng.* chap. 21) calls Pendergrass ' a Roman Catholic gentleman of known courage and honour.' Swift, attacking Prendergast's son, attacks Prendergast himself :—
'What ! thou, the spawn of him who shamed our isle,
Traitor, assassin, and informer vile.'
Swift's *On Noisy Tom, Works,*
1824, xii. 447.

when he is *loco parentis*. Yet, as good things become evil by excess, correction, by being immoderate, may become cruel. But when is correction immoderate ? When it is more frequent or more severe than is required *ad monendum et docendum*, for reformation and instruction. No severity is cruel which obstinacy makes necessary ; for the greatest cruelty would be to desist, and leave the scholar too careless for instruction, and too much hardened for reproof. Locke, in his treatise of Education, mentions a mother, with applause, who whipped an infant eight times before she had subdued it ; for had she stopped at the seventh act of correction, her daughter, says he, would have been ruined [1]. The degrees of obstinacy in young minds are very different ; as different must be the degrees of persevering severity. A stubborn scholar must be corrected till he is subdued. The discipline of a school is military. There must be either unbounded licence or absolute authority. The master, who punishes, not only consults the future happiness of him who is the immediate subject of correction ; but he propagates obedience through the whole school ; and establishes regularity by exemplary justice. The victorious obstinacy of a single boy would make his future endeavours of reformation or instruction totally ineffectual. Obstinacy, therefore, must never be victorious. Yet, it is well known, that there sometimes occurs a sullen and hardy resolution, that laughs at all common punishment, and bids defiance to all common degrees of pain. Correction must be proportioned to occasions. The flexible will be reformed by gentle discipline, and the refractory must be subdued by harsher methods. The degrees of scholastick, as of military punishment, no stated rules can ascertain. It must be enforced till it overpowers temptation ; till stubbornness becomes flexible, and perverseness regular. Custom and reason have, indeed, set some bounds to scholastick penalties. The schoolmaster inflicts no capital punishments ; nor enforces his edicts by either death or mutilation. The civil law has wisely determined, that a master who strikes at a scholar's eye shall be considered as criminal. But punishments, however severe, that produce no lasting evil, may be just and reasonable, because they may be necessary. Such have been the punishments used by the respondent. No scholar has gone from him

---

[1] Locke says :—' When once it comes to be a Trial of Skill, a Contest for Mastery betwixt you, and your child, you must be sure to carry it, whatever Blows it costs, if a Nod or Words will not prevail.' He continues :—' A prudent and kind Mother of my Acquaintance, was, on such an occasion, forced to whip her little Daughter, at her first coming home from Nurse, eight times successively the same Morning, before she could master her Stubbornness, and obtain a compliance in a very easy and indifferent matter. . . . As this was the first time, so I think, it was the last too she ever struck her.' *On Education* (ed. 1693), p. 84.

either blind or lame, or with any of his limbs or powers injured or impaired. They were irregular, and he punished them : they were obstinate, and he enforced his punishment. But, however provoked, he never exceeded the limits of moderation, for he inflicted nothing beyond present pain ; and how much of that was required, no man is so little able to determine as those who have determined against him ;—the parents of the offenders.—It has been said, that he used unprecedented and improper instruments of correction. Of this accusation the meaning is not very easy to be found. No instrument of correction is more proper than another, but as it is better adapted to produce present pain without lasting mischief. Whatever were his instruments, no lasting mischief has ensued ; and therefore, however unusual, in hands so cautious they were proper.—It has been objected, that the respondent admits the charge of cruelty, by producing no evidence to confute it. Let it be considered, that his scholars are either dispersed at large in the world, or continue to inhabit the place in which they were bred. Those who are dispersed cannot be found ; those who remain are the sons of his persecutors, and are not likely to support a man to whom their fathers are enemies. If it be supposed that the enmity of their fathers proves the justice of the charge, it must be considered how often experience shews us, that men who are angry on one ground will accuse on another ; with how little kindness, in a town of low trade, a man who lives by learning is regarded ; and how implicitly, where the inhabitants are not very rich, a rich man is hearkened to and followed. In a place like Campbelltown, it is easy for one of the principal inhabitants to make a party. It is easy for that party to heat themselves with imaginary grievances. It is easy for them to oppress a man poorer than themselves ; and natural to assert the dignity of riches, by persisting in oppression. The argument which attempts to prove the impropriety of restoring him to his [a] school, by alledging that he has lost the confidence of the people, is not the subject of juridical consideration ; for he is to suffer, if he must suffer, not for their judgement, but for his own actions. It may be convenient for them to have another master ; but it is a convenience of their own making. It would be likewise convenient for him to find another school ; but this convenience he cannot obtain.—The question is not what is now convenient, but what is generally right. If the people of Campbelltown be distressed by the restoration of the respondent, they are distressed only by their own fault ; by turbulent passions and unreasonable desires ; by tyranny, which law has defeated, and by malice, which virtue has surmounted.'

' This, Sir, (said he,) you are to turn in your mind, and make the best use of it you can in your speech.'

a his 1 : the 2, 3.

Of our friend Goldsmith he said, ' Sir, he is so much afraid of being unnoticed, that he often talks merely lest you should forget that he is in the company.' BOSWELL. ' Yes, he stands forward.' JOHNSON. ' True, Sir ; but if a man is to stand forward, he should wish to do it not in an aukward posture, not in rags, not so as that he shall only be exposed to ridicule.' BOSWELL. ' For my part, I like very well to hear honest Goldsmith talk away carelessly.' JOHNSON. ' Why yes, Sir ; but he should not like to hear himself.'

On Tuesday, April 14, the decree of the Court of Session in the schoolmaster's cause was reversed in the House of Lords, after a very eloquent speech by Lord Mansfield, who shewed himself an adept in school discipline, but I thought was too rigorous towards my client [1]. On the evening of the next day I supped with Dr. Johnson, at the Crown and Anchor tavern, in the Strand, in company with Mr. Langton and his brother-in-law, Lord Binning. I repeated a sentence of Lord Mansfield's speech, of which, by the aid of Mr. Longlands, the solicitor on the other side, who obligingly allowed me to compare his note with my own, I have a full copy : ' My Lords, severity is not the way to govern either boys or men.' ' Nay, (said Johnson,) it is the way to *govern* them. I know not whether it be the way to *mend* them.'

---

[1] Andrew Crosbie, arguing for the schoolmaster, had said :—' Supposing it true that the respondent had been provoked to use a little more severity than he wished to do, it might well be justified on account of the ferocious and rebellious behaviour of his scholars, some of whom cursed and swore at him, and even went so far as to wrestle with him, in which case he was under a necessity of subduing them as he best could.' *Scotch Appeal Cases*, xvii. p. 214. The judgement of the House of Lords is given in Paton's *Reports of Cases upon Appeal from Scotland*, ii. 277, as follows :—' A schoolmaster, appointed by the Magistrates and Town Council of Cambelton, without any mention being made as to whether his office was for life or at pleasure : Held that it was a public office, and that he was liable to be dismissed for a just and reasonable cause, and that acts of cruel chastisement of the boys were a justifiable cause for his dismissal ; reversing the judgment of the Court of Session. . . . The proof led before his dismission went to show that . . . scarce a day passed without some of the scholars coming home . . . with their heads cut, and their bodies discoloured. . . . He beat the pupils with wooden squares, . . . and sometimes with his fists, and used his feet by kicking them, . . . dragging them by the hair of the head. . . . He had also entered into the trade of cattle grazing and farming—dealt in black cattle—in the shipping business—and in herring fishing.'

I talked of the recent expulsion of six students from the University of Oxford, who were methodists,[a] and would not desist from publickly praying and exhorting [1]. JOHNSON. ' Sir, that expulsion was extremely just and proper [2]. What have they to do at an University who are not willing to be taught, but will presume to teach? Where is religion to be learnt but at an University? Sir, they were examined, and found to be mighty ignorant fellows.' BOSWELL. ' But, was it not hard, Sir, to expel them, for I am told they were good beings?' JOHNSON. ' Sir,[b] I believe they might be good beings; but they were not fit to be in the University of Oxford [3]. A cow is a very good animal in the field; but we turn her out of a garden.' Lord Elibank used to repeat this as an illustration uncommonly happy.

Desirous of calling Johnson forth to talk, and exercise his wit, though I should myself be the object of it, I resolutely ventured

[a] *comma omitted* 3.

[1] These six Methodists were in 1768 expelled St. Edmund Hall, by the Vice-Chancellor, acting as ' visitor.' Nominally they were expelled for their ignorance; in reality for their active Methodism. That they were ' mighty ignorant fellows ' was shown, but ignorance was tolerated at Oxford. One of their number confessed his ignorance, and declined all examination. But ' as he was represented to be a man of fortune, and declared that he was not designed for holy orders, the Vice-Chancellor did not think fit to remove him for this reason only, though he was supposed to be one of " the righteous overmuch." ' *Dr. Johnson : His Friends and his Critics*, pp. 51–57. Horace Walpole, Whig though he was, thought as Johnson. ' Oxford,' he wrote (*Letters*, vii. 183), ' has begun with these rascals, and I hope Cambridge will wake.'

[2] Much such an expulsion as this Johnson had justified in his *Life of Cheynel* (*Works*, vi. 415). ' A temper of this kind,' he wrote, ' is generally inconvenient and offensive in any society, but in a place of education is least to be tolerated. . . . Whoever endeavours to destroy subordination

[b] Sir, *omitted* 3.

. . . may be justly driven from a society, by which he thinks himself too wise to be governed, and in which he is too young to teach, and too opinionative to learn.'

[3] Johnson wrote far otherwise of the indulgence shown to Edmund Smith, the poet. ' The indecency and licentiousness of his behaviour drew upon him, Dec. 24, 1694, while he was yet only Batchelor, a publick admonition, entered upon record, in order to his expulsion. Of this reproof the effect is not known. He was probably less notorious. At Oxford, as we all know, much will be forgiven to literary merit. . . . Of his lampoon upon Dean Aldrich, [Smith was a Christ-Church man], I once heard a single line too gross to be repeated. But he was still a genius and a scholar, and Oxford was unwilling to lose him : he was endured, with all his pranks and his vices, two years longer ; but on Dec. 20, 1705, at the instance of all the canons, the sentence declared five years before was put in execution. The execution was, I believe, silent and tender.' *Life of Smith*, 30, 39, 40, 41.

to undertake the defence of convivial indulgence in wine, though he was not to-night in the most genial humour [1]. After urging the common plausible topicks, I at last had recourse to the maxim, *in vino veritas*;[a] a man who is well warmed with wine will speak truth [2]. JOHNSON. ' Why, Sir, that may be an argument for drinking, if you suppose men in general to be liars. But, Sir, I would not keep company with a fellow, who lyes as long as he is sober, and whom you must make drunk before you can get a word of truth out of him [3].'

Mr. Langton told us he was about to establish a school upon his estate, but it had been suggested to him, that it might have a tendency to make the people less industrious. JOHNSON. ' No, Sir. While learning to read and write is a distinction, the few who have that distinction may be the less inclined to work ; but when every body learns to read and write, it is no longer a distinction [4]. A man who has a laced waistcoat is too fine a man to work ; but if every body had laced waistcoats, we should have people working in laced waistcoats. There are no people whatever more industrious, none who work more, than our manufacturers [5] ; yet they have all learnt to read and write. Sir, you must not neglect doing a thing immediately good, from fear of remote evil ;— from fear of its being abused [6]. A man who has candles may sit

<hr>

[a] *veritas* ; 1, 2: *veritas*, 3.

[1] See *post*, ii. 193, note 1.

[2] ' Our bottle-conversation,' wrote Addison, ' is infected with party-lying.' *The Spectator*, No. 507.

[3] Mrs. Piozzi, in her ' Anecdotes,' p. 261, has given an erroneous account of this incident, as of many others. She pretends to relate it from recollection, as if she herself had been present ; when the fact is, that it was communicated to her by me. She has represented it as a personality, and the true point has escaped her. BOSWELL.

She tells the story against Boswell. ' I fancy Mr. B—— has not forgotten,' she writes. *John. Misc.* i. 321. See also *Ib.* ii. 16.

[4] See *post*, iii. 37.

[5] Johnson defines *manufacturer* as *a workman ; an artificer.*

[6] Johnson had no fear of popular education. In his attack on Jenyns's *Inquiry* (*ante*, i. 315), he wrote (*Works*, vi. 56) :—' Though it should be granted, that those who are *born to poverty and drudgery*, should not be *deprived*, by an *improper education*, of the *opiate* of *ignorance* ; even this concession will not be of much use to direct our practice, unless it be determined, who are those that are *born to poverty*. To entail irreversible poverty upon generation after generation, only because the ancestor happened to be poor, is, in itself, cruel, if not unjust. . . . I am always afraid of determining on the side of envy or cruelty. The privileges of education may, sometimes, be improperly bestowed, but I shall always fear to withhold them, lest I should be yielding

up too late, which he would not do if he had not candles ; but nobody will deny that the art of making candles, by which light is
continued to us beyond the time that the sun gives us light, is a
valuable art, and ought to be preserved.' BOSWELL. ' But, Sir,
would it not be better to follow Nature ; and go to bed and rise
just as Nature gives us light or with-holds it ? ' JOHNSON. ' No,
Sir ; for then we should have no kind of equality in the partition
of our time between sleeping and waking. It would be very
different in different seasons and in different places. In some of
the northern parts of Scotland how little light is there in the
depth of winter ! '

We talked of Tacitus [1], and I hazarded an opinion, that with all
his merit for penetration, shrewdness of judgement, and terse-
ness of expression, he was too compact, too much broken into
hints, as it were, and therefore too difficult to be understood.
To my great satisfaction Dr. Johnson sanctioned this opinion.
' Tacitus, Sir, seems to me rather to have made notes for an
historical work, than to have written a history [2].'

At this time it appears from his ' Prayers and Meditations,' that
he had been more than commonly diligent in religious duties,
particularly in reading the holy scriptures. It was Passion Week,
that solemn season which the Christian world has appropriated
to the commemoration of the mysteries of our redemption, and
during which, whatever embers of religion are in our breasts, will
be kindled into pious warmth.

I paid him short visits both on Friday and Saturday, and seeing
his large folio Greek Testament before him, beheld him with a
reverential awe, and would not intrude upon his time [3]. While

---

to the suggestions of pride, while I
persuade myself that I am following
the maxims of policy.' In *The Idler*,
No. 26, he attacked those who ' hold
it little less than criminal to teach
poor girls to read and write,' and
who say that ' they who are born to
poverty are born to ignorance, and will
work the harder the less they know.'

[1] Tacitus's *Agricola*, ch. xii, was
no doubt quoted in reference to the
shortness of the northern winter day.

[2] It is remarkable, that Lord
Monboddo, whom on account of his

resembling Dr. Johnson in some particulars, Foote called an Elzevir
edition of him, has, by coincidence,
made the very same remark. *Origin
and Progress of Language*, vol. iii.
2d edit. p. 219. BOSWELL. See Boswell's *Hebrides*, *post*, v. 74, n. 3, and
Mr. Chapman's edition, 1924, pp. 206,
466.

[3] On Saturday night Johnson recorded :—' I resolved, last Easter, to
read within the year, the whole Bible,
a very great part of which I had
never looked upon. I read the Greek

he was thus employed to such good purpose, and while his friends in their intercourse with him constantly found a vigorous intellect and a lively imagination, it is melancholy to read in his private register, ' My mind is unsettled and my memory confused. I have of late turned my thoughts with a very useless earnestness upon past incidents. I have yet got no command over my thoughts ; an unpleasing incident is almost certain to hinder my rest [1].' What philosophick heroism was it in him to appear with such manly fortitude to the world, while he was inwardly so distressed ! We may surely believe that the mysterious principle of being ' made perfect through suffering [2] ' was to be strongly exemplified in him.

On Sunday, April 19, being Easter-day, General Paoli and I paid him a visit before dinner. We talked of the notion that blind persons can distinguish colours by the touch. Johnson said, that Professor Sanderson [3] mentions his having attempted to do it, but that he found he was aiming at an impossibility ; that to be sure a difference in the surface makes the difference of colours ; but that difference is so fine, that it is not sensible to the touch. The General mentioned jugglers and fraudulent gamesters, who could know cards by the touch. Dr. Johnson

Testament without construing, and this day concluded the Apocalypse.' And on ' Easter day after 12 at night. The Day is now begun, on which I hope to begin a new course, ὥσπερ ἀφ' ὑσπλήγγων, [as if from the starting-place].

My hopes are from this time,

To rise early.

To waste less time.

To appropriate something to charity.' A week later he recorded :—' It is a comfort to me that, at last, in my sixty third year, I have attained to know, even thus hastily, confusedly, and imperfectly, what my Bible contains. . . . I have never yet read the apocrypha. . . . I have some time looked into the Maccabees, and read a chapter containing the question, *Which is the Strongest?* I think, in Esdras ' [1 Esdras, ch. iii. v. 10]. *Pr. and Med.* ¶¶ 94, 95, 97. ⟨See App. B, p. 495.⟩

[1] Prayers and Meditations, p. 111 [¶ 94]. BOSWELL.

[2] ' Perfect through sufferings.' *Hebrews*, ii. 10.

[3] ' I was always so incapable of learning mathematics,' wrote Walpole, 16 Aug.1796 (*Letters*, xv. 418), ' that I could not even get by heart the multiplication-table, as blind Professor Sanderson honestly told me, above threescore years ago, when I went to his lectures at Cambridge. After the first fortnight, he said to me, " Young man, it would be cheating you to take your money ; for you never can learn what I am trying to teach you." I was exceedingly mortified, and cried ; for, being a Prime Minister's son, I had firmly believed all the flattery with which I had been assured that my parts were capable of anything.' ⟨See N. Saunderson's *Algebra*, 1740, *Life*, i. p. xii.⟩

said, ' the cards used by such persons must be less polished than ours commonly are.'

We talked of sounds. The General said, there was no beauty in a simple sound, but only in an harmonious composition of sounds. I presumed to differ from this opinion, and mentioned the soft and sweet sound of a fine woman's voice. JOHNSON. ' No, Sir, if a serpent or a toad uttered it, you would think it ugly.' BOSWELL. ' So you would think, Sir, were a beautiful tune to be uttered by one of those animals.' JOHNSON. ' No, Sir, it would be admired. We have seen fine fiddlers whom we liked as little as toads,' (laughing).

Talking on the subject of taste in the arts, he said, that difference of taste was, in truth, difference of skill [1]. BOSWELL. ' But, Sir, is there not a quality called taste [2], which consists merely in perception or in liking ? For instance, we find people differ much as to what is the best style of English composition. Some think Swift's the best ; others prefer a fuller and grander way of writing.' JOHNSON. ' Sir, you must first define what you mean by style, before you can judge who has a good taste in style, and who has a bad. The two classes of persons whom you have mentioned don't differ as to good and bad. They both agree that Swift has a good neat style [3] ; but one loves a neat style,

[1] Reynolds said :—' Out of the great number of critics in this metropolis, who all pretend to knowledge in pictures, the greater part must be mere pretenders only. Taste does not come by chance : it is a long and laborious task to acquire it.' Northcote's *Reynolds*, i. 264.

[2] ' Jemmy Boswell,' wrote John Scott (afterwards Lord Eldon), ' called upon me . . ., desiring to know what would be my definition of *Taste*. I told him I must decline defining it, because I knew he would publish what I said would be my definition of it. . . . He continued his importunities in frequent calls, and, in one, complained much that I would not give him [it], as he had that morning got Henry Dundas's, Sir A. Macdonald's, and J. Anstruther's definitions. " Well, then," I said, " Boswell, we must have

an end of this. Taste, according to my definition, is the judgment which Dundas, Macdonald, Anstruther, and you, manifested, when you determined to quit Scotland, and to come into the south. You may publish this if you please." ' Twiss's *Eldon*, i. 303. ⟨Cf., however, Elwin's *18th-C. Men of Letters*, ii. 257.⟩ See *post*, iii. 261, note 2, for Lord Eldon.

[3] Johnson (*Life of Swift*, 112–114) says that ' Swift's delight was in simplicity. That he has in his works no metaphor, as has been said, is not true ; but his few metaphors seem to be received rather by necessity than choice. He studied purity. . . . His style was well suited to his thoughts. . . . He pays no court to the passions ; he excites neither surprise nor admiration ; he always understands himself, and his reader always under-

another loves a style of more splendour. In like manner, one loves a plain coat, another loves a laced coat ; but neither will deny that each is good in its kind.'

While I remained in London this spring, I was with him at several other times, both by himself and in company. I dined with him one day at the Crown and Anchor tavern, in the Strand, with Lord Elibank, Mr. Langton, and Dr. Vansittart of Oxford. Without specifying each particular day, I have preserved the following memorable things.

I regretted the reflection in his Preface to Shakspeare against Garrick, to whom we cannot but apply the following passage : ' I collated such copies as I could procure, and wished for more, but have not found the collectors of these rarities very communicative [1].' I told him, that Garrick had complained to me of it, and had vindicated himself by assuring me, that Johnson was made welcome to the full use of his collection, and that he left the key of it with a servant, with orders to have a fire and every convenience for him. I found Johnson's notion was, that Garrick wanted to be courted for them, and that, on the contrary, Garrick should have courted him, and sent him the plays of his own accord. But, indeed, considering the slovenly and careless manner in which books were treated by Johnson, it could not be expected that scarce and valuable editions should have been lent to him [2].

stands him ; the peruser of Swift wants little previous knowledge ; it will be sufficient that he is acquainted with common words and common things ; . . . [His style] instructs, but does not persuade.' Hume describes Swift's style as one which he ' can even approve, but surely can never admire. It has no harmony, no eloquence, no ornament ; and not much correctness, whatever the English may imagine.' J. H. Burton's *Hume*, ii. 413.

[1] Johnson's *Works*, v. 146.

[2] Dr. Warton wrote on Jan. 22, 1766 :—' Garrick is intirely off from Johnson, and cannot, he says, forgive him his insinuating that he withheld his old editions, which always were open to him ; nor, I suppose, his

never mentioning him in all his works.' Wooll's *Warton*, p. 313. Beauclerk wrote to Lord Charlemont in 1773 :— ' If you do not come here, I will bring all the club over to Ireland, to live with you, and that will drive you here in your own defence. Johnson *shall spoil your books*, Goldsmith pull your flowers, and Boswell talk to you : stay then if you can.' Charlemont's *Life*, i. 347. Yet Garrick had lent Johnson some books, for Johnson wrote to him on Oct. 10, 1766 :— ' I return you thanks for the present of the Dictionary, and will take care to return your other books.' Johnson's *Letters*, No. 186. Steevens, who had edited Johnson's *Shakespeare*, wrote to Garrick :—' I have taken the liberty to introduce your name,

A gentleman [1] having to some of the usual arguments for drinking added this : ' You know, Sir, drinking drives away care, and makes us forget whatever is disagreeable. Would not you allow a man to drink for that reason ? ' JOHNSON. ' Yes, Sir, if he sat next *you*.'

I expressed a liking for Mr. Francis Osborne's works, and asked him what he thought of that writer. He answered, ' A conceited fellow. Were a man to write so now, the boys would throw stones at him.' He however did not alter my opinion of a favourite authour, to whom I was first directed by his being quoted in ' The Spectator [2],' and in whom I have found much

because *I have found* no reason to say that the possessors of the old quartos were not sufficiently communicative.' *Garrick Corr.* i. 501. Mme. D'Arblay describes how ' Garrick, giving a thundering stamp . . . on some mark on the carpet that struck his eye—not with passion or displeasure, but merely as if from singularity ; . . . took off the voice of Dr. Johnson, in a short dialogue with himself that had passed the preceding week. " David !—Will you lend me your *Petrarca ?* " " Y-e-s, Sir ! " " David ! you sigh ? " " Sir —you shall have it certainly." " Accordingly," Mr. Garrick continued, " the book—stupendously bound—I sent to him that very evening. But scarcely had he taken the noble quarto in his hands, when, as Boswell tells me, he poured forth a Greek ejaculation and a couplet or two from Horace ; and then, in one of those fits of enthusiasm which always seem to require that he should spread his arms aloft in the air, he suddenly pounces my poor *Petrarca* over his head upon the floor ! And then, standing for several minutes lost in abstraction, he forgot, probably that he had ever seen it." ' *Memoirs of Dr. Burney*, i. 352. See *post*, iv. 371, note 2, ⟨and *John. Misc.* ii. 394⟩.

[1] The gentleman most likely is Boswell (*ante*, ii. 14, note 1). I suspect that this anecdote belongs to *ante*, ii. 188, when ' Johnson was

not in the most genial humour.' Boswell, while showing that Mrs. Piozzi misrepresented an incident of that evening ' as a personality,' would be afraid of weakening his case by letting it be seen that Johnson on that occasion was very personal. Since writing this I have noticed that Dr. T. Campbell records in his *Diary*, p. 53, that on April 1, 1775, he was dining at Mr. Thrale's with Boswell, when many of Johnson's ' bon mots were retailed. Boswell arguing in favour of a cheerful glass, adduced the maxim *in vino veritas*. " Well," says Johnson, " and what then, unless a man has lived a lye." B. then urged that it made a man forget all his cares. " That, to be sure," says Johnson, " might be of use, if a man sat by such a person as you." ' Campbell's account confirms what Boswell asserts (*ante*, ii. 188), that Mrs. Piozzi had the anecdote from him. ⟨Mrs. Piozzi, in her copy of the 1816 edit. of the *Life*, says : ' It was Boswell himself. Dr. Johnson said " The Man *compels* me to treat him so." ' ⟩

[2] No. 150. The quotation is from Francis Osborne's *Advice to a Son*. Swift, in *The Tatler*, No. 230, ranks Osborne with some other authors, who ' being men of the Court, and affecting the phrases then in fashion, are often either not to be understood, or appear perfectly ridiculous.' ⟨In *Refl. on Bankruptcies* and *Hypochondriack*, i and xxii, Boswell styles him ' Sir '

shrewd and lively sense, expressed indeed in a style somewhat quaint, which, however, I do not dislike. His book has an air of originality. We figure to ourselves an ancient gentleman talking to us.

When one of his friends endeavoured to maintain that a country gentleman might contrive to pass his life very agreeably, ' Sir (said he,) you cannot give me an instance of any man who is permitted to lay out his own time, contriving not to have tedious hours [1].' This observation, however, is equally applicable to gentlemen who live in cities, and are of no profession.

He said, ' there is no permanent national character ; it varies according to circumstances. Alexander the Great swept India : now the Turks sweep Greece.'

A learned gentleman who in the course of conversation wished to inform us of this simple fact, that the Counsel upon the circuit at Shrewsbury were much bitten by fleas, took, I suppose, seven or eight minutes in relating it circumstantially. He in a plenitude of phrase told us, that large bales of woollen cloth were lodged in the town-hall ;—that by reason of this, fleas nestled there in prodigious numbers ;—that the lodgings of the Counsel were near to the town-hall ;—and that those little animals moved from place to place with wonderful agility. Johnson sat in great impatience till the gentleman had finished his tedious narrative, and then burst out (playfully however,) ' It is a pity, Sir, that you have not seen a lion ; for a flea has taken you such a time, that a lion must have served you a twelvemonth [2].'

He would not allow Scotland to derive any credit from Lord Mansfield ; for he was educated in England. ' Much (said he,) may be made of a Scotchman, if he be *caught* young [3].'

<hr />

Francis (see F. A. Pottle, *Lit. Career Boswell*, No. 49).>

[1] See *post*, iii. 353 ; iv. 338 ; v. 108.

[2] Mrs. Piozzi, to whom I told this anecdote, has related it, as if the gentleman had given ' the *natural history* of the *mouse*.' Anecdotes, p. 191. BOSWELL. The gentleman was very likely Dr. Vansittart, who is mentioned just before. (See *ante*, i. 348, note 1.) Mrs. Thrale, in 1773, wrote to Johnson of ' the man that saw the mouse.' *Piozzi Letters*, i. 186. From Johnson's answer (*Letters*, No. 337) it seems that she meant Vansittart. Mr. Croker says ' this proves that Johnson himself sanctioned Mrs. Piozzi's version of the story—*mouse* versus *flea*.' Mr. Croker has an odd notion of what constitutes both a proof and a sanction.

[3] Lord Shelburne says that 'William Murray was sixteen years of age when he came out of Scotland, and spoke

Talking of a modern historian and a modern moralist [1], he said, ' There is more thought in the moralist than in the historian. There is but a shallow stream of thought in history.' BOSWELL. ' But surely, Sir, an historian has reflection.' JOHNSON. ' Why yes, Sir ; and so has a cat when she catches a mouse for her kitten. But she cannot write like ******* ; neither can *********.'

He said, ' I am very unwilling to read the manuscripts of authours, and give them my opinion [2]. If the authours who apply to me have money, I bid them boldly print without a name ; if they have written in order to get money, I tell them to go to the booksellers, and make the best bargain they can.' BOSWELL. ' But, Sir, if a bookseller should bring you a manu-script to look at ? ' JOHNSON. ' Why, Sir, I would desire the bookseller to take it away.'

I mentioned a friend of mine who had resided long in Spain, and was unwilling to return to Britain. JOHNSON. ' Sir, he is attached to some woman.' BOSWELL. ' I rather believe, Sir, it is the fine climate which keeps him there.' JOHNSON. ' Nay, Sir, how can you talk so ? What is *climate* to happiness [3] ? Place me in the heart of Asia †, should I not be exiled ? What proportion does climate bear to the complex system of human life ? You may advise me to go to live at Bologna to eat sausages. The sausages there, are the best in the world ; they lose much by being carried.'

On Saturday, May 9, Mr. Dempster [4] and I had agreed to dine by ourselves at the British Coffee-house. Johnson, on whom I happened to call in the morning, said, he would join us, which he did, and we spent a very agreeable day, though I recollect but little of what passed.

He said, ' Walpole was a minister given by the King to the

---

such broad Scotch that he stands entered in the University Books at Oxford as born at Bath, the Vice-Chancellor mistaking *Bath* for *Perth*.' Fitzmaurice's *Shelburne*, i. 67.

[1] The asterisks seem to show, as Croker stated, that Beattie and Robert-son are meant. This is rendered more probable from the fact that the last paragraph is about Scotchmen. ⟨In ed. 1 we find instead of the asterisks ' the moralist ' and ' the historian'.⟩

[2] See *ante*, ii. 51 ; *post*, iii. 373 ; iv. 121.

[3] Boswell's friend was very likely, as Croker suggested, his brother David, who had long resided in Valencia. In that case, Johnson came round to Boswell's opinion, for he wrote, ' he . . . will find Scotland but a sorry place after twelve years' residence in a happier climate ' ; *post*, iii. 434.

[4] See *ante*, i. 443, note 2.

† ⟨See *post*, v. 223.⟩

people : Pitt was a minister given by the people to the King,—as an adjunct.'

' The misfortune of Goldsmith in conversation is this : he goes on without knowing how he is to get off. His genius is great, but his knowledge is small. As they say of a generous man, it is a pity he is not rich, we may say of Goldsmith, it is a pity he is not knowing. He would not keep his knowledge to himself.'

Before leaving London this year, I consulted him upon a question purely of Scotch law. It was held of old, and continued for a long period, to be an established principle in that law, that whoever intermeddled with the effects of a person deceased, without the interposition of legal authority to guard against embezzlement, should be subjected to pay all the debts of the deceased, as having been guilty of what was technically called *vicious intromission*. The Court of Session had gradually relaxed the strictness of this principle, where the interference proved had been inconsiderable. In a case [1] which came before that Court the preceding winter, I had laboured to persuade the Judges to return to the ancient law. It was my own sincere opinion, that they ought to adhere to it ; but I had exhausted all my powers of reasoning in vain. Johnson thought as I did ; and in order to assist me in my application to the Court for a revision and alteration of the judgement, he dictated to me the following argument :

' THIS, we are told, is a law which has its force only from the long practice of the Court : and may, therefore, be suspended or modified as the Court shall think proper.

' Concerning the power of the Court to make or to suspend a law, we have no intention to inquire. It is sufficient for our purpose that every just law is dictated by reason ; and that the practice of every legal Court is regulated by equity. It is the quality of reason to be invariable and constant ; and of equity, to give to one man what, in the same case, is given to another. The advantage which humanity derives from law is this : that the law gives every man a rule of action, and prescribes a mode of conduct which shall entitle him to the support and protection of society. That the law may be a rule of action, it is necessary that it be known ; it is necessary that it be permanent and stable. The law is the measure of civil right ; but if the measure be changeable, the extent of the thing measured never can be settled.

---

[1] Wilson against Smith and Armour. 〈For a collation with Boswell's print BOSWELL. see App. B, p. 496.〉

' To permit a law to be modified at discretion, is to leave the community without law. It is to withdraw the direction of that publick wisdom, by which the deficiencies of private understanding are to be supplied. It is to suffer the rash and ignorant to act at discretion, and then to depend for the legality of that action on the sentence of the Judge. He that is thus governed, lives not by law, but by opinion : not by a certain rule to which he can apply his intention before he acts, but by an uncertain and variable opinion, which he can never know but after he has committed the act on which that opinion shall be passed. He lives by a law, (if a law it be,) which he can never know before he has offended it. To this case may be justly applied that important principle, *misera est servitus ubi jus est aut incognitum aut vagum.* If Intromission be not criminal till it exceeds a certain point, and that point be unsettled, and consequently different in different minds, the right of Intromission, and the right of the Creditor arising from it, are all *jura vaga*, and, by consequence, are *jura incognita* ; and the result can be no other than a *misera servitus*, an uncertainty concerning the event of action, a servile dependence on private opinion.

' It may be urged, and with great plausibility, that there may be Intromission without fraud ; which, however true, will by no means justify an occasional and arbitrary relaxation of the law. The end of law is protection as well as vengeance. Indeed, vengeance is never used but to strengthen protection. That society only is well governed, where life is freed from danger and from suspicion ; where possession is so sheltered by salutary prohibitions, that violation is prevented more frequently than punished. Such a prohibition was this, while it operated with its original force. The creditor of the deceased was not only without loss, but without fear. He was not to seek a remedy for an injury suffered ; for, injury was warded off.

' As the law has been sometimes administered, it lays us open to wounds, because it is imagined to have the power of healing. To punish fraud when it is detected, is the proper act of vindictive justice ; but to prevent frauds, and make punishment unnecessary, is the great employment of legislative wisdom. To permit Intromission, and to punish fraud, is to make law no better than a pitfall. To tread upon the brink is safe ; but to come a step further is destruction. But, surely, it is better to enclose the gulf, and hinder all access, than by encouraging us to advance a little, to entice us afterwards a little further, and let us perceive our folly only by our destruction.

' As law supplies the weak with adventitious strength, it likewise enlightens the ignorant with extrinsick understanding. Law teaches us to know when we commit injury, and when we suffer it. It fixes certain marks upon actions, by which we are admonished to do or to forbear them. *Qui sibi bene temperat in licitis*, says one of the fathers, *nunquam cadet in illicita.* He who never intromits at all, will never intromit with fraudulent intentions.

' The relaxation of the law against vicious intromission has been very favourably represented by a great master of jurisprudence [1], whose words have been exhibited with unnecessary pomp, and seem to be considered as irresistibly decisive. The great moment of his authority makes it necessary to examine his position. " Some ages ago, (says he,) before the ferocity of the inhabitants of this part of the island was subdued, the utmost severity of the civil law was necessary, to restrain individuals from plundering each other. Thus, the man who intermeddled irregularly with the moveables of a person deceased, was subjected to all the debts of the deceased without limitation. This makes a branch of the law of Scotland, known by the name of *vicious intromission* ; and so rigidly was this regulation applied in our Courts of Law, that the most trifling moveable abstracted *malâ fide*, subjected the intermeddler to the foregoing consequences, which proved in many instances a most rigorous punishment. But this severity was necessary, in order to subdue the undisciplined nature of our people. It is extremely remarkable, that in proportion to our improvement in manners, this regulation has been gradually softened, and applied by our sovereign Court with a sparing hand."

' I find myself under a necessity of observing, that this learned and judicious writer has not accurately distinguished the deficiencies and demands of the different conditions of human life, which, from a degree of savageness and independence, in which all laws are vain, passes or may pass, by innumerable gradations, to a state of reciprocal benignity, in which laws shall be no longer necessary. Men are first wild and unsocial, living each man to himself, taking from the weak, and losing to the strong. In their first coalitions of society, much of this original savageness is retained. Of general happiness, the product of general confidence, there is yet no thought. Men continue to prosecute their own advantages by the nearest way ; and the utmost severity of the civil law is necessary to restrain individuals from plundering each other. The restraints then necessary, are restraints from plunder, from acts of publick violence, and undisguised oppression. The ferocity of our ancestors, as of all other nations, produced not fraud, but rapine. They had not yet learned to cheat, and attempted only to rob. As manners grow more polished, with the knowledge of good, men attain likewise dexterity in evil. Open rapine becomes less frequent, and violence gives way to cunning. Those who before invaded pastures and stormed

[1] Lord Kames, in his ' Historical Law Tracts.' BOSWELL.

houses, now begin to enrich themselves by unequal contracts and fraudulent intromissions. It is not against the violence of ferocity, but the circumventions of deceit, that this law was framed ; and I am afraid the increase of commerce, and the incessant struggle for riches which commerce excites, gives us no prospect of an end speedily to be expected of artifice and fraud. It therefore seems to be no very conclusive reasoning, which connects those two propositions ;—" the nation is become less ferocious, and therefore the laws against fraud and *covin* ¹ shall be relaxed."

' Whatever reason may have influenced the Judges to a relaxation of the law, it was not that the nation was grown less fierce ; and, I am afraid, it cannot be affirmed, that it is grown less fraudulent.

' Since this law has been represented as rigorously and unreasonably penal, it seems not improper to consider what are the conditions and qualities that make the justice or propriety of a penal law.

' To make a penal law reasonable and just, two conditions are necessary, and two proper. It is necessary that the law should be adequate to its end ; that, if it be observed, it shall prevent the evil against which it is directed. It is, secondly, necessary that the end of the law be of such importance, as to deserve the security of a penal sanction. The other conditions of a penal law, which though not absolutely necessary, are to a very high degree fit, are, that to the moral violation of the law there are many temptations, and that of the physical observance there is great facility.

' All these conditions apparently concur to justify the law which we are now considering. Its end is the security of property ; and property very often of great value. The method by which it effects the security is efficacious, because it admits, in its original rigour, no gradations of injury ; but keeps guilt and innocence apart, by a distinct and definite limitation. He that intromits, is criminal ; he that intromits not, is innocent. Of the two secondary considerations it cannot be denied that both are in our favour. The temptation to intromit is frequent and strong ; so strong and so frequent, as to require the utmost activity of justice, and vigilance of caution, to withstand its prevalence ; and the method by which a man may entitle himself to legal intromission is so open and so facile, that to neglect it is a proof of fraudulent intention : for why should a man omit to do (but for reasons which he will not confess,) that which he can do so easily, and that which he knows to be required by the law ? If temptation were rare, a penal law might be deemed unnecessary. If the duty enjoined by the law were of difficult performance, omission, though it could not be justified,

---

¹ ' Covin. A deceitful agreement between two or more to the hurt [prejudice *Cowell*] of another.' Johnson's *Dictionary*, citing Cowell's *Interpreter*.

might be pitied. But in the present case, neither equity nor compassion operate against it. A useful, a necessary law is broken, not only without a reasonable motive, but with all the inducements to obedience that can be derived from safety and facility.

' I therefore return to my original position, that a law, to have its effect, must be permanent and stable. It may be said, in the language of the schools, *Lex non recipit majus et minus,*—we may have a law, or we may have no law, but we cannot have half a law. We must either have a rule of action, or be permitted to act by discretion and by chance. Deviations from the law must be uniformly punished, or no man can be certain when he shall be safe.

' That from the rigour of the original institution this Court has sometimes departed, cannot be denied. But, as it is evident that such deviations, as they make law uncertain, make life unsafe, I hope, that of departing from it there will now be an end ; that the wisdom of our ancestors will be treated with due reverence ; and that consistent and steady decisions will furnish the people with a rule of action, and leave fraud and fraudulent intromission no future hope of impunity or escape.'

With such comprehension of mind, and such clearness of penetration, did he thus treat a subject altogether new to him, without any other preparation than my having stated to him the arguments which had been used on each side of the question. His intellectual powers appeared with peculiar lustre, when tried against those of a writer of so much fame as Lord Kames, and that too in his Lordship's own department [1].

This masterly argument, after being prefaced and concluded

---

[1] Lord Kames (*Sketches of the History of Man*, iii. sk. 2. ii.) says :— ' The undisciplined manners of our forefathers in Scotland, made a law necessary, that whoever intermeddled irregularly with the goods of a deceased person, should be subjected to pay all his debts, however extensive. A due submission to legal authority, has in effect abrogated that severe law ; and it is now [1779] scarce ever heard of.' Scott introduces Lord Kames in *Redgauntlet*, at the end of chap. 1 of the *Narrative* :—' " What's the matter with the auld bitch next ? " said an acute metaphysical judge, though somewhat coarse in his manners, aside to his brethren.' In Boswell's poem *The Court of Session Garland*, where the Scotch judges each give judgement, we read :—

' Alemore the judgment as illegal blames,

" 'Tis equity, you bitch," replies my Lord Kames.'

Chambers's *Traditions of Edinburgh*, ii. 161. Mr. Chambers adds (p. 171) that when Kames retired from the Bench, ' after addressing his brethren in a solemn speech, . . . in going out at the door of the Court-Room, he turned about, and casting them a last look, cried, in his usual familiar tone, " Fare ye a' weel, ye bitches." '

with some sentences of my own, and garnished with the usual formularies, was actually printed and laid before the Lords of Session [1], but without success. My respected friend Lord Hailes, however, one of that honourable body, had critical sagacity enough to discover a more than ordinary hand in the *Petition*. I told him that [a] Dr. Johnson had favoured me with his pen. His Lordship, with wonderful *acumen*, pointed out exactly where his composition began, and where it ended [2]. But that I may do impartial justice, and conform to the great rule of Courts, *Suum cuique tribuito*, I must add, that their Lordships in general, though they were pleased to call this ' a well-drawn paper,' preferred the former very inferiour petition which I had written ; thus confirming the truth of an observation made to me by one of their number, in a merry mood : ' My dear Sir, give yourself no trouble in the composition of the papers you present to us ; for, indeed, it is casting pearls before swine.'

I renewed my solicitations that Dr. Johnson would this year accomplish his long-intended visit to Scotland.

' To JAMES BOSWELL, ESQ.

' DEAR SIR,

' THE regret has not been little with which I have missed a journey so pregnant with pleasing expectations, as that in which I could promise myself not only the gratification of curiosity, both rational and fanciful, but the delight of seeing those whom I love and esteem,[b] ***********. But such has been the course of things, that I could not come ; and such has been, I am afraid, the state of my body, that it would not well have seconded my inclination. My body, I think, grows better, and I refer my hopes to another year ; for I am very sincere in my design to pay the visit, and take the ramble. In the mean time, do not omit any opportunity of keeping up a favourable opinion of me in the minds of any of my friends. Beattie's book [3] is,

a that *om.* 2, 3.   b esteem, 1 : esteem. 2, 3.

[1] At this time there were no civil juries in Scotland. ' But this was made up for, to a certain extent, by the Supreme Court, consisting of no fewer than fifteen judges, who formed a sort of judicial jury, and were dealt with as such. . . . The great mass of the business was carried on by writing.' Cockburn's *Jeffrey*, i. 87. See *post*, ii. 291, note 6.

[2] In like manner, he had discovered the *Life of Cheynel* to be Johnson's. *Post*, v. 48.

[3] The *Essay on Truth*, published in May, 1770. Beattie wrote on Sept. 30, 1772 :—' The fourth edition of my essay is now in the press.' Forbes's *Life of Beattie*, 1806, i. 235. Three translations—French, Dutch, and German—had, it seems, already

I believe, every day more liked ; at least, I like it more, as I look more upon it.

' I am glad if you got credit by your cause, and am yet of opinion, that our cause was good, and that the determination ought to have been in your favour. Poor Hastie [1], I think, had but his deserts.

' You promised to get me a little Pindar, you may add to it a little Anacreon.

' The leisure which I cannot enjoy, it will be a pleasure to hear that you employ upon the antiquities of the feudal establishment. The whole system of ancient tenures is gradually passing away ; and I wish to have the knowledge of it preserved adequate and complete. For such an institution makes a very important part of the history of mankind. Do not forget a design so worthy of a scholar who studies the laws of his country, and of a gentleman who may naturally be curious to know the condition of his own ancestors †.

' I am, dear Sir,

' Yours with great affection,

' SAM. JOHNSON.'

' August 31, 1772 [2].'

appeared. *Ib.* p. 121. ' Mr. Johnson made Goldsmith a comical answer one day, when seeming to repine at the success of Beattie's Essay on Truth—" Here's such a stir (said he) about a fellow that has written one book, and I have written many." Ah, Doctor (says his friend), there go two-and-forty sixpences you know to one guinea.' Piozzi's *Anec.* p. 179 : John. Misc. i. 270. See *post*, v. 274. ⟨See also App. B, p. 496.⟩

[1] See *ante*, ii. 144, 183.

[2] On the same day he wrote to Dr. Taylor :—' Your uneasiness at the misfortunes of your Relations, I comprehend perhaps too well. It was an irresistible obtrusion of a disagreeable image, which you always wished away but could not dismiss, an incessant persecution of a troublesome thought neither to be pacified nor ejected. Such has of late been the state of my own mind. I had formerly great command of my attention, and what I did not like could

forbear to think on. But of this power, which is of the highest importance to the tranquillity of life, I have been so much exhausted, that I do not go into a company towards night, in which I foresee any thing disagreeable, nor enquire after any thing to which I am not indifferent, lest something, which I know to be nothing, should fasten upon my imagination, and hinder me from sleep.' *Letters*, No. 277. On Oct. 6 he wrote to Dr. Taylor :—' I am now within a few hours of being able to send the whole dictionary to the press [*ante*, ii. 155], and though I often went sluggishly to the work, I am not much delighted at the co[nclusion]. My purpose is to come down to Lichfield next week.' *Ib.* No. 278. ⟨He reached Lichfield on the 16th, stayed some weeks there and in Ashbourne, and returned to London on 11th Dec. *Ib.* Nos. 279–91.⟩

† ⟨See *post*, iii. 414, note 3.⟩

' To Dr. Johnson.

' My Dear Sir,

' Edinburgh, Dec. 25, 1772.

*   *   *   *   *   *

' I was much disappointed that you did not come to Scotland last autumn. However, I must own that your letter prevents me from complaining ; not only because I am sensible that the state of your health was but too good an excuse, but because you write in a strain which shews that you have agreeable views of the scheme which we have so long proposed.

*   *   *   *   *   *

' I communicated to Beattie what you said of his book in your last letter to me. He writes to me thus : " You judge very rightly in supposing that Dr. Johnson's favourable opinion of my book must give me great delight. Indeed it is impossible for me to say how much I am gratified by it ; for there is not a man upon earth whose good opinion I would be more ambitious to cultivate. His talents and his virtues I reverence more than any words can express. The extraordinary civilities [1], (the paternal attentions I should rather say,) and the many instructions I have had the honour to receive from him, will to me be a perpetual source of pleasure in the recollection,

' *Dum memor ipse mei, dum spiritus hos reget*[a] *artus* [2].'

" I had still some thoughts, while the summer lasted, of being obliged to go to London on some little business ; otherwise I should certainly have troubled him with a letter several months ago, and given some vent to my gratitude and admiration. This I intend to do, as soon as I am left a little at leisure. Mean time, if you have occasion to write to him, I beg you will offer him my most respectful compliments, and assure him of the sincerity of my attachment and the warmth of my gratitude."

*   *   *   *   *   *

' I am, &c.

' James Boswell.'

1773 : Ætat. 64.]—In 1773 his only publication was an edition of his folio Dictionary, with additions and corrections [3];

---

a *N. Heinsius* (1676) *reads* regit, *but some 18th-c. edd. retain* reget.

[1] See *ante*, ii. 141, note 3.

[2] ' While of myself I yet may think, while breath my body sways.' Morris's *Æneid*, iv. 336.

[3] It should seem that this dictionary work was not unpleasant to Johnson ; for Stockdale records (*Me-* moirs, ii. 179) that about 1774, having told him that he had declined to edit a new edition of Chambers's *Dictionary of the Arts and Sciences*, Johnson replied, ' that if I would not undertake it, he would. . . . I took the liberty to express my astonish-

nor did he, so far as is known, furnish any productions of his
fertile pen to any of his numerous friends or dependants, except
the Preface * [1] to his old amanuensis Macbean's ' Dictionary of
ancient Geography [2].' His Shakspeare, indeed, which had been
received with high approbation by the publick, and gone through
several editions, was this year re-published by George Steevens,
Esq. a gentleman not only deeply skilled in ancient learning,
and of very extensive reading in English literature, especially
the early writers, but at the same time of acute discernment and
elegant taste [3]. It is almost unnecessary to say, that by his
great and valuable additions to Dr. Johnson's work, he justly
obtained considerable reputation :

> ' *Divisum imperium cum Jove Cæsar habet* [4].'

' To JAMES BOSWELL, ESQ.

' DEAR SIR,

' I HAVE read your kind letter much more than the elegant

ment, that he, in his easy, and happy
circumstances, should think of preparing a new edition of a voluminous,
tedious, and scientifick dictionary.
" Sir," said he, " I like that *muddling*
work." He allowed some time to go
by, during which another editor was
found. Immediately after this intelligence, he called on me ; and his
first words were :—" It is gone, sir." '
See *ante*, i. 189, note 2.

[1] He, however, wrote, or partly
wrote, an Epitaph on Mrs. Bell, wife
of his friend John Bell, Esq. brother of
the Reverend Dr. Bell, Prebendary
of Westminster, which is printed in
his Works [i. 151]. It is in English
prose, and has so little of his manner,
that I did not believe he had any hand
in it, till I was satisfied of the fact by
the authority of Mr. Bell. BOSWELL.
⟨' They would have it English, not
Latin, which *vex'd* him.' MRS.
PIOZZI.⟩ The epitaph is ' now to be
seen in the parish church of Watford.'
Hawkins's *Johnson*, p. 471.

[2] See *ante*, i. 187. Mme. D'Arblay
(*Memoirs of Dr. Burney*, i. 271) says
that this year Goldsmith projected a
Dictionary of Arts and Sciences, in

which Johnson was to take the department of ethics, and that Dr.
Burney furnished the article *Musician*.
The scheme came to nothing. ⟨See
Davies's *Garrick*, ch. xli, Prior's *Goldsmith*, ii. 427 ff., and Cradock's *Mem.*,
i. 235.⟩

[3] We may doubt Steevens's taste.
Garrick ' produced *Hamlet* with alterations, rescuing,' as he said, ' that
noble play from all the rubbish of
the fifth act ' (*ante*, ii. 85, note 7).
Steevens wrote to Garrick :—' I expect
great pleasure from the perusal of
your altered *Hamlet*. It is a circumstance in favour of the poet which I
have long been wishing for. . . . You
had better throw what remains of the
piece into a farce, to appear immediately afterwards. No foreigner who
should happen to be present at the
exhibition, would ever believe it was
formed out of the loppings and ex-
crescences of the tragedy itself. You
may entitle it, *The Grave-Diggers ;
with the pleasant Humours of Osrick,
the Danish Macaroni.*' *Garrick Corres.*
i. 451.

[4] A line of an epigram in the *Life
of Virgil*, ascribed to Donatus.

Pindar which it accompanied. I am always glad to find myself not forgotten ; and to be forgotten by you would give me great uneasiness. My northern friends have never been unkind to me : I have from you, dear Sir, testimonies of affection, which I have not often been able to excite ; and Dr. Beattie rates the testimony which I was desirous of paying to his merit, much higher than I should have thought it reasonable to expect.

' I have heard of your masquerade [1]. What says your synod to such innovations ? I am not studiously scrupulous, nor do I think a masquerade either evil in itself, or very likely to be the occasion of evil ; yet as the world thinks it a very licentious relaxation of manners, I would not have been one of the *first* masquers in a country where no masquerade had ever been before [2].

' A new edition of my great Dictionary is printed, from a copy which I was persuaded to revise ; but having made no preparation, I was able to do very little. Some superfluities I have expunged, and some faults I have corrected, and here and there have scattered a remark ; but the main fabrick of the work remains as it was. I had looked very little into it since I wrote it, and, I think, I found it full as often better, as worse, than I expected.

' Baretti and Davies have had a furious quarrel [3] ; a quarrel, I think, irreconcileable. Dr. Goldsmith has a new comedy, which is expected in the spring. No name is yet given it [4]. The chief diversion arises

[1] Given by a lady at Edinburgh. BOSWELL. ⟨See App. B, p. 497.⟩

[2] There had been masquerades in Scotland ; but not for a very long time. BOSWELL. Johnson had no doubt seen an account of the masquerade in the *Gent. Mag.* for January, p. 43. It is stated there that ' it was the first masquerade ever seen in Scotland.' Boswell appeared as a Dumb Conjurer.

[3] Mrs. Thrale recorded in 1776, after her quarrel with Baretti :—' I had occasion to talk of him with Tom Davies, who spoke with horror of his ferocious temper ; " and yet," says I, " there is great sensibility about Baretti : I have seen tears often stand in his eyes." " Indeed," replies Davies, " I should like to have seen that sight vastly, when—even butchers weep." ' Hayward's *Piozzi* (ed. 2), i. 108. Davies said of Goldsmith :—' He, least of all mankind, approved Baretti's conversation ; he considered him as an insolent, overbearing foreigner.' Davies, in the same passage, speaks of Baretti as ' this unhappy Italian.' Davies's *Garrick*, ii. 168. As this was published in Baretti's life-time, the man could scarcely have been so ferocious as he was described.

[4] ' There were but a few days left before the comedy was to be acted, and no name had been found for it. " We are all in labour," says Johnson, whose labour of kindness had been untiring throughout, " for a name to Goldy's play." [See *post*, v. 308.] What now stands as the second title, *The Mistakes of a Night*, was originally the only one ; but it was thought undignified for a comedy. *The Old House a New Inn* was suggested in place of it, but dismissed as awkward. Sir Joshua offered a much

from a stratagem by which a lover is made to mistake his future father-in-law's house for an inn. This, you see, borders upon farce. The dialogue is quick and gay, and the incidents are so prepared as not to seem improbable.

' I am sorry that you lost your cause of Intromission, because I yet think the arguments on your side unanswerable. But you seem, I think, to say that you gained reputation even by your defeat; and reputation you will daily gain, if you keep Lord Auchinleck's precept in your mind, and endeavour to consolidate in your mind a firm and regular system of law, instead of picking up occasional fragments.

' My health seems in general to improve; but I have been troubled for many weeks with a vexatious catarrh, which is sometimes sufficiently distressful. I have not found any great effects from bleeding and physick; and am afraid, that I must expect help from brighter days and softer air.

' Write to me now and then; and whenever any good befalls you, make haste to let me know it, for no one will rejoice at it more than, dear Sir,

' Your most humble servant,

' London, Feb. 24, 1773.'   ' SAM. JOHNSON.'

' You continue to stand very high in the favour of Mrs. Thrale.'

While a former edition of my work was passing through the press, I was unexpectedly favoured with a packet from Philadelphia, from Mr. James Abercrombie, a gentleman of that country, who is pleased to honour me with very high praise of my ' Life of Dr. Johnson.' To have the fame of my illustrious friend, and his faithful biographer, echoed from the New World is extremely flattering; and my grateful acknowledgments shall be wafted across the Atlantick. Mr. Abercrombie has politely conferred on me a considerable additional obligation, by transmitting to me copies of two letters from Dr. Johnson to American gentlemen. ' Gladly, Sir, (says he,) would I have sent

better name to Goldsmith, saying, "You ought to call it *The Belle's Stratagem*, and if you do not I will damn it." This name was still under discussion . . . when Goldsmith, in whose ear perhaps a line of Dryden's lingered, hit upon *She Stoops to Conquer*.' Forster's *Goldsmith*, ii. 337, and Northcote's *Reynolds*, i. 285. ⟨The passage which it is suggested was remembered by Goldsmith was, doubtless:

' Th' offending Lover, when he lowest lies,
Submits, to conquer, and but kneels to rise.' (*Amphitryon*, iii.)⟩
In Chesterfield's *Letters*, ii. 107 the lover is ' prostrate ' and the last line is given,
' But stoops to conquer, and but kneels to rise.'
⟨See App. B, p. 498.⟩

you the originals ; but being the only relicks of the kind in America, they are considered by the possessors of such inestimable value, that no possible consideration would induce them to part with them. In some future publication of yours relative to that great and good man, they may perhaps be thought worthy of insertion.'

' To Mr. B——d [1].

' Sir,

' That in the hurry of a sudden departure you should yet find leisure to consult my convenience, is a degree of kindness, and an instance of regard, not only beyond my claims, but above my expectation. You are not mistaken in supposing that I set a high value on my American friends, and that you should confer a very valuable favour upon me by giving me an opportunity of keeping myself in their memory.

' I have taken the liberty of troubling you with a packet, to which I wish a safe and speedy conveyance, because I wish a safe and speedy voyage to him that conveys it. I am, Sir,

' Your most humble servant,
' Sam. Johnson.'

' London, Johnson's-court,
Fleet-street, March 4, 1773.'

' To the Reverend Mr. White [2].

' Dear Sir,

' Your kindness for your friends accompanies you across the Atlantick. It was long since observed by Horace [3], that no ship could leave care behind ; you have been attended in your voyage by other [a] powers,—by benevolence and constancy ; and I hope care did not often shew her face in their company.

' I received the copy of Rasselas [4]. The impression is not magnificent, but it flatters an authour, because the printer seems to have expected that it would be scattered among the people. The little book has

a better *orig.* (*Letters*, No. 298.).

[1] This gentleman, who now resides in America in a publick character of considerable dignity, desired that his name might not be transcribed at full length. Boswell. ⟨See App. B, p. 498.⟩

[2] Now Doctor White, and Bishop of the Episcopal Church in Pennsylvania. During his first visit to England in 1771, as a candidate for holy orders, he was several times in company with Dr. Johnson, who expressed a wish to see the edition of his Rasselas, which Dr. White told him had been printed in America. Dr. White, on his return, immediately sent him a copy. Boswell. ⟨See App. B, p. 499.⟩

[3] Horace. *Odes*, iii. 1. 34.

[4] ⟨See App. B, p. 499.⟩

been well received, and is translated into Italian [1], French [2], German, and Dutch [3]. It has now one honour more by an American edition.

'I know not that much has happened since your departure that can engage your curiosity. Of all publick transactions the whole world is now informed by the news-papers. Opposition seems to despond ; and the dissenters, though they have taken advantage of unsettled times, and a government much enfeebled, seem not likely to gain any immunities [4].

'Dr. Goldsmith has a new comedy in rehearsal at Covent-Garden, to which the manager predicts ill success [5]. I hope he will be mistaken. I think it deserves a very kind reception.

[1] ⟨See App. B, p. 499.⟩

[2] Malone had the following from Baretti :—' Baretti made a translation of *Rasselas* into French. . . . He never, however, could satisfy himself with the translation of the first sentence, which is uncommonly lofty. Mentioning this to Johnson, the latter said, after thinking two or three minutes, " Well, take up the pen, and if you can understand my pronunciation, I will see what I can do." He then dictated the sentence to the translator, which proved admirable, and was immediately adopted.' Prior's *Malone*, p. 161. Baretti, in a MS. note on his copy of *Piozzi Letters*, i. 225, says :—' Johnson never wrote true French, but when he translated for me the first paragraph of his *Rassellas*.' That Johnson's French was faulty, is shown by his letters in that language. *Ante*, ii. 82, and *post*, ii. 404. ⟨See App. B, p. 499.⟩

[3] ⟨For translations into these and other languages see Courtney, *Bibliography*, pp. 95-7, and *post*, App. B, p. 500. I find no record of a Dutch translation so early as 1773.⟩

[4] A motion in the House of Commons for a committee to consider of the subscription to the Thirty-nine Articles had, on Feb. 23 of this year, been rejected by 159 to 67. *Parl. Hist.* xvii. 742-58. A bill for the relief of Protestant Dissenters that passed the House of Commons by 65 to 14 on March 25, was rejected in the House of Lords by 86 to 28 on April 2. *Ib.* p. 790.

[5] See *post*, iii. 321, where Johnson says that ' Colman [the manager] was prevailed on at last by much solicitation, nay, a kind of force, to bring it on.' Mr. Forster (*Life of Goldsmith*, ii. 334-6) writes :—' The actors and actresses had taken their tone from the manager. Gentleman Smith threw up Young Marlow ; Woodward refused Tony Lumpkin ; Mrs. Abington . . . declined Miss Hardcastle [Gibbs points out, Goldsmith's *Wks.* ii. 291, that Mrs. Abington was not one of Colman's Company] ; and, in the teeth of his own misgivings, Colman could not contest with theirs. . . . He would not suffer a new scene to be painted for the play, he refused to furnish even a new dress, and was careful to spread his forebodings as widely as he could.' The play met with the greatest success. ' There was a new play by Dr. Goldsmith last night, which succeeded prodigiously,' wrote Walpole (*Letters*, viii. 256). The laugh was turned against the doubting manager. Ten days after the play had been brought out, Johnson wrote to Mrs. Thrale :—' C— is so distressed with abuse about his play, that he has solicited Goldsmith to *take him off the rack of the newspapers.*' *Letters*, No. 304. See *post*, iv. 325, for Mr. Steevens's account. ⟨See also App. B, p. 500.⟩

' I shall soon publish a new edition of my large Dictionary ; I have
been persuaded to revise it, and have mended some faults, but added
little to its usefulness.

' No book has been published since your departure, of which much
notice is taken. Faction only fills the town with pamphlets, and greater
subjects are forgotten in the noise of discord.

' Thus have I written, only to tell you how little I have to tell. Of
myself I can only add, that having been afflicted many weeks with a
very troublesome cough, I am now recovered.

' I take the liberty which you give me of troubling you with a letter †,
of which you will please to fill up the direction. I am, Sir,

' Your most humble servant,

' SAM. JOHNSON.'

' Johnson's-court, Fleet-street,
  London, March 4, 1773.'

On Saturday, April 3, the day after my arrival in London this
year, I went to his house late in the evening, and sat with Mrs.
Williams till he came home. I found in the London Chronicle,
Dr. Goldsmith's apology ¹ to the publick for beating Evans, a
bookseller, on account of a paragraph in a news-paper published
by him, which Goldsmith thought impertinent to him and to a
lady of his acquaintance ². The apology was written so much in
Dr. Johnson's manner, that both Mrs. Williams and I supposed
it to be his ; but when he came home, he soon undeceived us.
When he said to Mrs. Williams, ' Well, Dr. Goldsmith's *manifesto*
has got into your paper ³ ; ' I asked him if Dr. Goldsmith had

¹ It was anything but an apology,
unless *apology* is used in its old
meaning of *defence*.

² Nine days after *She Stoops to
Conquer* was brought out, a vile libel,
written, it is believed, by Kenrick
(*ante*, i. 497), was published by Evans
in *The London Packet*. The libeller
dragged in one of the Miss Hornecks,
' the Jessamy Bride ' of Goldsmith's
verse. Goldsmith, believing Evans
had written the libel, struck him with
his cane. The blow was returned, for
Evans was a strong man. He ' in-
dicted Goldsmith for the assault, but
consented to a compromise on his
paying fifty pounds to a Welsh charity.
. . . All the papers abused the . . . poet,
and all of them steadily turned aside

from the real point in issue. At last he
stated it himself ; in an *Address to the
Public* which was published in the
Daily Advertiser of the 31st of March.'
Forster's *Goldsmith*, ii. 347–351. The
libel is given in Goldsmith's *Misc.
Works* (1801), i. 103. ⟨See *ib.* 105 for
Goldsmith's ' unfinished relation of the
adventure '. For Thomas Evans, see
Nichols, *Lit. Anecd.* iii. 720. See also
App. B, p. 501.⟩

³ ' *Your* paper,' I suppose, because
the *Chronicle* was taken in at Bolt
Court. *Ante*, ii. 103. ⟨The ' manifesto ' was printed in the *London
Chronicle* for April 1–3.⟩

† ⟨It was addressed to the Rev.
William Samuel Johnson, LL.D. See
Johnson's *Letters*, No. 299.⟩

written it, with an air that made him see I suspected it was his, though subscribed by Goldsmith. JOHNSON. ' Sir, Dr. Goldsmith would no more have asked me to write such a thing as that for him, than he would have asked me to feed him with a spoon, or to do any thing else that denoted his imbecility. I as much believe that he wrote it, as if I had seen him do it. Sir, had he shewn it to any one friend, he would not have been allowed to publish it. He has, indeed, done it very well ; but it is a foolish thing well done. I suppose he has been so much elated with the success of his new comedy, that he has thought every thing that concerned him must be of importance to the publick.' BOSWELL. ' I fancy, Sir, this is the first time that he has been engaged in such an adventure.' JOHNSON. ' Why, Sir, I believe it is the first time he has *beat* ; he may have *been beaten* before [1]. This, Sir, is a new plume to him.'

I mentioned Sir John Dalrymple's ' Memoirs of Great-Britain and Ireland,' and his discoveries to the prejudice of Lord Russel and Algernon Sydney. JOHNSON. ' Why, Sir, every body who had just notions of government thought them rascals before. It is well that all mankind now see them to be rascals.' BOSWELL. ' But, Sir, may not those discoveries be true without their being rascals ? ' JOHNSON. ' Consider, Sir ; would any of them have been willing to have had it known that they intrigued with France ? Depend upon it, Sir, he who does what he is afraid should be known, has something rotten about him. This Dalrymple seems to be an honest fellow [2] ; for he tells equally what makes against both sides. But nothing can be poorer than his mode of writing:[a] it is the mere bouncing of a school-boy. Great He ! but greater She ! and such stuff [3].'

[a] writing: 1: writing; 2: writing, 3.

[1] See Forster's *Goldsmith*, i. 265, for a possible explanation of this sarcasm.

[2] Walpole is violent against Dalrymple and the King. ' What must,' he says, ' be the designs of this reign when George III. encourages a Jacobite wretch to hunt in France for materials for blackening the heroes who withstood the enemies of Protestantism and liberty ! ' *Journal of the Reign of George III*, i. 286.

[3] Mr. Hallam pointed out to Mr. Croker that Johnson was speaking of Dalrymple's description of the parting of Lord and Lady Russell :— ' With a deep and noble silence ; with a long and fixed look, in which respect and affection, unmingled with passion, were expressed ; Lord and Lady Russell parted for ever ; he great in this last act of his life, but she greater.' Dalrymple's *Memoirs*, i. 31. See *post*, ii. 237, for ' the foppery

I could not agree with him in this criticism; for though Sir John Dalrymple's style is not regularly formed in any respect, and one cannot help smiling sometimes at his affected *grandiloquence*, there is in his writing a pointed vivacity, and much of a gentlemanly spirit.

At Mr. Thrale's, in the evening, he repeated his usual paradoxical declamation against action in publick speaking [1]. ' Action can have no effect upon reasonable minds. It may augment noise, but it never can enforce argument. If you speak to a dog, you use action; you hold up your hand thus, because he is a brute; and in proportion as men are removed from brutes, action will have the less influence upon them.' MRS. THRALE. ' What then, Sir, becomes of Demosthenes's saying † ? " Action, action, action ! " ' JOHNSON. ' Demosthenes, Madam, spoke to an assembly of brutes; to a barbarous people [2].'

I thought it extraordinary, that he should deny the power of rhetorical action upon human nature, when it is proved by innumerable facts in all stages of society. Reasonable beings are not solely reasonable. They have fancies which may be pleased, passions which may be roused.

Lord Chesterfield being mentioned, Johnson remarked, that almost all of that celebrated nobleman's witty sayings were puns [3]. He, however, allowed the merit of good wit to his Lordship's saying of Lord Tyrawley [4] and himself, when both very old and infirm : ' Tyrawley and I have been dead these two years; but we don't choose to have it known.'

He talked with approbation of an intended edition of ' The

of Dalrymple '; and *post*, v. 403, for Johnson's imitation of Dalrymple's style.

[1] See *ante*, i. 334.

[2] See *ante*, ii. 171.

[3] Walpole says :—' It was not Chesterfield's fault if he had not wit; nothing exceeded his efforts in that point; and though they were far from producing the wit, they at least amply yielded the applause he aimed at.' *Memoirs of the Reign of George II*, 1846, i. 51.

[4] A curious account of Tyrawley is given in Walpole's *Reign of George II*,

iii. 108. He had been Ambassador at Lisbon, and he ' even affected not to know where the House of Commons was.' Walpole says (*Letters*, i. 308, note) that ' Pope has mentioned his and another Ambassador's seraglios in one of his Imitations of Horace.' He refers to the lines in the *Imitations*, i. 6. 120 :—

' Go dine with Chartres, in each vice
    outdo
K—l's lewd cargo, or Ty—y's crew.'
Kinnoul and Tyrawley, says Walpole, are meant.

† ⟨See App. B, p. 501.⟩

Spectator,' with notes ; two volumes of which had been prepared by a gentleman eminent in the literary world, and the materials which he had collected for the remainder had been transferred to another hand [1]. He observed, that all works which describe manners, require notes in sixty or seventy years, or less ; and told us, he had communicated all he knew that could throw light upon ' The Spectator.' He said, ' Addison had made his Sir Andrew Freeport a true Whig, arguing against giving charity to beggars, and throwing out other such ungracious sentiments ; but that he had thought better, and made amends by making him found an hospital for decayed farmers [2].' He called for the volume of ' The Spectator ', in which that account is contained, and read it aloud to us. He read so well, that every thing acquired additional weight and grace from his utterance [3].

The conversation having turned on modern imitations of ancient ballads, and some one having praised their simplicity, he treated them with that ridicule which he always displayed when this [a] subject was mentioned [4].

[a] this 1: that 2, 3.

[1] Mr. Chalmers (who, himself, has ably performed this task) informs me, that the first of these gentlemen was Dr. Percy, and the second Dr. John Calder. CROKER. ⟨See App. B, p. 501.⟩

[2] Sir Andrew Freeport, after giving money to some importunate beggars, says :—' I ought to give to an hospital of invalids, to recover as many useful subjects as I can ; but I shall bestow none of my bounties upon an alms-house of idle people ; and for the same reason I should not think it a reproach to me if I had withheld my charity from those common beggars.' *The Spectator*, No. 232. This paper is not by Addison. In No. 549, which is by Addison, Sir Andrew is made to found ' an almshouse for a dozen superannuated husbandmen.' I have before (ii. 119) contrasted the opinions of Johnson and Fielding as to alms-giving. A more curious contrast is afforded by the following passage in *Tom Jones*, book i. chap. iii :—' I have told my reader, that Mr. All-worthy inherited a large fortune ; that

he had a good heart, and no family. Hence, doubtless, it will be concluded by many, that he lived like an honest man, owed no one a shilling, took nothing but what was his own, kept a good house, entertained his neigh-bours with a hearty welcome at his table, and was charitable to the poor, i.e. to those who had rather beg than work, by giving them the offals from it ; that he dy'd immensely rich, and built an hospital.'

[3] Boswell says (*post*, v. 115) :— ' His recitation was grand and affect-ing, and, as Sir Joshua Reynolds has observed to me, had no more tone than it should have.' Mrs. Piozzi (*Anec.* p. 302 : John. Misc. i. 347) writes :—' His manner of repeating deserves to be described, though at the same time it defeats all power of description ; but whoever once heard him repeat an ode of Horace, would be long before they could endure to hear it repeated by another.' See *ante*, ii. 92, note 4.

[4] ' Some of the old legendary stories

He disapproved of introducing scripture phrases into secular discourse. This seemed to me a question of some difficulty. A scripture expression may be used, like a highly classical phrase, to produce an instantaneous strong impression ; and it may be done without being at all improper. Yet I own there is danger, that applying the language of our sacred book to ordinary subjects may tend to lessen our reverence for it. If therefore it be introduced at all, it should be with very great caution.

On Thursday, April 8, I sat a good part of the evening with him, but he was very silent. He said, ' Burnet's " History of his own Times " is very entertaining [1]. The style, indeed, is mere chit-chat [2]. I do not believe that Burnet intentionally lyed ; but he was so much prejudiced, that he took no pains to find out the truth. He was like a man who resolves to regulate his time by a certain watch ; but will not inquire whether the watch is right or not [3].'

Though he was not disposed to talk, he was unwilling that I should leave him ; and when I looked at my watch, and told him

put in verse by modern writers pro-voked him to caricature them thus one day at Streatham . . .

The tender infant, meek and mild,
   Fell down upon the stone ;
The nurse took up the squealing child,
   But still the child squeal'd on.

A famous ballad also, beginning *Rio verde, Rio verde*, when I commended the translation of it, he said he could do it better himself—as thus :

Glassy water, glassy water,
   Down whose current clear and
      strong,
Chiefs confus'd in mutual slaughter,
   Moor and Christian roll along.

But, Sir, said I, this is not ridiculous at all. " Why no (replied he), why should I always write ridiculously ? " ' Piozzi's *Anec.* p. 65 : John. Misc. i. 192. See *ante*, ii. 136, note 4. Neither Boswell nor Mrs. Piozzi mentions Percy by name as the subject of Johnson's ridicule.

[1] See *post*, v. 285.

[2] Rogers (*Table-Talk*, p. 88) said

that ' Fox considered Burnet's style to be perfect.'

[3] Johnson (*Milton*, 101) quotes ' Dalrymple's observation, who says, " that whenever Burnet's narrations are examined, he appears to be mis-taken." ' Bolingbroke (*Study Hist.*, 1752, ii. 172) wrote of party pamphlets and histories :—' Read them with suspicion, for they deserve to be sus-pected: pay no regard to the epithets given, nor to the judgments passed ; neglect all declamation, weigh the reasoning, and advert to fact. With such precautions, even Burnet's his-tory may be of some use.' Walpole, noticing an attack on Burnet, says (*Letters*, x. 118) :—' It shows his enemies are not angry at his telling falsehoods, but the truth . . . I will tell you what was said on the appear-ance of Burnet's *History*, by one whose testimony you yourself will not dis-pute. . . . That confessor said, " Damn him, he has told a great deal of truth, but where the devil did he learn it ? " This was Saint Atterbury's testimony.'

it was twelve o'clock, he cried, ' What's that to you and me ? ' and ordered Frank to tell Mrs. Williams that we were coming to drink tea with her, which we did. It was settled that we should go to church together next day.

On the 9th of April, being Good Friday, I breakfasted with him on tea and cross-buns [1] ; *Doctor* Levet, as Frank called him, making the tea. He carried me with him to the church of St. Clement Danes, where he had his seat ; and his behaviour was, as I had imaged to myself, solemnly devout [2]. I never shall forget the tremulous earnestness with which he pronounced the aweful petition in the Litany : ' In the hour of death, and at [3] the day of judgement, good LORD deliver us.'

We went to church both in the morning and evening. In the interval between the two services we did not dine ; but he read in the Greek New Testament, and I turned over several of his books.

In Archbishop Laud's Diary, I found the following passage, which I read to Dr. Johnson :

' 1623. February 1, Sunday. I stood by the most illustrious Prince Charles [4], at dinner. He was then very merry, and talked occasionally of many things with his attendants. Among other things, he said, that if he were necessitated to take any particular profession of life, he could not be a lawyer, adding his reasons : " I cannot (saith he,) defend a bad, nor yield in a good cause." '

JOHNSON. ' Sir, this is false reasoning ; because every cause has a bad side [5] : and a lawyer is not overcome, though the cause which he has endeavoured to support be determined against him.'

I told him that Goldsmith had said to me a few days before, ' As I take my shoes from the shoemaker, and my coat from the

---

[1] The cross-buns were for Boswell and Levet. Johnson recorded (*Pr. and Med.* ¶ 99) :—' On this whole day I took nothing of nourishment but one cup of tea without milk, but the fast was very inconvenient. Towards night I grew fretful, and impatient, unable to fix my mind or govern my thoughts.'

[2] It is curious to compare with this Johnson's own record :—' I found the service not burthensome nor tedious, though I could not hear the lessons. I hope in time to take pleasure in public Worship.' *Pr. and Med.* ¶ 99.

[3] In the original *in*.

[4] Afterwards Charles I. BOSWELL.

[5] See *ante*, ii. 47.

taylor, so I take my religion from the priest.' I regretted this loose way of talking. JOHNSON. ' Sir, he knows nothing ; he has made up his mind about nothing ¹.'

To my great surprize he asked me to dine with him on Easter-day. I never supposed that he had a dinner at his house ; for I had not then heard of any one of his friends having been entertained at his table. He told me, ' I generally have a meat pye on Sunday : it is baked at a publick oven, which is very properly allowed, because one man can attend it ; and thus the advantage is obtained of not keeping servants from church to dress dinners ².'

April 11, being Easter-Sunday, after having attended Divine Service at St. Paul's, I repaired to Dr. Johnson's. I had gratified my curiosity much in dining with JEAN JACQUES ROUSSEAU ³, while he lived in the wilds of Neufchatel : I had as great a curiosity to dine with DR. SAMUEL JOHNSON, in the dusky recess of a court in Fleet-street. I supposed we should scarcely have knives and forks, and only some strange, uncouth, ill-drest dish : but I found every thing in very good order. We had no other company but Mrs. Williams and a young woman whom I did not know. As a dinner here was considered as a singular phænomenon, and as I was frequently interrogated on the subject, my readers may perhaps be desirous to know our bill of fare. Foote, I remember, in allusion to Francis, the *negro*, was willing to suppose that our repast was *black broth*. But the fact was, that we had a very good soup, a boiled leg of lamb and spinach, a veal pye, and a rice pudding ⁴.

---

¹ See *post*, iii. 252, where Johnson said :—' Goldsmith had no settled notions upon any subject ; so he talked always at random.'

² The next day Johnson recorded : —' I have had some nights of that quiet and continual sleep, which I had wanted till I had almost forgotten it.' *Pr. and Med.* ¶ 100.

³ See *ante*, ii. 11.

⁴ We have the following account of Johnson's kitchen in 1778 : ' Mr. T⟨hrale⟩.—" And pray who is clerk of your kitchen, sir ? " Dr. J.— " Why, sir, I am afraid there is none ;

a general anarchy prevails in my kitchen, as I am told by Mr. Levat, who says it is not now what it used to be ! " Mr. T.—" But how do you get your dinners drest ? " Dr. J.— " Why, De Mullin has the chief management of the kitchen ; but our roasting is not magnificent, for we have no jack." Mr. T.—" No jack ? Why, how do they manage without ? " Dr. J.—" Small joints, I believe, they manage with a string, and larger are done at the tavern. I have some thoughts (with a profound gravity) of buying a jack, because I think a jack

Of Dr. John Campbell, the authour, he said, ' He is a very inquisitive and a very able man, and a man of good religious principles, though I am afraid he has been deficient in practice. Campbell is radically right ; and we may hope, that in time there will be good practice [1].'

He owned that he thought Hawkesworth was one of his imitators [2], but he did not think Goldsmith was. Goldsmith, he said, had great merit. BOSWELL. ' But, Sir, he is much indebted to you for his getting so high in the publick estimation.' JOHNSON. ' Why, Sir, he has, perhaps, got *sooner* to it by his intimacy with me.'

Goldsmith, though his vanity often excited him to occasional competition, had a very high regard for Johnson, which he at this time expressed in the strongest manner in the Dedication of his comedy, entitled, ' She stoops to conquer [3].'

Johnson observed, that there were very few books printed in Scotland before the Union. He had seen a complete collection of them in the possession of the Hon. Archibald Campbell, a non-juring Bishop [4]. I wish this collection had been kept entire. Many of them are in the library of the Faculty of Advocates at Edinburgh. I told Dr. Johnson that I had some intention to write the life of the learned and worthy Thomas Ruddiman [5]. He said, ' I should take pleasure in helping you to do honour to him. But his farewell letter to the Faculty of Advocates, when he resigned the office of their Librarian, should have been in Latin.'

I put a question to him upon a fact in common life, which he

<hr>

is some credit to a house." Mr. T.— " Well, but you'll have a spit, too ? " Dr. J.—" No, sir, no ; that would be superfluous ; for we shall never use it ; if a jack is seen, a spit will be presumed ! " ' Mme. D'Arblay's *Diary*, i. 115.

[1] See *ante*, i. 418.

[2] See *ante*, i. 252.

[3] ' By inscribing this slight performance to you, I do not mean so much to compliment you as myself. It may do me some honour to inform the publick, that I have lived many years in intimacy with you. It may

serve the interests of mankind also to inform them, that the greatest wit may be found in a character, without impairing the most unaffected piety.' BOSWELL.

[4] See an account of this learned and respectable gentleman, and of his curious work on the *Middle State*, ' Journal of a Tour to the Hebrides,' 3d edit. p. 371. BOSWELL. *Post*, v. 357. See also *post*, iv. 286.

[5] See *ante*, i. 225, n. 2, for Boswell's projected works, and i. 211, for Ruddiman. ⟨George Chalmers published his *Life of Ruddiman* in 1794.⟩

could not answer, nor have I found any one else who could. What is the reason that women servants, though obliged to be at the expense of purchasing their own clothes, have much lower wages than men servants, to whom a great proportion of that article is furnished, and when in fact our female house servants work much harder than the male [1] ?

He told me,[a] that he had twelve or fourteen times attempted to keep a journal of his life, but never could persevere [2]. He advised me to do it. ' The great thing to be recorded, (said he), is the state of your own mind [3] ; and you should write down every thing that you remember, for you cannot judge at first what is good or bad ; and write immediately while the impression is fresh, for it will not be the same a week afterwards [4].'

I again solicited him to communicate to me the particulars of his early life. He said, ' You shall have them all for twopence. I hope you shall know a great deal more of me before you write my Life.' He mentioned to me this day many circumstances, which I wrote down when I went home, and have interwoven in the former part of this narrative.

On Tuesday, April 13, he and Dr. Goldsmith and I dined at General Oglethorpe's. Goldsmith expatiated on the common topick, that the race of our people was degenerated, and that this was owing to luxury. JOHNSON. ' Sir, in the first place, I doubt the fact [5]. I believe there are as many tall men in England

a *comma omitted* 2, 3.

[1] ' When the efficiency [of men and women] is equal, but the pay unequal, the only explanation that can be given is custom.' J. S. Mill's *Political Economy*, Book ii. ch. xiv. § 5.

[2] The day before he told Boswell this he had recorded:—' My general resolution to which I humbly implore the help of God is to methodise my life ; to resist sloth. I hope from this time to keep a Journal.' *Pr. and Med.* ¶ 100. ⟨On nine other occasions he recorded the resolution, or the hope, to keep a journal. See *Ib.* ¶¶ 42, 43, 52, 66, 94, 104, 121, 139, 147. Cf. *Ib.* 48, where he resolves ' to write down his observations '.⟩ See *ante*, i. 433, and *post*, ii. 358.

[3] See *post*, iii. 228, where Johnson says :—' A man loves to review his

own mind. That is the use of a diary, or journal.'

[4] ' He who has not made the experiment, or who is not accustomed to require rigorous accuracy from himself, will scarcely believe how much a few hours take from certainty of knowledge, and distinctness of imagery. . . . To this dilatory notation must be imputed the false relations of travellers, where there is no imaginable motive to deceive. They trusted to memory, what cannot be trusted safely but to the eye, and told by guess what a few hours before they had known with certainty.' Johnson's *Journey Western Isl.* (1924), p. 133.

[5] Goldsmith, in his dedication to Reynolds of the *Deserted Village*, refers no doubt to Johnson's opinion

now, as ever there were. But, secondly, supposing the stature of our people to be diminished, that is not owing to luxury ; for, Sir, consider to how very small a proportion of our people luxury can reach. Our soldiery, surely, are not luxurious, who live on six-pence a day [1] ; and the same remark will apply to almost all the other classes. Luxury, so far as it reaches the poor, will do good to the race of people ; it will strengthen and multiply them. Sir, no nation was ever hurt by luxury ; for, as I said before, it can reach but to a very few. I admit that the great increase of commerce and manufactures hurts the military spirit of a people ; because it produces a competition for something else than martial honours,—a competition for riches. It also hurts the bodies of the people ; for you will observe, there is no man who works at any particular trade, but you may know him from his appearance to do so. One part or other of his body being more used than the rest, he is in some degree deformed : but, Sir, that is not luxury. A tailor sits cross-legged ; but that is not luxury. GOLDSMITH. ' Come, you're just going to the same place by another road.' JOHNSON. ' Nay, Sir, I say that is not *luxury*. Let us take a walk from Charing-cross to Whitechapel, through, I suppose, the greatest series of shops in the world ; what is there in any of these shops, (if you except gin-shops,) that can do any human being any harm ? ' GOLDSMITH. ' Well, Sir, I'll accept your challenge. The very next shop to Northumberland-house is a pickle-shop.' JOHNSON. ' Well, Sir : do we not know that

of luxury. He writes :—' I know you will object (and indeed *several of our best and wisest friends* concur in the opinion) that the depopulation it de-plores is no where to be seen, and the disorders it laments are only to be found in the poet's own imagination. . . . In regretting the depopulation of the country, I inveigh against the in-crease of our luxuries ; and here also I expect the shout of modern poli-ticians against me. For twenty or thirty years past, it has been the fashion to consider luxury as one of the greatest national advantages.' See *post*, iii. 55, 291.

[1] Johnson, in his *Parl. Debates* (*Works*, x. 418), makes General Handasyd say :—' The whole pay of a foot soldier is sixpence a-day, of which he is to pay fourpence to his landlord for his diet, or, what is very nearly the same, to carry fourpence daily to the market. . . . Twopence a-day is all that a soldier has to lay out upon cleanliness and decency, and with which he is likewise to keep his arms in order, and to supply himself with some part of his clothing. If, sir, after these deductions, he can, from twopence a-day, procure himself the means of enjoying a few happy moments in the year with his com-panions over a cup of ale, is not his economy much more to be envied than his luxury ? '

a maid can in one afternoon make pickles sufficient to serve a whole family for a year ? nay, that five pickle-shops can serve all the kingdom ? Besides, Sir, there is no harm done to any body by the making of pickles, or the eating of pickles.'

We drank tea with the ladies ; and Goldsmith sung Tony Lumpkin's song in his comedy, ' She stoops to conquer,' and a very pretty one, to an Irish tune [1], which he had designed for Miss Hardcastle ; but as Mrs. Bulkeley, who played the part, could not sing, it was left out. He afterwards wrote it down for me, by which means it was preserved, and now appears amongst his poems [2]. Dr. Johnson, in his way home, stopped at my lodgings in Piccadilly, and sat with me, drinking tea a second time, till a late hour.

I told him that Mrs. Macaulay said, she wondered how he could reconcile his political principles with his moral ; his notions of inequality and subordination with wishing well to the happiness of all mankind, who might live so agreeably, had they all their portions of land, and none to domineer over another. JOHNSON. ' Why, Sir, I reconcile my principles very well, because mankind are happier in a state of inequality and subordination [3]. Were they to be in this pretty state of equality, they would soon degenerate into brutes ;—they would become Monboddo's nation [4] ;—their tails would grow. Sir, all would be losers, were all to work for all :—they would have no intellectual improvement. All intellectual improvement arises from leisure : all leisure arises from one working for another.'

---

[1] The humours of Ballamagairy. BOSWELL.

[2] ' Ah me ! when shall I marry me ? Lovers are plenty ; but fail to relieve me.
He, fond youth, that could carry me, Offers to love, but means to deceive me.
But I will rally, and combat the ruiner : Not a look, not a smile shall my passion discover.
She that gives all to the false one pursuing her, Makes but a penitent—loses a lover.'

Boswell, in a letter which he published in *Lond. Mag.* June, 1774, xliii. 295, with the song, says :—'The tune is a pretty Irish air, called *The Humours of Balamagairy*, to which, he told me, he found it very difficult to adapt words ; but he has succeeded very happily in these few lines. As I could sing the tune, and was fond of them, he was so good as to give me them. . . . I preserve this little relic, in his own handwriting, with an affectionate care.' ⟨The MS. is no longer in the possession of the Boswell family, but was sold, with the other Boswell MSS., by Lord Talbot de Malahide to Lieut.-Col. R. H. Isham in 1927.⟩

[3] See *ante*, i. 408, and *post*, iii. 26.

[4] See *ante*, ii. 74.

Talking of the family of Stuart [1], he said, ' It should seem that the family at present on the throne has now established as good a right as the former family, by the long consent of the people ; and that to disturb this right might be considered as culpable. At the same time I own, that it is a very difficult question, when considered with respect to the house of Stuart. To oblige people to take oaths as to the disputed right, is wrong. I know not whether I could take them : but I do not blame those who do.' So conscientious and so delicate was he upon this subject, which has occasioned so much clamour against him.

Talking of law cases, he said, ' The English reports, in general, are very poor : only the half of what has been said is taken down ; and of that half, much is mistaken. Whereas, in Scotland, the arguments on each side are deliberately put in writing, to be considered by the Court. I think a collection of your cases upon subjects of importance, with the opinions of the Judges upon them, would be valuable.'

On Thursday, April 15, I dined with him and Dr. Goldsmith at General Paoli's. We found here Signor Martinelli †, of Florence, authour of a History of England in Italian, printed at London.

I spoke of Allan Ramsay's ' Gentle Shepherd,' in the Scottish dialect, as the best pastoral that had ever been written ; not only abounding with beautiful rural imagery, and just and pleasing sentiments, but being a real picture of manners ; and I offered to teach Dr. Johnson to understand it. ' No, Sir, (said he,) I won't learn it. You shall retain your superiority by my not knowing it.'

This brought on a question whether one man is lessened by another's acquiring an equal degree of knowledge with him [2]. Johnson asserted the affirmative. I maintained that the position might be true in those kinds of knowledge which produce wisdom, power, and force, so as to enable one man to have the government of others ; but that a man is not in any degree lessened by others knowing as well as he what ends in mere pleasure :— eating fine fruits, drinking delicious wines, reading exquisite poetry.

---

[1] See *ante*, i. 429.   † ⟨See App. B, p. 504.⟩
[2] See *ante*, ii. 169, for Johnson's ' half a guinea's worth of inferiority'.

The General observed, that Martinelli was a Whig. JOHNSON. 'I am sorry for it. It shows the spirit of the times : he is obliged to temporise.' BOSWELL. 'I rather think, Sir, that Toryism prevails in this reign.' JOHNSON. 'I know not why you should think so, Sir. You see your friend Lord Lyttelton [1], a nobleman, is obliged in his History to write the most vulgar Whiggism.'

An animated debate took place whether Martinelli should continue his History of England to the present day. GOLDSMITH. 'To be sure he should.' JOHNSON. 'No, Sir ; he would give great offence. He would have to tell of almost all the living great what they do not wish told.' GOLDSMITH. 'It may, perhaps, be necessary for a native to be more cautious ; but a foreigner who comes among us without prejudice, may be considered as holding the place of a Judge, and may speak his mind freely.' JOHNSON. 'Sir, a foreigner, when he sends a work from the press, ought to be on his guard against catching the errour and mistaken enthusiasm of the people among whom he happens to be.' GOLDSMITH. 'Sir, he wants only to sell his history, and to tell truth ; one an honest, the other a laudable motive.' JOHNSON. 'Sir, they are both laudable motives. It is laudable in a man to wish to live by his labours ; but he should write so as he may *live* by them, not so as he may be knocked on the head. I would advise him to be at Calais before he publishes his history of the present age. A foreigner who attaches himself to a political party in this country, is in the worst state that can be imagined : he is looked upon as a mere intermeddler. A native may do it from interest.' BOSWELL. 'Or principle.' GOLDSMITH. 'There are people who tell a hundred political lies every day, and are not hurt by it. Surely, then, one may tell truth with safety.' JOHNSON. 'Why, Sir, in the first place, he who tells a hundred lies has disarmed the force of his lies [2]. But besides ; a man had rather have a hundred lies told of him, than one truth which he does not wish should be

[1] ⟨Boswell printed a complimentary letter from Lyttelton in the third edition of his *Corsica*. See Boswell's *Letters*, No. 82, i. 148.⟩ See also *ante*, i. 256 ; ii. 38.

[2] Johnson has an interesting paper 'on lying' in *The Adventurer*, No. 50, which thus begins :—'When Aristotle was once asked, what a man could gain by uttering falsehoods ; he replied, "Not to be credited when he shall tell the truth." '

told.' GOLDSMITH. 'For my part, I'd tell truth, and shame the devil.' JOHNSON. 'Yes, Sir ; but the devil will be angry. I wish to shame the devil as much you do, but I should choose to be out of the reach of his claws.' GOLDSMITH. 'His claws can do you no harm, when you have the shield of truth.'

It having been observed that there was little hospitality in London ; JOHNSON. 'Nay, Sir, any man who has a name, or who has the power of pleasing, will be very generally invited in London. The man, Sterne, I have been told, has had engagements for three months [1].' GOLDSMITH. 'And a very dull fellow.' JOHNSON. 'Why no,[a] Sir [2].'

Martinelli told us, that for several years he lived much with Charles Townshend, and that he ventured to tell him he was a bad joker. JOHNSON. 'Why, Sir, thus much I can say upon the subject. One day he and a few more agreed to go and dine in the country, and each of them was to bring a friend in his carriage with him. Charles Townshend asked Fitzherbert to go with him, but told him, 'You must find somebody to bring you back : I can only carry you there.' Fitzherbert did not much like this arrangement. He however consented, observing sarcastically, ' It will do very well ; for then the same jokes will serve you in returning as in going [3].'

An eminent publick character [4] being mentioned ;—JOHNSON.

a Why no, 1 : Why, no, 2, 3.

[1] Johnson speaks of the past, for Sterne had been dead five years. Gray wrote on April 22, 1760 :— ' *Tristram Shandy* is still a greater object of admiration, the man as well as the book. One is invited to dinner, where he dines, a fortnight beforehand.' Gray's *Works*, ed. 1843, iii. 241.

[2] ' I was but once,' said Johnson, ' in Sterne's company, and then his only attempt at merriment consisted in his display of a drawing too indecently gross to have delighted even in a brothel.' Johnson's *Works* (1787), xi. 214.

[3] Townshend was not the man to make his jokes serve twice. Horace Walpole said of his *Champagne Speech*,—' It was Garrick writing and acting extempore scenes of Congreve.' *Memoirs of the Reign of*

George III, iii. 25. Sir G. Colebrooke says :—' When Garrick and Foote were present, he took the lead, and hardly allowed them an opportunity of showing their talents of mimicry, because he could excel them in their own art.' *Ib.* p. 101, note. ' " Perhaps," said Burke, " there never arose in this country, or in any country, a man of a more pointed and finished wit." ' Payne's *Burke*, i. 146.

[4] The ' eminent publick character ' is no doubt Burke, and the friend, as Mr. Croker suggests, probably Reynolds. See *post*, v. 36, for a like charge made by Johnson against Burke. Boswell commonly describes Burke as ' an eminent friend of ours ; ' but he could not do so as yet, for he first met him fifteen days later. (*Post*,

' I remember being present when he shewed himself to be so corrupted, or at least something so different from what I think right, as to maintain, that a member of parliament should go along with his party right or wrong. Now, Sir, this is so remote from native virtue, from scholastick virtue, that a good man must have undergone a great change before he can reconcile himself to such a doctrine. It is maintaining that you may lie to the publick ; for you lie when you call that right which you think wrong, or the reverse [1]. A friend of ours, who is too much an echo of that gentleman, observed, that a man who does not stick uniformly to a party, is only waiting to be bought. Why then, said I, he is only waiting to be what that gentleman is already.'

We talked of the King's coming to see Goldsmith's new play.—' I wish he would [2],' said Goldsmith ; adding, however, with an affected indifference, ' Not that it would do me the least good.' JOHNSON. ' Well then, Sir, let us say it would do *him* good, (laughing). No, Sir, this affectation will not pass ;— it is mighty idle. In such a state as ours, who would not wish to please the Chief Magistrate ? ' GOLDSMITH. ' I *do* wish to please him. I remember a line in Dryden,

>" And every poet is the monarch's friend."

It ought to be reversed.' JOHNSON. ' Nay, there are finer lines in Dryden on this subject :

>" For colleges on bounteous Kings depend,
>   And never rebel was to arts a friend [3]." '

General Paoli observed, that successful rebels might [4]. MARTIN-

---

ii. 240.) ⟨Sir James Mackintosh, Lord Wellesley, and Chalmers agreed with Croker that Burke and Sir Joshua were meant.⟩

[1] ' Party,' Burke wrote in 1770 (*Thoughts on the Present Discontents*), ' is a body of men united, for promoting by their joint endeavours the national interest, upon some particular principle in which they are all agreed. For my part, I find it impossible to conceive, that any one believes in his own politicks, or thinks them to be of any weight, who refuses to adopt the means of having them reduced into practice.' Payne's *Burke*, i. 86.

[2] On May 5, and again on Nov. 10, the play was commanded by the King and Queen. Prior's *Goldsmith*, ii. 394.

[3] *Absalom and Achitophel*, part i. l. 872.

[4] Paoli perhaps was thinking of himself. While he was still ' the successful rebel ' in Corsica, he had said to Boswell :—' The arts and sciences are like dress and ornament. You cannot expect them from us for

ELLI. 'Happy rebellions.' GOLDSMITH. 'We have no such phrase.' GENERAL PAOLI. 'But have you not the *thing*?' GOLDSMITH. 'Yes; all our *happy* revolutions. They have hurt our constitution, and will hurt it, till we mend it by another HAPPY REVOLUTION.'—I never before discovered that my friend Goldsmith had so much of the old prejudice in him.

General Paoli, talking of Goldsmith's new play, said, '*Il a fait un compliment très gracieux à une certaine grande dame*;' meaning a Duchess of the first rank [1].

I expressed a doubt whether Goldsmith intended it, in order that I might hear the truth from himself. It, perhaps, was not quite fair to endeavour to bring him to a confession, as he might not wish to avow positively his taking part against the Court. He smiled and hesitated. The General at once relieved him, by this beautiful image : '*Monsieur Goldsmith est comme la mer, qui jette des perles et beaucoup d'autres belle choses, sans s'en appercevoir.*' GOLDSMITH. '*Très bien dit, et très élégamment.*'

A person was mentioned, who it was said could take down in short hand the speeches in parliament with perfect exactness. JOHNSON. 'Sir, it is impossible. I remember one Angel, who came to me to write for him a Preface or Dedication to a book upon short hand [2], and he professed to write as fast as a man could speak. In order to try him, I took down a book, and read while he wrote ; and I favoured him, for I read more deliberately than usual. I had proceeded but a very little way, when he begged I would desist, for he could not follow me [3].' Hearing now for the first time of this Preface or Dedication, I said, ' What an expense, Sir, do you put us to in buying books,

some time. But come back twenty or thirty years hence, and we'll shew you arts and sciences.' Boswell's *Corsica*, p. 300.

[1] 'The Duke of Cumberland had been forbidden the Court on his marriage with . . . Mrs. Horton, a year before : but on the Duke of Gloucester's avowal of his marriage with . . . Lady Waldegrave, the King's indignation found vent in the Royal Marriage Act ; which was hotly opposed by the Whigs as an edict of tyranny . . .,

Goldsmith (perhaps for Burke's sake) helping to make it unpopular with the people. " We'll go to France," says Hastings to Miss Neville, " for there, even among slaves, the laws of marriage are respected." Said on the first night, this had directed repeated cheering . . . to the Duke of Gloucester, who sat in one of the boxes.' Forster's *Goldsmith*, ii. 358. See *ante*, ii. 152.

[2] ⟨See App. B, p. 504.⟩

[3] See *post*, iii. 270.

to which you have written Prefaces or Dedications.' JOHNSON. ' Why I have dedicated to the Royal Family all round ; that is to say, to the last generation of the Royal Family [1].' GOLDSMITH. ' And perhaps, Sir, not one sentence of wit in a whole Dedication.' JOHNSON. ' Perhaps not, Sir.' BOSWELL. ' What then is the reason for applying to a particular person to do that which any one may do as well ? ' JOHNSON. ' Why, Sir, one man has greater readiness at doing it than another.'

I spoke of Mr. Harris [2], of Salisbury, as being a very learned man, and in particular an eminent Grecian. JOHNSON. ' I am not sure of that. His friends give him out as such, but I know not who of his friends are able to judge of it.' GOLDSMITH. ' He is what is much better : he is a worthy humane man.' JOHNSON. ' Nay, Sir, that is not to the purpose of our argument [3] : that will as much prove that he can play upon the fiddle as well as Giardini, as that he is an eminent Grecian.' GOLDSMITH. ' The greatest musical performers have but small emoluments. Giardini, I am told, does not get above seven hundred a year.' JOHNSON. ' That is, indeed,[a] but little for a man to get, who does best that which so many endeavour to do.

[a] That is, indeed, 1 : That is indeed 2, 3.

[1] See *ante*, ii. 2.

[2] James Harris, father of the first Earl of Malmesbury, born 1709, died 1780. Two years later Boswell wrote to Temple : ' I am invited to a dinner . . . at Richard Owen Cambridge's where are to be Reynolds, Johnson, and Hermes Harris. " Do you think so ? said he. Most certainly, said I." Do you remember how I used to laugh at his style when we were in the Temple ? He thinks himself an ancient Greek from these little peculiarities, as the imitators of Shakspeare whom the Spectator mentions, thought they had done wonderfully when they had produced a line similar to

And so good morrow to ye good
    Master Lieutenant.'

Letters, No. 138, i. 220. It is not in the *Spectator*, but in *Martinus Scriblerus*, ch. ix (Swift's *Works*, 1824, xiii. 56),

that the imitators of Shakespeare are ridiculed. Harris got his name of Hermes from his *Hermes, or a Philosophical Inquiry concerning Universal Grammar*. Cradock (*Memoirs*, i. 208) says that, ' A gentleman applied to his friend to lend him some amusing book, and he recommended Harris's *Hermes*. On returning it, his friend asked him how he had been entertained. " Not much," he replied ; " he thought that all these imitations of *Tristram Shandy* fell far short of the original." ' See *post*, ii. 365 ; iii. 245 ; v. 377.

[3] Johnson suffers, in Cowper's epitaph on him, from the same kind of praise as Goldsmith gives Harris :—
' Whose verse may claim—grave, masculine, and strong,
    Superior praise to the mere poet's song.'
Cowper's *Poet. Works*, 1911, p. 363.

There is nothing, I think, in which the power of art is shown so much as in playing on the fiddle. In all other things we can do something at first. Any man will forge a bar of iron, if you give him a hammer ; not so well as a smith, but tolerably. A man will saw a piece of wood, and make a box, though a clumsy one ; but give him a fiddle and a fiddle-stick, and he can do nothing.'

On Monday, April 19, he called on me with Mrs. Williams, in Mr. Strahan's coach, and carried me out to dine with Mr. Elphinston ¹, at his academy at Kensington. A printer having acquired a fortune sufficient to keep his coach, was a good topick for the credit of literature ². Mrs. Williams said, that another printer, Mr. Hamilton, had not waited so long as Mr. Strahan, but had kept his coach several years sooner ³. JOHN-SON. ' He was in the right. Life is short. The sooner that a man begins to enjoy his wealth the better.'

Mr. Elphinston talked of a new book that was much admired, and asked Dr. Johnson if he had read it. JOHNSON. ' I have looked into it.' ' What (said Elphinston,) have you not read it through ? ' Johnson, offended at being thus pressed, and so obliged to own his cursory mode of reading, answered tartly, ' No, Sir ; do *you* read books *through* ⁴ ? '

He this day again defended duelling ⁵, and put his argument upon what I have ever thought the most solid basis ; that if publick war be allowed to be consistent with morality, private war must be equally so. Indeed we may observe what strained arguments are used, to reconcile war with the Christian religion.

---

¹ See *ante*, i. 210.

² Cave set up his coach about thirty years earlier (*ante*, i. 152, note 1). Dr. Franklin (*Writings*, 1907, ix. 262) wrote to Strahan in 1784 :—' I remember your observing once to me as we sat together in the House of Commons, that no two Journeymen Printers, within your Knowledge, had met with such Success in the World as ourselves. You were then at the head of your Profession, and soon afterwards became a Member of Parliament. I was an Agent for a few Provinces, and now act for them all.'

³ ' Hamilton made a large fortune out of Smollett's *History*.' Forster's *Goldsmith*, i. 149. He was also the proprietor of the *Critical Review*. ⟨Archibald Hamilton was for some time Strahan's manager. See Nichols, *Lit. Anecd.* iii. 398.⟩

⁴ See *ante*, i. 71, and *post*, iv. 308.

⁵ See *ante*, ii. 179, *post*, iv. 211, and v. 230. Horace Walpole wrote of the year 1773 :—' The rage of duelling had of late much revived, especially in Ireland, and many attempts were made in print and on the stage to curb so horrid and absurd a practice.'

But, in my opinion, it is exceedingly clear that duelling, having better reasons for its barbarous violence, is more justifiable than war, in which thousands go forth without any cause of personal quarrel, and massacre each other.

On Wednesday, April 21, I dined with him at Mr. Thrale's. A gentleman [1] attacked Garrick for being vain. JOHNSON. ' No wonder, Sir, that he is vain ; a man who is perpetually flattered in every mode that can be conceived. So many bellows have blown the fire, that one wonders he is not by this time become a cinder.' BOSWELL. ' And such bellows too. Lord Mansfield with his cheeks like to burst : Lord Chatham like an Æolus. I have read such notes from them to him, as were enough to turn his head [2].' JOHNSON. ' True. When he whom every body else flatters, flatters me, I then am truly happy.' MRS. THRALE. ' The sentiment is in Congreve, I think.' JOHNSON. ' Yes, Madam, in " The Way of the World : "

" If there's delight in love, 'tis when I see
    That heart which others bleed for, bleed for me [3]."

No, Sir, I should not be surprised though Garrick chained the ocean, and lashed the winds.' BOSWELL. ' Should it not be, Sir, lashed the ocean and chained the winds ? ' JOHNSON. ' No, Sir ; recollect the original :

" *In Corum atque Eurum solitus sævire flagellis*
    Barbarus, Æolio nunquam hoc in carcere passos,
    Ipsum compedibus qui vinxerat Ennosigæum [4]." '

Journal of the Reign of George III, i. 282.

[1] ⟨Murphy. On the 28th he attacked his acting and abused him to such an extent that Boswell ' was shocked to hear him.' See *Boswell Papers*, vi. 120, 125.⟩

[2] In the *Garrick Corres.* up to this date there is no letter from Lord Mansfield which answers Boswell's descriptions. To Lord Chatham Garrick had addressed some verses from Mount Edgecumbe. Chatham, on April 3, 1772, sent verses in return, and wrote :—' You have kindly settled upon me a lasting species of property I never dreamed of in that enchanting place : a far more able conveyancer than any in Chancery-land.' *Ib.* i. 459.

[3] ' Then I alone the Conquest prize, When I insult a Rival's Eyes : If there's, &c.' Act iii. sc. 12.

[4] ' But how did he return, this haughty brave, Who whipt the winds, and made the sea his slave ? (Tho' Neptune took unkindly to be bound ; And Eurus never such hard usage found In his Æolian Prisons under ground).'
    Dryden, *Juvenal*, x. 180.

This does very well, when both the winds and the sea are personified, and mentioned by their mythological names, as in Juvenal; but when they are mentioned in plain language, the application of the epithets suggested by me, is the most obvious; and accordingly my friend himself, in his imitation of the passage which describes Xerxes, has

'The waves he lashes, and enchains the wind.'

The modes of living in different countries, and the various views with which men travel in quest of new scenes, having been talked of, a learned gentleman [1] who holds a considerable office in the law, expatiated on the happiness of a savage life [2]; and mentioned an instance of an officer who had actually lived for some time in the wilds of America, of whom, when in that state, he quoted this reflection with an air of admiration, as if it had been deeply philosophical: 'Here am I, free and unrestrained, amidst the rude magnificence of Nature, with this Indian woman by my side, and this gun, with which I can procure food when I want it: what more can be desired for human happiness?' It did not require much sagacity to foresee that such a sentiment would not be permitted to pass without due animadversion. JOHNSON. 'Do not allow yourself, Sir, to be imposed upon by such gross absurdity. It is sad stuff; it is brutish. If a bull could speak, he might as well exclaim,— Here am I with this cow and this grass; what being can enjoy greater felicity?'

We talked of the melancholy end of a gentleman [3] who had destroyed himself. JOHNSON. 'It was owing to imaginary difficulties in his affairs, which, had he talked with any friend, would soon have vanished.' BOSWELL. 'Do you think, Sir, that all who commit suicide are mad?' JOHNSON. 'Sir, they are

---

[1] Most likely Mr. Pepys, a Master in Chancery, whom Johnson more than once roughly attacked at Streatham. See *post*, iv. 82, and Mme. D'Arblay's *Diary*, ii. 46.

[2] See *ante*, ii. 73.

[3] 'Jan. 5, 1772. Poor Mr. Fitzherbert hanged himself on Wednesday. He went to see the convicts executed that morning; and from thence, in his boots, to his son, having sent his groom out of the way. At three, his son said, "Sir, you are to dine at Mr. Buller's; it is time for you to go home and dress." He went to his own stable and hanged himself with a bridle. They say his circumstances were in great disorder.' Walpole's *Letters*, viii. 125. See *ante*, i. 82, and *post*, iii. 148.

often not universally disordered in their intellects, but one
passion presses so upon them, that they yield to it, and commit
suicide, as a passionate man will stab another.' He added, ' I
have often thought, that after a man has taken the resolution to
kill himself, it is not courage in him to do any thing, however
desperate, because he has nothing to fear.' GOLDSMITH. ' I
don't see that.' JOHNSON. ' Nay but,[a] my dear Sir, why should
not you see what every one else sees ? ' GOLDSMITH. ' It is for
fear of something that he has resolved to kill himself ; and will
not that timid disposition restrain him ? ' JOHNSON. ' It does
not signify that the fear of something made him resolve ; it is
upon the state of his mind, after the resolution is taken, that I
argue. Suppose a man, either from fear, or pride, or conscience,
or whatever motive, has resolved to kill himself ; when once the
resolution is taken, he has nothing to fear. He may then go
and take the King of Prussia by the nose, at the head of his
army. He cannot fear the rack, who is resolved to kill himself.
When Eustace Budgel [1] was walking down to the Thames,
determined to drown himself, he might, if he pleased, without
any apprehension of danger, have turned aside, and first set fire
to St. James's palace.'

On Tuesday, April 27, Mr. Beauclerk and I called on him in
the morning. As we walked up Johnson's-court, I said, ' I have
a veneration for this court ; ' and was glad to find that Beauclerk
had the same reverential enthusiasm [2]. We found him alone.
We talked of Mr. Andrew Stuart's elegant and plausible Letters
to Lord Mansfield [3] : a copy of which had been sent by the
authour to Dr. Johnson. JOHNSON. ' They have not answered
the end. They have not been talked of ; I have never heard
of them. This is owing to their not being sold. People seldom

---

[a] Nay but, 1: Nay, but 2, 3.

[1] Boswell, in his *Hebrides* (*post*, v.
54), says that ' Budgell was accused of
forging a will [Dr. Tindal's], and sunk
himself in the Thames, before the
trial of its authenticity came on.' Pope,
speaking of himself, says (1734) that he
' Let Budgel charge low Grubstreet
  on his quill,
And write whate'er he pleas'd, except his Will.'
Epistle to Arbuthnot, l. 378.

Budgell ' finished his Life by jumping
out of a Boat at London-bridge ' on
May 4, 1737, more than two years
after the publication of this Epistle
in January, 1735. *Gent. Mag.* vii.
315. See *post*, iii. 46.

[2] See *post*, ii. 427.

[3] On the Douglas Cause, published
in January this year. See *ante*, ii. 50,
and *post*, ii. 475.

read a book which is given to them ; and few are given. The way to spread a work is to sell it at a low price. No man will send to buy a thing that costs even sixpence, without an intention to read it.' BOSWELL. ' May it not be doubted, Sir, whether it be proper to publish letters, arraigning the ultimate decision of an important cause by the supreme judicature of the nation ? ' JOHNSON. ' No, Sir, I do not think it was wrong to publish these letters. If they are thought to do harm, why not answer them ? But they will do no harm. If[a] Mr. Douglas be indeed the son of Lady Jane, he cannot be hurt : if he be not her son, and yet has the great estate of the family of Douglas, he may well submit to have a pamphlet against him by Andrew Stuart. Sir, I think such a publication does good, as it does good to show us the possibilities of human life. And, Sir, you will not say that the Douglas cause was a cause of easy decision, when it divided your Court as much as it could do, to be determined at all. When your Judges were seven and seven, the casting vote of the President must be given on one side or other ; no matter, for my argument, on which ; one or the other *must* be taken ; as when I am to move, there is no matter which leg I move first. And then, Sir, it was otherwise determined here. No, Sir, a more dubious determination of any question cannot be imagined [1].'

<hr />

a harm. If 1, 2 : harm ; if 3.

[1] I regretted that Dr. Johnson never took the trouble to study a question which interested nations. He would not even read a pamphlet which I wrote upon it, entitled ' The Essence of the Douglas Cause ; ' which, I have reason to flatter myself, had considerable effect in favour of Mr. Douglas ; of whose legitimate filiation I was then, and am still, firmly convinced. Let me add, that no fact can be more respectably ascertained, than by the judgement of the most august tribunal in the world ; a judgement, in which Lord Mansfield and Lord Camden united in 1769, and from which only five of a numerous body entered a protest. BOSWELL. Boswell records, *post*, v. 362 :—' Dr. Johnson roused my zeal so much that

I took the liberty to tell him he knew nothing of the [Douglas] cause.' Lord Shelburne says : ' I conceived such a prejudice upon the sight of the present Lord Douglas's face and figure, that I could not allow myself to vote in this cause. If ever I saw a Frenchman, he is one.' Fitzmaurice's *Shelburne*, i. 7, note. Hume ' was struck,' he writes, ' with a very sensible indignation at the decision. The cause, though not in the least intricate, is so complicated, that it never will be reviewed by the public, who are besides perfectly pleased with the sentence ; being swayed by compassion and a few popular topics. To one who understands the cause as I do, nothing could appear more scandalous than the pleadings of the two law lords.' J. H. Burton's *Hume*,

He said, ' Goldsmith should not be for ever attempting to shine [1] in conversation : he has not temper for it, he is so much mortified when he fails. Sir, a game of jokes is composed partly of skill, partly of chance. A[a] man may be beat at times by one who has not the tenth part of his wit. Now Goldsmith's putting himself against another, is like a man laying a hundred to one who cannot spare the hundred. It is not worth a man's while. A man should not lay a hundred to one, unless he can easily spare it, though he has a hundred chances for him : he can get but a guinea, and he may lose a hundred. Goldsmith is in this state. When he contends, if he gets the better, it is a very little addition to a man of his literary reputation : if he does not get the better, he is miserably vexed.'

Johnson's own superlative power [b] of wit set him above any risk of such uneasiness. Garrick had remarked to me of him, a few days before, ' Rabelais and all other wits are nothing compared with him. You may be diverted by them ; but Johnson gives you a forcible hug, and shakes laughter out of you, whether you will or no.'

Goldsmith, however, was often very fortunate in his witty contests, even when he entered the lists with Johnson himself. Sir Joshua Reynolds was in company with them one day, when Goldsmith said, that he thought he could write a good fable, mentioned the simplicity which that kind of composition requires, and observed, that in most fables the animals introduced seldom talk in character. ' For instance, (said he,) the fable of the little fishes[2], who saw birds fly over their heads, and envying them, petitioned Jupiter to be changed into birds. The skill (continued he,) consists in making them talk like little fishes.' While he indulged himself in this fanciful reverie, he observed Johnson shaking his sides, and laughing. Upon which he smartly proceeded, ' Why, Dr. Johnson, this is not so easy as you seem to think ; for if you were to make little fishes talk, they would talk like WHALES.'

Johnson, though remarkable for his great variety of composition, never exercised his talents in fable, except we allow his

---

^a chance. A 1 : chance, a 2, 3.
ii. 423. In Campbell's *Chancellors*, v. 494, an account is given of a duel between Stuart and Thurlow that

^b power 1 : powers, 2, 3.
arose out of this suit.
[1] ⟨See *ante*, i. 423 ; *post*, ii. 253, 257.⟩
[2] ⟨See App. B, p. 505.⟩

beautiful tale [1] published in Mrs. Williams's Miscellanies [2] to be of that species. I have, however, found among his manuscript collections the following sketch of one :

' Glow-worm [3] lying in the garden saw a candle in a neighbouring palace,—and complained of the littleness of his own light ;—another observed—wait a little ;—soon dark ; [a]—have outlasted πολλ [*many*] of these glaring lights which are only brighter as they haste to nothing.'

On Thursday, April 29, I dined with him at General Oglethorpe's, where were Sir Joshua Reynolds, Mr. Langton, Dr. Goldsmith, and Mr. Thrale. I was very desirous to get Dr. Johnson absolutely fixed in his resolution to go with me to the Hebrides this year ; and I told him that I had received a letter from Dr. Robertson the historian, upon the subject, with which he was much pleased ; and now talked in such a manner of his long-intended tour, that I was satisfied he meant to fulfil his engagement.

The custom of eating dogs at Otaheite being mentioned, Goldsmith observed, that this was also a custom in China ; that a dog-butcher is as common there as any other butcher ; and that when he walks abroad all the dogs fall on him. JOHNSON. ' That is not owing to his killing dogs, Sir. I remember a butcher at Lichfield, whom a dog that was in the house where I lived, always attacked. It is the smell of carnage which provokes this, let the animals he has killed be what they may.' GOLDSMITH. ' Yes, there is a general abhorrence in animals at the signs of massacre. If you put a tub full of blood into a stable, the horses are like to go mad.' JOHNSON. ' I doubt that.' GOLDSMITH. ' Nay, Sir, it is a fact well authenticated.' THRALE. ' You had better prove it before you put it into your book on natural history. You may do it in my stable if you will.' JOHNSON. ' Nay, Sir, I would not have him prove it. If he is content to take his information from others, he may get through his book with little trouble, and without much endangering his reputation. But if he makes experiments for so comprehensive a book as his, there would be no end to

[a] dark ; 1 : dark, 2, 3.

[1] The Fountains. *Works*, ix. 176.
[2] See *ante*, ii. 25.
[3] It has already been observed (*ante*, ii. 55), that one of his first

Essays was a Latin Poem on a glow-worm ; but whether it be any where extant, has not been ascertained. MALONE.

them ; his erroneous assertions would then fall upon himself ; and he might be blamed for not having made experiments as to every particular.'

The character of Mallet having been introduced, and spoken of slightingly by Goldsmith ; JOHNSON. ' Why, Sir, Mallet had talents enough to keep his literary reputation alive as long as he himself lived [1] ; and that, let me tell you, is a good deal.' GOLDSMITH. ' But I cannot agree that it was so. His literary reputation was dead long before his natural death. I consider an authour's literary reputation to be alive only while his name will ensure a good price for his copy from the booksellers. I will get you (to Johnson,) a hundred guineas for any thing whatever that you shall write, if you put your name to it [2].'

Dr. Goldsmith's new play, ' She stoops to conquer,' being mentioned ; JOHNSON. ' I know of no comedy for many years that has so much exhilarated an audience, that has answered so much the great end of comedy—making an audience merry [3].'

Goldsmith having said, that Garrick's compliment to the Queen, which he introduced into the play of ' The Chances [4] ',

[1] ' His works are such as a writer, bustling in the world, shewing himself in publick, and emerging occasionally from time to time into notice, might keep alive by his personal influence ; but which, conveying little information and giving no great pleasure, must soon give way, as the succession of things produces new topicks of conversation and other modes of amusement.' Johnson's *Life of Mallet*, 25.

[2] Johnson made less money, because he never ' traded ' on his reputation. When he had made his name, he almost ceased to write.

[3] ' March 27, 1773. Dr. Goldsmith has written a comedy—no, it is the lowest of all farces. It is not the subject I condemn, though very vulgar, but the execution. The drift tends to no moral, no edification of any kind. The situations, however, are well imagined, and make one laugh, in spite of the grossness of the dialogue, the forced witticisms, and total improbability of the whole

plan and conduct. But what disgusts me most is, that though the characters are very low, and aim at low humour, not one of them says a sentence that is natural or marks any character at all. It is set up in opposition to sentimental comedy, and is as bad as the worst of them.' Walpole's *Letters*, viii. 260. Northcote (*Reynolds*, i. 286) says that Goldsmith gave him an order to see this comedy. ' The next time I saw him, he inquired of me what my opinion was of it. I told him that I would not presume to be a judge of its merits ; he asked, " Did it make you laugh ? " I answered, " Exceedingly." " Then," said the Doctor, " that is all I require." ' ⟨For Boswell's letter of congratulation see his *Letters*, No. 116, i. 192.⟩

[4] Garrick brought out his revised version of this play by Beaumont and Fletcher in 1754–5. Murphy's *Garrick*, p. 170. The compliment is in a speech by Don Juan, act v. sc. 3 :

which he had altered and revised this year, was mean and gross flattery ;—JOHNSON. 'Why, Sir, I would not *write*, I would not give solemnly under my hand, a character beyond what I thought really true ; but a speech on the stage, let it flatter ever so extravagantly, is formular[1]. It has always been formular to flatter Kings and Queens ; so much so, that even in our church-service we have " our most religious King," used indiscriminately, whoever is King. Nay, they even flatter themselves ;—" we have been graciously pleased to grant."—No modern flattery, however, is so gross as that of the Augustan age, where the Emperour was deified. " *Præsens Divus habebitur Augustus*[2]." And as to meanness, (rising into warmth,) how is it mean in a player,—a showman,—a fellow who exhibits himself for a shilling, to flatter his Queen[3] ? The attempt, indeed, was dangerous ; for if it had missed, what became of Garrick, and what became of the Queen ? As Sir William Temple says of a great General, it is necessary not only that his designs should[a] be formed in a masterly manner, but that they should be attended with success[4]. Sir, it is right, at a time when the Royal Family is not generally liked[5], to let it be seen that the people like at least one of them.' SIR JOSHUA REYNOLDS. 'I do not perceive why the profession of a player should be despised[6] ; for the great and ultimate end of all the employments of mankind is to produce amusement. Garrick produces more amusement than any body.' BOSWELL. 'You say, Dr. Johnson, that Garrick exhibits himself for a shilling.

<hr/>

[a] should *omitted* 2, 3.

'Ay, but when things are at the worst, they'll mend—example does every thing, ... and the fair sex will certainly grow better, whenever the greatest is the best woman in the kingdom.'

[1] *Formular* is not in Johnson's *Dictionary* ⟨and he is the sole authority for this sense⟩.

[2] 'On earth, a present god, shall Cæsar reign.'
FRANCIS. Horace, *Odes*, iii. 5. 2.

[3] See *ante*, i. 167.

[4] Johnson refers, I believe, to Temple's Essay *Of Heroic Virtue*, where he says that 'the excellency of genius' must not only 'be culti-

vated by education and instruction,' but also ' must be assisted by fortune, to preserve it to maturity ; because the noblest spirit or genius in the world, if it falls, though never so bravely, in its first enterprises, cannot deserve enough of mankind, to pretend to so great a reward, as the esteem of heroic virtue.' Temple's *Works*, iii. 306.

[5] See *post*, iii. 155.

[6] In an epitaph that Burke wrote for Garrick, he says : ' He raised the character of his profession to the rank of a liberal art.' Windham's *Diary*, p. 361.

In this respect he is only on a footing with a lawyer who exhibits himself for his fee, and even will maintain any nonsense or absurdity, if the case requires it. Garrick refuses a play or a part which he does not like ; a lawyer never refuses.' JOHNSON. ' Why, Sir, what does this prove ? only that a lawyer is worse. Boswell is now like Jack in " The Tale of a Tub [1]," who, when he is puzzled by an argument, hangs himself. He thinks I shall cut him down, but I'll let him hang,[a] ' (laughing vociferously.) SIR JOSHUA REYNOLDS. ' Mr. Boswell thinks that the profession of a lawyer being unquestionably honourable, if he can show the profession of a player to be more honourable, he proves his argument.'

On Friday, April 30, I dined with him at Mr. Beauclerk's, where were Lord Charlemont, Sir Joshua Reynolds, and some more members of the LITERARY CLUB, whom he had obligingly invited to meet me, as I was this evening to be balloted for as candidate for admission into that distinguished society. Johnson had done me the honour to propose me [2], and Beauclerk was very zealous for me.

Goldsmith being mentioned ; JOHNSON. ' It is amazing how little Goldsmith knows. He seldom comes where he is not more ignorant than any one else.' SIR JOSHUA REYNOLDS. ' Yet there is no man whose company is more liked.' JOHNSON. ' To be sure, Sir. When people find a man of the most

---

^a hang, 1: hang. 2, 3.

[1] ' The allusion,' as Mr. Lockhart pointed out, ' is not to the *Tale of a Tub*, but to the *History of John Bull*' (part ii. ch. 12 and 13). Jack, who hangs himself, is however the youngest of the three brothers of *The Tale of a Tub*, ' that have made such a clutter in the world ' (*ib.* chap. 2). Jack was unwillingly convinced by Habbakkuk's argument that to save his life he must hang himself. Sir Roger, he was promised, before the rope was well about his neck, would break in and cut him down.

[2] He wrote the following letter (*Letters*, No. 305) to Goldsmith, who filled the chair that evening. ' It is,' Mr. Forster says (*Life of Goldsmith*, ii. 367), ' the only fragment of correspondence between Johnson and Goldsmith that has been preserved.' ⟨See App. B, p. 505.⟩

' April 23, 1773.

' SIR,—I beg that you will excuse my Absence to the Club ; I am going this evening to Oxford.

' I have another favour to beg. It is that I may be considered as proposing Mr. Boswel for a candidate of our Society, and that he may be considered as regularly nominated.

I am, Sir,

Your most humble servant,

' SAM: JOHNSON.'

⟨See *post*, v. 76.⟩ If Johnson went to Oxford his stay there was brief, as on April 27 Boswell found him at home (*ante*, ii. 229).

distinguished abilities as a writer, their inferiour while he is with them, it must be highly gratifying to them. What Goldsmith comically says of himself is very true,—he always gets the better when he argues alone ; meaning, that he is master of a subject in his study, and can write well upon it ; but when he comes into company, grows confused, and unable to talk [1]. Take him as a poet, his " Traveller " is a very fine performance ; ay, and so is his " Deserted Village," were it not sometimes too much the echo of his " Traveller." Whether, indeed, we take him as a poet,—as a comick writer,—or as an historian, he stands in the first class.' BOSWELL. ' An historian ! My dear Sir, you surely will not rank his compilation of the Roman History with the works of other historians of this age ? ' JOHNSON. ' Why, who are before him [2] ? ' BOSWELL. ' Hume,—Robertson [3],—Lord Lyttelton.' JOHNSON. (His antipathy to the Scotch beginning to rise,). ' I have not read Hume ; but, doubtless, Goldsmith's History is better than the *verbiage* of Robertson [4], or the

[1] ' There are,' says Johnson, speaking of Dryden (*Life*, 167), ' men whose powers operate only at leisure and in retirement, and whose intellectual vigour deserts them in conversation.' See also *ante*, i. 413. ' No man,' he said of Goldsmith, ' was more foolish when he had not a pen in his hand, or more wise when he had ; ' *post*, iv. 29. Walpole (*Letters*, xiii. 276), who ' knew Hume personally and well,' said, ' Mr. Hume's writings were so superior to his conversation, that I frequently said he understood nothing till he had written upon it.'

[2] The age of great English historians had not long begun. The first volume of *The Decline and Fall* was published three years later. Addison had written in 1716 (*Freeholder*, No. 35), ' Our Country, which has produced Writers of the first Figure in every other kind of Work, has been very barren in good Historians.' Johnson, in 1751, repeated this observation in *The Rambler*, No. 122. Bolingbroke wrote in 1735 (*Study Hist.* 1752, i. 223), ' Our nation has furnished as ample and as important matter, good and bad, for history, as any nation under the sun : and yet we must yield the palm in writing history most certainly to the Italians and to the French, and I fear, even to the Germans.' ⟨See App. B, p. 505.⟩

[3] Gibbon, informing Robertson on March, 26, 1788, of the completion of *The Decline and Fall*, said :—' The praise which has ever been the most flattering to my ear, is to find my name associated with the names of Robertson and Hume ; and provided I can maintain my place in the triumvirate, I am indifferent at what distance I am ranked below my companions and masters.' Dugald Stewart's *Robertson*, p. 367.

[4] ' Sir,' said Johnson, ' if Robertson's style be faulty, he owes it me ; that is, having too many words, and those too big ones.' *Post*, iii. 173. Johnson was not singular among the men of his time in condemning Robertson's *verbiage*. Wesley (*Journal*, 28 Apr. 1772) wrote of vol. i. of *Charles the Fifth* :—' Here is a quarto volume of eight or ten shillings' price,

foppery of Dalrymple [1].' BOSWELL. 'Will you not admit the superiority of Robertson, in whose History we find such penetration—such painting?' JOHNSON. 'Sir, you must consider how that penetration and that painting are employed. It is not history, it is imagination. He who describes what he never saw, draws from fancy. Robertson paints minds as Sir Joshua paints faces in a history-piece : he imagines an heroick countenance. You must look upon Robertson's work as romance, and try it by that standard [2]. History it is not. Besides, Sir, it is the great excellence of a writer to put into his book as much as his book will hold. Goldsmith has done this in his History. Now Robertson might have put twice as much into his book. Robertson is like a man who has packed gold in wool : the wool takes up more room than the gold. No, Sir ; I always thought Robertson would be crushed by his own weight,—would be buried under his own ornaments. Goldsmith tells you shortly all you want to know : Robertson detains you a great deal too long. No man will read Robertson's cumbrous detail a second time ; but Goldsmith's plain narrative will please again and again. I would say to Robertson what an old tutor of a college said to one of his pupils : " Read over your compositions, and where ever you meet with a passage which you think is particularly fine, strike it out." Goldsmith's abridgement is better than that of Lucius Florus or Eutropius ; and I will venture to say, that if you compare him with Vertot [3], in the same places of the Roman History, you will find that he excels Vertot. Sir, he has the art of compiling, and of saying every thing he has to say in a pleasing manner [4]. He is now writing a Natural History and will make it as entertaining as a Persian Tale.'

containing dry, verbose dissertations on feudal government, the substance of all which might be comprised in half a sheet of paper !' ⟨Beattie wrote, 14 June 1773 : ' He [Burke] praises Robertson's style, but he says he writes like a man who composes in a dead language which he understands but cannot speak.' Margaret Forbes, *Beattie*, p. 81. For Johnson's help to Robertson see *Letters*, No. 499.⟩

[1] See *ante*, ii. 210.

[2] See *post*, iii. 404.

[3] ' Vertot, né en Normandie en 1655. Historien agréable et élégant. Mort en 1735.' Voltaire, *Siècle de Louis XIV* (*Œuvres*, 1878, xiv. 142).

[4] Even Hume had no higher notion of what was required in a writer of ancient history. He wrote to Robertson, who was, it seems, meditating a History of Greece :—' What can you do in most places with these authors but transcribe and translate

I cannot dismiss the present topick without observing, that it is probable that Dr. Johnson, who owned that he often ' talked for victory,' rather urged plausible objections to Dr. Robertson's excellent historical works, in the ardour of contest, than expressed his real and decided opinion ; for it is not easy to suppose, that he should so widely differ from the rest of the literary world [1].

JOHNSON. ' I remember once being with Goldsmith in Westminster-abbey. While we surveyed the Poets' Corner, I said to him,

" *Forsitan et nostrum nomen miscebitur istis* [2]."

When we got to Temple-bar he stopped me, pointed to the heads upon it [3], and slily whispered me,

" *Forsitan et nostrum nomen miscebitur* ISTIS [4]." '

Johnson praised John Bunyan highly. ' His " Pilgrim's Progress " has great merit, both for invention, imagination, and the conduct of the story ; and it has had the best evidence of its merit, the general and continued approbation of mankind. Few books, I believe, have had a more extensive sale. It is remarkable, that it begins very much like the poem of Dante ; yet there was no translation of Dante when Bunyan wrote. There is reason to think that he had read Spenser [5].'

them ? No letters or state papers from which you could correct their errors, or authenticate their narration, or supply their defects.' Burton's *Hume*, ii. 83.

[1] See *ante*, ii. 53. Southey, asserting that Robertson had never read the Laws of Alonso the Wise, says, that ' it is one of the thousand and one omissions for which he ought to be called rogue as long as his volumes last.' Southey's *Life*, ii. 318.

[2] Ovid. de Art. Amand. l. iii. v. 13 [339]. BOSWELL. ' It may be that our name too will mingle with those.'

[3] The *Gent. Mag.* for Jan. 1766 (p. 45) records, that ' a person was observed discharging musket-balls, from a steel cross-bow, at the two remaining heads upon Temple-Bar.' They were the heads of Scotch rebels

executed in 1746. ⟨ ' Yesterday ', says a news writer of the 1st of April, 1772, ' one of the rebels' heads on Temple Bar fell down.' P. Cunningham's *Handbook of London*, 1849, ii. 805.⟩ Samuel Rogers, who died at the end of 1855, said, ' I well remember one of the heads of the rebels upon a pole at Temple-Bar.' Rogers's *Table-Talk*, p. 2.

[4] In allusion to Dr. Johnson's supposed political principles, and perhaps his own. BOSWELL.

[5] ' The Doctor one day took Percy's little daughter upon his knee, and asked her what she thought of *Pilgrim's Progress*. The child answered that she had not read it. " No ! " replied the Doctor ; " then I would not give one farthing for you : " and he set her down and took no further

A proposition which had been agitated, that monuments to eminent persons should, for the time to come, be erected in St. Paul's church as well as in Westminster-abbey, was mentioned ; and it was asked, who should be honoured by having his monument first erected there [1]. Somebody suggested Pope. JOHNSON. ' Why, Sir, as Pope was a Roman Catholick, I would not have his to be first. I think Milton's rather should have the precedence [2]. I think more highly of him now than I did at twenty [3]. There is more thinking in him and in Butler, than in any of our poets.'

Some of the company expressed a wonder why the authour of so excellent a book as ' The Whole Duty of Man [4]' should conceal himself. JOHNSON. ' There may be different reasons assigned for this, any one of which would be very sufficient. He may have been a clergyman, and may have thought that his religious counsels would have less weight when known to come from a man whose profession was Theology. He may have been a man whose practice was not suitable to his principles, so that his character might injure the effect of his book, which he had written in a season of penitence. Or he may have been a man of rigid self-denial, so that he would have no reward for his pious labours while in this world, but refer it all to a future state.'

The gentlemen went away to their club, and I was left at

---

notice of her.' Croker's *Boswell*, p. 838. Mrs. Piozzi (*Anec.* p. 281 : John. Misc. i. 332) says, that Johnson once asked, ' Was there ever yet any thing written by mere man that was wished longer by its readers, excepting Don Quixote, Robinson Crusoe, and the Pilgrim's Progress ? '

[1] It was Johnson himself who was thus honoured. *Post*, iv. 423.

[2] Here is another instance of his high admiration of Milton as a Poet, notwithstanding his just abhorrence of that sour Republican's political principles. His candour and discrimination are equally conspicuous. Let us hear no more of his ' injustice to Milton.' BOSWELL.

[3] There was an exception to this.

In his criticism of *Paradise Lost* (*Milton*, 255), he says :—' The confusion of spirit and matter which pervades the whole narration of the war of heaven fills it with incongruity ; and the book in which it is related is, I believe, the favourite of children, and gradually neglected as knowledge is increased.'

[4] In the *Academy*, xxii. 348, 364, 382, Mr. C. E. Doble shews strong grounds for the belief that the author was Richard Allestree, D.D., Regius Professor of Divinity, Oxford, and Provost of Eton. Cowper spoke of it as ' that repository of self-righteousness and pharisaical lumber ; ' with which opinion Southey wholly disagreed. Southey's *Cowper*, i. 116.

Beauclerk's till the fate of my election should be announced to me. I sat in a state of anxiety which even the charming conversation of Lady Di Beauclerk could not entirely dissipate. In a short time I received the agreeable intelligence that I was chosen ¹. I hastened to the place of meeting, and was introduced to such a society as can seldom be found. Mr. Edmund Burke, whom I then saw for the first time, and whose splendid talents had long made me ardently wish for his acquaintance ; Dr. Nugent, Mr. Garrick, Dr. Goldsmith, Mr. (afterwards Sir William) Jones ², and the company with whom I had dined. Upon my entrance, Johnson placed himself behind a chair, on which he leaned as on a desk or pulpit, and with humorous formality gave me a *Charge*, pointing out the conduct expected from me as a good member of this club.

Goldsmith produced some very absurd verses which had been publickly recited to an audience for money ³. JOHNSON. ' I can match this nonsense. There was a poem called " Eugenio," which came out some years ago, and concludes thus :

" And now, ye trifling, self-assuming elves,
 Brimful of pride, of nothing, of yourselves,
 Survey Eugenio, view him o'er and o'er,
 Then sink into yourselves, and be no more ⁴."

¹ Johnson said to Boswell :—' Sir, they knew, that if they refused you, they'd probably never have got in another. I'd have kept them all out. Beauclerk was very earnest for you.' *Post*, v. 76.

² Garrick and Jones had been elected this same spring. See *ante*, i. 481, note 3.

³ Mr. Langton (*post*, iv. 13), mentions an ode brought by Goldsmith to the Club, which ıad been recited for money.

⁴ Dr. Johnson's memory here was not perfectly accurate : ' Eugenio ' does not conclude thus. There are eight more lines after the last of those quoted by him ; and the passage which he meant to recite is as follows :

' Say now ye fluttering, poor assuming elves,

Stark full of pride, of folly, of— yourselves ;
Say where's the wretch of all your impious crew
Who dares confront his character to view ?
Behold Eugenio, view him o'er and o'er,
Then sink into yourselves, and be no more.'

Mr. Reed informs me that the Authour of Eugenio, a Wine Merchant at Wrexham in Denbighshire, soon after its publication, viz. 17th May, 1737, cut his own throat ; and that it appears by Swift's Works, that the poem had been shewn to him, and received some of his corrections. Johnson had read ' Eugenio ' on his first coming to town, for we see it mentioned in one of his letters to Mr. Cave, which has been inserted in

Nay, Dryden in his poem on the Royal Society [1], has these lines:

> " Then we upon our globe's last verge shall go,
>   And see [a] the ocean leaning on the sky ;
> From thence our rolling neighbours we shall know,
>   And on the lunar world securely pry." '

Talking of puns, Johnson, who had a great contempt for that species of wit [2], deigned to allow that there was one good pun in ' Menagiana,' I think on the word *corps* [3].

Much pleasant conversation passed, which Johnson relished with great good humour. But his conversation alone, or

[a] view *orig. ed.*

this work [*ante*, i. 122]. BOSWELL. See Swift's *Works*, ed. 1824, xviii. 296, for his letter to this wine merchant, Thomas Beach by name.

[1] These lines are in the *Annus Mirabilis* (stanza 164) in a digression in praise of the Royal Society ; described by Johnson (*Life of Dryden*, 257) as ' an example seldom equalled of seasonable excursion and artful return.' *Ib.* 330, he says : ' Dryden delighted to tread upon the brink of meaning, where light and darkness begin to mingle. . . . This inclination sometimes produced nonsense, which he knew . . . ; and sometimes it issued in absurdities, of which perhaps he was not conscious.' He then quotes these lines, and continues : ' [They] have no meaning ; but may we not say, in imitation of Cowley on another book,

" 'Tis so like *sense*, 'twill serve the
        turn as well." '

Cowley's line is from his *Pindarique Ode to Mr. Hobbes* :—

' 'Tis so like *truth*, 'twill serve *our*
        turn as well.'

[2] In his *Dictionary*, he defines *punster* as *a low wit, who endeavours at reputation by double meaning.* See *post*, iii. 325 ; iv. 316.

[3] I formerly thought that I had perhaps mistaken the word, and imagined it to be *Corps*, from its similarity of sound to the real one. For an accurate and shrewd un-

known gentleman, to whom I am indebted for some remarks on my work, observes on this passage— ' Q. if not on the word *Fort* ? A vociferous French preacher said of Bourdaloue, " Il prêche *fort bien*, et moi *bien fort*."—Menagiana. See also Anecdotes Littéraires, Article Bourdaloue.' But my ingenious and obliging correspondent, Mr. Abercrombie of Philadelphia, has pointed out to me the following passage in ' Menagiana ' ; which renders the preceding conjecture unnecessary, and confirms my original statement :

' Mad[me] de Bourdonne, Chanoinesse de Remiremont, venoit d'entendre un discours plein de feu et d'esprit, mais fort peu solide, et très-irrégulier. Une de ses amies, qui y prenoit intérêt pour l'orateur, lui dit en sortant, " Eh bien, Mad[me] que vous semble-t-il de ce que vous venez d'entendre ?—Qu'il y a d'esprit ? "— " Il y [en] a tant, répondit Ma [me] de Bourdonne, que je n'y ai pas vû de *corps*." '—Menagiana, tome ii. p. 64. Amsterd. 1713. BOSWELL. *Ménagiana, ou Bons mots, rencontres agréables, pensées judicieuses, et observations curieuses, de M. Ménage*, was first published at Amsterdam in 1693. Gilles Ménage was born 1613, died 1692. ⟨The anecdote of the vociferous preacher, ' M. S. . . . Archidiacre d'Auxerre ', occurs in tome i, 1713, p. 159.⟩

what led to it, or was interwoven with it, is the business of this work [1].

On Saturday, May 1, we dined by ourselves at our old rendezvous, the Mitre tavern. He was placid, but not much disposed to talk. He observed that ' The Irish mix better with the English than the Scotch do ; their language is nearer to English ; as a proof of which, they succeed very well as players, which Scotchmen do not. Then, Sir, they have not that extreme nationality which we find in the Scotch. I will do you, Boswell, the justice to say, that you are the most *unscottified* of your countrymen. You are almost the only instance of a Scotchman that I have known, who did not at every other sentence bring in some other Scotchman [2].'

We drank tea with Mrs. Williams. I introduced a question which has been much agitated in the Church of Scotland, whether the claim of lay-patrons to present ministers to parishes be well founded ; and supposing it to be well founded, whether it ought to be exercised without the concurrence of the people ? That Church is composed of a series of judicatures : a Presbytery,—a Synod,—and,[a] finally, a General Assembly ; before all of which, this matter may be contended : and in some cases the Presbytery having refused to induct or *settle*, as they call it, the person presented by the patron, it has been found necessary to appeal to the General Assembly. He said, I might see the subject well treated in the ' Defence of Pluralities [3] ;' and although he thought that a patron should exercise his right with tenderness to the inclinations of the people of a parish, he was very clear as to his right. Then supposing the question to be pleaded before the General Assembly, he dictated to me what follows :

' AGAINST the right of patrons is commonly opposed, by the inferiour judicatures, the plea of conscience. Their conscience tells them, that the people ought to choose their pastor ; their conscience tells them that

[a] Synod,—and, 1 : Synod, and 2, 3.

[1] That Johnson only relished the conversation, and did not join in it, is most unlikely. In his *charge* to Boswell, he very likely pointed out that what was said within was not to be reported without. Boswell

gives only brief reports of the talk at the Club, and these not openly. See *post*, ii. 345, note 5 ; ⟨iii. 230, note 5⟩.

[2] See *post*, ii. 306.

[3] By the Rev. Henry Wharton, published in 1692.

they ought not to impose upon a congregation a minister ungrateful and unacceptable to his auditors. Conscience is nothing more than a conviction felt by ourselves of something to be done, or something to be avoided; and, in questions of simple unperplexed morality, conscience is very often a guide that may be trusted. But before conscience can determine, the state of the question is supposed to be completely known. In questions of law, or of fact, conscience is very often confounded with opinion. No man's conscience can tell him the rights [a] of another man [1]; they must be known by rational investigation or historical enquiry. Opinion, which he that holds it may call his conscience, may teach some men that religion would be promoted, and quiet preserved, by granting to the people universally the choice of their ministers. But it is a conscience very ill informed that violates the rights of one man, for the convenience of another. Religion cannot be promoted by injustice : and it was never yet found that a popular election was very quietly transacted.

' That justice would be violated by transferring to the people the right of patronage, is apparent to all who know whence that right had its original. The right of patronage was not at first a privilege torn by power from unresisting poverty. It is not an authority at first usurped in times of ignorance, and established only by succession and by precedents. It is not a grant capriciously made from a higher tyrant to a lower. It is a right dearly purchased by the first possessors, and justly inherited by those that succeeded them. When Christianity was established in this island, a regular mode of publick worship was prescribed. Publick worship requires a publick place ; and the proprietors of lands, as they were converted, built churches for their families and their vassals. For the maintenance of ministers, they settled a certain portion of their lands ; and a district, through which each minister was required to extend his care, was, by that circumscription, constituted a parish. This is a position so generally received in England, that the extent of a manor and of a parish are regularly received for each other. The churches which the proprietors of lands had thus built and thus endowed, they justly thought themselves entitled to provide with ministers ; and where the episcopal government prevails, the Bishop has no power to reject a man nominated by the patron, but for some crime that might exclude him from the priesthood. For the endowment of the church being the gift of the landlord, he was consequently at liberty to give it according to his choice, to any man capable of performing the holy offices. The people did not choose him, because the people did not pay him.

' We hear it sometimes urged, that this original right is passed out of

a rights 1: right 2, 3.
[1] See *ante*, ii. 126, for what Johnson said of the *inward light*.

memory, and is obliterated and obscured by many translations of property and changes of government ; that scarce any church is now in the hands of the heirs of the builders ; and that the present persons have entered subsequently upon the pretended rights by a thousand accidental and unknown causes. Much of this, perhaps, is true. But how is the right of patronage extinguished ? If the right followed the lands, it is possessed by the same equity by which the lands are possessed. It is, in effect, part of the manor, and protected by the same laws with every other privilege. Let us suppose an estate forfeited by treason, and granted by the Crown to a new family. With the lands were forfeited all the rights appendant to those lands ; by the same power that grants the lands, the rights also are granted. The right lost to the patron falls not to the people, but is either retained by the Crown, or, what to the people is the same thing, is by the Crown given away. Let it change hands ever so often, it is possessed by him that receives it with the same right as it was conveyed. It may, indeed, like all our possessions, be forcibly seized or fraudulently obtained. But no injury is still done to the people ; for what they never had, they have never lost. Caius may usurp the right of Titius ; but neither Caius nor Titius injure the people ; and no man's conscience, however tender or however active, can prompt him to restore what may be proved to have been never taken away. Supposing, what I think cannot be proved, that a popular election of ministers were to be desired, our desires are not the measure of equity. It were to be desired that power should be only in the hands of the merciful, and riches in the possession of the generous ; but the law must leave both riches and power where it finds them : and must often leave riches with the covetous, and power with the cruel. Convenience may be a rule in little things, where no other rule has been established. But as the great end of government is to give every man his own, no inconvenience is greater than that of making right uncertain. Nor is any man more an enemy to publick peace, than he who fills weak heads with imaginary claims, and breaks the series of civil subordination, by inciting the lower classes of mankind to encroach upon the higher.

'Having thus shown that the right of patronage, being originally purchased, may be legally transferred, and that it is now in the hands of lawful possessors, at least as certainly as any other right ;—we have left to the advocates of the people no other plea than that of convenience. Let us, therefore, now consider what the people would really gain by a general abolition of the right of patronage. What is most to be desired by such a change is, that the country should be supplied with better ministers. But why should we suppose that the parish will make a wiser choice than the patron ? If we suppose mankind actuated by interest, the patron is more likely to choose with caution, because he will suffer more by choosing wrong. By the deficiencies of his minister, or by his vices, he is equally offended with the rest of the congregation ; but he will have this reason more to lament them, that they will be imputed to his absurdity or corruption. The qualifications of a minister are well known to be learning and piety. Of his learning the patron is probably the only judge in the parish ; and of his piety not less a judge than others ; and is more likely to enquire minutely and diligently before he gives a presentation, than one of the parochial rabble, who can give nothing but a vote. It may be urged, that though the parish might not choose better ministers, they would at least choose ministers whom they like better, and who would therefore officiate with greater efficacy. That ignorance and per-verseness should always obtain what they like, was never considered as the end of government ; of which it is the great and standing benefit, that the wise see for the simple, and the regular act for the capricious. But that this argument supposes the people capable of judging, and resolute to act according to their best judgements, though this be sufficiently absurd, is not all its absurdity. It supposes not only wisdom, but unanimity in those, who upon no other occasions are unanimous or wise. If by some strange concurrence all the voices of a parish should unite in the choice of any single man, though I could not charge the patron with injustice for presenting a minister, I should censure him as unkind and injudicious. But, it is evident, that as in all other popular elections there will be contrariety of judgement and acrimony of passion, a parish upon every vacancy would break into factions, and the contest for the choice of a minister would set neigh-bours at variance, and bring discord into families. The minister would be taught all the arts of a candidate, would flatter some, and bribe others ; and the electors, as in all other cases, would call for holidays and ale, and break the heads of each other during the jollity of the canvas. The time must, however, come at last, when one of the factions must prevail, and one of the ministers get possession of the church. On what terms does he enter upon his ministry but those of enmity with half his parish ? By what prudence or what diligence can he hope to conciliate the affections of that party by whose defeat he has obtained his living ? Every man who voted against him will enter the church with hanging head and downcast eyes, afraid to encounter that neighbour by whose vote and influence he has been overpowered. He will hate his neighbour for opposing him, and his minister for having prospered by the opposition ; and, as he will never see him but with pain, he will never see him but with hatred. Of a minister presented by the patron, the parish has seldom any thing worse to say than that they do not know him. Of a minister chosen by a popular contest, all those who do not favour him, have nursed up in their bosoms principles of hatred and reasons of rejection. Anger is excited principally by pride. The pride of a common man is very little exasperated by the supposed usurpation of an acknowledged superior. He bears only his little share of a general evil, and suffers in common with the whole parish : but when the contest is between equals, the defeat has many aggravations ; and he that is defeated by his next neighbour, is seldom satisfied without some revenge : and it is hard to say what bitterness of malignity would prevail in a parish where these elections should happen to be frequent, and the enmity of opposition should be re-kindled before it had cooled.'

Though I present to my readers Dr. Johnson's masterly thoughts on this [a] subject, I think it proper to declare, that notwithstanding I am myself a lay patron, I do not entirely subscribe to his opinion.

On Friday, May 7, I breakfasted with him at Mr. Thrale's in the Borough. While we were alone, I endeavoured as well as I could to apologise for a lady[1] who had been divorced from her husband by act of Parliament. I said, that he had used her very ill, had behaved brutally to her, and that she could not continue to live with him without having her delicacy contaminated ; that all affection for him was thus destroyed ; that the essence of conjugal union being gone, there remained only a cold form, a mere civil obligation ; that she was in the prime of life, with qualities to produce happiness ; that these ought not to be lost ; and, that the gentleman on whose account she was divorced had gained her heart while thus unhappily situated.

[a] this 1 : the 2, 3.

[1] Lady Diana Beauclerk. In 1768 Beauclerk married the eldest daughter of the second Duke of Marlborough, two days after her divorce from her first husband, Viscount Bolingbroke, the nephew of the famous Lord Bolingbroke. She was living when her story, so slightly veiled as it is, was thus published by Boswell. The marriage was not a happy one. Two years after Beauclerk's death, Mr. Burke, looking at his widow's house, said in Miss Burney's presence :—' I am extremely glad, to see her at last so well housed ; poor woman ! the bowl has long rolled in misery ; I rejoice that it has now found its balance. I never, myself, so much enjoyed the sight of happiness in another, as in that woman when I first saw her after the death of her husband.' He then drew Beauclerk's character ' in strong and marked expressions, describing the misery he gave his wife, his singular ill-treatment of her, and the necessary relief the death of such a man must give.' Mme. D'Arblay's *Diary*, ii. 147.

Seduced, perhaps, by the charms of the lady in question, I thus attempted to palliate what I was sensible could not be justified ; for,[a] when I had finished my harangue, my venerable friend gave me a proper check : ' My dear Sir, never accustom your mind to mingle virtue and vice. The woman's a whore, and there's an end on't.'

He described the father [1] of one of his friends thus : ' Sir, he was so exuberant a talker at publick meetings, that the gentlemen of his county were afraid of him. No business could be done for his declamation.'

He did not give me full credit when I mentioned that I had carried on a short conversation by signs with some Esquimaux, who were then in London, particularly with one of them who was a priest. He thought I could not make them understand me. No man was more incredulous as to particular facts, which were at all extraordinary [2] ; and therefore no man was more scrupulously inquisitive, in order to discover the truth.

I dined with him this day at the house of my friends, Messieurs Edward and Charles Dilly [3], booksellers in the Poultry : there were present, their elder brother Mr. Dilly of Bedfordshire, Dr. Goldsmith, Mr. Langton, Mr. Claxton †, Reverend Dr. Mayo a dissenting minister, the Reverend Mr. Toplady [4], and my friend the Reverend Mr. Temple.

Hawkesworth's compilation of the voyages to the South Sea being mentioned ;—JOHNSON. ' Sir, if you talk of it as a subject of commerce, it will be gainful [5] ; if as a book that is to increase human knowledge, I believe there will not be much of that. Hawkesworth can tell only what the voyagers have told him ; and they have found very little, only one new animal, I think.' BOSWELL. ' But many insects, Sir.' JOHNSON. ' Why, Sir, as to

[a] *comma omitted* 2, 3.

[1] Old Mr. Langton. CROKER. See *post*, iii. 47.

[2] See *post*, iii. 188 ⟨and 229 ; v. 331⟩.

[3] See *post*, iii. 67.

[4] The writer of hymns.

[5] Malone says that ' Hawkesworth ... was introduced by Garrick to Lord Sandwich, who, thinking to put a few hundred pounds into his pocket, appointed him to revise and publish Cook's *Voyages*. He scarcely did any-thing to the MSS., yet sold it to Cadell and Strahan . . . for 6,000*l*.' Prior's *Malone*, p. 441. Thurlow, in his speech on copy-right on March 24, 1774, said ' that Hawkesworth's book, which was a mere composition of trash, sold for three guineas by the booksellers' monopolizing.' *Parl. Hist.* xvii. 1086. See *ante*, i. 253, note 1, and *post*, v. 282.

† ⟨John Claxton, F.S.A., ' worthy Claxton', Boswell's *Letters, passim*.⟩

insects, Ray reckons of British insects twenty thousand species. They might have staid at home and discovered enough in that way.'

Talking of birds, I mentioned Mr. Daines Barrington's ingenious Essay against the received notion of their migration. JOHNSON. ' I think we have as good evidence for the migration of woodcocks as can be desired. We find they disappear at a certain time of the year, and appear again at a certain time of the year ; and some of them, when weary in their flight, have been known to alight on the rigging of ships far out at sea.' One of the company observed, that there had been instances of some of them found in summer in Essex. JOHNSON. ' Sir, that strengthens our argument. *Exceptio probat regulam.* Some being found shews, that, if all remained, many would be found. A few sick or lame ones may be found.' GOLDSMITH. ' There is a partial migration of the swallows ; the stronger ones migrate, the others do not [1].'

BOSWELL. ' I am well assured that the people of Otaheite who have the bread tree, the fruit of which serves them for bread, laughed heartily when they were informed of the tedious process necessary with us to have bread ;—plowing, sowing, harrowing, reaping, threshing, grinding, baking.' JOHNSON. ' Why, Sir, all ignorant savages will laugh when they are told of the advantages of civilized life. Were you to tell men who live without houses, how we pile brick upon brick, and rafter upon rafter, and that after a house is raised to a certain height, a man tumbles off a scaffold, and breaks his neck, he [a] would laugh heartily at our folly in building ; but it does not follow that men are better without houses. No, Sir, (holding up a slice of a good loaf,) this is better than the bread tree [2].'

He repeated an argument, which is to be found in his ' Rambler [3],' against the notion that the brute creation is endowed

[a] neck, he 1 : neck ; he 2, 3.   *Grammar demands* they.

[1] Gilbert White held ' that, though most of the swallow kind may migrate, yet some do stay behind, and hide with us during the winter.' White's *Selborne*, Letter xii. See *ante*, ii. 55.

[2] See *ante*, ii. 73.

[3] No. 41. ' The sparrow that was hatched last spring makes her first nest the ensuing season, of the same materials, and with the same art, as in any following year ; and the hen conducts and shelters her first brood of chickens with all the prudence that she ever attains.'

with the faculty of reason : ' birds build by instinct ; they
never improve ; they build their first nest as well as any one that [a]
they ever build.' GOLDSMITH. ' Yet we see if you take away
a bird's nest with the eggs in it, she will make a slighter nest
and lay again.' JOHNSON. ' Sir, that is because at first she has
full time and makes her nest deliberately.   In the case you
mention she is pressed to lay, and must therefore make her nest
quickly, and consequently it will be slight.' GOLDSMITH. ' The
nidification of birds is what is least known in natural history,
though one of the most curious things in it.'

I introduced the subject of toleration [1].   JOHNSON. ' Every
society has a right to preserve publick peace and order, and
therefore has a good right to prohibit the propagation of
opinions which have a dangerous tendency.   To say the *magistrate* has this right, is using an inadequate word : it is the *society*
for which the magistrate is agent.   He may be morally or theo-
logically wrong in restraining the propagation of opinions which
he thinks dangerous, but he is politically right.' MAYO. ' I am
of opinion, Sir, that every man is entitled to liberty of conscience
in religion ; and that the magistrate cannot restrain that right.'
JOHNSON. ' Sir, I agree with you.   Every man has a right to
liberty of conscience, and with that the magistrate cannot
interfere.   People confound liberty of thinking with liberty of
talking ; nay, with liberty of preaching.   Every man has a
physical right to think as he pleases ; for it cannot be discovered
how he thinks.   He has not a moral right ; [b] for he ought to
inform himself, and think justly.   But, Sir, no member of a
society has a right to *teach* any doctrine contrary to what that [c]
society holds to be true.   The magistrate, I say, may be wrong
in what he thinks : but,[d] while he thinks himself right, he may,[d]
and ought to enforce what he thinks [2].' MAYO. ' Then, Sir,

---

a that *om.* 2, 3.   b right ; 1 : right 2, 3.   c that 1 : the 2, 3.   d *comma om.* 2, 3.

[1] See *post*, iii. 11, 380 ; iv. 12,
216.
[2] Rousseau went further than Johnson in this.   About eleven years
earlier he had, in his *Contrat Social*,
iv. 8, laid down certain ' simple
dogmas,' such as the belief in a God
and a future state, and said :—' Sans
pouvoir obliger personne à les croire,

il [le souverain] peut bannir de l'état
quiconque ne les croit pas : . . . Que
si quelqu'un, après avoir reconnu
publiquement ces mêmes dogmes, se
conduit comme ne les croyant pas,
qu'il soit puni de mort ; il a commis
le plus grand des crimes, il a menti
devant les lois.'

we are to remain always in errour, and truth never can prevail ; and the magistrate was right in persecuting the first Christians.' JOHNSON. ' Sir, the only method by which religious truth can be established is by martyrdom. The magistrate has a right to enforce what he thinks ; and he who is conscious of the truth has a right to suffer. I am afraid there is no other way of ascertaining the truth, but by persecution on the one hand and enduring it on the other [1].' GOLDSMITH. ' But how is a man to act, Sir ? Though firmly convinced of the truth of his doctrine, may he not think it wrong to expose himself to persecution ? Has he a right to do so ? Is it not, as it were, committing voluntary suicide ? ' JOHNSON. ' Sir, as to voluntary suicide, as you call it, there are twenty thousand men in an army who will go without scruple to be shot at, and mount a breach for five-pence a day.' GOLDSMITH. ' But have they a moral right to do this ? ' JOHNSON. ' Nay, Sir, if you will not take the universal opinion of mankind, I have nothing to say. If mankind cannot defend their own way of thinking, I cannot defend it. Sir, if a man is in doubt whether it would be better for him to expose himself to martyrdom or not, he should not do it. He must be convinced that he has a delegation from heaven.' GOLDSMITH. ' I would consider whether there is the greater chance of good or evil upon the whole. If I see a man who has fallen into a well, I would wish to help him out ; but if there is a greater probability that he shall pull me in, than that I shall pull him out, I would not attempt it. So were I to go to Turkey, I might wish to convert the Grand Signor to the Christian faith ; but when I considered that I should probably be put to death without effectuating my purpose in any degree, I should keep myself quiet.' JOHNSON. ' Sir, you must consider that we have perfect and imperfect obligations. Perfect obligations, which are generally not to do something, are clear and positive ; as, " thou shalt not kill." But charity, for instance, is not definable by limits. It is a duty to give to the poor ; but no man can say how much another should give to the poor, or when a man has given too little to save his soul. In the same manner,[a] it is a duty to instruct the ignorant, and of con-

---

[a] *comma omitted* 3.

[1] See *post*, iv. 12.

sequence to convert infidels to Christianity ; but no man in the common course of things is obliged to carry this to such a degree as to incur the danger of martyrdom, as no man is obliged to strip himself to the shirt in order to give charity. I have said, that a man must be persuaded that he has a particular delegation from heaven.' GOLDSMITH. ' How is this to be known ? Our first reformers, who were burnt for not believing bread and wine to be CHRIST '—JOHNSON. (interrupting him,) ' Sir, they were not burnt for not believing bread and wine to be CHRIST, but for insulting those who did believe it. And, Sir, when the first reformers began, they did not intend to be martyred : as many of them ran away as could.' BOSWELL. ' But, Sir, there was your countryman, Elwal [1], who you told me challenged King George with his black-guards, and his red-guards.' JOHNSON. ' My countryman, Elwal, Sir, should have been put in the stocks ; a proper pulpit for him ; and he'd have had a numerous audience. A man who preaches in the stocks will always have hearers enough.' BOSWELL. ' But Elwal thought himself in the right.' JOHNSON. ' We are not providing for mad people ; there are places for them in the neighbourhood,[a] ' (meaning Moorfields.) MAYO. ' But, Sir, is it not very hard that I should not be allowed to teach my children what I really believe to be the truth ? ' JOHNSON, ' Why, Sir, you might contrive to teach your children *extrà scandalum* ; but, Sir, the magistrate, if he knows it, has a right to restrain you. Suppose you teach your children to be thieves ? ' MAYO. ' This is making a joke of the subject.' JOHNSON. ' Nay, Sir, take it thus :—that you teach them the community of goods ; for which there are as many plausible arguments as for most erroneous doctrines. You teach them that all things at first were in common, and that no man had a right to any thing but as he laid his hands upon it ; and that this still is, or ought to be, the rule amongst mankind. Here, Sir, you sap a great principle in society,—property. And don't you think the magistrate would have a right to prevent you ? Or, suppose you should teach your children the notions [b] of the Adamites, and they should run naked into the streets, would not the magistrate have a right to flog 'em into

a neighbourhood, 1: neighbourhood. 2, 3.   b notions 1: notion 2, 3.
[1] Boswell calls Elwall Johnson's   from the same county. ⟨Cf. the
countryman, because they both came   Oxford Dictionary s.v. *Country* 7 and

their doublets ? ' MAYO. ' I think the magistrate has no right
to interfere till there is some overt act.' BOSWELL. ' So, Sir,
though he sees an enemy to the state charging a blunderbuss, he is
not to interfere till it is fired off ? ' MAYO. ' He must be sure of
its direction against the state.' JOHNSON. ' The magistrate is to
judge of that.—He has no right to restrain your thinking,
because the evil centers in yourself. If a man were sitting at
this table, and chopping off his fingers, the magistrate, as
guardian of the community, has no authority to restrain him,
however he might do it from kindness as a parent.—Though,
indeed, upon more consideration, I think he may ; as it is
probable, that he who is chopping off his own fingers, may
soon proceed to chop off those of other people. If I think
it right to steal Mr. Dilly's plate, I am a bad man ; but he can
say nothing to me. If I make an open declaration that I think
so, he will keep me out of his house. If I put forth my hand, I
shall be sent to Newgate. This is the gradation of thinking,
preaching, and acting : if a man thinks erroneously, he may
keep his thoughts to himself, and nobody will trouble him ;
if he preaches erroneous doctrine, society may expel him ;
if he acts in consequence of it, the law takes place, and he is
hanged [1].' MAYO. ' But, Sir, ought not Christians to have
liberty of conscience ? ' JOHNSON. ' I have already told you so,
Sir. You are coming back to where you were.' BOSWELL. ' Dr.
Mayo is always taking a return post-chaise, and going the stage
over again. He has it at half price.' JOHNSON. ' Dr. Mayo,
like other champions for unlimited toleration, has got a set of
words [2]. Sir, it is no matter, politically, whether the magistrate
be right or wrong. Suppose a club were to be formed, to drink
confusion to King George the Third, and a happy restoration

Jane Austen's use (*Novels*, ed. Chapman, 1926, i. 396).⟩ See *ante*, ii. 164.

[1] Baretti, in a MS. note on *Piozzi Letters*, i. 219, says :—' Johnson would have made an excellent Spanish inquisitor : To his shame be it said, he always was tooth and nail against toleration.'

[2] Dr. Mayo's calm temper and steady perseverance, rendered him an admirable subject for the exercise of Dr. Johnson's powerful abilities. He never flinched : but, after reiterated blows, remained seemingly unmoved as at the first. The scintillations of Johnson's genius flashed every time he was struck, without his receiving any injury. Hence he obtained the epithet of THE LITERARY ANVIL. BOSWELL.

See *post*, iii. 284 *et seq.*, for an

to Charles the Third [1] ; this would be very bad with respect to the State ; but every member of that club must either conform to its rules, or be turned out of it. Old Baxter †, I remember, maintains, that the magistrate should " tolerate all things that are tolerable." This is no good definition of toleration upon any principle ; but it shews that he thought some things were not tolerable.' TOPLADY. ' Sir, you have untwisted this difficult subject with great dexterity [2].'

During this argument, Goldsmith sat in restless agitation, from a wish to get in and *shine* [3]. Finding himself excluded, he had taken his hat to go away [4], but remained for some time with it in his hand, like a gamester, who at the close of a long night, lingers for a little while, to see if he can have a favourable opening to finish with success. Once when he was beginning to speak, he found himself overpowered by the loud voice of Johnson, who was at the opposite end of the table, and did not perceive Goldsmith's attempt. Thus disappointed of his wish to obtain the attention of the company, Goldsmith in a passion threw down his hat, looking angrily at Johnson, and exclaiming in a bitter tone, ' *Take it.*' When Toplady was going to speak, Johnson uttered some sound, which led Goldsmith to think that he was beginning again, and taking the words from Toplady.

account of another dinner at Mr. Dilly's, where Johnson and Mayo met.

[1] The Young Pretender, Charles Edward.

[2] ⟨Mrs. Piozzi printed as a postscript to Johnson's letter to her of 20 May, 1775, the following sentence : ' I dined in a large company at a dissenting bookseller's yesterday, and disputed against toleration with one Doctor Meyer.' Croker, who was probably right in assuming that ' this must have been the dinner noted in the text,' was unable to reconcile the dates, and the mention in the body of the letter of the death of the Queen of Denmark (10 May, 1775). He thought that Boswell had ' misdated and misplaced his note of this conversation.' Mrs. Piozzi, however, was the culprit, for she cut the sentence from another letter and pasted it on to this one. The name in the original, now in the Adam Collection, is not easily decipherable, but Malone in his annotated copy of the *Piozzi Letters* said it was ' Mayo '. We have no record that Johnson ever met a ' Doctor Meyer'.⟩

[3] See *ante*, i. 423 and ii. 231.

[4] ' It is very possible he had to call at Covent-garden on his way, and that for this, and not for Boswell's reason, he had taken his hat early. The actor who so assisted him in Young Marlow, Lee Lewes, was taking his benefit this seventh of May ; and, for an additional attraction, Goldsmith had written him the "occasional" epilogue.' Forster's *Goldsmith*, ii. 376.

† ⟨See App. B, p. 505.⟩

Upon which, he seized this opportunity of venting his own envy and spleen, under the pretext of supporting another person : ' Sir, (said he to Johnson,) the gentleman has heard you patiently for an hour ; pray allow us now to hear him [1].' JOHNSON. (sternly,) ' Sir, I was not interrupting the gentleman. I was only giving him a signal of my attention. Sir, you are impertinent.' Goldsmith made no reply, but continued in the company for some time.

A gentleman present [2] ventured to ask Dr. Johnson if there was not a material difference as to toleration of opinions which lead to action, and opinions merely speculative ; for instance, would it be wrong in the magistrate to tolerate those who preach against the doctrine of the TRINITY ? Johnson was highly offended, and said, ' I wonder, Sir, how a gentleman of your piety can introduce this subject in a mixed company.' He told me afterwards, that the impropriety was, that perhaps some of the company might have talked on the subject in such terms as would [a] have shocked him [3] ; or he might have been forced to appear in their eyes a narrow-minded man. The gentleman, with submissive deference, said, he had only hinted at the question from a desire to hear Dr. Johnson's opinion upon it. JOHNSON. ' Why then, Sir, I think that permitting men to preach any opinion contrary to the doctrine of the established church, tends,[b] in a certain degree, to lessen the authority of the church, and,[b] consequently, to lessen the influence of religion.' ' It may be considered, (said the gentleman,) whether it would not be politick to tolerate in such a case.' JOHNSON. ' Sir, we have been talking of *right :* this is another question. I [c] think it is *not* politick to tolerate in such a case.'

Though he did not think it fit that so aweful a subject should be introduced in a mixed company, and therefore at this time waved the theological question ; yet his own orthodox belief in

[a] would 1 : might 2, 3.　　[b] *comma omitted* 3.　　[c] *I* 1, 2: I 3.

[1] Johnson was not given to interrupting a speaker. Hawkins (*Life*, p. 164), describing his conversation, says :—' For the pleasure he communicated to his hearers, he expected not the tribute of silence : on the contrary, he encouraged others, particularly young men, to speak, and paid a due attention to what they said.' See *post*, iii. 54, note 1.

[2] That this was Langton can be seen from Boswell's *Hebrides*, Aug. 22, *post*, v. 89, and from Johnson's letters, *post*, ii. 265, 282, 292. ⟨Mrs. Piozzi's note confirms the identification.⟩

[3] See *post*, iv. 216.

the sacred mystery of the TRINITY is evinced beyond doubt, by the following passage in his private devotions :

' O LORD, hear my prayers [a], for JESUS CHRIST'S sake ; to whom with thee and the HOLY GHOST, *three persons and one* GOD, be all honour and glory, world without end.[b] Amen [1].'

BOSWELL. ' Pray, Mr. Dilly, how does Dr. Leland's [2] " History of Ireland " sell ? ' JOHNSON. (bursting forth with a generous indignation,) ' The Irish are in a most unnatural state ; for we see there the minority prevailing over the majority [3]. There is no instance, even in the ten persecutions [4], of such severity as that which the Protestants of Ireland have exercised against the Catholicks. Did we tell them we have conquered them, it would be above board : to punish them by confiscation and other penalties, as rebels, was monstrous injustice [5]. King William was not their lawful sovereign : he had not been acknowledged by the Parliament of Ireland, when they appeared in arms against him.'

I here suggested something favourable of the Roman Catholicks. TOPLADY. ' Does not their invocation of saints suppose omnipresence in the saints ? ' JOHNSON. ' No, Sir ; it supposes only pluri-presence ; [c] and when spirits are divested of matter, it seems probable that they should see with more extent than when in an embodied state. There is, therefore, no approach to an invasion of any of the divine attributes, in the invocation of saints. But I think it is will-worship, and presumption. I see no command for it, and therefore think it is safer not to practise it [6].'

He and Mr. Langton and I went together to THE CLUB, where we found Mr. Burke, Mr. Garrick, and some other members, and

a prayers 1, *orig.*: prayer 2, 3.   b end. 1, *orig.*: end, 2, 3.   c *semicolon omitted* 3.

[1] Pr. and Med. p. 40. ⟨¶ 40.⟩ BOSWELL.

[2] See *ante*, i. 489.

[3] ' In England,' wrote Burke, ' the Roman Catholics are a sect ; in Ireland they are a nation.' Burke's *Corres.* iv. 89.

[4] ' The celebrated number of *ten* persecutions has been determined by the ecclesiastical writers of the fifth century, who possessed a more distinct view of the prosperous or adverse fortunes of the church, from the age of Nero to that of Diocletian. The ingenious parallels of the *ten* plagues of Egypt, and of the *ten* horns of the Apocalypse, first suggested this calculation to their minds.' Gibbon's *Decline and Fall*, ch. xvi, first edit. i. 555.

[5] See *ante*, ii. 121, 130.

[6] See *ante*, ii. 105.

amongst them our friend Goldsmith, who sat silently brooding over Johnson's reprimand to him after dinner. Johnson perceived this, and said aside to some of us, ' I'll make Goldsmith forgive me ; ' and then called to him in a loud voice, ' Dr. Goldsmith,—something passed to-day where you and I dined ; I ask your pardon [1].' Goldsmith answered placidly, ' It must be much from you, Sir, that I take ill.' And so at once the difference was over, and they were on as easy terms as ever, and Goldsmith rattled away as usual [2].

In our way to the club to-night, when I regretted that Goldsmith would, upon every occasion, endeavour to shine, by which he often exposed himself, Mr. Langton observed, that he was not like Addison, who was content with the fame of his writings, and did not aim also at excellency in conversation, for which he found himself unfit ; and that he said to a lady,[a] who complained of his having talked little in company, ' Madam, I have but ninepence in ready money, but I can draw for a thousand pounds [3].'

[a] *comma omitted* 3.

[1] Reynolds said :—' He had one virtue which I hold one of the most difficult to practise. After the heat of contest was over, if he had been informed that his antagonist resented his rudeness, he was the first to seek after a reconciliation.' Leslie and Taylor's *Reynolds*, ii. 457. He wrote to Dr. Taylor, 18 Nov. 1756 :—' When I am musing alone, I feel a pang for every moment that any human being has by my peevishness or obstinacy spent in uneasiness.' *Letters*, No. 106. More than twenty years later he said in Miss Burney's hearing :—' I am always sorry when I make bitter speeches, and I never do it, but when I am insufferably vexed.' Mme. D'Arblay's *Diary*, i. 130. ' When the fray was over,' writes Murphy (*Life*, p. 140), ' he generally softened into repentance, and, by conciliating measures, took care that no animosity should be left rankling in the breast of his antagonist.' See *ante*, ii. 109, and *post*, iv. 321.

[2] Johnson had offended Langton as well as Goldsmith this day, yet of Goldsmith only did he ask pardon. Perhaps this fact increased Langton's resentment, which lasted certainly more than a year. See *post*, ii. 282, 292.

[3] ' Addison, speaking of his own deficience in conversation, used to say of himself, that, with respect to intellectual wealth, " he could draw bills for a thousand pounds, though he had not a guinea in his pocket." ' Johnson's *Life of Addison*, 106. Somewhat the same thought may be found in *The Tatler*, No. 30, where it is said that ' a man endowed with great perfections without good-breeding, is like one who has his pockets full of gold, but always wants change for his ordinary occasions.' I have traced it still earlier, for Burnet in his *History of his own Times*, i. 210, says, that ' Bishop Wilkins used to say, Lloyd had the most learning in ready cash of any he ever knew.' Later authors have used the same image. Lord Chesterfield (*Letters*, i. 517) in 1749 wrote of Lord Bolingbroke :—' He has an in-

I observed, that Goldsmith had a great deal of gold in his cabinet, but, not content with that, was always taking out his purse. JOHNSON. ' Yes, Sir, and that so often an empty purse ! '

Goldsmith's incessant desire of being conspicuous in company, was the occasion of his sometimes appearing to such disadvantage as one should hardly have supposed possible in a man of his genius ¹. When his literary reputation had risen deservedly high, and his society was much courted, he became very jealous of the extraordinary attention which was every where paid to Johnson. One evening, in a circle of wits, he found fault with me for talking of Johnson as entitled to the honour of unquestionable superiority. ' Sir, (said he,) you are for making a monarchy of what should be a republick.'

He was still more mortified, when talking in a company with fluent vivacity, and, as he flattered himself, to the admiration of all who were present ; a German who sat next him, and perceived Johnson rolling himself, as if about to speak, suddenly stopped him, saying, ' Stay, stay,—Toctor Shonson is going to say something.' This was, no doubt, very provoking, especially to one so irritable as Goldsmith, who frequently mentioned it with strong expressions of indignation ².

finite fund of various and almost universal knowledge, which, from the clearest and quickest conception, and happiest memory, that ever man was blessed with, he always carries about him. It is his pocket-money, and he never has occasion to draw upon a book for any sum.' Southey wrote in 1816 (*Life and Corres.* iv. 206) :—' I wish to avoid a conference which will only sink me in Lord Liverpool's judgment : what there may be in me is not payable at sight ; give me leisure and I feel my strength.' Rousseau was in want of readiness like Addison :—' Je fais d'excellents impromptus à loisir ; mais sur le temps je n'ai jamais rien fait ni dit qui vaille. Je ferois une fort jolie conversation par la poste, comme on dit que les Espagnols jouent aux échecs. Quand je lus le trait d'un duc de Savoie qui se retourna, faisant

route, pour crier, *A votre gorge, marchand de Paris*, je dis, Me voilà.' *Confessions*, livre iii. See also *post*, iii. 339, and Johnson's *Lives Poets* (ed. Hill), ii. 156.

¹ ' Among the many inconsistencies which folly produces, or infirmity suffers in the human mind, there has often been observed a manifest and striking contrariety between the life of an author and his writings ; and Milton, in a letter to a learned stranger, by whom he had been visited, with great reason congratulates himself upon the consciousness of being found equal to his own character, and having preserved in a private and familiar interview that reputation which his works had procured him.' *The Rambler*, No. 14.

² Prior (*Life of Goldsmith*, ii. 459) says that it was not a German who

It may also be observed, that Goldsmith was sometimes content to be treated with an easy familiarity, but, upon occasions, would be consequential and important. An instance of this occurred in a small particular. Johnson had a way of contracting the names of his friends ; as, Beauclerk, Beau ; Boswell, Bozzy ; Langton, Lanky ; Murphy, Mur ; Sheridan, Sherry [1]. I remember one day, when Tom Davies was telling that Dr. Johnson said, ' We are all in labour for a name to *Goldy's* play,' Goldsmith seemed displeased that such a liberty should be taken with his name, and said, ' I have often desired him not to call me *Goldy* [2].' Tom was remarkably attentive to the most minute circumstance about Johnson. I recollect his telling me once, on my arrival in London, ' Sir, our great friend has made an improvement on his appellation of old Mr. Sheridan. He calls him now *Sherry derry.*'

' To the Reverend Mr. Bagshaw, at Bromley [3].

' Sir,

' I return you my sincere thanks for your additions to my Dictionary ; but the new edition has been published some time, and therefore

interrupted Goldsmith but a Swiss, Mr. Moser, the keeper of the Royal Academy (*post*, iv. 227). He adds that at a Royal Academy dinner Moser interrupted another person in the same way, when Johnson seemed preparing to speak, whereupon Goldsmith said, ' Are you sure that *you* can comprehend what he says ? '

[1] Edmund Burke he called Mund ; Dodsley, Doddy ; Derrick, Derry ; Cumberland, Cumbey ; Monboddo, Monny ; Stockdale, Stockey. Mrs. Piozzi represents him in his youth as calling Edmund Hector ' dear Mund.' *Ante*, i. 92, note 2. Sheridan's father had been known as Sherry among Swift and his friends. Swift's *Works*, ed. 1824, xv. 100.

[2] Mr. Forster (*Life of Goldsmith*, ii. 103) on this remarks :—' It was a courteous way of saying, " I wish *you* [Davies] wouldn't call me Goldy, whatever Mr. Johnson does." ' That he is wrong in this is shown by Boswell, in his letter to Johnson of Feb.

14, 1777, where he says :—' You remember poor Goldsmith, when he grew important, and wished to appear *Doctor Major*, could not bear your calling him *Goldy*.' *Post*, iii. 101. See also *post*, v. 308.

[3] The Reverend Thomas Bagshaw, M.A. who died on November 20, 1787, in the seventy-seventh year of his age, Chaplain of Bromley College, in Kent, and Rector of Southfleet. He had resigned the cure of Bromley Parish some time before his death. For this, and another letter from Dr. Johnson in 1784, to the same truly respectable man, I am indebted to Dr. John Loveday, of the Commons [*ante*, i. 462, note 1], a son of the late learned and pious John Loveday, Esq. of Caversham in Berkshire, who obligingly transcribed them for me from the originals in his possession. This worthy gentleman, having retired from business, now lives in Warwickshire. The world has been lately

I cannot now make use of them. Whether I shall ever revise it more, I know not. If many readers had been as judicious, as diligent, and as communicative as yourself, my work had been better. The world must at present take it as it is. I am, Sir,

'Your most obliged
'And most humble servant,
'SAM. JOHNSON.'

'May 8, 1773.'

On Sunday, May 8 [1], I dined with Johnson at Mr. Langton's [2], with Dr. Beattie and some other company. He descanted on the subject of Literary Property. 'There seems, (said he,) to be in authours a stronger right of property than that by occupancy; a metaphysical [3] right, a right, as it were, of creation, which should from its nature be perpetual; but the consent of nations is against it, and indeed reason and the interests of learning are against it; for were it to be perpetual, no book, however useful, could be universally diffused amongst mankind, should the proprietor take it into his head to restrain its circulation. No book could have the advantage of being edited with notes, however necessary to its elucidation, should the proprietor perversely oppose it. For the general good of the world, therefore, whatever valuable work has once been created by an authour, and issued out by him, should be understood as no longer in his power, but as belonging to the publick; at the same time the authour is entitled to an adequate reward. This he should have by an exclusive right to his work for a considerable number of years [4].'

He attacked Lord Monboddo's strange speculation on the primitive state of human nature [5]; observing, 'Sir, it is all

obliged to him as the Editor of the late Rev. Dr. Townson's excellent work, modestly entitled 'A Discourse on the Evangelical History, from the Interment to the Ascension of our Lord and Saviour Jesus Christ'; to which is prefixed, a truly interesting and pleasing account of the authour, by the Reverend Mr. Ralph Churton. BOSWELL.

[1] Sunday was May 9.

[2] As Langton was found deeply to resent Johnson's hasty expression at the dinner on the 7th, we must assume that he had invited Johnson to dine with him before the offence had been given.

[3] In the *Dictionary* Johnson, as the second definition of *metaphysical*, says: 'In Shakespeare it means *supernatural* or *preternatural*.' 'Creation' being beyond the nature of man, the right derived from it is preternatural or metaphysical.

[4] See *ante*, i. 437 ⟨and Johnson's letter to Strahan, *Letters*, No. 349 (*John. Misc.* ii. 442–5)⟩.

[5] Hume, on Feb. 24 of this year, mentioned to Adam Smith as a late publication Lord Monboddo's *Origin*

conjecture about a thing useless, even were it known to be true. Knowledge of all kinds is good. Conjecture, as to things useful, is good ; but conjecture as to what it would be useless to know, such as whether men went upon all four, is very idle.'

On Monday, May 9 [1], as I was to set out on my return to Scotland next morning, I was desirous to see as much of Dr. Johnson as I could. But I first called on Goldsmith to take leave of him. The jealousy and envy which, though possessed of many most amiable qualities, he frankly avowed, broke out violently at this interview. Upon another occasion, when Goldsmith confessed himself to be of an envious disposition, I contended with Johnson that we ought not to be angry with him, he was so candid in owning it. ' Nay, Sir, (said Johnson,) we must be angry that a man has such a superabundance of an odious quality, that he cannot keep it within his own breast, but it boils over.' In my opinion, however, Goldsmith had not more of it than other people have, but only talked of it freely [2].

He now seemed very angry that Johnson was going to be a traveller ; said,[a] ' he would be a dead weight for me to carry, and that I should never be able to lug him along through the Highlands and Hebrides.' Nor would he patiently allow me to enlarge upon Johnson's wonderful abilities ; but exclaimed, ' Is he like Burke, who winds into a subject like a serpent ? ' ' But, (said I,) Johnson is the Hercules who strangled serpents in his cradle.'

I dined with Dr. Johnson at General Paoli's. He was obliged, by indisposition, to leave the company early ; he appointed me, however, to meet him in the evening at Mr. (now Sir Robert) Chambers's in the Temple, where he accordingly came, though he continued to be very ill. Chambers, as is common on such occasions, prescribed various remedies to him. JOHNSON. (fretted by pain,) ' Pr'ythee don't teaze me. Stay till I am

[a] *comma omitted* 3.

and Progress of Language :—' It contains all the absurdity and malignity which I expected ; but is writ with more ingenuity and in a better style than I looked for.' J. H. Burton's *Hume*, ii. 467. See *ante*, ii. 74.

[1] Monday was May 10.

[2] See *ante*, i. 413. Percy wrote of Goldsmith's envy :—' Whatever appeared of this kind was a mere momentary sensation, which he knew not how like other men to conceal.' Goldsmith's *Misc. Works*, i. 117. ⟨See App. B, p. 506.⟩

well, and then you shall tell me how to cure myself.' He grew better, and talked with a noble enthusiasm of keeping up the representation of respectable families. His zeal on this subject was a circumstance in his character exceedingly remarkable, when it is considered that he himself had no pretensions to blood. I heard him once say, ' I have great merit in being zealous for subordination and the honours of birth ; for I can hardly tell who was my grandfather [1].' He maintained the dignity and propriety of male succession, in opposition to the opinion of one of our friends [2], who had that day employed Mr. Chambers to draw his will, devising his estate to his three sisters, in preference to a remote heir male. Johnson called them ' three *dowdies*,' and said, with as high a spirit as the boldest Baron in the most perfect days of the feudal system, ' An ancient estate should always go to males. It is mighty foolish to let a stranger have it because he marries your daughter, and takes your name. As for an estate newly acquired by trade, you may give it, if you will, to the dog *Towser*, and let him keep his *own* name.'

I have known him at times exceedingly diverted at what seemed to others a very small sport [3]. He now laughed immoderately, without any reason that we could perceive, at our friend's making his will ; called him the *testator*, and added, ' I dare say, he thinks he has done a mighty thing. He won't stay till he gets home to his seat in the country, to produce this wonderful deed : he'll call up the landlord of the first inn on the road ; and, after a suitable preface upon mortality and the uncertainty

---

[1] He might have applied to himself his own version of Ovid's lines, *Genus et proavos*, &c., the motto to *The Rambler*, No. 46 :—
' Nought from my birth or ancestors
  I claim ;
 All is my own, my honour and my
  shame.'
See *ante*, ii. 153. ⟨For Cornelius Ford, ' gentleman,' Johnson's grandfather, see A. L. Reade, *Reades of Blackwood Hill*, p. 132.⟩
[2] That Langton is meant is shewn by Johnson's letter of July 5 (*post*, ii. 265). The man who is there described as leaving the town in deep dudgeon was certainly Langton.

' Where is now my legacy ? ' writes Johnson. He is referring, I believe, to the last part of his playful and boisterous speech, where he says :—
' I hope he has left me a legacy.' Mr. Croker, who is great at suspicions, ridiculously takes the mention of a legacy seriously, and suspects ' some personal disappointment at the bottom of this strange obstreperous and sour merriment.' He might as well accuse Falstaff of sourness in his mirth. ⟨Mrs. Piozzi's note in her copy (1816) of the *Life* confirms the identification.⟩
[3] See *post*, v. 249, where Boswell makes the same remark.

of life, will tell him that he should not delay making his will ;
and here, Sir, will he say, is my will, which I have just made,
with the assistance of one of the ablest lawyers in the kingdom ;
and he will read it to him (laughing all the time). He believes
he has made this will ; but he did not make it : you, Chambers,
made it for him. I trust you have had more conscience than
to make him say, " being of sound understanding ; " ha, ha, ha !
I hope he has left me a legacy. I'd have his will turned into
verse, like a ballad.'

In this playful manner did he run on, exulting in his own
pleasantry, which certainly was not such as might be expected
from the authour of ' The Rambler,' but which is here preserved,
that my readers may be acquainted even with the slightest occasional characteristicks of so eminent a man.

Mr. Chambers did not by any means relish this jocularity
upon a matter of which *pars magna fuit* [1], and seemed impatient
till he got rid of us. Johnson could not stop his merriment, but
continued it all the way till we got without the Temple-gate.
He then burst into such a fit of laughter, that he appeared to be
almost in a convulsion ; and, in order to support himself, laid
hold of one of the posts at the side of the foot pavement, and
sent forth peals so loud, that in the silence of the night his voice
seemed to resound from Temple-bar to Fleet-ditch.

This most ludicrous exhibition of the aweful, melancholy, and
venerable Johnson [2], happened well to counteract the feelings of

---

[1] ' Et quorum pars magna fui.'
' Yea, and was no small part
thereof.'
Morris, *Æneids*, ii. 6.

[2] Johnson, as drawn by Boswell, is
too ' aweful, melancholy, and venerable.' Such ' admirable fooling ' as
he describes here is but rarely shown
in his pages. Yet he must often have
seen equally ' ludicrous exhibitions.'
Hawkins (*Life*, p. 258) says, that ' in
the talent of humour there hardly
ever was Johnson's equal, except
perhaps among the old comedians.'
Murphy writes (*Life*, p. 139) :—' Johnson was surprized to be told, but it is
certainly true, that, with great powers
of mind, wit and humour were his

shining talents.' Mrs. Piozzi confirms
this. ' Mr. Murphy,' she writes (*Anec.*
p. 205 : John. Misc. i. 287), ' always
said, he was incomparable at buffoonery.' She adds (p. 298 : i. 345) :—
' He would laugh at a stroke of genuine
humour, or sudden sally of odd absurdity, as heartily and freely as I
ever yet saw any man ; and though
the jest was often such as few felt
besides himself, yet his laugh was
irresistible, and was observed immediately to produce that of the company, not merely from the notion
that it was proper to laugh when he
did, but purely out of want of power
to forbear it.' Miss Burney records :—
'Dr. Johnson has more fun, and

sadness which I used to experience when parting with him for a considerable time. I accompanied him to his door, where he gave me his blessing.

He records of himself this year, ' Between Easter and Whitsuntide, having always considered that time as propitious to study, I attempted to learn the Low Dutch language [1].' It is to be observed, that he here admits an opinion of the human mind being influenced by seasons, which he ridicules in his writings [2]. His progress, he says, ' was interrupted by a fever, which, by the imprudent use of a small print, left an inflammation in his useful eye [3].' We cannot but admire his spirit when we know, that amidst a complication of bodily and mental distress, he was still animated with the desire of intellectual improvement [4]. Various notes of his studies appear on different days, in his manuscript diary of this year ; such as,

' *Inchoavi lectionem Pentateuchi—Finivi lectionem Gonf. Fab. Burdonum* [5].*—Legi primum actum Troadum.—Legi Dissertationem Clerici postremam de Pent.—*2 *of Clark's Sermons.—L. Appolonii pugnam Betriciam* †.*—L. centum versus Homeri.*'

Let this serve as a specimen of what accessions of literature he was perpetually infusing into his mind, while he charged himself with idleness.

This year died Mrs. Salusbury, (mother of Mrs. Thrale,) a lady whom he appears to have esteemed much, and whose memory he honoured with an Epitaph [6].

comical humour, and love of nonsense about him, than almost anybody I ever saw.' *Diary*, i. 204. See Boswell's own account, *post*, iv. 428.

[1] Pr. and Med. p. 129 ⟨¶ 103⟩. BOSWELL. See *post*, iv. 21, for Johnson's study of Low Dutch.

[2] 'Those that laugh at the portentous glare of a comet, and hear a crow with equal tranquillity from the right or left, will yet talk of times and situations proper for intellectual performances,' &c. *The Idler*, No. xi. See *ante*, i. 332.

[3] ' He did not see at all with one of his eyes ' (*ante*, i. 41). ⟨See App. B, p. 506.⟩

[4] Not six months before his death,

he wished me to teach him the Scale of Musick :—' Dr. Burney, teach me at least the alphabet of your language.' BURNEY.

[5] Confutatio Burdonum [i. e. Scaligerorum] Fabulæ (auctore I. R). ⟨First printed in the second edition of D. Heinsius's *Hercules tuam fidem*. See App. B, p. 507.⟩

† ⟨*Bebriciam*. The reference is to the fight of Polydeuces with Amycus, king of the Bebryces, in book ii of the *Argonautica*. See *John. Misc.* i. 69, n. 5.⟩

[6] Mrs. Piozzi's Anecdotes of Johnson, p. 131. BOSWELL. Mrs. Piozzi (*Anec.* p. 129 : John. Misc. i. 235) describes her mother and Johnson as

In a letter from Edinburgh, dated the 29th of May, I pressed him to persevere in his resolution to make this year the projected visit to the Hebrides, of which he and I had talked for many years, and which I was confident would afford us much entertainment.

' To James Boswell, Esq.

' Dear Sir,

' When your letter came to me, I was so darkened by an inflammation in my eye, that I could not for some time read it. I can now write without trouble, and can read large prints. My eye is gradually growing stronger ; and I hope will be able to take some delight in the survey of a Caledonian loch.

' Chambers is going a Judge, with six thousand a year, to Bengal [1]. He and I shall come down together as far as Newcastle, and thence I shall easily get to Edinburgh. Let me know the exact time when your Courts intermit. I must conform a little to Chambers's occasions, and he must conform a little to mine. The time which you shall fix, must be the common point to which we will come as near as we can. Except this eye, I am very well.

' Beattie is so caressed, and invited, and treated, and liked, and flattered, by the great, that I can see nothing of him. I am in great hope that he will be well provided for, and then we will live upon him at the Marischal College, without pity or modesty [2].

'excellent . . ., far beyond the excellence of any other man and woman I ever yet saw. As her conduct . . . extorted his truest esteem, her cruel illness excited all his tenderness. . . . He acknowledged himself improved by her piety, and astonished at her fortitude, and hung over her bed with the affection of a parent, and the reverence of a son.' Baretti, in a MS. note on *Piozzi Letters*, i. 81, says that ' Johnson could not much bear Mrs. Salusbury, nor Mrs. Salusbury him, when they first knew each other. But her cancer moved his compassion, and made them friends.' Johnson, recording her death, says 18 June :—'Yesterday as I touched her hand and kissed it, she pressed my hand between her two hands, which she probably intended as the parting caress. . . . This morning being called about nine to feel her pulse, I said at parting, " God bless you ; for Jesus Christ's sake." She smiled, as pleased.' *Pr. and Med.* p. 128 : ¶ 102.

[1] Johnson wrote to Dr. Taylor July 22, 1782 :—' Sir Robert Chambers slipped this session through the fingers of revocation, but I am in doubt of his continuance. Shelburne seems to be his enemy. Mrs. Thrale says they will do him no harm. She perhaps thinks there is no harm without hanging. The mere act of recall strips him of eight thousand a year.' *Letters*, No. 795.

[2] Beattie was Professor of Moral Philosophy. For some years his English friends had tried to procure for him a permanent provision beyond the very moderate emoluments arising from his office. Just before Johnson wrote, Beattie had been pri-

' —— ¹ left the town without taking leave of me, and is gone in deep dudgeon to —— ². Is not this very childish ? Where is now my legacy ³ ?

' I hope your dear lady and her dear baby are both well. I shall see them too when I come ; and I have that opinion of your choice, as to suspect that when I have seen Mrs. Boswell, I shall be less willing to go away. I am, dear Sir,

' Your affectionate humble servant,

' SAM. JOHNSON.'

' Johnson's-court, Fleet-street,
      July 5, 1773.'

' Write to me as soon as you can. Chambers is now at Oxford.'

I again wrote to him, informing him that the Court of Session rose on the twelfth of August, hoping to see him before that time, and expressing, perhaps in too extravagant terms, my admiration of him, and my expectation of pleasure from our intended tour.

' To JAMES BOSWELL, ESQ.

' DEAR SIR,

' I SHALL set out from London on Friday the sixth ⁴ of this month, and purpose not to loiter much by the way. Which day I shall be at Edinburgh, I cannot exactly tell. I suppose I must drive to an inn, and send a porter to find you.

' I am afraid Beattie will not be at his College soon enough for

vately informed that he was to have a pension of £200 a year. Forbes's *Beattie*, 1806, i. 254, 264. When Johnson heard of this ' he clapped his hands, and cried, " O brave we ! " ' ' *Post*, v. 360.

¹ Langton. See *ante*, ii. 254, note 2, and 259.

² Langton—his native village.

³ See *ante*, ii. 261, note 2.

⁴ That he set out on this day is shewn by his letter dated 12 Aug. to Mrs. Thrale. *Letters*, No. 318. The following anecdote in the Percy Memoir prefixed to Goldsmith's *Misc. Works* (i. 110), is therefore inaccurate :—' I was dining at Sir Joshua Reynolds's, August 7, 1773, where, amongst other company, were the Archbishop of Tuam and Mr. (now Lord) Eliot, when the latter making use of some sarcastical reflections on Goldsmith, Johnson broke out warmly in his defence, and, in the course of a spirited eulogium, said, " Is there a man, Sir, now who can pen an essay with such ease and elegance as Goldsmith ? " ' Johnson did in August, 1783, dine at Reynolds's, and meet there the Archbishop of Tuam, ' a man coarse of voice and inelegant of language.' *Letters*, No. 876. ⟨This anecdote is an interpolation by S. Rose, whose informant was Dr. W. Farr. Balderston, *Hist. Percy's Memoir*, p. 60.⟩

us, and I shall be sorry to miss him ; but there is no staying for the concurrence of all conveniences. We will do as well as we can.

' I am, Sir,

' Your most humble servant,

' August 3, 1773.' ' SAM. JOHNSON.'

TO THE SAME.

' DEAR SIR,

' NOT being at Mr. Thrale's when your letter came, I had written the inclosed paper and sealed it ; bringing it hither for a frank, I found yours. If any thing could repress my ardour, it would be such a letter as yours. To disappoint a friend is unpleasing : and he that forms expectations like yours, must be disappointed. Think only when you see me, that you see a man who loves you, and is proud and glad that you love him.

' I am, Sir,

' Your most affectionate

' August 3, 1773.' ' SAM. JOHNSON.'

TO THE SAME.

' Newcastle, Aug. 11, 1773 [a].

' DEAR SIR,

' I CAME hither last night, and hope, but do not absolutely promise, to be in Edinburgh on Saturday. Beattie will not come so soon.

' I am, Sir,

' Your most humble servant,

' SAM. JOHNSON.'

' My compliments to your lady.'

TO THE SAME.

' MR. JOHNSON sends his compliments to Mr. Boswell, being just arrived at Boyd's.'

' Saturday night.'

His stay in Scotland was from the 18th of August [1], on which day he arrived, till the 22d of November, when he set out on his return to London ; and I believe ninety-four days [2] were never passed by any man in a more vigorous exertion.

He came by the way of Berwick upon Tweed to Edinburgh,

[a] 1771 *editions* 1, 2, 3.

[1] It was on Saturday the 14th of August that he arrived. ⟨See *post*, v. 21.⟩

[2] From Aug. 14 to Nov. 22 is one hundred days.

where he remained a few days, and then went by St. Andrew's, Aberdeen, Inverness, and Fort Augustus, to the Hebrides, to visit which was the principal object he had in view. He visited the isles of Sky, Rasay, Col, Mull, Inchkenneth, and Icolmkill. He travelled through Argyleshire by Inverary, and from thence by Lochlomond and Dunbarton to Glasgow, then by Loudon to Auchinleck in Ayrshire, the seat of my family, and then by Hamilton, back to Edinburgh, where he again spent some time. He thus saw the four Universities of Scotland [1], its three principal cities, and as much of the Highland and insular life as was sufficient for his philosophical contemplation. I had the pleasure of accompanying him during the whole of this journey. He was respectfully entertained by the great, the learned, and the elegant, wherever he went ; nor was he less delighted with the hospitality which he experienced in humbler life [2].

His various adventures, and the force and vivacity of his mind, as exercised during this peregrination, upon innumerable topicks, have been faithfully, and to the best of my abilities, displayed in my ' Journal of a Tour to the Hebrides,' to which, as the publick has been pleased to honour it by a very extensive circulation [3], I beg leave to refer, as to a separate and remarkable portion of his life [4], which may be there seen in detail, and which exhibits as striking a view of his powers in conversation, as his works do of his excellence in writing. Nor can I deny to myself the very

---

[1] It is strange that not one of the four conferred on him an honorary degree. This same year Beattie had been thus honoured at Oxford. Gray, who visited Aberdeen eight years before Johnson, was offered the degree of doctor of laws, ' which, having omitted to take it at Cambridge, he thought it decent to refuse.' Johnson's *Life of Gray*, 18. ⟨See App. B.⟩

[2] He was long remembered amongst the lower orders of Hebrideans by the title of the *Sassenach More*, the *big Englishman*. WALTER SCOTT.

[3] The first edition was published on 1 October, 1785. In the following August, in his preface to the third edition, Boswell speaks of the first two editions as ' large impressions.' ⟨See Mr. F. A. Pottle's *Bibliography*, p. 122.⟩

[4] The authour was not a small gainer by this extraordinary Journey ; for Dr. Johnson thus writes to Mrs. Thrale, Nov. 3, 1773 : ' Boswell will praise my resolution and perseverance, and I shall in return celebrate his good humour and perpetual cheerfulness. He has better faculties than I had imagined ; more justness of discernment, and more fecundity of images. It is very convenient to travel with him ; for there is no house where he is not received with kindness and respect.' Let. 90, to Mrs. Thrale. MALONE. Johnson's *Letters*, No. 337. ⟨See *post*, v. 52, n. 6.⟩

flattering gratification of inserting here the character which my
friend Mr. Courtenay has been pleased to give of that work :

> ' With Reynolds' pencil, vivid, bold, and true,
> So fervent Boswell gives him to our view :
> In every trait we see his mind expand ;
> The master rises by the pupil's hand ;
> We love the writer, praise his happy vein,
> Grac'd with the naiveté of the sage Montaigne.
> Hence not alone are brighter parts display'd,
> But e'en the specks of character pourtray'd :
> We *see* the Rambler with fastidious smile
> Mark the lone tree, and note the heath-clad isle ;
> But when th' heroick tale of Flora [a] [1] charms,
> Deck'd in a kilt, he wields a chieftain's arms :
> The tuneful piper sounds a martial strain,
> And Samuel sings, " The King shall have his *ain*." '

During his stay at Edinburgh, after his return from the
Hebrides, he was at great pains to obtain information concerning
Scotland ; and it will appear from his subsequent letters, that he
was not less solicitous for intelligence on this subject after his
return to London.

'To James Boswell, Esq.

' Dear Sir,

' I came home last night, without any incommodity, danger,
or weariness, and am ready to begin a new journey. I shall go
to Oxford on Monday [2]. I know Mrs. Boswell wished me well to

[a] Flora 1 (*and orig.*): Flora's 2, 3.

[1] ' The celebrated Flora Macdonald. See Boswell's *Tour*.' Courtenay.

[2] Lord Eldon (at that time Mr.
John Scott) has the following reminiscences of this visit :—' I had
a walk in New Inn Hall Garden,
with Dr. Johnson, [and] Sir Robert
Chambers. . . . Sir Robert was gather-
ing snails, and throwing them over the
wall into his neighbour's garden. The
Doctor reproached him very roughly,
and stated to him that this was un-
mannerly and unneighbourly. " Sir,"
said Sir Robert, " my neighbour is a
Dissenter." " Oh ! " said the Doctor,
" if so, Chambers, toss away, toss away,

as hard as you can." The Doctor was
frequently . . . very absent. I have seen
him standing for a very long time,
without moving, with a foot on each
side the kennel which was then in the
middle of the High Street, with his
eyes fixed on the water running in it. . . .
In the common room of University
College, he was dilating upon some
subject, and the then head of Lincoln
College, Dr. Mortimer, . . . occasionally
interrupted him, saying, "I deny that."
This was often repeated, and observed
upon by Johnson, . . . in terms expressive of increasing displeasure and
anger. At length, upon the Doctor's
repeating the words, " I deny that,"

go [1]; her wishes have not been disappointed. Mrs. Williams has received Sir A's [2] letter.

' Make my compliments to all those to whom my compliments may be welcome.

' Let the box [3] be sent as soon as it can, and let me know when to expect it.

' Enquire, if you can, the order of the Clans : Macdonald is first, Maclean second ; further I cannot go. Quicken Dr. Webster [4].

' I am, Sir,
' Yours affectionately,
' SAM. JOHNSON.'

' Nov. 27, 1773.'

' MR. BOSWELL TO DR. JOHNSON.

' Edinburgh, Dec. 2, 1773.

* * * * * *

' YOU shall have what information I can procure as to the order of the Clans. A gentleman of the name of Grant tells me, that there

---

" Sir," said Johnson, " you must have forgot that an author has said, *Plus negabit unus asinus in una hora quam centum philosophi probaverint in centum annis.*" ' [Dr. Fisher, who related this story to Mr. Croker, described Dr. Mortimer ⟨, who became Rector of Lincoln in Sept. 1781,⟩ as ' a Mr. Mortimer, a shallow under-bred man, who had no sense of Johnson's superiority. . . . He flatly contradicted some assertion which Johnson had pronounced to be as clear as that two and two make four.' Croker's *Boswell*, p. 483. See also ed. 1835, x. 138.]
' Mrs. John Scott used . . . to relate that she had herself helped Dr. Johnson one evening to fifteen cups of tea.' Twiss's *Eldon*, i. 87.

[1] In this he showed a very acute penetration. My wife paid him the most assiduous and respectful attention, while he was our guest ; so that I wonder how he discovered her wishing for his departure. The truth is, that his irregular hours and uncouth habits, such as turning the candles with their heads downwards,

when they did not burn bright enough, and letting the wax drop upon the carpet, could not but be disagreeable to a lady. Besides, she had not that high admiration of him which was felt by most of those who knew him ; and what was very natural to a female mind, she thought he had too much influence over her husband. She once in a little warmth, made, with more point than justice, this remark upon that subject : ' I have seen many a bear led by a man ; but I never before saw a man led by a bear.' BOSWELL. See *ante*, ii. 66.

[2] Sir Alexander Gordon, one of the Professors at Aberdeen. BOSWELL.

[3] This was a box containing a number of curious things which he had picked up in Scotland, particularly some horn spoons. BOSWELL.

[4] The Reverend Dr. Alexander Webster, one of the ministers of Edinburgh, a man of distinguished abilities, who had promised him information concerning the Highlands and Islands of Scotland. BOSWELL.

is no settled order among them ; and he says, that the Macdonalds were not placed upon the right of the army at Culloden [1] ; the Stuarts were. I shall, however, examine witnesses of every name that I can find here. Dr. Webster shall be quickened too. I like your little memorandums ; they are symptoms of your being in earnest with your book of northern travels.

' Your box shall be sent next week by sea. You will find in it some pieces of the broom bush, which you saw growing on the old castle of Auchinleck. The wood has a curious appearance when sawn across. You may either have a little writing-standish made of it, or get it formed into boards for a treatise on witchcraft, by way of a suitable binding.'

*   *   *   *   *   *

' MR. BOSWELL TO DR. JOHNSON.

' Edinburgh, Dec. 18, 1773.

*   *   *   *   *   *

' YOU promised me an inscription for a print to be taken from an historical picture of Mary Queen of Scots being forced to resign her crown, which Mr. Hamilton at Rome has painted for me. The two following have been sent to me :

" *Maria Scotorum Regina meliori seculo digna, jus regium civibus seditiosis invita resignat.*"

" *Cives seditiosi Mariam Scotorum Reginam sese muneri abdicare invitam cogunt.*"

' Be so good as to read the passage in Robertson, and see if you cannot give me a better inscription [2]. I must have it both in Latin and English ; so if you should not give me another Latin one, you will at least choose the best of these two, and send a translation of it.'

*   *   *   *   *   *

His humane forgiving disposition was put to a pretty strong test on his return to London, by a liberty which Mr. Thomas Davies had taken with him in his absence, which was, to publish two volumes, entitled, ' Miscellaneous and fugitive Pieces,' which

---

[1] The Macdonalds always laid claim to be placed on the right of the whole clans, and those of that tribe assign the breach of this order at Culloden as one cause of the loss of the day. The Macdonalds, placed on the left wing, refused to charge, and positively left the field unassailed and unbroken. Lord George Murray in vain endeavoured to urge them on by saying, that their behaviour would make the left the right, and that he himself would take the name of Macdonald. WALTER SCOTT.

[2] ⟨See *post*, ii. 293, note 2, and App. B, p. 510.⟩

he advertised in the news-papers, ' By the Authour of the Rambler.' In this collection, several of Dr. Johnson's acknowledged writings, several of his anonymous performances, and some which he had written for others, were inserted ; but there were also some in which he had no concern whatever [1]. He was at first very angry, as he had good reason to be. But, upon consideration of his poor friend's narrow circumstances, and that he had only a little profit in view, and meant no harm, he soon relented, and continued his kindness to him as formerly [2].

In the course of his self-examination with retrospect to this year, he seems to have been much dejected ; for he says, January 1, 1774, ' This year has passed with so little improvement, that I doubt whether I have not rather [a] impaired than increased my learning ' [3] ; and yet we have seen how he *read*, and we know how he *talked* during that period.

He was now seriously engaged in writing an account of our travels in the Hebrides, in consequence of which I had the pleasure of a more frequent correspondence with him.

' To JAMES BOSWELL, ESQ.

' DEAR SIR,

' MY operations have been hindered by a cough ; at least I flatter myself, that if the [b] cough had not come, I should have been further advanced. But I have had no intelligence from Dr. W——, [Webster,] nor from the Excise-office, nor from you. No account of the little borough [4]. Nothing of the Erse language. I have yet heard nothing of my box.

[a] rather *not in orig. MS.*   [b] the 1 : my 2, 3.

[1] The whole of the first volume is Johnson's and three-quarters of the second. A second edition was published the following year, with a third volume added, which also contained pieces by Johnson, but no apology from Davies.

[2] ' When Davies printed the *Fugitive Pieces* without his knowledge or consent ; How, said I, would Pope have raved, had he been served so ? " We should never (replied he) have heard the last on't, to be sure ; but then Pope was a narrow man : I will however (added he) storm and bluster *myself* a little this time ; "— so went to London in all the wrath he could muster up. At his return I asked how the affair ended : " Why (said he), I was a fierce fellow, and pretended to be very angry, and Thomas was a good-natured fellow, and pretended to be very sorry: so *there* the matter ended : I believe the dog loves me dearly. Mr. Thrale (turning to my husband), what shall you and I do that is good for Tom Davies ? We will do something for him, to be sure." ' Piozzi's *Anec.* p. 55 : John. Misc. i. 184.

[3] Prayers and Meditations, p. 129. BOSWELL.

[4] The ancient Burgh of Prestick, in Ayrshire. BOSWELL.

' You must make haste and gather me all you can, and do it quickly, or I will and shall do without it.

' Make my compliments to Mrs. Boswell, and tell her that I do not love her the less for wishing me away. I gave her trouble enough, and shall be glad, in recompence, to give her any pleasure.

' I would send some porter into the Hebrides, if I knew which way it could be got to my kind friends there. Enquire, and let me know.

' Make my compliments to all the Doctors of Edinburgh, and to all my friends, from one end of Scotland to the other.

' Write to me, and send me what intelligence you can : and if any thing is too bulky for the post, let me have it by the carrier. I do not like trusting winds and waves.

' I am, dear Sir,
' Your most, &c.

' Jan. 29, 1774.'   ' SAM. JOHNSON.'

TO THE SAME.

' DEAR SIR,

' IN a day or two after I had written the last discontented letter, I received my box, which was very welcome. But still I must entreat you to hasten Dr. Webster, and continue to pick up what you can that may be useful.

' Mr. Oglethorpe was with me this morning. You ᵃ know his errand. He was not unwelcome.

' Tell Mrs. Boswell that my good intentions towards her still continue. I should be glad to do any thing that would either benefit or please her.

' Chambers is not yet gone, but so hurried, or so negligent, or so proud, that I rarely see him. I have, indeed, for some weeks past, been very ill of a cold and cough, and have been at Mrs. Thrale's, that I might be taken care of. I am much better : *novæ redeunt in prælia vires* [1] ; but I am yet tender, and easily disordered. How happy it was that neither of us were ill in the Hebrides.

' The question of Literary Property is this day before the Lords [2].

ᵃ morning. You 1: morning. you 2: morning, you 3.

[1] Perhaps Johnson imperfectly remembered, ' *novæ rediere in pristina vires.*' *Æneid,* xii. 424.

[2] See *ante,* i. 437 ; ii. 259. The decision was given on Feb. 22 against the perpetual right. ' By the above decision . . . near 200,000*l.* worth of what was honestly purchased at public sale, and which was yesterday thought property, is now reduced to nothing.

. . . The English booksellers have now no other security in future for any literary purchase they may make, but the statute of the 8th of Queen Anne, which secures to the author's assigns an exclusive property for 14 years, to revert again to the author, and vest in him for 14 years more.' *Ann. Reg.* 1774, xvii. i. 95.

Murphy [1] drew up the Appellants' case, that is, the plea against the perpetual right. I have not seen it, nor heard the decision. I would not have the right perpetual.

' I will write to you as any thing occurs, and do you send me something about my Scottish friends. I have very great kindness for them. Let me know likewise how fees come in, and when we are to see you.

' I am, Sir,

' Yours affectionately,

' London, Feb. 7, 1774.'   ' SAM. JOHNSON.'

He at this time wrote the following letters to Mr. Steevens, his able associate in editing Shakspeare :

' To GEORGE STEEVENS, ESQ. IN HAMPSTEAD.

' SIR,

' IF I am asked when I have seen Mr. Steevens, you know what answer I must give ; if I am asked when I shall see him, I wish you would tell me what to say.

' If you have " Lesley's History of Scotland," or any other book about Scotland, except Boetius and Buchanan, it will be a kindness if you send them to, Sir,

' Your humble servant,

' Feb. 7, 1774.'   ' SAM. JOHNSON.'

TO THE SAME.

SIR,

' WE are thinking to augment our club, and I am desirous of nominating you, if you care to stand the ballot, and can attend on Friday nights at least twice in five weeks : less than that [a] is too little, and rather more will be expected. Be pleased to let me know before Friday.

' I am, Sir,

' Your most, &c.

' Feb. 21, 1774.'   ' SAM. JOHNSON.'

TO THE SAME.

' SIR,

' LAST night you became a member of the club ; if you call on me on Friday, I will introduce you. A gentleman [2], proposed after you, was rejected.

a that 1 : this 2, 3.

[1] Murphy was a barrister as well as an author.

[2] ⟨His identity is disclosed by a letter, dated 8 March, 1774, from Garrick to Steevens printed by Mr. H. Murdock in the *Proc. Massachu-* *setts Hist. Soc.*, Mar. 1919, p. 150 : ' Do you know a gentleman whose name is *Gibbon*, propos'd by Dr. Goldsmith, and who was blackball'd the same evening you was elected ? '⟩

' I thank you for Neander, but wish he were not so fine [1]. I will take care of him.

'   ' I am, Sir,
'   ' Your humble servant,
' March 5, 1774.'   ' SAM. JOHNSON.'

' To JAMES BOSWELL, ESQ.
' DEAR SIR,
' DR. WEBSTER'S informations were much less exact and much less determinate than I expected : they are, indeed, much less positive than, if he can trust his own book [2] which he laid before me, he is able to give. But I believe it will always be found, that he who calls much for information will advance his work but slowly.

' I am, however, obliged to you, dear Sir, for your endeavours to help me, and hope, that between us something will some time be done, if not on this, on some occasion.

' Chambers is either married, or almost married, to Miss Wilton, a girl of sixteen, exquisitely beautiful, whom he has, with his lawyer's tongue, persuaded to take her chance with him in the East.

' We have added to the club [3], Charles Fox [4], Sir Charles Bunbury [5], Dr. Fordyce [6], and Mr. Steevens [7].

[1] See the Catalogue of Mr. Steevens's Library, No. 265 :—' Neandri (Mich.) Opus Aureum, Gr. et Lat. 2 tom. 4to. Corio turcico, foliis deauratis. Lipsiæ, 1577.' This was doubtless the book . . . MALONE (1811).

[2] A manuscript account drawn up[a] by Dr. Webster of all the parishes in Scotland, ascertaining their length, breadth, number of inhabitants, and distinguishing Protestants and Roman Catholicks. This book had been transmitted to government, and Dr. Johnson saw a copy of it in Dr. Webster's possession. BOSWELL.

[3] Beauclerk, three weeks earlier, had written to Lord Charlemont :—' Our club has dwindled away to nothing. Nobody attends but Mr. Chambers, and he is going to the East Indies. Sir Joshua and Goldsmith have got into such a round of pleasures, that they have no time.' Charlemont's *Life*, i. 350. Johnson, no doubt, had been kept away by illness (*ante*, ii. 272).

[4] Mr. Fox, as Sir James Mackintosh informed me, was brought in by Burke. CROKER.

[5] Sir C. Bunbury was the brother of Mr. H. W. Bunbury, the caricaturist, who married Goldsmith's friend, the elder Miss Horneck— ' Little Comedy ' as she was called. Forster's *Goldsmith*, ii. 147.

[6] Rogers (*Table-Talk*, p. 23) tells how Dr. Fordyce, who sometimes drank a good deal, was summoned to a lady patient when he was conscious that he had had too much wine. ' Feeling her pulse, and finding himself unable to count its beats, he muttered, " Drunk, by God ! " Next morning . . . a letter from her was put into his hand. " She too well knew," she wrote, " that he had discovered the unfortunate condition in which she was when he last visited her ; and she entreated him to keep the matter secret in consideration of the enclosed (a hundred-pound bank-note)." '

[7] Steevens wrote to Garrick on

a up *omitted* 2, 3.

' Return my thanks to Dr. Webster. Tell Dr. Robertson that I have not much to reply to his censure of my negligence ; and tell Dr. Blair, that since he has written hither what I said to him, we must now consider ourselves as even, forgive one another, and begin again [1]. I care not how soon, for he is a very pleasing man. Pay my compliments to all my friends, and remind Lord Elibank of his promise to give me all his works.

' I hope Mrs. Boswell and little Miss are well.—When shall I see them again ? She is a sweet lady, only she was so glad to see me go, that I have almost a mind to come again, that she may again have the same pleasure.

' Enquire if it be practicable to send a small present of a cask of porter to Dunvegan, Rasay, and Col. I would not wish to be thought forgetful of civilities.

' I am, Sir,

' Your humble servant,

' SAM. JOHNSON.'

' March 5, 1774.'

On the 5th of March I wrote to him, requesting his counsel whether I should this spring come to London. I stated to him on the one hand some pecuniary embarrassments, which, together with my wife's situation at that time, made me hesitate ; and, on the other, the pleasure and improvement which my annual visit to the metropolis always afforded me ; and particularly mentioned a peculiar satisfaction which I experienced in celebrating the festival of Easter in St. Paul's cathedral ; that to my fancy it appeared like going up to Jerusalem at the feast of the Passover ; and that the strong devotion which I felt on that occasion diffused its influence on my mind through the rest of the year [2].

March 6 :—' Mr. C. Fox pays you but a bad compliment ; as he appears, like the late Mr. Secretary Morris, to enter the Society at a time when he has *nothing else to do*. If the *bon ton* should prove a contagious disorder among us, it will be curious to trace its progress. I have already seen it breaking out in Dr. G[oldsmith] under the form of many a waistcoat : but I believe Dr. J[ohnson] will be the last man in whom the symptoms of it will be detected.' *Proc.*

Massachusetts Hist. Soc., Mar. 1919, p. 149. In less than a month poor Goldsmith was dead. Fox, just before his election to the club, had received through one of the door-keepers of the House of Commons the following note :—' SIR,—His Majesty has thought proper to order a new commission of the Treasury to be made out, in which I do not perceive your name. NORTH.'

[1] See Boswell's answer, *post*, ii. 278.
[2] See *post*, ii. 360.

'To James Boswell, Esq.

[*Not dated* [1], *but written about the* 15th *of March.*]

' Dear Sir,

' I am ashamed to think that since I received your letter I have passed so many days without answering it.

' I think there is no great difficulty in resolving your doubts. The reasons for which you are inclined to visit London, are, I think, not of sufficient strength to answer the objections. That you should delight to come once a year to the fountain of intelligence and pleasure, is very natural ; but both information and pleasure must be regulated by propriety. Pleasure, which cannot be obtained but by unseasonable or unsuitable expence, must always end in pain ; and pleasure, which must be enjoyed at the expence of another's pain, can never be such as a worthy mind can fully delight in.

' What improvement you might gain by coming to London, you may easily supply, or easily compensate, by enjoining yourself some particular study at home, or opening some new avenue to information. Edinburgh is not yet exhausted ; and I am sure you will find no pleasure here which can deserve either that you should anticipate any part of your future fortune, or that you should condemn yourself and your lady to penurious frugality for the rest of the year.

' I need not tell you what regard you owe to Mrs. Boswell's entreaties ; or how much you ought to study the happiness of her who studies yours with so much diligence, and of whose kindness you enjoy such good effects. Life cannot subsist in society but by reciprocal concessions. She permitted you to ramble last year, you must permit her now to keep you at home.

' Your last reason is so serious, that I am unwilling to oppose it. Yet you must remember, that your image of worshipping once a year in a certain place, in imitation of the Jews, is but a comparison ; and *simile non est idem ;* if the annual resort to Jerusalem was a duty to the Jews, it was a duty because it was commanded ; and you have no such command, therefore no such duty. It may be dangerous to receive too readily, and indulge too fondly, opinions, from which, perhaps, no pious mind is wholly disengaged, of local sanctity and local devotion. You know what strange effects they have produced over a great part of the Christian world. I am now writing, and you, when you read this, are reading under the Eye of Omnipresence.

' To what degree fancy is to be admitted into religious offices, it

[1] For Johnson on the importance of dating letters see *ante*, i. 122, note 2.

would require much deliberation to determine. I am far from intending totally to exclude it. Fancy is a faculty bestowed by our Creator, and it is reasonable that all his gifts should be used to his glory, that all our faculties should co-operate in his worship ; but they are to co-operate according to the will of him that gave them, according to the order which his wisdom has established. As ceremonies prudential or convenient are less obligatory than positive ordinances, as bodily worship is only the token to others or ourselves of mental adoration, so Fancy is always to act in subordination to Reason. We may take Fancy for a companion, but must follow Reason as our guide. We may allow Fancy to suggest certain ideas in certain places ; but Reason must always be heard, when she tells us, that those ideas and those places have no natural or necessary relation. When we enter a church we habitually recall to mind the duty of adoration, but we must not omit adoration for want of a temple ; because we know, and ought to remember, that the Universal Lord is every where present ; and that, therefore, to come to Jona [1], or to Jerusalem, though it may be useful, cannot be necessary.

' Thus I have answered your letter, and have not answered it negligently. I love you too well to be careless when you are serious.

' I think I shall be very diligent next week about our travels, which I have too long neglected.

' I am, dear Sir,

' Your most, &c.

' SAM. JOHNSON.'

' Compliments to Madam and Miss.'

TO THE SAME.

' DEAR SIR,

' THE lady who delivers [2] this has a lawsuit, in which she desires to make use of your skill and eloquence, and she seems to think that she shall have something more of both for a recommendation from me ; which, though I know how little you want any external incitement to your duty, I could not refuse her, because I know that at least it will not hurt her, to tell you that I wish her well.

' I am, Sir,

' Your most humble servant,

' SAM. JOHNSON.'

' May 10, 1774.'

[1] ⟨In his *Journey to the Western Islands* Johnson uses ' Jona ' and ' Iona ' indifferently.⟩

[2] ⟨Johnson himself tells us that this letter was ' by mistake given to the post'. See the fragment of a second letter to Boswell on the same subject. *Letters*, No. 355.⟩

' MR. BOSWELL TO DR. JOHNSON.

' Edinburgh, May 12, 1774.

' LORD HAILES has begged of me to offer you his best respects, and to transmit to you specimens of " Annals of Scotland, from the Accession of Malcolm Kenmore to the Death of James V." in drawing up which, his Lordship has been engaged for some time. His Lordship writes to me thus : " If I could procure Dr. Johnson's criticisms, they would be of great use to me in the prosecution of my work, as they would be judicious and true. I have no right to ask that favour of him. If you could, it would highly oblige me."

' Dr. Blair requests you may be assured that he did not write to London what you said to him, and that neither by word nor letter has he made the least complaint of you ; but, on the contrary, has a high respect for you, and loves you much more since he saw you in Scotland. It would both divert and please you to see his eagerness about this matter.'

' TO JAMES BOSWELL, ESQ.

' Streatham, June 21, 1774.

' DEAR SIR,

' YESTERDAY I put the first sheets of the " Journey to the Hebrides " to the press. I have endeavoured to do you some justice in the first paragraph [1]. It will be one volume in octavo, not thick.

' It will be proper to make some presents in Scotland. You shall tell me to whom I shall give ; and I have stipulated twenty-five for you to give in your own name [2]. Some will take the present better from me, others better from you. In this, you who are to live in the place ought to direct. Consider it. Whatever you can get for my purpose, send me ; and make my compliments to your lady and both the young ones.

' I am, Sir, your, &c.

' SAM. JOHNSON.'

---

[1] ' I was induced,' he says, ' to undertake the journey, by finding in Mr. Boswell a companion, whose acuteness would help my inquiry, and whose gaiety of conversation and civility of manners are sufficient to counteract the inconveniencies of travel, in countries less hospitable than we have passed.' The passage was quoted by Boswell in his *Hebrides*, *post*, v. 52.

[2] See *post*, iii. 94.

'Mr. Boswell to Dr. Johnson.

'Edinburgh, June 24 ª, 1774.

'You do not acknowledge the receipt of the various packets which I have sent to you. Neither can I prevail with you to *answer* my letters, though you honour me with *returns* [1]. You have said nothing to me about poor Goldsmith [2], nothing about Langton [3].

'I have received for you, from the Society for propagating Christian Knowledge in Scotland [4], the following Erse books :—" The New Testament; "—"Baxter's Call; "—" The Confession of Faith of the Assembly of Divines at Westminster; "—" The Mother's Catechism; "—" A Gaelick and English Vocabulary [5]." '

'To James Boswell, Esq.

'Dear Sir,

'I wish you could have looked over my book before the printer, but it could not easily be. I suspect some mistakes ; but as I deal, perhaps, more in notions than in facts, the matter is not great, and the second edition will be mended, if any such there be. The press will go on slowly for a time, because I am going into Wales to-morrow.

'I should be very sorry if I appeared to treat such a character as that of ᵇ Lord Hailes otherwise than with high respect. I return the sheets [6], to which I have done what mischief I could ; and finding it so little, thought not much of sending them. The narrative is clear, lively, and short.

'I have done worse to Lord Hailes than by neglecting his sheets : I have run him in debt. Dr. Horne, the President of Magdalen College in Oxford, wrote to me about three months ago, that he purposed to reprint Walton's Lives, and desired me to contribute to the work : my answer [7] was, that Lord Hailes intended the same publication ; and Dr.

ª June 25 *edit.* 1.

[1] Boswell wrote to Temple on May 8, 1779 :—' I think Dr. Johnson never *answered* but three of my letters, though I have had numerous *returns* from him.' *Letters*, No. 193, ii. 288. See *post*, iii. 209.

[2] Dr. Goldsmith died April 4, this year. Boswell.

Boswell wrote to Garrick on April 11, 1774 :—' Dr. Goldsmith's death would affect all the Club much. I have not been so much affected with any event that has happened of a long time. I wish you would give me who are at a distance, . . . some particulars

ᵇ that of *om.* 2, 3.

with regard to his last appearances, *Letters*, No. 124, i. 201.

[3] See *ante*, ii. 265.

[4] See *ante*, ii. 27, and *post*, v. 370.

[5] These books Dr. Johnson presented to the Bodleian Library. Boswell. ⟨See *post*, ii. 285 and App. B, p. 508.⟩

[6] On the cover enclosing them, Dr. Johnson wrote, ' If my delay has given any reason for supposing that I have not a very deep sense of the honour done me by asking my judgement, I am very sorry.' Boswell.

[7] ⟨This letter, dated 30 April 1774,

Horne has resigned it to him [1]. His Lordship must now think seriously about it.

' Of poor dear Dr. Goldsmith there is little to be told, more than the papers have made publick. He died of a fever, made, I am afraid, more violent by uneasiness of mind. His debts began to be heavy, and all his resources were exhausted. Sir Joshua [2] is of opinion that he owed not less than two thousand pounds [3]. Was ever poet so trusted before ?

' You may, if you please, put the inscription thus :

" *Maria Scotorum Regina nata* 15—, *a suis in exilium acta* 15—, *ab hospitâ neci data* 15—." You must find the years.

' Of your second daughter you certainly gave the account yourself, though you have forgotten it. While Mrs. Boswell is well, never doubt of a boy. Mrs. Thrale brought, I think, five girls running, but while I was with you she had a boy.

' I am obliged to you for all your pamphlets, and of the last I hope to make some use. I made some of the former.

' I am, dear Sir,

' Your most affectionate servant,

' July 4, 1774.'   ' SAM. JOHNSON.'

' My compliments to all the three ladies.'

' To BENNET LANGTON, ESQ. AT LANGTON, NEAR SPILSBY,
LINCOLNSHIRE.

' DEAR SIR,

' YOU have reason to reproach me that I have left your last letter so long unanswered, but I had nothing particular to say. Chambers, you find, is gone far, and poor Goldsmith is gone much further. He died of a fever, exasperated, as I believe, by the fear of distress.

is printed in Mr. R. B. Adam's *Catalogue*. Johnson says : ' You are reviving him [Walton] at Oxford, Lord Hail . . . appears to have the same design. I once had it too.'>

[1] See *post*, ii. 283, 445 ; iii. 107.

[2] ' Sir Joshua was much affected by the death of Goldsmith, to whom he had been a very sincere friend. He did not touch the pencil for that day, a circumstance most extraordinary for him, who passed *no day without a line*.' Northcote's *Reynolds*, i. 325.

[3] He owed his tailor £79, though he had paid him £110 in 1773. In this payment was included £35 for

his nephew's clothes. We find such entries in his own bills as—

<table>
<tr><td></td><td>£</td><td>s.</td><td>d.</td></tr>
<tr><td>' To Tyrian bloom satin grain and garter blue silk breeches . . .</td><td>8</td><td>2</td><td>7</td></tr>
<tr><td>To Queen's-blue dress suit . . . . .</td><td>11</td><td>17</td><td>0</td></tr>
<tr><td>To your blue velvet suit .</td><td>21</td><td>10</td><td>9 '</td></tr>
</table>

(See *ante*, ii. 83.) Filby's son said to Mr. Prior :—' My father attributed no blame to Goldsmith ; he had been a good customer ; and had he lived would have paid every farthing.' Prior's *Goldsmith*, ii. 232.

He had raised money and squandered it, by every artifice of acquisition, and folly of expence. But let not his frailties be remembered ; he was a very great man [1].

' I have just begun to print my Journey to the Hebrides, and am leaving the press to take another journey into Wales, whither Mr. Thrale is going, to take possession of, at least, five hundred a year, fallen to his lady. All at Streatham, that are alive [2], are well.

' I have never recovered from the last dreadful illness [3], but flatter myself that I grow gradually better ; much, however, yet remains to mend. Κύριε ἐλέησον [4].

' If you have the Latin version of *Busy, curious, thirsty fly* [5], be so kind as to transcribe and send it ; but you need not be in haste, for I

---

[1] ' Soon after Goldsmith's death, certain persons dining with Sir Joshua were commenting rather freely on some part of his works, which, in their opinion, neither discovered talent nor originality. To this, Dr. Johnson listened in his usual growling manner, for some time ; when, at length, his patience being exhausted, he rose, with great dignity, looked them full in the face, and exclaimed, " If nobody was suffered to abuse poor Goldy, but those who could write as well, he would have few censors." ' Northcote's *Reynolds*, i. 327. To Goldsmith might be applied the words that Johnson wrote of Savage (*Savage*, 343) :—' Vanity may surely readily be pardoned in him, to whom life afforded no other comforts than barren praises, and the consciousness of deserving them. Those are no proper judges of his conduct .who have slumbered away their time on the down of plenty ; nor will any wise man presume to say, " Had I been in Savage's condition, I should have lived or written better than Savage." '

[2] Mrs. Thrale's mother died the summer before (*ante*, ii. 263). Most of her children died early. By 1777 she had lost seven out of eleven. *Post*, iii. 109.

[3] Johnson had not seen Langton since early in the summer of 1773. He was then suffering from a fever

and an inflammation in the eye, for which he was twice copiously bled. (*Pr. and Med.* 22 July, ¶ 103.) The following winter he was distressed by a cough. (*Ib.* 9 Jan., ¶ 106.) Neither of these illnesses was severe enough to be called dreadful. In the spring of 1770 he was very ill. (*Ib.* 14 Apr., ¶ 85.) On Sept. 18, 1771, he records : —' For the last year I have been slowly recovering . . . from the violence of my last illness.' (*Ib.* ¶ 91.) On April 18, 1772, in reviewing the last year, he writes :—' An unpleasing incident is almost certain to hinder my rest. This is the remainder of my last illness.' (*Ib.* ¶ 94.) In the winter of 1772–3, he suffered from a cough. (*Ib.* ¶ 100.) I think that he must mean the illness of 1770, though it is to be noticed that he wrote to Boswell on July 5, 1773 :—' Except this eye [the inflamed eye], I am very well.' (*Ante*, ii. 264.)

[4] ' Lord have mercy upon us.'

[5] See Johnson's *Works*, i. 172, for his Latin version. D'Israeli (*Curiosities of Literature*, ed. 1859, iii. 496) says ' that Oldys [*ante*, i. 175] always asserted that he was the author of the well-known song—*Busy* [etc.], and, as he was a rigid lover of truth, I doubt not that he wrote it. . . . I have traced this popular song through a dozen of collections since the year 1740, the first in which I find it.'

shall be I know not where, for at least five weeks. I wrote the following tetrastick on poor Goldsmith :

Τὸν τάφον εἰσοράᾳς τὸν Ὀλιβάροιο, κονίην
Ἄφροσι μὴ σεμνὴν, Ξεῖνε, πόδεσσι πάτει·
Οἷσι μέμηλε φύσις, μέτρων χάρις, ἔργα παλαιῶν,
Κλαίετε ποιητὴν, ἱστορικὸν, φυσικόν [1].

' Please to make my most respectful compliments to all the ladies, and remember me to young George and his sisters. I reckon George begins to shew a pair of heels.

' Do not be sullen now [2], but let me find a letter when I come back.

' I am, dear Sir,

' Your affectionate, humble servant,

' SAM. JOHNSON.'

' July 5, 1774.'

' TO MR. ROBERT LEVET.

' Llewenny [3], in Denbighshire, Aug. 16, 1774.

' DEAR SIR,

' MR. THRALE'S affairs have kept him here a great while, nor do I know exactly when we shall come hence. I have sent you a bill upon Mr. Strahan.

' I have made nothing of the Ipecacuanha, but have taken abundance of pills, and hope that they have done me good.

' Wales, so far as I have yet seen of it, is a very beautiful and rich country, all enclosed, and planted. Denbigh is not a mean town. Make my compliments to all my friends, and tell Frank I hope he remembers my advice. When his money is out, let him have more.

' I am, Sir,

' Your humble servant,

' SAM. JOHNSON.'

[1] Mr. Seward (*Anec.*, 1798, ii. 466) gives the following version of these lines :
' Whoe'er thou art, with reverence tread
Where Goldsmith's letter'd dust is laid.
If nature and the historic page,
If the sweet muse thy care engage,
Lament him dead, whose powerful mind
Their various energies combin'd.'
[2] See *ante*, ii. p. 265.
[3] At Lleweney, the house of Mrs. Thrale's cousin, Mr. Cotton, Dr. Johnson stayed nearly three weeks.

Post, v. 435. ⟨The Hon. Thomas Fitzmaurice, who had purchased the house (Pennant, *Tour Wales*, 1784, ii. 25), invited Johnson to visit him in 1780. Johnson's *Letters*, No. 664. ' Aristotle ' Twining describes the house in 1785 as ' a large but irregular building, containing a noble hall, in the true antique style, with galleries, a huge chimney, great beams, and weapons of all sorts stuck around it.' *Select. fr. Papers Twining Family*, 1887, pp. 116 ff. See also A. M. Broadley, *Dr. Johnson and Mrs. Thrale*, 1910, pp. 182, 229.⟩

'Mr. Boswell to Dr. Johnson.

'Edinburgh, Aug. 30, 1774.

' You have given me an inscription for a portrait of Mary Queen of Scots, in which you, in a short and striking manner, point out her hard fate. But you will be pleased to keep in mind, that my picture is a representation of a particular scene in her history ; her being forced to resign her crown, while she was imprisoned in the castle of Loch-levin. I must, therefore, beg that you will be kind enough to give me an inscription † suited to that particular scene ; or determine which of the two formerly transmitted to you is the best ; and, at any rate, favour me with an English translation. It will be doubly kind if you comply with my request speedily.

' Your critical notes on the specimen of Lord Hailes's "Annals of Scot-land," are excellent. I agreed with you in every one of them. He himself objected only to the alteration of *free* to *brave*, in the passage where he says that Edward " departed with the glory due to the con-querour of a free people." He says, " to call the Scots brave would only add to the glory of their conquerour." You will make allowance for the national zeal of our annalist. I now send a few more leaves of the Annals, which I hope you will peruse, and return with observations, as you did upon the former occasion. Lord Hailes writes to me thus : " Mr. Boswell will be pleased to express the grateful sense which Sir David Dalrymple [1] has of Dr. Johnson's attention to his little specimen. The further specimen will show, that

" Even in an *Edward* he can see desert [2]."

' It gives me much pleasure to hear that a re-publication of Isaac Walton's Lives is intended. You have been in a mistake in thinking that Lord Hailes had it in view. I remember one morning [3], while he sat with you in my house, he said, that there should be a new edition of Walton's Lives ; and you said,[a] that " they should be benoted a little." This was all that passed on that subject. You must, there-fore, inform Dr. Horne, that he may resume his plan. I enclose a

[a] *comma omitted* [3].

[1] Lord Hailes was Sir David Dal-rymple. See *ante*, i. 267. He is not to be confounded with Sir John Dalrymple, mentioned *ante*, ii. 210.

[2] ' Ev'n in a Bishop I can spy Desert ;
Secker is decent, Rundel has a Heart.'
Pope's *Epilogue to the Satires*, ii. 70.

[3] In the first two editions *forenoon*.

Boswell, in three other passages, made the same change in the third edition. *Forenoon* perhaps he considered a Scotticism. ⟨The change was also made once in the second edition (*post*, iv. 328). Boswell did not hesitate to alter his own letters included in the *Life* : see his *Letters*, No. 111, i. 185.⟩

† ⟨See *ante*, ii. 270 ; *post*, ii. 293, note 2, 445 ; iii. 107.⟩

note concerning it ; and if Dr. Horne will write to me, all the attention that I can give shall be cheerfully bestowed, upon what I think a pious work, the preservation and elucidation of Walton, by whose writings I have been most pleasingly edified.'

* * * * * *

' MR. BOSWELL TO DR. JOHNSON.

' Edinburgh, Sept. 16, 1774.

' WALES has probably detained you longer than I supposed. You will have become quite a mountaineer, by visiting Scotland one year and Wales another. You must next go to Switzerland. Cambria will complain, if you do not honour her also with some remarks. And I find *concessere columnæ* [1], the booksellers expect another book. I am impatient to see your " Tour to Scotland and the Hebrides [2]." Might you not send me a copy by the post as soon as it is printed off ? '

* * * * * *

' TO JAMES BOSWELL, ESQ.

' DEAR SIR,

' YESTERDAY I returned from my Welch journey. I was sorry to leave my book suspended so long ; but having an opportunity of seeing, with so much convenience, a new part of the island, I could not reject it. I have been in five of the six counties of North Wales ; and have seen St. Asaph and Bangor, the two seats of their Bishops ; have been upon Penmanmaur [3] and Snowden [4], and passed over into Anglesea. But Wales is so little different from England, that it offers nothing to the speculation of the traveller.

' When I came home, I found several of your papers, with some pages of Lord Hailes's Annals, which I will consider. I am in haste

---

[1] Horace, *Ars Poet.* l. 373.

[2] ' Do not you long to hear the roarings of the old lion, over the bleak mountains of the North ? ' wrote Steevens to Garrick. *Garrick Corres.* ii. 122. ⟨The *Journey* was not published till Jan. 1775: see *post*, ii. 287, 288, 290.⟩

[3] ' Aug. 18. We came to Penman mawr by day light, and found a way, lately made, very easy and very safe. It was cut smooth, and inclosed between parallel walls ; the outer of which secures the passenger from the precipice, which is deep and dreadful. . . . The sea beats at the bottom of the way. At Evening the Moon shone eminently bright, and our thoughts of danger being now past, the rest of our journey was very pleasant. At an hour somewhat late we came to Bangor, where we found a very mean Inn, and had some difficulty to obtain lodging. I lay in a room where the other bed had two men.' Johnson's *Journey into North Wales* (*post*, v. 447).

[4] He did not go to the top of Snowdon. He says :—' On the side of Snowden are the remains of a large fort, to which we climbed with great labour. I was breathless and harrassed.' *Ib.* Aug. 26 (*post*, v. 451).

to give you some account of myself, lest you should suspect me of
negligence in the pressing business which I find recommended to my
care, and which I knew nothing of till now, when all care is vain [1].

' In the distribution of my books I purpose to follow your advice,
adding such as shall occur to me. I am not pleased with your notes
of remembrance added to your names, for I hope I shall not easily
forget them.

' I have received four Erse books, without any direction, and suspect
that they are intended for the Oxford library. If that is the intention,
I think it will be proper to add the metrical psalms, and whatever else
is printed in Erse, that the present may be complete. The donor's
name should be told.

' I wish you could have read the book before it was printed, but our
distance does not easily permit it.

' I am sorry Lord Hailes does not intend to publish Walton ; I am
afraid it will not be done so well, if it be done at all.

' I purpose now to drive the book forward. Make my compliments
to Mrs. Boswell, and let me hear often from you.

' I am, dear Sir,

' Your affectionate humble servant,

' London, Octob. 1, 1774.'   ' SAM. JOHNSON.'

This tour to Wales, which was made in company with Mr. and
Mrs. Thrale, though it no doubt contributed to his health
and amusement, did not give occasion [a] to such a discursive
exercise of his mind as our tour to the Hebrides. I do not find
that he kept any journal or notes of what he saw there [2]. All
that I heard him say of it was, that ' instead of bleak and barren
mountains, there were green and fertile ones ; and that one of
the castles in Wales would contain all the castles that he had
seen in Scotland.'

Parliament having been dissolved [3], and his friend Mr. Thrale,

a give occasion 1 : give an occasion 2, 3.

[1] I had written to him, to request
his interposition in behalf of a convict, who I thought was very unjustly condemned. BOSWELL.

⟨See App. B, p. 508.⟩

[2] He had kept a journal which was
edited by Mr. Duppa in 1816. It
will be found *post*, in vol. v. 427 foll.

[3] ' When . . . the general election
. . . broke up the delightful society in
which we had spent some time at

Beconsfield, Dr. Johnson shook the
hospitable master of the house [Burke]
kindly by the hand, and said, " Fare-
wel my dear Sir, and remember that
I wish you all the success which ought
to be wished you, which can possibly
be wished you indeed—*by an honest
man.*" ' Piozzi's *Anec.* p. 242 : John.
Misc. i. 309. The dissolution was on
Sept. 30. ⟨Johnson, with the Thrales,
had arrived at Beaconsfield on the

who was a steady supporter of government, having again to encounter the storm of a contested election, he wrote a short political pamphlet, entitled ' The Patriot,' * addressed to the electors of Great-Britain ; a title which, to factious men, who consider a patriot only as an opposer of the measures of government, will appear strangely misapplied. It was, however, written with energetick vivacity ; and, except those passages in which it endeavours to vindicate the glaring outrage of the House of Commons in the case of the Middlesex election, and to justify the attempt to reduce our fellow-subjects in America to unconditional submission, it contained an admirable display of the properties of a real patriot, in the original and genuine sense ;— a sincere, steady, rational, and unbiassed friend to the interests and prosperity of his King and country. It must be acknowledged, however, that both in this and his two former pamphlets, there was, amidst many powerful arguments, not only a considerable portion of sophistry, but a contemptuous ridicule of his opponents, which was very provoking.

' To Mr. Perkins [1].

' Sir,

' You may do me a very great favour. Mrs. Williams, a gentlewoman whom you may have seen at Mr. Thrale's, is a petitioner for Mr. Hetherington's charity : petitions are this day issued at Christ's Hospital.

' I am a bad manager of business in a crowd ; and if I should send a mean man, he may be put a away without his errand. I must therefore intreat that you will go, and ask for a petition for Anna Williams, whose paper of enquiries was delivered with answers at the counting-house of

a sent *in the original.*

28th. See Broadley, *Dr. Johnson and Mrs. Thrale*, 1910, p. 217.⟩ See *ante*, ii. 222, for Johnson's opinion of Burke's honesty.

[1] Mr. Perkins was for a number of years the worthy superintendant of Mr. Thrale's great brewery, and after his death became one of the proprietors of it ; and now resides in Mr. Thrale's house in Southwark, which was the scene of so many literary meetings, and in which he continues the liberal hospitality for which it was eminent. Dr. Johnson esteemed him much. He hung up in the counting-house a fine proof of the admirable mezzotinto of Dr. Johnson, by Doughty ; and when Mrs. Thrale asked him somewhat flippantly, ' Why do you put him up in the counting-house ? ' he answered, ' Because, Madam, I wish to have one wise man there.' ' Sir,' (said Johnson,) ' I thank you. It is a very handsome compliment, and I believe you speak sincerely.' Boswell.

the hospital on Thursday the 20th. My servant will attend you thither, and bring the petition home ᵃ when you have it.

' The petition, which they are to give us, is a form which they deliver to every petitioner, and which the petitioner is afterwards to fill up, and return to them again. This we must have, or we cannot proceed according to their directions. You need, I believe, only ask for a petition ; if they enquire for whom you ask, you can tell them.

' I beg pardon for giving you this trouble ; but it is a matter of great importance.

' I am, Sir,
' Your most humble servant,
' SAM. JOHNSON.'

' October 25, 1774.'

' To JAMES BOSWELL, ESQ.

' DEAR SIR,

' THERE has appeared lately in the papers an account of a boat overset between Mull and Ulva, in which many passengers were lost, and among them Maclean of Col. We, you know, were once drowned ¹ ; I hope, therefore, that the story is either wantonly or erroneously told. Pray satisfy me by the next post.

' I have printed two hundred and forty pages. I am able to do nothing much worth doing to dear Lord Hailes's book. I will, however, send back the sheets ; and hope, by degrees, to answer all your reasonable expectations.

' Mr. Thrale has happily surmounted a very violent and acrimonious opposition² ; but all joys have their abatements ᵇ : Mrs. Thrale has fallen from her horse, and hurt herself very much. The rest of our friends, I believe, are well. My compliments to Mrs. Boswell.

' I am, Sir,
' Your most affectionate servant,
' SAM. JOHNSON.'

' London, Octob. 27, 1774.'

ᵃ to me *orig.*   ᵇ abatements 1 : abatement 2, 3.

¹ In the news-papers. BOSWELL.

² ' Oct. 16, 1774. In Southwark there has been outrageous rioting ; but I neither know the candidates, their connections, nor success.' Walpole's *Letters*, ix. 71. Of one Southwark election Mrs. Piozzi writes (*Anec.* p. 214 : John. Misc. i. 293) :— ' A borough election once shewed me his toleration of boisterous mirth. . . . A rough fellow . . ., a hatter by trade, seeing Mr. Johnson's beaver in a state of decay, seized it suddenly with one hand, and clapping him on the back with the other ; Ah, Master Johnson (says he), this is no time to be thinking about *hats*. " No, no, Sir (replies our Doctor in a cheerful tone), hats are of no use now, as you say, except to throw up in the air and huzza with ; " accompanying his words with the true election halloo.'

This letter, which shews his tender concern for an amiable young gentleman to whom we ª had been very much obliged in the Hebrides, I have inserted according to its date, though before receiving it I had informed him of the melancholy event that the young Laird of Col was unfortunately drowned ¹.

'To JAMES BOSWELL, ESQ.

'DEAR SIR,

'LAST night I corrected the last page of our "Journey to the Hebrides." The printer has detained it all this time, for I had, before I went into Wales, written all except two sheets. "The Patriot" was called for by my political friends on Friday, was written on Saturday, and I have heard little of it. So vague are conjectures at a distance ². As soon as I can, I will take care that copies be sent to you, for I would wish that they might be given before they are bought ; but I am afraid that Mr. Strahan will send to you and to the booksellers at the same time. Trade is as diligent as courtesy. I have mentioned all that you recommended. Pray make my compliments to Mrs. Boswell and the younglings. The club has, I think, not yet met.

'Tell me, and tell me honestly, what you think and what others say of our travels. Shall we touch the continent ³ ?

'I am, dear Sir,

'Your most humble servant,

'Nov. 26, 1774.'   'SAM. JOHNSON.'

In his manuscript diary of this year, there is the following entry :

'Nov. 27. Advent Sunday. I considered that this day, being the beginning of the ecclesiastical year, was a proper time for a new course of life. I began to read the Greek Testament regularly at 160 verses every Sunday. This day I began the Acts.

'In this week I read Virgil's Pastorals. I learned to repeat the Pollio and Gallus. I read carelessly the first Georgick.'

ª we 1: he 2, 3.

¹ See *post*, v. 331. Johnson thus mentions him (*Journey Western Islands*, p. 132) :—'Here we had the last embrace of this amiable man, who, while these pages were preparing to attest his virtues, perished in the passage between Ulva and Inch Kenneth.'

² Alluding to a passage in a letter of mine, where speaking of his ' Jour-

ney to the Hebrides,' I say, ' But has not " The Patriot " been an interruption, by the time taken to write it, and the time luxuriously spent in listening to its applauses ? ' BOSWELL.

³ We had projected a voyage together up the Baltick, and talked of visiting some of the more northern regions. BOSWELL. See *post*, iii. 134 and v. 215.

Such evidences of his unceasing ardour, both for ' divine and human lore,' when advanced into his sixty-fifth year, and not-withstanding his many disturbances from disease, must make us at once honour his spirit, and lament that it should be so grievously clogged by its material tegument. It is remarkable, that he was very fond of the precision which calculation pro-duces[1]. Thus we find in one of his manuscript diaries, ' 12 pages in 4to. Gr. Test. and 30 pages in Beza's folio, comprize the whole in 40 days.'

' DR. JOHNSON TO JOHN HOOLE, ESQ.[2]

' DEAR SIR,

' I HAVE returned your play[3], which you will find underscored with red, where there was a word which I did not like. The red will be washed off with a little water.

' The plot is so well framed, the intricacy so artful, and the dis-entanglement so easy, the suspense so affecting, and the passionate parts so properly interposed, that I have no doubt of its success.

                        ' I am, Sir,
                            ' Your most humble servant,
' December 19, 1774.'   ' SAM. JOHNSON.'

1775 : ÆTAT. 66.]—The first effort of his pen in 1775, was, ' Proposals for publishing the Works of Mrs. Charlotte Lennox[4],'† in three volumes quarto. In his diary, January 2, I find this entry : ' Wrote Charlotte's Proposals.' But, indeed, the internal evidence would have been quite sufficient. Her claim to the favour of the publick was thus enforced :

' Most of the pieces, as they appeared singly, have been read with approbation, perhaps above their merit[a], but of no great advan-tage to the writer. She hopes, therefore, that she shall not be

                    a merit 1 : merits 2, 3.

[1] See *ante*, i. 72.

[2] John Hoole, the son of a London watchmaker, was born in Dec. 1727, and died on Aug. 2, 1803. At the age of seventeen he was placed as a clerk in the East-India House ; but, like ⟨Charles Lamb and⟩ James and John Stuart Mill, he was an author as well as a clerk. See *ante*, i. 383 ; *post*, iv. 70.

[3] ' Cleonice.' BOSWELL.

Nichols (*Lit. Anec.* ii. 407) says that as *Cleonice* was a failure on the stage Mr. Hoole returned ' a considerable part of the money which he had re-ceived for the copy-right, alledging, that, as the piece was not successful on the stage, it could not be very profitable to the bookseller, and ought not to be a loss.'

[4] See *ante*, i. 255. ⟨See App. B, p. 509.⟩

considered as too indulgent to vanity, or too studious of interest, if, from that labour which has hitherto been chiefly gainful to others, she endeavours to obtain at last some profit for herself and her children. She cannot decently enforce her claim by the praise of her own performances ; nor can she suppose, that, by the most artful and laboured address, any additional notice could be procured to a publication, of which HER MAJESTY has condescended to be the PATRONESS.'

He this year also wrote the Preface to Baretti's ' Easy Lessons in Italian and English ¹.' †

> ' TO JAMES BOSWELL, ESQ.
>
> ' DEAR SIR,
>
>   ' YOU never did ask for a book by the post till now, and I did not think on it. You see now it is done. I sent one to the King, and I hear he likes it ².
>
>   ' I shall send a parcel into Scotland for presents, and intend to give to many of my friends. In your catalogue you left out Lord Auchinleck.
>
>   ' Let me know, as fast as you read it, how you like it ; and let me know if any mistake is committed, or any thing important left out. I wish you could have seen the sheets. My compliments to Mrs. Boswell, and to Veronica ³, and to all my friends.
>
> > ' I am, Sir,
> >
> > ' Your most humble servant,
>
> ' January 14, 1775.'   ' SAM. JOHNSON.'

> ' MR. BOSWELL TO DR. JOHNSON.
>
> > ' Edinburgh, Jan. 19, 1775.
>
>   ' BE pleased to accept of my best thanks for your " Journey to the Hebrides," which came to me by last night's post. I did really ask the favour twice ; but you have been even with me by granting it so speedily. BIS *dat qui cito dat* ⁴. Though ill of a bad cold, you kept me up the greatest part of the last night ; for I did not stop till I had read every word of your book. I looked back to our first talking of

---

¹ ⟨*Easy Phraseology, for the use of Young Ladies, who intend to learn the colloquial part of the Italian Language.*⟩ See *post*, ii. 449. ⟨See App. B, p. 509.⟩

² ' The King,' wrote Walpole on Jan. 21, 1775 (*Letters*, ix. 146), ' sent for the book in MS., and then wondering, said, " I protest, Johnson seems to be a Papist and a Jacobite ! " —so he did not know why he had been made to give him a pension ! '

³ Boswell's daughter. *Post*, v. 25.

⁴ ⟨' Memini, nisi fallor, apud Senecam alicubi legere : Bis dat qui cito dat.' *Adagia*, 1508, 92 verso. Erasmus was possibly thinking of Seneca *Ben.* ii. i. ' Sic demus, quomodo vellemus accipere, ante omnia libenter, cito', etc. But the proverb is apparently a modification of Publilius Syrus, 266, ' Inopi beneficium bis dat, qui dat celeriter.' E. BENSLY.⟩

a visit to the Hebrides, which was many years ago, when sitting by ourselves in the Mitre tavern [1], in London, I think about *witching time o' night* [2] ; and then exulted in contemplating our scheme fulfilled, and a *monumentum perenne* [3] of it erected by your superiour abilities. I shall only say, that your book has afforded me a high gratification. I shall afterwards give you my thoughts on particular passages. In the mean time, I hasten to tell you of your having mistaken two names, which you will correct in London, as I shall do here, that the gentlemen who deserve the valuable compliments which you have paid them, may enjoy their honours. In page 106, for *Gordon* read *Murchison ;* and in page 357, for *Maclean* read *Macleod* [4].

* * * * * *

' But I am now to apply to you for immediate aid in my profession, which you have never refused to grant when I requested it. I enclose you a petition for Dr. Memis, a physician at Aberdeen, in which Sir John Dalrymple has exerted his talents, and which I am to answer as Counsel for the managers of the Royal Infirmary in that city. Mr. Jopp, the Provost, who delivered to you your freedom [5], is one of my clients, and, *as a citizen of Aberdeen*, you will support him.

' The fact is shortly this. In a translation of the charter of the Infirmary from Latin into English, made under the authority of the managers, the same phrase in the original is in one place rendered *Physician*, but when applied to Dr. Memis is rendered *Doctor of Medicine*. Dr. Memis complained of this before the translation was printed, but was not indulged with having it altered ; and he has brought an action for damages, on account of a supposed injury, as if the designation given to him were [a] an inferiour one, tending to make it be supposed he is *not* a *Physician*, and, consequently, to hurt his practice. My father has dismissed the action as groundless, and now he has appealed to the whole Court [6].'

[a] were 1 : was 2, 3.

[1] It was at the Turk's Head coffee-house in the Strand. See *ante*, i. 450.

[2] *Hamlet*, act iii. sc. 2.

[3] ' Exegi monumentum ære perennius.'

Horace, *Odes*, iii. 30. 1.

[4] ⟨These and other mistakes pointed out by Boswell remain uncorrected in both the second impression (1775) and the second edition (1785). See Mr. R. W. Chapman's edition, 1924.⟩

[5] See *post*, v. 90.

[6] In the Court of Session of Scotland an action is first tried by one of the Judges, who is called the Lord Ordinary ; and if either party is dissatisfied, he may appeal to the whole Court, consisting of fifteen, the Lord President and fourteen other Judges, who have both in and out of Court the title of Lords, from the name of their estates ; as, Lord Auchinleck, Lord Monboddo, &c. BOSWELL. See *ante*, ii. 201, note 1. ⟨See also App. B.⟩

'To James Boswell, Esq.

'Dear Sir,

'I LONG to hear how you like the book ; it is, I think, much liked here. But Macpherson is very furious [1] ; can you give me any more intelligence about him, or his Fingal ? Do what you can,[a] and do it quickly. Is Lord Hailes on our side ?

'Pray let me know what I owed you when I left you, that I may send it to you.

'I am going to write about the Americans [2]. If you have picked up any hints among your lawyers, who are great masters of the law of nations, or if your own mind suggests any thing, let me know. But mum, it is a secret.

'I will send your parcel of books as soon as I can ; but I cannot do as I wish. However, you find every thing mentioned in the book which you recommended.

'Langton is here ; we are all that ever we were [3]. He is a worthy fellow, without malice, though not without resentment.

'Poor Beauclerk is so ill, that his life is thought to be in danger [4]. Lady Di nurses him with very great assiduity.

'Reynolds has taken too much to strong liquor [5], and seems to delight in his new character.

[a] *comma omitted* 3.

[1] Johnson had thus written of him (*Journey Western Islands*, p. 107) :—'I suppose my opinion of the poems of Ossian is already discovered. I believe they never existed in any other form than that which we have seen. The editor, or author, never could shew the original ; nor can it be shewn by any other ; to revenge reasonable incredulity, by refusing evidence, is a degree of insolence, with which the world is not yet acquainted ; and stubborn audacity is the last refuge of guilt.' See *ante*, ii. 126.

[2] *Taxation no Tyranny*. See *post*, ii. 312.

[3] See *ante*, ii. 265.

[4] In Tickell's *Epistle from the Hon. Charles Fox to the Hon. John Townshend* (1779) are the following lines (p. 11) :—

'Soon as to Brooks's thence thy footsteps bend,
What gratulations thy approach attend !

. . . .

See Beauclerk's cheek a tinge of red surprise,
And Friendship give what cruel Health denies.'

[5] It should be recollected, that this fanciful description of his friend was given by Johnson after he himself had become a water-drinker. Boswell.

Johnson, *post*, ii. 362, describes one of his friends as *muddy*. On April 12, 1776 (*post*, iii. 41), in a discussion about wine, when Reynolds said to him, ' You have sat by, quite sober, and felt an envy of the happiness of those who were drinking,' he replied, ' Perhaps, contempt.' On April 28, 1778 (*Ib.* 329), he said to Reynolds : ' I won't argue any more with you, Sir. You are too far gone.' See also *ante*, i. 313, note 3, where he said to him : ' Sir, I did not count your glasses of wine, why should you number up my cups of tea ? '

' This is all the news that I have ; but as you love verses, I will send you a few which I made upon Inchkenneth [1] ; but remember the condition, that [a] you shall not show them, except to Lord Hailes, whom I love better than any man whom I know so little. If he asks you to transcribe them for him, you may do it, but I think he must promise not to let them be copied again, nor to show them as mine.

' I have at last sent back Lord Hailes's sheets. I never think about returning them, because I alter nothing. You will see that I might as well have kept them. However, I am ashamed of my delay ; and if I have the honour of receiving any more, promise punctually to return them by the next post. Make my compliments to dear Mrs. Boswell, and to Miss Veronica.

' I am, dear Sir,

' Yours most faithfully,

' SAM. JOHNSON [2].'

' Jan. 21, 1775.'

' MR. BOSWELL TO DR. JOHNSON.

' Edinburgh, Jan. 27, 1775.

* * * * * *

' YOU rate our lawyers here too high, when you call them great masters of the law of nations.

* * * * * *

' As for myself, I am ashamed to say that [b] I have read little and thought little on the subject of America. I will be much obliged to you, if you will direct me where I shall find the best information of what is to be

---

a that *om.* 2, 3.

b that *om.* 2, 3.

[1] See them in ' Journal of a Tour to the Hebrides,' 3d edit. p. 337. BOSWELL. *Post*, v. 325–6.

[2] He now sent me a Latin inscription for my historical picture of Mary Queen of Scots, and afterwards favoured me with an English translation. Mr. Alderman Boydell, that eminent Patron of the Arts, has subjoined them to the engraving from my picture.

' Maria Scotorum Regina,
Hominum seditiosorum
Contumeliis lassata,
Minis territa, clamoribus victa,
Libello, per quem

Regno cedit,
Lacrimans trepidansque
Nomen apponit.'

' Mary Queen of Scots,
Harrassed, terrified, and overpowered
By the insults, menaces,
And clamours
Of her rebellious subjects,
Sets her hand,
With tears and confusion,
To a resignation of the kingdom.'
BOSWELL.

Northcote (*Life of Reynolds*, ii. 234) calls Boydell the ' truest and greatest encourager of English art that England ever saw'. ⟨See App. B, p. 510.⟩

said on both sides. It is a subject vast in its present extent and future consequences. The imperfect hints which now float in my mind, tend rather to the formation of an opinion that our government has been precipitant and severe in the resolutions taken against the Bostonians [1]. Well do you know that I have no kindness for that race. But nations, or bodies of men, should, as well as individuals, have a fair trial, and not be condemned on character alone. Have we not express contracts with our colonies, which afford a more certain foundation of judgement, than general political speculations on the mutual rights of States and their provinces or colonies ? Pray let me know immediately what to read, and I shall diligently endeavour to gather for you any thing that I can find. Is Burke's speech on American taxation published by himself ? Is it authentick ? I remember to have heard you say, that you had never considered East-Indian affairs ; though, surely, they are of much importance to Great-Britain. Under the recollection of this, I shelter myself from the reproach of ignorance about the Americans. If you write upon the subject, I shall certainly understand it. But, since you seem to expect that I should know something of it, without your instruction, and that my own mind should suggest something, I trust you will put me in the way.

*   *   *   *   *   *

' What does Becket [2] mean by the *Originals* of Fingal and other poems of Ossian, which he advertises to have lain in his shop ? '

*   *   *   *   *   *

' To James Boswell, Esq.

' Dear Sir,

' You sent me a case to consider, in which I have no facts but what are against us, nor any principles on which to reason. It is vain to try to write thus without materials. The fact seems to be against you ; at least I cannot know nor say any thing to the contrary. I am glad that you like the book so well. I hear no more of Macpherson. I shall long to know what Lord Hailes says of it. Lend it him privately. I shall send the parcel as soon as I can. Make my compliments to Mrs. Boswell.

' I am, Sir, &c.

' Sam. Johnson.'

' Jan. 28, 1775.'

---

[1] By the Boston Port-Bill, passed in 1774, Boston had been closed as a port for the landing and shipping of goods. *Ann. Reg.* xvii. 64.

[2] Becket, the publisher of *Ossian*. ⟨See App. B, p. 510.⟩

' MR. BOSWELL TO DR. JOHNSON.
' Edinburgh, Feb. 2, 1775.

*   *   *   *   *   *

' As to Macpherson, I am anxious to have from yourself a full and pointed account of what has passed between you and him. It is confidently told here, that before your book came out he sent to you, to let you know that he understood you meant to deny the authenticity of Ossian's poems ; that the originals were in his possession ; that you might have inspection of them, and might take the evidence of people skilled in the Erse language ; and that he hoped, after this fair offer, you would not be so uncandid as to assert that he had refused reasonable proof. That you paid no regard to his message, but published your strong attack upon him ; that[a] then he wrote a letter to you, in such terms as he thought suited to one who had not acted as a man of veracity. You may believe it gives me pain to hear your conduct represented as unfavourable, while I can only deny what is said, on the ground that your character refutes it, without having any information to oppose. Let me, I beg it of you, be furnished with a sufficient answer to any calumny upon this occasion.

' Lord Hailes writes to me, (for we correspond more than we talk together,) " As to Fingal, I see a controversy arising, and purpose to keep out of its way. There is no doubt that I might mention some circumstances ; but I do not choose to commit them to paper [1]." What his opinion is, I do not know. He says, " I am singularly obliged to Dr. Johnson for his accurate and useful criticisms. Had he given some strictures on the general plan of the work, it would have added much to his favours." He is charmed with your verses on Inchkenneth, says they are very elegant, but bids me tell you he doubts whether

" *Legitimas faciunt pectora pura preces* [2] "

a that 1 : and 2, 3.

[1] His Lordship, notwithstanding his resolution, did commit his sentiments to paper, and in one of his notes affixed to his Collection of Old Scottish Poetry, he says, that ' to doubt the authenticity of those poems is a refinement in Scepticism indeed.' J. BLAKEWAY.

[2] Mr. Croker writes (*Boswell*, p. 378, note) :—' The original draft of these verses in Johnson's autograph is now before me. He had first written

" Sunt pro legitimis pectora pura sacris ; "

he then wrote

" Legitimas faciunt pura labella preces ; "

which more nearly approaches Mr. Boswell's version, and alludes, happily I think, to the prayers having been read by the young lady. . . . The line as it stands in the *Works* [Sint pro legitimis pura labella sacris, i. 167], is substituted in *Mr. Langton's hand*. . . . As I have reason to believe that Mr. Langton assisted in editing these Latin *poemata*, I conclude that these alterations were his own while superintending the press.'

be according to the rubrick : but that is your concern ; for, you know, he is a Presbyterian.'

* * * * * *

'To Dr. Lawrence [1].

'Feb. 7, 1775.

' Sir,

' One of the Scotch physicians is now [a] prosecuting a corporation that in some publick instrument have stiled him *Doctor of Medicine* instead of *Physician*. Boswell desires, being advocate for the corporation, to know whether *Doctor of Medicine* is [b] not a legitimate title, and whether it may [c] be considered as a disadvantageous distinction. I am to write to-night ; be pleased to tell me.

'I am, Sir, your most, &c.

'Sam. Johnson.'

'To James Boswell, Esq.

'My dear Boswell,

' I am surprised that, knowing as you do the disposition of your countrymen to tell lies in favour of each other [2], you can be at all affected by any reports that circulate among them. Macpherson never in his life offered me the [d] sight of any original or of any evidence of any kind ; but thought only of intimidating me by noise and threats, till my last answer,— that I would not be deterred from detecting what I thought a cheat, by the menaces of a ruffian,—put an end to our correspondence.

' The state of the question is this. He, and Dr. Blair, whom I consider as deceived, say, that he copied the poem from old manuscripts. His copies, if he had them, and I believe him to have none, are nothing. Where are the manuscripts ? They can be shown if they exist, but they were never shown. *De non existentibus et non apparentibus*, says our law, *eadem est ratio*. No man has a claim to credit upon his own word, when better evidence, if he had it, may be

[a] here *orig*.   [b] be *orig*.   [c] can *orig*.   [d] the 1: a 2, 3.

[1] The learned and worthy Dr. Lawrence, whom Dr. Johnson respected and loved as his physician and friend. Boswell.

Dr. Lawrence was descended, as Sir Egerton Brydges informs me, from Milton's friend [' Lawrence, of virtuous father virtuous son.' Milton's *Sonnets*, xx.]. Croker (*Boswell*, p. 734). See *post*, iv. 143.

[2] My friend has, in this letter, relied upon my testimony, with a confidence, of which the ground has escaped my recollection. Boswell. Lord Shelburne said : ' Like the generality of Scotch, Lord Mansfield had no regard to truth whatever.' Fitzmaurice's *Shelburne*, i. 68. ⟨Lord Fitzmaurice points out that ' notwithstanding this sweeping condemnation Lord Shelburne selected two Scotchmen (Richard Oswald and Caleb Whitefoord) to negociate the peace with the American Colonies '. *Ibid*. note.⟩

easily produced. But, so far as we can find, the Erse language was never written till very lately for the purposes of religion. A nation that cannot write, or a language that was never written, has no manuscripts.

' But whatever he has,ª he never offered to show. If old manuscripts should now be mentioned, I should, unless there were more evidence than can be easily had, suppose them another proof of Scotch conspiracy in national falsehood.

' Do not censure the expression ; you know it to be true.

' Dr. Memis's question is so narrow as to allow no speculation ; and I have no facts before me but those which his advocate has produced against you.

' I consulted this morning the President of the London College of Physicians ¹, who says, that with us, *Doctor of Physick* (we do not say *Doctor of Medicine*) is the highest title that a practicer of physick can have ; that *Doctor* implies not only *Physician*, but teacher of physick ; that every *Doctor* is legally a *Physician* ; but no man, not a *Doctor*, can *practice physick* but by *licence* particularly granted. The Doctorate is a licence of itself. It seems to us a very slender cause of prosecution.

*   *   *   *   *   *

' I am now engaged, but in a little time I hope to do all you would have. My compliments to Madam and Veronica.

' I am, Sir,

' Your most humble servant,

' SAM. JOHNSON.'

' February 7, 1775.'

What words were used by Mr. Macpherson in his letter to the venerable Sage, I have never heard ; but they are generally said to have been of a nature very different from the language of literary contest. Dr. Johnson's answer appeared in the newspapers of the day, and has since been frequently re-published ; but not with perfect accuracy. I give it as dictated to me by himself, written down in his presence, and authenticated by a note in his own hand-writing, ' *This, I think, is a true copy* ².'

ª *comma omitted* 2, 3.

¹ Dr. Lawrence. See Johnson's letter to Warren Hastings of Dec. 20, 1774. *Post*, iv. 70.

² I have deposited it in the British Museum. BOSWELL. Mr. P. Cunningham says :—' Of all the MSS. which Boswell says he *had deposited* in the British Museum, only the copy of the letter to Lord Chesterfield has been found, and that was *not* deposited by him, but after his death, " pursuant to the intentions of the late James Boswell, Esq." ' Croker's *Boswell*, p. 430. ⟨The original letter to Macpherson is now in the Adam collection. It will be seen that it differs materially from the copy printed by Boswell:—' Mr. James Macpherson

' MR. JAMES MACPHERSON,

' I RECEIVED your foolish and impudent letter. Any violence offered me I shall do my best to repel ; and what I cannot do for myself, the law shall do for me. I hope I shall never be deterred from detecting what I think a cheat, by the menaces of a ruffian.

' What would you have me retract ? I thought your book an imposture ; I think it an imposture still. For this opinion I have given my reasons to the publick, which I here dare you to refute. Your rage I defy. Your abilities, since your Homer [1], are not so formidable ; and what I hear of your morals inclines me to pay regard not to what you shall say, but to what you shall prove. You may print this if you will.

' SAM. JOHNSON [2].'

Mr. Macpherson little knew the character of Dr. Johnson, if he supposed that he could be easily intimidated ; for no man was ever more remarkable for personal courage. He had, indeed, an aweful dread of death, or rather, ' of something after death [3] ; ' and what rational man, who seriously thinks of quitting all that he has ever known, and going into a new and unknown state of being, can be without that dread ? But his fear was from reflection ; his courage natural. His fear, in that one instance, was the result of philosophical and religious consideration. He feared death, but he feared nothing else, not even what might occasion death [4]. Many instances of his resolution may be

—I received your foolish and impudent note. Whatever insult is offered me I will do my best to repel, and what I cannot do for myself the law will do for me. I will not desist from detecting what I think a cheat from any fear of the menaces of a Ruffian.

You want me to retract. What shall I retract ? I thought your book an imposture from the beginning. I think it upon yet surer reasons an imposture still. For this opinion I give the publick my reasons which I here dare you to refute.

But however I may despise you, I reverence truth and if you can prove the genuineness of the work I will confess it. Your rage I defy, your abilities since your Homer are not so formidable, and what I have heard of your morals disposes me to pay regard not to what you shall say, but to what you can prove.

You may print this if you will.

SAM: JOHNSON.

Jan 20. 1775.'

See also App. B, p. 511.〉

[1] In the *Gent. Mag.* for 1773, p. 192, is announced : ' The Iliad of Homer. Translated by James Macpherson, Esq. ; 2 vols. 4to. 2*l*. 2*s*. Becket.' See *post*, App. B, p. 513.

[2] ' Within a few feet of Johnson lay (by one of those singular coincidences in which the Abbey abounds) his deadly enemy, James Macpherson.' Stanley's *Westm. Abbey*, p. 298.

[3] *Hamlet*, act iii. sc. 1.

[4] ' Fear was indeed a sensation to which Mr. Johnson was an utter stranger, excepting when some sudden apprehensions seized him that he

mentioned.   One day, at Mr. Beauclerk's house in the country †,
when two large dogs were fighting, he went up to them, and
beat them till they separated [1] ; and at another time, when told
of the danger there was that a gun might burst if charged with
many balls, he put in six or seven, and fired it off against
a wall.   Mr. Langton told me, that when they were swimming
together near Oxford, he cautioned Dr. Johnson against a pool,
which was reckoned particularly dangerous ; upon which Johnson
directly swam into it.   He told me himself that one night he
was attacked in the street by four men, to whom he would not
yield, but kept them all at bay, till the watch came up, and
carried both him and them to the round-house [2].   In the play-
house at Lichfield, as Mr. Garrick informed me, Johnson having
for a moment quitted a chair which was placed for him between
the side-scenes, a gentleman took possession of it, and when
Johnson on his return civilly demanded his seat, rudely refused
to give it up ; upon which Johnson laid hold of it, and tossed
him and the chair into the pit.   Foote, who so successfully
revived the old comedy, by exhibiting living characters, had
resolved to imitate Johnson on the stage, expecting great profits
from his ridicule of so celebrated a man.   Johnson being informed of his intention, and being at dinner at Mr. Thomas
Davies's the bookseller, from whom I had the story, he asked
Mr. Davies ' what was the common price of an oak stick ; ' and
being answered six-pence, ' Why then, Sir, (said he,) give me
leave to send your servant to purchase me a shilling one.   I'll
have a double quantity ; for I am told Foote means to *take me
off*, as he calls it, and I am determined the fellow shall not do
it with impunity.'   Davies took care to acquaint Foote of this,
which effectually checked the wantonness of the mimick [3].   Mr.
Macpherson's menaces made Johnson provide himself with the

was going to die.'   Piozzi's *Anec.*
p. 277 : John. Misc. i. 330.   In this
respect his character might be likened
to that of Fearing, in *Pilgrim's Progress*
(Part ii, ed. 1693, p. 104), as described
by Great-Heart :—' When we came at
the Hill Difficulty, he made no stick
at that, nor did he much fear the
Lyons.   For you must know, that his
Trouble was not about such things as

those, his Fear was about his Accep-
tance at last.'
    [1] See *post*, v. 329.
    [2] See *ante*, i. 249, where Garrick
humorously foretold the Round-house
for Johnson.
    [3] See *ante*, ii. 95.
    † ⟨Beauclerk's house was near the
top of Muswell Hill, N. London.   See
post, ii. 378 n. 1.⟩

same implement of defence [1] ; and had he been attacked, I have no doubt that, old as he was, he would have made his corporal prowess be felt as much as his intellectual.

His ' Journey to the Western Islands of Scotland [2] ' * is a most valuable performance. It abounds in extensive philosophical views of society, and in ingenious sentiments[a] and lively description. A considerable part of it, indeed, consists of speculations, which many years before he saw the wild regions which we visited together, probably had employed his attention, though the actual sight of those scenes undoubtedly quickened and augmented them. Mr. Orme, the very able historian [3], agreed with me in this opinion, which he thus strongly expressed :— ' There are in that book thoughts, which, by long revolution in the great mind of Johnson, have been formed and polished like pebbles rolled in the ocean ! '

That he was to some degree of excess a *true-born Englishman* [4], so as to have ever [b] entertained an undue prejudice against both the country and the people of Scotland, must be allowed [5].

***

[a] sentiments 1: sentiment 2, 3.   [b] to have entertained 2, 3.

[1] ' It was,' writes Hawkins (*Life*, p. 491), ' an oak-plant of a tremendous size ; a plant, I say, and not a shoot or branch, for it had had a root, which being trimmed to the size of a large orange, became the head of it. Its height was upwards of six feet, and from about an inch in diameter at the lower end, increased to near three : this he kept in his bedchamber, so near the chair in which he constantly sat, as to be within reach.' Macpherson, like Johnson, was a big man. Dr. A. Carlyle says (*Auto.* p. 398) :—' He was good-looking, of a large size, with very thick legs, to hide which he generally wore boots, though not then the fashion. He appeared to me proud and reserved.'

[2] Boswell wrote to Temple on April 4 :—' Mr. Johnson has allowed me to write out a supplement to his *Journey*.' *Letters*, No. 137, i. 218. On May 10 he wrote :—' I have not written out another line of my *Remarks* on the Hebrides. I found it impossible to do it in London. Besides Dr. Johnson does not seem very desireous that I should publish any supplement. Between ourselves, he is not apt to encourage one to *share* reputation with himself.' *Ib.* No. 140, i. 222.

[3] Colonel Newcome, when a lad, ' was for ever talking of India, and the famous deeds of Clive and Lawrence. His favourite book was a history of India—the history of Orme.' Thackeray's *Newcomes*, ch. 76. See *post*, iii. 284 ; v. 408, note 4.

[4] *Richard II*, act i. sc. 3, l. 309. See *ante*, i. 129.

[5] A passage in the *North Briton*, No. 34, shews how wide-spread this prejudice was. The writer gives his ' real, fair, and substantial objections to the administration of this *Scot* [Lord Bute]. The first is, that he is a *Scot*. . . . I am certain, that reason could never believe that a *Scot* was fit to have the management of *English* affairs. . . . A *Scot* hath no more

But it was a prejudice of the head, and not of the heart. He had no ill will to the Scotch ; for, if he had been conscious of that, he would never have thrown himself into the bosom of their country, and trusted to the protection of its remote inhabitants with a fearless confidence. His remark upon the nakedness of the country, from its being denuded of trees [1], was made after having travelled two hundred miles along the eastern coast, where certainly trees are not to be found near the road ;

right to preferment in *England* than a *Hanoverian* or a *Hottentot*.' In *Humphry Clinker* (Letter of July 13) we read :—' From Doncaster northwards, all the windows of all the inns are scrawled with doggrel rhimes in abuse of the Scotch nation.' Walpole, writing of the contest between the House of Commons and the city in 1771, says of the Scotch courtiers :— ' The Scotch wanted to come to blows, and were at least not sorry to see the House of Commons so contemptible.' *Memoirs of the Reign of George III*, iv. 301. ' What a nation is Scotland,' he wrote at the end of the Gordon Riots, ' in every reign engendering traitors to the State, and false and pernicious to the kings that favour it the most !' *Letters*, xi. 222. See *post*, iv. 169. Lord Shelburne, a man of a liberal mind, wrote :—' I can scarce conceive a Scotchman capable of liberality, and capable of impartiality.' After calling them ' a sad set of innate cold-hearted, impudent rogues,' he continues :—' It's a melancholy thing that there is no finding any other people that will take pains, or be amenable even to the best purposes.' Fitzmaurice's *Shelburne*, ii. 308. Hume wrote to his countryman, Gilbert Elliot, in 1764 :—' I do not believe there is one Englishman in fifty, who, if he heard I had broke my neck to-night, would be sorry. Some, because I am not a Whig ; some, because I am not a Christian ; and all, because I am a Scotsman. Can you seriously talk of my continuing an

Englishman ? Am I, or are you, an Englishman ?' Elliot replies :—' Notwithstanding all you say, we are both Englishmen ; that is, true British subjects, entitled to every emolument and advantage that our happy constitution can bestow.' Burton's *Hume*, ii. 238, 240. Hume, in his prejudice against England, went far beyond Johnson in his prejudice against Scotland. In 1769 he wrote : —' I am delighted to see the daily and hourly progress of madness and folly and wickedness in England. The consummation of these qualities are the true ingredients for making a fine narrative in history, especially if followed by some signal and ruinous convulsion,—as I hope will soon be the case with that pernicious people !' *Ib.* p. 431. In 1770 he wrote :—' Our government has become a chimera, and is too perfect, in point of liberty, for so rude a beast as an Englishman ; who is a man, a bad animal too, corrupted by above a century of licentiousness.' *Ib.* p. 434. ⟨See also *post*, iv. 169 and v. 19.⟩

[1] ' The love of planting,' wrote Sir Walter Scott, ' which has become almost a passion, . . . is much to be ascribed to Johnson's sarcasms.' *Croker Corres.* ii. 34. Lord Jeffrey wrote from Watford in 1833 :—' What a country this old England is. In a circle of twenty miles from this spot (leaving out London and its suburbs), there is more old timber . . . than in all Scotland.' Cockburn's *Jeffrey*, i. 348. See *post*, ii. 311.

and he said it was ' a map of the road ¹ ' which he gave. His disbelief of the authenticity of the poems ascribed to Ossian, a Highland bard, was confirmed in the course of his journey, by a very strict examination of the evidence offered for it ; and although their authenticity was made too much a national point by the Scotch, there were many respectable persons in that country, who did not concur in this ; so that his judgement upon the question ought not to be decried, even by those who differ from him. As to myself, I can only say, upon a subject now become very uninteresting, that when the fragments of Highland poetry first came out, I was much pleased with their wild peculiarity, and was one of those who subscribed to enable their editor, Mr. Macpherson, then a young man, to make a search in the Highlands and Hebrides for a long poem in the Erse language, which was reported to be preserved somewhere in those regions. But when there came forth an Epick Poem in six books, with all the common circumstances of former compositions of that nature ; and when, upon an attentive examination of it, there was found a perpetual recurrence of the same images which appear in the fragments ; and when no ancient manuscript, to authenticate the work, was deposited in any publick library, though that was insisted on as a reasonable proof, *who* could forbear to doubt ² ?

¹ See *post*, v. 69.

² Even David Hume subscribed to the fund. He wrote in 1760 :— ' Certain it is, that these poems are in every body's mouth in the Highlands, have been handed down from father to son, and are of an age beyond all memory and tradition. . . . Adam Smith . . . told me, that the piper of the Argyleshire militia repeated to him all those poems which Mr. Macpherson had translated. . . . We have therefore set about a subscription of a guinea, or two guineas a-piece, in order to enable Mr. Macpherson to undertake a mission into the Highlands to recover more of these fragments.' *European Mag.*, May, 1784, v. 327. Hume changed his opinion. ' On going to London,'

writes Dr. A. Carlyle (*Auto.* p. 276), ' he went over to the other side, and loudly affirmed the poems to be inventions of Macpherson. I happened to say one day, when he was declaiming against Macpherson, that I had met with nobody of his opinion but William Caddel of Cockenzie, and President Dundas, which he took ill, and was some time of forgetting.' Gibbon, in the *Decline and Fall* (vol. i. ch. 6), quoted Ossian, but added :— ' Something of a doubtful mist still hangs over these Highland traditions ; nor can it be entirely dispelled by the most ingenious researches of modern criticism.' On this Hume wrote to him on March 18, 1776 :—' I see you entertain a great doubt with regard to the authenticity of the poems of

Johnson's grateful acknowledgements of kindnesses received
in the course of this tour, completely refute the brutal reflections
which have been thrown out against him, as if he had made an
ungrateful return ; and his delicacy in sparing in his book those
who we find from his letters to Mrs. Thrale, were just objects
of censure [1], is much to be admired. His candour and amiable
disposition is conspicuous from his conduct, when informed by
Mr. Macleod, of Rasay, that he had committed a mistake,
which gave that gentleman some uneasiness. He wrote him a
courteous and kind letter, and inserted in the news-papers an
advertisement, correcting the mistake [2].

The observations of my friend Mr. Dempster in a letter [3]
written to me, soon after he had read Dr. Johnson's book, are
so just and liberal, that they cannot be too often repeated :

*   *   *   *   *   *

' There is nothing in the book, from beginning to end, that a
Scotchman need to take amiss. What he says of the country
is true ; and his observations on the people are what must naturally
occur to a sensible, observing, and reflecting inhabitant of a convenient
metropolis, where a man on thirty pounds a year may be better
accommodated with all the little wants of life, than Col or Sir Allan.

' I am charmed with his researches concerning the Erse language,
and the antiquity of their manuscripts. I am quite convinced ; and I
shall rank Ossian, and his Fingals and Oscars, amongst the nursery
tales, not the true history of our country, in all time to come.

' Upon the whole, the book cannot displease, for it has no pretensions.

Ossian. . . . Where a supposition is so
contrary to common sense, any positive evidence of it ought never to be
regarded. Men run with great avidity to give their evidence in favour
of what flatters their passions and
their national prejudices. You are
therefore over and above indulgent
to us in speaking of the matter with
hesitation.' Gibbon's *Misc. Works*,
i. 225. So early as 1763 Hume had
asked Dr. Blair for ' proof that these
poems . . . were not forged within
these five years by James Macpherson.
*These proofs must not be arguments, but
testimonies.*' J. H. Burton's *Hume*, i.
466. Smollett, it should seem, believed
in Ossian to the end. In *Humphry Clin-*
ker, in the letter dated Sept. 3, he makes
one of his characters write :—' The
poems of Ossian are in every mouth. A
famous antiquarian of this country, the
laird of Mackfarlane, at whose house
we dined . . ., can repeat them all in
the original Gaelick.' See *post*, v. 387.

[1] I find in his letters only Sir A.
Macdonald (*ante*, ii. 157) of whom
this can be said. ⟨From Inverary he
wrote to Mrs. Thrale of Macquarry of
Ulva's (*post*, iii. 126, v. 319) ' negligence and folly.' *Letters*, No. 332.⟩

[2] See ' Journal of a Tour to the
Hebrides,' 3d edit. p. 520 [p. 431].
BOSWELL. ⟨See *post*, v. 412.⟩

[3] For the letter, see *post*, v. 407.

The authour neither says he is a geographer, nor an antiquarian, nor very learned in the history of Scotland, nor a naturalist, nor a fossilist [1]. The manners of the people, and the face of the country, are all he attempts to describe, or seems to have thought of. Much were it to be wished, that they who have travelled into more remote, and of course more curious regions, had all possessed his good sense. Of the state of learning, his observations on Glasgow University show he has formed a very sound judgement. He understands our climate too ; and he has accurately observed the changes, however slow and imperceptible to us, which Scotland has undergone, in consequence of the blessings of liberty and internal peace.'

*　*　*　*　*　*

Mr. Knox [†], another native of Scotland, who has since made the same tour, and published an account of it, is equally liberal.

' I have read (says he,) his book again and again, travelled with him from Berwick to Glenelg, through countries with which I am well acquainted ; sailed with him from Glenelg to Rasay, Sky, Rum, Col, Mull, and Icolmkill, but have not been able to correct him in any matter of consequence. I have often admired the accuracy, the precision, and the justness of what he advances, respecting both the country and the people.

' The Doctor has every where delivered his sentiments with freedom, and in many instances with a seeming regard for the benefit of the inhabitants, and the ornament of the country. His remarks on the want of trees and hedges for shade, as well as for shelter to the cattle, are well founded, and merit the thanks, not the illiberal censure [a] of the natives. He also felt for the distresses of the Highlanders, and explodes,[b] with great propriety,[b] the bad management of the grounds, and the neglect of timber in the Hebrides.'

Having quoted Johnson's just compliments on the Rasay family [2], he says,

' On the other hand, I found this family equally lavish in their encomiums upon the Doctor's conversation, and his subsequent civilities to a young gentleman of that country, who, upon waiting upon him at London, was well received, and experienced all the attention

---

[a] censures *Knox*.

[1] *Fossilist* is not in Johnson's *Dictionary*. ⟨He uses it in the *Journey*, 1924, p. 44.⟩

[2] ' Raasay has little that can detain a traveller, except the Laird and his family ; but their power wants no

[b] *commas omitted* 2, 3.

auxiliaries. Such a seat of hospitality, amidst the winds and waters, fills the imagination with a delightful contrariety of images.' *Journey Western Isl.*, 1924, p. 59.

[†] ⟨John Knox's *Tour through the*

and regard that a warm friend could bestow. Mr. Macleod having also been in London, waited upon the Doctor, who provided a magnificent and expensive entertainment in honour of his old Hebridean acquaintance.'

And talking of the military road by Fort Augustus, he says,

' By this road, though one of the most rugged in Great Britain, the celebrated Dr. Johnson passed from Inverness to the Hebride Isles. His observations on the country and people are extremely correct, judicious, and instructive [1].'

Mr. Tytler, the acute and able vindicator of Mary Queen of Scots, in one of his letters to Mr. James Elphinstone, published in that gentleman's ' Forty Years' Correspondence,' says,

' I read Dr. Johnson's Tour with very great pleasure. Some few errours he has fallen into, but of no great importance, and those are lost in the numberless beauties of his work.
' If I had leisure, I could perhaps point out the most exceptionable places ; but at present I am in the country, and have not his book at hand. It is plain he meant to speak well of Scotland ; and he has in my apprehension done us great honour in the most capital article, the character of the inhabitants.'

His private letters to Mrs. Thrale, written during the course of his journey, which therefore may be supposed to convey his genuine feelings at the time, abound in such benignant sentiments towards the people who showed him civilities [2], that no man whose temper is not very harsh and sour, can retain a doubt of the goodness of his heart.
It is painful to recollect with what rancour he was assailed by numbers of shallow irritable North Britons, on account of his supposed injurious treatment of their country and country-men, in his ' Journey.' Had there been any just ground for such a charge, would the virtuous and candid Dempster [3] have given his opinion of the book, in the terms which I have quoted ?

Highlands of Scotland and the Hebride Isles in 1786 was published in 1787 at London. The passages quoted occur on pp. lxviii–ix.⟩
    [1] Page 103. BOSWELL.
    [2] From Skye he wrote, 30 Sept. :—

' The hospitality of this remote region is like that of the golden age. We have found ourselves treated at every house as if we came to confer a benefit.' *Letters*, No. 329, i. 267.
    [3] See *ante*, i. 443, note 2.

Would the patriotick Knox [1] have spoken of it as he has done ?
Would Mr. Tytler, surely

'—— a *Scot*, if ever *Scot* there were,'

have expressed himself thus ? And let me add, that, citizen of
the world as I hold myself to be, I have that degree of predilection for my *natale solum*, nay, I have that just sense of the
merit of an ancient nation, which has been ever renowned for
its valour, which in former times maintained its independence
against a powerful neighbour, and in modern times has been
equally distinguished for its ingenuity and industry in civilized
life, that I should have felt a generous indignation at any injustice done to it. Johnson treated Scotland no worse than he
did even his best friends, whose characters he used to give as
they appeared to him, both in light and shade. Some people,
who had not exercised their minds sufficiently, condemned him
for censuring his friends. But Sir Joshua Reynolds, whose
philosophical penetration and justness of thinking were not
less known to those who lived with him, than his genius in
his art is admired by the world, explained his conduct thus :
' He was fond of discrimination, which he could not show
without pointing out the bad as well as the good in every
character ; and as his friends were those whose characters he
knew best, they afforded him the best opportunity for showing
the acuteness of his judgement.'

He expressed to his friend Mr. Windham of Norfolk, his
wonder at the extreme jealousy of the Scotch, and their resentment at having their country described by him as it really
was ; when, to say that it was a country as good as England,
would have been a gross falsehood. ' None of us, (said he,)
would be offended if a foreigner who has travelled here should
say, that vines and olives don't grow in England.' And as to
his prejudice against the Scotch, which I always ascribed to
that nationality which he observed in *them*, he said to the
same gentleman, ' When I find a Scotchman, to whom an
Englishman is as a Scotchman, that Scotchman shall be as
an Englishman to me [2].' His intimacy with many gentlemen

---

[1] I observed with much regret,
while the first edition of this work
was passing through the press (August
1790,) that this ingenious gentleman
was dead. BOSWELL.

[2] See *ante*, ii. 242.

of Scotland, and his employing so many natives of that country as his amanuenses [1], prove that his prejudice was not virulent ; and I have deposited in the British Museum, amongst other pieces of his writing, the following note in answer to one from me, asking if he would meet me at dinner at the Mitre, though a friend of mine, a Scotchman, was to be there :—

' Mr. Johnson does not see why Mr. Boswell should suppose a Scotchman less acceptable than any other man. He will be at the Mitre.'

My much-valued friend Dr. Barnard, now Bishop of Killaloe, having once expressed to him an apprehension, that if he should visit Ireland he might treat the people of that country more un-favourably than he had done the Scotch, he answered, with strong pointed double-edged wit, ' Sir, you have no reason to be afraid of me. The Irish are not in a conspiracy to cheat the world by false representations of the merits of their countrymen [2]. No, Sir ; the Irish are a FAIR PEOPLE ;—they never speak well of one another.'

Johnson told me an instance of Scottish nationality, which made a very unfavourable impression upon his mind. A Scotch-man, of some consideration in London, solicited him to recom-mend, by the weight of his learned authority, to be master of an English school, a person of whom he who recommended him confessed he knew no more but that he was his countryman. Johnson was shocked at this unconscientious conduct [3].

All the miserable cavillings against his ' Journey,' in news-papers [4], magazines, and other fugitive publications, I can speak

---

[1] See *ante*, i. 187, 536.

[2] See *ante*, ii. 121, 297, and *post*, iv. 186.

[3] Johnson (*Journey Western Islands*, p. 146) says that ' the mediocrity of knowledge ' obtained in the Scotch universities, ' countenanced in general by a national combination so invidious, that their friends cannot defend it, and actuated in particulars by a spirit of enterprise, so vigorous, that their enemies are constrained to praise it, enables them to find, or to make their

way to employment, riches, and dis-tinction.' ⟨See App. B, p. 514.⟩

[4] Macpherson had great influence with the newspapers. Walpole wrote in February, 1776 :—' Macpherson, the Ossianite, had a pension of £600 a year from the Court, to supervise the newspapers.' In Dec. 1781, Wal-pole mentions the difficulty of getting ' a vindicatory paragraph ' inserted in the papers. ' This was one of the great grievances of the time. Mac-pherson had a pension of £800 a year

from certain knowledge, only furnished him with sport. At last there came out a scurrilous volume, larger than Johnson's own, filled with malignant abuse, under a name, real or fictitious, of some low man in an obscure corner of Scotland, though supposed to be the work of another Scotchman, who has found means to make himself well known both in Scotland and England. The effect which it had upon Johnson was, to produce this pleasant observation to Mr. Seward, to whom he lent the book : ' This fellow must be a blockhead. They don't know how to go about their abuse. Who will read a five shilling book against me ? No, Sir, if they had wit, they should have kept pelting me with pamphlets 1.'

' MR. BOSWELL TO DR. JOHNSON.

' Edinburgh, Feb. 18, 1775.

' YOU would have been very well pleased if you had dined with me to-day. I had for my guests, Macquharrie, young Maclean of Col, the successor of our friend, a very amiable man, though not marked with such active qualities as his brother ; Mr. Maclean of Torloisk in Mull, a gentleman of Sir Allan's family ; and two of the clan Grant ; so that the Highland and Hebridean genius reigned. We had a great deal of conversation about you, and drank your health in a bumper. The toast was not proposed by me, which is a circumstance to be remarked, for I am now so connected with you, that any thing that I can say or do to your honour has not the value of an additional compliment. It is only giving you a guinea out of that treasure of admiration which already belongs to you, and which is no hidden treasure ; for I suppose my admiration of you is co-existent with the knowledge of my character.

' I find that the Highlanders and Hebrideans in general are much fonder of your " Journey " than the low-country or *hither* Scots. One of the Grants said to-day, that he was sure you were a man of a good heart, and a candid man, and seemed to hope he should be able to

from Court for inspecting newspapers, and inserted what lies he pleased, and prevented whatever he disapproved of being printed.' *Journal of the Reign of George III*, ii. 17, 483. ⟨See *post*, ii. 363.⟩

1 This book was published in 1779 under the title of ' *Remarks on Dr. Samuel Johnson's Journey to the Hebrides*, by the Rev. Donald M'Nicol, A.M., Minister of Lismore in Argyleshire.' In 1817 it was reprinted at Glasgow together with Johnson's *Journey*. The *Remarks* are a few pages shorter than the *Journey*. By ' another Scotchman,' Boswell certainly meant Macpherson. ⟨The question of Macpherson's participation in M'Nicol's book is discussed by Mr. Chapman in his ed. of Johnson's *Journey*, p. 484.⟩

convince you of the antiquity of a good proportion of the poems of Ossian.   After all that has passed, I think the matter is capable of being proved to a certain degree.   I am told that Macpherson got one old Erse MS.† from Clanranald, for the restitution of which he executed a formal obligation ; and it is affirmed, that the Gaelick (call it Erse or call it Irish,) has been written in the Highlands and Hebrides for many centuries.   It is reasonable to suppose, that such of the inhabitants as acquired any learning, possessed the art of writing as well as their Irish neighbours, and Celtick cousins ; and the question is, can sufficient evidence be shewn of this ?

' Those who are skilled in ancient writings can determine the age of MSS. or at least can ascertain the century in which they were written ; and if men of veracity, who are so skilled, shall tell us that MSS. in the possession of families in the Highlands and isles, are the works of a remote age, I think we should be convinced by their testimony.

' There is now come to this city, Ranald Macdonald§ from the Isle of Egg, who has several MSS. of Erse poetry, which he wishes to publish by subscription.   I have engaged to take three copies of the book, the price of which is to be six shillings, as I would subscribe for all the Erse that can be printed,[a] be it old or new, that the language may be preserved.   This man says, that some of his manuscripts are ancient ; and, to be sure, one of them which was shewn to me does appear to have the duskyness of antiquity.

*   *   *   *   *   *

' The enquiry is not yet quite hopeless, and I should think that the exact truth may be discovered, if proper means be used.   I am, &c.   ' JAMES BOSWELL.'

' To JAMES BOSWELL, ESQ.

' DEAR SIR,

' I AM sorry that I could get no books for my friends in Scotland. Mr. Strahan has at last promised to send two dozen to you.   If they come, put the names of my friends into them ; you may cut them out [1], and paste them with a little starch in the book.

' You then are going wild about Ossian.   Why do you think any part can be proved ?   The dusky manuscript of Egg is probably not fifty years old ; if it be an hundred, it proves nothing.   The tale of Clanranald has [b] no proof.   Has Clanranald told it ?   Can he prove it ? There are, I believe, no Erse manuscripts.   None of the old families had a single letter in Erse that we heard of.   You say it is likely that they could write.   The learned, if any learned there were, could ; but

---

[a] *comma omitted* 3.   [b] has 1 : is 2, 3.

[1] From a list in his hand-writing.   BOSWELL.   †§ ⟨See App. B, p. 514.⟩

knowing by that learning, some written language, in that language they wrote, as letters had never been applied to their own. If there are manuscripts, let them be shewn, with some proof that they are not forged for the occasion. You say many can remember parts of Ossian. I believe all those parts are versions of the English ; at least there is no proof of their antiquity.

' Macpherson is said to have made some translations himself ; and having taught a boy to write it, ordered him to say that he had learnt it of his grandmother. The boy, when he grew up, told the story. This Mrs. Williams heard at Mr. Strahan's table. Do not [a] be credulous ; you know how little a Highlander can be trusted [1]. Macpherson is, so far as I know, very quiet. Is not that proof enough ? Every thing is against him. No visible manuscript ; no inscription in the language : no correspondence among friends : no transaction of business, of which a single scrap remains in the ancient families. Macpherson's pretence is, that the character was Saxon. If he had not talked unskilfully of *manuscripts*, he might have fought with oral tradition much longer. As to Mr. Grant's information, I suppose he knows much less of the matter than ourselves.

' In the mean time, the bookseller says that the sale [2] is sufficiently quick. They printed four thousand. Correct your copy wherever it is wrong, and bring it up. Your friends will all be glad to see you. I think of going myself into the country about May.

' I am sorry that I have not managed to send the books [b] sooner. I have left four for you, and do not restrict you absolutely to follow my directions in the distribution. You must use your own discretion.

' Make my compliments to Mrs. Boswell : I suppose she is now just beginning to forgive me.

' I am, dear Sir, your humble servant,

' Feb. 25, 1775.'   ' SAM. JOHNSON.'

---

[a] Do not : 1 Don't 2, 3.

[1] ' Such is the laxity of Highland conversation, that the inquirer is kept in continual suspense, and by a kind of intellectual retrogradation, knows less as he hears more.' Johnson's *Journey*, p. 45. The Highlanders ' are not much accustomed to be interrogated by others ; and seem never to have thought upon interrogating themselves ; so that if they do not know what they tell to be true, they likewise do not distinctly perceive it to be false.' *Ib.*, p. 106.

[2] Of his ' Journey to the Western Islands of Scotland.' BOSWELL.

[b] books 1 : book 2, 3.

It was sold at five shillings a copy. It did not reach a second edition till 1785, when perhaps a fresh demand for it was caused by the publication of Boswell's *Hebrides*. Boswell, in a note, *post*, iii. 325, n. 5, says that 4,000 copies were sold very quickly. Hannah More (*Memoirs*, i. 39) says that Cadell told her that he had sold 4,000 copies the first week. This, I think, must be an exaggeration. ⟨There were two impressions of the 1775 edition and three unauthorized reprints.⟩

On Tuesday, March 21, I arrived in London [1] ; and on repair-
ing to Dr. Johnson's before dinner, found him in his study, sitting
with Mr. Peter Garrick, the elder brother of David, strongly resembling him in countenance and voice, but of more sedate and
placid manners [2]. Johnson informed me, that ' though Mr. Beauclerk was in great pain, it was hoped he was not in danger [3], and
that he now wished to consult Dr. Heberden to try the effect of
a *new understanding.*' Both at this interview, and in the evening
at Mr. Thrale's, where he and Mr. Peter Garrick and I met again,
he was vehement on the subject of the Ossian controversy ; observing, ' We do not know that there are any ancient Erse
manuscripts ; and we have no other reason to disbelieve that
there are men with three heads, but that we do not know that
there are any such men.' He also was outrageous, upon his
supposition that my countrymen ' loved Scotland better than
truth [4],' saying, ' All of them,—nay not all,—but *droves* of
them, would come up, and attest any thing for the honour of
Scotland.' He also persevered in his wild allegation, that he
questioned if there was a tree between Edinburgh and the
English border older than himself [5]. I assured him he was
mistaken, and suggested that the proper punishment would be
that he should receive a stripe at every tree above a hundred
years old, that was found within that space. He laughed, and
said, ' I believe I might submit to it for a *baubee* ! '

The doubts which, in my correspondence with him, I had

---

[1] Boswell, on the way to London,
wrote, 18 March, to Temple :—' I
have continual schemes of publication ; but cannot fix. I am still very
unhappy with my father. We are so
totally different that a good understanding is scarcely possible. He
looks on my going to London just
now as an *expedition*—as idle and
extravagant ; when in reality it is
highly improving to me, considering
the company which I enjoy.' *Letters*,
No. 136, i. 215.

[2] See *post*, ii. 462. ⟨See Broadley,
Dr. Johnson and Mrs. Thrale, p. 163.⟩

[3] See *ante*, ii. 292.

[4] ' A Scotchman must be a very
sturdy moralist, who does not love

Scotland better than truth : he will
always love it better than inquiry ;
and if falsehood flatters his vanity,
will not be very diligent to detect it.'
Johnson's *Journey Western Islands*,
1924, p. 108.

[5] At Slanes Castle in Aberdeen-
shire he wrote :—' I had now travelled two hundred miles in Scotland, and seen only one tree not
younger than myself.' *Journey*, p. 18.
Goldsmith wrote from Edinburgh on
Sept. 26, 1753 :—' Every part of the
country presents the same dismall
landscape, no grove nor brook lend
their musick to cheer the stranger, or
make the inhabitants forget their
poverty.' *Letters*, 1928, p. 10.

ventured to state as to the justice and wisdom of the conduct
of Great-Britain towards the American colonies, while I at the
same time requested that he would enable me to inform myself
upon that momentous subject, he had altogether disregarded ;
and had recently published a pamphlet, entitled, ' Taxation no
Tyranny ; an Answer to the Resolutions and Address of the
American Congress ¹.' *

He had long before indulged most unfavourable sentiments
of our fellow-subjects in America ². For, as early as 1769,
I was told by Dr. John Campbell, that he had said of them,
' Sir, they are a race of convicts ³, and ought to be thankful
for any thing we allow them short of hanging.'

Of this performance I avoided to talk with him ; for I had
now formed a clear and settled opinion ⁴, that the people of
America were well warranted to resist a claim that their fellow-
subjects in the mother-country should have the entire command
of their fortunes, by taxing them without their own consent ;
and the extreme violence which it breathed, appeared to me
so unsuitable to the mildness of a Christian philosopher,
and so directly opposite to the principles of peace which he had
so beautifully recommended in his pamphlet respecting Falkland's Islands ⁵, that I was sorry to see him appear in so unfavourable a light. Besides, I could not perceive in it that

¹ This, like his pamphlet on *Falkland's Islands*, was published without
his name. ⟨Four editions were published in 1775. See App. B, p. 515.⟩

² See Appendix A, p. 476.

³ Convicts were sent to nine of
the American settlements. According to one estimate about 2,000 had
been for many years sent annually.
' Dr. Lang, after comparing different
estimates, concludes that the number
sent there might be about fifty
thousand altogether.' *Penny Cycl.*
xxv. 138.

⁴ This ' clear and settled opinion '
must have been formed in three
days, and between Grantham and
London. For from that Lincolnshire town he had written to Temple
on March 18 :—' As to American affairs, I have really not studied the

subject. It is too much for me perhaps ; or I am too indolent or frivolous. From the smattering which
newspapers have given me, I have
been of different minds several
times. That I am a Tory, a lover of
power in monarchy, and a discour-
ager of much liberty in the people I
avow. But it is not clear to me that
our colonies are compleatly our subjects.' *Letters*, No. 136, i. 213. Four
years later, 3 May, 1779, he wrote to
Temple :—' I must candidly tell you
that I think you should not puzzle
yourself with political speculations
more than I do. Neither of us is fit
for that sort of mental labour.' *Ib.*
No. 193, ii. 288. See *post*, iii. 205-7,
for a contest between Johnson and
Boswell on this subject.

⁵ See *ante*, ii. 134.

ability of argument, or that felicity of expression, for which he
was, upon other occasions, so eminent. Positive assertion, sarcastical severity, and extravagant ridicule, which he himself
reprobated as a test of truth, were united in this rhapsody.

That this pamphlet was written at the desire of those who
were then in power, I have no doubt; and, indeed, he owned
to me, that it had been revised and curtailed by some of them.†
He told me, that they had struck out one passage, which was
to this effect :

‘ That the Colonists could with no solidity argue from their not
having been taxed while in their infancy, that they should not now
be taxed. We do not put a calf into the plow ; we wait till he is
an ox.’

He said, ‘ They struck it out either critically as too ludicrous,
or politically as too exasperating. I care not which. It was
their business. If an architect says, I will build five stories,
and the man who employs him says, I will have only three,
the employer is to decide.’ ‘ Yes, Sir, (said I,) in ordinary
cases. But should it be so when the architect gives his skill
and labour *gratis* ? ’

Unfavourable as I am constrained to say my opinion of this
pamphlet was, yet, since it was congenial with the sentiments
of numbers at that time, and as every thing relating to the
writings of Dr. Johnson is of importance in literary history,
I shall therefore insert some passages which were struck out,
it does not appear why, either by himself or those who revised it. They appear printed in a few proof leaves of it in my
possession, marked with corrections in his own hand-writing.
I shall distinguish them by *Italicks*.

In the paragraph where he says, the Americans were incited
to resistance by European intelligence from

‘ Men whom they thought their friends, but who were friends only
to themselves [1],’

there followed,—

‘ and made, by their selfishness, the enemies of their country.’

[1] Johnson's *Works*, vi. 261. † ⟨See App. B, p. 515.⟩

And the next paragraph ran thus :

' On the original contrivers of mischief, *rather than on those whom they have deluded*, let an insulted nation pour out its vengeance.'

The paragraph which came next was in these words :

' *Unhappy is that country in which men can hope for advancement by favouring its enemies. The tranquillity of stable government is not always easily preserved against the machinations of single innovators ; but what can be the hope of quiet, when factions hostile to the legislature can be openly formed and openly avowed ?* '

After the paragraph which now concludes the pamphlet, there followed this, in which he certainly means the great Earl of Chatham [1], and glances at a certain popular Lord Chancellor [2]: '

' *If, by the fortune of war, they drive us utterly away, what they will do next can only be conjectured. If a new monarchy is erected, they will want a* KING. *He who first takes into his hand the sceptre of America, should have a name of good omen.* WILLIAM *has been known both as conqueror and deliverer ; and perhaps England, however contemned, might yet supply them with* ANOTHER WILLIAM. *Whigs, indeed, are not willing to be governed ; and it is possible that* KING WILLIAM *may be strongly inclined to guide their measures : but Whigs have been cheated like other mortals, and suffered their leader to become their tyrant, under the name of their* PROTECTOR. *What more they will receive from England, no man can tell. In their rudiments of empire they may want a* CHANCELLOR.'

Then came this paragraph :

' *Their numbers are, at present, not quite sufficient for the greatness which, in some form of government or other, is to rival the ancient monarchies ; but, by Dr. Franklin's rule of progression*[3], *they will, in*

---

[1] Four years earlier he had also attacked him. *Ante*, ii. 134, note 4.

[2] Lord Camden, formerly Chief Justice Pratt. See *ante*, ii. 72, note 3 ; and *post*, ii. 353, note 2.

[3] ' Our People,' wrote Franklin in 1751 (*Writings*, iii. 65), ' must at least be doubled every 20 Years.' The population he reckoned at upwards of one million. Johnson referred to this rule also in the following passage :—
' We are . . . told . . . that the continent of North America contains three millions, not of men merely, but of whigs, of whigs fierce for liberty, and disdainful of dominion ; that they multiply with the fecundity of their own rattlesnakes, so that every quarter of a century doubles their numbers.' *Works*, vi. 227. Burke, in his *Speech on Conciliation with America*, a fortnight after Johnson's pamphlet appeared, said, ' your children do not grow faster from infancy to manhood,

a century and a quarter, be more than equal to the inhabitants of Europe. When the Whigs of America are thus multiplied, let the Princes of the earth tremble in their palaces. If they should continue to double and to double, their own hemisphere will[a] *not contain them. But let not our boldest oppugners of authority look forward with delight to this futurity of Whiggism.'*

How it ended I know not, as it is cut off abruptly at the foot of the last of these proof pages [1].

His pamphlets in support of the measures of administration were published on his own account, and he afterwards collected them into a volume, with the title of 'Political Tracts, by the Authour of the Rambler,' with this motto :

> *' Fallitur egregio quisquis sub Principe credit*
> *Servitium ; nunquam libertas gratior extat*
> *Quam sub Rege pio.'*   CLAUDIANUS [2].

These pamphlets drew upon him numerous attacks [3]. Against the common weapons of literary warfare he was hardened ; but

a will 1, 2: would 3.

than they spread from families to communities, and from villages to nations.' Payne's *Burke*, i. 169.

[1] Dr. T. Campbell records on April 20, 1775 (*Diary*, p. 74 : John. Misc. ii. 53), that ' Johnson said the first thing he would do, would be to quarter the army on the citys, and if any refused free quarters, he would pull down that person's house, if it was joyned to other houses, but would burn it if it stood alone. This and other schemes he proposed in the manuscript of *Taxation no Tyranny*, but these, he said, the Ministry expunged.' See *post*, iii. 290, where, talking of the Americans, Johnson exclaimed, ' he'd burn and destroy them.' On June 11, 1781, Campbell records (*ib.* p. 88 : John. Misc. ii. 55) that Johnson said to him :—' Had we treated the Americans as we ought, and as they deserved, we should have at once razed all their towns—and let them enjoy their forests.' Campbell justly describes this talk as ' wild rant.' ⟨See also App. A, p. 476.⟩

[2] ' He errs who deems obedience
    to a prince
Slav'ry—a happier freedom
    never reigns
Than with a pious Monarch.'
    Stil. iii. 113. CROKER.
This volume was published in 1776. The copy in the library of Pembroke College, Oxford, bears the inscription in Johnson's hand : ' To Sir Joshua Reynolds from the Authour.' On the title-page Sir Joshua has written his own name. ⟨See App. B, p. 515.⟩

[3] ⟨For a list of these see Courtney, pp. 126–7.⟩ R. B. Sheridan thought of joining in these attacks. In his *Life* by Moore (i. 135) fragments of his projected answer are given. He intended to attack Johnson on the side of his pension. One thought he varies three times. ' Such pamphlets,' he writes, ' will be as trifling and insincere as the venal quit-rent of a birth-day ode.' This again appears as ' The easy quit-rent of refined panegyric,' and yet again as ' The miserable quit-rent of an annual

there were two instances of animadversion which I communicated to him, and from what I could judge, both from his silence and his looks, appeared to me to impress him much.

One was, ' A Letter to Dr. Samuel Johnson, occasioned by his late political Publications.' It appeared previous to his ' Taxation no Tyranny,' and was written by Dr. Joseph Towers [1]. In that performance, Dr. Johnson was treated with the respect due to so eminent a man, while his conduct as a political writer was boldly and pointedly arraigned, as inconsistent with the character of one, who, if he did employ his pen upon politicks,

' It might reasonably be expected should distinguish himself, not by party violence and rancour, but by moderation and by wisdom.'

It concluded thus :

' I would, however, wish you to remember, should you again address the publick under the character of a political writer, that luxuriance of imagination or energy of language will ill compensate for the want of candour, of justice, and of truth. And I shall only add, that should I hereafter be disposed to read, as I heretofore have done, the most excellent of all your performances, " THE RAMBLER," the pleasure which I have been accustomed to find in it will be much diminished by the reflection that the writer of so moral, so elegant, and so valuable a work, was capable of prostituting his talents in such productions as " The False Alarm," the " Thoughts on the Transactions respecting Falkland's Islands," and " The Patriot." '

I am willing to do justice to the merit of Dr. Towers, of whom I will say, that although I abhor his Whiggish democratical notions and propensities, (for I will not call them principles,) I esteem him as an ingenious, knowing, and very convivial man.

The other instance was a paragraph of a letter to me, from my old and most intimate friend, the Reverend Mr. Temple, who wrote the character of Gray, which has had the honour to be adopted both by Mr. Mason and Dr. Johnson in their accounts of that poet [2]. The words were,

' How can your great, I will not say your *pious*, but your *moral* friend, support the barbarous measures of administration, which

pamphlet.' ⟨See also the biographies by Rae (i. 308) and Sichel (i. 76, 472).⟩
[1] See *post*, iv. 40.

[2] See *ante*, i. 436 ; *post*, iv. 153, note 2 ; ⟨and App. B to this volume, p. 515⟩.

they have not the face to ask even their infidel pensioner Hume to defend [1].'

However confident of the rectitude of his own mind, Johnson may have felt sincere uneasiness that his conduct should be erroneously imputed to unworthy motives, by good men ; and that the influence of his valuable writings should on that account be in any degree obstructed or lessened [2].

He complained to a Right Honourable friend [3] of distinguished talents and very elegant manners, with whom he maintained a long intimacy, and whose generosity towards him will afterwards appear [4], that his pension having been given to him as a literary character, he had been applied to by administration to write political pamphlets ; and he was even so much irritated, that he declared his resolution to resign his pension. His friend shewed him the impropriety of such a measure, and he afterwards expressed his gratitude, and said he had received good advice. To that friend he once signified a wish to have his pension secured to him for his life ; but he neither asked nor

---

[1] Boswell wrote to Temple on June 19, 1775 :—' Mr. Hume and Lord Kames joined in attacking Dr. Johnson to an absurd pitch. Mr. Hume said he would give me half a crown for every page of his Dictionary in which he could not find an absurdity, if I would give him half a crown for every page in which he did find one. He talked so insolently, really, that I calmly determined to be at him. So I repeated, by way of telling that Dr. Johnson *could* be touched, the admirable passage in your letter how the ministry had set him to write in a way that they could not ask *even their infidel pensioner Hume* to write. . . . When Hume asked if it was from an American, I said, " No, it was from an English gentleman." " Would a *gentleman* write so ? " said he.—In short, Davy was finely punished for his treatment of my revered friend ; and he deserved it richly, both for his petulance to so great a character ; and for his talking so before *me*.'

Letters, No. 147, i. 233–4. Hume's pension was £400. He obtained it through Lord Hertford, the English ambassador in Paris, under whom he had served as secretary to the embassy. J. H. Burton's *Hume*, ii. 289.

[2] Dr. T. Campbell records on March 16 of this year (*Diary*, p. 36 : John. Misc. ii. 42) :—' Thrale asked Dr. Johnson what Sir Joshua Reynolds said of *Taxation no Tyranny*. Sir Joshua, quoth the Doctor, has not read it. I suppose, quoth Thrale, he has been very busy of late ; no, says the Doctor, but I never look at his pictures, so he won't read my writings. . . . Thrale then asked him if he had got Miss Reynolds' opinion, for she it seems is a politician ; as to that, quoth the Doctor, it is no great matter, for she could not tell after she had read it, on which side of the question Mr. Burke's speech was.'

[3] William Gerard Hamilton.

[4] See *post*, iv. 245.

received from government any reward whatsoever for his political labours [1].

On Friday, March 24, I met him at the LITERARY CLUB, where were Mr. Beauclerk, Mr. Langton, Mr. Colman, Dr. Percy, Mr. Vesey, Sir Charles Bunbury, Dr. George Fordyce, Mr. Steevens, and Mr. Charles Fox. Before he came in, we talked of his ' Journey to the Western Islands,' and of his coming away, ' willing to believe the second sight [2],' which seemed to excite some ridicule. I was then so impressed with the truth of many of the stories of it which I had been told, that I avowed my conviction, saying, ' He is only *willing* to believe : I *do* believe. The evidence is enough for me, though not for his great mind. What will not fill a quart bottle will fill a pint bottle. I am filled with belief [3].' ' Are you ? (said Colman,) then cork it up.'

I found his ' Journey ' the common topick of conversation in London at this time, wherever I happened to be. At one of Lord Mansfield's formal Sunday evening conversations, strangely called *Levées*, his Lordship addressed me, ' We have all been reading your travels, Mr. Boswell.' I answered, ' I was but the humble attendant of Dr. Johnson.' The Chief Justice replied, with that air and manner which none, who ever saw and heard him, can forget, ' He speaks ill of nobody but Ossian.'

Johnson was in high spirits this evening at the club, and talked with great animation and success. He attacked Swift, as he used to do upon all occasions. ' The " Tale of a Tub " is so much superiour to his other writings, that one can hardly

---

[1] Sixteen days after this pamphlet was published, Lord North, as Chancellor of the University of Oxford, proposed that the degree of Doctor in Civil Law should be conferred on Johnson (*post*, ii. 331). Perhaps the Chancellor in this was cheaply rewarding the service that had been done to the Minister. See *ante*, i. 373.

[2] Johnson's ' Journey to the Western Islands of Scotland,' edit. 1785, p. 256. BOSWELL. Edit. 1924, p. 100 : see *ante*, ii. 10, note 3.

[3] He had written to Temple on the

18th :—' The *second sight* . . . pleases my superstition, which you know is not small, and being not of the gloomy but the grand species, is an enjoyment ; and I go further than Mr. Johnson, for the facts which I heard convinced me.' *Letters*, No. 136, i. 212. When ten years later he published his *Tour*, he said (Nov. 10) that he had returned from the Hebrides with a considerable degree of faith ; ' but,' he added, ' since that time, my belief in those stories has been much weakened ' (*post*, v. 390).

believe he was the authour of it [1].   There [a] is in it such a vigour of mind, such a swarm of thoughts, so much of nature, and art, and life [2].'   I wondered to hear him say of " Gulliver's Travels," ' When once you have thought of big men and little men, it is very easy to do all the rest.'   I endeavoured to make a stand for Swift, and tried to rouse those who were much more able to defend him ; but in vain.   Johnson at last, of his own accord, allowed very great merit to the inventory of articles found in the pockets [b] of the Man Mountain, particularly the description of his watch, which it was conjectured was his GOD, as he consulted it upon all occasions.   He observed, that ' Swift put his name to but two things, (after he had a name to put,) " The Plan for the Improvement of the English Language," and the last " Drapier's Letter [3]." '

a it. There 1, 2: it: ' there 3.   b pockets 1: pocket 2, 3.

[1] This doubt has been much agitated on both sides, I think without good reason. See Addison's ' Freeholder,' May 4, 1714 [*The Freeholder* was published from Dec. 1715 to June 1716. In the number for May 4 there is no mention of *The Tale of a Tub*] ; An Apology for the Tale of a Tub [Swift's *Prose Works*, 1897, i. 13] ;—Dr. Hawkesworth's Preface to Swift's Works, and Swift's Letter to Tooke the Printer, and Tooke's Answer, in that collection ;—Sheridan's Life of Swift ;—Mr. Courtenay's note on p. 3 of his ' Poetical Review of the Literary and Moral Character of Dr. Johnson ; ' and Mr. Cooksey's ' Essay on the Life and Character of John Lord Somers, Baron of Evesham.'

Dr. Johnson here speaks only to the *internal evidence*. I take leave to differ from him, having a very high estimation of the powers of Dr. Swift. His ' Sentiments of a Church-of-England-man,' his ' Sermon on the Trinity,' and other serious pieces, prove his learning as well as his acuteness in logick and metaphysicks ; and his various compositions of a different cast exhibit not only wit, humour, and ridicule ; but a knowledge ' of nature, and art, and life : ' a combination

therefore of those powers, when (as the ' Apology ' says,) ' the authour was young, his invention at the heighth, and his reading fresh in his head,' might surely produce ' *The Tale of a Tub*.' BOSWELL.

[2] ' His *Tale of a Tub* has little resemblance to his other pieces. It exhibits a vehemence and rapidity of mind, a copiousness of images, and vivacity of diction such as he afterwards never possessed or never exerted. It is of a mode so distinct and peculiar that it must be considered by itself ; what is true of that is not true of any thing else which he has written.' Johnson's *Swift*, 111. At the conclusion of the *Life of Swift* (141), Johnson allows him one great merit :—' It was said, in a Preface to one of the Irish editions, that Swift had never been known to take a single thought from any writer, ancient or modern. This is not literally true ; but perhaps no writer can easily be found that has borrowed so little, or that in all his excellences and all his defects has so well maintained his claim to be considered as original.' See *ante*, i. 452.

[3] ⟨The fact that Johnson does not, in his *Dictionary*, give Swift's name to

From Swift, there was an easy transition to Mr. Thomas Sheridan.—JOHNSON. ' Sheridan is a wonderful admirer of the tragedy of Douglas, and presented its authour with a gold medal. Some years ago, at a coffee-house in Oxford, I called to him, " Mr. Sheridan, Mr. Sheridan, how came you to give a gold medal to Home, for writing that foolish play [1] ? " This, you see, was wanton and insolent ; but I *meant* to be wanton and insolent. A medal has no value but as a stamp of merit. And was Sheridan to assume to himself the right of giving that stamp ? If Sheridan was magnificent enough to bestow a gold medal as an honorary reward of dramatick excellence, he should have requested one of the Universities to choose the person on whom it should be conferred. Sheridan had no right to give a stamp of merit : it was counterfeiting Apollo's coin [2].'

the quotations from *Gulliver's Travels*, has no significance. He treated *Clarissa*, the *Faerie Queene*, *Hudibras*, and other works similarly.⟩

[1] See *post*, v. 360. David Hume wrote of Home's *Agis* :—' I own, though I could perceive fine strokes in that tragedy, I never could in general bring myself to like it : the author, I thought, had corrupted his taste by the imitation of Shakspere, whom he ought only to have admired.' J. H. Burton's *Hume*, i. 392. About *Douglas* he wrote :—' I am persuaded it will be esteemed the best, and by French critics the only tragedy of our language ! ' *Ib*. ii. 17. Hume perhaps admired it the more as it was written, to use his own words, ' by a namesake of mine.' *Ib*. i. 316. *Home* is pronounced *Hume*. He often wrote of his friend as ' Mr. John Hume, *alias* Home.' A few days before his death he added the following codicil to his will :—' I leave to my friend Mr. John Home of Kilduff, ten dozen of my old claret, at his choice ; and one single bottle of that other liquor called port. I also leave to him six dozen of port, provided that he attests under his hand, signed John *Hume*, that he has himself alone

finished that bottle at two sittings. By this concession, he will at once terminate the only two differences that ever arose between us concerning temporal matters.' *Ib*. ii. 506. Sir Walter Scott wrote in his *Diary* in 1827 :—' I finished the review of John Home's works, which, after all, are poorer than I thought them. Good blank verse, and stately sentiment, but something luke-warmish, excepting *Douglas*, which is certainly a master-piece. Even that does not stand the closet. Its merits are for the stage ; and it is certainly one of the best acting plays going.' Lockhart's *Scott*, edit. 1828, vii. 29.

[2] Sheridan, says Mr. S. Whyte (*Misc.* p. 46), brought out *Douglas* at the Dublin Theatre. The first two nights it had great success. The third night was as usual to be the author's. It had meanwhile got abroad that he was a clergyman. This play was considered a profanation of the clerical character, a faction was raised against it, and the third night did not pay its expenses. It was Whyte who suggested that, by way of consolation, Sheridan should give Home a gold medal. The inscription said that he presented it to him ' for having en-

On Monday, March 27, I breakfasted with him at Mr. Strahan's. He told us, that he was engaged to go that evening to Mrs. Abington's benefit. ' She was visiting some ladies whom I was visiting, and begged that I would come to her benefit. I told her I could not hear : but she insisted so much on my coming, that it would have been brutal to have refused her.' This was a speech quite characteristical. He loved to bring forward his having been in the gay circles of life ; and he was, perhaps, a little vain of the solicitations of this elegant and fashionable actress. He told us, the play was to be ' The Hypocrite,' altered from Cibber's ' Nonjuror 1,' so as to satirize the Methodists. ' I do not think (said he,) the character of the Hypocrite justly applicable to the Methodists, but it was very applicable to the Nonjurors 2. I once said to Dr. Madan 3, a clergyman of Ireland, who was a great Whig, that perhaps a Nonjuror would have been less criminal in taking the oaths imposed by the ruling power, than refusing them ; because refusing them, necessarily laid him under almost an irresistible temptation to be more criminal ; for, a man *must* live, and if he precludes himself from the support furnished by the establishment, will probably be reduced to very wicked shifts to maintain himself 4.'

riched the Stage with a Perfect Tragedy.' Whyte took the medal to London. When he was close at his journey's end, ' I was,' he writes, ' stopped by highwaymen, and preserved the well-meant offering, by the sacrifice of my purse, at the imminent peril of my life.'

1 ' No merit now the dear Nonjuror claims,
    Molière's old stubble in a moment flames.'
The *Nonjuror* was ' a comedy threshed out of Molière's *Tartuffe*.' *The Dunciad*, i. 253.

2 See *post*, iv. 286–8 ; also Macaulay's *England*, ch. xiv. (ed. 1874, v. 94), for remarks on what Johnson here says.

3 See *ante*, i. 318, *post*, iv. 205, where his name is spelt *Madden*.

4 This was not merely a cursory remark ; for in his Life of Fenton [2]

he observes, ' With many other wise and virtuous men, who at that time of discord and debate [about the beginning of this century,] consulted conscience well or ill informed a, more than interest, he doubted the legality of the government ; and refusing to qualify himself for publick employment, by taking b the oaths required, left the University without a degree.' This conduct Johnson calls ' perverseness of integrity.'

The question concerning the morality of taking oaths, of whatever kind, imposed by the prevailing power at the time, rather than to be excluded from all consequence, or even any considerable usefulness in society, has been agitated with all the acuteness of casuistry. It is related, that he who devised the oath of abjuration, profligately boasted, that he had

a whether well or ill informed *Johnson*.   b taking *not in Johnson*.

BOSWELL. ' I should think, Sir, that a man who took the oaths contrary to his principles, was a determined wicked man, because he was sure he was committing perjury ; whereas a Nonjuror might be insensibly led to do what was wrong, without being so directly conscious of it.' JOHNSON. ' Why, Sir, a man who goes to bed to his patron's wife is pretty sure that he is committing wickedness.' BOSWELL. ' Did the nonjuring clergymen do so, Sir ? ' JOHNSON. ' I am afraid many of them did.'

I was startled at his argument, and could by no means think it convincing. Had not his own father complied with the requisition of government [1], (as to which he once observed to me, when I pressed him upon it, ' *That*, Sir, he was to settle with himself,') he would probably have thought more unfavourably of a Jacobite who took the oaths :

> ' ———— had he not resembled
> My father as he *swore*——— [2].'

Mr. Strahan talked of launching into the great ocean of London, in order to have a chance for rising into eminence ; and, observing that many men were kept back from trying their fortunes there, because they were born to a competency,

framed a test which should ' damn one half of the nation, and starve the other.' Upon minds not exalted to inflexible rectitude, or minds in which zeal for a party is predominant to excess, taking that oath against conviction, may have been palliated under the plea of necessity, or ventured upon in heat, as upon the whole producing more good than evil.

At a county election in Scotland, many years ago, when there was a warm contest between the friends of the Hanoverian succession, and those against it, the oath of abjuration having been demanded, the freeholders upon one side rose to go away. Upon which a very sanguine gentleman, one of their number, ran to the door to stop them, calling out with much earnestness, ' Stay, stay, my friends, and let us swear the rogues out of it ! ' BOSWELL.

Johnson, writing of the oaths re-

quired under the Militia Bill of 1756, says :—' The frequent imposition of oaths has almost ruined the morals of this unhappy nation, and of a nation without morals it is of small importance who shall be king.' *Lit. Mag.* 1756, i. 59.

[1] Dr. Harwood sent me the following extract from the book containing the proceedings of the corporation of Lichfield : ' 19th July, 1712. Agreed that Mr. Michael Johnson be, and he is hereby elected a magistrate and brother of their incorporation ; a day is given him to Thursday next to take the oath of fidelity and allegiance, and the oath of a magistrate. Signed, &c.'—' 25th July, 1712. Mr. Johnson took the oath of allegiance, and that he believed there was no transubstantiation in the sacrament of the Lord's Supper before, &c.'—CROKER. ⟨See App. B, p. 516.⟩

[2] A parody on *Macbeth*, act ii. sc. 2.

said, ' Small certainties are the bane of men of talents [1] ; ' which
Johnson confirmed. Mr. Strahan put Johnson in mind of a
remark which he had made to him ; ' There are few ways in
which a man can be more innocently employed than in getting
money.' ' The more one thinks of this, (said Strahan,) the juster
it will appear.'

Mr. Strahan had taken a poor boy from the country as an
apprentice, upon Johnson's recommendation. Johnson having
enquired after him, said, ' Mr. Strahan, let me have five guineas on
account, and I'll give this boy one. Nay, if a man recommends a
boy, and does nothing for him, it is sad work. Call him down.'

I followed him into the court-yard [2], behind Mr. Strahan's
house ; and there I had a proof of what I had heard him
profess, that he talked alike to all. ' Some people (said he),[a]
tell you that they let themselves down to the capacity of their
hearers. I never do that. I speak uniformly, in as intelligible a
manner as I can [3].'

' Well, my boy, how do you go on ? '—' Pretty well, Sir ; but
they are afraid I an't strong enough for some parts of the
business.' JOHNSON. ' Why I shall be sorry for it ; for when
you consider with how little mental power and corporeal labour
a printer can get a guinea a week, it is a very desirable occupation for you. Do you hear,—take all the pains you can ;
and if this does not do, we must think of some other way of
life for you. There's a guinea.'

---

^a Some people (said he,) 1: Some people 2, 3.

[1] Lord Southampton asked Bishop
Watson of Llandaff ' " how am I to
bring up my son so as to make him
get forwards in the world ? " " I know
of but one way," replied the Bishop ;
" give him parts and poverty." " Well,
then," replied Lord S., " if God has
given him parts, I will manage as to the
poverty." ' H. C. Robinson's *Diary*,
i. 337. Lord Eldon said that Thurlow
promised to give him a post worth
about £160 a year, but he never did.
' In after life,' said Eldon, ' I inquired
[of him] why he had not fulfilled his
promise ; and his answer was curious :
—" It would have been your ruin.

Young men are very apt to be content
when they get something to live upon ;
so when I saw what you were made
of, I determined to break my promise
to make you work ; " and I dare
say he was right, for there is nothing
does a young lawyer so much good as
to be half starved.' Twiss's *Eldon*,
i. 134.

[2] In New Street, near Gough
Square, in Fleet Street, whither, in
February, 1770, the King's printing-
house was removed from what is
still called Printing House Square.
CROKER.

[3] See *post*, iv. 184.

Here was one of the many, many instances of his active benevolence. At the same time, the slow and sonorous solemnity with which, while he bent himself down, he addressed a little thick short-legged boy, contrasted with the boy's aukwardness and awe, could not but excite some ludicrous emotions [1].

I met him at Drury-lane play-house in the evening. Sir Joshua Reynolds, at Mrs. Abington's request, had promised to bring a body of wits to her benefit ; and having secured forty places in the front boxes, had done me the honour to put me in the group. Johnson sat on the seat directly behind me [2] ; and as he could neither see nor hear at such a distance from the stage, he was wrapped up in grave abstraction, and seemed quite a cloud, amidst all the sunshine of glitter and gaiety [3].

[1] Johnson wrote to Dr. Taylor on April 8 of this year :—' I have placed young Davenport in the greatest printing house in London, and hear no complaint of him but want of size, which will not hinder him much. He may when he is a journeyman always get a guinea a week.' *Letters*, No. 387. Mr. Jewitt in the *Gent. Mag.* for Dec. 1878, pp. 694, 698, gives an account of this lad. He was the orphan son of a clergyman, a friend of the Rev. W. Langley, Master of Ashbourne School (see *post*, iii. 138). Mr. Langley asked Johnson's help ' in procuring him a place in some eminent printing office.' Davenport wrote to Mr. Langley nearly eight years later :—' According to your desire, I consulted Dr. Johnson about my future employment in life, and he very laconically told me " to work hard at my trade, as others had done before me." I told him my size and want of strength prevented me from getting so much money as other men. " Then," replied he, " you must get as much as you can." ' The boy was nearly sixteen when he was apprenticed, and had learnt enough Latin to quote Virgil, so that there was nothing in Johnson's speech beyond his understanding. ⟨See also Johnson's *Letters*, Nos. 368, 387·2, and

Nichols, *Lit. Anec.* iii. 287.⟩
[2] Seven years afterwards, Johnson described this evening. Miss Monckton had told him that he must see Mrs. Siddons. ' Well, Madam,' he answered, ' if you desire it, I will go. See her I shall not, nor hear her ; but I'll go, and that will do. The last time I was at a play, I was ordered there by Mrs. Abington, or Mrs. Somebody, I do not well remember who ; but I placed myself in the middle of the first row of the front boxes, to show that when I was called I came.' Mme. D'Arblay's *Diary*, ii. 199. At Fontainebleau he went to a comedy (*post*, ii. 394), so that it was not ' the last time he was at a play.'
[3] ' One evening in the oratorio season of the year 1771,' writes Mrs. Piozzi (*Anec.* 72 : John. Misc. i. 196), ' Mr. Johnson went with me to Covent-Garden theatre ; . . . he sat surprisingly quiet, and I flattered myself that he was listening to the music. When we were got home, however, he repeated these verses, which he said he had made at the oratorio.'
' In Theatro, March 8, 1771.
Tertii verso quater orbe lustri,
Quid theatrales tibi, Crispe, pompae ?
Quam decet canos male literatos
                      Sera voluptas

I wondered at his patience in sitting out a play of five acts, and a farce of two. He said very little ; but after the prologue to ' Bon Ton ¹ ' had been spoken, which he could hear pretty well from the more slow and distinct utterance, he talked of prologue-writing, and observed, ' Dryden has written prologues superiour to any that David Garrick has written ; but David Garrick has written more good prologues than Dryden has done. It is wonderful that he has been able to write such a variety ᵃ of them ².'

At Mr. Beauclerk's, where I supped, was Mr. Garrick, whom I made happy with Johnson's praise of his prologues ; and I suppose, in gratitude to him, he took up one of his favourite topicks, the nationality of the Scotch, which he maintained in his ᵇ pleasant manner, with the aid of a little poetical fiction. ' Come, come, don't deny it : they are really national. Why, now, the Adams ³ are as liberal-minded men as any in the world : but, I don't know how it is, all their workmen are

ᵃ a variety 1 : variety 2, 3.　　　ᵇ his 1 : a 2, 3.

Tene mulceri fidibus canoris ?
Tene cantorum modulis stupere ?
Tene per pictas, oculo elegante,
　　　　Currere formas ?
Inter aequales, sine felle liber,
Codices veri studiosus inter
Rectius vives.　Sua quisque carpat
　　　　Gaudia gratus.
Lusibus gaudet puer otiosis,
Luxus oblectat juvenem theatri,
At seni fluxo sapienter uti
　　　　Tempore restat.'
　　　　(*Works*, i. 166.)

¹ *Bon Ton, or High Life above Stairs*, by Garrick. He made King the comedian a present of this farce, and it was acted for the first time on his benefit—a little earlier in the month. Murphy's *Garrick*, pp. 330, 332.

² ' August, 1778. An epilogue of Mr. Garrick's to *Bonduca* was . . . mentioned, and Dr. Johnson said it was a miserable performance . . . " I don't know what is the matter with David ; I am afraid he is grown superannuated, for his prologues and epilogues used to be incomparable." '

Mme. D'Arblay's *Diary*, i. 65.

³ ' Scottish brethren and architects, who had bought Durham Yard, and erected a large pile of buildings with dwellings and warehouses, under the affected name of the Adelphi. These men, of great taste in their profession, were attached particularly to Lord Bute and Lord Mansfield, and thus by public and private nationality zealous politicians.' Walpole's *Memoirs of the Reign of George III*, iv. 173. Hume wrote to Adam Smith in June 1772, at a time when there was ' a universal loss of credit ' :—
' Of all the sufferers, I am the most concerned for the Adams. . . . But their undertakings were so vast, that nothing could support them. They must dismiss 3000 workmen, who, comprehending the materials, must have expended above £100,000 a-year. . . . To me the scheme of the Adelphi always appeared so imprudent, that my wonder is how they could have gone on so long.' J. H. Burton's *Hume*, ii. 460. Garrick lived in the Adelphi (*post*, iv. 96).

Scotch. You are, to be sure, wonderfully free from that nationality : but so it happens, that you employ the only Scotch
shoe-black in London.' He imitated the manner of his old
master with ludicrous exaggeration ; repeating, with pauses and
half-whistlings interjected,

> ' *Os homini sublime dedit,—cœlumque tueri*
> *Jussit,—et erectos ad sidera—tollere vultus* [1]';

looking downwards all the time, and, while pronouncing the
four last words, absolutely touching the ground with a kind of
contorted gesticulation.

Garrick, however, when he pleased, could imitate Johnson
very exactly [2]; for that great actor, with his distinguished powers
of expression which were so universally admired, possessed also
an admirable talent of mimickry. He was always jealous that
Johnson spoke lightly of him [3]. I recollect his exhibiting him to
me one day, as if saying, ' Davy has some convivial pleasantry
about him, but 'tis a futile fellow [4] ; ' which he uttered perfectly
with the tone and air of Johnson.

I cannot too frequently request of my readers, while they
peruse my account of Johnson's conversation, to endeavour to
keep in mind his deliberate and strong utterance. His mode of
speaking was indeed very impressive [5] ; and I wish it could be

[1] ' Man looks aloft, and with erected
eyes
     Beholds his own hereditary
     skies.'
          DRYDEN, Ovid, *Meta.* i. 85.
[2] Hannah More (*Memoirs*, i. 213)
says that she was made ' the um-
pire in a trial of skill between Garrick
and Boswell, which could most nearly
imitate Dr. Johnson's manner. I remember I gave it for Boswell in
familiar conversation, and for Garrick
in reciting poetry.'
[3] ' Gesticular mimicry and buffoonery he hated, and would often
huff Garrick for exercising it in his
presence.' Hawkins's *Johnson*, p. 386.
[4] In editions 1 and 2 Johnson
is represented as only saying, ' Davy
is futile.' ⟨Mrs. Piozzi in her copy
of the 1816 edition inserts ' little '
between ' futile ' and ' fellow '.⟩

[5] My noble friend Lord Pembroke
said once to me at Wilton, with a
happy pleasantry and some truth,
that, ' Dr. Johnson's sayings would
not appear so extraordinary, were it
not for his *bow-wow way*.' The sayings
themselves are generally of sterling
merit ; but, doubtless, his *manner*
was an addition to their effect ; and
therefore should be attended to as
much as may be. It is necessary,
however, to guard those who were
not acquainted with him, against
overcharged imitations or caricatures
of his manner, which are frequently
attempted, and many of which are
second-hand copies from the late
Mr. Henderson the actor, who, though
a good mimick of some persons, did
not represent Johnson correctly.
BOSWELL. ⟨See *post*, v. 18.⟩

preserved as musick is written, according to the very ingenious method of Mr. Steele [1], who has shown how the recitation of Mr. Garrick, and other eminent speakers, might be transmitted to posterity _in score_ [2].

Next day I dined with Johnson at Mr. Thrale's. He attacked Gray, calling him ' a dull fellow.' BOSWELL. ' I understand he was reserved, and might appear dull in company ; but surely he was not dull in poetry.' JOHNSON. ' Sir, he was dull in company, dull in his closet, dull every where [3]. He was dull in a new way, and that made many people think him GREAT. He was a mechanical poet.' He then repeated some ludicrous lines, which have escaped my memory, and said, ' Is not that GREAT, like his Odes ? ' Mrs. Thrale maintained that his Odes were melodious ; upon which he exclaimed,

' Weave the warp, and weave the woof ; '—

I added, in a solemn tone,

' The winding-sheet of Edward's race.'

' _There_ is a good line.'—' Ay, (said he), and the next line is a good one,' (pronouncing it contemptuously ;)

' Give ample verge and room enough.'— [4]

[1] See ' _Prosodia Rationalis_ ; or, an Essay towards establishing the Melody and Measure of Speech, to be expressed and perpetuated by peculiar Symbols.' London, 1779. BOSWELL. ⟨This book was first published in 1775.⟩

[2] I use the phrase _in score_, as Dr. Johnson has explained it in his Dictionary. ' _A song in_ SCORE, the words with the musical notes of a song annexed.' But I understand that in scientifick propriety it means all the parts of a musical composition noted down in the characters by which it is exhibited to the eye of the skilful. BOSWELL. It was _declamation_ that Steele pretended to reduce to notation by new characters. This he called the _melody_ of speech, not the harmony, which the term in _score_ implies. BURNEY.

[3] Johnson, in his _Life of Gray_

(24), spoke better of him. ' What has occurred to me, from the slight inspection of his letters in which my undertaking has engaged me, is, that his mind had a large grasp ; that his curiosity was unlimited, and his judgement cultivated.' Walpole (_Letters_, ii. 339) allowed that he was bad company. ' Sept. 3, 1748. I agree with you most absolutely in your opinion about Gray: he is the worst company in the world—from a melancholy turn, from living reclusely, and from a little too much dignity, he never converses easily—all his words are measured and chosen, and formed into sentences ; his writings are admirable ; he himself is not agreeable.' ⟨See App. B, p. 516.⟩

[4] In the original, ' Give ample room and verge enough.' In the _Life of Gray_ (46) Johnson says that

' No, Sir, there are but two good [1] stanzas in Gray's poetry, which are in his " Elegy in a Country Church-yard." ' ' He then repeated the stanza,

' For who to dumb forgetfulness a prey,' &c.

mistaking one word ; for instead of *precincts* he said *confines*. He added, ' The other stanza I forget [2].'

A young lady [3] who had married a man much her inferiour in rank being mentioned, a question arose how a woman's relations should behave to her in such a situation ; and, while I recapitulate the debate, and recollect what has since happened [4], I cannot but be struck in a manner that delicacy forbids me to express. While I contended that she ought to be treated with an inflexible steadiness of displeasure, Mrs. Thrale was all for mildness and forgiveness, and, according to the vulgar phrase, ' making the best of a bad bargain.' JOHNSON. ' Madam, we must distinguish. Were I a man of rank, I would not let a daughter starve who had made a mean marriage ; but having voluntarily degraded herself from the station which she was originally entitled to hold, I would support her only in that which she herself had chosen ; and would not put her on a level with my other daughters. You are to consider, Madam, that it is our duty to maintain the

the slaughtered bards ' are called upon to " Weave the warp, and weave the woof," perhaps with no great propriety ; for it is by crossing the woof with the warp that men weave the web or piece ; and the first line was dearly bought by the admission of its wretched correspondent, " Give ample room and verge enough." He has, however, no other line as bad.' See *ante*, i. 402.

[1] This word, which is in the first edition, is not in the second or third.

[2] ' The *Church-yard* abounds with images which find a mirrour in every mind, and with sentiments to which every bosom returns an echo. The four stanzas beginning " Yet even these bones," are to me original : I have never seen the notions in any other place ; yet he that reads them here, persuades himself that he has always felt them. Had Gray written

often thus, it had been vain to blame, and useless to praise him.' Johnson's *Life of Gray*, 51. Goldsmith, in his *Life of Parnell* (*Works*, 1885, iv. 176), thus seems to sneer at *The Elegy* :— 'The " NightPiece on Death " deserves every praise, and I should suppose, with very little amendment, might be made to surpass all those night pieces and church-yard scenes that have since appeared.'

[3] Mr. Croker says, ' no doubt Lady Susan Fox . . . who, in 1773, married Mr. William O'Brien, an actor.' It was in 1764 that she was married, so that it is not likely that she was the subject of this talk. See Walpole's *Letters*, vi. 47. ⟨For O'Brien's colonial and home appointments, see the *D.N.B.*⟩

[4] Mrs. Thrale's marriage with Mr. Piozzi.

subordination of civilized society ; and when there is a gross and shameful deviation from rank, it should be punished so as to deter others from the same perversion.'

After frequently considering this subject, I am more and more confirmed in what I then meant to express, and which was sanctioned by the authority, and illustrated by the wisdom, of Johnson ; and I think it of the utmost consequence to the happiness of Society, to which subordination is absolutely necessary [1]. It is weak, and contemptible, and unworthy, in a parent to relax in such a case. It is sacrificing general advantage to private feelings. And let it be considered, that the claim of a daughter who has acted thus, to be restored to her former situation, is either fantastical or unjust. If there be no value in the distinction of rank, what does she suffer by being kept in the situation to which she has descended ? If there be a value in that distinction, it ought to be steadily maintained. If indulgence be shewn to such conduct, and the offenders know that in a longer or shorter time they shall be received as well as if they had not contaminated their blood by a base alliance, the great check upon that inordinate caprice which generally occasions low marriages, will be removed, and the fair and comfortable order of improved life will be miserably disturbed [2].

Lord Chesterfield's letters being mentioned, Johnson said, ' It was not to be wondered at that they had so great a sale, considering that they were the letters of a statesman, a wit, one who had been so much in the mouths of mankind, one long accustomed *virûm volitare per ora* [3].'

---

[1] See *ante*, i. 408.

[2] Boswell was of the same way of thinking as Squire Western, who ' did indeed consider a parity of fortune and circumstances to be physically as necessary an ingredient in marriage, as difference of sexes, or any other essential ; and had no more apprehension of his daughter's falling in love with a poor man, than with any animal of a different species.' *Tom Jones*, bk. vi. ch. 9.

[3] ' Temptanda via est, qua me quoque possim

Tollere humo victorque virum volitare per ora.'

' New ways I must attempt, my grovelling name
To raise aloft, and wing my flight to fame.'

DRYDEN, Virgil, *Georg*. iii. 9. ⟨Walpole writes that Chesterfield had from the time of his retirement in 1748 ' lived at White's, gaming, and pronouncing witticisms among the boys of quality. . . . He was so accustomed to see people laugh at the most trifling things he said, that he would be dis-

On Friday, March 31, I supped with him and some friends at a tavern [1]. One of the company [2] attempted, with too much forwardness, to rally him on his late appearance at the theatre ; but had reason to repent of his temerity. ' Why, Sir, did you go to Mrs. Abington's benefit ? Did you see ? ' JOHNSON. ' No, Sir.' ' Did you hear ? ' JOHNSON. ' No, Sir.' ' Why then, Sir, did you go ? ' JOHNSON. ' Because, Sir, she is a favourite of the publick ; and when the publick cares the thousandth part for you that it does for her, I will go to your benefit too [3].'

Next morning I won a small bet from Lady Diana Beauclerk, by asking him as to one of his particularities, which her Ladyship laid I durst not do. It seems he had been frequently observed at the Club to put into his pocket the Seville oranges, after he had squeezed the juice of them into the drink which he made for himself. Beauclerk and Garrick talked of it to me, and seemed to think that he had a strange unwillingness to be discovered. We could not divine what he did with them ; and this was the bold question to be put. I saw on his table the spoils of the preceding night, some fresh peels nicely scraped and cut into pieces. ' O, Sir, (said I,) I now partly see what you do with the squeezed oranges which you put into your pocket at the Club.' JOHNSON. ' I have a great love for them.' BOSWELL. ' And pray, Sir, what do you do with them ? You scrape them, it seems, very neatly, and what next ? ' JOHNSON. ' I [a] let them dry, Sir.' BOSWELL. ' And what next ? ' JOHNSON. ' Nay, Sir, you shall know their fate no further.' BOSWELL. ' Then the world must be left in the dark. It must be said (assuming a mock solemnity,) he scraped them, and let them dry, but what he did

a I *omitted* 2, 3.

appointed at finding nobody smile before they knew what he was going to say.' *Mem. Reign Geo. II*, i. 44.⟩ ' Chesterfield was at once the most distinguished orator in the Upper House, and the undisputed sovereign of wit and fashion.' Macaulay's *Life*, i. 325.

[1] With the Literary Club, as is shewn by Boswell's letter of April 4, 1775, in which he says :—' I dine . . . Friday at the Turk's Head, Gerrard Street, with our Club, . . . who now *dine* once a month, and sup every Friday.' *Letters*, No. 137, i. 218. The meeting of Friday, March 24, is described *ante*, ii. 318, and that of Friday, April 7, *post*, ii. 345.

[2] Very likely Boswell (*ante*, ii. 84, note 3). ⟨Mrs. Piozzi thought so too.⟩

[3] In the *Garrick Corres.* (ii. 141) is a letter dated March 4, 1776, from (to use Garrick's own words) ' that worst of bad women, Mrs. Abington, to ask my playing for her benefit.' It is endorsed by Garrick :—' A copy of Mother Abington's letter about leaving the stage.'

with them next, he never could be prevailed upon to tell.'
JOHNSON. ' Nay, Sir, you should say it more emphatically :—he
could not be prevailed upon, even by his dearest friends, to
tell ¹.'

He had this morning received his Diploma as Doctor of Laws
from the University of Oxford. He did not vaunt of his new
dignity, but I understood he was highly pleased with it. I shall
here insert the progress and completion of that high academical
honour, in the same manner as I have traced his obtaining that
of Master of Arts.

To the Reverend Dr. FOTHERGILL, *Vice-Chancellor of the University of*
Oxford, *to be communicated to the Heads of Houses, and proposed in*
Convocation.

' MR. VICE-CHANCELLOR AND GENTLEMEN ²,

' THE honour of the degree of M.A. by diploma, formerly conferred
upon MR. SAMUEL JOHNSON, in consequence of his having eminently
distinguished himself by the publication of a series of Essays, ex-
cellently calculated to form the manners of the people, and in which
the cause of religion and morality has been maintained and recommended by the strongest powers of argument and elegance of language,
reflected an equal degree of lustre upon the University itself.

' The many learned labours which have since that time employed the
attention and displayed the abilities of that great man, so much to the
advancement of literature and the benefit of the community, render
him worthy of more distinguished honours in the Republick of letters :
and I persuade myself, that I shall act agreeably to the sentiments of
the whole University, in desiring that it may be proposed in Convocation to confer on him the degree of Doctor in Civil Law by
diploma, to which I readily give my consent ; and am,

' Mr. Vice-Chancellor and Gentlemen,
' Your affectionate friend and servant,
' NORTH ³.'

' Downing-street,
     March 23, 1775.'

---

¹ Twenty years earlier he had recommended to Miss Boothby as a
remedy for indigestion dried orange-
peel finely powdered, taken in a glass
of hot red port. ' I would not,' he
adds, ' have you offer it to the Doctor
as my medicine. Physicians do not
love intruders.' *Letters*, No. 79. See
post, iv. 204, note 5.

² The misprint of *Chancellor* for
Gentlemen is found in both the second
and third editions. It is not in the first.

³ Extracted from the Convocation
Register, Oxford. BOSWELL.

Diploma.

'*CANCELLARIUS, Magistri, et Scholares Universitatis Oxoniensis omnibus ad quos præsentes Literæ pervenerint, Salutem in Domino Sempiternam.*

'*Sciatis, virum illustrem, Samuelem Johnson, in omni humaniorum literarum genere eruditum, omniumque scientiarum comprehensione felicissimum, scriptis suis, ad popularium mores formandos summâ verborum elegantiâ ac sententiarum gravitate compositis, ita olim inclaruisse, ut dignus videretur cui ab Academiâ suâ eximia quædam laudis præmia deferentur*[a] *quique [in] venerabilem Magistrorum Ordinem summâ cum dignitate cooptaretur :*

'*Cùm verò eundem clarissimum virum tot posteà tantique labores, in patriâ præsertim linguâ ornandâ et stabiliendâ feliciter impensi, ita insigniverint, ut in Literarum Republicâ Princeps jam et Primarius jure habeatur ; Nos Cancellarius, Magistri, et Scholares Universitatis Oxoniensis, quò*[b] *talis viri merita pari honoris remuneratione exæquentur, et perpetuum suæ simul laudis, nostræque ergà literas propensissimæ voluntatis extet monumentum, in solenni Convocatione Doctorum et Magistrorum Regentium, et non Regentium, prædictum Samuelem Johnson Doctorem in Jure Civili renunciavimus et constituimus, eumque virtute præsentis Diplomatis singulis juribus, privilegiis et honoribus, ad istum gradum quàquà pertinentibus, frui et gaudere jussimus. In cujus rei testimonium commune Universitatis Oxoniensis sigillum præsentibus apponi fecimus.*

'*Datum in Domo nostræ*[c] *Convocationis die tricesimo Mensis Martii, Anno Domini Millesimo septingentesimo, septuagesimo quinto*[1].'

[a] *deferrentur* Register. [b] *ut* Register. [c] *nostra* Register.

[1] The original is in my possession. He shewed me the Diploma, and allowed me to read it, but would not consent to my taking a copy of it, fearing perhaps that I should blaze it abroad in his life-time. His objection to this appears from his 99th letter to Mrs. Thrale, whom in that letter he thus scolds for the grossness of her flattery of him :—' The other Oxford news is, that they have sent me a degree of Doctor of Laws, with such praises in the Diploma as perhaps ought to make me ashamed : they are very like your praises. I wonder whether I shall ever shew it [*them* in the original] to you.'

It is remarkable that he never, so far as I know, assumed his title of *Doctor*, but called himself *Mr.* Johnson, as appears from many of his cards or notes to myself, and I have seen many from him to other persons, in which he uniformly takes that designation.—I once observed on his table a letter directed to him with the addition of *Esquire*, and objected to it as being a designation inferiour to that of Doctor ; but he checked me, and seemed pleased with it, because, as I conjectured, he liked to be sometimes taken out of the class of literary men, and to be merely *genteel,—un gentilhomme com⟨m⟩e un autre.* Bos-

' *Viro Reverendo* Thomæ Fothergill, *S.T.P. Universitatis Oxoniensis Vice-Cancellario.*

' *S. P. D.*

' Sam. Johnson.

' *MULTIS non est opus, ut testimonium quo, te præside, Oxonienses nomen meum posteris commendârunt, quali animo acceperim compertum faciam. Nemo sibi placens non lætatur* [1] *; nemo sibi non placet, qui vobis, literarum arbitris, placere potuit. Hoc tamen habet incommodi tantum beneficium, quod mihi nunquam posthâc sine vestræ famæ detrimento vel labi liceat vel cessare ; semperque sit timendum, ne quod mihi tam eximiæ laudi est, vobis aliquando fiat opprobrio. Vale* [2]*.'*

7 Id. Apr. 1775.'

He revised some sheets of Lord Hailes's ' Annals of Scotland,' and wrote a few notes on the margin with red ink, which he bade me tell his Lordship did not sink into the paper, and might be wiped off with a wet sponge, so that he did not spoil his manuscript.—I observed to him that there were very few of his friends so accurate as that I could venture to put down in writing what they told me as his sayings. Johnson. ' Why should you write down *my* sayings ? ' Boswell. ' I write them when they are good.' Johnson. ' Nay, you may as well write down the sayings of any one else that are good.' But *where*, I might with great propriety have added, can I find such ?

I visited him by appointment in the evening, and we drank tea with Mrs. Williams. He told me that he had been in the company of a gentleman [3] whose extraordinary travels had been much the subject of conversation. But I found that he had not listened to him with that full confidence, without which there is little satisfaction in the society of travellers. I was curious to hear what opinion so able a judge as Johnson had formed of his abilities, and I asked if he was not a man of sense. Johnson. ' Why, Sir, he is not a distinct relater ; and I should say, he is

---

well. See *post*, iv. 79, where Johnson applies the title to himself in speaking, and iv. 268, note 1, where he does in writing, and v. 37, note 2.

[1] ' To make a man pleased with himself, let me tell you, is doing a very great thing.' *Post*, iii. 328.

[2] ' The original is in the hands of Dr. Fothergill, then Vice-Chancellor, who made this transcript.' T. Warton.—Boswell.

[3] Bruce, the Abyssinian traveller, as is shewn by Johnson's *Letters*, No. 386. ⟨For Johnson's varying opinion of Bruce's veracity see *Johnsonian Miscellanies*, ii. 12.⟩

neither abounding nor deficient in sense. I did not perceive any superiority of understanding.' BOSWELL. 'But will you not allow him a nobleness of resolution, in penetrating into distant regions?' JOHNSON. 'That, Sir, is not to the present purpose: we are talking of his sense. A fighting cock has a nobleness of resolution.'

Next day, Sunday, April 2, I dined with him at Mr. Hoole's. We talked of Pope. JOHNSON. 'He wrote his "Dunciad" for fame. That was his primary motive. Had it not been for that, the dunces might have railed against him till they were weary, without his troubling himself about them. He delighted to vex them, no doubt; but he had more delight in seeing how well he could vex them [1].'

The 'Odes to Obscurity and Oblivion,' in ridicule of 'cool Mason and warm Gray [2],' being mentioned, Johnson said, 'They are Colman's best things.' Upon its being observed that it was believed these Odes were made by Colman and Lloyd jointly;— JOHNSON. 'Nay, Sir, how can two people make an Ode? Perhaps one made one of them, and one the other [3].' I observed that two people had made a play, and quoted the anecdote of Beaumont and Fletcher, who were brought under suspicion of

---

[1] 'That the design [of the *Dunciad*] was moral, whatever the author might tell either his readers or himself, I am not convinced. The first motive was the desire of revenging the contempt with which Theobald had treated his *Shakespeare*, and regaining the honour which he had lost, by crushing his opponent.' Johnson's *Life of Pope*, 357.

[2] 'Daughter of Chaos and old Night,
Cimmerian Muse, all hail!
That wrapt in never-twinkling gloom canst write,
And shadowest meaning with thy dusky veil!
What Poet sings, and strikes the strings?
It was the mighty Theban spoke.
He from the ever-living lyre
With magick hand elicits fire.

Heard ye the din of modern rhimers bray?
It was cool M—n; or warm G—y,
Involv'd in tenfold smoke.'
Colman's *Prose on Several Occasions*, ii. 273.

[3] 'These Odes,' writes Colman, 'were indeed a piece of boys' play with my schoolfellow Lloyd, with whom they were written in concert.' *Ib.* i. xi. In the *Connoisseur (ante,* i. 420) they had also written in concert. 'Their humour and their talents were well adapted to what they had undertaken; and Beaumont and Fletcher present what is probably the only parallel instance of literary cooperation so complete, that the portions written by the respective parties are undistinguishable.' Southey's *Cowper*, i. 47.

treason, because while concerting the plan of a tragedy when sitting together at a tavern, one of them was overheard saying to the other, ' I'll kill the King.' JOHNSON. ' The first of these Odes is the best : but they are both good. They exposed a very bad kind of writing.' BOSWELL. ' Surely, Sir, Mr. Mason's " Elfrida " is a fine poem : at least you will allow there are some good passages in it.' JOHNSON. ' There are now and then some good imitations of Milton's bad manner.'

I often wondered at his low estimation of the writings of Gray and Mason. Of Gray's poetry I have, in a former part of this work,[1] expressed my high opinion ; and for that of Mr. Mason I have ever entertained a warm admiration [2]. His ' Elfrida ' is exquisite, both in poetical description and moral sentiment ; and his ' Caractacus ' is a noble drama [3]. Nor can I omit paying my tribute of praise to some of his smaller poems, which I have read with pleasure, and which no criticism shall persuade me not to like. If I wondered at Johnson's not tasting the works of Mason and Gray, still more have I wondered at their not tasting his works ; that they should be insensible to his energy of diction, to his splendour of images, and comprehension of thought. Tastes may differ as to the violin, the flute, the hautboy, in short, all the lesser instruments : but who can be insensible to the powerful impressions of the majestick organ ?

His ' Taxation no Tyranny ' being mentioned, he said, ' I think I have not been attacked enough for it. Attack is the re-action ; I never think I have hit hard, unless it rebounds [4].' BOSWELL. ' I don't know, Sir, what you would be at. Five or six shots of small arms in every newspaper, and repeated cannonading in

[1] *Ante*, i. 404.

[2] Boswell, writing to Temple two days later, recalled the time ' when you and I sat up all night at Cambridge and read Gray with a noble enthusiasm, when we first used to read Mason's *Elfrida*, and when we talked of that elegant knot of worthies, Gray, Mason, Walpole, &c.' *Letters*, No. 137, i. 217.

[3] ' I have heard Mr. Johnson relate how he used to sit in some coffee-house [at Oxford], and turn M—'s C-r-ct-u-s into ridicule for the diver-sion of himself and of chance comers-in. " The Elf—da (says he) was too exquisitely pretty ; I could make no fun out of that." ' Piozzi's *Anec.*, p. 37 : John. Misc. i. 169. I doubt whether Johnson used the word *fun*, which he describes in his *Dictionary* as ' a low cant word.'

[4] See *post*, iii. 375; v. 273, 400. According to Dr. T. Campbell (*Diary*, p. 36 : John. Misc. ii. 42), Johnson, on March 16, had said that *Taxation no Tyranny* did not sell. ⟨See, however, *ante*, ii. 312, note 1.⟩

pamphlets, might, I think, satisfy you [1]. But, Sir, you'll never make out this match, of which we have talked, with a certain political lady, since you are so severe against her principles [2].' JOHNSON. ' Nay, Sir, I have the better chance for that. She is like the Amazons of old ; she must be courted by the sword. But I have not been severe upon her.' BOSWELL. ' Yes, Sir, you have made her ridiculous.' JOHNSON. ' That was already done, Sir. To endeavour to make *her* ridiculous, is like blacking the chimney.'

I put him in mind that the landlord at Ellon [3] in Scotland said, that he heard he was the greatest man in England,—next to Lord Mansfield. ' Ay, Sir, (said he,) the exception defined the idea. A Scotchman could go no farther :

" The force of Nature could no farther go [4]." '

Lady Miller's collection of verses by fashionable people, which were put into her Vase at Batheaston villa [5], near Bath, in competition for honorary prizes, being mentioned, he held them very cheap : ' *Bouts rimés* (said he,) is a mere conceit, and an *old* conceit *now* ; I wonder how people were persuaded to write in that manner for this lady [6].' I named a gentleman of his acquaintance

[1] Six days later he wrote to Dr. Taylor :—' The patriots pelt me with answers. Four pamflets, I think, already, besides newspapers and reviews, have been discharged against me. I have tried to read two of them, but did not go through them.' *Letters*, No. 387.

[2] ' Mrs. Macaulay,' says Mr. Croker, who quotes *Taxation no Tyranny*, Johnson's *Works*, vi. 258, where she is described as ' a female patriot, bewailing the miseries of her friends and fellow-citizens.' See *ante*, i. 447. ⟨Mrs. Piozzi agrees (1816 edit.).⟩

[3] See *post*, v. 96; and *post*, iii. 209, for another landlord's account of Johnson.

[4] From Dryden's lines on Milton.

[5] Walpole wrote on Jan. 15, 1775 (*Letters*, ix. 134) :—' They [the Millers] hold a Parnassus fair every Thursday, give out rhymes and themes, and all the flux of quality at Bath contend for the prizes. A Roman vase dressed with pink ribbons and myrtles receives the poetry, which is drawn out every festival ; six judges of these Olympic games retire and select the brightest compositions, which the respective successful acknowledge, kneel to Mrs. Calliope Miller, kiss her fair hand, and are crowned by it with myrtle, with—I don't know what.' ⟨See App. B, p. 517.⟩

[6] Miss Burney wrote, in 1780 :—' Do you know now that, notwithstanding Bath Easton is so much laughed at in London, nothing here is more tonish than to visit Lady Miller. . . . She is a round, plump, coarse-looking dame of about forty, and while all her aim is to appear an elegant woman of fashion, all her success is to seem an ordinary woman in very common life, with fine clothes on.' Mme. D'Arblay's *Diary*, i. 364. ⟨See App. B, p. 517.⟩

who wrote for the Vase. JOHNSON. ' He was a blockhead for his pains.' BOSWELL. ' The Duchess of Northumberland wrote [1].' JOHNSON. ' Sir, the Duchess of Northumberland may do what she pleases : nobody will say any thing to a lady of her high rank. But I should be apt to throw ******'s [2] verses in his face.'

I talked of the chearfulness of Fleet-street, owing to the constant quick succession of people which we perceive passing through it. JOHNSON. ' Why, Sir, Fleet-street has a very animated appearance ; but I think the full tide of human existence is at Charing-cross [3].'

He made the common remark on the unhappiness which men who have led a busy life experience, when they retire in expectation of enjoying themselves at ease, and that they generally languish for want of their habitual occupation, and wish to return to it. He mentioned as strong an instance of this as can well be imagined. ' An eminent tallow-chandler in London, who had acquired a considerable fortune, gave up the trade in favour of his foreman, and went to live at a country-house near town. He soon grew weary, and paid frequent visits to his old shop, where he desired they might let him know their *melting-days*, and he would come and assist them ; which he accordingly did. Here, Sir, was a man, to whom the most disgusting circumstance in the business to which he had been used, was a relief from idleness [4].'

[1] ' Yes, on my faith ! There are *bouts-rimés* on a buttered muffin, made by her Grace the Duchess of Northumberland.' Walpole's *Letters*, ix. 134. ' She was,' Walpole writes, ' a jovial heap of contradictions. . . . She was familiar with the mob, while stifled with diamonds ; and yet was attentive to the most minute privileges of her rank, while almost shaking hands with a cobbler.' *Memoirs of the Reign of George III*, i. 419. Dr. Percy showed her Goldsmith's ballad of *Edwin and Angelina* in MS., and she had a few copies privately printed. Forster's *Goldsmith*, i. 379.

[2] Perhaps Mr. Seward, who was something of a literary man, and who visited Bath (*post*, iv. 180).

⟨Croker suggests Richard Graves : see App. B, p. 517.⟩

[3] ' — rerum
Fluctibus in mediis et tempestatibus urbis.'
Horace, *Epistles*, ii. 2. 84. See *ante*, i. 461, and *post*, iii. 302.

[4] ' Qui semel adspexit quantum dimissa petitis
Præstent, mature redeat repetatque relicta.'
Horace, *Epistles*, i. 7. 96.
' To his first state let him return with speed,
Who sees how far the joys he left exceed
His present choice.' FRANCIS.
Malone says that ' Walpole, after he ceased to be minister, endeavoured to amuse his mind with reading. . . .

On Wednesday, April 5, I dined with him at Messieurs Dilly's, with Mr. John Scott of Amwell [1], the Quaker, Mr. Langton, Mr. Miller, (now Sir John,) and Dr. Thomas Campbell [2], an

But one day when the present Mr. Welbore Ellis was in his library, he heard him say, with tears in his eyes, after having taken up several books and at last thrown away a folio just taken down from a shelf, " Alas ! it is all in vain ; *I* CANNOT *read.*" ' Prior's *Malone*, p. 379. Lord Eldon, after his retirement, said to an inn-keeper who was thinking of giving up business :—' Believe me, for I speak from experience, when a man, who has been much occupied through life, arrives at having nothing to do, he is very apt not to know what to do *with himself.*' Later on, he said :—' It was advice given by me in the spirit of that Principal of Brasenose, who, when he took leave of young men quitting college, used to say to them, " Let me give you one piece of advice : *Cave de resignationibus.*" And very good advice too.' Twiss's *Eldon*, iii. 246. ⟨See Johnson's *Letters*, No. 483, Piozzi, *Anec.*, p. 254 : John. Misc. i. 316, and *post*, iii. 176.⟩

[1] See *post*, ii. 351. He had but lately begun to visit London. ' Such . . . was his constant apprehension of the small-pox, that he lived for twenty years within twenty miles of London, without visiting it more than once.' At the age of thirty-five he was inoculated, and henceforth was oftener in town. Campbell's *British Poets*, p. 569. ⟨See *John. Misc.* ii. 47.⟩

[2] Mr. S. Raymond, Prothonotary of the Supreme Court of New South Wales, published in Sydney in 1854 *A Diary of a Visit to England in 1775, by an Irishman* (*The Rev. Dr. Thomas Campbell,*) *with Notes.* The MS., the editor says, was discovered behind an old press in one of the offices of his Court. The name of the writer nowhere appears in the MS. It is clear, however, that if it

is not a forgery, the author was Campbell. In the *Edinburgh Review* for Oct., 1859, its authenticity is examined, and is declared to be beyond a doubt. Lord Macaulay aided the Reviewer in his investigation. *Ib.*, p. 323. He could scarcely, however, have come to his task with a mind altogether free from bias, for the editor ' has contrived,' we are told, ' to expose another of Mr. Croker's blunders.' Faith in him cannot be wrong who proves that Croker is not in the right. The value of this *Diary* is rated too highly by the Reviewer. The Master of Balliol College has pointed out to me that it adds but very little to Johnson's sayings. So far as he is concerned, we are told scarcely anything of mark that we did not know already. This makes the Master doubt its genuineness. I have noticed one suspicious passage. An account is given of a dinner at Mr. Thrale's on April 1, at which Campbell met Murphy, Boswell, and Baretti. ' Johnson's *bons mots* were retailed in such plenty that they, like a surfeit, could not lie upon my memory.' In one of the stories told by Murphy, Johnson is made to say, ' Damn the rascal.' Murphy would as soon have made the Archbishop of Canterbury swear as Johnson ; much sooner the Archbishop of York. It was Murphy who ' paid him the highest compliment that ever was paid to a layman, by asking his pardon for repeating some oaths in the course of telling a story ' (*post*, iii. 41). Even supposing that at this time he was ignorant of his character, though the supposition is a wild one, he would at once have been set right by Boswell and the Thrales (*post*, ii. 433). It is curious, that this anecdote imputing profanity to Johnson is not

Irish Clergyman, whom I took the liberty of inviting to Mr.
Dilly's table, having seen him at Mr. Thrale's, and been told
that he had come to England chiefly with a view to see Dr.
Johnson, for whom he entertained the highest veneration. He
has since published ' A Philosophical Survey of the South of
Ireland,' a very entertaining book, which has, however, one fault ;
—that it assumes the fictitious character of an Englishman.

We talked of publick speaking.—JOHNSON. ' We must not
estimate a man's powers by his being able or not able to deliver
his sentiments in publick. Isaac Hawkins Browne [1], one of the
first wits of this country, got into Parliament, and never opened
his mouth. For my own part, I think it is more disgraceful
never to try to speak, than to try it and fail ; as it is more
disgraceful not to fight, than to fight and be beaten.' This
argument appeared to me fallacious ; for if a man has not
spoken, it may be said that he would have done very well if
he had tried ; whereas, if he has tried and failed, there is nothing
to be said for him. ' Why then, (I asked,) is it thought disgraceful for a man not to fight, and not disgraceful not to
speak in publick ? ' JOHNSON. ' Because there may be other
reasons for a man's not speaking in publick than want of resolution : he may have nothing to say, (laughing.) Whereas,
Sir, you know courage is reckoned the greatest of all virtues ;
because, unless a man has that virtue, he has no security for
preserving any other.'

He observed, that ' the statutes against bribery were intended
to prevent upstarts with money from getting into Parliament [2] ; '

quoted by the Edinburgh reviewer.
On the whole I think that the *Diary*
is genuine, and accordingly I have
quoted it more than once. ⟨See
App . B, p. 518.⟩

[1] Mrs. Piozzi (*Anec.*, p. 173 : John.
Misc. i. 266) says that Johnson spoke
of Browne as ' of all conversers the
most delightful with whom he ever
was in company.' Pope's bathos, in
his lines to Murray :—
' Grac'd as thou art with all the pow'r
    of words,
So known, so honour'd, at the house
    of Lords,'

was happily parodied by Browne :—
' Persuasion tips his tongue whene'er
    he talks,
And he has chambers in the King's
    Bench Walks.'
Pattison's *Satires of Pope*, pp. 57, 134.
See *post*, v. 156.

[2] Walpole says of Beckford's Bribery Bill of 1768 :—' Grenville, to
flatter the country-gentlemen, who
can ill afford to combat with great
lords, nabobs, commissaries, and
West-Indians, declaimed in favour
of the bill.' *Memoirs of the Reign of
George III*, iii. 159.

adding, that ' if he were a gentleman of landed property, he would turn out all his tenants who did not vote for the candidate whom he supported [1].' LANGTON. ' Would not that, Sir, be checking the freedom of election ? ' JOHNSON. ' Sir, the law does not mean that the privilege of voting should be independent of old family interest ; of the permanent property of the country.'

On Thursday, April 6, I dined with him at Mr. Thomas Davies's, with Mr. Hicky [2], the painter, and my old acquaintance Mr. Moody, the player.

Dr. Johnson, as usual, spoke contemptuously of Colley Cibber. ' It is wonderful that a man, who for forty years had lived with the great and the witty, should have acquired so ill the talents of conversation : and he had but half to furnish ; for one half of what he said was oaths [3].' He, however, allowed considerable merit to some of his comedies, and said there was no reason to believe that ' The Careless Husband ' was not written by himself [4]. Davies said, he was the first dramatick writer who introduced genteel ladies upon the stage. Johnson refuted this observation by instancing several such characters in comedies before his time. DAVIES. (trying to defend himself from a charge of ignorance,) ' I mean genteel moral characters.' ' I think (said Hicky,) gentility and morality are inseparable.' BOSWELL. ' By no means, Sir. The genteelest characters are often the most immoral. Does not Lord Chesterfield give precepts for uniting wickedness and the graces ? A man, indeed, is not genteel when he gets drunk ; but most vices may be committed very

---

[1] See *ante*, ii. 167, where he said much the same. Another day, however, he agreed that a landlord ought to give leases to his tenants, and not wish ' to keep them in a perpetual wretched dependence on his will. " It is a man's duty," he said, " to extend comfort and security among as many people as he can. He should not wish to have his tenants mere *Ephemeræ*,—mere beings of an hour." ' *Post*, v. 304.

[2] ' Thomas Hickey . . . is now best remembered by a characteristic portrait of his friend Tom Davies,

engraved with Hickey's name to it.' P. CUNNINGHAM.

[3] See *ante*, ii. 92. In the *Life of Pope* (238), Johnson says that ' the shafts of satire were directed in vain against Cibber . . ., being repelled by ⟨his⟩ impenetrable impudence.' Pope speaks of Cibber's ' impenetrability.' Elwin's *Pope*, ix. 231.

[4] He alludes perhaps to a note on the *Dunciad*, ii. 140, in which it is stated that ' the author has celebrated even Cibber himself (presuming him to be the author of the *Careless Husband*).' See *post*, iii. 72, note 4.

genteelly : a man may debauch his friend's wife genteelly : he may
cheat at cards genteelly.' HICKY. ' I do not think *that* is
genteel.' BOSWELL. ' Sir, it may not be like a gentleman, but
it may be genteel.' JOHNSON. ' You are meaning two different
things. One means exteriour grace ; the other honour. It is
certain that a man may be very immoral with exteriour grace.
Lovelace, in " Clarissa," is a very genteel and a very wicked
character. Tom Hervey [1], who died t'other day, though a vicious
man, was one of the genteelest men that ever lived.' Tom
Davies instanced Charles the Second. JOHNSON, (taking fire
at any attack upon that Prince, for whom he had an extraordinary partiality [2],) ' Charles the Second was licentious in his
practice ; but he always had a reverence for what was good.
Charles the Second knew his people, and rewarded merit [3]. The
Church was at no time better filled than in his reign. He was
the best King we have had from his time till the reign of his
present Majesty, except James the Second, who was a very good
King, but unhappily believed that it was necessary for the
salvation of his subjects that they should be Roman Catholicks.
He had the merit of endeavouring to do what he thought was for
the salvation of the souls of his subjects, till he lost a great
Empire. *We*, who thought that we should *not* be saved if we
were Roman Catholicks, had the merit of maintaining our religion,
at the expence of submitting ourselves to the government of
King William [4], (for it could not be done otherwise,)—to the

---

[1] See *ante*, ii. 32.

[2] Burke told Malone that ' Hume,
in compiling his history, did not give
himself a great deal of trouble in
examining records, &c. ; and that the
part he most laboured at was the
reign of King Charles II, for whom
he had an unaccountable partiality.'
Prior's *Malone*, p. 368.

[3] Yet Johnson wrote of Otway
(*Life*, 15), who was nine years old
when Charles II. came to the throne,
and who outlived him by only a few
weeks :—' He had what was in those
times the common reward of loyalty ;
he lived and died neglected.' Hawkins (*Life*, p. 51) says that he heard

Johnson speak of Dr. Hodges, who, in
the height of the Great Plague of
1665, continued in London, ' and
was almost the only one of his profession that had the courage to oppose
his art to the spreading of the con-
tagion. It was the hard fate of this
person, a short time after, to die a
prisoner for debt, in Ludgate : Johnson related this circumstance to us,
with the tears ready to start from his
eyes ; and, with great energy, said,
" Such a man would not have been
suffered to perish in these times." '

[4] Johnson in 1742 said that William
III. ' was arbitrary, insolent, gloomy,
rapacious, and brutal ; that he was, at

government of one of the most worthless scoundrels that ever existed. No ; Charles the Second was not such a man as ——, (naming another King). He did not destroy his father's will [1]. He took money, indeed, from France : but he did not betray those over whom he ruled [2] : he did not let the French fleet pass ours. George the First knew nothing, and desired to know nothing ; did nothing, and desired to do nothing : and the only good thing that is told of him is, that he wished to restore the crown to its hereditary successor [3].' He roared with prodigious violence against George the Second. When he ceased, Moody interjected, in an Irish tone, and with a comick look, ' Ah ! poor George the Second.'

I mentioned that Dr. Thomas Campbell had come from Ireland to London, principally to see Dr. Johnson. He seemed angry at this observation. DAVIES. ' Why, you know, Sir, there came a man from Spain to see Livy [4] ; and Corelli came to

all times, disposed to play the tyrant ; that he had, neither in great things, nor in small, the manners of a gentleman ; that he was capable of gaining money by mean artifices, and that he only regarded his promise when it was his interest to keep it.' *Review Acc. Conduct Duchess of Marlb., Works*, vi. 6. Nearly forty years later, in his *Life of Rowe* (5), he aimed a fine stroke at that King. ' The fashion . . . of the time,' he wrote, ' was to accumulate upon Lewis all that can raise horror and detestation ; and whatever good was withheld from him, that it might not be thrown away, was bestowed upon king William.' Yet in the *Life of Prior* (13) he allowed him great merit. ' His whole life had been action, and none ever denied him the resplendent qualities of steady resolution and personal courage.' See *post*, v. 255.

[1] ' The fact of suppressing the will is indubitably true,' wrote Walpole (*Letters*, x. 335). ' When the news arrived of the death of George the First, my father carried the account from Lord Townshend to the then Prince of Wales. . . . The Council

met as soon as possible. . . . There Archbishop Wake, with whom one copy of the will had been deposited, . . . advanced, and delivered the will to the King, who put it into his pocket, and went out of Council without opening it, the Archbishop not having courage or presence of mind to desire it to be read, as he ought to have done. . . . I was once talking to the late Lady Suffolk, the former mistress, on that extraordinary event. She said, " I cannot justify the deed to the legatees, but towards his father, the late King was justifiable : for George the First had burnt two wills made in favour of George the Second." '

[2] ' Charles the second, by his affability and politeness, made himself the idol of the nation, which he betrayed and sold.' Johnson's *Review Acc. Conduct Duchess of Marlb., Works*, vi. 7.

[3] ' It was maliciously circulated, that he was indifferent to his own succession, and scarcely willing to stretch out a hand to grasp the crown within his reach.' Coxe's *Walpole*, i. 57. ⟨See Johnson's *Addison*, 93.⟩

[4] Plin. Epist. Lib. ii. Ep. 3. BOSWELL.

England to see Purcell [1], and, when he heard he was dead, went
directly back again to Italy.' JOHNSON. 'I should not have
wished to be dead to disappoint Campbell, had he been so
foolish as you represent him ; but I should have wished to have
been a hundred miles off.' This was apparently perverse ; and
I do believe it was not his real way of thinking : he could not
but like a man who came so far to see him. He laughed with
some complacency, when I told him Campbell's odd expression
to me concerning him : ' That having seen such a man, was a
thing to talk of a century hence,'—as if he could live so long [2].

We got into an argument whether the Judges who went to
India might with propriety engage in trade. Johnson warmly
maintained that they might. ' For why (he urged) should not
Judges get riches, as well as those who deserve them less ? ' I
said, they should have sufficient salaries, and have nothing to
take off their attention from the affairs of the publick. JOHNSON.
' No Judge, Sir, can give his whole attention to his office ; and it
is very proper that he should employ what time he has to
himself, for [a] his own advantage, in the most profitable manner.'
' Then, Sir, (said Davies, who enlivened the dispute by making
it somewhat dramatick,) he may become an insurer ; and when
he is going to the bench, he may be stopped,—" Your Lordship
cannot go yet : here is a bunch of invoices : several ships are
about to sail." ' JOHNSON. ' Sir, you may as well say a Judge
should not have a house ; for they may come and tell him,
" Your Lordship's house is on fire ; " and so, instead of minding
the business of his Court, he is to be occupied in getting the
engine with the greatest speed. There is no end of this. Every
Judge who has land, trades to a certain extent in corn or in
cattle ; and in the land itself, undoubtedly. His steward acts

[a] for 1: to 2, 3.

[1] Mr. Davies was here mistaken.
Corelli never was in England. BUR-
NEY.

[2] Mr. Croker is wrong in saying
that the Irishman in Mrs. Thrale's
letter of May 16, 1776 (*Piozzi Letters*,
i. 329), is Dr. Campbell. The man
mentioned there had never met
Johnson, though she wrote more than
a year after this dinner at Davies's.
She certainly quotes one of ' Dr.

C—l's phrases,' but she might also
have quoted Shakspeare. I have no
doubt that Mrs. Thrale's Irishman
was a Mr. Musgrave (*post*, iv. 323,
note 1), who is humorously described
in Mme. D'Arblay's *Diary*, ii. 83.
Since writing this note I have seen
that the Edinburgh reviewer (Oct.
1859, p. 326) had come to the same
conclusion. ⟨See App. B, p. 519.⟩

for him, and so do clerks for a great merchant. A Judge may be a farmer ; but he is not to geld his own pigs [1]. A Judge may play a little at cards for his amusement ; but he is not to play at marbles, or at chuck-farthing in the Piazza. No, Sir ; there is no profession to which a man gives a very great proportion of his time. It is wonderful, when a calculation is made, how little the mind is actually employed in the discharge of any profession. No man would be a Judge, upon the condition of being obliged to be totally [a] a Judge. The best employed lawyer has his mind at work but for a small proportion of his time : a great deal of his occupation is merely mechanical [2].—I once wrote for a magazine : I made a calculation, that if I should write but a page a day, at the same rate, I should, in ten years, write nine volumes in folio, of an ordinary size and print.' BOSWELL. ' Such as Carte's History ? ' JOHNSON. ' Yes, Sir. When a man writes from his own mind, he writes very rapidly [3]. The greatest part of a writer's time is spent in reading, in order to write : a man will turn over half a library to make one book.'

I argued warmly against the Judges trading, and mentioned Hale as an instance of a perfect Judge, who devoted himself entirely to his office. JOHNSON. ' Hale, Sir, attended to other things beside law : he left a great estate.' BOSWELL. ' That was, because what he got, accumulated without any exertion and anxiety on his part.'

While the dispute went on, Moody once tried to say something upon our side. Tom Davies clapped him on the back, to encourage him. Beauclerk, to whom I mentioned this circumstance, said, ' that he could not conceive a more humiliating situation than to be clapped on the back by Tom Davies.'

We spoke of Rolt, to whose Dictionary of Commerce, Dr. Johnson wrote the Preface [4]. JOHNSON. ' Old Gardner the

[a] being obliged to be totally 1 : being totally 2, 3.

[1] See *post*, v. 111, where Johnson said that ' he did not approve of a judge's calling himself *Farmer* Burnett, and going about with a little round hat.'

[2] ' If all the employment of life were crowded into the time which it really occupied, perhaps a few weeks, days, or hours, would be sufficient for

its accomplishment, so far as the mind was engaged in the performance.' *The Rambler*, No. 8.

[3] Johnson certainly did, who had a mind stored with knowledge, and teeming with imagery : but the observation is not applicable to writers in general. BOSWELL. See *post*, iv. 214.

[4] See *ante*, i. 358.

bookseller employed Rolt and Smart to write a monthly miscellany, called " The Universal Visitor [1]." There was a formal
written contract, which Allen the printer saw. Gardner thought
as you do of the Judge. They were bound to write nothing
else ; they were to have, I think, a third of the profits of this
sixpenny pamphlet ; and the contract was for ninety-nine years.
I wish I had thought of giving this to Thurlow, in the cause
about Literary Property. What an excellent instance would it
have been of the oppression of booksellers towards poor
authours [2] ! ' (smiling). Davies, zealous for the honour of *the
Trade* [3], said, Gardner was not properly a bookseller. JOHNSON.
' Nay, Sir ; he certainly was a bookseller. He had served his
time regularly, was a member of the Stationers' company, kept
a shop in the face of mankind, purchased copyright, and was a
bibliopole [4], Sir, in every sense. I wrote for some months in " The
Universal Visitor," for poor Smart, while he was mad, not then
knowing the terms on which he was engaged to write, and
thinking I was doing him good. I hoped his wits would soon
return to him. Mine returned to me, and I wrote in " The
Universal Visitor " no longer.'

Friday, April 7, I dined with him at a tavern, with a
numerous company [5]. JOHNSON. ' I have been reading " Twiss's

[1] See *ante*, i. 306.

[2] There has probably been some
mistake as to the terms of this supposed extraordinary contract, the re-
cital of which from hearsay afforded
Johnson so much play for his sportive
acuteness. Or if it was worded as he
supposed, it is so strange that I
should conclude it was a joke. Mr.
Gardner, I am assured, was a worthy
and a liberal man. BOSWELL.
⟨This contract was discovered in the
Public Museum, Reading, by Mr.
Stuart Pigott. See *Times Lit. Suppl.*,
13 June 1929. The agreement was
between Smart and Rolt as editors,
Allen as printer, and Gardner as
publisher : the editors were to receive
' one full fourth part of the clear
profits ' as payment, and all the parties
were prohibited from engaging in ' any
work or undertaking of a like nature '
as long as the agreement remained in
force.⟩

[3] See *post*, iii. 285, note 2.

[4] *Bibliopole* is not in Johnson's
Dictionary.

[5] The Literary Club. ⟨See *post*,
App. B, p. 519.⟩ Mr. Croker says that
the records of the Club show that, after
the first few years, Johnson very
rarely attended, and that he and
Boswell never met there above seven
or eight times. It may be observed,
he adds, how very rarely Boswell
records the conversation at the club.
Except in one instance (*post*, iii. 230),
he says, Boswell confines his report
to what Johnson or himself may have
said. That this is not strictly true is
shewn by his report of the dinner
recorded above, where we find reported remarks of Beauclerk and Gibbon. Seven meetings besides this are

Travels in Spain," which are just come out. They are as good as the first book of travels that you will take up. They are as good as those of Keysler [1] or Blainville [2] ; nay, as Addison's, if you except the learning. They are not so good as Brydone's [3], but they are better than Pococke's [4]. I have not, indeed, cut the leaves yet ; but I have read in them where the pages are open, and I do not suppose that what is in the pages which are closed is worse than what is in the open pages.—It would seem (he added,) that Addison had not acquired much Italian learning, for we do not find it introduced into his writings [5]. The only instance that I recollect, is his quoting " *Stavo bene ; per star meglio, sto qui* [6]." '

I mentioned Addison's having borrowed many of his classical remarks from Leandro Alberti [7]. Mr. Beauclerk said, ' It was alledged that he had borrowed also from another Italian authour.' JOHNSON. ' Why, Sir, all who go to look for what the Classicks have said of Italy, must find the same passages ; and I should think it would be one of the first things the Italians would do on the revival of learning, to collect all that the Roman authours have said of their country.'

mentioned by Boswell. See *ante*, ii. 240, 255, 318, 330 ; and *post*, iii. 230, 384, and iv. 326. Of all but the last there is some report, however brief, of something said. When Johnson was not present, Boswell would have nothing to record in this book.

[1] *Travels through Germany, &c.*, 1756–7.

[2] *Travels through Holland, &c. Translated from the French*, 1743.

[3] ⟨*A Tour through Sicily and Malta*, 1773.⟩ See *post*, ii. 468, and iii. 356.

[4] *Description of the East*, 1743–5.

[5] Johnson had made the same remark, and Boswell had mentioned Leandro Alberti, when they were talking in an inn in the Island of Mull. *Post*, v. 310. ⟨See App. B, p. 519.⟩

[6] Addison does not mention where this epitaph, which has eluded a very diligent inquiry, is found. MALONE. Croker found it in Howell: 'The Italian saying may be well applyed to poor

England, *I was well, I would be better, I took physic, and dyed*.' Howell's *Lett*. bk. iii. no. 12. It is quoted by Addison in *The Spectator*, No. 25 :— ' This letter puts me in mind of an Italian epitaph written on the monument of a Valetudinarian : *Stavo ben, ma per star meglio sto qui* ; which it is impossible to translate.' ⟨See also Dryden, *Wks*. xiv. 149.⟩

[7] Lord Chesterfield, as Mr. Croker points out, makes the same observation in one of his *Letters to his Son* (i. 564). Boswell, however, does not get it from him, for he had said the same in the *Hebrides* (*post*, v. 310), six months before the publication of Chesterfield's *Letters*. Addison, in the preface to his *Remarks*, says :— ' Before I enter'd on my Voyage I took care to refresh my Memory among the Classic Authors, and to make such Collections out of 'em as I might afterwards have Occasion for.'

Ossian being mentioned ;—JOHNSON. ' Supposing the Irish and Erse languages to be the same, which I do not believe [1], yet as there is no reason to suppose that the inhabitants of the Highlands and Hebrides ever wrote their native language, it is not to be credited that a long poem was preserved among them. If we had no evidence of the art of writing being practised in one of the counties of England, we should not believe that a long poem was preserved *there*, though in the neighbouring counties, where the same language was spoken, the inhabitants could write.' BEAUCLERK. ' The ballad of Lilliburlero was once in the mouths of all the people of this country, and is said to have had a great effect in bringing about the Revolution [2]. Yet I question whether any body can repeat it now; which shews how improbable it is that much poetry should be preserved by tradition.'

One of the company † suggested an internal objection to the antiquity of the poetry said to be Ossian's, that we do not find the wolf in it, which must have been the case had it been of that age.

The mention of the wolf had led Johnson to think of other wild beasts ; and while Sir Joshua Reynolds and Mr. Langton were carrying on a dialogue about something which engaged them earnestly, he, in the midst of it, broke out, ' Pennant tells of Bears—' [what he added, I have forgotten.] They went on, which he being dull of hearing, did not perceive, or, if he did, was not willing to break off his talk ; so he continued to vociferate his remarks, and *Bear* (' like a word in a catch ', as Beauclerk said,) was repeatedly heard at intervals, which coming from him who, by those who did not know him, had been so often assimilated to that ferocious animal [3], while we who were sitting around could hardly stifle laughter, produced a very ludicrous

[1] See *ante*, ii. 156.

[2] ' It made an impression on the army, that cannot be well imagined by those who saw it not. The whole army, and at last all people both in city and country, were singing it perpetually. And perhaps never had so slight a thing so great an effect.' Burnet's *Own Time*, ed. 1833, iii. 336. In *Tristram Shandy*, vol. i. chap. 21, when Mr. Shandy advanced one of his hypotheses :—' My uncle Toby,' we read, ' would never offer to answer this by any other kind of argument, than that of whistling half-a-dozen bars of *Lillabullero*.'

[3] See *ante*, ii. 66. ⟨Mason, in a letter dated 26 June 1782, calls Johnson a ' bear upon stilts'. *Adam Catalogue*.⟩

† ⟨See App. B, p. 519, note to p. 345.⟩

effect. Silence having ensued, he proceeded : ' We are told, that the black bear is innocent ; but I should not like to trust myself with him.' Mr. Gibbon muttered, in a low tone of voice, ' I should not like to trust myself with *you*.' This piece of sarcastick pleasantry was a prudent resolution, if applied to a competition of abilities [1].

Patriotism having become one of our topicks, Johnson suddenly uttered, in a strong determined tone, an apophthegm, at which many will start : ' Patriotism is the last refuge of a scoundrel [2].' But let it be considered, that he did not mean a real and generous love of our country, but that pretended patriotism which so many, in all ages and countries, have made a cloak for self-interest. I maintain, that certainly all patriots were not scoundrels. Being urged (not by Johnson), to name one exception, I mentioned an eminent person [3], whom we all greatly admired. JOHNSON. ' Sir, I do not say that he is *not* honest ; but we have no reason to conclude from his political conduct that he *is* honest. Were he to accept of a place from this ministry, he would lose that character of firmness which he has, and might be turned out of his place in a year. This ministry is neither stable [4], nor grateful to their friends, as Sir Robert Walpole was : so that he may think it more for his interest to take his chance of his party coming in.'

Mrs. Pritchard being mentioned, he said, ' Her playing was quite mechanical. It is wonderful how little mind she had. Sir,

[1] ' Of Gibbon, Mackintosh neatly remarked, that he might have been cut out of a corner of Burke's mind without his missing it.' *Life of Mackintosh*, i. 92. It is worthy of notice that Gibbon scarcely mentions Johnson in his writings. Moreover, in the names that he gives of the members of the Literary Club, who ' form a large and luminous constellation of British stars,' though he mentions eighteen of them, he passes over Boswell. Gibbon's *Memoirs*, p. 311. See also *post*, ii. 366.

[2] We may compare with this Dryden's line :—

' Usurp'd a patriot's all-atoning name.'

Absalom and Achitophel, i. l. 179. Hawkins (*Life*, p. 506) says that ' to party-opposition Johnson ever expressed great aversion ; and, of the pretences of patriots, always spoke with indignation and contempt.' Hawkins adds, ' he partook of the short-lived joy that infatuated the public ' when Walpole fell ; but a few days convinced him that the patriotism of the opposition had been either hatred or ambition. For *patriots*, see *ante*, i. 295, note 1, and *post*, iv. 87.

[3] No doubt Mr. Burke. CROKER. See *ante*, ii. 222, note 4.

[4] Lord North's ministry lasted from 1770 to 1782.

she had never read the tragedy of Macbeth all through. She no more thought of the play out of which her part was taken, than a shoemaker thinks of the skin, out of which the piece of leather, of which he is making a pair of shoes, is cut [1].'

On Saturday, May 8 [2], I dined with him at Mr. Thrale's, where we met the Irish Dr. Campbell [3]. Johnson had supped the night before at Mrs. Abington's, with some fashionable people whom he named ; and he seemed much pleased with having made one in so elegant a circle. Nor did he omit to pique his *mistress* [4] a little with jealousy of her housewifery ; for he said, (with a smile,) ' Mrs. Abington's jelly, my dear Lady, was better than yours.'

Mrs. Thrale, who frequently practised a coarse mode of flattery, by repeating his *bon mots* in his hearing [5], told us that he had said, a certain celebrated actor was just fit to stand at the door of an auction-room with a long pole, and cry ' Pray gentlemen, walk in ; ' and that a certain authour, upon hearing this, had said, that another still more celebrated actor was fit for nothing better than that, and would pick your pocket after you came out [6]. JOHNSON. ' Nay, my dear lady, there is no wit in what our friend added ; there is only abuse. You may as well say of any man that he will pick a pocket. Besides, the man who is stationed at the door does not pick people's pockets ; that is done within, by the auctioneer.'

Mrs. Thrale told us, that Tom Davies repeated, in a very bald manner, the story of Dr. Johnson's first repartee to me, which

---

[1] Perhaps Johnson had this from Davies, who says (*Life of Garrick*, i. 153) :—' Mrs. Pritchard read no more of the play of Macbeth than her own part, as written out and delivered to her by the prompter.' She played the heroine in *Irene* (*ante*, i. 197). See *post*, iv. 243, and v. 126.

[2] A misprint for April 8.

[3] Boswell calls him the ' Irish Dr. Campbell,' to distinguish him from the Scotch Dr. Campbell mentioned *ante*, i. 417.

[4] See *ante*, i. 494.

[5] Baretti, in a MS. note in his copy of *Piozzi Letters*, i. 374, says :—' Johnson was often fond of saying silly things in strong terms, and the silly Madam never failed to eccho that beastly kind of wit.' ⟨See App B, p. 519.⟩

[6] According to Dr. T. Campbell, who was present at the dinner (*Diary*, p. 66 : John. Misc. ii. 50), Barry and Garrick were the two actors, and Murphy the author. If Murphy said this in the heat of one of his quarrels with Garrick, he made amends in his *Life* of that actor (p. 362) :—' It was with Garrick a fixed principle, that authors were intitled to the emolument of their labours, and by that generous way of thinking, he held out an invitation to men of genius.' ⟨Mrs. Piozzi identifies the ' celebrated actor ' as Barry and the ' certain authour ' as Murphy. *Marg. note* (1816).⟩

I have related exactly [1]. He made me say, ' I *was born* in Scotland,' instead of ' I *come from* Scotland ; ' so that Johnson's saying, ' That, Sir, is what a great many of your countrymen cannot help,' had no point, or even meaning : and that upon this being mentioned to Mr. Fitzherbert, he observed, ' It is not every man that can *carry* a *bon mot.*'

On Monday, April 10, I dined with him at General Oglethorpe's, with Mr. Langton and the Irish Dr. Campbell, whom the General had obligingly given me leave to bring with me. This learned gentleman was thus gratified with a very high intellectual feast, by not only being in company with Dr. Johnson, but with General Oglethorpe, who had been so long a celebrated name both at home and abroad [2].

I must, again and again, intreat of my readers not to suppose that my imperfect record of conversation contains the whole of what was said by Johnson, or other eminent persons who lived with him. What I have preserved, however, has the value of the most perfect authenticity.

He this day enlarged upon Pope's melancholy remark,

　　' Man never *is*, but always *to be* blest [3].'

He asserted, that *the present* was never a happy state to any

---

[1] Page 392, Vol. i. BOSWELL.

[2] Let me here be allowed to pay my tribute of most sincere gratitude to the memory of that excellent person, my intimacy with whom was the more valuable to me, because my first acquaintance with him was unexpected and unsolicited. Soon after the publication of my ' Account of Corsica,' he did me the honour to call on me, and approaching me with a frank courteous air, said, ' My name, Sir, is Oglethorpe, and I wish to be acquainted with you.' I was not a little flattered to be thus addressed by an eminent man, of whom I had read in Pope, from my early years,

' Or [a], driven by strong benevolence of soul,
Will [b] fly, like Oglethorpe, from pole to pole.'

[a] One *Pope.*

I was fortunate enough to be found worthy of his good opinion, insomuch, that I not only was invited to make one in the many respectable companies whom he entertained at his table, but had a cover at his hospitable board every day when I happened to be disengaged ; and in his society I never failed to enjoy learned and animated conversation, seasoned with genuine sentiments of virtue and religion. BOSWELL.

See *ante*, i. 127, and ii. 59, note 1. The couplet from Pope is from *Imitations of Horace, Epist.* ii. 2. 276.

[3] ' Hope springs eternal in the human breast :
Man never Is, but always To be blest.'
　　　　Essay on Man, i. 95.

[b] Shall *Pope.*

human being ; but that, as every part of life, of which we are
conscious, was at some point of time a period yet to come, in
which felicity was expected, there was some happiness produced
by hope [1]. Being pressed upon this subject, and asked if he
really was of opinion, that though, in general, happiness was very
rare in human life, a man was not sometimes happy in the
moment that was present, he answered, ' Never, but when he is
drunk [2].'

He urged General Oglethorpe to give the world his Life. He
said, ' I know no man whose Life would be more interesting.
If I were furnished with materials, I should be very glad to
write it [3].'

Mr. Scott [4] of Amwell's Elegies were lying in the room. Dr.
Johnson observed, ' They are very well ; but such as twenty
people might write.' Upon this I took occasion to controvert
Horace's maxim,

> '———— *mediocribus esse poetis*
> *Non Di, non homines, non concessêre columnæ* [5].'

for here (I observed,) was a very middle-rate poet, who pleased
many readers, and therefore poetry of a middle sort was entitled
to some esteem ; nor could I see why poetry should not, like
every thing else, have different gradations of excellence, and
consequently of value. Johnson repeated the common remark,
that ' as there is no necessity for our having poetry at all, it
being merely a luxury, an instrument of pleasure, it can have

[1] ' The natural flights of the human mind are not from pleasure to pleasure, but from hope to hope.' *The Rambler*, No. 2. See *post*, iii. 53, and iv. 303. Swift defined happiness as ' a perpetual possession of being well deceived.' *Tale of a Tub*, Sect. ix, *Prose Works*, ed. 1897, i. 119.

[2] See *post*, iii. 5.

[3] The General seemed unwilling to enter upon it at this time ; but upon a subsequent occasion he communicated to me a number of particulars, which I have committed to writing ; but I was not sufficiently diligent in obtaining more from him, not apprehending that his friends

were so soon to lose him ; for notwithstanding his great age, he was very healthy and vigorous, and was at last carried off by a violent fever, which is often fatal at any period of life. BOSWELL.
⟨According to Dr. Campbell, on Oglethorpe's excusing himself from writing his life, ' Boswell desired him only to furnish the skeleton, and that Dr. Johnson would supply bones and sinews '. *John. Misc.* ii. 51.⟩

[4] See *ante*, ii. 338.

[5]   ' Mediocribus esse poetis
Non homines, non Di, non concessere
     columnae.'
          Horace, *Ars Poet.* l. 372.

no value, unless when exquisite in its kind.' I declared myself not satisfied. ' Why then, Sir, (said he,) Horace and you must settle it.' He was not much in the humour of talking †.

No more of his conversation for some days appears in my journal [1], except that when a gentleman told him he had bought a suit of laces[a] for his lady, he said, ' Well, Sir, you have done a good thing and a wise thing.' ' I have done a good thing, (said the gentleman,) but I do not know that I have done a wise thing.' JOHNSON. ' Yes, Sir ; no money is better spent than what is laid out for domestick satisfaction. A man is pleased that his wife is drest as well as other people ; and a wife is pleased that she is drest.'

On Friday, April 14, being Good-Friday, I repaired to him in the morning, according to my usual custom on that day, and breakfasted with him. I observed that he fasted so very strictly [2], that he did not even taste bread, and took no milk with his tea ; I suppose because it is a kind of animal food.

He entered upon the state of the nation, and thus discoursed : ' Sir, the great misfortune now is, that government has too little power. All that it has to bestow,[b] must of necessity be given to support itself ; so that it cannot reward merit. No man, for instance, can now be made a Bishop for his learning and piety [3] ; his only chance for promotion is his being connected

---

a laces 1 : lace 2, 3.

b *comma omitted* 2, 3.

[1] Why he failed to keep his journal may be guessed from his letter to Temple :—' I am,' he wrote on April 17, ' indeed enjoying this metropolis to the full according to my taste, except that I cannot, I see, have a plenary indulgence from you for Asiatic multiplicity. Be not afraid of me, except when I take too much claret ; and then indeed there is a *furor brevis* as dangerous as anger. . . . I have rather had too much dissipation since I came last *to Town*. I try to keep a journal, and shall shew you that I have done tollerably. But it is hardly credible what ground I go over, and what a variety of men and manners I contemplate in a day ; and all the time I myself am *pars magna*, for my exuberant spirits will not let me listen enough.' *Letters*, No. 138.

[2] Johnson, in *The Rambler*, No. 110, published on Easter Eve, 1751, thus justifies fasting :—' Austerity is the proper antidote to indulgence ; the diseases of mind as well as body are cured by contraries, and to contraries we should readily have recourse, if we dreaded guilt as we dread pain.'

[3] From this too just observation there are some eminent exceptions. BOSWELL.

Dr. Johnson said :—' Few bishops are now made for their learning. To be a bishop, a man must be learned in a learned age,—factious in a factious age ; but always of eminence.' *Post*, v. 80.

† ⟨He was irritated by Boswell's questioning. See *John. Misc.* ii. 52.⟩

with somebody who has parliamentary interest. Our several ministries in this reign have outbid each other in concessions to the people. Lord Bute, though a very honourable man,—a man who meant well,—a man who had his blood full of prerogative,—was a theoretical statesman,—a book-minister [1],—and thought this country could be governed by the influence of the Crown alone. Then, Sir, he gave up a great deal. He advised the King to agree that the Judges should hold their places for life, instead of losing them at the accession of a new King. Lord Bute, I suppose, thought to make the King popular by this concession; but the people never minded it; and it was a most impolitick measure. There is no reason why a Judge should hold his office for life, more than any other person in publick trust. A Judge may be partial otherwise than to the Crown: we have seen Judges partial to the populace [2]. A Judge may become corrupt, and yet there may not be legal evidence against him. A Judge may become froward from age. A Judge may grow unfit for his office in many ways. It was desirable that there should be a possibility of being delivered from him by a new King. That is now gone by an act of Parliament *ex gratiâ* of the Crown [3]. Lord Bute advised the King to give up a very large sum of money [4], for which nobody

[1] Lord Shelburne wrote of him :— ' He panted for the Treasury, having a notion that the King and he understood it from what they had read about revenue and funds while they were at Kew.' Fitzmaurice's *Shelburne*, i. 111.

[2] Chief Justice Pratt (afterwards Lord Camden) became popular by his conduct as a judge in Wilkes's case. In 1764 he received the freedom of the guild of merchants in Dublin in a gold box, and from Exeter the freedom of the city. The city of London gave him its freedom in a gold box, and had his portrait painted by Reynolds. *Gent. Mag.* 1764, pp. 44, 96, 144. See *ante*, ii. 72, note 3, and 314.

[3] The King, on March 3, 1761, recommended this measure to Parlia-

ment. *Parl. Hist.* xv. 1007. ' This,' writes Horace Walpole, ' was one of Lord Bute's strokes of pedantry. The tenure of the judges had formerly been a popular topic ; and had been secured, as far as was necessary. He thought this trifling addition would be popular now, when nobody thought or cared about it.' *Memoirs of the Reign of George III*, i. 41.

[4] The money arising from the property of the prizes taken before the declaration of war, which were given to his Majesty by the peace of Paris, and amounted to upwards of 700,000 l., and from the lands in the ceded islands, which were estimated at 200,000 l. more. Surely, there was a noble munificence in this gift from a Monarch to his people. And let it be remembered, that during the Earl

thanked him. It was of consequence to the King, but nothing to the publick, among whom it was divided. When I say Lord Bute advised, I mean, that such acts were done when he was minister, and we are to suppose that he advised them.—Lord Bute shewed an undue partiality to Scotchmen. He turned out Dr. Nichols [1], a very eminent man, from being physician to the King, to make room for one of his countrymen, a man very low in his profession [2]. He had *********** [3] and **** [4] to go on

of Bute's administration, the King was graciously pleased to give up the hereditary revenues of the Crown, and to accept, instead of them, of the limited sum of 800,000 l. a year ; upon which Blackstone observes, that ' The hereditary revenues, being put under the same management as the other branches of the publick patrimony, will produce more, and be better collected than heretofore ; and the publick is a gainer of upwards of 100,000 l. *per annum*, by this disinterested bounty of his Majesty.' Book I. Chap. viii. p. 330. BOSWELL. Lord Bolingbroke (*Dissert. upon Parties*, xviii), in 1734, pointed out that ' if the Funds appropriated produce the double of that immense Revenue of 800,000 l. a Year, which hath been so liberally given the King for Life, the whole is his without Account ; but if they fail in any Degree to produce it, the Entire national Fund is engaged to make up the Difference.' Blackstone (edit. of 1778, i. 331) says :—'£800,000 being found insufficient, was increased in 1777 to £900,000.' He adds, ' the public is still a gainer of near £100,000.'

[1] ⟨Dr. Frank Nicholls.⟩ See *post*, iii. 163.

[2] Lord Eldon says that Dundas, ' in broken phrases,' asked the King to confer a baronetcy on ' an eminent Scotch apothecary who had got from Scotland the degree of M.D. The King said :—" What, what, is that all ? It shall be done. I was afraid you meant to ask me to make the Scotch apothecary a physician :— that's more difficult." ' He added :— ' They may make as many Scotch apothecaries Baronets as they please, but I shall die by the College.' Twiss's *Eldon*, ii. 354. A Dr. Duncan was appointed physician to the King in 1760. Croker's *Boswell*, p. 448. ⟨William Duncan, M.D., physician extraordinary to the King, was created a baronet 14 Aug. 1764. Burke's *Extinct Baronetcies*.⟩

[3] Wedderburne, afterwards Lord Chancellor Loughborough, and Earl of Rosslyn. One of his ' errands ' had been to bring Johnson bills in payment of his first quarter's pension. *Ante*, i. 376.

[4] Home, the author of *Douglas*. Boswell says that ' Home showed the Lord Chief Baron Orde a pair of pumps he had on, and desired his lordship to observe how well they were made, telling him at the same time that they had been made for Lord Bute, but were rather too little for him, so his lordship had made John a present of them. " I think," said the Lord Chief Baron, " you have taken the measure of Lord Bute's foot." ' *Boswelliana*, p. 252. Dr. A. Carlyle (*Auto.* p. 335), writes :—' With Robertson and Home in London I passed the time very agreeably ; for though Home was now [1758] entirely at the command of Lord Bute, whose nod made him break every engagement—for it was not given above an hour or two before dinner—yet as he was sometimes at liberty when the noble lord was to dine abroad, like a

SAMUEL JOHNSON
from the painting by JAMES BARRY, R.A., *c.* 1775
in the National Portrait Gallery

errands for him. He had occasion for people to go on errands for him ; but he should not have had Scotchmen ; and, certainly, he should not have suffered them to have access to him before the first people in England.'

I told him, that the admission of one of them before the first people in England, which had given the greatest offence, was no more than what happens at every minister's levee, where those who attend are admitted in the order that they have come, which is better than admitting them according to their rank ; for if that were to be the rule, a man who has waited all the morning might have the mortification to see a peer, newly come, go in before him, and keep him waiting still. JOHNSON. ' True, Sir ; but **** should not have come to the levee, to be in the way of people of consequence. He saw Lord Bute at all times ; and could have said what he had to say at any time, as well as at the levee. There is now no Prime Minister : there is only an agent for government in the House of Commons [1]. We are governed by the Cabinet : but there is no one head there, as in [a] Sir Robert Walpole's time.' BOSWELL. ' What then, Sir, is the use of Parliament ? ' JOHNSON. ' Why, Sir, Parliament is a larger council to the King ; and the advantage of such a council is, having a great number of men of property concerned in the legislature, who, for their own interest, will not consent to bad laws. And you must have observed, Sir, that administration is feeble and timid, and cannot act with that authority and resolution which is necessary. Were I in power, I would turn out every man who dared to oppose me. Government has the distribution of offices, that it may be enabled to maintain its authority [2].'

[a] there, as in 1 : there since 2, 3.

horse loosened from his stake, he was more sportful than usual.'

[1] Lord North was merely the King's agent. The King was really his own minister at this time, though he had no seat in his own cabinet councils.

[2] Only thirty-four years earlier, on the motion in the Lords for the removal of Walpole, the Duke of Argyle said :—' If my father or brother took upon him the office of a sole minister, I would oppose it as inconsistent with

the constitution, as a high crime and misdemeanour. I appeal to your consciences whether he [Walpole] hath not done this . . . He hath turned out men lately for differing with him.' Lord Chancellor Hardwicke replied :—' A sole minister is so illegal an office, that it is none. Yet a noble lord says, *Superior respondeat*, which is laying down a rule for a prime minister ; whereas the noble duke was against any.' *The Secker*

' Lord Bute (he added,) took down too fast, without building
up something new.' BOSWELL. ' Because, Sir, he found a rotten
building. The political coach was drawn by a set of bad
horses : it was necessary to change them.' JOHNSON. ' But he
should have changed them one by one.'

I told him that I had been informed by Mr. Orme [1], that many
parts of the East-Indies were better mapped than the Highlands of Scotland. JOHNSON. ' That a country may be mapped,
it must be travelled over.' ' Nay, (said I, meaning to laugh with
him at one of his prejudices,) can't you say, it is not *worth*
mapping ? '

As we walked to St. Clement's church, and saw several shops
open upon this most solemn fast-day of the Christian world,
I remarked, that one disadvantage arising from the immensity
of London, was, that nobody was heeded by his neighbour ;
there was no fear of censure for not observing Good-Friday, as
it ought to be kept, and as it is kept in country-towns. He
said, it was, upon the whole, very well observed even in London.
He, however, owned, that London was too large ; but added,
' It is nonsense to say the head is too big for the body. It
would be as much too big, though the body were ever so large ;
that is to say, though the country were ever so extensive. It
has no similarity to a head connected with a body.'

Dr. Wetherell, Master of University College, Oxford, accompanied us home from church [2]; and after he was gone, there

MS. in *Parl. Hist.* xi. 1056–7. In
the Protest against the rejection of
the motion it was stated :—' We are
persuaded that a sole, or even a first
minister, is an officer unknown to the
law of Britain,' &c. *Ib.* p. 1215.
Johnson reports the Chancellor as
saying :—' It has not been yet pretended that he assumes the title of
prime minister, or indeed, that it is
applied to him by any but his
enemies. . . . The first minister can, in
my opinion, be nothing more than
a formidable illusion, which, when
one man thinks he has seen it, he
shows to another, as easily frighted
as himself,' &c. Johnson's *Works*,
x. 214–15. In his *Dictionary, premier*
is only given as an adjective, and
prime minister is not given at all.
When the Marquis of Rockingham
was forming his cabinet in March
1782, Burke wrote to him :—' Stand
firm on your ground,—but *one* ministry. I trust and hope that your lordship will not let *one*, even but *one*
branch of the state . . . out of your
own hands, or those which you can
entirely rely on.' Burke's *Corres.* ii.
462. See also *post*, iii. 46, iv. 81, and
139, 200.

[1] See *ante*, ii. 300.

[2] ⟨'We . . . saw Dr. Wetherel in the
pew, and by his desire took him home
with us. He did not go very soon.'
Pr. and Med. ¶ 109.⟩

came two other gentlemen †, one of whom uttered the common-place complaints, that by the increase of taxes, labour would be dear, other nations would undersell us, and our commerce would be ruined. JOHNSON, (smiling). ' Never fear, Sir. Our commerce is in a very good state ; and suppose we had no commerce at all, we could live very well on the produce of our own country.' I cannot omit to mention, that I never knew any man who was less disposed to be querulous than Johnson. Whether the subject was his own situation, or the state of the publick, or the state of human nature in general, though he saw the evils, his mind was turned to resolution, and never to whining or complaint [1].

We went again to St. Clement's in the afternoon. He had found fault with the preacher in the morning for not choosing a text adapted to the day. The preacher in the afternoon had chosen one extremely proper : ' It is finished.'

After the evening service, he said, ' Come, you shall go home with me, and sit just an hour.' But he was better than his word ; for after we had drunk tea [2] with Mrs. Williams, he asked me to go up to his study with him, where we sat a long while together in a serene undisturbed frame of mind, sometimes in silence, and sometimes conversing, as we felt ourselves inclined, or more properly speaking, as *he* was inclined ; for during all the course of my long intimacy with him, my respectful attention never abated, and my wish to hear him was such, that I constantly watched every dawning of communication from that great and illuminated mind.

He observed, ' All knowledge is of itself of some value. There is nothing so minute or inconsiderable, that I would not rather know it than not. In the same manner, all power, of whatever sort, is of itself desirable. A man would not submit to learn to hem a ruffle, of his wife, or his wife's maid ; but if a mere wish could attain it, he would rather wish to be able to hem a ruffle.'

---

[1] ' As he liberally confessed that all his own disappointments proceeded from himself, he hated to hear others complain of general injustice.' Piozzi's *Anec.* p. 251 : John. Misc. i. 315. See *post*, iv. 116, 172, 383 note.

[2] ' Boswel and I went to Church, but came very late. We then took tea, by Boswel's desire, and I eat one bun, I think, that I might not seem to fast ostentatiously.' *Pr. and Med.* ¶ 109.

† ⟨See App. B, p. 519.⟩

He again advised me to keep a journal [1] fully and minutely, but not to mention such trifles as, that meat was too much or too little done, or that the weather was fair or rainy. He had, till very near his death, a contempt for the notion that the weather affects the human frame [2].

I told him that our friend Goldsmith had said to me, that he had come too late into the world, for that Pope and other poets had taken up the places in the Temple of Fame ; so that as but a few at any period can possess poetical reputation, a man of genius can now hardly acquire it. JOHNSON. ' That is one of the most sensible things I have ever heard of Goldsmith [3]. It is difficult to get literary fame, and it is every day growing more difficult. Ah, Sir, that should make a man think of securing happiness in another world, which all who try sincerely for it may attain. In comparison of that, how little are all other things ! The belief of immortality is impressed upon all men, and all men act under an impression of it, however they may talk, and though, perhaps, they may be scarcely sensible of it.' I said, it appeared to me that some people had not the least notion of immortality ; and I mentioned a distinguished gentleman of our

---

[1] See *ante*, i. 433 ; ii. 217 note 2.

[2] See *ante*, i. 332.

[3] The following passages shew that the thought, or something like it, was not new to Johnson :— ' Bruyere ⟨*Les Caractères*, i. 1⟩ declares that we are come into the world too late to produce any thing new, that nature and life are preoccupied, and that description and sentiment have been long exhausted.' *The Rambler*, No. 143. ' Some advantage the antients might gain merely by priority, which put them in possession of the most natural sentiments, and left us nothing but servile repetition or forced conceits.' *Ib*. No. 169. ' My earlier predecessors . . . had the whole field of life before them, untrodden and unsurveyed ; characters of every kind shot up in their way, and those of the most luxuriant growth, or most conspicuous colours, were naturally cropt by the first sickle. They that follow are forced to peep into neglected corners.' *The Idler*, No. 3. ' The first writers took possession of the most striking objects for description, and the most probable occurrences for fiction.' *Rasselas*, ch. x. Some years later he wrote :—' Whatever can happen to man has happened so often, that little remains for fancy or invention.' *Dryden*, 231. See also *The Rambler*, No. 86. In *The Adventurer*, No. 95, he wrote :—' The complaint . . . that all topicks are preoccupied, is nothing more than the murmur of ignorance or idleness.' See *post*, iv. 236. ⟨Cf. Ménage, *Antibaillet*, 1690, ii, p. 208, ' St. Jérome dit que son Maître Donat expliquant ce mot de Térence, *Nihil est dictum, quod non sit dictum prius*, pestoit contre les Anciens qui lui avoient pris ses pensées. *Pereant qui ante nos nostra dixerunt*.'⟩

acquaintance. JOHNSON. ' Sir, if it were not for the notion of immortality, he would cut a throat to fill his pockets.' When I quoted this to Beauclerk, who knew much more of the gentleman than we did, he said, in his acid manner, ' He would cut a throat to fill his pockets, if it were not for fear of being hanged.'

Dr. Johnson proceeded : ' Sir, there is a great cry about infidelity [1] ; but there are, in reality, very few infidels. I have heard a person, originally a Quaker, but now, I am afraid, a Deist, say, that he did not believe there were, in all England, above two hundred infidels.'

He was pleased to say, ' If you come to settle here, we will have one day in the week on which we will meet by ourselves. That is the happiest conversation where there is no competition, no vanity, but a calm quiet interchange of sentiments [2].' In his private register this evening is thus marked, ' Boswell sat with me till night ; we had some serious talk [3].' It also appears from the same record, that after I left him he was occupied in religious duties, in ' giving Francis, his servant, some directions for preparation to communicate ; in reviewing his life, and resolving on better conduct [4].' The humility and piety which he

---

[1] Warburton, in the Dedication of his *Divine Legation* to the Freethinkers (vol. i, p. ii), says:—'Nothing, I believe, strikes the serious observer with more surprize, in this age of novelties, than that strange propensity to infidelity, so visible in men of almost every condition : amongst whom the advocates of Deism are received with all the applauses due to the inventers of the arts of life, or the deliverers of oppressed and injured nations.' See *ante*, ii. 81.

[2] In *The Rambler*, No. 89, Johnson writes of ' that interchange of thoughts which is practised in free and easy conversation ; where suspicion is banished by experience, and emulation by benevolence ; where every man speaks with no other restraint than unwillingness to offend, and hears with no other disposition than desire to be pleased.' In *The*

Idler, No. 34, he says ' that companion will be oftenest welcome, whose talk flows out with inoffensive copiousness, and unenvied insipidity.' He wrote, 13 Aug. 1777, to Mrs. Thrale :—' Such tattle as filled your last sweet letter prevents one great inconvenience of absence, that of returning home a stranger and an enquirer. The variations of life consist of little things. Important innovations are soon heard, and easily understood. Men that meet to talk of physicks or metaphysicks, or law or history, may be immediately acquainted. We look at each other in silence, only for want of petty talk upon slight occurrences.' *Letters*, No. 537.

[3] Prayers and Meditations, p. 138. BOSWELL.

[4] This line is not, as appears, a quotation, but an abstract of p. 139 of *Pr. and Med.* ⟨¶¶ 109, 110⟩.

discovers on such occasions, is truely edifying. No saint, however, in the course of his religious warfare, was more sensible of the unhappy failure of pious resolves, than Johnson. He said one day, talking to an acquaintance on this subject, ' Sir, Hell is paved with good intentions [1].'

On Sunday, April 16, being Easter-day, after having attended the solemn service at St. Paul's [2], I dined with Dr. Johnson and Mrs. Williams. I maintained that Horace was wrong in placing happiness in *Nil admirari* [3], for that I thought admiration one of the most agreeable of all our feelings [4] ; and I regretted that I had lost much of my disposition to admire, which people generally do as they advance in life. JOHNSON. ' Sir, as a man advances in life, he gets what is better than admiration—judgement, to estimate things at their true value.' I still insisted that admiration was more pleasing than judgement, as love is more pleasing than friendship. The feeling of friendship is like that of being comfortably filled with roast beef ; love, like being enlivened with champagne. JOHNSON. ' No, Sir ; admiration and love are like being intoxicated with champagne ; judgement and friendship like being enlivened. Waller has hit upon the same thought with you [5] : but I don't believe you have borrowed from Waller. I wish you would enable yourself to borrow more [6].'

[1] This is a proverbial sentence. ' Hell (says Herbert) is full of good meanings and wishings.' *Jacula Prudentum*, No. 170, edit. 1651. MALONE.

[2] Boswell wrote, 17 April 1775, to Temple :—' I have only to tell you, as my *divine*, that I yesterday received the Holy Sacrament in St. Paul's Church, and was exalted in piety.' It was in the same letter that he mentioned ' Asiatic multiplicity ' (*ante*, ii. 352, note 1). *Letters*, No. 138, i. 220.

[3] ' Nil admirari prope res est una, Numici,
Solaque, quae possit facere et servare beatum.'
Horace, *Epis*. i. 6. 1.
' Not to admire, is all the art I know,
To make men happy, and to keep them so.'
Pope's *Imitations*, adapted from Creech.

[4] ' We live by Admiration, Hope, and Love ;
And, even as these are well and wisely fixed,
In dignity of being we ascend.
Wordsworth's *Excursion*, iv. 763–5.

[5] ' Amoret's as sweet and good
As the most delicious food ;
Which but tasted does impart
Life and gladness to the heart.
Sacharissa's beauty's wine,
Which to madness does incline [a] ;
Such a liquor as no brain
That is mortal can sustain.'
[Waller's *Epistles*, xii.] BOSWELL.

[6] Not that he would have wished Boswell ' to talk from books.' ' You and I,' he once said to him, ' do not talk from books.' *Post*, v. 378. ⟨See *post*, iii. 108, note 1, for Boswell's criticism of himself for neglecting to read.⟩

[a] incline 1, 2 : decline 3.

He then took occasion to enlarge on the advantages of reading, and combated the idle superficial notion, that knowledge enough may be acquired in conversation. ' The foundation (said he,) must be laid by reading. General principles must be had from books, which, however, must be brought to the test of real life. In conversation you never get a system. What is said upon a subject is to be gathered from a hundred people. The parts of a truth, which a man gets thus, are at such a distance from each other, that he never attains to a full view.'

' To BENNET LANGTON, ESQ.

' DEAR SIR,

' I HAVE enquired more minutely about the medicine for the rheumatism, which I am sorry to hear that you still want. The receipt is this :

' Take equal quantities of flour of sulphur, and *flour* of mustard-seed, make them an electuary with honey or treacle ; and take a bolus as big as a nutmeg several times a day, as you can bear it : drinking after it a quarter of a pint of the infusion of the root of Lovage.

' Lovage, in Ray's " Nomenclature," is Levisticum : perhaps the Botanists may know the Latin name.

' Of this medicine I pretend not to judge. There is all the appearance of its efficacy, which a single instance can afford : the patient was very old, the pain very violent, and the relief, I think, speedy and lasting.

' My opinion of alterative medicine is not high, but *quid tentasse nocebit ?* if it does harm, or does no good, it may be omitted ; but that it may do good, you have, I hope, reason to think is desired by,

' Sir, your most affectionate,

' Humble servant,

' SAM. JOHNSON.'

' April 17, 1775.'

On Tuesday, April 18, he and I were engaged to go with Sir Joshua Reynolds to dine with Mr. Cambridge [1], at his beautiful villa on the banks of the Thames, near Twickenham. Dr. Johnson's tardiness was such, that Sir Joshua, who had an appointment at Richmond, early in the day, was obliged to go by himself on horseback, leaving his coach to Johnson and me. Johnson was in such good spirits, that every thing seemed to please him as we drove along.

[1] See *post*, iv. 196.

Our conversation turned on a variety of subjects. He thought portrait-painting an improper employment for a woman[1]. ' Publick practice of any art, (he observed,) and staring in men's faces, is very indelicate in a female.' I happened to start a question of propriety[a], whether, when a man knows that some of his intimate friends are invited to the house of another friend, with whom they are all equally intimate, he may join them without an invitation. JOHNSON. ' No, Sir ; he is not to go when he is not invited. They may be invited on purpose to abuse him ',(smiling).†

As a curious instance how little a man knows, or wishes to know, his own character in the world, or, rather, as a convincing proof that Johnson's roughness was only external, and did not proceed from his heart, I insert the following dialogue. JOHNSON. ' It is wonderful, Sir, how rare a quality good humour is in life. We meet with very few good humoured men.' I mentioned four of our friends[2], none of whom he would allow to be good humoured. One was *acid*, another was *muddy*[3], and to the others he had objections which have escaped me. Then, shaking his head and stretching himself at his[b] ease in the coach, and smiling with much complacency, he turned to me and said, ' I look upon *myself* as a good humoured fellow.' The epithet *fellow*, applied to the great Lexicographer, the stately Moralist, the masterly Critick, as if he had been *Sam* Johnson, a mere pleasant companion, was highly diverting ; and this light notion of himself struck me with wonder. I answered, also smiling, ' No, no, Sir ; that will *not* do. You are good natured, but not

---

[a] of propriety *omitted* 2, 3.

[b] his *omitted* 2, 3.

[1] ⟨Boswell wrote in his journal, ' [In the] Coach : " JOHNSON. Miss Reynolds ought not to paint. Publick practice of staring in men's faces inconsistent with delicacy ".' *Boswell Papers*, vi. 41.⟩ Yet he sat to Miss Reynolds, as he tells us, perhaps ten times (*Letters*, Nos. 682 and 876), and ' Miss Reynolds's mind,' he said, ' is very near to purity itself.' Piozzi, *Anecd.* p. 88 : John. Misc. i. 207.

[2] ⟨Boswell's journal shows that the four were Reynolds, Burke, Beauclerk, and Langton. No specific objections are recorded against Reynolds and Burke, but Beauclerk is described as

' acid ' and Langton ' muddy '. *Boswell Papers*, vi. 41, 46.⟩ Boswell mentions Beauclerk's ' acid manner '. *Ante*, ii. 359. ⟨See App. B, p. 519.⟩

[3] In his *Dictionary*, Johnson defines *muddy* as *cloudy in mind, dull* ; and quotes *The Winter's Tale*, act i. sc. 2. Wesley (*Journal*, 27 Feb. 1747) writes : —' Honest, *muddy* M. B. conducted me to his house.' Johnson (*post*, ii. 460), after telling how an acquaintance of his drank, adds, ' not that he gets drunk, for he is a very pious man, but he is always *muddy*.'

† ⟨Boswell's record of this dialogue is : ' JOHNSON. You're not to go where

good humoured [1] : you are irascible.   You have not patience
with folly and absurdity.   I believe you would pardon them, if
there were time to deprecate your vengeance ; but punishment
follows so quick after sentence, that they cannot escape.'

I had brought with me a great bundle of Scotch magazines
and news-papers †, in which his ' Journey to the Western Islands '
was attacked in every mode ; and I read a great part of them
to him, knowing they would afford him entertainment.   I wish
the writers of them had been present : they would have been
sufficiently vexed.   One ludicrous imitation of his style, by
Mr. Maclaurin [2], now one of the Scotch Judges, with the title
of Lord Dreghorn, was distinguished by him from the rude
mass. ' This (said he,) is the best.   But I could caricature my
own style much better myself.'   He defended his remark upon
the general insufficiency of education in Scotland ; and confirmed to me the authenticity of his witty saying on the learning
of the Scotch ;—' Their learning is like bread in a besieged
town : every man gets a little, but no man gets a full meal [3].'
' There is (said he,) in Scotland a diffusion of learning, a certain
portion of it widely and thinly spread.   A merchant there has
as much learning as one of their clergy [4].'

He talked of Isaac Walton's Lives, which was one of his most
favourite books.   Dr. Donne's Life, he said, was the most perfect
of them.   He observed, that ' it was wonderful that Walton, who

others are invited. BOSWELL. Not I to
Thrale's when you and Langton are
there? JOHNSON. No, we may be invited
to abuse you.' *Boswell Papers*, vi. 41.⟩
[1] In *The Rambler*, No. 72, Johnson defines good-humour as ' a habit
of being pleased ; a constant and per-
ennial softness of manner, easiness of
approach, and suavity of disposition.'
  † ⟨Cf. *ante*, ii. 308 ; Courtney, 120.⟩
[2] See *post*, v. 48.
[3] ' It is with their learning as with
provisions in a besieged town, every
one has a mouthful, and no one a
bellyful.' Johnson's *Works* (1787),
xi. 200. ⟨See Piozzi, *Anecd.*, p. 263
(John. Misc. i. 321) and App. B, p. 520⟩.
[4] ' Men bred in the universities of
Scotland cannot be expected to be

often decorated with the splendours
of ornamental erudition, but they
obtain a mediocrity of knowledge,
between learning and ignorance, not
inadequate to the purposes of common life, which is, I believe, very
widely diffused among them.' Johnson's *Western Islands*, 146. Lord Shelburne said that the Earl of Bute had
' a great deal of superficial knowledge, such as is commonly to be met
with in France and Scotland, chiefly
upon matters of Natural Philosophy,
Mines, Fossils, a smattering of Me-
chanicks, a little Metaphysicks, and a
very false taste in everything.' Fitzmaurice's *Shelburne*, i. 110. ' A gentleman who had heard that Bentley
was born in the north, said to Porson,

was in a very low situation in life, should have been familiarly received by so many great men, and that at a time when the ranks of society were kept more separate than they are now.' He supposed that Walton had then given up his business as a linen-draper and sempster, and was only an authour [1] ; and added, ' that he was a great panegyrist.' BOSWELL. ' No quality will get a man more friends than a disposition to admire the qualities of others. I do not mean flattery, but a sincere admiration.' JOHNSON. ' Nay, Sir, flattery pleases very generally [2]. In the first place, the flatterer may think what he says to be true : but, in the second place, whether he thinks so or not, he certainly thinks those whom he flatters of consequence enough to be flattered.'

No sooner had we made our bow to Mr. Cambridge, in his library, than Johnson ran eagerly to one side of the room, intent on poring over the backs of the books [3]. Sir Joshua observed,

" Wasn't he a Scotchman ? "—" No, sir," replied Porson ; " Bentley was a great Greek scholar." ' Rogers's *Table Talk*, p. 322. See *post*, v. 57.

[1] Walton did not retire from business till 1643. But in 1664, Dr. King, Bishop of Chichester, in a letter prefixed to his *Lives*, mentions his having been familiarly acquainted with him for forty years ; and in 1631 he was so intimate with Dr. Donne, that he was one of the friends who attended him on his death bed. J. BOSWELL, jun. His first wife's uncle was George Cranmer, the grandson of the Archbishop's brother. His second wife was half-sister of Bishop Ken.

[2] Johnson himself, as Boswell twice tells us, ' was somewhat susceptible of flattery.' *Post*, iv. 427 ; v. 17.

[3] The first time he dined with me, he was shewn into my book-room, and instantly pored over the lettering of each volume within his reach. My collection of books is very miscellaneous, and I feared there might be some among them that he would not like. But seeing the number of volumes very considerable, he said, ' You are an honest man, to have

formed so great an accumulation of knowledge.' BURNEY. Miss Burney describes this visit (*Memoirs of Dr. Burney*, ii. 90, 93) :—' Every body rose to do him honour ; and he returned the attention with the most formal courtesie. My father ... whispered to him that music was going forward ; which he would not, my father thinks, have found out ; and placing him on the best seat vacant, told his daughters to go on with the duet ; while Dr. Johnson, intently rolling towards them one eye—for they say he does not see with the other—made a grave nod, and gave a dignified motion with one hand, in silent approvance of the proceeding.' He was next introduced to Miss Burney, but ' his attention was not to be drawn off two minutes longer from the books, to which he now strided his way. . . . He pored over them, shelf by shelf, almost brushing them with his eye-lashes from near examination. At last, fixing upon something that happened to hit his fancy, he took it down, and, standing aloof from the company, which he seemed clean and clear to forget, he began, ... very composedly, (aside,) ' He runs to the books, as I do to the pictures : but I have the advantage. I can see much more of the pictures than he can of the books.' Mr. Cambridge, upon this, politely said, ' Dr. Johnson, I am going, with your pardon, to accuse myself, for I have the same custom which I perceive you have. But it seems odd that one should have such a desire to look at the backs of books.' Johnson, ever ready for contest, instantly started from his reverie, wheeled about, and answered, ' Sir, the reason is very plain. Knowledge is of two kinds. We know a subject ourselves, or we know where we can find information upon it. When we enquire into any subject, the first thing we have to do is to know what books have treated of it. This leads us to look at catalogues, and at [a] the backs of books in libraries.' Sir Joshua observed to me the extraordinary promptitude with which Johnson flew upon an argument. ' Yes, (said I,) he has no formal preparation, no flourishing with his sword ; he is through your body in an instant [1].'

Johnson was here solaced with an elegant entertainment, a very accomplished family, and much good company ; among whom was Mr. Harris [2] of Salisbury, who paid him many compliments on his ' Journey to the Western Islands.'

The common remark as to the utility of reading history being made ;—JOHNSON. ' We must consider how very little history there is ; I mean real authentick history. That certain Kings reigned, and certain battles were fought, we can depend upon as true ; but all the colouring, all the philosophy,[b] of history is

[a] at *omitted* 2, 3.　　　　　[b] *comma omitted* 2, 3.

to read to himself ; and as intently as if he had been alone in his own study. We were all excessively provoked : for we were languishing, fretting, expiring to hear him talk.' Dr. Burney, taking up something that Mrs. Thrale had said, ventured to ask him about Bach's concert. ' The Doctor, comprehending his drift, good-naturedly put away his book, and, see-sawing, with a very humorous smile, drolly repeated, " Bach, sir ? Bach's concert ? And pray, sir, who is Bach ? Is he a piper ? " '

[1] Reynolds, noting down ' such qualities as Johnson's works cannot convey,' says that ' the most distin-

guished was his possessing a mind which was, as I may say, always ready for use. Most general subjects had undoubtedly been already discussed in the course of a studious thinking life. In this respect few men ever came better prepared into whatever company chance might throw him, and the love which he had to society gave him a facility in the practice of applying his knowledge of the matter in hand, in which I believe he was never exceeded by any man.' Leslie and Taylor's *Reynolds*, ii. 454. ⟨See Piozzi, *Anec.* 201 : John. Misc. i. 285.⟩

[2] See *ante*, ii. 225 ⟨and App. B, p. 520.⟩

conjecture [1].' BOSWELL. ' Then, Sir, you would reduce all history to no better than an almanack [2], a mere chronological series of remarkable events.' Mr. Gibbon, who must at that time have been employed upon his history [3], of which he published the first volume in the following year, was present ; but did not step forth in defence of that species of writing. He probably did not like to *trust* himself with JOHNSON [4] !

Johnson observed, that the force of our early habits was so great, that though reason approved, nay, though our senses relished a different course, almost every man returned to them. I do not believe there is any observation upon human nature better founded than this ; and, in many cases, it is a very painful truth ; for where early habits have been mean and wretched, the joy and elevation resulting from better modes of life, must be damped by the gloomy consciousness of being under an almost inevitable doom to sink back into a situation which we recollect

[1] ' Our silly things called " histories," ' wrote Burke (*Corres.* i. 337). ' The Duke of Richmond, Fox, and Burke,' said Rogers (*Table-Talk*, p. 82), ' were conversing about history, philosophy, and poetry. The Duke said, " I prefer history to philosophy or poetry, because history is *truth*." Both Fox and Burke disagreed with him : they thought that poetry was *truth*, being a representation of human nature.' Lord Bolingbroke had said (*Study Hist.*, ii) that the child ' in riper years applies himself to history, or to that which he takes for history, to authorized romance.'

[2] Mr. Plunket made a great sensation in the House of Commons (Feb. 28, 1825) by saying that history, if not judiciously read, ' was no better than an old almanack,'—which Mercier had already said in his *Nouveau Tableau de Paris*—' Malet du Pan's and such-like histories of the revolution are no better than an old almanack.' Boswell, we see, had anticipated both. CROKER.

[3] ' It was at Rome, on the 15th of October, 1764,' says Gibbon in a famous passage, ' that the idea of

writing the decline and fall of the city first started to my mind.' It was not till towards the end of 1772 that he ' undertook the composition of the first volume.' Gibbon's *Memoirs*, 1900, pp. 167, 189.

[4] See p. 348. BOSWELL. Gibbon, when with Johnson, perhaps felt that timidity which kept him silent in Parliament. ' I was not armed by Nature and education,' he writes, ' with the intrepid energy of mind and voice,

Vincentem strepitus, et natum rebus agendis.

⟨Horace, *Ars Poet.* l. 82.⟩ Timidity was fortified by pride, and even the success of my pen discouraged the trial of my voice.' Gibbon's *Memoirs*, 191. Some years before he entered Parliament, he said that his genius was ' better qualified for the deliberate compositions of the Closet, than for the extemporary discourses of the Parliament. An unexpected objection would disconcert me ; and as I am incapable of explaining to others what I do not thoroughly understand myself, I should be meditating, while I ought to be answering.' *Private Letters*, 1896, i. 23.

with disgust. It surely may be prevented, by constant attention
and unremitting exertion to establish contrary habits of superiour
efficacy.

'The Beggar's Opera,' and the common question, whether it
was pernicious in its effects, having been introduced ;—JOHNSON.
'As to this matter, which has been very much contested, I
myself am of opinion, that more influence has been ascribed to
"The Beggar's Opera," than it in reality ever had ; for I do not
believe that any man was ever made a rogue by being present
at its representation. At the same time I do not deny that it
may have some influence, by making the character of a rogue
familiar, and in some degree pleasing [1].' Then collecting himself, as it were, to give a heavy stroke : 'There is in it such a
labefactation of all principles, as may be injurious to morality.'

While he pronounced this response, we sat in a comical sort
of restraint, smothering a laugh, which we were afraid might
burst out. In his Life of Gay, he has been still more decisive
as to the inefficiency of 'The Beggar's Opera' in corrupting
society [2]. But I have ever thought somewhat differently ; for,
indeed, not only are the gaiety and heroism of a highwayman
very captivating to a youthful imagination, but the arguments
for adventurous depredation are so plausible, the allusions so
lively, and the contrasts with the ordinary and more painful
modes of acquiring property are so artfully displayed, that it
requires a cool and strong judgement to resist so imposing an

---

[1] A very eminent physician, whose
discernment is as acute and penetrating in judging of the human character as it is in his own profession,
remarked once at a club where I was,
that a lively young man, fond of
pleasure, and without money, would
hardly resist a solicitation from his
mistress to go upon the highway,
immediately after being present at
the representation of 'The Beggar's
Opera.' I have been told of an ingenious observation by Mr. Gibbon,
that '"The Beggar's Opera" may, perhaps, have sometimes increased the
number of highwaymen ; but that it
has had a beneficial effect in refining
that class of men, making them less
ferocious, more polite, in short, more
like gentlemen.' Upon this Mr.
Courtenay said, that 'Gay was the
Orpheus of highwaymen.' BOSWELL.

[2] 'The play, like many others, was
plainly written only to divert, without
any moral purpose, and is therefore
not likely to do good ; nor can it be
conceived, without more speculation
than life requires or admits, to be pro-
ductive of much evil. Highwaymen
and house-breakers seldom frequent
the play-house, or mingle in any
elegant diversion ; nor is it possible
for any one to imagine that he may
rob with safety, because he sees Macheath reprieved upon the stage.' *Life
of Gay*, 22. ⟨Sir John Fielding and

aggregate : yet, I own, I should be very sorry to have ' The Beggar's Opera ' suppressed ; for there is in it so much of real London life, so much brilliant wit, and such a variety of airs, which, from early association of ideas, engage, soothe, and enliven the mind, that no performance which the theatre exhibits, delights me more.

The late ' *worthy* ' Duke of Queensberry [1], as Thomson, in his ' Seasons,' justly characterises him, told me, that when Gay first shewed him ' The Beggar's Opera,' his Grace's observation was, ' This is a very odd thing, Gay ; I am satisfied that it is either a very good thing, or a very bad thing.' It proved the former, beyond the warmest expectations of the authour or his friends. Mr. Cambridge, however, shewed us to day, that there was good reason enough to doubt concerning its success. He was told by Quin, that during the first night of its appearance it was long in a very dubious state ; that there was a disposition to damn it, and that it was saved by the song [2],

> ' Oh ponder well ! be not severe ! '

the audience being much affected by the innocent looks of Polly, when she came to those two lines, which exhibit at once a painful and ridiculous image,

> ' For on the rope that hangs my Dear,
> Depends poor Polly's life.'

Quin himself had so bad an opinion of it, that he refused the part of Captain Macheath, and gave it to Walker [3], who

Sir John Hawkins, both magistrates, reported that the play had caused an increase in crime. See Dr. Hill's notes on this passage.⟩

[1] ' The worthy Queensb'ry yet laments his Gay.'
The Seasons. Summer, l. 1422. Pope (*Epistle to Arbuthnot*, l. 260) says :—
' Of all thy blameless life the sole return
My Verse, and Queensb'ry weeping o'er thy urn ! '
Johnson (*Life of Gay*, 24) mentions ' the affectionate attention of the duke and dutchess of Queensberry, into whose

house he was taken, and with whom he passed the remaining part of his life.' Smollett, in *Humphry Clinker*, in the letters of Sept. 12 and 15, speaks of the Duke as ' one of the best men that ever breathed,' ' one of those few noblemen whose goodness of heart does honour to human nature.' He died in 1778.

[2] The twelfth air in act i.

[3] ' In several parts of tragedy,' writes Tom Davies, ' Walker's look, deportment, and action gave a distinguished glare to tyrannic rage.' Davies's *Garrick*, i. 24.

acquired great celebrity by his grave yet animated performance of it [1].

We talked of a young gentleman's marriage with an eminent singer [2], and his determination that she should no longer sing in publick, though his father was very earnest she should, because her talents would be liberally rewarded, so as to make her a good fortune. It was questioned whether the young gentleman, who had not a shilling in the world [3], but was blest with very uncommon talents, was not foolishly delicate, or foolishly proud, and his father truely rational without being mean. Johnson, with all the high spirit of a Roman senator, exclaimed, ' He resolved wisely and nobly to be sure. He is a brave man. Would not a gentleman be disgraced by having his wife singing publickly for hire? No, Sir, there can be no doubt here. I know not if I should not *prepare* myself for a publick singer, as readily as let my wife be one.'

Johnson arraigned the modern politicks of this country, as entirely devoid of all principle of whatever kind. ' Politicks (said he) are now nothing more than means of rising in the world. With this sole view do men engage in politicks, and their whole conduct proceeds upon it. How different in that respect is the state of the nation now from what it was in the time of Charles the First, during the Usurpation, and after the Restoration, in the time of Charles the Second. Hudibras affords a strong proof how much hold political principles had then upon the minds of men. There is in Hudibras a great deal of bullion which will always last. But to be sure the brightest

---

[1] Pope said of himself and Swift: —' Neither of us thought it would succeed. We shewed it to Congreve, who . . . said, " It would either take greatly, or be damned confoundedly." We were all at the first night of it, in great uncertainty of the event ; till we were very much encouraged by over-hearing the Duke of Argyle . . . say, " It will do,—it must do !—I see it in the eyes of them ! " This was a good while before the first act was over, and so gave us ease soon ; for the duke . . . has a more particular knack than any one now living, in discover-

ing the taste of the public. He was quite right in this, as usual ; the good nature of the audience appeared stronger and stronger every act, and ended in a clamour of applause.' Spence's *Anec.* p. 159. See *The Dunciad*, iii. 330, and *post*, iii. 321.

[2] ⟨Sheridan & his 1st Wife. Mrs. Piozzi. Marg. note in 1816 ed.⟩ R. B. Sheridan married Miss Linley on 13 April, 1773. ⟨See App. B, p. 521.⟩

[3] His wife had £3000, settled on her by ' an old gentleman of considerable fortune ' to whom she had been engaged. Moore's *Sheridan*, i. 41.

strokes of his wit owed their force to the impression of the characters, which was upon men's minds at the time ; to their knowing them, at table and in the street ; in short, being familiar with them ; and above all, to his satire being directed against those whom a little while before they had hated and feared [1]. The nation in general has ever been loyal, has been at all times attached to the monarch, though a few daring rebels have been wonderfully powerful for a time. The murder of Charles the First was undoubtedly not committed with the approbation or consent of the people. Had that been the case, Parliament would not have ventured to consign the regicides to their deserved punishment. And we know what exuberance of joy there was when Charles the Second was restored. If Charles the Second had bent all his mind to it, had made it his sole object, he might have been as absolute as Louis the Fourteenth.' A gentleman observed he would have done no harm if he had. JOHNSON. ' Why, Sir, absolute princes seldom do any harm. But they who are governed by them are governed by chance. There is no security for good government.' CAMBRIDGE. ' There have been many sad victims to absolute power [a].' JOHNSON. ' So, Sir, have there been to popular factions.' BOSWELL. ' The question is, which is worst, one wild beast or many ? '

Johnson praised ' THE SPECTATOR,' particularly the character of Sir Roger de Coverley. He said, ' Sir Roger did not die a violent death, as has been generally fancied. He was not killed ; he died only because others were to die, and because his death afforded an opportunity to Addison for some very fine writing. We have the example of Cervantes making Don Quixote die [2].—I never could see why Sir Roger is represented

---

[a] power 1 : government (*by parablepsy*) 2, 3.

[1] ' Those who had felt the mischiefs of discord, and the tyranny of usurpation, read *Hudibras* with rapture, for every line brought back to memory something known, and gratified resentment, by the just censure of something hated. But the book which was once quoted by Princes, and which supplied conversation to all the assemblies of the gay and witty, is now seldom mentioned, and even by those that affect to mention it, is seldom read.' *Idler*, No. 59.

[2] In his *Life of Addison*, 48, Johnson says :—' The reason which induced Cervantes to bring his hero to the grave, *para mi solo nacio Don Quixote, y yo para el* [for me alone was Don Quixote born, and I for him], made Addison declare, with undue vehemence of expression, that he would kill Sir Roger ; being of

as a little cracked. It appears to me that the story of the widow was intended to have something superinduced upon it : but the superstructure did not come [1].'

Somebody found fault with writing verses in a dead language, maintaining that they were merely arrangements of so many words, and laughed at the Universities of Oxford and Cambridge, for sending forth collections of them not only in Greek and Latin, but even in Syriack, Arabick, and other more unknown tongues. JOHNSON. ' I would have as many of these as possible ; I would have verses in every language that there are the means of acquiring. Nobody imagines that an University is to have at once two hundred poets ; but it should be able to show two hundred scholars. Pieresc's [2] death was lamented, I think, in forty languages. And I would have [a] at every coronation, and every death of a King, every *Gaudium*, and every *Luctus*, University-verses, in as many languages as can be acquired. I would have the world to be thus told, " Here is a school where every thing may be learnt." '

Having set out next day on a visit to the Earl of Pembroke, at Wilton [3], and to my friend, Mr. Temple [4], at Mamhead, in Devonshire, and not having returned to town till the second of May, I did not see Dr. Johnson for a considerable time, and during the remaining part of my stay in London, kept very

[a] have 1: have had 2, 3.

opinion that they were born for one another, and that any other hand would do him wrong.'

[1] ' It may be doubted whether Addison ever filled up his original delineation. He describes his Knight as having his imagination somewhat warped ; but of this perversion he has made very little use.' *Ibid*. 49.

[2] ' The Papers left in the closet of Pieresc supplied his heirs with a whole winter's fuel.' *The Idler*, No. 65. ' A chamber in his house filled with letters from the most eminent scholars of the age was discovered : the learned in Europe had addressed Pieresc in their difficulties, who was hence called " the Avocat general of the republic of letters." Such was the disposition of his niece, that

although entreated to permit them to be published, she preferred to regale herself occasionally with burning these learned epistles to save the expense of fire-wood.' D'Israeli's *Curios. Lit.* i. 78. ⟨See App. B, p. 521.⟩

[3] Boswell was accompanied by Paoli. To justify his visit to London, he said :—' I think it is also for my interest, as in time I may get something. Lord Pembroke was very obliging to me when he was in Scotland, and has corresponded with me since. I have hopes from him.' *Letters*, No. 136, i. 215. See*ib.*,No. 138, p. 220, and *post*, iii. 122, note 2. Walpole described Lord Pembroke in 1764 as ' a young profligate.' *Memoirs of the Reign of George III*, i. 415.

[4] Page 316. BOSWELL.

imperfect notes of his conversation, which had I according to my usual custom written out at large soon after the time †, much might have been preserved, which is now irretrievably lost. I can now only record some particular scenes, and a few fragments of his *memorabilia*. But to make some amends for my relaxation of diligence in one respect, I have to present my readers with arguments upon two law cases, with which he favoured me.

On Saturday, the sixth of May, we dined by ourselves at the Mitre, and he dictated to me what follows, to obviate the complaint already mentioned [1], which had been made in the form of an action in the Court of Session, by Dr. Memis, of Aberdeen, that in the same translation of a charter in which *physicians* were mentioned, he was called *Doctor of Medicine*.

' THERE are but two reasons for which a physician can decline the title of *Doctor of Medicine*, because he supposes himself disgraced by the doctorship, or supposes the doctorship disgraced by himself. To be disgraced by a title which he shares in common with every illustrious name of his profession, with Boerhaave, with Arbuthnot, and with Cullen, can surely diminish no man's reputation. It is, I suppose, to the doctorate, from which he shrinks, that he owes his right of practising physick. A Doctor of Medicine is a physician under the protection of the laws, and by the stamp of authority. The physician who is not a Doctor, usurps a profession, and is authorised only by himself to decide upon health and sickness, and life and death. That this gentleman is a Doctor, his diploma makes evident ; a diploma not obtruded upon him, but obtained by solicitation, and for which fees were paid. With what countenance any man can refuse the title which he has either begged or bought, is not easily discovered.

' All verbal injury must comprise in it either some false position, or some unnecessary declaration of defamatory truth. That in calling him Doctor, a false appellation was given him, he himself will not pretend, who at the same time that he complains of the title, would be offended if we supposed him to be not a Doctor. If the title of Doctor be a defamatory truth, it is time to dissolve our colleges ; for why should the publick give salaries to men whose approbation is reproach ? It may likewise deserve the notice of the publick to consider what help can be given to the professors of physick, who all share with this unhappy gentleman the ignominious appellation, and of whom the very boys in the street are not afraid to say, *There goes the Doctor*.

† ⟨See *Boswell Papers*, vi. 24.⟩   [1] Page 291. BOSWELL.

' What is implied by the term Doctor is well known. It distinguishes him to whom it is granted, as a man who has attained such knowledge of his profession as qualifies him to instruct others. A Doctor of Laws is a man who can form lawyers by his precepts. A Doctor of Medicine is a man who can teach the art of curing diseases. There is an old axiom which no man has yet thought fit to deny, *Nil dat quod non habet*. Upon this principle to be Doctor implies skill, for *nemo docet quod non didicit*. In England, whoever practises physick, not being a Doctor, must practise by a licence : but the doctorate conveys a licence in itself.

' By what accident it happened that he and the other physicians were mentioned in different terms, where the terms themselves were equivalent, or where in effect that which was applied to him was the more[a] honourable, perhaps they who wrote the paper cannot now remember. Had they expected a lawsuit to have been the consequence of such petty variation, I hope they would have avoided it [1]. But, probably, as they meant no ill, they suspected no danger, and, therefore, consulted only what appeared to them propriety or convenience.'

A few days afterwards I consulted him upon a cause, *Paterson and others* against *Alexander and others*, which had been decided by a casting vote in the Court of Session, determining that the Corporation of Stirling was corrupt, and setting aside the election of some of their officers, because it was proved that three of the leading men who influenced the majority, had entered into an unjustifiable compact, of which, however, the majority were ignorant. He dictated to me, after a little consideration, the following sentences upon the subject :

' THERE is a difference between majority and superiority ; majority is applied to number, and superiority to power ; and power, like many other things, is to be estimated *non numero sed pondere*. Now though the greater *number* is not corrupt, the greater *weight* is corrupt, so that corruption predominates in the borough, taken *collectively*, though, perhaps, taken *numerically*, the greater part may be uncorrupt. That borough, which is so constituted as to act corruptly, is in the eye of reason corrupt, whether it be by the uncontrolable power of a few, or by an accidental pravity of the multitude. The objection, in which is urged the injustice of making the innocent suffer with the guilty, is an objection not only against society, but against the possibility of society.

<hr>

[a] more 1 : most 2, 3.

[1] In justice to Dr. Memis, though I was against him as an Advocate, I must mention, that he objected to the variation very earnestly, before the translation was printed off. BOSWELL.

All societies, great and small, subsist upon this condition ; that as the individuals derive advantages from union, they may likewise suffer inconveniences ; that as those who do nothing, and sometimes those who do ill, will have the honours and emoluments of general virtue and general prosperity, so those likewise who do nothing, or perhaps do well, must be involved in the consequences of predominant corruption.'

This in my opinion was a very nice case ; but the decision was affirmed in the House of Lords.

On Monday, May 8, we went together and visited the mansions of Bedlam [1]. I had been informed that he had once been there before with Mr. Wedderburne, (now Lord Loughborough,) Mr. Murphy, and Mr. Foote ; and I had heard Foote give a very entertaining account of Johnson's happening to have his attention arrested by a man who was very furious, and who, while beating his straw [2], supposed it to be [a] William Duke of Cumberland, whom he was punishing for his cruelties in Scotland, in

a to be 1 ; was 2, 3.

[1] Croker quotes *The World* of June 7, 1753, p. 137, where a Londoner writes, ' to gratify the curiosity of a country friend, I accompanied him a few weeks ago to Bedlam.... It was in the Easter week . . . ; when to my great surprise, I found a hundred people at least, who, having paid their twopence a piece, were suffered unattended to run rioting up and down the wards, making sport . . . of the miserable inhabitants. . . . I saw the spectators in a loud laugh of triumph at the ravings they had occasioned.' Young (*Universal Passion*, Sat. v. ll. 17–24) describes Britannia's daughters
' As unreserv'd, and beauteous, as the sun,
Through every sign of vanity they run ;
Assemblies, parks, coarse feasts in city halls,
Lectures, and trials, plays, committees, balls ;
Wells, Bedlams, executions, Smithfield scenes,
And fortune-tellers' caves, and lions' dens.'

In 1749, William Hutton walked from Nottingham to London, passed three days there in looking about, and returned on foot. The whole journey cost him ten shillings and eight-pence. He says :—' I wished to see a number of curiosities, but my shallow pocket forbade. *One penny, to see Bedlam, was all I could spare.*' Hutton's *Life*, pp. 71, 74. Richardson (*Familiar Letters*, No. 153) makes a young lady describe her visit to Bedlam :—' The distemper'd fancies of the miserable patients most unaccountably provoked mirth, and loud laughter ; nay, so shamefully inhuman were some, among whom (I am sorry to say it !) were several of my own sex, as to endeavour to provoke the patients into rage to make them sport.' ⟨For ' the beautiful new buildings ' near it, see *post*, iv. 208.⟩

[2] In the *Life of Dryden*, 206, Johnson writes :—' Virgil would have been too hasty if he had condemned him [Statius] to straw for one sounding line.' In *Humphry Clinker* (Letter

1746.[1] There was nothing peculiarly remarkable this day ; but the general contemplation of insanity was very affecting. I accompanied him home, and dined and drank tea with him.

Talking of an acquaintance of ours [2], distinguished for knowing an uncommon variety of miscellaneous articles both in antiquities and polite literature, he observed, ' You know, Sir, he runs about with little weight upon his mind.' And talking of another very ingenious gentleman [3], who from the warmth of his temper was at variance with many of his acquaintance, and wished to avoid them, he said, ' Sir, he leads the life of an outlaw.'

On Friday, May 12 [4], as he had been so good as to assign

---

iii. of June 10), Mr. Bramble says to Clinker :—' The sooner you lose your senses entirely, the better for yourself and the community. In that case, some charitable person might provide you with a dark room and clean straw in Bedlam.' Churchill, in *Independence* (lines 317–18), writes :—

' To Bethlem with him—give him whips and straw—
I'm very sensible he's mad in Law.'

[1] My very honourable friend General Sir George Howard, who served in the Duke of Cumberland's army, has assured me that the cruelties were not imputable to his Royal Highness. BOSWELL.

Walpole shews the Duke's cruelty to his own soldiers. ' In the late Rebellion, some recruits had been raised under a positive engagement of dismission at the end of three years. When the term was expired, they thought themselves at liberty, and some of them quitted the corps. . . . The Duke ordered them to be tried as deserters ; and not having received a legal discharge, they were condemned. Nothing could mollify him ; two were executed.' *Memoirs of the Reign of George II*, ii. 203.

[2] Mr. Croker suggested that this is Dr. Percy (see *ante*, i. 486), but Percy was more than ' an acquaintance of ours,' he was a friend.

[3] No doubt Mr. George Steevens. CROKER. See *post*, iii. 281 ; iv. 178, 274.

[4] On this day Johnson wrote to Mrs. Thrale :—' Boswell has made me promise not to go to Oxford till he leaves London ; I had no great reason for haste, and therefore might as well gratify a friend. I am always proud and pleased to have my company desired. Boswell would have thought my absence a loss, and I knew not who else would have considered my presence as profit. He has entered himself at the Temple, and I joined in his bond. He is to plead before the Lords, and hopes very nearly to gain the cost of his journey. He lives much with his friend Paoli.' *Letters*, No. 390. Boswell wrote to Temple on June 6 : —' For the last fortnight that I was in London . . . I lay at Paoli's house, and had the command of his coach. . . . I felt more dignity when I had several servants at my devotion, a large apartment, and the convenience and state of a coach. I recollected that this *dignity in London* was honourably acquired by my travels abroad and my pen after I came home ; so I could enjoy it with my own approbation.' *Letters*, No. 146, i. 230. A year later he records, that henceforth, while in London, he was Paoli's constant guest

me a room in his house, where I might sleep occasionally, when I happened to sit with him to a late hour, I took possession of it this night, found every thing in excellent order, and was attended by honest Francis with a most civil assiduity. I asked Johnson whether I might go to a consultation with another lawyer upon Sunday, as that appeared to me to be doing work as much in my way, as if an artisan should work on the day appropriated for religious rest. JOHNSON. ' Why, Sir, when you are of consequence enough to oppose the practice of consulting upon Sunday, you should do it : but you may go now. It is not criminal, though it is not what one should do, who is anxious for the preservation and increase of piety, to which a peculiar observance of Sunday is a great help. The distinction is clear between what is of moral and what is of ritual obligation.'

On Saturday, May 13, I breakfasted with him by invitation, accompanied by Mr. Andrew Crosbie [1], a Scotch Advocate, whom he had seen at Edinburgh, and the Hon. Colonel (now General) Edward Stopford, brother to Lord Courtown, who was desirous of being introduced to him. His tea and rolls and butter, and whole breakfast apparatus were all in such decorum, and his behaviour was so courteous, that Colonel Stopford was quite surprized, and wondered at his having heard so much said of Johnson's slovenliness and roughness. I have preserved nothing of what passed, except that Crosbie pleased him much by talking learnedly of alchymy, as to which Johnson was not a positive unbeliever, but rather delighted in considering what progress had actually been made in the transmutation of metals, what near approaches there had been to the making of gold ; and

---

till he had a house of his own there (*post*, iii. 34).

[1] Lord Stowell told Mr. Croker that, among the Scottish *literati*, Mr. Crosbie was the only man who was disposed to *stand up* to Johnson. Croker's *Boswell*, p. 270. It is said that he was the original of Mr. Counsellor Pleydell in Scott's novel of *Guy Mannering*. Dr. A. Carlyle (*Auto*. p. 420) says of ' the famous club called The Poker,' which was

founded in Edinburgh in 1762 :—' In a laughing humour, Andrew Crosbie was chosen Assassin, in case any officer of that sort should be needed ; but David Hume was added as his Assessor, without whose assent nothing should be done, so that between *plus* and *minus* there was likely to be no bloodshed.' See *post*, v. 45. ⟨Crosbie was distantly related to Boswell, his uncle-in-law, Charles Erskine, Lord Tinwald, being the uncle of Boswell's told us that it was affirmed, that a person in the Russian dominions had discovered the secret, but died without revealing it, as imagining it would be prejudicial to society. He added, that it was not impossible but it might in time be generally known.

It being asked whether it was reasonable for a man to be angry at another whom a woman had preferred to him ;— JOHNSON. ' I do not see, Sir, that it is reasonable for a man to be angry at another, whom a woman has preferred to him : but angry he is, no doubt ; and he is loath to be angry at himself.'

Before setting out for Scotland on the 23d [1], I was frequently in his company at different places, but during this period have recorded only two remarks : one concerning Garrick : ' He has not Latin enough. He finds out the Latin by the meaning,[a] rather than the meaning by the Latin [2].' And another concerning writers of travels, who, he observed, ' were more defective than any other writers [3].'

[a] *comma omitted* 2, 3.

mother. See F. Miller, *Andrew Crosbie*, 1925. John Ramsay of Ochtertyre has left a good account of him. See *Scotland and Scotsmen in the 18th C.*, 1888, i. 449 ff.〉

[1] He left on the 22nd. ' Boswel,' wrote Johnson to Mrs. Thrale on May 22, ' went away at two this morning. . . . He got two-and-forty guineas in fees while he was here. He has, by his Wife's persuasion and mine, taken down a present for his Mother-in-law.' *Letters*, No. 395. Boswell, the evening of the same day, wrote to Temple from Grantham :— ' I have now eat a term's commons in the Inner Temple. You cannot imagine what satisfaction I had in the form and ceremony of *the Hall*. . . . After breakfasting with PAOLI, and worshipping at St. Paul's, I dined *tête-à-tête* with my charming Mrs. Stuart. . . . We talked with unreserved freedom, as we had nothing to fear. We were *philosophical*, upon honour— not deep, but feeling. We were pious. We drank tea, and bid each other

adieu as finely as romance paints. She is my wife's dearest friend. So you see how beautiful our intimacy is. I then went to Mr. Johnson and he accompanied me to Dilly's, where we supt, and then he went with me to the inn in Holborn, whence the Newcastle fly sets out. We were warmly affectionate. He is to buy for me a chest of books of his chusing off stalls, and I am to read more and drink less. That was his counsel.' *Boswell's Letters*, No. 142, i. 226.

[2] Yet Gilbert Walmesley had called him in his youth ' a good scholar.' *Garrick Corres.* i. 1 ; and Boswell wrote to him (11 April 1774) :—' Mr. Johnson is ready to bruise any one who calls in question your classical knowledge and your happy application of it.' *Boswell's Letters*, No. 124, i. 202.

[3] ' Those whose lot it is to ramble can seldom write, and those who know how to write very seldom ramble.' Johnson to Mrs. Thrale. *Letters*, No. 236. See *post*, iii. 301.

I passed many hours with him on the 17th [1], of which I find all my memorial is, ' much laughing.' It should seem he had that day been in a humour for jocularity and merriment, and upon such occasions I never knew a man laugh more heartily. We may suppose, that the high relish of a state so different from his habitual gloom, produced more than ordinary exertions of that distinguishing faculty of man, which has puzzled philosophers so much to explain [2]. Johnson's laugh was as remarkable as any circumstance in his manner. It was a kind of good humoured growl. Tom Davies described it drolly enough : ' He laughs like a rhinoceros.'

[1] A letter from Boswell to Temple on this day helps to fill up the gap in his journal :—' It gives me acute pain that I have not written more to you since we parted last. But I have been like a skiff on the sea, driven about by a multiplicity of waves. I am now at Mr. Thrale's villa at Streatham—a delightful spot. Dr. Johnson is here too. I came yesterday to dinner, and this morning Dr. Johnson and I return to London, and I go with Mr. Beauclerc to see his elegant villa and library, worth £3,000, at Muswell Hill . . ., and return and dine with him. I hope Dr. Johnson will dine with us. I am in that dissipated state of mind that I absolutely cannot write. I at least imagine so. But while I glow with gayety, I feel friendship for you, nay, admiration of some of your qualities, as strong as you could wish. My excellent friend ! let us ever cultivate that mutual regard which, as it has lasted till now, will, I trust, never fail. . . . On Saturday last, I dined with John Wilkes and his daughter and nobody else at the Mansion-House. It was a most pleasant scene. I had that day breakfasted with Dr. Johnson. I drank tea with Lord Bute's daughter-in-law, and I supped with Miss Bosville. What variety ! Mr. Johnson went with me to Beauclerc's villa, Beauclerc having been ill. It is delightful. Just as at Highgate. He has one of the most numerous and splen-

did private libraries that I ever saw. Greenhouses, hothouse, observatory, laboratory for chymical experiments— in short every thing princely. We dined with him at his house in the Adelphi. . . . I have promised to Dr. Johnson to read when I get to Scotland and to keep an account of what I read. I shall let you know how I go on. My mind must be nourished.' *Letters*, No. 141, i. 223–4.

[2] Swift did not laugh. ' He had a countenance sour and severe, which he seldom softened by any appearance of gaiety. He stubbornly resisted any tendency to laughter.' Johnson's *Life of Swift*, 122. Neither did Pope laugh. ' By no merriment, either of others or his own, was he ever seen excited to laughter.' Ib. *Pope*, 266. Lord Chesterfield wrote (*Letters*, i. 269) :—' How low and unbecoming a thing laughter is. . . . I am sure that, since I have had the full use of my reason, nobody has ever heard me laugh.' Mrs. Piozzi records (*Anec.* p. 298 : John. Misc. i. 345) that ' Mr. Johnson used to say " that the size of a man's understanding might always be justly measured by his mirth ; " ' and his own was never contemptible.' ⟨Hannah More, writing in 1776, says : ' Johnson and Garrick began a close encounter, telling old stories, " e'en from their boyish days," at Lichfield. We all stood round them above an hour,

' To BENNET LANGTON, ESQ.

' DEAR SIR,
  ' I HAVE an old amanuensis [1] in great distress. I have given what
I think I can give, and begged till I cannot tell where to beg again. I
put into his hands this morning four guineas. If you could collect
three guineas more, it would clear him from his present difficulty.
                              ' I am, Sir,
                                  ' Your most humble servant,
                                        ' SAM. JOHNSON.'

' May 21, 1775.'
                          ' To JAMES BOSWELL, ESQ.

' DEAR SIR,
  ' I MAKE no doubt but you are now safely lodged in your own
habitation, and have told all your adventures to Mrs. Boswell and Miss
Veronica. Pray teach Veronica to love me. Bid her not mind
mamma.
  ' Mrs. Thrale has taken cold, and been very much disordered, but I
hope is grown well. Mr. Langton went yesterday to Lincolnshire, and
has invited Nicolaida [2] to follow him. Beauclerk talks of going to
Bath. I am to set out on Monday; so there is nothing but
dispersion.
  ' I have returned Lord Hailes's entertaining sheets [3], but must stay till
I come back for more, because it will be inconvenient to send them
after me in my vagrant state.

laughing in defiance of every rule of
decorum and Chesterfield.' *Memoirs*,
i. 70.⟩ See *ante*, ii. 231, 262.
  [1] The day before he wrote to Mrs.
Thrale :—' Peyton and Macbean
[*ante*, i. 187] are both starving, and
I cannot keep them.' *Letters*, No.
393. On April 1, 1776, he wrote :—
' Poor Peyton expired this morning.
He probably during many years, for
which he sat starving by the bed of
a wife, not only useless but almost
motionless, condemned by poverty to
personal attendance, and by the necessity of such attendance chained down
to poverty—he probably thought often
how lightly he should tread the path
of life without his burthen. Of this
thought the admission was unavoid-
able, and the indulgence might be
forgiven to frailty and distress. His
wife died at last, and before she was

buried he was seized by a fever, and
is now going to the grave. Such
miscarriages, when they happen to
those on whom many eyes are fixed,
fill histories and tragedies ; and tears
have been shed for the sufferings, and
wonder excited by the fortitude of
those who neither did nor suffered
more than Peyton.' *Ib.* No. 467.
Baretti, in a marginal note on the first
letter, writes :—' Peyton was a fool
and a drunkard. I never saw so
nauseous a fellow.' But Baretti was
a harsh judge.
  [2] A learned Greek. BOSWELL.
Parr became acquainted with ' Mr.
Nicoläides, a learned Greek, nephew
of the Patriarch of Constantinople,
who fled from some massacre of the
Greeks.' Johnstone's *Life of Parr*,
i. 84. ⟨See *Johnsonian Misc.* i. 103.⟩
  [3] See *ante*, ii. 278.

' I promised Mrs. Macaulay [1] that I would try to serve her son at Oxford. I have not forgotten it, nor am unwilling to perform it. If they desire to give him an English education, it should be considered whether they cannot send him for a year or two to an English school. If he comes immediately from Scotland, he can make no figure in our Universities. The schools in the north, I believe, are cheap ; and, when I was a young man, were eminently good.

' There are two little books published by the Foulis [2], Telemachus and Collins's Poems, each a shilling ; I would be glad to have them.

' Make my compliments to Mrs. Boswell, though she does not love me. You see what perverse things ladies are, and how little fit to be trusted with feudal estates. When she mends and loves me, there may be more hope of her daughters.

' I will not send compliments to my friends by name, because I would be loath to leave any out in the enumeration. Tell them, as you see them, how well I speak of Scotch politeness, and Scotch hospitality, and Scotch beauty, and of every thing Scotch, but Scotch oat-cakes, and Scotch prejudices.

' Let me know the answer of Rasay [3], and the decision relating to Sir Allan [4].

<blockquote>
' I am, my dearest Sir, with great affection,
' Your most obliged, and
' Most humble servant,
' SAM. JOHNSON.'
</blockquote>

' May 27, 1775.'

After my return to Scotland, I wrote three letters to him, from which I extract the following passages :

' I have seen Lord Hailes since I came down. He thinks it wonderful that you are pleased to take so much pains in revising his " Annals ". I told him that you said you were well rewarded by the entertainment which you had in reading them.'

' There has been a numerous flight of Hebrideans in Edinburgh this summer, whom I have been happy to entertain at my house. Mr. Donald Macqueen [5] and Lord Monboddo supped with me one evening.

---

[1] Wife of the Reverend Mr. Kenneth Macaulay, authour of ' The History of St. Kilda.' BOSWELL. See *post*, v. 122.

[2] ' The Elzevirs of Glasgow,' as Boswell called them. *Post*, v. 370.

[3] See *post*, v. 412.

[4] A law-suit carried on by Sir Allan Maclean, Chief of his Clan, to recover certain parts of his family estates from the Duke of Argyle. BOSWELL.

[5] A very learned minister in the Isle of Sky, whom both Dr. Johnson and I have mentioned with regard. BOSWELL.
See *post*, v. 150, and Johnson's *Journey Western Isl.*, 1924, 52. Johnson in another passage, (*ib.* 107), speaks of

They joined in controverting your proposition, that the Gaelick of the Highlands and Isles of Scotland was not written till of late.'

' My mind has been somewhat dark this summer [1]. I have need of your warming and vivifying rays ; and I hope I shall have them frequently. I am going to pass some time with my father at Auchinleck.'

' To JAMES BOSWELL, ESQ.

' DEAR SIR,

' I AM now [a] returned from the annual ramble into the middle counties [2].

a now *omitted* 2, 3.

him as ' a very learned Minister. . . . He wished me to be deceived [as regards Ossian], for the honour of his country ; but would not directly and formally deceive me.' Johnson told him this to his face. *Post*, v. 240. His credulity is shewn by the belief he held, that the name of a place called *Ainnit* in Skye was the same as the *Anaitidis delubrum* in Lydia. *Ib.* 220.

[1] This darkness is seen in his letters. He wrote ' June 3, 1775. It required some philosophy to bear the change from England to Scotland. The unpleasing tone, the rude familiarity, the barren conversation of those whom I found here, in comparison with what I had left, really hurt my feelings. . . . The General Assembly is sitting; and I practise at its bar. There is *de facto* something low and coarse in such employment, though *upon paper*, it is a *Supreme Judicature*. But guineas must be had. . . . Do you know it requires more than ordinary spirit to do what I am to do this very morning ? I am to go to the General Assembly and arraign a judgement pronounced last year by Dr. Robertson, John Home, and a good many more of them ; and they are to appear on the other side. To speak well, when I despise both the cause and the judges, is difficult. But I believe I shall do wonderfully. I look forward with aversion to the dull labour of the Court of Session. You see, Temple,

I have my troubles as well as you have. My promise under the venerable yew has kept me sober.' *Letters*, No. 145, i. 229. On June 19, he is ' vexed to think myself a coarse labourer in an obscure corner. . . . Mr. Hume says there will in all probability be a change of the ministry soon, which he regrets. O Temple, while they change so often, how does one feel an ambition to have a share in the great department. . . . My father is most unhappily dissatisfied with me. . . . He harps on my going over Scotland with a *brute* (think how *shockingly* erroneous), and wandering (or some such phrase) to London.' *Ib.* No. 147, p. 231. 'Aug. 12. I have had a pretty severe return this summer of that melancholy or hypochondria, which is inherent in my constitution. . . . While afflicted with melancholy, all the doubts which have ever disturbed thinking men, come upon me. I awake in the night, dreading annihilation or being thrown into some horrible state of being.' He recounts a complimentary letter he had received from Lord Mayor Wilkes, and continues :—' Tell me, my dear Temple, if a man who receives so many marks of more than ordinary consideration can be satisfied to drudge in an obscure corner, where the manners of the people are disagreeable to him?' *Ib.* No. 148, pp. 236 ff.

[2] He was absent from the end of May till some time in August. He

Having seen nothing I had not seen before, I have nothing to relate. Time has left that part of the island few antiquities ; and commerce has left the people no singularities. I was glad to go abroad, and, perhaps, glad to come home ; which is, in other words, I was, I am afraid, weary of being at home, and weary of being abroad. Is not this the state of life ? But, if we confess this weariness, let us not lament it ; for all the wise and all the good say, that we may cure it.

' For the black fumes which rise in your mind, I can prescribe nothing but that you disperse them by honest business or innocent pleasure, and by reading, sometimes easy and sometimes serious. Change of place is useful ; and I hope that your residence at Auchinleck will have many good effects [1]. * * * * * *

' That I should have given pain to Rasay [2], I am sincerely sorry ; and wrote from Oxford on June 1 :— ' Don't suppose that I live here as we live at Streatham. I went this morning to the chapel at six.' *Letters*, No. 399. He was the guest of Mr. Coulson, a Fellow of University College. On June 6, he wrote :— ' Such is the uncertainty of all human things, that Mr. C⟨oulson⟩ has quarrelled with me. He says, I raise the laugh upon him, and he is an independent man, and all he has is his own, and he is not used to such things.' *Ib.* No. 401. An eye-witness * told Mr. Croker that ' Coulson was going out on a country living, and talking of it with the same pomp, as to Lord Stowell.' [He had expressed to him ' his doubts whether, after living so long in the *great world*, he might not grow weary of the comparative retirement of a country parish'. Croker's *Boswell*, p. 425.] Johnson chose to imagine his becoming an archdeacon, and made himself merry —at Coulson's expense ; at last they got to warm words, and Johnson concluded the debate by exclaiming emphatically—' Sir, having meant you no offence, I will make you no apology.' *Ib.* p. 458. The quarrel was made up, for the next day he wrote :—' C⟨oulson⟩ and I are pretty well again.' *Letters*, No. 403.

2 :—' It is hardly credible how difficult it is for a man of my sensibility to support existence in the family where I now am. My father, whom I really both respect and *affectionate* (if that is a word ; for it is a different feeling from that which is expressed by *love*, which I can say of you from my soul), is so different from me— we *divaracate* so much, as Dr. Johnson said—that I am often hurt, when, I dare say, he means no harm, and he has a method of treating me, which makes me *feel* myself like *a timid boy*, which to *Boswell* (comprehending all that my character does, in my own imagination and in that of a wonderful number of mankind) is intollerable. His wife, too, whom in my conscience I cannot condemn for any capital bad quality, is so narrow-minded, and, I don't know how, so set upon keeping him totally under her own management, and so suspicious, and so sowrishly tempered, that it requires the utmost exertion of practical philosophy to keep myself quiet. I, however, have done so all this week, to admiration, nay, I have appeared good-humoured ; but it has cost me drinking a considerable quantity of strong beer to dull my faculties.' *Letters*, No. 149, i. 240.

2 ⟨See *post*, v. 412, n. 2, and Johnson's *Letters*, No. 390.⟩

1 Boswell wrote to Temple on Sept.

* Dr. Philip Fisher (*ante*, ii. 268 n. 2).

am therefore very much pleased that he is no longer uneasy. He still thinks that I have represented him as personally giving up the Chieftainship. I meant only that it was no longer contested between the two houses, and supposed it settled, perhaps, by the cession of some remote generation, in the house of Dunvegan. I am sorry the advertisement was not continued for three or four times in the papers.

' That Lord Monboddo and Mr. Macqueen should controvert a position contrary to the imaginary interest of literary or national prejudice, might be easily imagined ; but of a standing fact there ought to be no controversy : If there are men with tails, catch an *homo caudatus* ; if there was writing of old in the Highlands or Hebrides, in the Erse language, produce the manuscripts. Where men write, they will write to one another, and some of their letters, in families studious of their ancestry, will be kept. In Wales there are many manuscripts.

' I have now three parcels of Lord Hailes's history, which I purpose to return all the next week : that his respect for my little observations should keep his work in suspense, makes one of the evils of my journey. It is in our language, I think, a new mode of history, which tells all that is wanted, and, I suppose, all that is known, without laboured splendour of language, or affected subtilty of conjecture. The exactness of his dates raises my wonder. He seems to have the closeness of Henault [1] without his constraint.

' Mrs. Thrale was so entertained with your " Journal [2]," that she almost read herself blind. She has a great regard for you.

' Of Mrs. Boswell, though she knows in her heart that she does not love me, I am always glad to hear any good, and hope that she and the little dear ladies will have neither sickness nor any other affliction. But she knows that she does not care what becomes of me, and for that she may be sure that I think her very much to blame.

' Never, my dear Sir, do you take it into your head to think that I

---

[1] Voltaire wrote of Président Hénault : ' Il a été dans l'histoire ce que Fontenelle a été dans la philosophie. Il l'a rendue familière.' *Œuvres*, xiv. 80. ⟨He often spoke in the highest terms of his *Nouvel Abrégé chronologique de l'histoire de France*. M. H. Lion, in a full account of this work, says : ' Jamais auteur n'avait fait entrer plus de matière en un espace si limité et dans un cadre aussi étroit.' *Le Président Hénault*, 1903, p. 300. First published in 1744, editions and continuations followed down to 1836.⟩

[2] My ' Journal of a Tour to the Hebrides,' which that lady read in the original manuscript. BOSWELL. Johnson wrote to Mrs. Thrale, ' May 22, 1775 :—I am not sorry that you read Boswel's journal. Is it not a merry piece ? There is much in it about poor me.' *Letters*, No. 395. ' June 11, 1775. You never told me, and I omitted to enquire, how you were entertained by Boswell's Journal. One would think the man had been hired to be a spy upon me. He was very diligent, and caught opportuni-

do not love you ; you may settle yourself in full confidence both of my
love and my esteem ; I love you as a kind man, I value you as a
worthy man, and hope in time to reverence you as a man of exemplary
piety. I hold you as Hamlet has it, " in my heart of heart [1]," and
therefore, it is little to say, that I am, Sir,

'Your affectionate humble servant,

'London, August 27, 1775.'   'SAM. JOHNSON.'

TO THE SAME.

'SIR,

'IF in these papers,[2] there is little alteration attempted, do not
suppose me negligent. I have read them perhaps more closely than
the rest ; but I find nothing worthy of an objection.

'Write to me soon, and write often, and tell me all your honest
heart.

'I am, Sir,

'Your's affectionately,

'August 30, 1775.'   'SAM. JOHNSON.'

TO THE SAME.

'MY DEAR SIR,

'I NOW write to you, lest in some of your freaks and humours you
should fancy yourself neglected. Such fancies I must entreat you
never to admit, at least never to indulge ; for my regard for you is so
radicated and fixed, that it is become part of my mind, and cannot be
effaced but by some cause uncommonly violent ; therefore, whether I
write or not, set your thoughts at rest. I now write to tell you that
I shall not very soon write again, for I am to set out to-morrow on
another journey.

*   *   *   *   *   *

'Your friends are all well at Streatham, and in Leicester-fields [3].
Make my compliments to Mrs. Boswell, if she is in good humour
with me.

'I am, Sir, &c.

'September 14, 1775.'   'SAM. JOHNSON.'

What he mentions in such light terms as, 'I am to set out
to-morrow on another journey,' I soon afterwards discovered
was no less than a tour to France with Mr. and Mrs. Thrale.

---

ties of writing from time to time.' *Ib.*
No. 405.

[1] *Hamlet*, act iii. sc. 2. ⟨Edd. 2, 3
of the *Life* read ' heart of hearts '.⟩

[2] Another parcel of Lord Hailes's
'Annals of Scotland.' BOSWELL.

[3] Where Sir Joshua Reynolds lived.
BOSWELL.

This was the only time in his life that he went upon the Continent.

' To Mr. Robert Levet.

' Sept. 18 [1], 1775.
Calais.

' Dear Sir,

' We are here in France, after a very pleasing passage of no more than six hours. I know not when I shall write again, and therefore I write now, though you cannot suppose that I have much to say. You have seen France yourself [2]. From this place we are going to Rouen, and from Rouen to Paris, where Mr. Thrale designs to stay about five or six weeks. We have a regular recommendation to the English resident, so we shall not be taken for vagabonds. We think to go one way and return another, and for [a] as much as we can. I will try to speak a little French [3]; I tried hitherto but little, but I spoke sometimes. If I heard better, I suppose I should learn faster. I am, Sir,

' Your humble servant,

' Sam. Johnson.'

To the Same.

' Paris, Oct. 22, 1775.

' Dear Sir,

' We are still here, commonly very busy in looking about us. We have been to-day at Versailles. You have seen it, and I shall not describe it. We came yesterday from Fontainbleau, where the Court is now. We went to see the King and Queen at dinner, and the Queen was so impressed by Miss [4], that she sent one of the Gentlemen to enquire who she was. I find all true that you have ever told me of Paris. Mr. Thrale is very liberal, and keeps us two coaches, and a very fine table; but I think our cookery very bad [5]. Mrs. Thrale got into a convent of English nuns, and I talked with her through the grate, and I am very kindly used by the English Benedictine friars. But upon the whole I cannot make much acquaintance here; and though the churches, palaces, and some private houses are very magnificent, there is no very great pleasure after having seen many, in

[a] *Dr. Birkbeck Hill suggests* see.

[1] Johnson's birthday. In *Pr. and Med.* ¶ 113, is a prayer which was, he writes, ' composed at Calais in a sleepless night, and used before the morn at Nôtre Dame.'

[2] See *ante*, i. 243, note 3.

[3] ' While Johnson was in France, he was generally very resolute in speaking Latin.' *Post*, ii. 404. ⟨See also *ante*, ii. 81, 208, note 2.⟩

[4] Miss Thrale. Boswell.

[5] In his *Journal* he records ' their meals are gross ' (*post*, ii. 389). We may doubt therefore Mrs. Piozzi's statement that he said of the French : ' They have few sentiments, but they express them neatly; they have little meat too, but they dress it well.' Piozzi's *Anec.* p. 102 : John. Misc. i. 216.

seeing more ; at least the pleasure, whatever it be, must some time have an end, and we are beginning to think when we shall come home. Mr. Thrale calculates that as we left Streatham on the fifteenth of September, we shall see it again about the fifteenth of November.

' I think I had not been on this side of the sea five days before I found a sensible improvement in my health. I ran a race † in the rain this day, and beat Baretti. Baretti is a fine fellow, and speaks French, I think, quite as well as English [1].

' Make my compliments to Mrs. Williams ; and give my love to Francis ; and tell my friends that I am not lost.

' I am, dear Sir,

' Your affectionate humble, &c.

' SAM. JOHNSON.'

' TO DR. SAMUEL JOHNSON.

' Edinburgh, Oct. 24, 1775.

' MY DEAR SIR,

' IF I had not been informed that you were at Paris, you should have had a letter from me by the earliest opportunity, announcing the birth of my Son, on the 9th instant ; I have named him Alexander [2], after my father. I now write, as I suppose your fellow traveller, Mr. Thrale, will return to London this week, to attend his duty in Parliament, and that you will not stay behind him.

' I send another parcel of Lord Hailes's "Annals." I have undertaken to solicit you for a favour to him, which he thus requests in a letter to me : " I intend soon to give you ' The Life of Robert Bruce,' which you will be pleased to transmit to Dr. Johnson. I wish that you could assist me in a fancy which I have taken, of getting Dr. Johnson to draw a character of Robert Bruce, from the account that I give of that prince. If he finds materials for it in my work, it will be a proof that I have been fortunate in selecting the most striking incidents."

' I suppose by " *The Life of Robert Bruce*," his Lordship means that part of his " Annals " which relates the history of that prince, and not a separate work.

' Shall we have " *A Journey to Paris* " from you in the winter ? You will, I hope, at any rate be kind enough to give me some account of your French travels very soon, for I am very impatient. What a

---

[1] See *ante*, i. 362, note 1.

[2] Boswell wrote to Temple 10 Oct. : —' You know, my dearest friend, of what importance this is to me ; of what importance it is to the Family of Auchinleck, which, you may be well convinced, is my supreme object in

this world.' *Letters*, No. 150, i. 242. Alexander Boswell was killed in a duel in 1822. ⟨See Cockburn's *Mem.*, 1910, p. 370.⟩

† ⟨For two other races which Johnson ran and won, see *John. Misc.* ii. 278, 396.⟩

different scene have you viewed this autumn, from that which you viewed in autumn 1773 ! I ever am, my dear Sir,

'Your much obliged and
'Affectionate humble servant,
'JAMES BOSWELL.'

'To JAMES BOSWELL, ESQ.

'DEAR SIR,

'I AM glad that the young Laird is born, and an end, as I hope, put to the only difference that you can ever have with Mrs. Boswell [1]. I know that she does not love me ; but I intend to persist in wishing her well till I get the better of her.

'Paris is, indeed, a place very different from the Hebrides, but it is to a hasty traveller not so fertile of novelty, nor affords so many opportunities of remark. I cannot pretend to tell the publick any thing of a place better known to many of my readers than to myself. We can talk of it when we meet.

'I shall go next week to Streatham, from whence I purpose to send a parcel of the " History " every post. Concerning the character of Bruce, I can only say, that I do not see any great reason for writing it ; but I shall not easily deny what Lord Hailes and you concur in desiring.

'I have been remarkably healthy all the journey, and hope you and your family have known only that trouble and danger which has so happily terminated. Among all the congratulations that you may receive, I hope you believe none more warm or sincere, than those of, dear Sir,

'Your most affectionate,
'November 16, 1775 [2].'   'SAM. JOHNSON.'

'To MRS. LUCY PORTER, IN LICHFIELD [3].

'DEAR MADAM,

'THIS week I came home from Paris. I have brought you a little box, which I thought pretty ; but I know not whether it is properly a

---

[1] This alludes to my old feudal principle of preferring male to female succession. BOSWELL. See *post*, ii. 414.

[2] He wrote to Dr. Taylor on the same day :—' I came back last Tuesday from France. Is not mine a kind of life turned upside down ? Fixed to a spot when I was young, and roving the world when others are contriving to sit still, I am wholly unsettled. I am a kind of ship with a wide sail, and without an anchor.' *Letters*, No. 440.

[3] There can be no doubt that many years previous to 1775, he corresponded with this lady, who was his step-daughter, but none of his earlier letters to her have been preserved. BOSWELL. Many of these earlier letters were printed by Malone and Croker in later editions. See i. 512.

snuff-box, or a box for some other use. I will send it, when I can find an opportunity. I have been through the whole journey remarkably well. My fellow-travellers were the same whom you saw at Lichfield[1], only we took Baretti with us. Paris is not so fine a place as you would expect. The palaces and churches, however, are very splendid and magnificent ; and what would please you, there are many very fine pictures ; but I do not think their way of life commodious or pleasant [2].

' Let me know how your health has been all this while. I hope the fine summer has given you strength sufficient to encounter the winter.

' Make my compliments to all my friends ; and, if your fingers will let you, write to me, or let your maid write, if it be troublesome to you. I am, dear Madam,

'   ' Your most affectionate humble servant,

' Nov. 16, 1775.'   ' SAM. JOHNSON.'

To the Same.

' Dear Madam,

' Some weeks ago I wrote to you, to tell you that I was just come home from a ramble, and hoped that I should have heard from you. I am afraid winter has laid hold on your fingers, and hinders you from writing. However, let somebody write, if you cannot, and tell me how you do, and a little of what has happened at Lichfield among our friends. I hope you are all well.

' When I was in France, I thought myself growing young, but am afraid that cold weather will take part of my new vigour from me. Let us, however, take care of ourselves, and lose no part of our health by negligence.

' I never knew whether you received the Commentary on the New Testament, and the Travels, and the glasses.

' Do, my dear love, write to me ; and do not let us forget each other. This is the season of good wishes, and I wish you all good. I have not lately seen Mr. Porter[3], nor heard of him. Is he with you ?

' Be pleased to make my compliments to Mrs. Adey[4], and Mrs. Cobb[4], and all my friends ; and when I can do any good, let me know.

'   ' I am, dear Madam,

'   ' Yours most affectionately,

' December, 1775.'   ' SAM. JOHNSON.'

---

[1] When on their way to Wales, July 7, 1774, *post*, v. 428.

[2] Smollett wrote (*Travels*, i. 88) :— ' Notwithstanding the gay disposition of the French, their houses are all gloomy. . . . After all it is in England only, where we must look for cheerful apartments, gay furniture, neatness, and convenience.'

[3] Son of Mrs. Johnson, by her first husband. BOSWELL.

[4] ⟨For these ladies, see App. B, p. 522.⟩

It is to be regretted, that he did not write an account of his travels in France ; for as he is reported to have once said, that ' he could write the Life of a Broomstick [1],' so, notwithstanding so many former travellers have exhausted almost every subject for remark in that great kingdom, his very accurate observation, and peculiar vigour of thought and illustration, would have produced a valuable work. During his visit to it, which lasted but about two months, he wrote notes or minutes of what he saw. He promised to show me them, but I neglected to put him in mind of it ; and the greatest part of them has been lost, or, perhaps, destroyed in a precipitate burning of his papers a few days before his death, which must ever be lamented. One small paper-book, however, entitled ' FRANCE II,' has been preserved, and is in my possession. It is a diurnal register of his life and observations, from the 10th of October to the 4th of November, inclusive, being twenty-six days, and shows an extraordinary attention to various minute particulars. Being the only memorial of this tour that remains, my readers, I am confident, will peruse it with pleasure, though his notes are very short, and evidently written only to assist his own recollection.

' OCT. 10. Tuesday. We saw the *Ecole Militaire*, in which one hundred and fifty young boys are educated for the army. They have arms of different sizes, according to the age ;—flints [a] of wood. The building is very large, but nothing fine, except the council-room. The French have large squares in the windows ;—they make good iron palisades. Their meals are gross.

' We visited the Observatory, a large building of a [b] great height. The upper stones of the parapet very large, but not cramped with iron. The flat on the top is very extensive ; but on the insulated part there is no parapet. Though it was broad enough, I did not care to go upon it. Maps were printing in one of the rooms.

' We walked to a small convent of the Fathers of the Oratory. In the reading-desk of the refectory lay the lives of the Saints.

' Oct. 11. Wednesday. We went to see *Hôtel de Chatlois* [c][2], a house

[a] think (?) *MS.* [b] *a blot in the MS.* [c] Chatelet *MS.*

[1] Johnson in his *Life of Swift*, 73, quotes from Delany's *Obs. upon Lord Orrery's Remarks*, 1754, p. 58, Stella's reply to a gentleman's remark ' Surely that Vanessa must be an extraordinary woman that could inspire the Dean to write so finely upon her. Mrs. Johnston, smiled, and answered, that she thought that point not quite so clear ; for it was well known, the Dean could write finely upon a broomstick.'

[2] Walpole wrote from Paris 9 Sept. 1775 :—' I have not yet had time to see the Hôtel du Châtelet.' *Letters*, ix. 252.

not very large, but very elegant. One of the rooms was gilt to a degree that I never saw before. The upper part for servants and their masters was pretty.

' Thence we went to Mr. Monville's, a house divided into small apartments, furnished with effeminate and minute elegance.—Porphyry.

' Thence we went to St. Roque's church, which is very large ;—the lower part of the pillars incrusted with marble.—Three chapels behind the high altar ;—the last a mass of low arches.—Altars, I believe, all round.

' We passed through *Place de Vendôme*, a fine square, about as big as Hanover-square.—Inhabited by the high families.—Lewis XIV. on horse-back in the middle.

' Monville is the son of a farmer-general. In the house of Chatlois [a] is a room furnished with japan, fitted up in Europe.

' We dined with Boccage [b] [1], the Marquis Blanchetti, and his lady.— The sweetmeats taken by the Marchioness Blanchetti, after observing that they were dear.—Mr. Le Roy, Count Manucci, the Abbé, the Prior [2], and Father Wilson, who staid with me, till I took him home in the coach.

' Bathiani is gone.

' The French have no laws for the maintenance of their poor.—Monk not necessarily a priest.—Benedictines rise at four ;—are at church an hour and half ; at church again half an hour before, half an hour after, dinner ; and again from half an hour after seven to eight. They may sleep eight hours.—Bodily labour wanted in monasteries.

' The poor taken to hospitals, and miserably kept.—Monks in the convent fifteen :—accounted poor.

' Oct. 12. Thursday. We went to the Gobelins.—Tapestry makes a good picture ;—imitates flesh exactly.—One piece with a gold ground ; —the birds not exactly coloured.—Thence we went to the King's cabinet ;—very neat, not, perhaps, perfect.—Gold ore [c].—Candles of the candle-tree.—Seeds.—Woods.—Thence to Gagnier's [d] house, where I saw rooms nine, furnished with a profusion of wealth and elegance which I never have [e] seen before.—Vases.—Pictures.—The dragon china.—The lustre said to be of crystal, and to have cost 3,500l.— The whole furniture said to have cost 125,000l.—Damask hangings covered with pictures.—Porphyry.—This house struck me.—Then we

[a] Chatelet *MS*.   [b] Bocage *MS*.   [c] oar *MS*.   [d] Gagni's *MS*.
[e] have 1, *MS*.: had 2, 3.

On 31 July, 1789, writing of the violence of the mob, he says :—' The hôtel of the Duc de Châtelet, lately built and superb, has been assaulted, and the furniture sold by auction.' *Ib.* xiv. 173.

[1] See *post*, ii. 403, note, and iv. 331.
[2] The Prior of the Convent of the Benedictines where Johnson had a cell appropriated to him. *Post*, ii. 399 and 402.

waited on the ladies to Monville's.—Captain Irwin with us [1].—Spain. County towns all beggars.—At Dijon he could not find the way to Orleans.—Cross roads of France very bad.—Five soldiers.—Woman.— Soldiers escaped [a].——The Colonel would not lose five men for the death of one woman.—The magistrate cannot seize a soldier but by the Colonel's permission.—Good inn at Nismes.—Moors of Barbary fond of Englishmen.—Gibraltar eminently healthy;—it has beef from Barbary. —There is a large garden.—Soldiers sometimes fall from the rock.

' Oct. 13. Friday. I staid at home all day, only went to find the Prior, who was not at home.—I read something in Canus [2].—*Nec admiror, nec multum laudo.*

' Oct. 14. Saturday. We went to the house of Mr. Argenson, which was almost wainscotted with looking-glasses, and covered with gold.— The ladies' closet wainscotted with large squares of glass over painted paper. They always place mirrours to reflect their rooms.

' Then we went to Julien's, the Treasurer of the Clergy :—30,000l. a year.—The house has no very large room, but is set with mirrours, and covered with gold.—Books of wood here, and in another library.

' At D********'s [3] I looked into the books in the lady's closet, and, in contempt, shewed them to Mr. T.—*Prince Titi* [4] ; *Bibl. des Fées*, and other books.—She was offended, and shut up, as we heard after-wards, her apartment.

' Then we went to Julien Le Roy, the King's watch-maker, a man of character in his business, who shewed a small clock made to find the longitude [5].—A decent man [b].

' Afterwards we saw the *Palais Marchand* [6], and the Courts of

[a] *MS. illegible.*   [b] His wife was *and another word heavily erased in MS.*

[1] The rest of this paragraph appears to be a minute of what was told by Captain Irwin. BOSWELL.

[2] Melchior Canus, a celebrated Spanish Dominican, who died at Toledo, in 1560. He wrote a treatise *De Locis Theologicis*, in twelve books. BOSWELL.

[3] D'Argenson's. ⟨MS.⟩

[4] See Macaulay's *Lit. Essays*, 1923, p. 207, and Mr. Croker's answer in his note on this passage. His notion that ' the work was exhibited purposely on the lady's table, in the expectation that her English visitors would think it a literary curiosity,' seems absurd. He does not choose to remember the ' *Bibl. des Fées* and other books.' Since I wrote this note Mr. Napier has published an edition of Boswell, in which this question is carefully examined (ii. 550–9). He sides with Macaulay. ⟨The work, *Histoire du Prince Titi*, 1735, was by Thémiseul de Saint-Hyacinthe.⟩

[5] ' Si quelque invention peut suppléer à la connaissance qui nous est refusée des longitudes sur la mer, c'est celle du plus habile horloger de France (M. Leroi), qui dispute cette invention à l'Angleterre.' Voltaire, *Siècle de Louis XV*, ch. 43. ⟨See App. B.⟩

[6] The *Palais Marchand* was properly only the stalls . . . which were placed along some of the galleries of the Palais. They have been all swept away in Louis Philippe's restoration of the Palais. CROKER.

Justice, civil and criminal.—Queries [a] on the *Sellette* [1].—This building has the old Gothick passages, and a great appearance of antiquity.—Three hundred prisoners sometimes in the gaol [2].

' Much disturbed ;—hope no ill will be [3].

' In the afternoon I visited Mr. Freron the journalist [4]. He spoke Latin very scantily, but seemed to understand me.—His house not splendid, but of commodious size.—His family, wife, son, and daughter, not elevated but decent.—I was pleased with my reception.—He is to translate my book [b], which I am to send him with notes.

' Oct. 15. Sunday.   At Choisi, a royal palace on the banks of the Seine, about 7 m. from Paris.—The terrace noble along the river.—The rooms numerous and grand, but not discriminated from other palaces.—The chapel beautiful, but small.—China globes.—Inlaid table [c].—Labyrinth.—Sinking table [5].—Toilet tables.

' Oct. 16. Monday.   The Palais Royal very grand, large, and lofty.—A very great collection of pictures.—Three of Raphael.—Two Holy Family.—One small piece of M. Angelo.—One room of Rubens.—I thought the pictures of Raphael fine [6].

' The Thuilleries [d].—Statues.—Venus.—Æn. and Anchises in his arms.—Nilus.—Many more.—The walks not open to mean persons.—Chairs at night hired for two sous apiece.—Pont tournant [7].

' Austin Nuns.—Grate.—Mrs. Fermor, Abbess [8].—She knew Pope,

a Queeney *MS.*   b book 1, *MS.* : books 2, 3.   c table 1, *MS.*: tables 2, 3.
d Tuilleries *MS.*

1 ' Petit siège de bois sur lequel on faisait asseoir, pour les interroger, ceux qui étaient accusés d'un délit pouvant faire encourir une peine afflictive.' LITTRÉ.

2 The Conciergerie, before long to be crowded with the victims of the Revolution.

3 This passage, which some may [a] think superstitious, reminds me of Archbishop Laud's Diary. BOSWELL. Laud, for instance, on Oct. 27, 1640, records :—' In my upper study hung my picture taken by the life ; and coming in, I found it fallen down upon the face, and lying on the floor, the string being broken by which it was hanged against the wall. I am almost every day threatened with my ruin in Parliament. God grant this be no omen.' Perhaps there was nothing superstitious in Johnson's entry. He may have felt ill in mind or

body, and dreaded to become worse.

4 ⟨For an account of Fréron, see Cornou, *Élie Fréron*, 1922.⟩

5 A round table, the centre of which descended by machinery to a lower floor ; so that supper might be served and removed without the presence of servants. It was invented by Louis XV. during the favour of Madame du Barri. CROKER.

6 See *ante*, i. 363, note 3.

7 Before the revolution the passage from the garden of the Thuilleries into the Place Louis XV. was over a *pont tournant*. CROKER.

8 The niece of Arabella Fermor, the Belinda of the *Rape of the Lock*. Johnson thus mentions this lady (*Life of Pope*, 54) :—' At Paris, a few years ago, a niece of Mrs. Fermor, who presided in an English Convent, mentioned Pope's work with very little gratitude, rather as an insult

a some may 1 : so many 2, 3.

and thought him disagreeable.—Mrs. —— has many books ¹ ;—has seen life.—Their frontlet disagreeable.—Their hood.—Their life easy. —Rise about five ; hour and half in chapel.—Dine at ten.—Another hour and half at chapel ; half an hour about three, and half an hour more at seven :—four hours in chapel.—A large garden.—Thirteen pensioners ².—Teacher complained.

' At the Boulevards ᵃ saw nothing, yet was glad to be there.—Rope-dancing and farce.—Egg dance.

' N ᵇ. [Note.] Near Paris, whether on week-days or Sundays, the roads empty.

' Oct. 17. Tuesday. At the Palais Marchand.—I bought

A snuff-box ³,	24 L.
——————	6
Table book	15
Scissars 3 p [pair]	18
	63—2 12 6 ⁴

' We heard the lawyers plead.—N ᵇ. As many killed at Paris as there are days in the year. *Chambre de question* ⁵.—Tournelle ⁶ at the Palais Marchand.—An old venerable building.

' The Palais Bourbon, belonging to the Prince of Condé. Only one small wing shown ;—lofty ;—splendid ;—gold and glass.—The battles of the great Condé are painted in one of the rooms. The present Prince a grandsire at thirty-nine ⁷.

' The sight of palaces, and other great buildings, leaves no very distinct images, unless to those who talk of them ᶜ and impress them ᶜ. As I entered, my wife was in my mind ⁸ : she would have been pleased. Having now nobody to please, I am little pleased.

ᵃ Boulevard *MS*.   ᵇ *looks like* R *in MS*.   ᶜ and impress them 1, *MS*.: omitted 2, 3.

than an honour.' She is no doubt the Lady Abbess mentioned *post*, ii. 435. She told Mrs. Piozzi in 1784 ' that she believed there was but little comfort to be found in a house that harboured *poets* ; for that she remembered Mr. Pope's praise made her aunt very troublesome and conceited, while his numberless caprices would have employed ten servants to wait on him.' Piozzi's *Journey*, i. 20.

¹ Mrs. Thrale wrote, on Sept. 18, 1777 :—' When Mr. Thrale dismisses me, I am to take refuge among the Austin Nuns, and study Virgil with dear Miss Canning.' *Piozzi Letters*, i. 374.

² *Pensionnaires*, pupils who boarded in the convent.

³ He brought back a snuff-box for Miss Porter. *Ante*, ii. 387.

⁴ 63 livres = £2 12s. 6d.

⁵ See *ante*, i. 467, note 1.

⁶ ' Ce nom de tournelle, étant devenu le nom de plusieurs châteaux, se conserva au parlement de Paris pour signifier la chambre chargée des affaires criminelles.' LITTRÉ.

⁷ The grandson was the Duke d'Enghien who was put to death by Napoleon Bonaparte in 1804.

⁸ His tender affection for his departed wife, of which there are many evidences in his ' Prayers and Medi-

' N ª. In France there is no middle rank ¹.

' So many shops open, that Sunday is little distinguished at Paris.—The palaces of Louvre and Thuilleries ᵇ granted out in lodgings.

' In the *Palais de Bourbon*, gilt globes of metal at the fire-place.

' The French beds commended.—Much of the marble, only paste.

' The Colosseum a mere wooden building, at least much of it.

' Oct. 18. Wednesday. We went to Fontainebleau, which we found a large mean town, crouded with people.—The forest thick with woods, very extensive.—Manucci ² secured us lodging ᶜ.—The appearance of the country pleasant.—No hills, few streams, only one hedge.—I remember no chapels nor crosses on the road.—Pavement still, and rows of trees.

' N ª. Nobody but mean people walk in Paris ³.

' Oct. 19. Thursday. At court, we saw the apartments ;—the King's bed-chamber and council-chamber extremely splendid.—Persons of all ranks in the external ᵈ rooms through which the family passes ;—servants and masters.—Brunet with us the second time.

' The introductor came to us ;—civil to me.—Presenting.—I had scruples.—Not necessary.—We went and saw the King ⁴ and Queen at dinner.—We saw the other ladies at dinner—Madame Elizabeth ⁵, with the Princess of Guimené.—At night we went to a comedy. I neither saw nor heard.—Drunken women.—Mrs. Th. preferred one to the other.

' Oct. 20. Friday. We saw the Queen mount in the forest.—Brown habit; rode aside: one lady rode aside.—The Queen's horse light grey; —martingale.—She galloped.—We then went to the apartments, and admired them.—Then wandered through the palace.—In the passages, stalls and shops.—Painting in fresco by a great master, worn out.—We saw the King's horses and dogs.—The dogs almost all English.—Degenerate.

' The horses not much commended.—The stables cool ; the kennel filthy.

' At night the ladies went to the opera. I refused, but should have been welcome.

ª *looks like* R *in MS.*   ᵇ Tuillleries *MS.*   ᶜ lodging 1, *MS.*: lodgings 2, 3.
ᵈ outward *MS.*

tations,' appears very feelingly in this passage. BOSWELL.

' On many occasions I think what she would have said or done. When I saw the sea at Brighthelmston, I wished for her to have seen it with me.' *Pr. and Med.* 28 Mar. 1770, ¶ 83.

¹ See *post*, ii. 402.
² See *post*, iii. 89.
³ Dr. Moore (*View of Society & Manners in France*, 1779, i. 33) says

that in Paris, ' foot passengers skulk behind pillars, or run into shops, to avoid being crushed by the coaches, which are driven as near the wall as the coachman pleases.' Only on the Pont Neuf, and the Pont Royal, and the quays between them were there, he adds, foot-ways.

⁴ Lewis XVI.
⁵ The King's sister, who was guillotined in the Reign of Terror.

' The King fed himself with his left hand as we.

' Saturday, 21. In the night I got ground.—We came home to Paris.
—I think we did not see the chapel.—Tree broken by the wind.—
The French chairs made all of boards painted.

' N ᵃ. Soldiers at the court of justice.—Soldiers not amenable to the
magistrates.—Dijon woman ¹.

' Faggots ᵇ in the palace.—Every thing slovenly, except in the chief
rooms.—Trees in the roads, some tall, none old, many very young and
small.

' Women's saddles seem ill made.—Queen's bridle woven with silver.
—Tags to strike the horse.

' Sunday, Oct. 22. To Versailles ², a mean town. Carriages of business
passing.—Mean shops against the wall.—Our way lay through Sêve ᶜ,
where the China manufacture.—Wooden bridge at Sêve ᶜ, in the way to
Versailles.—The palace of great extent.—The front long ; I saw it not
perfectly.—The Menagerie. Cygnets dark ; their black feet ; on the
ground ; tame.—Halcyons, or gulls.—Stag and hind, young.—Aviary,
very large : the net, wire.—Black stag of China, small.—Rhinoceros, the
horn broken and pared away, which, I suppose, will grow ; the basis, I
think, four inches cross ; the skin folds like loose cloth doubled over his
body, and cross his hips ; a vast animal, though young ; as big, perhaps,
as four oxen.—The young elephant, with his tusks just appearing.—The
brown bear put out his paws ;—all very tame.—The lion.—The tigers I
did not well view.—The camel, or dromedary with two bunches called the
Huguin³, taller than any horse.—Two camels with one bunch.—Among
the birds was a pelican, who being let out, went to a fountain, and swam
about to catch fish. His feet well webbed : he dipped his head, and turned
his long bill sidewise. He caught two or three fish, but did not eat them.

' Trianon is a kind of retreat appendant to Versailles. It has an open
portico ; the pavement, and, I think, the pillars, of marble.—There are
many rooms, which I do not distinctly remember.—A table of porphyry,
about five feet long, and between two and three broad, given to
Lewis ᵈ XIV. by the Venetian State.—In the council-room almost all
that was not door or window, was, I think, looking-glass.—Little Trianon
is a small palace like a gentleman's house.—The upper floor paved with
brick.—Little Vienne.—The court is ill paved.—The rooms at the top

ᵃ *Looks like* R *in MS.*   ᵇ Fagot *MS.*   ᶜ Sevre *MS.*   ᵈ Lewis 1, *MS.*: Louis 2, 3.

¹ See p. 391. BOSWELL.
² ' When at Versailles the people
shewed us the theatre. As we stood
on the stage looking at some machinery for playhouse purposes : Now
we are here, what shall we act, Mr.
Johnson,—The Englishman in Paris ?

" No, no (replied he), we will try
to act Harry the Fifth." ' Piozzi's
Anec. p. 101 : John. Misc. i. 216. *The
Englishman in Paris* is by Foote.
³ This epithet should be applied to
this animal with one bunch. Bos-
WELL. ⟨See App. B, p. 523.⟩

are small, fit to sooth the imagination with privacy. In the front of Versailles are small basons of water on the terrace, and other basons, I think, below them.—There are little courts.—The great gallery is wainscotted with mirrors, not very large, but joined by frames. I suppose the large plates were not yet made.—The play-house was very large.—The chapel I do not remember if we saw—We saw one chapel, but I am not certain whether there or at Trianon.—The foreign office paved with bricks.— The dinner half a Louis ᵃ each, and, I think, a Louis ᵃ over.—Money given at Menagerie, three livres ; at palace ᵇ, six livres.

'Oct. 23. Monday. Last night I wrote to Levet.——We went to see the looking-glasses wrought. They come from Normandy in cast plates, perhaps the third of an inch thick. At Paris they are ground upon a marble table, by rubbing one plate on ᶜ another with grit between them. The various sands, of which there are said to be five, I could not learn. The handle, by which the upper glass is moved, has the form of a wheel, which may be moved in all directions. The plates are sent up with their surfaces ground, but not polished, and so continue till they are bespoken, lest time should spoil the surface, as we were told. Those that are to be polished, are laid on a table covered with several thick cloths, hard strained, that the resistance may be equal ; they are then rubbed with a hand rubber, held down hard by a contrivance which I did not well understand. The powder which is used last seemed to me to be iron dissolved in aqua fortis : they called it, as Baretti said, *marc* ᵈ *de l'eau forte*, which he thought was dregs. They mentioned vitriol and saltpetre. The cannon ball swam in the quicksilver. To silver them, a leaf of beaten tin is laid, and rubbed with quicksilver, to which it unites. Then more quicksilver is poured upon it, which, by its mutual [attraction] rises very high. Then a paper is laid at the nearest end of the plate, over which the glass is slided till it lies upon the plate, having driven much of the quicksilver before it. It is then, I think, pressed upon cloths, and then set sloping to drop the superfluous mercury ; the slope is daily heightened towards a perpendicular.

'In the way I saw the Grêve, the mayor's house, and the Bastile.

'We then went to Sans-terre, a brewer ¹. He brews with about as much malt as Mr. Thrale, and sells his beer at the same price, though he pays no duty for malt, and little more than half as much for beer. Beer is sold retail at 6d. a bottle. He brews 4,000 barrels a year. There are seventeen brewers in Paris, of whom none is supposed to brew more than he :—reckoning them at 3,000 each, they make 51,000 a year.—They make their malt, for malting is here no trade.

'The moat of the Bastile is dry.

ᵃ Lewis *MS*.   ᵇ elsewhere *MS*.   ᶜ on 1, *MS*. : upon 2, 3.   ᵈ Mar *MS*.
  ¹ He who commanded the troops at the execution of Lewis XVI.

' Oct. 24. Tuesday. We visited the King's library—I saw the *Speculum humanæ Salvationis*, rudely printed, with ink, sometimes pale, sometimes black ; part supposed to be with wooden types, and part with pages cut on boards.—The Bible, supposed to be older than that of Mentz, in 62 [1] : it has no date ; it is supposed to have been printed with wooden types.—I am in doubt ; the print is large and fair, in two folios.—Another book was shown me, supposed to have been printed with wooden types ;—I think, *Durandi Sanctuarium* [2] in 58. This is inferred from the difference of form sometimes seen in the same letter, which might be struck with different puncheons.—The regular similitude of most letters proves better that they are metal.—I saw nothing but the *Speculum* which I had not seen, I think, before.

' Thence to the Sorbonne.—The library very large, not in lattices like the King's. *Marbone* [a] and *Durandi* [b], q. collection 14 vol.[c] *Scriptores de rebus Gallicis*, many folios.—*Histoire Généalogique of France*, 9 vol.[c]—*Gallia Christiana*, the first edition, 4to.[d] the last, f. 12 vol.[c]— The Prior and Librarian dined [with us] :—I waited on them home.— Their garden pretty, with covered walks, but small ; yet may hold many students.—The Doctors of the Sorbonne are all equal ;—choose those who succeed to vacancies.—Profit little.

' Oct. 25. Wednesday. I went with the Prior to St. Cloud, to see Dr. Hooke.—We walked round the palace, and had some talk.—I dined with our whole company at the Monastery.—In the library, *Beroald,—Cymon, Titus*, from Boccace.—*Oratio Proverbialis* to the Virgin, from Petrarch ; Falkland to Sandys ; Dryden's Preface to the third vol. of Miscellanies [3].

' Oct. 26. Thursday. We saw the china at Sêve [e], cut, glazed, painted. Bellevue, a pleasing house, not great : fine prospect.—Meudon, an old palace.—Alexander, in Porphyry : hollow between eyes and nose, thin cheeks.—Plato and Aristotle.—Noble terrace overlooks the town.—St. Cloud.—Gallery not very high, nor grand, but pleasing.—In the rooms, Michael Angelo, drawn by himself, Sir Thomas More, Des Cartes, Bochart, Naudæus, Mazarine.—Gilded wainscot, so common that it is not minded.—Gough and Keene.—Hooke came to us at the inn.—A message from Drumgould.

' Oct. 27. Friday. I staid at home.—Gough and Keene, and Mrs. S——'s friend dined with us.—This day we began to have a fire.—

---

[a] Martene *MS.*   [b] Durand's *MS.*   [c] fol. *MS.*   [d] 4. *MS.*   [e] Sevre *MS.*

[1] 1462. ⟨See App. B., p. 524.⟩
[2] I cannot learn of any book of this name. Perhaps Johnson saw *Durandi Rationale Officiorum Divinorum*, which was printed in 1459. A copy of this he had seen at Blenheim in 1774. See *post*, v. 459.
[3] He means, I suppose, that he read these different pieces while he remained in the library. Boswell.

The weather is grown very cold, and I fear, has a bad effect upon my breath, which has grown much more free and easy in this country.

' Sat. Oct. 28. I visited the Grand Chartreux ᵃ built by St. Louis ᵇ.— It is built for forty, but contains only twenty-four, and will not maintain more. The friar that spoke to us had a pretty apartment ¹.— Mr. Baretti says four rooms ; I remember but three.—His books seemed to be French.—His garden was neat ; he gave me grapes.— We saw the Place de Victoire, with the statues of the King, and the captive nations.

' We saw the palace and gardens of Luxembourg, but the gallery was shut.—We climbed to the top stairs.—I dined with Colbrooke, who had much company :—Foote, Sir George Rodney, Motteux, Udson, Taaf.—Called on the Prior, and found him in bed.

' Hotel—a guinea a day.—Coach, three guineas a week.—Valet de place ², three 1. 3 a day.—*Avantcoureur*, a guinea a week.—Ordinary dinner, six 1. a head.—Our ordinary seems to be about five guineas a day.—Our extraordinary expences, as diversions, gratuities, clothes, I cannot reckon.—Our travelling is ten guineas a day.

' White stockings ᶜ, 18 1.—Wig.—Hat.

' Sunday, Oct. 29. We saw the boarding-school.—The *Enfans trouvés* ⁴.—A room with about eighty-six children in cradles, as sweet as a parlour.—They lose a third ⁵ ; take in to perhaps more than seven [years old] ; put them to trades ; pin to them the papers sent with them.—Want nurses.—Saw their chapel.

' Went to St. Eustatia ; saw an innumerable company of girls catechised, in many bodies, perhaps 100 to a catechist.—Boys taught at one time, girls at another.—The sermon ; the preacher wears a cap, which he takes off at the name :—his action uniform, not very violent.

ᵃ Chartreuse *MS*.   ᵇ St. Lewis *MS*.   ᶜ stockens *MS*.

¹ Johnson in his *Dictionary* defines *Apartment* as *A room ; a set of rooms*.

² Smollett (*Travels*, i. 85) writes of these temporary servants :—' You cannot conceive with what eagerness and dexterity these rascally valets exert themselves in pillaging strangers. There is always one ready in waiting on your arrival, who begins by assisting your own servant to unload your baggage, and interests himself in your own affairs with such artful officiousness, that you will find it difficult to shake him off.'

³ Livres—francs we should now say.

⁴ It was here that Rousseau got rid of his children. ' Je savois que l'éducation pour eux la moins périlleuse étoit celle des Enfants-Trouvés, et je les y mis.' *Les Rêveries*, ixᵐᵉ promenade.

⁵ Dr. Franklin, in 1785, wrote :— ' I am credibly inform'd, that nine-tenths of them die there pretty soon.' *Writings*, ix. 335. Lord Kames (*Sk. of the History of Man*, ii. 49) says :— ' The Paris almanack for the year 1768, mentions, that there were baptized 18,576 infants, of whom the foundling-hospital received 6025.'

' Oct. 30. Monday.   We saw the library of St. Germain [1].—A very noble collection.—*Codex Divinorum Officiorum*, 1459 :—a letter, square like that of the *Offices*, perhaps the same.—The *Codex*, by Fust and Gernsheym.—*Meursius*, 12 v. fol.—*Amadis*, in French, 3 v. fol.— CATHOLICON *sine colophone*, but of 1460.—Two other editions [2], one by   *Augustin. de Civitate Dei*, without name, date, or place, but of Fust's square letter as it seems.

' I dined with Col. Drumgould ;—had a pleasing afternoon.

' Some of the books of St. Germain's stand in presses from the wall, like those at Oxford.

' Oct. 31. Tuesday.   I lived at the Benedictines ; meagre day ; soup meagre, herrings, eels, both with sauce ; fryed fish ; lentils, tasteless in themselves.   In [a] the library ; where I found *Maffeus's* [b] *de Historiâ Indicâ : Promontorium flectere, to double the Cape*.   I parted very tenderly from the Prior and Friar Wilkes [3].

Maitre es [c] *Arts*, 2 y.—*Bacc. Theol.* 3 y.—*Licentiate*, 2 y.—*Doctor Th.* 2 y. in all 9 years.—For the Doctorate three disputations, *Major*, *Minor*, *Sorbonica*.—Several colleges suppressed, and transferred to that which was the Jesuit's College.

' Nov. 1. Wednesday.   We left Paris.—St. Denis, a large town ; the church not very large, but the middle isle is very lofty and aweful. —On the left are chapels built beyond the line of the wall, which destroy the symmetry of the sides.—The organ is higher above the pavement than any [d] I have ever seen.—The gates are of brass.—On the middle gate is the history of our Lord.—The painted windows are historical, and said to be eminently beautiful.—We were at another church belonging to a convent, of which the portal is a dome ; we could not enter further, and it was almost dark.

---

a To *MS.*   b Maffeus *MS.*   c es 1, *MS.*: *des* 2, 3.   d any *not in MS.*

[1] St. Germain-des-Prés. ⟨See App. B, p. 526.⟩

[2] I have looked in vain into De Bure, Meerman, Mattaire, and other typographical books, for the two editions of the 'Catholicon', which Dr. Johnson mentions here, with *names* which I cannot make out. I read ' one by *Latinius*, one by *Boedinus*.' I have deposited the original MS. in the British Museum, where the curious may see it. My grateful acknowledgements are due to Mr. Planta for the trouble he was pleased to take in aiding my researches. BOSWELL. ⟨Mr. Planta was successively Assistant Librarian, 1773, Under Li-brarian, 1775, and Principal Librarian, 1799, of the British Museum.⟩

[3] Friar Wilkes visited Johnson in May 1776. Johnson's *Letters*, No. 483. On Sept. 18, 1777, Mrs. Thrale wrote to Johnson :—' I have got some news that will please you now. Here is an agreeable friend come from Paris, whom you were very fond of when we were there—the Prior of our English Benedictine Convent, Mr. Cowley. . . . He enquires much for you ; and says, Wilkes is very well, No. 45, as they call him in the Convent. A cell is always kept ready for your use, he tells me.' *Piozzi Letters*, i. 373.

' Nov. 2. Thursday. We came this day to Chantilly, a seat belonging to the Prince of Condé.—This place is eminently beautified by all varieties of waters ^a starting up in fountains, falling in cascades, running in streams, and spread in lakes.—The water seems to be too near the house.—All this water is brought from a source or river^b three leagues off, by an artificial canal, which for one league is carried under ground.—The house is magnificent.—The cabinet seems well stocked : what I remember was, the jaws of a hippopotamus, and a young hippopotamus preserved, which, however, is so small, that I doubt its reality.—It seems too hairy for an abortion, and too small for a mature birth.—Nothing was in spirits ^c ; all was dry.—The dog ; the deer ; the ant-bear with long snout.—The toucan, long broad beak. —The stables were of very great length.—The kennel had no scents.— There was a mockery of a village.—The Menagerie had few animals ¹. —Two faussans ^{d 2}, or Brasilian weasels, spotted, very wild.—There is a forest, and, I think, a park.—I walked till I was very weary, and next morning felt my feet battered, and ^e with pains in the toes.

' Nov. 3. Friday. We came to Compiegne, a very large town, with a royal palace built round a pentagonal court.—The court is raised upon vaults, and has, I suppose, an entry on one side by a gentle rise. —Talk of painting ³.—The church is not very large, but very elegant and splendid.—I had at first great difficulty to walk, but motion grew continually easier.—At night we came to Noyon, an episcopal city.— The cathedral is very beautiful, the pillars alternately Gothick and Corinthian.—We entered a very noble parochial church.—Noyon is walled, and is said to be three miles round.

^a water *MS*. ^b a river *MS*. ^c spirit *MS*. ^d fausans *MS*. ^e and sore, with pains *MS*.

¹ The writing is so bad here, that the names of several of the animals could not be decyphered without much more acquaintance with natural history than I possess.—Dr. Blagden, with his usual politeness, most obligingly examined the MS. To that gentleman, and to Dr. Gray, of the British Museum, who also very readily assisted me, I beg leave to express my best thanks. BOSWELL. For Dr. Blagden see *post*, iv. 30. ⟨Dr. E. W. Gray was the Keeper of Natural History and Antiquities. See *D.N.B.*⟩

² It is thus written by Johnson, from the French pronunciation of *fossane*. It should be observed, that the person who shewed this Menagerie was mistaken in supposing the *fossane* and the Brasilian weasel to be the same, the *fossane* being a different animal, and a native of Madagascar. I find them, however, upon one plate in Pennant's ' Synopsis of Quadrupeds.' BOSWELL.

³ How little Johnson relished this talk is shewn by his letter to Mrs. Thrale of May 1, 1780, and by her answer. He wrote :—' The exhibition, how will you do, either to see or not to see ! The exhibition is eminently splendid. There is contour, and keeping, and grace, and expression, and all the varieties of artificial excellence.' *Letters*, No. 663. She answered: —' When did I ever plague you about contour, and grace, and expression ? I have dreaded them all three since

' Nov. 4. Saturday. We rose very early, and came through St. Quintin [a] to Cambray, not long after three.—We went to an English nunnery, to give a letter to Father Welch, the confessor, who came to visit us in the evening.

' Nov. 5. Sunday. We saw the cathedral.—It is very beautiful, with chapels on each side.—The choir splendid.—The balustrade in one part brass.—The Neff [1] very high and grand.—The altar silver as far as it is seen.—The vestments very splendid.——At the Benedictines church—— '

Here his Journal [2] ends abruptly. Whether he wrote any more after this time, I know not ; but probably not much, as he arrived in England about the 12th of November. These short notes of his tour, though they may seem minute taken singly, make together a considerable mass of information, and exhibit such an ardour of enquiry and acuteness of examination, as, I believe, are found in but few travellers, especially at an advanced age. They completely refute the idle notion which has been propagated, *that he could not see* [3] ; and, if he had taken the trouble to revise and digest them, he undoubtedly could have expanded them into a very entertaining narrative.

When I met him in London the following year, the account which he gave me of his French tour, was, ' Sir, I have seen all the visibilities of Paris, and around it ; but to have formed an acquaintance with the people there, would have required more time than I could stay. I was just beginning to creep into acquaintance [4] by means of Colonel Drumgould, a very high

[a] St. Quentin *MS*.

[1] ' *Nef*, (old French, from *nave*) the body of a church.' Johnson's *Dictionary*.

[2] My worthy and ingenious friend, Mr. Andrew Lumisden, by his accurate acquaintance with France, enabled me to make out many proper names, which Dr. Johnson had written indistinctly, and sometimes spelt erroneously. BOSWELL. Lumisden is mentioned *post*, v. 194.

[3] Baretti, in a marginal note on *Piozzi Letters*, i. 142, says that ' Johnson did not think Paris worth seeing a second time, though he had seen that hapless day at Compeigne, when you teized me so.' *Piozzi Lett*. ii. 116.

[1] ' *Nef*, (old French, from *nave*) the body of a church.' Johnson's *Dictionary*. next to nothing of it during the few days he had been there.' On p. 159 he adds :—' He noticed the country so little, that he scarcely spoke of it ever after.' He shews, however, his ignorance of Johnson's doings by saying that ' in France he never touched a pen.'

[4] Hume's reception in 1763 was very different. He wrote to Adam Smith :—' I have been three days at Paris, and two at Fontainebleau, and have everywhere met with the most extraordinary honours, which the most exorbitant vanity could wish or desire.' The Dauphin's three children, afterwards Lewis XVI, Lewis

man, Sir, head of *L'Ecole Militaire*, a most complete character, for he had first been a professor of rhetorick, and then became a soldier †. And, Sir, I was very kindly treated by the English Benedictines, and have a cell appropriated to me in their convent.'

He observed, ' The great in France live very magnificently, but the rest very miserably. There is no happy middle state as in England ¹. The shops of Paris are mean ; the meat in the markets is such as would be sent to a gaol in England ² :

XVIII, and Charles X, had each to make to him a set speech of congratulation. He was the favourite of the most exclusive coteries. Burton's *Hume*, ii. 168, 177, 208. But at that date, sceptical philosophy was the rage.

† ⟨See App. B, pp. 526–7.⟩

¹ Walpole wrote from Paris in 1771 (*Letters*, viii. 61, 63) :—' The distress here is incredible, especially at court. ... The middling and common people are not much richer than Job when he had lost everything but his patience.' Rousseau wrote of the French in 1777 : —' Cette nation, qui se prétend si gaie, montre peu cette gaieté dans ses jeux. Souvent j'allois jadis aux guinguettes, pour y voir danser le menu peuple ; mais ses danses étoient si maussades, son maintien si dolent, si gauche, que j'en sortois plutôt contristé que réjoui.' *Les Rêveries*, ixᵐᵉ promenade. Baretti (*Journey to Genoa*, iv. 146) denies that the French ' are entitled to the appellation of chearful.' ' Provence,' he says (*ib.* 148), ' is the only province in which you see with some sort of frequency the rustick assemblies roused up to chearfulness by the *Fifre* and the *Tambourin*.' Mrs. Piozzi describes the absence of ' the happy middle state ' abroad. ' As soon as Dover is left behind, every man seems to belong to some other man, and no man to himself.' Piozzi's *Journey*, ii. 341. Voltaire in 1764, in his review of *Julia Mandeville* (*Œuvres*, xxv. 182), says :—' Pour peu qu'un roman, une tragédie, une comédie ait

de succès à Londres, on en fait trois et quatre éditions en peu de mois ; c'est que l'état mitoyen est plus riche et plus instruit en Angleterre qu'en France, &c.' But Barry, the painter, in 1766, described to Burke, ' the crouds of busy contented people, which cover (as one may say) the whole face of the country.' But he was an Irishman comparing France with Ireland. ' They make a strong, but melancholy contrast to a miserable —— which I cannot help thinking of sometimes. You will not be at any loss to know that I mean Ireland.' Barry's *Works*, i. 57. Hume in his essay on *The Parties of Great Britain*, published in 1741, alludes to the absence of a middle class in Scotland. He says: ' there are only two Ranks of Men among us ; Gentlemen, who have some Fortune and Education, and the meanest slaving Poor ; without any considerable Number of that middling Rank of Men, which abounds more in England, both in Cities and in the Country, than in any other Part of the World.' *Essays, Moral & Political*, 139. ⟨This passage was omitted in the third edition, 1748.⟩

² Yet Smollett wrote in 1763 :— ' All manner of butcher's meat and poultry are extremely good in Paris. The beef is excellent.' He adds, ' I can by no means relish their cookery.' Smollett's *Travels*, i. 86. Walpole, on 11 Sept. 1765, writing from Amiens, said he was ' almost famished for want of clean victuals and comfortable tea

and Mr. Thrale justly observed, that the cookery of the French was forced upon them by necessity ; for they could not eat their meat, unless they added some taste to it. The French are an indelicate people ; they will spit upon any place [1]. At Madame ———————'s [2], a literary lady of rank, the footman took the sugar in his fingers [3], and threw it into my coffee. I was going to put it aside ; but hearing it was made on purpose for me, I e'en tasted Tom's fingers. The same lady would needs make tea à l'Angloise. The spout of the tea-pot did not pour freely : she bad the footman blow into it [4]. France is worse than Scotland in every thing but climate. Nature has done more for the French ; but they have done less for themselves than the Scotch have done.'

It happened that Foote was at Paris at the same time with Dr. Johnson, and his description of my friend while there, was abundantly ludicrous. He told me, that the French were quite astonished at his figure and manner, and at his dress, which he obstinately continued exactly as in London [5] ;—his brown clothes,

and bread and butter.' *Letters*, vi. 291. Goldsmith, in 1770, wrote from Paris :—' As for the meat of this country I can scarce eat it, and though we pay two good shillings an head for our dinner, I find it all so tough, that I have spent less time with my knife than my pick-tooth.' Forster's *Goldsmith*, ii. 219.

[1] Walpole calls Paris ' the ugliest beastly town in the universe,' and describes the indelicacy of the talk of women of the first rank. *Letters*, vi. 351. See *post*, iii. 352 ; iv. 237.

[2] ⟨Madame du Boccage, according to Mrs. Piozzi. *Marg. note in* 1816 *ed.* See also *Johnsonian Misc.* ii. 291.⟩

[3] In Edinburgh, Johnson threw a glass of lemonade out of the window because the waiter had put the sugar into it ' with his greasy fingers.' *Post*, v. 22. ⟨See also Johnson's *Letters*, No. 326, i. 253.⟩

[4] Mrs. Thrale wrote to Johnson in 1782 :—' When we were in France we could form little judgment [of the spread of refinement], as our

time was passed chiefly among English ; yet I recollect that one fine lady, who entertained us very splendidly, put her mouth to the teapot, and blew in the spout when it did not pour freely.' *Piozzi Letters*, ii. 247. ⟨See *Johnsonian Misc.* ii. 291.⟩

[5] ' That he did not continue exactly as in London is stated by Boswell himself. ' He was furnished with a Paris-made wig, of handsome construction.' (*Post*, iii. 325.) His *Journal* shews that he bought articles of dress (*ante*, ii. 398). Hawkins (*Life*, p. 517) says that ' he yielded to the remonstrances of his friends so far as to dress in a suit of black and a Bourgeois wig, but resisted their importunity to wear ruffles. . . . By a note in his diary it appears, that he laid out near thirty pounds in cloaths for this journey.' A story told by Foote we may believe as little as we please. ' Foote is quite impartial,' said Johnson, ' for he tells lies of every body. *Post*, ii. 434.

black stockings, and plain shirt. He mentioned, that an Irish gentleman said to Johnson, ' Sir, you have not seen the best French players.' JOHNSON. ' Players, Sir ! I look on them as no better than creatures set upon tables and joint-stools to make faces and produce laughter, like dancing dogs.'— ' But, Sir, you will allow that some players are better than others ? ' JOHNSON. ' Yes, Sir, as some dogs dance better than others †.'

While Johnson was in France, he was generally very resolute in speaking Latin. It was a maxim with him that a man should not let himself down, by speaking a language which he speaks imperfectly. Indeed, we must have often observed how inferiour, how much like a child a man appears, who speaks a broken tongue. When Sir Joshua Reynolds, at one of the dinners of the Royal Academy, presented him to a Frenchman of great distinction, he would not deign to speak French, but talked Latin, though his Excellency did not understand it, owing, perhaps, to Johnson's English pronunciation [1] : yet upon another occasion he was observed to speak French to a Frenchman of high rank, who spoke English ; and being asked the reason, with some expression of surprise,—he answered, ' because I think my French is as good as his English.' Though Johnson understood French perfectly, he could not speak it readily, as I have observed at his first interview with General Paoli, in 1769 [2] ; yet he wrote it, I imagine, pretty [a] well, as appears from some of his letters in Mrs. Piozzi's collection, of which I shall transcribe one :

[a] very 1: pretty 2, 3.

[1] If Johnson's Latin was understood by foreigners in France, but not in England, the explanation may be found in his *Life of Milton*, 107, where he says :—' He who travels, if he speaks Latin, may so soon learn the sounds which every native gives it, that he need make no provision before his journey ; and if strangers visit us, it is their business to practise such conformity to our modes as they expect from us in their own countries.' Johnson was so sturdy an Englishman that likely enough, as he was in London, he would not alter his pronunciation to suit his Excellency's ear. In Priestley's *Works*, xxiii. 233, a conversation is reported in which Dr. Johnson argued for the Italian method of pronouncing Latin. ⟨For other instances of Johnson's colloquial Latin see *ante*, ii. 125, *post*, ii. 406, and Piozzi, *Anecd.*, p. 101 : John. Misc. i. 216.⟩

[2] See *ante*, ii. 80.

† ⟨For Johnson's contempt of actors, see *ante*, i. 167 ; ii. 234 ; *post*, iii. 184.⟩

A Madame La Comtesse de ——— [1].

'July 16, 1771 [2].

' OUI, *Madame, le moment est arrivé, et il faut que je parte. Mais pourquoi faut il partir? Est ce que je m'ennuye? Je m'ennuyerai ailleurs. Est ce que je cherche ou quelque plaisir, ou quelque soulagement? Je ne cherche rien, je n'espere rien. Aller voir ce que jai vû, etre un peu rejoué, un peu degouté, me resouvenir que la vie se passe,* ᵃ *et qu'elle se passe* ᵃ *en vain, me plaindre de moi, m'endurcir aux dehors ; voici le tout de ce qu'on compte pour les delices de l'année. Que Dieu vous donne, Madame, tous les agrémens de la vie, avec un esprit qui peut en jouir sans s'y livrer trop.'*

Here let me not forget a curious anecdote, as related to me by Mr. Beauclerk, which I shall endeavour to exhibit as well as I can in that gentleman's lively manner ; and in justice to him it is proper to add, that Dr. Johnson told me I might rely both on the correctness of his memory, and the fidelity of his narrative. ' When Madame de Boufflers was first in England [3], (said Beauclerk,) she was desirous to see Johnson. I accordingly went with her to his chambers in the Temple, where she was entertained with his conversation for some time. When our visit was over, she and I left him, and were got into Inner Temple-lane, when all at once I heard a noise like thunder. This was occasioned by Johnson, who it seems, upon a little recollection, had taken it into his head that he ought to have done the honours of his literary residence to a foreign lady of quality, and eager to show himself a man of gallantry, was hurrying down the stair-case in violent agitation. He overtook us before we reached the Temple-gate, and brushing in between

---

ᵃ et qu'elle se passe *omitted* 2, 3.

[1] Mme. de Boufflers. MRS. PIOZZI. She was the mistress of the Prince of Conti. She understood English, and was the correspondent of Hume ⟨and Walpole. Her full name and style was Marie Charlotte Hippolyte, Comtesse de Boufflers-Rouverel (1724– c. 1800)⟩.

[2] In the *Piozzi Letters* (i. 34), this letter is dated May 16, 1771 ; in Boswell's first and second editions, July 16, 1771 ;. in the third edition, July 16, 1775. In May, 1771, Johnson,

so far as there is anything to shew, was in London. On July 16, both in 1771 and 1775, he was at Ashbourne. One of Hume's Letters (*Private Corres.*, p. 283), dated April 17, 1775, shews that Mme. de Boufflers was at that time ' speaking of coming over to England.' ⟨The original letter is dated May 16, 1771, according to Maggs Bros.' *Catal.* No. 433.⟩

[3] She was in England in the summer of 1763. Jesse's *Selwyn*, i. 235.

me and Madame de Boufflers, seized her hand, and conducted her to her coach. His dress was a rusty brown morning suit, a pair of old shoes by way of slippers, a little shrivelled wig sticking on the top of his head, and the sleeves of his shirt and the knees of his breeches hanging loose. A considerable crowd of people gathered round, and were not a little struck by this singular appearance.'

He spoke Latin with wonderful fluency and elegance †. When Pere Boscovich [1] was in England, Johnson dined in company with him at Sir Joshua Reynolds's, and at Dr. Douglas's, now Bishop of Salisbury. Upon both occasions that celebrated foreigner expressed his astonishment at Johnson's Latin conversation. When at Paris, Johnson thus characterised Voltaire to Freron the Journalist: ' *Vir est acerrimi ingenii et paucarum literarum.'*

' To Dr. Samuel Johnson.

' Edinburgh, Dec. 5, 1775.

' My dear Sir,

' Mr. Alexander Maclean, the young Laird [a] of Col, being to set out to-morrow for London, I give him this letter to introduce him to your acquaintance. The kindness which you and I experienced from his brother, whose unfortunate death we sincerely lament [2], will make us always desirous to shew attention to any branch of the family. Indeed, you have so much of the true Highland cordiality, that I am sure you would have thought me to blame if I had neglected to recommend to you this Hebridean prince, in whose island we were hospitably entertained. I ever am with respectful attachment, my dear Sir,

' Your most obliged
' And most humble servant,
' James Boswell.'

Mr. Maclean returned with the most agreeable accounts of the polite attention with which he was received by Dr. Johnson.

In the course of this year Dr. Burney informs me,[b] that ' he very frequently met Dr. Johnson at Mr. Thrale's, at Streatham, where

---

[a] present young Laird 1.

[b] *comma omitted* 2, 3.

[1] Boscovich, a learned Jesuit, was born at Ragusa in 1711, and died in 1787. He visited London in 1760, and was elected a Fellow of the Royal Society. Chalmers's *Biog. Dict.* vi. 149–58. See *ante*, ii. 125.

[2] See *ante*, ii. 288.

† ⟨' He spoke Latin with great fluency and elegance. He said, indeed, he had taken great pains about it.' Johnson's *Works*, 1787, xi. 199. See *ante*, ii. 404.⟩

they had many long conversations, often sitting up as long as the fire and candles lasted, and much longer than the patience of the servants subsisted [1].'

A few of Johnson's sayings, which that gentleman recollects, shall here be inserted.

' I never take a nap after dinner but when I have had a bad night, and then the nap takes me.'

' The writer of an epitaph should not be considered as saying nothing but what is strictly true. Allowance must be made for some degree of exaggerated praise. In lapidary inscriptions a man is not upon oath [2].'

' There is now less flogging in our great schools than formerly, but then less is learned there ; so that what the boys get at one end,[a] they lose at the other [3].'

' More is learned in publick than in private schools [4], from emulation ; there is the collision of mind with mind, or the radiation of many minds pointing to one centre. Though few boys make their own exercises, yet if a good exercise is given up, out of a great number of boys, it is made by somebody.'

' I hate by-roads in education. Education is as well known, and has long been as well known, as ever it can be [5]. En-

[a] *comma omitted* 2, 3.

[1] Four years later Johnson thus spoke to Miss Burney of her father :—
' " I love Burney : my heart goes out to meet him ! " " He is not ungrateful, sir," cried I ; " for most heartily does he love you." " Does he, madam ? I am surprised at that." " Why, sir ? why should you have doubted it ? " " Because, madam, Dr. Burney is a man for all the world to love : it is but natural to love him." I could have almost cried with delight at this cordial, unlaboured *éloge*.' Mme. D'Arblay's *Diary*, i. 196.

[2] ' Though a sepulchral inscription is professedly a panegyrick, and, therefore, not confined to historical impartiality, yet it ought always to be written with regard to truth. No man ought to be commended for virtues which he never possessed, but whoever is curious to know his faults must inquire after them in other

places.' Johnson's *Essay on Epitaphs, Works*, v. 265. See *post*, iii. 387.

[3] See *ante*, i. 46.

[4] See *post*, iii. 12, and v. 85.

[5] Johnson's Dick Wormwood, in *The Idler*, No. 83, a man ' whose sole delight is to find every thing wrong, . . . triumphs when he talks on the present system of education, and tells us with great vehemence, that we are learning words when we should learn things.' In the *Life of Milton*, 37, Johnson writes :—' It is told that in the art of education he [Milton] performed wonders, and a formidable list is given of the authors, Greek and Latin, that were read in Aldersgate-street by youth between ten and fifteen or sixteen years of age. Those who tell or receive these stories should consider that nobody can be taught faster than he can learn. The speed of the horseman must be

deavouring to make children prematurely wise is useless labour.
Suppose they have more knowledge at five or six years old
than other children, what use can be made of it ? It will be
lost before it is wanted, and the waste of so much time and
labour of the teacher can never be repaid. Too much is expected from precocity, and too little performed. Miss ——— 1 was
an instance of early cultivation, but in what did it terminate ?
In marrying a little Presbyterian parson, who keeps an infant
boarding-school, so that all her employment now is,

"To suckle fools, and chronicle small-beer 2."

She tells the children, "This is a cat, and that is a dog, with
four legs and a tail ; see there ! you are much better than a
cat or a dog, for you can speak 3." If I had bestowed such an

limited by the power of his horse.'
He advised Boswell ' not to *refine* in
the education of his children. . . .
"You must do as other people do ".'
Post, iii. 169. Yet, in his *Life of
Barretier* (*Works*, vi. 380), he says :—
' The first languages which he learned
were the French, German, and Latin,
which he was taught, not in the common way, by a multitude of definitions,
rules, and exceptions, which fatigue
the attention and burden the memory,
without any use proportionate to the
time which they require, and the
disgust which they create. The
method by which he was instructed
was easy and expeditious, and, therefore, pleasing. He learned them all in
the same manner, and almost at the
same time, by conversing in them
indifferently with his father.'

1 Miss Aikin, better known as Mrs.
Barbauld. Johnson uses *Presbyterian*
where we should use *Unitarian*. ' The
Unitarians of the present day [1843]
are chiefly the . . . representatives of
that branch of the early Non-con-
formists who received the denomina-
tion of Presbyterians ; and they are
still known by that name.' *Penny
Cycl.* xxvi. 6.

2 *Othello*, act ii. sc. 1, line 160.

3 He quotes Barbauld's *Lessons for
Children* (p. 68, ed. of 1878). Mrs.
Piozzi (*Anec.*, p. 16 : John. Misc. i.
157), speaking of books for children
says :—' Mrs. Barbauld . . . had his
best praise . . . ; no man was more
struck than Mr. Johnson with voluntary descent from possible splendour
to painful duty.' Mrs. Piozzi alludes
to Johnson's praise of Dr. Watts (*Life*,
23) :—' Every man, acquainted with
the common principles of human
action, will look with veneration on
the writer who is at one time com-
bating Locke, and at another making
a catechism for children in their fourth
year. A voluntary descent from the
dignity of science is perhaps the hard-
est lesson that humility can teach.'
He praised Milton (*Life*, 106) also,
who, when ' writing *Paradise Lost*,
could descend from his elevation to
rescue children from the perplexity
of grammatical confusion, and the
trouble of lessons unnecessarily repeated.' Mrs. Barbauld did what
it was said Gay had shown could be
done. ' One may write things to a
child without being childish.' Swift's
Works, xvii. 21. In her *Advertisement*, she says :—' The task is humble,
but not mean ; to plant the first idea

education on a daughter, and had discovered that she thought of
marrying such a fellow, I would have sent her to the *Congress*.'

'After having talked slightingly of musick, he was observed
to listen very attentively while Miss Thrale played on the
harpsichord, and with eagerness he called to her, " Why don't
you dash away like Burney ? " Dr. Burney upon this said to
him, " I believe, Sir, we shall make a musician of you at last."
Johnson with candid complacency replied, " Sir, I shall be glad
to have a new sense given to me [1]." '

in a human mind can be no dishonour
to any hand.' ' Ethicks, or morality,'
wrote Johnson, ' is one of the studies
which ought to begin with the first
glimpse of reason, and only end with
life itself.' *Works*, v. 243. This
might have been the motto of her
book. As the *Advertisement* was not
published till 1778 (Barbauld's *Works*,
ii. 19) it is possible that Johnson's
criticism had reached her, and that
it was meant as an answer. Among
her pupils were William Taylor of
Norwich, Sir William Gell, and the
first Lord Denman (*ib.* i. xxv–xxx).
Mrs. Barbauld bore Johnson no ill-
will. In her *Eighteen Hundred and
Eleven*, p. 14, she describes some future
pilgrims ' from the blue Mountains
or Ontario's lake,' coming to view
' London's faded glories.'

' With throbbing bosoms shall the
    wanderers tread
The hallowed mansions of the silent
    dead,
Shall enter the long isle and vaulted
    dome
Where Genius and where Valour find
    a home ;
Bend at each antique shrine, and
    frequent turn
To clasp with fond delight some
    sculptured urn,
The ponderous mass of Johnson's
    form to greet,
Or breathe the prayer at Howard's
    sainted feet.'

  [1] According to Mme. D'Arblay he
said :—' Sir, I shall be very glad to

have a new sense put into me.' He
had been wont to speak slightingly
of music and musicians. ' The first
symptom that he shewed of a tendency to conversion . . . was upon hearing the following paragraph read aloud
from the preface to Dr. Burney's
History of Music while it was yet in
manuscript :—" The love of leng-
thened tones and modulated sound,
seems a passion implanted in human
nature throughout the globe ; as we
hear of no people, however wild and
savage in other particulars, who have
not music of some kind or other, with
which they seem greatly delighted."
" Sir," cried Dr. Johnson, after a little
pause, " this assertion I believe may
be right." And then, see-sawing a
minute or two on his chair, he forcibly
added : " All animated nature loves
music—except myself ! " ' *Dr. Burney's Memoirs*, ii. 77. Hawkins records : ' Of music in general, he has
been heard to say, " it excites in my
mind no ideas, and hinders me from
contemplating my own." . . . I have
sometimes thought that music was
positive pain to him. Upon his hearing a celebrated performer go through
a hard composition, and hearing it
remarked that it was very difficult,
Johnson said, " I would it had been
impossible." ' *Life*, p. 319. Yet he had
once bought a flageolet, though he
had never made out a tune. ' Had
I learnt to fiddle,' he said, ' I should
have done nothing else ' (*post*, iii.
242, and v. 314). Not six months
before his death he asked Dr. Burney

' He had come down one morning to the breakfast-room, and been a considerable time by himself before any body appeared. When on a subsequent day, he was twitted by Mrs. Thrale for being very late, which he generally was, he defended himself by alluding to the extraordinary morning, when he had been too early,[a] " Madam, I do not like to come down to *vacuity*." '

' Dr. Burney having remarked that Mr. Garrick was beginning to look old, he said, " Why, Sir, you are not to wonder at that ; no man's face has had more wear and tear [1]." '

Not having heard from him for a longer time than I supposed he would be silent, I wrote to him December 18, not in good spirits,[a]

' Sometimes I have been afraid that the cold which has gone over Europe this year like a sort of pestilence [2] has seized you severely :

[a] *comma* 1, 2 : *full stop* 3.

to teach him the scale of music (*ante*, ii. 263, note 4). That ' he appeared fond of the bagpipe, and used often to stand for some time with his ear close to the great drone ' (*post*, v. 315), does not tell for much either way. In his *Western Islands* (p. 53), he shews his pleasure in singing. ' After supper,' he writes, ' the ladies sung Erse songs, to which I listened as an English audience to an Italian opera, delighted with the sound of words which I did not understand.' Boswell records (*post*, v. 265) that another day a lady ' pleased him much, by singing Erse songs, and playing on the guittar.' Johnson himself shews that if his ear was dull to music, it was by no means dead to sound. He thus describes a journey by night in the Highlands (*Western Islands*, p. 143) :—' The wind was loud, the rain was heavy, and the whistling of the blast, the fall of the shower, the rush of the cataracts, and the roar of the torrent, made a nobler chorus of the rough musick of nature than it had ever been my chance to hear before.' In 1783, when he was in his seventy-fourth

year, he said, on hearing the music of a funeral procession :—' This is the first time that I have ever been affected by musical sounds.' *Post*, iv. 22. See also iii. 197.

[1] Miss Burney, in 1778, records that he said :—' David, madam, looks much older than he is ; for his face has had double the business of any other man's ; it is never at rest ; when he speaks one minute, he has quite a different countenance to what he assumes the next ; I don't believe he ever kept the same look for half an hour together, in the whole course of his life ; and such an eternal, restless, fatiguing play of the muscles, must certainly wear out a man's face before its real time.' Mme. D'Arblay's *Diary*, i. 64. ⟨Malone records ' when some one observed to Foote that Garrick's features still had great effect notwithstanding his age, " Yes," said Foote, " wonderfully so, considering all the wear and tear they have gone through ".' Prior's *Malone*, p. 369.⟩

[2] On Nov. 2 of this year, a proposal was made to Garrick by the proprietors of Covent-Garden

sometimes my imagination, which is upon occasions prolifick of evil, hath figured that you may have somehow taken offence at some part of my conduct.'

'To James Boswell, Esq.

'Dear Sir,

'Never dream of any offence. How should you offend me? I consider your friendship as a possession, which I intend to hold till you take it from me, and to lament if ever by my fault I should lose it. However, when such suspicions find their way into your mind, always give them vent; I shall make haste to disperse them; but hinder their first ingress if you can. Consider such thoughts as morbid.

'Such illness as may excuse my omission to Lord Hailes, I cannot honestly plead. I have been hindered, I know not how, by a succession of petty obstructions. I hope to mend immediately, and to send next post to his Lordship. Mr. Thrale would have written to you if I had omitted; he sends his compliments and wishes to see you.

'You and your lady will now have no more wrangling about feudal inheritance [1]. How does the young Laird of Auchinleck? I suppose Miss Veronica is grown a reader and discourser.

'I have just now got a cough, but it has never yet hindered me from sleeping: I have had quieter nights than are common with me.

'I cannot but rejoice that Joseph [2] has had the wit to find the way back. He is a fine fellow, and one of the best travellers in the world.

'Young Col brought me your letter. He is a very pleasing youth. I took him two days ago to the Mitre, and we dined together. I was as civil as I had the means of being.

'I have had a letter from Rasay, acknowledging, with great appearance of satisfaction, the insertion in the Edinburgh paper [3]. I am very glad that it was done.

'My compliments to Mrs. Boswell, who does not love me; and of

---

Theatre, 'that now in the time of dearth and sickness' they should open their theatres only five nights in each week. *Garrick Corres.* ii. 108.

[1] Mrs. Boswell no doubt had disliked her husband's wish to pass over his daughters in entailing the Auchinleck estate, in favour of heirs-male however remote. *Post*, ii. 414. Johnson, on Feb 9, 1776, opposing this

intention, wrote:—'I hope I shall get some ground now with Mrs. Boswell.' *Post*, ii. 420.

[2] Joseph Ritter, a Bohemian, who was in my service many years, and attended Dr. Johnson and me in our Tour to the Hebrides. After having left me for some time, he had now returned to me. Boswell. See *ante*, ii. 103, and *post*, iii. 216.

[3] See *post*, v. 411–12.

all the rest, I need only send them to those that do : and I am afraid it will give you very little trouble to distribute them.

> ' I am, my dear, dear Sir,
>> ' Your affectionate humble servant,
>>> ' SAM. JOHNSON.'

' December 23, 1775 †.'

1776 : ÆTAT. 67.]—IN 1776, Johnson wrote, so far as I can discover, nothing for the publick : but that his mind was still ardent, and fraught with generous wishes to attain to still higher degrees of literary excellence, is proved by his private notes of this year, which I shall insert in their proper place.

' To JAMES BOSWELL, ESQ.

' DEAR SIR,

' I HAVE at last sent you all Lord Hailes's papers. While I was in France, I looked very often into Henault[1] ; but Lord Hailes, in my opinion, leaves him far and far behind. Why I did not dispatch so short a perusal sooner, when I look back, I am utterly unable to discover : but human moments are stolen away by a thousand petty impediments which leave no trace behind them. I have been afflicted, through the whole Christmas, with the general disorder, of which the worst effect was a cough, which is now much mitigated, though the country, on which I look from a window at Streatham, is now covered with a deep snow. Mrs. Williams is very ill : every body else is as usual.

' Among the papers, I found a letter to you, which I think you had not opened ; and a paper for " The Chronicle," which I suppose it not necessary now to insert. I return them both.

' I have, within these few days, had the honour of receiving Lord Hailes's first volume, for which I return my most respectful thanks.

' I wish you, my dearest friend, and your haughty lady, (for I know she does not love me,) and the young ladies, and the young Laird, all happiness. Teach the young gentleman, in spite of his mamma, to think and speak well of,

> ' Sir,
>> ' Your affectionate humble servant,
>>> ' SAM. JOHNSON.'

' Jan. 10, 1776.'

At this time was in agitation a matter of great consequence to me and my family, which I should not obtrude upon the world, were it not that the part which Dr. Johnson's friendship

---

[1] See *ante*, ii. 383.

† ⟨The first volume of the first edition ends with this letter.⟩

for me made him take in it, was the occasion of an exertion of his abilities, which it would be injustice to conceal. That what he wrote upon the subject may be understood, it is necessary to give a state of the question, which I shall do as briefly as I can.

In the year 1504, the barony or manour of Auchinleck, (pronounced *Affléck* [1],) in Ayrshire, which belonged to a family of the same name with the lands, having fallen to the Crown by forfeiture, James the Fourth, King of Scotland, granted it to Thomas Boswell, a branch of an ancient family in the county of Fife, stiling him in the charter, ' *dilecto familiari nostro ;* ' and assigning, as the cause of the grant, ' *pro bono et fideli servitio nobis præstito.*' Thomas Boswell was slain in battle, fighting along with his Sovereign, at the fatal field of Floddon, in 1513 [2].

From this very honourable founder of our family, the estate was transmitted, in a direct series of heirs male, to David Boswell, my father's great grand uncle, who had no sons, but four daughters, who were all respectably married, the eldest to Lord Cathcart.

David Boswell, being resolute in the military feudal principle of continuing the male succession, passed by his daughters, and settled the estate on his nephew by his next brother, who approved of the deed, and renounced any pretensions which he might possibly have, in preference to his son. But the estate having been burthened with large portions to the daughters, and other debts, it was necessary for the nephew to sell a considerable part of it, and what remained was still much encumbered.

The frugality of the nephew preserved, and, in some degree, relieved the estate. His son, my grandfather, an eminent lawyer, not only re-purchased a great part of what had been sold, but acquired other lands ; and my father, who was one of the Judges of Scotland, and had added considerably to the

[1] Mr. Croker says that he was informed by Boswell's grand-daughter, Teresa, Lady Eliot, who died in 1836, that it had come to be pronounced Auchinleck. The Rev. James Chrystal, the minister of Auchinleck, in answer to my inquiry, politely informs me that ' the name " Affleck " is still quite common as applied to the parish, and even Auchinleck House is as often called Place Affleck as otherwise.' ⟨' Affleck ' is still, 1930, in use.⟩

[2] See *post*, v. 379. ⟨Also App. B, p. 527.⟩

estate, now signified his inclination to take the privilege allowed by our law [1], to secure it to his family in perpetuity by an entail, which, on account of marriage [a] articles, could not be done without my consent.

In the plan of entailing the estate, I heartily concurred with him, though I was the first to be restrained by it ; but we unhappily differed as to the series of heirs which should be established, or in the language of our law, called to the succession. My father had declared a predilection for heirs general, that is, males and females indiscriminately. He was willing, however, that all males descending from his grandfather should be preferred to females ; but would not extend that privilege to males deriving their descent from a higher source. I, on the other hand, had a zealous partiality for heirs male, however remote, which I maintained by arguments which appeared to me to have considerable weight [2]. And in the particular case

[a] marriage 1 : his marriage 2, 3.

[1] Acts of Parliament of Scotland, 1685, Cap. 22. BOSWELL.
Cockburn (*Life of Jeffrey*, i. 372) mentions ' the statute (11 and 12 Victoria, chap. 36) which dissolves the iron fetters by which, for about 160 years, nearly three-fourths of the whole land in Scotland was made permanently unsaleable, and unattachable for debt, and every acre in the kingdom might be bound up, throughout all ages, in favour of any heirs, or any conditions, that the caprice of each unfettered owner might be pleased to proscribe.'

[2] As first, the opinion of some distinguished naturalists, that our species is transmitted through males only, the female being all along no more than a *nidus*, or nurse, as Mother Earth is to plants of every sort ; which notion seems to be confirmed by that text of scripture, ' He was yet *in the loins of his* FATHER when Melchisedeck met him ' (Heb. vii. 10) ; and consequently, that a man's grandson by a daughter, instead of being his *surest* descendant, as is vulgarly said, has, in reality, no connection whatever with his blood. —And secondly, independent of this theory, (which, if true, should completely exclude heirs general,) that if the preference of a male to a female, without regard to primogeniture, (as a son, though much younger, nay, even a grandson by a son, to a daughter,) be once admitted, as it universally is, it must be equally reasonable and proper in the most remote degree of descent from an original proprietor of an estate, as in the nearest ; because,—however distant from the representative at the time,—that remote heir male, upon the failure of those nearer to the *original proprietor* than he is, becomes in fact the nearest male to *him*, and is, therefore, preferable as *his* representative, to a female descendant.—A little extension of mind will enable us easily to perceive that a son's son, in continuation to whatever length of time, is preferable to a son's daughter, in the succession to an ancient inheritance ; in which regard should be had to the representation of the original proprietor,

of our family, I apprehended that we were under an implied
obligation, in honour and good faith, to transmit the estate by
the same tenure which we held it, which was as heirs male, excluding nearer females. I therefore, as I thought conscientiously,
objected to my father's scheme.

My opposition was very displeasing to my father, who was
entitled to great respect and deference ; and I had reason to
apprehend disagreeable consequences from my non-compliance
with his wishes [1].   After much perplexity and uneasiness, I
wrote to Dr. Johnson, stating the case, with all its difficulties,
at full length, and earnestly requesting that he would consider
it at leisure, and favour me with his friendly opinion and
advice.

' To James Boswell, Esq.

' Dear Sir,

' I was much impressed by your letter, and,[a] if I can form upon your
case any resolution satisfactory to myself, will very gladly impart it : but
whether I am quite equal to it, I do not know. It is a case compounded
of law and justice, and requires a mind versed in juridical disquisitions.
Could you not [b] tell your whole mind to Lord Hailes ? He is, you know,
both a Christian and a Lawyer. I suppose he is above partiality, and
above loquacity : and, I believe, he will not think the time lost in
which he may quiet a disturbed, or settle a wavering mind. Write to
me, as any thing occurs to you ; and if I find myself stopped by want
of facts necessary to be known, I will make enquiries of you as my
doubts arise.

[a] *comma omitted* 2, 3.   [b] Could you not 1 : Could not you 2, 3.

and not to that of one of his descendants.

I am aware of Blackstone's admirable demonstration of the reason-
ableness of the legal succession,
upon the principle of there being the
greatest probability that the nearest
heir of the person who last dies proprietor of an estate, is of the blood
of the first purchaser. But supposing
a pedigree to be carefully authenticated through all its branches, instead
of mere *probability* there will be a
certainty, that *the nearest heir male,
at whatever period*, has the same
right of blood with the first heir male,

namely, *the original purchaser's eldest
son.* Boswell.

[1] Boswell wrote to Temple on Sept.
2, 1775 :—' What a discouraging reflection is it, that my father has in
his possession a renunciation of my
birthright, which I *madly* granted
to him, and which he has not the
generosity to restore, now that I am
doing beyond his utmost hopes ; and
that he may incommode and disgrace
me by some strange settlements,
while, all this time, not a shilling is
secured to my wife and children, in
case of my death.' *Letters*, No. 149,
i. 241.

' If your former resolutions should be found only fanciful, you decide rightly in judging that your father's fancies may claim the preference ; but whether they are fanciful or rational, is the question. I really think Lord Hailes could help us.

' Make my compliments to dear Mrs. Boswell ; and tell her, that I hope to be wanting in nothing that I can contribute to bring you all out of your troubles.

' I am, dear Sir, most affectionately,

' Your humble servant,

' London, Jan. 15, 1776.'   ' SAM. JOHNSON.'

TO THE SAME.

' DEAR SIR,

' I AM going to write upon a question which requires more know-ledge of local law, and more acquaintance with the general rules of inheritance, than I can claim ; but I write, because you request it.

' Land is, like any other possession, by natural right wholly in the power of its present owner ; and may be sold, given, or bequeathed, absolutely or conditionally, as judgement shall direct, or passion incite.

' But natural right would avail little without the protection of law ; and the primary notion of law is restraint in the exercise of natural right. A man is therefore, in society, not fully master of what he calls his own, but he still retains all the power which law does not take from him.

' In the exercise of the right which law either leaves or gives, regard is to be paid to moral obligations.

' Of the estate which we are now considering, your father still retains such possession, with such power over it, that he can sell it, and do with the money what he will, without any legal impediment. But when he extends his power beyond his own life, by settling the order of succession, the law makes your consent necessary.

' Let us suppose that he sells the land to risk the money in some specious adventure, and in that adventure loses the whole ; his posterity would be disappointed ; but they could not think themselves injured or robbed. If he spent it upon vice or pleasure, his successors could only call him vicious and voluptuous ; they could not say that he was injurious or unjust.

' He that may do more,[a] may do less. He that, by selling [b] or squander-ing, may disinherit a whole family, may certainly disinherit part, by a partial settlement.

' Laws are formed by the manners and exigencies of particular times, and it is but accidental that they last longer than their causes : the

a comma omitted 2, 3.   b comma inserted 2, 3.

limitation of feudal succession to the male arose from the obligation of
the tenant to attend his chief in war.

'As times and opinions are always changing, I know not whether it
be not usurpation to prescribe rules to posterity, by presuming to judge
of what we cannot know ; and I know not whether I fully approve either
your design or your father's, to limit that succession which descended to
you unlimited. If we are to leave *sartum tectum* [1] to posterity, what we
have without any merit of our own received from our ancestors, should
not choice and free-will be kept unviolated ? Is land to be treated
with more reverence than liberty ?—If this consideration should restrain
your father from disinheriting some of the males, does it leave you the
power of disinheriting all the females ?

'Can the possessor of a feudal estate make any will ? Can he appoint,
out of the inheritance, any portions to his daughters ? There seems to be
a very shadowy difference between the power of leaving land, and of
leaving money to be raised from land ; between leaving an estate to
females, and leaving the male heir, in effect, only their steward.

'Suppose at one time a law that allowed only males to inherit, and
during the continuance of this law many estates to have descended,
passing by the females, to remoter heirs. Suppose afterwards the law
repealed in correspondence with a change of manners, and women made
capable of inheritance ; would not then the tenure of estates be changed?
Could the women have no benefit from a law made in their favour ?
Must they be passed by upon moral principles for ever, because they
were once excluded by a legal prohibition ? Or may that which passed
only to males by one law, pass likewise to females by another ?

'You mention your resolution to maintain the right of your brothers [2] :
I do not see how any of their rights are invaded.

'As your whole difficulty arises from the act of your ancestor, who
diverted the succession from the females, you enquire, very properly,
what were his motives, and what was his intention ; for you certainly are
not bound by his act more than he intended to bind you, nor hold
your land on harder or stricter terms than those on which it was
granted.

'Intentions must be gathered from acts. When he left the estate to
his nephew, by excluding his daughters, was it, or was it not, in his power
to have perpetuated the succession to the males ? If he could have done
it, he seems to have shown, by omitting it, that he did not desire it to
be done ; and, upon your own principles, you will not easily prove your
right to destroy that capacity of succession which your ancestors have
left.

[1] The technical term in Roman law
for a building in good repair.

[2] Which term I applied to all the
heirs male. BOSWELL.

' If your ancestor had not the power of making a perpetual settlement ; and if, therefore, we cannot judge distinctly of his intentions, yet his act can only be considered as an example ; it makes not an obligation. And, as you observe, he set no example of rigorous adherence to the line of succession. He that overlooked a brother, would not wonder that little regard is shown to remote relations.

' As the rules of succession are, in a great part, purely legal, no man can be supposed to bequeath any thing, but upon legal terms ; he can grant no power which the law denies ; and if he makes no special and definite limitation, he confers all the powers a which the law allows.

' Your ancestor, for some reason, disinherited his daughters ; but it no more follows that he intended his b act as a rule for posterity, than the disinheriting of his brother.

' If therefore, you ask by what right your father admits daughters to inheritance, ask yourself, first, by what right you require them to be excluded ?

' It appears, upon reflection, that your father excludes nobody ; he only admits nearer females to inherit before males more remote ; and the exclusion is purely consequential.

' These, dear Sir, are my thoughts, immethodical and deliberative ; but, perhaps, you may find in them some glimmering of evidence.

' I cannot, however, but again recommend to you a conference with Lord Hailes, whom you know to be both a Lawyer and a Christian.

' Make my compliments to Mrs. Boswell, though she does not love me.

                              ' I am, Sir,
                              ' Your affectionate servant,
' Feb. 3, 1773 ¹.'   ' SAM. JOHNSON.'

I had followed his recommendation and consulted Lord Hailes, who upon this subject had a firm opinion contrary to mine. His Lordship obligingly took the trouble to write me a letter, in which he discussed with legal and historical learning, the points in which I saw much difficulty, maintaining that ' the succession of heirs general was the succession, by the law of Scotland, from the throne to the cottage, as far as we can learn it by record ; ' observing that the estate of our family had not been limited to heirs male ; and that though an heir male had in one instance been chosen in preference to nearer females, that had been an arbitrary act, which had seemed to be best

a powers 1: power 2, 3.   b his 1: this 2, 3.
¹ A misprint in editions 1, 2, 3 for 1776.

in the embarrassed state of affairs at that time ; and the fact was, that upon a fair computation of the value of land and money at the time, applied to the estate and the burthens upon it, there was nothing given to the heir male but the skeleton of an estate, ' The plea of conscience (said his Lordship,) which you put, is a most respectable one, especially when *conscience* and *self* are on different sides. But I think that conscience is not well informed, and that *self* and *she* ought on this occasion to be of a side.'

This letter, which had considerable influence upon my mind, I sent to Dr. Johnson, begging to hear from him again, upon this interesting question.

' To JAMES BOSWELL, ESQ.

' DEAR SIR,

' HAVING not any acquaintance with the laws or customs of Scotland, I endeavoured to consider your question upon general principles, and found nothing of much validity that I could oppose to this position : " He who inherits a fief unlimited by his ancestor [a], inherits the power of limiting it according to his own judgement or opinion." If this be true, you may join with your father.

' Further consideration produced [b] another conclusion : " He who receives a fief unlimited by his ancestors, gives his heirs some reason to complain, if he does not transmit it unlimited to posterity. For why should he make the state of others worse than his own, without a reason ? " If this be true, though neither you nor your father are about to do what is quite right, but as your father violates (I think) the legal succession least, he seems to be nearer the right than yourself.

' It cannot but occur that " Women have natural and equitable claims as well as men, and these claims are not to be capriciously or lightly superseded or infringed." When fiefs implied military service, it is easily discerned why females could not inherit them ; but that reason is now at an end. As manners make laws, manners likewise repeal them.

' These are the general conclusions which I have attained. None of them are very favourable to your scheme of entail, nor perhaps to any scheme. My observation, that only he who acquires an estate may bequeath it capriciously [1], if it contains any conviction, includes this position likewise, that only he who acquires an estate may entail

---

 a ancestor 1: ancestors 2, 3.   b produced 1: produces 2, 3.

[1] I had reminded him of his observation mentioned, ii. 261. BOSWELL.

it capriciously. But I think it may be safely presumed, that " he who inherits an estate, inherits all the power legally concomitant ; " and that " He who gives or leaves unlimited an estate legally limitable, must be presumed to give that power of limitation which he omitted to take away, and to commit future contingencies to future prudence." In these two positions I believe Lord Hailes will advise you to rest ; every other notion of possession seems to me full of difficulties, and embarrassed with scruples.

' If these axioms be allowed, you have arrived now at full liberty without the help of particular circumstances, which, however, have in your case great weight. You very rightly observe, that he who passing by his brother gave the inheritance to his nephew, could limit no more than he gave ; and by Lord Hailes's estimate of fourteen years' purchase, what he gave was no more than you may easily entail according to your own opinion, if that opinion should finally prevail.

' Lord Hailes's suspicion that entails are encroachments on the dominion of Providence, may be extended to all hereditary privileges and all permanent institutions ; I do not see why it may not be extended to any provision but a for the present hour, since all care about futurity proceeds upon a supposition, that we know at least in some degree what will be future. Of the future we certainly know nothing ; but we may form conjectures from the past ; and the power of forming conjectures, includes, in my opinion, the duty of acting in conformity to that probability which we discover. Providence gives the power, of which reason teaches the use.

' I am, dear Sir,

' Your most faithful servant,

' SAM. JOHNSON.'

' Feb. 9, 1776.'

' I hope I shall get some ground now with Mrs. Boswell ; make my compliments to her, and to the little people.

' Don't burn papers ; they may be safe enough in your own box,— you will wish to see them hereafter.'

TO THE SAME.

' DEAR SIR,

' To the letters which I have written about your great question I have nothing to add. If your conscience is satisfied, you have now only your prudence to consult. I long for a letter, that I may know how this troublesome and vexatious question is at last decided [1]. I hope

---

a but *omitted* 2, 3.

[1] The entail framed by my father with various judicious clauses, was   executed a by him and me, settling the estate upon the heirs male of his

a executed 1 : settled 2, 3.

that it will at last end well. Lord Hailes's letter was very friendly, and very seasonable, but I think his aversion from entails has something in it like superstition. Providence is not counteracted by any means which Providence puts into our power. The continuance and propagation of families makes a great part of the Jewish law, and is by no means prohibited in the Christian institution, though the necessity of it continues no longer. Hereditary tenures are established in all civilised countries, and are accompanied in most with hereditary authority. Sir William Temple considers our constitution as defective, that there is not an unalienable estate in land connected with a peerage [1] : and Lord Bacon mentions as a proof that the Turks are Barbarians, their want of *Stirpes*, as he calls them, or hereditary rank [2]. Do not let your mind, when it is freed from the supposed necessity of a rigorous entail, be entangled with contrary objections, and think all entails unlawful, till you have cogent arguments, which I believe you will never find. I am afraid of scruples [3].

' I have now sent all Lord Hailes's papers ; part I found hidden in a drawer in which I had laid them for security, and had forgotten them. Part of these are written twice ; I have returned both the copies. Part I had read before.

' Be so kind as to return Lord Hailes my most respectful thanks for his first volume ; his accuracy strikes me with wonder ; his narrative is far superiour to that of Henault, as I have formerly mentioned.

grandfather, which I found had been already done by my grandfather, imperfectly, but so as to be defeated only by selling the lands. I was freed by Dr. Johnson from scruples of conscientious obligation, and could, therefore, gratify my father. But my opinion and partiality for male succession, in its full extent, remained unshaken. Yet let me not be thought harsh or unkind to daughters ; for my notion is, that they should be treated with great affection and tenderness, and always participate of the prosperity of the family. Boswell.

[1] Temple, in *Popular Discontents* (*Works*, 1720, i. 269), examines the general dissatisfaction with the judicature of the House of Lords. Till the end of Elizabeth's reign, he states, the peers, who were few in number, were generally possessed of great estates which rendered them less subject to corruption. As one remedy for the evil existing in his time, he suggests that the Crown shall create ' no Baron, who shall not, at the same time, entail Four thousand Pounds a Year upon that Honour whilst it continues in his Family ; a Viscount, Five ; an Earl, Six ; a Marquis, Seven ; and a Duke, Eight.'

[2] ' A cruel tyranny, bathed in the blood of their emperors upon every succession ; a heap of vassals and slaves ; no nobles, no gentlemen, no freemen, no inheritance of land, no stirp of ancient families, [nullæ stirpes antiquæ].' Spedding's *Bacon*, vii. 22.

[3] ' Let me warn you very earnestly against scruples,' he wrote on March 5 (*post*, ii. 423) :—' I am no friend to scruples,' he had said at St. Andrews. *Post*, v. 62. During his last illness he said :—' Scruples made many men

' I am afraid that the trouble, which my irregularity and delay has cost him, is greater, far greater, than any good that I can do him will ever recompense ; but if I have any more copy, I will try to do better.

' Pray let me know if Mrs. Boswell is friends with me, and pay my respects to Veronica, and Euphemia, and Alexander.

' I am, Sir,
' Your most humble servant,

' February 15, 1776 a.'   ' SAM. JOHNSON.'

' MR. BOSWELL TO DR. JOHNSON.
' Edinburgh, Feb. 20, 1776.

*   *   *   *   *   *

' YOU have illuminated my mind and relieved me from imaginary shackles of conscientious obligation.   Were it necessary, I could immediately join in an entail upon the series of heirs approved by my father ; but it is better not to act too suddenly.'

' DR. JOHNSON TO MR. BOSWELL.

' DEAR SIR,

' I AM glad that what I could think or say has at all contributed to quiet your thoughts.   Your resolution not to act, till your opinion is confirmed by more deliberation, is very just.   If you have been scrupulous, do not now be rash.   I hope that as you think more, and take opportunities of talking with men intelligent in questions of property, you will be able to free yourself from every difficulty.

' When I wrote last, I sent, I think, ten packets.   Did you receive them all ?

' You must tell Mrs. Boswell that I suspected her to have written without your knowledge [1], and therefore did not return any answer, lest a clandestine correspondence should have been perniciously discovered.   I will write to her soon. *   *   *   *   *   *.

' I am, dear Sir,
' Most affectionately yours,

' Feb. 24, 1776.'   ' SAM. JOHNSON.

Having communicated to Lord Hailes what Dr. Johnson wrote concerning the question which perplexed me so much,

a 1775 1, 2, 3 *in error.*

miserable, but few men good.' Hoole's *Narrative* : John. Misc. ii. 152. ⟨' Good Friday, March 28, 1766. Scruples distract me, but at Church I had hopes to conquer them.' *Prayers*

& *Med.* ¶ 62 ; *Ib.* i. 38.⟩

[1] A letter to him on the interesting subject of the family settlement, which I had read. BOSWELL.

his Lordship wrote to me : ' Your scruples have produced more fruit than I ever expected from them ; an excellent dissertation on general principles of morals and law.'

I wrote to Dr. Johnson on the 20th of February, complaining of melancholy, and expressing a strong desire to be with him ; informing him that the ten packets came all safe ; that Lord Hailes was much obliged to him, and said he had almost wholly removed his scruples against entails.

' TO JAMES BOSWELL, ESQ.

' DEAR SIR,

' I HAVE not had your letter half an hour ; as you lay so much weight upon my notions, I should think it not just to delay my answer.

' I am very sorry that your melancholy should return, and should be sorry likewise if it could have no relief but from my company. My counsel you may have when you are pleased to require it ; but of my company you cannot in the next month have much, for Mr. Thrale will take me to Italy, he says, on the first of April.

' Let me warn you very earnestly against scruples. I am glad that you are reconciled to your settlement, and think it a great honour to have shaken Lord Hailes's opinion of entails. Do not, however, hope wholly to reason away your troubles ; do not feed them with attention, and they will die imperceptibly away. Fix your thoughts upon your business, fill your intervals with company, and sunshine will again break in upon your mind [1]. If you will come to me, you must come very quickly ; and even then I know not but we may scour the country together, for I have a mind to see Oxford and Lichfield, before I set out on this long journey. To this I can only add, that I am, dear Sir,

' Your most affectionate humble servant,

' SAM. JOHNSON.'

' March 5, 1776.'

---

[1] Paoli had given Boswell much the same advice. ' I told him that I had almost become for ever incapable of taking a part in active life. " All this," said Paoli, " is melancholy. I have also studied metaphysicks. I know the arguments for fate and free-will, for the materiality and immateriality of the soul, and even the subtile arguments for and against the existence of matter. *Ma lasciamo queste dispute ai oziosi.* But let us leave these disputes to the idle. *Io tengo sempre fermo un gran pensiero.* I hold always firm one great object. I never feel a moment of despondency." ' Boswell's *Corsica*, p. 327. See *post*, iv. 71.

To the Same.

'Dear Sir,

'Very early in April we leave England, and in the beginning
of the next week I shall leave London for a short time; of this I
think it necessary to inform you, that you may not be disappointed
in any of your enterprises. I had not fully resolved to go into the
country before this day.

'Please to make my compliments to Lord Hailes; and mention
very particularly to Mrs. Boswell my hope that she is reconciled to, Sir,

'Your faithful servant,

'Sam. Johnson.'

'March 12, 1776.'

Above thirty years ago, the heirs of Lord Chancellor Clarendon presented the University of Oxford with the continuation
of his History, and such other of his Lordship's manuscripts as
had not been published, on condition that the profits arising
from their publication should be applied to the establishment of
a *Manège* in the University. The gift was accepted in full
convocation. A person being now recommended to Dr. Johnson, as fit to superintend this proposed riding-school, he exerted
himself with that zeal for which he was remarkable upon every
similar occasion [1]. But, on enquiry into the matter, he found
that the scheme was not likely to be soon carried into execution; the profits arising from the Clarendon press being, from
some mismanagement, very scanty. This having been explained to him by a respectable dignitary of the church, who
had good means of knowing it, he wrote a letter upon the
subject, which at once exhibits his extraordinary precision and
acuteness, and his warm attachment to his Alma Mater.

'To the Reverend Dr. Wetherell, Master of
University-College, Oxford.

'Dear Sir,

'Few things are more unpleasant than the transaction of
business with men who are above knowing or caring what they have

---

[1] Johnson, in his letters to the
Thrales during the year 1775, mentions this riding-school frequently.
The person recommended was named
Carter. Gibbon (*Memoirs*, p. 81)
erroneously says 'the profit of the
second part of Lord Clarendon's
History has been applied to the
establishment of a riding-school, that
the polite exercises might be taught,
I know not with what success, in the
university.' ⟨See App. B, p. 527.⟩

to do ; such as the trustees for Lord Cornbury's institution will,
perhaps, appear, when you have read Dr. *******'s letter.

'The last part of the Doctor's letter is of great importance. The
complaint [1] which he makes I have heard long ago, and did not know
but it was redressed. It is unhappy that a practice so erroneous has
not yet been altered ; for altered it must be, or our press will be useless
with all its privileges. The booksellers, who, like all other men, have
strong prejudices in their own favour, are enough inclined to think
the practice of printing and selling books by any but themselves, an
encroachment on the rights of their fraternity ; and have need of
stronger inducements to circulate academical publications than those
of one another ; for, of that mutual co-operation by which the general
trade is carried on, the University can bear no part. Of those whom
he neither loves nor fears, and from whom he expects no reciprocation
of good offices, why should any man promote the interest but for
profit ? I suppose, with all our scholastick ignorance of mankind, we
are still too knowing to expect that the booksellers will erect themselves into patrons, and buy and sell under the influence of a disinterested zeal for the promotion of learning.

'To the booksellers, if we look for either honour or profit from
our press, not only their common profit, but something more must
be allowed ; and if books, printed at Oxford, are expected to be rated
at a high price, that price must be levied on the publick, and paid by
the ultimate purchaser, not by the intermediate agents. What price
shall be set upon the book, is, to the booksellers, wholly indifferent,
provided that they gain a proportionate profit by negociating the sale.

'Why books printed at Oxford should be particularly dear, I am,
however, unable to find. We pay no rent ; we inherit many of our
instruments and materials ; lodging and victuals are cheaper than at
London ; and, therefore, workmanship ought, at least, not to be dearer.
Our expences are naturally less than those of booksellers ; and, in
most cases, communities are content with less profit than individuals.

'It is, perhaps, not considered through how many hands a book often
passes, before it comes into those of the reader ; or what part of the
profit each hand must retain, as a motive for transmitting it to the next.

'We will call our primary agent in London, Mr. Cadell [2], who
receives our books from us, gives them room in his warehouse, and

---

[1] I suppose the complaint was,
that the trustees of the Oxford press
did not allow the London booksellers
a sufficient profit upon vending their
publications. BOSWELL.

[2] Cadell published *The False Alarm*

and Johnson's other political pamphlets, and, with Strahan, *The Journey
to the Western Islands*. Gibbon
described him as ' That honest and
liberal bookseller.' Stewart's *Life of
Robertson*, p. 366.

issues them on demand ; by him they are sold to Mr. Dilly, a wholesale bookseller, who sends them into the country ; and the last seller is the country bookseller. Here are three profits to be paid between the printer and the reader, or in the style of commerce, between the manufacturer and the consumer ; and if any of these profits is too penuriously distributed, the process of commerce is interrupted.

' We are now come to the practical question, what is to be done ? You will tell me, with reason, that I have said nothing, till I declare how much, according to my opinion, of the ultimate price ought to be distributed through the whole succession of sale.

' The deduction, I am afraid, will appear very great : but let it be considered before it is refused. We must allow, for profit, between thirty and thirty-five *per cent*. between six and seven shillings in the pound ; that is, for every book which costs the last buyer twenty shillings, we must charge Mr. Cadell with something less than fourteen. We must set the copies at fourteen shillings each, and superadd what is called the quarterly-book, or for every hundred books so charged we must deliver an hundred and four.

' The profits will then stand thus :

' Mr. Cadell, who runs no hazard, and gives no credit, will be paid for warehouse room and attendance by a shilling profit on each book, and his chance of the quarterly-book.

' Mr. Dilly, who buys the book for fifteen shillings, and who will expect the quarterly-book if he takes five and twenty, will sell [a] it to his country customer at sixteen and sixpence, by which, at the hazard of loss, and the certainty of long credit, he gains the regular profit of ten *per cent*. which is expected in the wholesale trade.

' The country bookseller, buying at sixteen and sixpence, and commonly trusting a considerable time, gains but three and sixpence, and,[b] if he trusts a year, not much more than two and sixpence ; otherwise than as he may, perhaps, take as long credit as he gives.

' With less profit than this, and more you see he cannot have, the country bookseller cannot live ; for his receipts are small, and his debts sometimes bad.

' Thus, dear Sir, I have been incited by Dr. *******'s letter to give you a detail of the circulation of books, which, perhaps, every man has not had opportunity of knowing ; and which those who know it, do not, perhaps, always distinctly consider.

' I am, &c.

' March 12, 1776.'　　　　　　　　　　　' SAM. JOHNSON [1].'

---

a sell 1 : send 2, 3.　　　　　b *comma omitted* 3.

[1] I am happy in giving this full and clear statement to the publick, to vindicate, by the authority of the greatest authour of his age, that

Having arrived in London late on Friday, the 15th of March, I hastened next morning to wait on Dr. Johnson, at his house ; but found he was removed from Johnson's-court, No. 7, to Bolt-court, No. 8 [1], still keeping to his favourite Fleet-street. My reflection at the time upon this change as marked in my Journal, is as follows : ' I felt a foolish regret that he had left a court which bore his name [2] ; but it was not foolish to be affected with some tenderness of regard for a place in which I had seen him a great deal, from whence I had often issued a better and a happier man than when I went in, and which had often appeared to my imagination while I trod its pavement [a], in the solemn darkness of the night, to be sacred to wisdom and piety [3].' Being informed that he was at Mr. Thrale's, in the Borough, I hastened thither, and found Mrs. Thrale and him at breakfast. I was kindly welcomed. In a moment he was in a full glow of conversation, and I felt myself elevated as if brought into another state of being. Mrs. Thrale and I looked to each other while he talked, and our looks expressed our congenial admiration and affection for him. I shall ever recollect this scene with great pleasure. I exclaimed to her, ' I am now, intellectually, *Hermippus redivivus*, I am quite restored by him, by transfusion of *mind* [4].' ' There are many (she replied) who admire and respect Mr. Johnson ; but you and I *love* him.'

a pavement 1 : pavements 2, 3.

respectable body of men, the Booksellers of London, from vulgar reflections, as if their profits were exorbitant, when, in truth, Dr. Johnson has here allowed them more than they usually demand. BOSWELL.

[1] ' Behind ⟨the house⟩ was a garden, which he took delight in watering; a room on the ground-floor was assigned to Mrs. Williams, and the whole of the two pair of stairs floor was made a repository for his books ; one of the rooms thereon being his study. Here, in the intervals of his residence at Streatham, he received the visits of his friends, and, to the most intimate of them, sometimes gave, not inelegant dinners.' Hawkins's *Johnson* p. 531. He wrote to

Mrs. Thrale on Aug. 14, 1780 :— ' This . . . is all that I have to tell you, except that I have three bunches of grapes on a vine in my garden ; at least, this is all that I will now tell of my garden.' *Letters*, No. 692. ⟨See *post*, iii. 398.⟩ This house was burnt down in 1819. *Notes and Queries*, 1st S., v. 233, and 9th S., ii. 7.

[2] He said, when in Scotland, that he was *Johnson of that Ilk*. BOSWELL. See *post*, iii. 326, note 4.

[3] See *ante*, ii. 229.

[4] See vol. i. p. 417. BOSWELL. Boswell refers to the work of Dr. Cohausen of Coblentz, *Hermippus Redivivus*, 1742. Dr. John Campbell ⟨imitated⟩ it, under the title of *Hermippus Redivivus, or the Sage's Triumph over Old Age and the*

He seemed very happy in the near prospect of going to Italy with Mr. and Mrs. Thrale. ' But, (said he,) before leaving England I am to take a jaunt to Oxford, Birmingham, my native city Lichfield, and my old friend, Dr. Taylor's, at Ashbourn, in Derbyshire. I shall go in a few days, and you, Boswell, shall go with me.' I was ready to accompany him ; being willing even to leave London to have the pleasure of his conversation.

I mentioned with much regret the extravagance of the representative of a great family in Scotland, by which there was danger of its being ruined ; and as Johnson respected it for its antiquity, he joined with me in thinking it would be happy if this person should die. Mrs. Thrale seemed shocked at this, as feudal barbarity ; and said, ' I do not understand this preference of the estate to its owner ; of the land to the man who walks upon that land.' JOHNSON. ' Nay, Madam, it is not a preference of the land to its owner ; it is the preference of a family to an individual. Here is an establishment in a country, which is of importance for ages, not only to the chief but to his people ; an establishment which extends upwards and downwards ; that this should be destroyed by one idle fellow is a sad thing.'

He said, ' Entails [1] are good, because it is good to preserve in a country, serieses of men, to whom the people are accustomed to look up as to their leaders. But I am for leaving a quantity of land in commerce, to excite industry, and keep money in the country ; for if no land were to be bought in a country [a],

---

[a] a country 1 : the country 2, 3.

Grave. Cohausen maintained that life might be prolonged to 115 years by breathing the breath of healthy young women. He founded his theory ' on a Roman inscription— —*Æsculapio et Sanitati L. Colodius Hermippus qui vixit annos cxv. dies v. puellarum anhelitu.*' He maintained that one of the most eligible conditions of life was that of a Confessor of youthful nuns. *Lowndes's Bibl. Man.* p. 488, and *Gent. Mag.* xiii. 279. I. D'Israeli (*Curiosities of Literature*, ed. 1834, ii. 102) describes Campbell's book as a ' curious banter on the hermetic philosophy, and the universal medicine ; the grave irony is so closely kept up, that it deceived for a length of time the most learned. . . . Campbell assured a friend it was a mere *jeu-d'-esprit.*' Lord E. Fitzmaurice (*Life of Shelburne*, ii. 314) says that Ingenhousz, a Dutch physician who lived with Shelburne, combated in one of his works the notion held by certain schoolmasters, that it was ' wholesome to inhale the air which has passed through the lungs of their pupils, closing the windows, in order purposely to facilitate that operation.'

[1] See *post*, v. 101.

there would be no encouragement to acquire wealth, because a family could not be founded there ; or if it were acquired, it must be carried away to another country where land may be bought. And although the land in every country will remain the same, and be as fertile where there is no money, as where there is, yet all that portion of the happiness of civil life, which is produced by money circulating in a country, would be lost.' BOSWELL. ' Then, Sir, would it be for the advantage of a country that all its lands were sold at once ? ' JOHNSON. 'So far, Sir, as money produces good, it would be an advantage ; for, then that country would have as much money circulating in it as it is worth. But to be sure this would be counterbalanced by disadvantages attending a total change of proprietors.'

I expressed my opinion that the power of entailing should be limited thus : ' That there should be one third, or perhaps one half of the land of a country kept free for commerce ; that the proportion allowed to be entailed, should be parcelled out so that no family could entail above a certain quantity. Let a family according to the abilities of its representatives, be richer or poorer in different generations, or always rich if its representatives be always wise : but let its absolute permanency be moderate. In this way we should be certain of there being always a number of established roots ; and as in the course of nature, there is in every age an extinction of some families, there would be continual openings for men ambitious of perpetuity, to plant a stock in the entail ground ¹.' JOHNSON. ' Why, Sir, mankind will be better able to regulate the system of entails, when the evil of too much land being locked up by them is felt, than we can do at present when it is not felt.'

I mentioned Dr. Adam Smith's book on ' The Wealth of

¹ The privilege of perpetuating in a family an estate and arms *indefeasibly* fro mgeneration to generation, is enjoyed by none of his Majesty's subjects except in Scotland, where the legal fiction of *fine and recovery* is unknown. It is a privilege so proud, that I should think it would be proper to have the exercise of it dependent on the royal prerogative. It seems absurd to permit the power of perpetuating their representation, to men, who having had no eminent merit, have truly no name. The King, as the impartial father of his people, would never refuse to grant the privilege to those who deserved it. BOSWELL.

Nations ¹,' which was just published, and that Sir John Pringle had observed to me, that Dr. Smith, who had never been in trade, could not be expected to write well on that subject any more than a lawyer upon physick. JOHNSON. ' He is mistaken, Sir : a man who has never been engaged in trade himself may undoubtedly write well upon trade, and there is nothing which requires more to be illustrated by philosophy than trade does. As to mere wealth, that is to say, money, it is clear that one nation or one individual cannot increase its store but by making another poorer : but trade procures what is more valuable, the reciprocation of the peculiar advantages of different countries. A merchant seldom thinks but of his own particular trade. To write a good book upon it, a man must have extensive views. It is not necessary to have practised, to write well upon a subject.' I mentioned law as a subject on which no man could write well without practice. JOHNSON. ' Why, Sir, in England, where so much money is to be got by the practice of the law, most of our writers upon it have been in practice ; though Blackstone had not been much in practice when he published his " Commentaries." But upon the Continent, the great writers on law have not all been in practice : Grotius, indeed,ᵃ was ; but Puffendorf was not, Burlamaqui was not.'

When we had talked of the great consequence which a man acquired by being employed in his profession, I suggested a doubt of the justice of the general opinion, that it is improper in a lawyer to solicit employment ; for why, I urged, should it not be equally allowable to solicit that as the means of consequence, as it is to solicit votes to be elected a member of Parliament ? Mr. Strahan had told me,ᵃ that a countryman of his and mine ², who had risen to eminence in the law, had, when first making his way, solicited him to get him employed in city causes. JOHNSON. ' Sir, it is wrong to stir up law-suits ; but

ᵃ *comma omitted* 2, 3.

¹ Boswell wrote to Temple, 28 April :—' Murphy says he has read thirty pages of Smith's *Wealth* but shall read no more. Smith, too, is now of our Club. It has lost its select merit.' *Letters*, No. 160, i. 250.

Johnson can scarcely have read Smith ; if he did, it made no impression on him. His ignorance on many points as to what constitutes the wealth of a nation remained as deep as ever.

² Mr. Wedderburn. CROKER.

when once it is certain that a law-suit is to go on, there is nothing wrong in a lawyer's endeavouring that he shall have the benefit, rather than another.' BOSWELL. 'You would not solicit employment, Sir, if you were a lawyer.' JOHNSON. ' No, Sir; but not because I should think it wrong, but because I should disdain it.' This was a good distinction, which will be felt by men of just pride. He proceeded : 'However, I would not have a lawyer to be wanting to himself in using fair means. I would have him to inject a little hint now and then, to prevent his being overlooked.'

Lord Mountstuart's bill for a Scotch Militia [1], in supporting which his Lordship had made an able speech in the House of Commons, was now a pretty general topick of conversation. —JOHNSON. ' As Scotland contributes so little land-tax [2] towards the general support of the nation, it ought not to have a militia paid out of the general fund, unless it should be thought for the general interest, that Scotland should be protected from an invasion, which no man can think will happen ; for what enemy would invade Scotland, where there is nothing to be got ? No, Sir ; now that the Scotch have not the pay of English soldiers spent among them, as so many troops are sent abroad, they are trying to get money another way, by having a militia paid. If they are afraid, and seriously desire to have an armed force to defend them, they should pay for it. Your scheme is to retain a part of your little [a] land-tax, by making us pay and clothe your militia.' BOSWELL. 'You should not talk of *we* and *you*, Sir : there is now an *Union*.' JOHNSON. ' There must be a

[a] *little omitted* 2, 3.

[1] A similar bill had been thrown out sixteen years earlier by 194 to 84. ' A bill for a Militia in Scotland was less successful ; nor could the disaffected there obtain this mode of having their arms restored. Pitt had acquiesced ; but . . . the young Whigs attacked it with all their force.' Walpole's *Reign of George II*, iii. 280. Lord Mountstuart's bill was thrown out by 112 to 95, the Ministry being in the minority. The arguments for and against it are stated in the *Ann. Reg.* xix. 140. See *post*, iii. 1. Henry

Mackenzie (*Life of John Home*, i. 26) says :—' The Poker Club [was] instituted in 1762, at a time when Scotland was refused a militia, and thought herself affronted by the refusal. . . . The name . . . was chosen from a quaint sort of allusion to the principles it was originally meant to excite, as a club to stir up the fire and spirit of the country.' See *ante*, ii. 376.

[2] ' Scotland only paid one-fortieth to the land-tax, the very specific tax, out of which all the expences of a militia were to be drawn.' *Ann. Reg.* xix. 141.

distinction of interest, while the proportions of land-tax are so unequal. If Yorkshire should say, " Instead of paying our land-tax, we will keep a greater number of militia," it would be unreasonable.' In this argument my friend was certainly in the wrong. The land-tax is as unequally proportioned between different parts of England, as between England and Scotland ; nay, it is considerably unequal in Scotland itself. But the land-tax is but a small part of the numerous branches of publick revenue, all of which Scotland pays precisely as England does. A French invasion made in Scotland would soon penetrate into England.

He thus discoursed upon supposed obligations [a] in settling estates :—' Where a man gets the unlimited property of an estate, there is no obligation upon him in *justice* to leave it to one person rather than to another. There is a motive of preference from *kindness*, and this kindness is generally entertained for the nearest relation. If I *owe* a particular man a sum of money, I am obliged to let that man have the next money I get, and cannot in justice let another have it : but if I owe money to no man, I may dispose of what I get as I please. There is not a *debitum justitiæ* to a man's next heir ; there is only a *debitum caritatis*. It is plain, then, that I have morally a choice, according to my liking. If I have a brother in want, he has a claim from affection to my assistance ; but if I have also a brother in want, whom I like better, he has a preferable claim. The right of an heir at law is only this, that he is to have the succession to an estate, in case no other person is appointed to it by the owner. His right is merely preferable to that of the King.'

We got into a boat to cross over to Black-friars ; and as we moved along the Thames, I talked to him of a little volume, which, altogether unknown to him, was advertised to be published in a few days, under the title of ' *Johnsoniana*, or *Bon Mots* of Dr. Johnson [1].' JOHNSON. ' Sir, it is a mighty impudent thing.' BOSWELL. ' Pray, Sir, could you have no redress if

---

[a] obligations 1 : obligation 2, 3.

[1] *Johnsoniana ; or a Collection of Bon Mots. By Dr. Johnson and Others. Together with the Choice Sentences of Publius Syrius, now first translated into English*. Printed for J. Ridley, 1776, 8vo. In a new edition of this book, which was published in the following year, the editor states, that either ' through hurry or inattention some obscene jests had unluckily found a place in the first edition.' See *post*, iii. 325.

you were to prosecute a publisher for bringing out, under your name, what you never said, and ascribing to you dull stupid nonsense, or making you swear profanely, as many ignorant relaters of your *bon mots* do [1] ? ' JOHNSON. ' No, Sir ; there will always be some truth mixed with the falsehood, and how can it be ascertained how much is true and how much is false ? Besides, Sir, what damages would a jury give me for having been represented as swearing ? ' BOSWELL. ' I think, Sir, you should at least disavow such a publication, because the world and posterity might with much plausible foundation say, " Here is a volume which was publickly advertised and came out in Dr. Johnson's own time, and, by his silence, was admitted by him to be genuine." ' JOHNSON. ' I shall give myself no trouble about the matter.'

He was, perhaps, above suffering from such spurious publications ; but I could not help thinking, that many men would be much injured in their reputation, by having absurd and vicious sayings imputed to them ; and that redress ought in such cases to be given.

He said, ' The value of every story depends on its being true. A story is a picture either of an individual or of human nature in general : if it be false, it is a picture of nothing. For instance : suppose a man should tell that Johnson, before setting out for Italy, as he had to cross the Alps, sat down to make himself wings. This many people would believe ; but it would be a picture of nothing. ******* [2] (naming a worthy friend of ours,) used to think a story, a story, till I shewed him that truth

[1] See *ante*, ii. 338, note 2.
[2] The number of the asterisks, taken with the term *worthy friend*, renders it almost certain that Langton was meant. The story might, however, have been told of Reynolds, for he wrote of Johnson :—' Truth, whether in great or little matters, he held sacred. From the violation of truth, he said, in great things your character or your interest was affected, in lesser things your pleasure is equally destroyed. I remember, on his relating some incident, I added something to his relation which I supposed might likewise have happened : " It would have been a better story," says he, " if it had been so ; but it was not." ' Leslie and Taylor's *Reynolds*, ii. 457. Mrs. Piozzi records (*Anec.* p. 116 : John. Misc. i. 225) :— ' A story (says he) is a specimen of human manners, and derives its sole value from its truth. When Foote has told me something, I dismiss it from my mind like a passing shadow : when Reynolds tells me something, I consider myself as possessed of an idea the more.' ⟨Croker thought that Langton was meant. Ed. 1831, iii. 320. In Boswell's journal Langton's name is given in full. *Boswell Papers*, vi. 252.⟩

was essential to it [1].' I observed, that Foote entertained us with stories which were not true ; but that, indeed, it was properly not as narratives that Foote's stories pleased us, but as collections of ludicrous images. JOHNSON. ' Foote is quite impartial, for he tells lies of every body †.'

The importance of strict and scrupulous veracity cannot be too often inculcated. Johnson was known to be so rigidly attentive to it, that even in his common conversation the slightest circumstance was mentioned with exact precision [2]. The knowledge of his having such a principle and habit made his friends have a perfect reliance on the truth of every thing that he told, however it might have been doubted if told by many others. As an instance of this, I may mention an odd incident which he related as having happened to him one night in Fleet-street. ' A gentlewoman (said he) begged I would give her my arm to assist her in crossing the street, which I accordingly did ; upon which she offered me a shilling, supposing me to be the watchman. I perceived that she was somewhat in liquor.' This, if told by most people, would have been thought an invention ; when told by Johnson, it was believed by his friends as much as if they had seen what passed.

We landed at the Temple-stairs, where we parted.

I found him in the evening in Mrs. Williams's room. We talked of religious orders. He said, ' It is as unreasonable for

[1] Boswell felt this when, more than eight years earlier, he wrote :—' As I have related Paoli's remarkable sayings, I declare upon honour, that I have neither added nor diminished ; nay so scrupulous have I been, that I would not make the smallest variation even when my friends thought it would be an improvement. I know with how much pleasure we read what is perfectly authentick.' Boswell's *Corsica*, Pref. See *post*, iii. 209.

[2] In his *Life of Browne* (edit. 1927, p. 8) he says of ' innocent frauds ':— ' But ... no fraud is innocent ; for the confidence which makes the happiness of society, is in some degree diminished by every man, whose practice is at variance with his words.' ' Mr. Tyers,' writes Murphy (*Life*, p. 146), ' observed, " that Dr. Johnson always talked as if he was talking upon oath." ' Compared with Johnson's strictness, Rousseau's laxity is striking. After describing ' ces gens qu'on appelle vrais dans le monde,' he continues :—' L'homme que j'appelle *vrai* fait tout le contraire. En choses parfaitement indifférentes, la vérité, qu'alors l'autre respecte si fort, le touche fort peu, et il ne se fera guère de scrupule d'amuser une compagnie par des faits controuvés, dont il ne résulte aucun jugement injuste, ni pour ni contre qui que ce soit vivant ou mort.' *Les Rêveries*, ivme promenade.

† ⟨According to Cradock, Johnson said of Foote : ' If we venture to come into company with Foote, we have no

a man to go into a Carthusian convent for fear of being immoral, as for a man to cut off his hands for fear he should steal.
There is, indeed, great resolution in the immediate act of dis-
membering himself ; but when that is once done, he has no
longer any merit : for though it is out of his power to steal, yet
he may all his life be a thief in his heart. So when a man has
once become a Carthusian, he is obliged to continue so, whether
he chooses it or not. Their silence, too, is absurd. We read in
the Gospel of the apostles being sent to preach, but not to hold
their tongues. All severity that does not tend to increase good,
or prevent evil, is idle. I said to the Lady Abbess [1] of a convent, " Madam, you are here, not for the love of virtue, but the
fear of vice." She said, " She should remember this as long as
she lived." ' I thought it hard to give her this view of her
situation, when she could not help it ; and, indeed, I wondered
at the whole of what he now said ; because, both in his ' Rambler [2]'
and ' Idler [3],' he treats religious austerities with much solemnity of
respect [4].

Finding him still persevering in his abstinence from wine, I
ventured to speak to him of it.—JOHNSON. ' Sir, I have no
objection to a man's drinking wine, if he can do it in moderation. I found myself apt to go to excess in it, and therefore,
after having been for some time without it, on account of illness, I thought it better not to return to it [5]. Every man is to
judge for himself, according to the effects which he experiences.
One of the fathers tells us, he found fasting made him so
peevish [6] that he did not practise it.'

Though he often enlarged upon the evil of intoxication [7], he

---

right . . . to look for Truth.' *Memoirs*,
1826, i, 95.>

[1] No doubt Mrs. Fermor (*ante*, ii.
392).

[2] No. 110.   [3] No. 52.

[4] But see *ante*, i. 365 ; *post*, v. 62.

[5] See *ante*, ii. 8, and *post*, iii. 245.

[6] Three weeks later, at his usual
fast before Easter, Johnson recorded :
—' I felt myself very much disordered by emptiness, and called for
tea with peevish and impatient eagerness.' *Pr. and Med.* ¶ 115.

[7] Of the use of spirituous liquors,
he wrote in his second notice of
Hanway's *Journal* (*Works*, vi. 26) :—
' The mischiefs arising, on every side,
from this compendious mode of
drunkenness, are enormous and in-
supportable ; equally to be found
among the great and the mean ; filling
palaces with disquiet, and distraction,
harder to be borne, as it cannot be mentioned; and overwhelming multitudes
with incurable diseases, and unpitied
poverty.' Stockdale (*Memoirs*, ii. 189)

was by no means harsh and unforgiving to those who indulged in occasional excess in wine. One of his friends [1], I well remember, came to sup at a tavern with him and some other gentlemen, and too plainly discovered that he had drunk too much at dinner. When one who loved mischief, thinking to produce a severe censure, asked Johnson, a few days afterwards, ' Well, Sir, what did your friend say to you, as an apology for being in such a situation ? ' Johnson answered, ' Sir, he said all that a man *should* say : he said he was sorry for it.'

I heard him once give a very judicious practical advice upon this subject : ' A man, who has been drinking wine at all freely, should never go into a new company. With those who have partaken of wine with him, he may be pretty well in unison ; but he will probably be offensive, or appear ridiculous, to other people.'

He allowed very great influence to education. ' I do not deny, Sir, but there is some original difference in minds ; but it is nothing in comparison of what is formed by education.

says that he heard Mrs. Williams ' wonder what pleasure men can take in making beasts of themselves. "I wonder, Madam," replied the Doctor, " that you have not penetration enough to see the strong inducement to this excess ; for he who makes a *beast* of himself, gets rid of the pain of being a *man*." '

[1] Very likely Boswell. See *post*, iv. 112, for a like instance. In 1775, under a yew tree, he promised Temple to be sober. On Aug. 12, 1775, he wrote :—' My promise under the solemn yew I have observed wonderfully, having never infringed it till the other day, that a very jovial company of us dined superbly at a tavern ; and I unwarily exceeded my bottle of old hock ; and, having once broke over the pale, I run wild. But I did not get drunk. I was, however, intoxicated, and very ill next day.' *Letters*, No. 148, i. 236. During his present visit to London he wrote :— ' My promise under the solemn yew at Mamhead was not religiously kept ;

because a little wine hurried me on too much. The General has taken my word of honour that I shall not taste fermented liquor for a year, that I may recover sobriety. I have kept this promise now about three weeks. I was really growing a drunkard.' *Ib*. No. 160, p. 251. In 1778 he was for a short time a water drinker. *Post*, iii. 328. His intemperance grew upon him, and at last carried him off. On Dec. 4, 1790, he wrote to Malone :—' Courtenay . . . took my word and honour that, till the 1st of March, my allowance of wine *per diem* should not exceed four good glasses at dinner, and a pint after it : and this I have kept, though I have dined with Jack Wilkes,' &c. *Letters*, No. 286, ii. 405. On March 8, 1791, he wrote :— ' Your friendly admonition as to excess in wine *has* been often too applicable. . . . As I am now free from my restriction to Courtenay, I shall be much upon my guard ; for, to tell the truth, I did go too deep the day before yesterday.' *Ib*. No. 296, p. 427.

We may instance the science of *numbers*, which all minds are equally capable of attaining [1] ; yet we find a prodigious difference in the powers of different men, in that respect, after they are grown up, because their minds have been more or less exercised in it : and I think the same cause will explain the difference of excellence in other things, gradations admitting always some difference in the first principles [2].'

[1] ' Mathematics are, perhaps, too much studied at our universities. This seems a science, to which the meanest intellects are equal. I forget who it is that says, " All men might understand mathematics, if they would." ' Goldsmith's *Present State of Polite Learning*, ch. 13.

[2] ' No, Sir,' he once said, ' people are not born with a particular genius for particular employments or studies, for it would be like saying that a man could see a great way east, but could not west. It is good sense applied with diligence to what was at first a mere accident, and which, by great application, grew to be called, by the generality of mankind, a particular genius.' Miss Reynolds's *Recollections* in *John. Misc.* ii. 287. Perhaps this is Miss Reynolds's recollection of the following, in Boswell's *Hebrides* (*post*, v. 35) :—*Johnson.* ' I could as easily apply to law as to tragick poetry.' —*Boswell.* ' Yet, sir, you did apply to tragick poetry, not to law.'—*Johnson.* ' Because, sir, I had not money to study law. Sir, the man who has vigour, may walk to the east, just as well as to the west, if he happens to turn his head that way.' ' The true Genius,' he wrote (*Life of Cowley*, 3), ' is a mind of large general powers, accidentally determined to some particular direction.' Reynolds held the same doctrine, having got it no doubt from Johnson. He held ' that the superiority attainable in any pursuit whatever does not originate in an innate propensity of the mind to that pursuit in particular, but depends on the general strength of the intellect, and on the intense and constant application of that strength to a specific purpose. He regarded ambition as the *cause* of eminence, but accident as pointing out the *means*.' Northcote's *Reynolds*, i. 11. ' Porson insisted that all men are born with abilities nearly equal. " Any one," he would say, " might become quite as good a critic as I am, if he would only take the trouble to make himself so. I have made myself what I am by intense labour." ' Rogers's *Table Talk*, p. 305. Hume maintained the opposite. ' This forenoon,' wrote Boswell on June 19, 1775, ' Mr. Hume came in. . . . He did not say much : I only remember his remark, that characters depend more on original formation than on the way we are educated ; " for," said he, " princes are educated uniformly ; and yet how different they are. How different was James II from Charles II ".' *Letters*, No. 147, i. 234. Boswell recorded, two years earlier (*post*, v. 214) :—' Dr. Johnson denied that any child was better than another, but by difference of instruction ; though, in consequence of greater attention being paid to instruction by one child than another, and of a variety of imperceptible causes, such as instruction being counteracted by servants, a notion was conceived, that of two children, equally well educated, one was naturally much worse than another.'

This is a difficult subject ; but it is best to hope that diligence may do a great deal. We are *sure* of what it can do, in increasing our mechanical force and dexterity.

I again visited him on Monday. He took occasion to enlarge, as he often did, upon the wretchedness of a sea-life [1]. ' A ship is worse than a gaol. There is, in a gaol, better air, better company, better conveniency of every kind ; and a ship has the additional disadvantage of being in danger. When men come to like a sea-life, they are not fit to live on land [2].'—' Then (said I) it would be cruel in a father to breed his son to the sea.' JOHNSON. ' It would be cruel in a father who thinks as I do. Men go to sea, before they know the unhappiness of that way of life ; and when they have come to know it, they cannot escape from it, because it is then too late to choose another profession ; as indeed is generally the case with men, when they have once engaged in any particular way of life.'

On Tuesday, March 19, which was fixed for our proposed jaunt, we met in the morning at the Somerset coffee-house in the Strand, where we were taken up by the Oxford coach. He was accompanied by Mr. Gwyn [3], the architect ; and a gentleman of Merton College, whom we did not know, had the fourth seat. We soon got into conversation ; for it was very remarkable of Johnson, that the presence of a stranger was [a] no restraint upon his talk. I observed that Garrick, who was about to quit the stage, would soon have an easier life. JOHNSON. ' I doubt that, Sir.' BOSWELL. ' Why, Sir, he will be Atlas with the burthen off his back.' JOHNSON. ' But I know not, Sir, if he will be so steady without his load. However, he should never play any more, but be entirely the gentleman, and not partly the player : he should no longer subject himself to be hissed by a mob, or to be insolently treated by performers, whom he

[a] was 1 : had 2, 3.

[1] See *ante*, i. 348 ; *post*, v. 137, 249.
[2] The grossness of naval men is shewn in Captain Mirvan, in Miss Burney's *Evelina*. In her *Diary*, i. 358, she records :—' The more I see of sea captains, the less reason I have to be ashamed of Captain Mirvan ; for they have all so irresistible a propensity to wanton mischief,—to roast-

ing beaus, and detesting old women, that I quite rejoice I showed the book to no one ere printed, lest I should have been prevailed upon to soften his character.'
[3] Baretti, in a MS. note in *Piozzi Letters*, i. 349, describes Gwyn as ' the Welsh architect that built the bridge at Oxford.' He built Magdalen Bridge.

used to rule with a high hand, and who would gladly retaliate.'
BOSWELL. 'I think he should play once a year for the benefit
of decayed actors, as it has been said he means to do.' JOHNSON.
'Alas, Sir ! he will soon be a decayed actor himself.'

Johnson expressed his disapprobation of ornamental architecture, such as magnificent columns supporting a portico, or
expensive pilasters supporting merely their own capitals, 'because it consumes labour disproportionate to its utility.' For
the same reason he satyrised statuary. 'Painting (said he)
consumes labour not disproportionate to its effect ; but a fellow
will hack half a year at a block of marble to make something
in stone that hardly resembles a man. The value of statuary
is owing to its difficulty. You would not value the finest head
cut upon a carrot [1].' Here he seemed to me to be strangely
deficient in taste ; for surely statuary is a noble art of imitation,
and preserves a wonderful expression of the varieties of the
human frame ; and although it must be allowed that the circumstances of difficulty enhance the value of a marble head,
we should consider, that if it requires a long time in the performance, it has a proportionate value in durability.

Gwyn was a fine lively rattling fellow. Dr. Johnson kept
him in subjection, but with a kindly authority. The spirit of
the artist, however, rose against what he thought a Gothick
attack, and he made a brisk defence. 'What, Sir, will you allow
no value to beauty in architecture or in statuary ? Why should
we allow it then in writing ? Why do you take the trouble to
give us so many fine allusions, and bright images, and elegant
phrases ? You might convey all your instruction without these
ornaments.' Johnson smiled with complacency ; but said, 'Why,
Sir, all these ornaments are useful, because they obtain an easier
reception for truth ; but a building is not at all more convenient
for being decorated with superfluous carved work.'

Gwyn at last was lucky enough to make one reply to Dr.

[1] 'Whence,' asks Goldsmith, 'has proceeded the vain magnificence of expensive architecture in our col-leges ? Is it, that men study to more advantage in a palace than in a cell ? One single performance of taste, or genius, confers more real honours on its parent university, than all the labours of the chissel.' *Present State of Polite Learning*, ch. 13. Newton used to say of his friend, the Earl of Pembroke, 'that he was a lover of stone dolls.' Brewster's *Newton*, ed. 1855, ii. 411.

Johnson, which he allowed to be excellent. Johnson censured him for taking down a church which might have stood many years, and building a new one at a different place, for no other reason but that there might be a direct road to a new bridge ; and his expression was, ' You are taking a church out of the way, that the people may go in a straight line to the bridge.'— ' No, Sir, (said Gwyn,) I am putting the church *in* the way, that the people may not *go out of the way*.' JOHNSON. (with a hearty loud laugh of approbation,) ' Speak no more. Rest your colloquial fame upon this.'

Upon our arrival at Oxford, Dr. Johnson and I went directly to University College, but were disappointed on finding that one of the fellows, his friend Mr. Scott [1], who accompanied him from Newcastle to Edinburgh, was gone to the country. We put up at the Angel inn, and passed the evening by ourselves in easy and familiar conversation. Talking of constitutional melancholy, he observed, ' A man so afflicted, Sir, must divert distressing thoughts, and not combat with them.' BOSWELL. ' May not he think them down, Sir ? ' JOHNSON. ' No, Sir. To attempt to *think them down* is madness. He should have a lamp constantly burning in his bed-chamber during the night, and if wakefully disturbed, take a book, and read, and compose himself to rest. To have the management of the mind is a great art, and it may be attained in a considerable degree by experience and habitual exercise.' BOSWELL. ' Should not he provide amusements for himself ? Would it not, for instance, be right for him to take a course of chymistry ? ' JOHNSON. ' Let him take a course of chymistry, or a course of rope-dancing, or a course of any thing to which he is inclined at the time. Let him contrive to have as many retreats for his mind as he can, as many things to which it can fly from itself [2]. Burton's " Anatomy of Melancholy [3] " is a valuable work. It is, perhaps, overloaded with quotation. But there is great spirit and great power in what Burton says, when he writes from his own mind.'

Next morning we visited Dr. Wetherell, Master of University College, with whom Dr. Johnson conferred on the most ad-

---

[1] Afterwards Lord Stowell. See *post*, v. 16.

[2] See *ante*, i. 446.

[3] See *ante*, ii. 121, and *post*, iii. 415.

vantageous mode of disposing of the books printed at the
Clarendon press, on which subject his letter has been inserted
in a former page [1]. I often had occasion to remark, Johnson
loved business [2], loved to have his wisdom actually operate on
real life. Dr. Wetherell and I talked of him without reserve
in his own presence. WETHERELL. ' I would have given him
a hundred guineas if he would have written a preface to his
" Political Tracts [3]," by way of a Discourse on the British Constitution.' BOSWELL. ' Dr. Johnson, though in his writings,
and upon all occasions a great friend to the constitution both
in church and state, has never written expressly in support of
either. There is really a claim upon him for both. I am sure
he could give a volume of no great bulk upon each, which would
comprise all the substance, and with his spirit would effectually
maintain them. He should erect a fort on the confines of each.'
I could perceive that he was displeased with this dialogue. He
burst out, ' Why should *I* be always writing [4] ? ' I hoped he was
conscious that the debt was just, and meant to discharge it,
though he disliked being dunned.

We then went to Pembroke College, and waited on his old
friend Dr. Adams, the master of it, whom I found to be a most
polite, pleasing, communicative man. Before his advancement
to the headship of his college, I had intended to go and visit
him at Shrewsbury, where he was rector of St. Chad's, in order
to get from him what particulars he could recollect of Johnson's
academical life. He now † obligingly gave me part of that
authentick information, which, with what I afterwards owed
to his kindness, will be found incorporated in its proper place
in this work.

Dr. Adams had distinguished himself by an able answer to
David Hume's ' Essay on Miracles.' He told me he had once
dined in company with Hume in London [5] ; that Hume shook

---

[1] See *ante*, ii. 424.
[2] See *post*, iv. 86–7.
[3] See *ante*, ii. 315.
[4] See *ante*, i. 398 ; ii. 15, 35.
[5] ' Hume told Cadell the bookseller that he had a great desire to
be introduced to as many of the persons who had written against him as
could be collected. . . . Accordingly,

Dr. Douglas, Dr. Adams, &c. &c., were
invited by Cadell to dine at his house,
in order to meet Hume. They came ;
and Dr. Price, who was of the party,
assured me that they were all delighted with David.' Rogers's *Table
Talk*, p. 106.
    † ⟨See Boswell's *Note Book*, 1925,
p. 8.⟩

hands with him, and said, ' You have treated me much better than I deserve ; ' and that they exchanged visits. I took the liberty to object to treating an infidel writer with smooth civility. Where there is a controversy concerning a passage in a classick authour, or concerning a question in antiquities, or any other subject in which human happiness is not deeply interested, a man may treat his antagonist with politeness and even respect. But where the controversy is concerning the truth of religion, it is of such vast importance to him who maintains it, to obtain the victory, that the person of an opponent ought not to be spared. If a man firmly believes that religion is an invaluable treasure [1], he will consider a writer who endeavours to deprive mankind of it as a *robber* ; he will look upon him as *odious*, though the Infidel might think himself in the right. A robber who reasons as the gang do in the ' Beggar's Opera,' who call themselves *practical* philosophers [2], and may have as much sincerity as pernicious *speculative* philosophers, is not the less an object of just indignation. An abandoned profligate may think that it is not wrong to debauch my wife ; but shall I, therefore, not detest him ? And if I catch him in making an attempt, shall I treat him with politeness ? No, I will kick him down stairs, or run him through the body ; that is, if I really love my wife, or have a true rational notion of honour. An Infidel then shall not be treated handsomely by a Christian, merely because he endeavours to rob with ingenuity. I do declare, however, that I am exceedingly unwilling to be provoked to anger, and could I be persuaded that truth would not suffer from a cool moderation in its defenders, I should wish to preserve good humour, at least, in every controversy ; nor, indeed, do I see why a man should lose his temper while he does all he

---

[1] Boswell, in his *Corsica*, p. 275, uses a strange argument against infidelity. ' Belief is favourable to the human mind, were it for nothing else but to furnish it entertainment. An infidel I should think, must frequently suffer from ennui.' In his *Hebrides, post*, v. 30, note 3, he attacks Adam Smith for being ' so forgetful of human comfort as to give any countenance to that dreary infidelity which would " make us poor indeed." '

[2] ' JEMMY TWITCHER. Are we more dishonest than the rest of Mankind ? What we win, Gentlemen, is our own, by the Law of Arms, and the Right of Conquest.

' CROOK-FINGER'D JACK. Where shall we find such another Set of practical Philosophers, who to a Man are above the Fear of Death ? ' *The Beggar's Opera*, act ii. sc. 1.

can to refute an opponent. I think ridicule may be fairly used against an infidel ; for instance, if he be an ugly fellow, and yet absurdly vain of his person [1], we may contrast his appearance with Cicero's beautiful image of Virtue, could she be seen [2]. Johnson coincided with me and said, ' When a man voluntarily engages in an important controversy, he is to do all he can to lessen his antagonist, because authority from personal respect has much weight with most people, and often more than reasoning [3]. If my antagonist writes bad language, though that may not be essential to the question, I will attack him for his bad language.' ADAMS. ' You would not jostle a chimney-sweeper.' JOHNSON. ' Yes, Sir, if it were necessary to jostle him *down*.'

Dr. Adams told us, that in some of the Colleges at Oxford, the fellows had excluded the students from social intercourse with them in the common room [4]. JOHNSON. ' They are in the right, Sir, for there[a] can be no real conversation, no fair exertion of mind amongst them, if the young men are by ; for a man who

a Sir, for there 1, 2: Sir: there 3.

[1] Boswell, I think, here aims a blow at Gibbon. He says (*post*, iv. 73), that Johnson had talked ' with some disgust ' of Mr. Gibbon's ugliness. He wrote to Temple on May 8, 1779 :— ' He [Gibbon] is an ugly, affected, disgusting fellow and poisons our literary club to me.' He had, 28 Apr., 1776, classed him among ' infidel wasps or venomous insects.' *Letters*, No. 160, i. 250 ; No. 287, ii. 287. The younger Colman describes Gibbon as dressed ' in a suit of flower'd velvet, with a bag and sword.' *Random Records*, i. 121. ⟨Walpole says : ' I well knew his vanity, even about his ridiculous face and person.' *Letters*, ii. 376.⟩

[2] ' Formam quidem ipsam, Marce fili, et tamquam faciem honesti vides, " quæ si oculis cerneretur, mirabiles amores," ut ait Plato, " excitaret sapientiae." ' Cicero, *De Off.* i. 5.

[3] Of Beattie's attack on Hume, he said :—' Treating your adversary with respect, is striking soft in a battle.' *Post*, v. 29.

[4] When Gibbon entered Magdalen College in 1752, the ordinary commoners were already excluded. ' As a gen-tleman commoner,' he writes, ' I was admitted to the society of the fellows, and fondly expected that some questions of literature would be the amusing and instructive topics of their discourse. Their conversation stagnated in a round of college business, Tory politics, personal anecdotes, and private scandal : their dull and deep potations excused the brisk intemperance of youth ; and their constitutional toasts were not expressive of the most lively loyalty for the house of Hanover.' Gibbon's *Memoirs*, p. 57. In Jesse's edition of White's *Selborne*, p. 11, it is stated that ' White, as long as his health allowed him, always attended the annual election of Fellows at Oriel College, where the gentlemen commoners were allowed the use of the common-room after dinner. This liberty they seldom availed themselves of, except on the occasion of Mr. White's visits ; for such was his happy and, indeed, inimitable manner of . . . telling a story, that the room was always filled when he was there.' He died in 1793.

has a character does not choose to stake it in their presence.' BOSWELL. ' But, Sir, may there not be very good conversation without a contest for superiority ? ' JOHNSON. ' No animated conversation, Sir, for it cannot be but one or other will come off superiour. I do not mean that the victor must have the better of the argument, for he may take the weak side ; but his superiority of parts and knowledge will necessarily appear : and he to whom he thus shews himself superiour is lessened in the eyes of the young men [1]. You know it was said, ' *Mallem cum Scaligero errare quam cum Clavio rectè sapere* [2].' In the same manner take Bentley's and Jason de Nores' Comments upon Horace, you will admire Bentley more when wrong, than Jason when right.'

We walked with Dr. Adams into the master's garden, and into the common room. JOHNSON. (after a reverie of meditation,) ' Ay ! Here I used to play at draughts with Phil. Jones [3] and Fludyer †. Jones loved beer, and did not get very forward in the church. Fludyer turned out a scoundrel [4], a Whig, and said he was ashamed of having been bred at Oxford. He had a living at Putney, and got under the eye of some retainers to the court at that time, and so became a violent Whig : but he had been a scoundrel all along,[a] to be sure.' BOSWELL. ' Was he a scoundrel, Sir, in any other way than that of being a political scoundrel ? Did he cheat at draughts ? ' JOHNSON. ' Sir, we never played for *money*.'

[a] *comma omitted* 2, 3.

[1] ' So different are the colours of life, as we look forward to the future, or backward to the past ; and so different the opinions and sentiments which this contrariety of appearance naturally produces, that the conversation of the old and young ends generally with contempt or pity on either side. . . . One generation is always the scorn and wonder of the other, and the notions of the old and young are like liquors of different gravity and texture which never can unite.' *The Rambler*, No. 69.

[2] ' It was said of a dispute between two mathematicians, " malim cum Scaligero errare, quam cum Clavio recte sapere ; " that " it was more eligible to go wrong with one than right with the other." A tendency of the same kind every mind must feel at the perusal of Dryden's prefaces and Rymer's discourses.' Johnson's *Life of Dryden*, 200. ⟨See Johnson's *Lives Poets*, ed. Hill, i. 413, n. 1.⟩

[3] ' There is evidence of Phil. Jones's love of beer ; for we find scribbled at the end of the college buttery-books, " O yes, O yes, come forth, Phil Jones, and answer to your charge for exceeding the batells." His excess, perhaps, was in liquor.' *Dr. Johnson : His Friends, &c.*, p. 23. ⟨See App. B, p. 529.⟩

[4] See *post*, iii. 1.

† ⟨For Fludyer or Fludger see App. B, p. 529.⟩

He then carried me to visit Dr. Bentham, Canon of Christ-Church, and Divinity Professor, with whose learned and lively conversation we were much pleased. He gave us an invitation to dinner, which Dr. Johnson told me was a high honour. ' Sir, it is a great thing to dine with the Canons of Christ-Church.' We could not accept his invitation, as we were engaged to dine at University College. We had an excellent dinner there, with the Master and Fellows, it being St. Cuthbert's day, which is kept by them as a festival, as he was a saint of Durham, with which this college is much connected [1].

We drank tea with Dr. Horne [2], late President of Magdalen College, and Bishop of Norwich, of whose abilities, in different respects, the publick has had eminent proofs, and the esteem annexed to whose character was increased by knowing him personally. He had talked of publishing an edition of Walton's Lives [3], but had laid aside that design, upon Dr. Johnson's telling him, from mistake, that Lord Hailes intended to do it. I had wished to negociate between Lord Hailes and him, that one or other should perform so good a work. JOHNSON. ' In order to do it well, it will be necessary to collect all the editions of Walton's Lives. By way of adapting the book to the taste of the present age, they have, in a later edition, left out a vision which he relates Dr. Donne had [4], but it should be restored ;

[1] Dr. Fisher, who was present, told Mr. Croker that ' he recollected one passage of the conversation. Boswell quoted *Quem Deus vult perdere, prius dementat*, and asked where it was. A pause. At last Dr. Chandler said, in Horace. Another pause. Then Fisher remarked that he knew of no metre in Horace to which the words could be reduced : and Johnson said dictatorially, " The young man is right." ' See *post*, iv. 181. For another of Dr. Fisher's anecdotes, see *ante*, ii. 269. Mark Pattison recorded in his *Diary* in 1843 (*Memoirs*, p. 203), on the authority of Mr. (later Cardinal) Newman :—' About 1770, the worst time in the University, a head of Oriel then, who was continually obliged to be assisted to bed

by his butler. Gaudies, a scene of wild license. At Christ Church they dined at three, and sat regularly till chapel at nine.' A gaudy is such a festival as the one in the text.

[2] The author of the *Commentary on the Psalms*. See *post*, v. 30, note 3.

[3] See *ante*, ii. 279, 283.

[4] ' I have seen,' said Mr. Donne to Sir R. Drewry, ' a dreadful vision since I saw you ; I have seen my dear wife pass twice by me through this room with her hair hanging about her shoulders, and a dead child in her arms.' He learnt that on the same day, and about the very hour, after a long and dangerous labour, she had been delivered of a dead child. Walton's *Lives*, Donne, ed. 1796, p. 46. ⟨See App. B, p. 530.⟩

and there should be a critical catalogue given of the works of the different persons whose lives were written by Walton, and therefore their works must be carefully read by the editor.'

We then went to Trinity College, where he introduced me to Mr. Thomas Warton, with whom we passed a part of the evening. We talked of biography.—JOHNSON. ' It is rarely well executed ¹. They only who live with a man can write his life with any genuine exactness and discrimination ; and few people who have lived with a man know what to remark about him. The chaplain of a late Bishop ², whom I was to assist in writing some memoirs of his Lordship, could tell me scarcely any thing ³.'

I said, Mr. Robert Dodsley's life should be written, as he had been so much connected with the wits of his time ⁴, and by his literary merit had raised himself from the station of a footman. Mr. Warton said, he had published a little volume under the title of ' The Muse in Livery ⁵.' JOHNSON. ' I doubt whether

¹ Biographers ' so little regard the manners or behaviour of their heroes, that more knowledge may be gained of a man's real character, by a short conversation with one of his servants, than from a formal and studied narrative, begun with his pedigree, and ended with his funeral.' *The Rambler*, No. 60. See *post*, iii. 71.

² See *post*, iii. 112–13.

³ It has been mentioned to me, by an accurate English friend, that Dr. Johnson could never have used the phrase *almost nothing*, as not being English ; and therefore I have put another in its place. At the same time, I am not quite convinced it is not good English. For the best writers use the phrase ' *little or nothing* ; ' i.e. almost so little as to be nothing. BOSWELL ⟨ed. 2, 1793⟩.

Boswell might have left *almost nothing* in his text. Johnson used it in his writings, certainly twice. ' [It] will add almost nothing to the expense.' *Works*, v. 307. ' I have

read little, almost nothing.' *Pr. and Med.* ¶ 130. Moreover, in a letter to Mrs. Aston, written on Nov. 5, 1779 (*Letters*, No. 643), he says :— ' Nothing almost is purchased.' In *King Lear*, act. ii. sc. 2, l. 172, we have :—

' Nothing almost sees miracles
But misery.' ⟨See App. B, p. 530.⟩

⁴ ' Pope's fortune did not suffer his charity to be splendid and conspicuous, but he assisted Dodsley with a hundred pounds that he might open a shop.' Johnson's *Life of Pope*, 286. ⟨Dodsley's life was written by Mr. Ralph Straus in 1910.⟩

⁵ *A Muse in Livery : or, The Footman's Miscellany*. Printed for the Author, 1732. A rhyme in the motto on the title-page shows what a Cockney muse Dodsley's was. He writes:—
' But when I mount behind the Coach,
And bear aloft a flaming Torch.'
The Preface is written with much good feeling.

Dodsley's brother [1] would thank a man who should write his life : yet Dodsley himself was not unwilling that his original low condition should be recollected. When Lord Lyttelton's " Dialogues of the Dead " came out, one of which is between Apicius, an ancient epicure, and Dartineuf †, a modern epicure, Dodsley said to me, " I knew Dartineuf well, for I was once his footman [2]." '

Biography led us to speak of Dr. John Campbell [3], who had written a considerable part of the ' *Biographia Britannica.*' Johnson, though he valued him highly, was of opinion that there was not so much in his great work, ' A Political Survey of Great Britain,' as the world had been taught to expect [4] ; and had said to me, that he believed Campbell's disappointment, on account of the bad success of that work, had killed him. He this evening observed of it, ' That work was his death.' Mr. Warton, not adverting to his meaning, answered, ' I believe so ; from the great attention he bestowed on it.' JOHNSON. ' Nay, Sir, he died of *want* of attention, if he died at all by that book.'

We talked of a work much in vogue at that time, written in a very mellifluous style, but which, under pretext of another subject, contained much artful infidelity [5]. I said it was not

---

[1] James Dodsley, many years a bookseller in Pall Mall. He died Feb. 19, 1797. P. CUNNINGHAM. He was living, therefore, when this anecdote was published.

[2] Walpole (*Letters*, iv. 136) says :— ' You know how decent, humble, inoffensive a creature Dodsley is ; how little apt to forget or disguise his having been a footman.' Johnson seems to refer to Dodsley in the following passage, written in 1756 (*Project for Employment of Authors* : *Works*, v. 358) :—' The last century imagined, that a man, composing in his chariot, was a new object of curiosity ; but how much would the wonder have been increased by a footman studying behind it ! '

[3] See *ante*, i. 417. ⟨See App. B, p. 531.⟩

[4] Yet surely it is a very useful

work, and of wonderful research and labour for one man to have executed. BOSWELL. See *post*, v. 324.

[5] Two days earlier, Hume congratulated Gibbon on the first volume of his *Decline and Fall* :—' I own, that if I had not previously had the happiness of your personal acquaintance, such a performance, from an Englishman in our age, would have given me some surprise. You may smile at this sentiment ; but as it seems to me that your countrymen, for almost a whole generation, have given themselves up to barbarous and absurd faction, and have totally neglected all polite letters, I no longer expected any valuable production ever to come from them.' J. H. Burton's *Hume*, ii. 484.

† ⟨For Dartineuf see App. B, p. 530.⟩

fair to attack us thus unexpectedly ; he should have warned us
of our danger, before we entered his garden of flowery eloquence,
by advertising, ' Spring-guns and man-traps set here [1].' The
authour had been an Oxonian, and was remembered there for
having ' turned Papist.' I observed, that as he had changed
several times—from the Church of England to the Church of
Rome,—from the Church of Rome to infidelity,—I did not
despair yet of seeing him a methodist preacher. JOHNSON.
(laughing.) ' It is said, that his range has been more extensive,
and that he has once been Mahometan [2]. However, now that
he has published his infidelity, he will probably persist in it.'
BOSWELL. ' I am not quite sure of that, Sir.'

I mentioned Sir Richard Steele having published his ' Christian
Hero,' with the avowed purpose of obliging himself to lead a
religious life [3] ; yet, that his conduct was by no means strictly

[1] Five weeks later Boswell used a
different metaphor. ' I think it is
right that as fast as infidel wasps or
venomous insects, whether creeping
or flying, are hatched, they should be
crushed.' *Letters*, No. 160, i. 250. If
the infidels were wasps to the orthodox, the orthodox were hornets to the
infidels. Gibbon wrote (*Memoirs*, p.
242) :—' The freedom of my writings
has indeed provoked an implacable
tribe ; but, as I was safe from the
stings, I was soon accustomed to the
buzzing of the hornets.'

[2] Macaulay thus examines this
report (*Lit. Essays*, 1923, p. 210) :—
' To what then, it has been asked,
could Johnson allude ? Possibly to
some anecdote or some conversation
of which all trace is lost. One conjecture may be offered, though with
diffidence. Gibbon tells us in his
memoirs [*Memoirs*, p. 62], that at
Oxford he took a fancy for studying
Arabic, and was prevented from doing
so by the remonstrances of his tutor.
Soon after this, the young man fell in
with Bossuet's controversial writings,
and was speedily converted by them
to the Roman Catholic faith. The
apostasy of a gentleman commoner

would of course be for a time the
chief subject of conversation in the
common room of Magdalen. His
whim about Arabic learning would
naturally be mentioned, and would
give occasion to some jokes about
the probability of his turning Mussul-
man. If such jokes were made,
Johnson, who frequently visited Oxford, was very likely to hear of
them.' I have little doubt that in the
following lines Gibbon refers to the
attack thus made on him by Boswell
and Johnson. ' Many years afterwards, when the name of Gibbon was
become as notorious as that of Middleton, it was industriously whispered at
Oxford that the historian had formerly
" turned Papist ; " my character stood
exposed to the reproach of incon-
stancy.' Gibbon's *Memoirs*, p. 73.
⟨This passage occurs in the latest
and most perfect of Gibbon's autobiographical sketches, ' Memoir F ' :
it was written in 1792–3. See John
Murray's edition, 1897, p. 88.⟩

[3] Steele, in his *Apology for Himself
and his Writings* (ed. 1714, p. 80),
says of himself :—' He first became
an author when an ensign of the
Guards, a way of life exposed to much

suitable. JOHNSON. ' Steele, I believe, practised the lighter vices.'

Mr. Warton, being engaged, could not sup with us at our inn ; we had therefore another evening by ourselves. I asked Johnson, whether a man's [1] being forward in making [a] himself known to eminent people, and seeing as much of life, and getting as much information as he could in every way, was not yet lessening himself by his forwardness. JOHNSON. ' No, Sir ; a man always makes himself greater as he increases his knowledge.'

I censured some ludicrous fantastick dialogues between two coach-horses,[b] and other such stuff, which Baretti had lately published [2]. He joined with me, and said, ' Nothing odd will do long. " Tristram Shandy " did not last [3].' I expressed a desire to be acquainted with a lady who had been much talked of,

<hr>

[a] in making 1: to make 2, 3.   [b] *comma omitted* 2, 3.

irregularity ; and being thoroughly convinced of many things, of which he often repented, and which he more often repeated, he writ, for his own private use, a little book called the *Christian Hero*, with a design principally to fix upon his own mind a strong impression of virtue and religion, in opposition to a stronger propensity towards unwarrantable pleasures. This secret admonition was too weak ; he therefore printed the book with his name, in hopes that a standing testimony against himself, and the eyes of the world (that is to say) of his acquaintance, upon him in a new light, might curb his desires, and make him ashamed of understanding and seeming to feel what was virtuous, and living so quite contrary a life.'

[1] ' A man,' no doubt, is Boswell himself.

[2] ⟨See *ante*, ii. 290.⟩ ' " I was sure, when I read it, that the preface to Baretti's *Dialogues* was Dr. Johnson's ; and that I made him confess." " Baretti's *Dialogues* ?—What are they about ? " " A thimble, and a spoon, and a knife, and a fork ! They are the most absurd, and yet the most laughable things you ever saw. They were

written for Miss Thrale, and all the dialogues are between her and him, except now and then, a shovel and a poker, or a goose and a chair, happen to step in." ' Mme. D'Arblay's *Diary*, ii. 263.

[3] ' April 4, 1760. At present, nothing is talked of, nothing admired, but what I cannot help calling a very insipid and tedious performance : it is a kind of novel called *The Life and Opinions of Tristram Shandy* ; the great humour of which consists in the whole narration always going backwards.' Walpole's *Letters*, iv. 369. ' March 7, 1761. The second and third volumes of *Tristram Shandy*, the dregs of nonsense, have universally met the contempt they deserve.' *Ib.* v. 32. ' " My good friend," said Dr. Farmer (*ante*, i. 368), one day in the parlour at Emanuel College, " you young men seem very fond of this Tristram Shandy ; but mark my words, . . . however much it may be talked about at present, yet, depend upon it, in the course of twenty years, should any one wish to refer to the book in question, he will be obliged to go to an antiquary to inquire for it." ' Nichols's *Lit. Hist.* vi. 156. See *ante*, ii. 173, note 2, and 222.

and universally celebrated for extraordinary address and insinuation [1]. JOHNSON. ' Never believe extraordinary characters which you hear of people. Depend upon it, Sir, they are exaggerated. You do not see one man shoot a great deal higher than another.' I mentioned Mr. Burke. JOHNSON. ' Yes ; Burke *is* an extraordinary man. His stream of mind is perpetual [2].' It is very pleasing to me to record, that Johnson's high estimation of the talents of this gentleman was uniform from their early acquaintance. Sir Joshua Reynolds informs me, that when Mr. Burke was first elected a member of Parliament, and Sir John Hawkins expressed a wonder at his attaining a seat, Johnson said, ' Now we who know Burke [a], know, that he will be one of the first men in this country [3].' And once, when Johnson was ill, and unable to exert himself as much as usual without fatigue, Mr. Burke having been mentioned, he said, ' That fellow calls forth all my powers. Were I to see Burke now,[b] it would kill me [4].' So much was he accustomed to consider conversation as a contest [5], and such was his notion of Burke as an opponent.

[a] Burke 1: Mr. Burke 2, 3.   [b] *comma omitted* 2, 3.

[1] Mrs. Rudd. She and the two brothers Perreau were charged with forgery. She was tried first and acquitted, the verdict of the jury being ' not guilty, according to the evidence before us.' The *Ann. Reg.* xviii. 231, adds :—' There were the loudest applauses on this acquittal almost ever known in a court of justice.' ' The issue of Mrs. Rudd's trial was thought to involve the fate of the Perreaus ; and the popular fancy had taken the part of the woman as against the men.' They were convicted and hanged, protesting their innocence. *Letters of Boswell*, ed. 1857, pp. 223–230. Boswell wrote to Temple on April 28, 1776 :—' You know my curiosity and love of adventure. I have got acquainted with the celebrated Mrs. Rudd.' *Ib.*, ed. Tinker, No. 160. Three days later, he wrote :—' Perhaps the adventure with Mrs. Rudd is very foolish, notwithstanding Dr. Johnson's approbation.' *Ib.* No. 161. See *post*, iii. 79, 330, ⟨and App. B, p. 531⟩.

[2] ⟨After altering the phrase to ' His vigour of mind is incessant ', Boswell says in his revise ' I restore, I find the exact words as to Burke.' *Johnson & Boswell Revised*, 1928, p. 41.⟩ See *post*, iv. 275, where Johnson says that Mrs. Montagu has 'a constant stream of conversation,' and a second time allows that Burke ' is an extraordinary man.' Johnson writes of ' a stream of melody.' *Hammond*, 8. ⟨See *O.E.D.* s.v. STREAM, *sb.* 6.⟩ For Burke's conversation see *post*, iii. 247 ; iv. 19, 167 ; v. 32 ff.

[3] See *ante*, ii. 16.

[4] According to Boswell's record in *Boswelliana*, p. 273, two sayings are here united. He there writes, on the authority of Mr. Langton :—' Dr. Johnson had a very high opinion of Edmund Burke. He said, " That fellow calls forth all my powers " ; and once, when he was out of spirits and rather dejected, he said, " Were I to see Burke now 'twould kill me." '

[5] See *ante*, ii. 100, iii. 24, iv. 111, v. 17.

Next morning, Thursday, March 21, we set out in a post-chaise to pursue our ramble. It was a delightful day, and we drove [a] through Blenheim Park. When I looked at the magnificent bridge built by John Duke of Marlborough, over a small rivulet, and recollected the Epigram made upon it—

> ' The lofty arch his high ambition shows,
> The stream, an emblem of his bounty flows [1] : '

and saw that now, by the genius of Brown [2], a magnificent body of water was collected, I said, ' They have *drowned* the Epigram.' I observed to him, while in the midst of the noble scene around us, ' You and I, Sir, have, I think, seen together the extremes of what can be seen in Britain :—the wild rough island of Mull, and Blenheim Park.'

We dined at an excellent inn at Chapel-house, where he expatiated on the felicity of England in its taverns and inns, and triumphed over the French for not having, in any perfection, the tavern life. ' There is no private house, (said he,) in which people can enjoy themselves so well, as at a capital tavern. Let there be ever so great plenty of good things, ever so much grandeur, ever so much elegance, ever so much desire that every body should be easy ; in the nature of things it cannot be : there must always be some degree of care and anxiety. The master of the house is anxious to entertain his guests ; the guests are anxious to be agreable to him : and no man, but a very impudent dog indeed, can as freely command what is in another man's house, as if it were his own [3]. Whereas, at a tavern, there is a general freedom from anxiety. You are sure you are welcome : and the more noise you make, the more

---

[a] drove 1 : rode 2, 3.

[1] In a note on the *Dunciad*, ii. 50, the author of this epigram is said to be Dr. ⟨Abel⟩ Evans.

[2] Capability Brown, as he was called. See *post*, iii. 400.

[3] Such an ' impudent dog ' had Boswell himself been in Corsica. ' Before I was accustomed to the Corsican hospitality,' he wrote, ' I sometimes forgot myself, and imagining I was in a publick house, called for what I wanted with the tone which one uses in calling to the waiters at a tavern. I did so at Pino, asking for a variety of things at once ; when Signora Tomasi perceiving my mistake, looked in my face and smiled, saying with much calmness and good-nature, " Una cosa dopo un altra, Signore. One thing after another, Sir." ' Boswell's *Corsica*, p. 275. A Corsican gentleman, who knows the Tomasi family, told me that this reply is preserved among them by tradition.

trouble you give, the more good things you call for, the welcomer you are. No servants will attend you with the alacrity which waiters do, who are incited by the prospect of an immediate reward in proportion as they please. No, Sir ; there is nothing which has yet been contrived by man, by which so much happiness is produced as by a good tavern or inn [1].' He then repeated, with great emotion, Shenstone's lines :

> ' Whoe'er has travell'd life's dull round,
>   Where'er his stages may have been,
> May sigh to think he still has found
>   The warmest welcome at an inn [2].'

My illustrious friend, I thought, did not sufficiently admire Shenstone [3]. That ingenious and elegant gentleman's opinion of Johnson appears in one of his letters to Mr. Graves [4], dated Feb. 9, 1760. ' I have lately been reading one or two volumes of the Rambler ; who, excepting against some few hardnesses [5] in his manner, and the want of more examples to enliven, is one of the most nervous, most perspicuous, most concise, most [a]

---

[a] and most *orig*.

[1] Sir John Hawkins has preserved very few *Memorabilia* of Johnson. There is, however, to be found, in his bulky tome [p. 87], a very excellent one upon this subject. ' In contradiction to those, who, having a wife and children, prefer domestick enjoyments to those which a tavern affords, I have heard him assert, *that a tavern chair was the throne of human felicity.*—" As soon (said he) as I enter the door of a tavern, I experience an oblivion of care, and a freedom from solicitude : when I am seated, I find the master courteous, and the servants obsequious to my call ; anxious to know and ready to supply my wants : wine there exhilarates my spirits, and prompts me to free conversation and an interchange of discourse with those whom I most love : I dogmatise and am contradicted, and in this conflict of opinions and sentiments I find delight." ' BOSWELL. ⟨See App. B, p. 531.⟩

[2] We happened to lie this night at the inn at Henley, where Shenstone wrote these lines *. BOSWELL. ⟨See App. B, p. 531.⟩

[3] See *ante*, i. 555 ; *post*, v. 267.

[4] See Shenstone's *Works*, 1769, iii. 353. Rev. Richard Graves, author of *The Spiritual Quixote*. He and Shenstone were fellow-students at Pembroke College, Oxford. ⟨See App. B.⟩

[5] ' He too often makes use of the *abstract* for the *concrete*.' SHENSTONE. BOSWELL.

* I give them as they are found in the corrected edition of his Works, published after his death. In Dodsley's collection [vol. v, 1766, p. 52] the stanza ran thus :

> ' Whoe'er has travell'd life's dull round,
>   Whate'er his *various tour has* been,
> May sigh to think *how oft* he found
>   *His* warmest welcome at an Inn.' BOSWELL ⟨ed. 2, 1793⟩.

harmonious prose writers I know. A learned diction improves by time.'

In the afternoon, as we were driven rapidly along in the post-chaise, he said to me, ' Life has not many things better than this ¹.'

We stopped at Stratford-upon-Avon, and drank tea and coffee ; and it pleased me to be with him upon the classick ground of Shakspeare's native place.

He spoke slightingly of Dyer's ' Fleece ².'—' The subject, Sir, cannot be made poetical. How can a man write poetically of serges and druggets ? Yet you will hear many people talk to you gravely of that *excellent* poem, " THE FLEECE." ' Having talked of Dr. Grainger's ' Sugar-Cane,' I mentioned to him Mr. Langton's having told me, that this poem, when read in manuscript at Sir Joshua Reynolds's, had made all the assembled wits burst into a laugh, when, after much blank-verse pomp, the poet began a new paragraph thus :

' Now, Muse, let's sing of *rats*.'

And what increased the ridicule was, that one of the company, who slily overlooked the reader, perceived that the word had

¹ ' I asked him why he doated on a coach so ? and received for answer, "That in the first place, the company was shut in with him *there* ; and could not escape, as out of a room : in the next place, he heard all that was said in a carriage, where it was my turn to be deaf".' Piozzi's *Anec.* p. 276 : John. Misc. i. 329. ⟨' He loved indeed the very act of travelling, and I cannot tell how far one might have taken him in a carriage before he would have wished for refreshment.' *Ib.* p. 169 : John. Misc. i. 263.⟩ See *post*, iii. 5, 162. Gibbon wrote (*Misc. Works*, i. 408) :—' Were not the expense enormous, I would travel every year some hundred miles, more especially in England.'

² Johnson (*Life of Dyer*, 7) tells the following ' ludicrous story ' of *The Fleece*. ' Dodsley the bookseller was one day mentioning it to a critical visiter, with more expectation of suc-

cess than the other could easily admit. In the conversation the author's age was asked ; and being represented as advanced in life, " He will," said the critick, " be buried in woollen." ' To encourage the trade in wool, an Act was passed requiring the dead to be buried in woollen. Burke refers to this when he says of Lord Chatham, who was swathed in flannel owing to the gout :—' Like a true obeyer of the laws, *he* will be buried in woollen.' Burke's *Corres.* ii. 201. Hawkins (*Life*, p. 232) says :—' A portrait of Samuel Dyer [see *post*, iv. 11] was painted by Sir Joshua Reynolds, and from it a mezzotinto was scraped, the print whereof, as he was little known, sold only to his friends ; a singular use was made of it : Bell, the publisher of the English poets, caused an engraving to be made from it, and prefixed it to the poems of Mr. John Dyer.'

been originally *mice*, and had been altered to *rats*, as more dignified [1].

This passage does not appear in the printed work. Dr. Grainger, or some of his friends, it should seem, having become sensible that introducing even *Rats*, in a grave poem, might be liable to banter. He, however, could not bring himself to relinquish the idea ; for they are thus, in a still more ludicrous manner, periphrastically exhibited in his poem as it now stands :

> ' Nor with less waste the whisker'd vermin race
> A countless clan despoil the lowland cane.'

Johnson said, that Dr. Grainger was an agreeable man ; a man who would do any good that was in his power. His translation of Tibullus, he thought, was very well done ; but ' The Sugar-Cane, a Poem,' did not please him [2] ; for, he exclaimed, ' What could he make of a sugar-cane ? One might as well write " The Parsley-bed, a Poem ; " or, " The Cabbage-garden, a Poem." ' BOSWELL. ' You must then *pickle* your cabbage with the *sal atticum*.' JOHNSON. ' You know there is already " The Hop-Garden, a Poem [3] ": and, I think, one could say a great deal

---

[1] Such is this little laughable incident, which has been often related. Dr. Percy, the Bishop of Dromore, who was an intimate friend of Dr. Grainger, and has a particular regard for his memory, has communicated to me the following explanation :

' The passage in question was originally not liable to such a perversion ; for the authour having occasion in that part of his work to mention the havock made by rats and mice, had introduced the subject in a kind of mock heroick, and a parody of Homer's battle of the frogs and mice, invoking the Muse of the old Grecian bard in an elegant and well-turned manner. In that state I had seen it ; but afterwards, unknown to me and other friends, he had been persuaded, contrary to his own better judgement, to alter it, so as to produce the unlucky effect above-mentioned.'

The above was written by the Bishop when he had not the Poem it. self to recur to ; and though the account

given was true of it at one period, yet as Dr. Grainger afterwards altered the passage in question ; the remarks in the text do not now apply to the printed poem.

The Bishop gives this character of Dr. Grainger :—' He was not only a man of genius and learning, but had many excellent virtues ; being one of the most generous, friendly, and benevolent men I ever knew.' BOSWELL. ⟨See App. B, pp. 532–4.⟩

[2] Dr. Johnson said to me, ' Percy, Sir, was angry with me for laughing at the Sugar-cane : for he had a mind to make a great thing of Grainger's rats.' BOSWELL.

Johnson helped Percy in writing a review of this poem (*ante*, i. 481, 553).

[3] In *Poems* by Christopher Smart, ed. 1752, p. 100. One line may serve as a sample of the whole poem. Writing of ' Bacchus, God of hops,' the poet says :—

' 'Tis he shall gen'rate the buxom
  beer.'

about cabbage. The poem might begin with the advantages of civilized society over a rude state, exemplified by the Scotch, who had no cabbages till Oliver Cromwell's soldiers introduced them [1]; and one might thus shew how arts are propagated by conquest, as they were by the Roman arms.' He seemed to be much diverted with the fertility of his own fancy.

I told him, that I heard Dr. Percy was writing the history of the wolf in Great-Britain. JOHNSON. ' The wolf, Sir! why the wolf? Why does he not write of the bear, which we had formerly? Nay, it is said we had the beaver. Or why does he not write of the grey rat, the Hanover rat, as it is called, because it is said to have come into this country about the time that the family of Hanover came? I should like to see " *The History of the Grey Rat, by Thomas Percy, D.D. Chaplain in Ordinary to His Majesty,*" ' (laughing immoderately). BOSWELL. ' I am afraid a court chaplain could not decently write of the grey rat.' JOHNSON. ' Sir, he need not give it the name of the Hanover rat.' Thus could he indulge a luxuriant sportive imagination, when talking of a friend whom he loved and esteemed.

He mentioned to me the singular history of an ingenious acquaintance [2]. ' He had practised physick in various situations with no great emolument. A West-India gentleman, whom he delighted by his conversation, gave him a bond for a handsome annuity during his life, on the condition of his accompanying him to the West-Indies, and living with him there for two years. He accordingly embarked with the gentleman; but upon the voyage fell in love with a young woman who happened to be one of the passengers, and married the wench. From the imprudence of his disposition he quarrelled with the gentleman, and declared he would have no connection with him. So he forfeited the annuity. He settled as a physician in one of the Leeward Islands. A man was sent out to him merely to compound his medicines. This fellow set up as a rival to him in his practice of physick, and got so much the better of him in the opinion of the people of the island, that he carried away all the business; upon which he returned to England, and soon after died.'

[1] See *post*, v. 84.   [2] ⟨See App. B, p. 534.⟩

On Friday, March 22, having set out early from Henley [1], where we had lain the preceding night, we arrived at Birmingham about nine o'clock, and, after breakfast, went to call on his old schoolfellow Mr. Hector [2]. A very stupid maid, who opened the door, told us, that ' her master was gone out ; he was gone to the country ; she could not tell when he would return.' In short, she gave us a miserable reception ; and Johnson observed, ' She would have behaved no better to people who wanted him in the way of his profession.' He said to her, ' My name is Johnson ; tell him I called. Will you remember the name ? ' She answered with rustick simplicity, in the Warwickshire pronunciation, ' I don't understand you, Sir.'—' Blockhead, (said he,) I'll write.' I never heard the word *blockhead* applied to a woman before, though I do not see why it should not, when there is evident occasion for it [3]. He, however, made another attempt to make her understand him, and roared loud in her ear, ' *Johnson*,' and then she catched the sound.

We next called on Mr. Lloyd [4], one of the people called Quakers. He too was not at home ; but Mrs. Lloyd was, and received us courteously, and asked us to dinner. Johnson said to me, ' After the uncertainty of all human things at Hector's, this invitation came very well.' We walked about the town, and he was pleased to see it increasing.

I talked of legitimation by subsequent marriage, which obtained in the Roman law, and still obtains in the law of Scot-

---

[1] Thirteen miles from Birmingham.

[2] Mr. Hector's house was in the Square—now known as the Old Square. It afterwards formed part of the Stork Hotel, but it was pulled down when Corporation Street was made. A marble tablet had been placed on the house at the suggestion of the late Mr. George Dawson, marking the spot where ' Samuel Johnson was the guest, Edmund Hector was the host.' This tablet, together with the wainscoting, the door, and the mantelpiece of one of the rooms, was set up in Aston Hall, at the Johnson Centenary, in a room that is to be known as Dr. Johnson's Memorial Room. ⟨See J. Hill and R. K. Dent, *Mem.*

of the Old Square, 1897, pp. 21–32.⟩

[3] My worthy friend Mr. Langton, to whom I am under innumerable obligations in the course of my Johnsonian History, has furnished me with a droll illustration of this question. An honest carpenter, after giving some anecdote, in his presence, of the ill treatment which he had received from a clergyman's wife, who was a noted termagant, and whom he accused of unjust dealing in some transaction with him, added, ' I took care to let her know what I thought of her.' And being asked, ' What did you say ? ' answered, ' I told her she was a *scoundrel*.' BOSWELL.

[4] ⟨Mr. Sampson Lloyd, the banker : see App. B, p. 535.⟩

land. JOHNSON. ' I think it a bad thing ; because the chastity of women being of the utmost importance, as all property depends upon it, they who forfeit it should not have any possibility of being restored to good character ; nor should the children, by an illicit connection, attain the full rights [a] of lawful children, by the posteriour consent of the offending parties.' His opinion upon this subject deserves consideration. Upon his principle there may, at times, be a hardship, and seemingly a strange one, upon individuals ; but the general good of society is better secured. And, after all, it is unreasonable in an individual to repine that he has not the advantage of a state which is made different from his own, by the social institution under which he is born. A woman does not complain that her brother, who is younger than her, gets their common father's estate. Why then should a natural son complain that a younger brother, by the same parents lawfully begotten, gets it ? The operation of law is similar in both cases. Besides, an illegitimate son, who has a younger legitimate brother by the same father and mother, has no stronger claim to the father's estate, than if that legitimate brother had only the same father, from whom alone the estate descends.

Mr. Lloyd joined us in the street ; and in a little while we met *Friend Hector*, as Mr. Lloyd called him. It gave me pleasure to observe the joy which Johnson and he expressed on seeing each other again. Mr. Lloyd and I left them together, while he obligingly shewed me some of the manufactures of this very curious assemblage of artificers. We all met at dinner at Mr. Lloyd's, where we were entertained with great hospitality. Mr. and Mrs. Lloyd had been married the same year with their Majesties, and,[b] like them, had been blessed with a numerous family of fine children, their numbers being exactly the same. Johnson said, ' Marriage is the best state for man [c] in general ; and every man is a worse man, in proportion as he is unfit for the married state.'

I have always loved the simplicity of manners, and the spiritual-mindedness of the Quakers ; and talking with Mr. Lloyd, I observed, that the essential part of religion was piety, a devout intercourse with the Divinity ; and that many a man was a Quaker without knowing it.

As Dr. Johnson had said to me in the morning, while we walked together, that he liked individuals among the Quakers, but not the sect ; when we were at Mr. Lloyd's, I kept clear of introducing any question [a] concerning the peculiarities of their faith. But I having asked to look at Baskerville's edition of ' Barclay's Apology,' Johnson laid hold of it ; and the chapter on baptism happening to open, Johnson remarked, ' He says there is neither precept nor practice for baptism, in the scriptures ; that is false.' Here he was the aggressor, by no means in a gentle manner ; and the good Quakers had the advantage of him ; for he had read negligently, and had not observed that Barclay speaks of *infant* baptism [1] ; which they calmly made him perceive. Mr. Lloyd, however, was in as great a mistake ; for when insisting that the rite of baptism by water was to cease, when the *spiritual* administration of CHRIST began, he maintained, that John the Baptist said, ' *My baptism* shall decrease, but *his* shall increase.' Whereas the words are, ' *He* must increase, but *I* must decrease [2].'

One of them having objected to the ' observance of days, and months, and years,' Johnson answered, ' The Church does not superstitiously observe days, merely as days, but as memorials of important facts. Christmas might be kept as well upon one day of the year as another ; but there should be a stated day for commemorating the birth of our Saviour, because there is danger that what may be done on any day, will be neglected.'

He said to me at another time, ' Sir, the holidays observed by our church are of great use in religion.' There can be no doubt of this, in a limited sense, I mean if the number of such consecrated portions of time be not too extensive. The excellent Mr. Nelson's [3] ' Festivals and Fasts,' which has, I understand, the greatest sale of any book ever printed in England, except the Bible, is a most valuable help to devotion ; and in addition to it I would recommend two sermons on the same subject, by

[a] question 1 : questions 2, 3.

[1] ' As to the Baptism of Infants, it is a mere human Tradition, for which neither Precept nor Practice is to be found in all the Scripture.' Barclay's *Apology*, Proposition xii, ed. 1765, (Baskerville), p. 355. ⟨See App. B, p. 535.⟩

[2] John iii. 30. BOSWELL.

[3] Mr. Seward (*Anec.* ii. 104) says that ' Dr. Johnson always supposed that Mr. Richardson had Mr. Nelson in his thoughts, when he delineated the character of Sir Charles Grandison.' ⟨Boswell's copy of Nelson's *Companion for the Festivals and Fasts of the Church of England*, 1782, bore Johnson's notes.⟩

Mr. Pott, Archdeacon of St. Alban's, equally distinguished for piety and elegance. I am sorry to have it to say, that Scotland is the only Christian country, Catholick or Protestant, where the great events of our religion are not solemnly commemorated by its ecclesiastical establishment, on days set apart for the purpose.

Mr. Hector was so good as to accompany me to see the great works of Mr. Bolton, at a place which he has called Soho, about two miles from Birmingham, which the very ingenious proprietor shewed me himself to the best advantage. I wish that[a] Johnson had been with us : for it was a scene which I should have been glad to contemplate by his light [1]. The vastness and the contrivance of some of the machinery would have ' matched his mighty mind.' I shall never forget Mr. Bolton's expression to me : ' I sell here, Sir, what all the world desires to have—POWER.' He had about seven hundred people at work. I contemplated him as an *iron chieftain*, and he seemed to be a father to his tribe. One of them came to him, complaining grievously of his landlord for having distrained his goods. ' Your landlord is in the right, Smith, (said Bolton). But I'll tell you what : find you a friend who will lay down one half of your rent, and I'll lay down the other half ; and you shall have your goods again.'

From Mr. Hector I now learnt many particulars of Dr. Johnson's early life, which, with others that he gave me at different times since, have contributed to the formation of this work.

Dr. Johnson said to me in the morning, ' You will see, Sir, at Mr. Hector's, his sister, Mrs. Careless [2], a clergyman's widow.

a that *om.* 2, 3.

[1] ' Mr. Arkwright pronounced Johnson to be the only person who, on a first view, understood both the principle and powers of his most complicated pieces of machinery.' Johnson's *Works* (1787), xi. 215. Arthur Young, who visited Birmingham in 1768, writes :—' I was no where more disappointed than at Birmingham ; where I could not gain any intelligence even of the most common nature, through the excessive jealousy of the manufacturers. It seems the French have carried off several of their fabricks, and there-by injured the town not a little : This makes them so cautious, that they will show strangers scarce any thing.' *Tour through the North of England*, iii. 279.

[2] Johnson wrote to Mrs. Thrale, July 1770 :—' I have passed one day at Birmingham with my old friend Hector—there's a name—and his sister, an old love. My mistress is grown much older than my friend.

—" O quid habes illius, illius
Quæ spirabat amores,
Quæ me surpuerat mihi." '

[' Of her, of her what now remains

She was the first woman with whom I was in love. It dropt out of my head imperceptibly ; but she and I shall always have a kindness for each other.' He laughed at the notion that a man never can be really in love but once, and considered it as a mere romantick fancy.

On our return from Mr. Bolton's, Mr. Hector took me to his house, where we found Johnson sitting placidly at tea [1], with his *first love* ; who, though now advanced in years, was a genteel woman, very agreeable, and well-bred.

Johnson lamented to Mr. Hector the state of one of their school-fellows, Mr. Charles Congreve, a clergyman, which he thus described : ' He obtained, I believe, considerable preferment in Ireland, but now lives in London, quite as a valetudinarian, afraid to go into any house but his own. He takes a short airing in his post-chaise every day. He has an elderly woman, whom he calls cousin, who lives with him, and jogs his elbow, when his glass has stood too long empty, and encourages him in drinking, in which he is very willing to be encouraged ; not that he gets drunk, for he is a very pious man, but he is always muddy [2]. He confesses to one bottle of port every day, and he probably drinks more. He is quite unsocial ; his conversation is monosyllabical [a] : and when, at my last visit, I asked him what a clock it was ? that signal of my departure had so pleasing an effect on him, that he sprung up to look at his watch, like a greyhound bounding at a hare.' When Johnson took leave of Mr. Hector, he said, ' Don't grow like Congreve ; nor let me grow like him, when you are near me [3].'

[a] monosyllabical 1: quite monosyllabical 2, 3.

Who breath'd the loves, who charm'd the swains,
And snatch'd me from my heart ? '
FRANCIS, Horace, *Odes*, iv. 13. 18.]
Letters, No. 235.

[1] Some years later (20 Oct. 1781) he wrote :—' Mrs. Careless took me under her care, and told me when I had tea enough.' *Ib*. No. 742. ⟨See App. B, p. 537.⟩

[2] See *ante*, ii. 362, note 3.

[3] Johnson, in a letter to Hector, on March 7 of this year, described Congreve as ' very dull, very valetu-dinary, and very recluse, willing, I am afraid, to forget the world, and content to be forgotten by it, to repose in that sullen sensuality, into which men naturally sink, who think disease a justification of indulgence, and converse only with those who hope to prosper by indulging them. . . . Infirmity will come, but let us not invite it; indulgence will allure us, but let us turn resolutely away. Time cannot always be defeated, but let us not yield till we are conquered.' *Letters*, No. 460. ⟨See *ante*, i. 45 and *post*, ii. App. B, p. 537.⟩

When he again talked of Mrs. Careless to-night, he seemed
to have had his affection revived ; for he said, ' If I had married
her, it might have been as happy for me [1].' BOSWELL. ' Pray,
Sir, do you not suppose that there are fifty women in the world,
with any one of whom a man may be as happy, as with any
one woman in particular.' JOHNSON. ' Ay, Sir, fifty thousand.'
BOSWELL. ' Then, Sir, you are not of opinion with some who
imagine that certain men and certain women are made for each
other ; and that they cannot be happy if they miss their counter-
parts.' JOHNSON. ' To be sure not, Sir. I believe marriages
would in general be as happy, and often more so, if they were
all made by the Lord Chancellor, upon a due consideration of
characters and circumstances, without the parties having any
choice in the matter.'

I wished to have staid at Birmingham to-night, to have talked
more with Mr. Hector ; but my friend was impatient to reach
his native city : so we drove on that stage in the dark, and were
long pensive and silent. When we came within the focus of
the Lichfield lamps, ' Now (said he,) we are getting out of a
state of death.' We put up at the Three Crowns, not one of
the great inns, but a good old fashioned one, which was kept by
Mr. Wilkins, and was the very next house to that in which
Johnson was born and brought up, and which was still his own
property [2]. We had a comfortable supper, and got into high
spirits. I felt all my Toryism glow in this old capital of Staffordshire. I could have offered incense *genio loci* ; and I indulged in libations of that ale, which Boniface, in ' The Beaux
Stratagem,' recommends with such an eloquent jollity [3].

[1] In the same letter he said :—'I
hope dear Mrs. Careless is well, and
now and then does not disdain to
mention my name. It is happy
when a Brother and Sister live to
pass their time at our age together.
I have nobody to whom I can talk of
my first years—when I go to Lichfield I see the old places, but find
nobody that enjoyed them with me.'

[2] I went through the house where
my illustrious friend was born, with
a reverence with which it doubtless
will long be visited. An engraved

view of it, with the adjacent buildings,
is in ' The Gentleman's Magazine '
for February, 1785. BOSWELL. ⟨See
post, iv. 372, n. 2.⟩

[3] The scene of Farquhar's *Beaux
Stratagem* is laid in Lichfield. The
passage in which the ale is praised
begins as follows :—

' *Aimwell.* I have heard your town
of Litchfield much fam'd for ale,
I think I'll taste that.

' *Boniface.* Sir, I have now in my
cellar ten tun of the best ale in
Staffordshire ; 'tis smooth as oil,

Next morning he introduced me to Mrs. Lucy Porter, his step-daughter. She was now an old maid, with much simplicity of manner. She had never been in London. Her brother, a Captain in the navy, had left her a fortune of ten thousand pounds ; about a third of which she had laid out in building a stately house, and making a handsome garden, in an elevated situation in Lichfield. Johnson, when here by himself, used to live at her house. She reverenced him, and he had a parental tenderness for her [1].

We then visited Mr. Peter Garrick, who had that morning received a letter from his brother David, announcing our coming to Lichfield. He was engaged to dinner, but asked us to tea, and to sleep at his house. Johnson, however, would not quit his old acquaintance Wilkins, of the Three Crowns. The family likeness of the Garricks was very striking [2] ; and Johnson thought that David's vivacity was not so peculiar to himself as was supposed. ' Sir, (said he,) I don't know but if Peter had cultivated all the arts of gaiety as much as David has done, he might have been as brisk and lively. Depend upon it, Sir, vivacity is much an art, and depends greatly on habit.' I believe there is a good deal of truth in this, notwithstanding a ludicrous story told me by a lady abroad, of a heavy German baron, who had lived much with the young English at Geneva,

sweet as milk, clear as amber, and strong as brandy ; and will be just fourteen year old the fifth day of next March, old stile.' Act i. sc. 1. See *post*, iv. 97. ⟨See also ii. App. B, p. 538.⟩

[1] Though his letters to her are very affectionate, yet what he wrote of her to Mrs. Thrale shews that her love for him was not strong. Thus he writes :—' July 20, 1767. Miss Lucy is more kind and civil than I expected.' *Letters*, No. 190. ' July 17, 1771. Lucy is a philosopher ; and considers me as one of the external and accidental things that are to be taken and left without emotion. If I could learn of Lucy would it be better ? Will you teach me ? ' *Ib.* No. 260. ' Aug. 1, 1775. This was to have been my last letter from this

place, but Lucy says I must not go this week. Fits of tenderness with Mrs. Lucy are not common ; but she seems now to have a little paroxysm, and I was not willing to counteract it.' *Ib.* No. 427. ' Oct. 27, 1781. Poor Lucy's illness has left her very deaf, and, I think, very inarticulate. . . . But she seems to like me better than she did.' *Ib.* No. 744. ' Oct. 31, 1781. Poor Lucy's health is very much broken. . . . Her mental powers are not impaired, and her social virtues seem to increase. She never was so civil to me before.' *Ib.* No. 745. On his mother's death he had written to her :—' Every heart must lean to somebody, and I have nobody but you.' *Ib.* No. 127. ⟨See *John. Misc.* i. 298.⟩

[2] See *ante*, ii. 311.

and was ambitious to be as lively as they ; with which view,
he, with assiduous exertion, was jumping over the tables and
chairs in his lodgings ; and when the people of the house ran
in and asked, with surprize, what was the matter, he answered,
' *Sh' apprens t'etre fif.*'

We dined at our inn, and had with us a Mr. Jackson ¹, one of
Johnson's schoolfellows, whom he treated with much kindness,
though he seemed to be a low man, dull and untaught. He had
a coarse grey coat, black waistcoat, greasy leather breeches, and
a yellow uncurled wig ; and his countenance had the ruddiness
which betokens one who is in no haste to ' leave his can.' He
drank only ale. He had tried to be a cutler at Birmingham, but
had not succeeded ; and now he lived poorly at home, and had
some scheme of dressing leather in a better manner than
common ; to his indistinct account of which, Dr. Johnson listened with patient attention, that he might assist him with his
advice. Here was an instance of genuine humanity and real
kindness in this great man, who has been most unjustly represented as altogether harsh and destitute of tenderness. A
thousand such instances might have been recorded in the course
of his long life ; though,ᵃ that his temper was warm and hasty,
and his manner often rough, cannot be denied.

I saw here, for the first time, *oat ale* ; and oat cakes not hard
as in Scotland, but soft like a Yorkshire cake, were served at
breakfast. It was pleasant to me to find, that ' *Oats,*' the ' *food
of horses* ²,' were so much used as the *food of the people* in Dr.
Johnson's own town. He expatiated in praise of Lichfield and
its inhabitants, who, he said, were ' the most sober, decent
people 3 in England, the genteelest in proportion to their wealth,
and spoke the purest English 4.' I doubted as to the last article

ᵃ *comma omitted* 2, 3.

¹ See *post*, iii. 131, ⟨and Johnson's
Letters, Nos. 455, 460, 537⟩.

² Boswell varies Johnson's definition, which was ' a grain, which in
England is generally given to horses,
but in Scotland supports the people.'
Ante, i. 294, note 8.

3 ' " I remember," said Dr. John-
son, " when all the *decent* people in
Lichfield got drunk every night." '
Post, v. 59. See *post*, iii. 77 ⟨and

John. Misc. ii. 410 for Johnson's praise
of Lichfield⟩.

4 Nearly four years after the publication of *Evelina*, he wrote :—' Whatever Burney [by Burney he meant Miss
Burney] may think of the celerity of
fame, the name of Evelina had never
been heard at Lichfield till I brought
it. I am afraid my dear townsmen
will be mentioned in future days as
the last part of this nation that was

of this eulogy: for they had several provincial sounds; as,[a] *there*, pronounced like *fear*, instead of like *fair*; *once* pronounced *woonse*, instead of *wunse*, or *wonse*. Johnson himself never got entirely free of those provincial accents [b] [1]. Garrick sometimes used to take him off, squeezing a lemon into a punch-bowl, with uncouth gesticulations, looking round the company, and calling out, ' Who's for *poonsh*? [2] '

Very little business appeared to be going forward in Lichfield. I found however two strange manufactures for so inland a place, sail-cloth and streamers for ships; and I observed them making some saddle-cloths, and dressing sheepskins: but upon the whole, the busy hand of industry seemed to be quite slackened. ' Surely, Sir, (said I,) you are an idle set of people.' ' Sir, (said Johnson,) we are a city of philosophers: [c] we work with our heads, and make the boobies of Birmingham [3] work for us with their hands.'

There was at this time a company of players performing at Lichfield. The manager, Mr. Stanton, sent his compliments, and begged leave to wait on Dr. Johnson. Johnson received him very courteously, and he drank a glass of wine with us. He was a plain decent well-behaved man, and expressed his gratitude to Dr. Johnson for having once got him permission from Dr. Taylor at Ashbourne to play there upon moderate terms. Garrick's name was soon introduced. JOHNSON. ' Garrick's conversation is gay and grotesque. It is a dish of all sorts, but all good things. There is no solid meat in it: there is a want of sentiment in it. Not but that he has sentiment sometimes, and sentiment too very powerful and very pleasing: but it has not its full proportion in his conversation.'

When we were by ourselves he told me, ' Forty years ago, Sir, I was in love with an actress here, Mrs. Emmet, who acted

[a] *comma omitted* 3.   [b] his provincial accent 1: those provincial accents 2, 3.
[c] *colon* 1, 2: *comma* 3.

civilised. But the days of darkness are soon to be at an end; the reading society ordered it to be procured this week.' *Letters*, No. 747.

[1] See *ante*, ii. 159.

[2] Garrick himself, like the Lichfieldians, always said—*shupreme, shuperior*. BURNEY. ⟨Johnson said *He* cured him of saying Feyther for *Father*. MRS. PIOZZI. Marg. note in 1816 edition of the *Life*.⟩

[3] Johnson did not always speak so disrespectfully of Birmingham. In his *Taxation no Tyranny* (*Works*, vi. 228), he wrote :—' The traders of Birmingham have rescued themselves from all imputation of narrow selfishness, by a manly recommendation to parliament of the rights and dignity of their native country.' ⟨In *Letters*, No. 560, he describes it as ' the seat of the mechanick arts '.⟩

Flora, in " Hob in the Well [1] ".' What merit this lady had as an actress, or what was her figure, or her manner, I have not been informed : but, if we may believe Mr. Garrick, his old master's taste in theatrical merit was by no means refined [2] ; he was not an *elegans formarum spectator* [3]. Garrick used to tell, that Johnson said of an actor, who played Sir Harry Wildair [4] at Lichfield, ' There is a courtly vivacity about the fellow ; ' when in fact, according to Garrick's account, ' he was the most vulgar ruffian that ever went upon *boards*.'

We had promised Mr. Stanton to be at his theatre on Monday. Dr. Johnson jocularly proposed me to write a Prologue for the occasion : ' A Prologue, by James Boswell, Esq. from the Hebrides.' I was really inclined to take the hint. Methought, ' Prologue, spoken before Dr. Samuel Johnson, at Lichfield, 1776 ; ' would have sounded as well as, ' Prologue, spoken before the Duke of York, at Oxford,' in Charles the Second's time. Much might have been said of what Lichfield had done for Shakspeare, by producing Johnson and Garrick. But I found he was averse to it.

We went and viewed the museum of Mr. Richard Green [5], apothecary here, who told me he was proud of being a relation of Dr. Johnson's. It was, truely, a wonderful collection, both of antiquities and natural curiosities, and ingenious works of art. He had all the articles accurately arranged, with their names upon labels, printed at his own little press ; and on the staircase leading to it was a board, with the names of contributors marked in gold letters. A printed catalogue of the collection was to be had at a bookseller's. Johnson expressed his admiration of the activity and diligence and good fortune of Mr. Green, in getting together, in his situation, so great a variety of things ; and Mr. Green told me that Johnson once said to him, ' Sir, I should as soon have thought of building a man of war, as of collecting such a museum.' Mr. Green's obliging alacrity in shewing it

---

[1] This play was Cibber's *Hob ; or The Country Wake*, with additions, which in its turn was Dogget's *Country Wake* reduced. Baker's *Biog. Dram.* 1782, ii. 155.

[2] Boswell says, *post*, iv. 243, that ' Johnson . . . had thought more upon the subject of acting than might be generally supposed.'

[3] A nice observer of the female form. Terence, *Eun.* iii. 5. CROKER.

[4] In Farquhar's Comedy of *Sir Harry Wildair* ⟨or the more popular first part *The Constant Couple*.⟩

[5] ⟨The nature of the relationship between Johnson and Green or Greene is unknown. See Reade, *Reades of Blackwood Hill*, p. 145.⟩

was very pleasing. His engraved portrait, with which he has favoured me, has a motto truely characteristical of his disposition, ' *Nemo sibi vivat.*'

A physician being mentioned who had lost his practice, because his whimsically changing his religion had made people distrustful of him, I maintained that this was unreasonable, as religion is unconnected with medical skill. JOHNSON. ' Sir, it is not unreasonable ; for when people see a man absurd in what they understand, they may conclude the same of him in what they do not understand. If a physician were to take to eating of horse-flesh, nobody would employ him ; though one may eat horse-flesh, and be a very skilful physician. If a man were educated in an absurd religion, his continuing to profess it would not hurt him, though his changing to it would.'

We drank tea and coffee at Mr. Peter Garrick's, where was Mrs. Aston, one of the maiden sisters of Mrs. Walmsley, wife of Johnson's first friend [1], and sister also of the lady of whom Johnson used to speak with the warmest admiration, by the name of Molly Aston [2], who was afterwards married to Captain Brodie of the navy.

On Sunday, March 24, we breakfasted with Mrs. Cobb, a widow lady, who lived in an agreeable sequestered place close by the town, called the Friary, it having been formerly a religious house. She and her niece, Miss Adey, were great admirers of Dr. Johnson ; and he behaved to them with a kindness and easy pleasantry, such as we see between old and intimate acquaintance. He accompanied Mrs. Cobb to St. Mary's church, and I went to the cathedral, where I was very much delighted with the musick, finding it to be peculiarly solemn, and accordant with the words of the service.

We dined at Mr. Peter Garrick's, who was in a very lively humour, and verified Johnson's saying, that if he had cultivated gaiety as much as his brother David, he might have equally excelled in it. He was to-day quite a London narrator, telling us a variety of anecdotes with that earnestness and attempt at mimickry which we usually find in the wits of the metropolis. Dr. Johnson went with me to the cathedral in the afternoon [3].

---

[1] Gilbert Walmesley, *ante*, i. 81.
[2] See *ante*, i. 83.

[3] Cradock (*Memoirs*, i. 74) says that in the Cathedral porch, a gentle-

It was grand and pleasing to contemplate this illustrious writer, now full of fame, worshipping in ' the solemn temple [1] ' of his native city.

I returned to tea and coffee at Mr. Peter Garrick's, and then found Dr. Johnson at the Reverend Mr. Seward's [2], Canon Residentiary, who inhabited the Bishop's palace [3], in which Mr. Walmsley lived, and which had been the scene of many happy hours in Johnson's early life. Mr. Seward had, with ecclesiastical hospitality and politeness, asked me in the morning, merely as a stranger, to dine with him ; and in the afternoon, when I was introduced to him, he asked Dr. Johnson and me to spend the evening and sup with him. He was a genteel well-bred dignified clergyman, had travelled with Lord Charles Fitzroy, uncle of the present Duke of Grafton, who died when abroad, and he had lived much in the great world. He was an ingenious and literary man, had published an edition of Beaumont and Fletcher, and written verses in Dodsley's collection. His lady was the daughter of Mr. Hunter, Johnson's first schoolmaster. And now, for the first time, I had the pleasure of seeing his celebrated daughter, Miss Anna Seward, to whom I have since been indebted for many civilities, as well as some obliging communications concerning Johnson [4].

Mr. Seward mentioned to us the observations which he had made upon the strata of earth in volcanos, from which it appeared, that they were so very different in depth at different periods, that no calculation whatever could be made as to the time required for their formation. This fully refuted an anti-

man, who ' might, perhaps, be too ambitious to be thought an acquaintance of the great Literary Oracle, . . . ventured to say, " Dr. Johnson, we have had a most excellent discourse to day ; " to which he instantly replied, " That may be, Sir, but it is impossible for you to know it." '

He said that he was forced to examine these communications ' with much caution.' ' They were tinctured with a strong prejudice against Johnson.' His book, he continued, was meant to be ' a *real history*, and not a *novel*,' so that he had ' to suppress all erroneous particulars, however entertaining.' He accused her of attacking Johnson with malevolence. *Gent. Mag.* 1793, p. 1009. ⟨For this malevolence see Miss Seward's *Letters*, 1811, *passim*.⟩ For Boswell's second meeting with her, see *post*, iii. 284. ⟨See also Boswell's *Letters*, No. 252, ii. 348.⟩

[1] *The Tempest*, act iv. sc. 1.

[2] See *post* ⟨App. B, p. 539⟩: iii. 151.

[3] Johnson, in 1763, advising Miss Porter to rent a house, said :—' You might have the Palace for twenty pounds.' *Letters*, No. 154.

[4] Boswell, after his book was published, quarrelled with Miss Seward.

mosaical remark introduced into Captain Brydone's entertaining
Tour, I hope heedlessly, from a kind of vanity which is too
common in those who have not sufficiently studied the most
important of all subjects. Dr. Johnson, indeed, had said before,
independent of this observation, ' Shall all the accumulated
evidence of the history of the world ;—shall the authority of
what is unquestionably the most ancient writing, be overturned
by an uncertain remark such as this [1] ? '

On Monday, March 25, we breakfasted at Mrs. Lucy Porter's.
Johnson had sent an express to Dr. Taylor's, acquainting him
of our being at Lichfield [2], and Taylor had returned an answer
that his post-chaise should come for us this day. While we sat
at breakfast, Dr. Johnson received a letter by the post, which
seemed to agitate him very much. When he had read it, he
exclaimed, ' One of the most dreadful things that has happened
in my time.' The phrase *my time*, like the word *age*, is usually
understood to refer to an event of a publick or general nature.
I imagined something like an assassination of the King—like
a gunpowder plot carried into execution—or like another fire
of London. When asked, ' What is it, Sir ? ' he answered, ' Mr.
Thrale has lost his only son [3] ! ' This was, no doubt, a very
great affliction to Mr. and Mrs. Thrale, which their friends
would consider accordingly ; but from the manner in which the
intelligence of it was communicated by Johnson, it appeared for
the moment to be comparatively small. I, however, soon felt a
sincere concern, and was curious to observe, how Dr. Johnson
would be affected. He said, ' This is a total extinction to their

[1] A Signor Recupero had noticed
on Etna, the thickness of each stra-
tum of earth between the several strata
of lava. ' Recupero tells me,' wrote
Brydone, ' he is exceedingly embarrassed by these discoveries, in
writing the history of the mountain.
That Moses hangs like a dead weight
upon him, and blunts all his zeal for
inquiry ; for that really he has not
the conscience to make his mountain
so young as that prophet makes the
world. . . . The bishop, who is strenuously orthodox—for it is an excellent
see—has already warned him to be

upon his guard, and not to pretend to
be a better natural historian than
Moses.' Brydone's *Tour*, i. 68.
[2] He wrote, 23 March :—' Mr.
Boswel is with me, but I will take
care that he shall hinder no business,
nor shall he know more than you
would have him.' *Letters*, No. 464.
[3] ' March 23, 1776. Master Thrale,
son of Mr. Thrale, member for the
Borough, suddenly before his father's
door.' *Gent. Mag.* 1776, p. 142. ⟨His
other son, Ralph, had died in July
1775. Johnson's *Letters*, No. 422.⟩

family, as much as if they were sold into captivity.' Upon my mentioning that Mr. Thrale had daughters, who might inherit his wealth ;—' Daughters, (said Johnson, warmly,) he'll no more value his daughters than— ' I was going to speak.—' Sir, (said he,) don't you know how you yourself think ? Sir, he wishes to propagate his name [1].' In short, I saw male succession strong in his mind, even where there was no name, no family of any long standing. I said, it was lucky he was not present when this misfortune happened. JOHNSON. ' It is lucky for *me*. People in distress never think that you feel enough.' BOSWELL. ' And Sir, they will have the hope of seeing you, which will be a relief in the mean time ; and when you get to them, the pain will be so far abated, that they will be capable of being consoled by you, which, in the first violence of it, I believe, would not be the case.' JOHNSON. ' No, Sir ; violent pain of mind, like violent pain of body, *must* be severely felt.' BOSWELL. ' I own, Sir, I have not so much feeling for the distress of others, as some people have, or pretend to have : but I know this, that I would do all in my power to relieve them.' JOHNSON. ' Sir, it is affectation to pretend to feel the distress of others, as much as they do themselves. It is equally so, as if one should pretend to feel as much pain while a friend's leg is cutting off, as he does. No, Sir ; you have expressed the rational and just nature of sympathy. I would have gone to the extremity of the earth to have preserved this boy [2].'

He was soon quite calm. The letter was from Mr. Thrale's clerk, and concluded, ' I need not say how much they wish to see you in London.' He said, ' We shall hasten back from Taylor's.'

Mrs. Lucy Porter and some other ladies of the place talked a great deal of him when he was out of the room, not only with veneration but affection. It pleased me to find that he was so much *beloved* in his native city.

Mrs. Aston, whom I had seen the preceding night [3], and her

[1] See *post*, iii. 95.

[2] ' Sir,' he said, ' I would walk to the extent of the diameter of the earth to save Beauclerk ' (*post*, iv. 10). He had written of the boy the previous summer :—' Pray give my service to my dear friend Harry, and tell him that Mr. Murphy does not love him better than I do.' *Letters*, No. 415.

[3] ⟨Boswell had met Mrs. Aston two days before (*ante*, ii. 466).⟩

sister, Mrs. Gastrel, a widow lady, had each a house and garden, and pleasure-ground, prettily situated upon Stowhill, a gentle eminence [a] adjoining to Lichfield. Johnson walked away to dinner there, leaving me by myself without any apology ; I wondered at this want of that facility of manners, from which a man has no difficulty in carrying a friend to a house where he is intimate ; I felt it very unpleasant to be thus left in solitude in a country town, where I was an entire stranger, and began to think myself unkindly deserted : but I was soon relieved, and convinced that my friend, instead of being deficient in delicacy, had conducted the matter with perfect propriety, for I received the following note in his hand-writing : ' Mrs. Gastrel, at the lower house on Stowhill, desires Mr. Boswell's company to dinner at two.' I accepted of the invitation, and had here another proof how amiable his character was in the opinion of those who knew him best. I was not informed, till afterwards, that Mrs. Gastrel's husband was the clergyman who, while he lived at Stratford upon Avon, where he was proprietor of Shakspeare's garden, with Gothick barbarity cut down his mulberry-tree [1], and, as Dr. Johnson told me, did it to vex his neighbours. His lady, I have reason to believe, on the same authority [2], participated in the guilt of what the enthusiasts for our immortal bard deem almost a species of sacrilege.

After dinner Dr. Johnson wrote a letter to Mrs. Thrale on the death of her son [3]. I said it would be very distressing to Thrale, but she would soon forget it, as she had so many things to think of. JOHNSON. ' No, Sir, Thrale will forget it first. *She* has many things that she *may* think of. *He* has many things that he *must* think of [4].' This was a very just remark upon the different effect of those light pursuits which occupy a vacant and easy mind, and those serious engagements which arrest attention, and keep us from brooding over grief.

He observed of Lord Bute, ' It was said of Augustus, that it would have been better for Rome that he had never been born,

[a] eminence 1 : eminence, 2, 3.

[1] See an accurate and animated statement of Mr. Gastrel's barbarity, by Mr. Malone, in a note on ' Some account of the Life of William Shakspeare,' prefixed to his admirable edition of that Poet's works, Vol. i. p. 118. BOSWELL. ⟨See App. B, pp. 540–1.⟩

[2] See Prior's *Life of Malone*, p. 142.
[2] Johnson's *Letters*, No. 465.
[4] See *post.*, iii. 18, note 1.

or had never died.   So it would have been better for this nation
if Lord Bute had never been minister, or had never resigned.'

In the evening we went to the Town-hall, which was converted into a temporary theatre, and saw ' Theodosius,' with ' The
Stratford Jubilee.' I was happy to see Dr. Johnson sitting in a
conspicuous part of the pit, and receiving affectionate homage
from all his acquaintance. We were quite gay and merry. I
afterwards mentioned to him that I condemned myself for being
so, when poor Mr. and Mrs. Thrale were in such distress.
JOHNSON. ' You are wrong, Sir ; twenty years hence Mr. and
Mrs. Thrale will not suffer much pain from the death of their
son. Now, Sir, you are to consider, that distance of place, as
well as distance of time, operates upon the human feelings. I
would not have you be gay in the presence of the distressed,
because it would shock them ; but you may be gay at a
distance. Pain for the loss of a friend, or of a relation whom
we love, is occasioned by the want which we feel. In time the
vacuity is filled with something else ; or,ᵃ sometimes the vacuity
closes up of itself.'

Mr. Seward and Mr. Pearson, another clergyman here, supt
with us at our inn, and after they left us, we sat up late as we
used to do in London.

Here I shall record some fragments of my friend's conversation during this jaunt.

' Marriage, Sir, is much more necessary to a man than to a
woman ; for he is much less able to supply himself with domestick
comforts. You will recollect my saying to some ladies the other
day, that I had often wondered why young women should
marry, as they have so much more freedom, and so much more
attention paid to them while unmarried, than when married. I
indeed did not mention the *strong* reason for their marrying—
the *mechanical* reason.' BOSWELL. ' Why that *is* a strong one.
But does not imagination make it seemᵇ much more important than
it is in reality ? Is it not, to a certain degree, a delusion in us
as well as in women ? ' JOHNSON. ' Why yes, Sir ; but it is a
delusion that is always beginning again.' BOSWELL. ' I don't
know but there is upon the whole more misery than happiness
produced by that passion.' JOHNSON. ' I don't think so, Sir.'

ᵃ *comma omitted* 2, 3.   ᵇ seem *omitted* 2, 3.

' Never speak of a man in his own presence. It is always indelicate, and may be offensive.'

' Questioning is not the mode of conversation among gentlemen [1]. It is assuming a superiority, and it is particularly wrong to question a man concerning himself. There may be parts of his former life which he may not wish to be made known to other persons, or even brought to his own recollection.'

' A man should be careful never to tell tales of himself to his own disadvantage. People may be amused and laugh at the time, but they will be remembered, and brought out against him upon some subsequent occasion.'

' Much may be done if a man puts his whole mind to a particular object. By doing so, Norton [2] has made himself the great lawyer that he is allowed to be.'

I mentioned an acquaintance of mine [3], a sectary, who was a very religious man, who not only attended regularly on publick worship with those of his communion, but made a particular study of the Scriptures, and even wrote a commentary on some

---

[1] Mr. Hoole wrote of Johnson's last days :—' Being asked unnecessary and frivolous questions, he said he often thought of Macbeth [act iii. sc. 4, l. 118]—" Question enrages him." ' *John. Misc.* ii. 151. ⟨See App. B, p. 541.⟩

[2] Sir Fletcher Norton, afterwards Speaker of the House of Commons, and in 1782 created Baron Grantley. MALONE. For Norton's ignorance, see *ante*, ii. 91. Walpole (*Letters*, v. 385) described him as ' a tough enemy ; I don't mean in parts or argument, but one that makes an excellent bull-dog.' When in 1770 he was made Speaker, Walpole wrote : —' Nothing can exceed the badness of his character even in this bad age.' *Ib.* vii. 354. In his *Memoirs of the Reign of George III*, i. 240, Walpole says :—' It was known that in private causes he took money from both parties.' Horne (afterwards Horne Tooke) charged Norton with this practice ; *Parl. Hist.* xvii. 1010 ; and so did Junius in his *Letter* xxxix.

Churchill, in *The Duellist* (*Poems*, ed. 1766, ii. 87), writing of him, says :—
' How often . . . . . .
Hath he ta'en briefs on false pretence,
And undertaken the defence
Of trusting Fools, whom in the end
He meant to ruin, not defend ? '
Lord Eldon said that ' he was much known by the name of Sir Bull-face Double Fee.' He added that ' he was not a lawyer.' Twiss's *Eldon*, iii. 98. ' Acting, it was supposed from resentment, having been refused a peerage,' he made on May 7, 1777, a bold speech to the King on presenting the Civil List Bill. ' He told him that his faithful Commons, labouring under burthens almost too heavy to be borne, had granted him a very great additional revenue—great beyond example, great beyond his Majesty's highest wants.' Walpole's *Journal of the Reign of George III*, ii. 113, and *Parl. Hist.* xix. 213.

[3] ⟨He has not been identified.⟩

parts of them, yet was known to be very licentious in indulging himself with women ; maintaining that men are to be saved by faith alone, and that the Christian religion had not prescribed any fixed rule for the intercourse between the sexes. JOHNSON. ' Sir, there is no trusting to that crazy piety.'

I observed that it was strange how well Scotchmen were known to one another in their own country, though born in very distant counties ; for we do not find that the gentlemen of neighbouring counties in England are mutually known to each other. Johnson, with his usual acuteness, at once saw and explained the reason of this ; ' Why, Sir, you have Edinburgh, where the gentlemen from all your counties meet, and which is not so large but that[a] they are all known. There is no such common place of collection in England, except London, where from its great size and diffusion, many of those who reside in contiguous counties of England, may long remain unknown to each other.'

On Tuesday, March 26, there came for us an equipage properly suited to a wealthy well-beneficed clergyman ;—Dr. Taylor's large roomy post-chaise, drawn by four stout plump horses, and driven by two steady jolly postillions, which conveyed us to Ashbourne ; where I found my friend's schoolfellow living upon an establishment perfectly corresponding with his substantial creditable equipage : his house, garden, pleasure-grounds, table, in short every thing good, and no scantiness appearing. Every man should form such a plan of living as he can execute completely. Let him not draw an outline wider than he can fill up. I have seen many skeletons of shew and magnificence which excite at once ridicule and pity. Dr. Taylor had a good estate of his own, and good preferment in the church [1], being a prebendary of Westminster, and rector of Bosworth. He was a diligent justice of the peace, and presided over the town of Ashbourne, to the inhabitants of which I was told he was very liberal ; and as a proof of this it was mentioned to me, he had the preceding winter, distributed two hundred pounds among such of them as stood in need of his assistance. He had

a that *om.* 2, 3.

[1] Johnson, on May 16, wrote of him to Mrs. Thrale :—' The Doctor . . . has his head as full as yours at an election. Livings and preferments, as if he were in want with twenty children, run in his head. But a man must have his head on something, small or great.' *Letters*, No. 479. ⟨See App. B, p. 542.⟩

consequently a considerable political interest in the county of Derby, which he employed to support the Devonshire family ; for though the schoolfellow and friend of Johnson, he was a Whig. I could not perceive in his character much congeniality of any sort with that of Johnson, who, however, said to me, ' Sir, he has a very strong understanding [1].' His size, and figure, and countenance, and manner, were that of a hearty English 'Squire, with the parson super-induced : and I took particular notice of his upper servant, Mr. Peters, a decent grave man, in purple clothes, and a large white wig, like the butler or *major domo* of a Bishop.

Dr. Johnson and Dr. Taylor met with great cordiality ; and Johnson soon gave him the same sad account of their school-fellow, Congreve, that he had given to Mr. Hector [2] ; adding a remark of such moment to the rational conduct of a man in the decline of life, that it deserves to be imprinted upon every mind : ' There is nothing against which an old man should be so much upon his guard as putting himself to nurse [3].' Innumerable have been the melancholy instances of men once distinguished for firmness, resolution, and spirit, who in their latter days have been governed like children, by interested female artifice.

Dr. Taylor commended a physician who was known to him and Dr. Johnson, and said, ' I fight many battles for him, as many people in the country dislike him.' JOHNSON. ' But you should consider, Sir, that by every one of your victories he is a loser ; for, every man of whom you get the better, will be very angry, and will [a] resolve not to employ him ; whereas if people get the better of you in argument about him, they'll think, " We'll

---

[a] will *omitted* 2, 3.

[1] Johnson wrote on May 25, 1780 (*Letters*, No. 672) : ' —— is come to town, brisk and vigorous, fierce and fell, to drive on his lawsuit. Nothing in all life now can be more *profligater* than what he is ; and if, in case, that so be, that they persist for to resist him, he is resolved not to spare no money, nor no time.' Taylor is meant, and Baretti, in a marginal note, says :— ' This was the elegant phraseology of that Doctor.' See *post*, iii. 180.

[2] See *ante*, ii. 460.

[3] He did not hold with Steele, who in *The Spectator*, No. 153, writes :— ' It was prettily said, " He that would be long an old man, must begin early to be one." ' Mrs. Piozzi (*Anec.* p. 275 : John. Misc. i. 329) says that ' the saying of the old philosopher, ... That he who wants least is most like the gods, who want nothing ; was a favourite sentence with Dr. Johnson, who ... required less attendance, sick or well, than ever I saw any human creature.' ⟨For Johnson's dislike of valetudinarianism, see *Ib.* 197 : John. Misc. i. 282.⟩

send for Dr. ****** [1] nevertheless." ' This was an observation deep and sure in human nature.

Next day we talked of a book [2] in which an eminent judge was arraigned before the bar of the publick, as having pronounced an unjust decision in a great cause. Dr. Johnson maintained that this publication would not give any uneasiness to the Judge. ' For (said he,) either he acted honestly, or he meant to do injustice. If he acted honestly, his own consciousness will protect him ; if he meant to do injustice, he will be glad to see the man who attacks him, so much vexed.'

Next day, as Dr. Johnson had acquainted Dr. Taylor of the reason for his returning speedily to London, it was resolved that we should set out after dinner. A few of Dr. Taylor's neighbours were his guests that day.

Dr. Johnson talked with approbation of one who had attained to the state of the philosophical wise man, that is, to have no want of any thing. ' Then, Sir, (said I,) the savage is a wise man.' ' Sir, (said he,) I do not mean simply being without,— but not having a want.' I maintained, against this proposition, that it was better to have fine clothes, for instance, than not to feel the want of them. JOHNSON. ' No, Sir ; fine clothes are good only as they supply the want of other means of procuring respect. Was Charles the Twelfth, think you, less respected for his coarse blue coat and black stock [3] ? And you find the King of Prussia dresses plain, because the dignity of his character is sufficient.' I here brought myself into a scrape, for I heedlessly said, ' Would not *you*, Sir, be the better for velvet and embroidery ? ' JOHNSON. ' Sir, you put an end to all argument when you introduce your opponent himself. Have you no better manners ? There is *your want*.' I apologised by saying, I had mentioned him as an instance of one who wanted as little as any man in the world, and yet, perhaps, might receive some additional lustre from dress.

[1] Dr. Butter, of Derby, is mentioned *post*, iii. 1, 154, 163 ; iv. 110, 399.

[2] Andrew Stuart's *Letters to Lord Mansfield* (*ante*, ii. 229).

[3] Johnson was thinking of Charles's meeting with the King of Poland.

' Charles XII était en grosses bottes, ayant pour cravate un taffetas noir qui lui serrait le cou ; son habit était, comme à l'ordinaire, d'un gros drap bleu, avec des boutons de cuivre doré.' Voltaire's *Œuvres*, xvi. 218.

APPENDIX A.

(*Page* 312.)

JOHNSON'S sentiments towards his fellow-subjects in America have never, so far as I know, been rightly stated. It was not because they fought for liberty that he had come to dislike them. A man who, ' bursting forth with a generous indignation, had said :—"The Irish are in a most unnatural state ; for we see there the minority prevailing over the majority " ' (*ante*, ii. 255), was not likely to wish that our plantations should be tyrannically governed. The man who, ' in company with some very grave men at Oxford,' gave as his toast, ' Here's to the next insurrection of the negroes in the West Indies ' (*post*, iii. 200), was not likely to condemn insurrections in general. The key to his feelings is found in his indignant cry, ' How is it that we hear the loudest *yelps* for liberty among the drivers of negroes ? ' (*Ib.* 201.) He hated slavery as perhaps no man of his time hated it. While the Quakers, who were almost the pioneers in the Anti-slavery cause, were still slave-holders and slave-dealers, he lifted up his voice against it. So early as 1740, when Washington was but a child of eight, he had in his *Life of Sir Francis Drake* maintained ' the natural right of the negroes to liberty and independence.' (*Works*, vi. 313.) In 1756 he described Jamaica as ' a place of great wealth and dreadful wickedness, a den of tyrants and a dungeon of slaves.' (*Introd. Pol. St. Gt. Britain, Ib.* vi. 130.) In 1759 he wrote :—' Of black men the numbers are too great who are now repining under English cruelty.' (*Idler*, No. 87.) In the same year, in describing the cruelty of the Portuguese discoverers, he said :—' We are openly told, that they had the less scruple concerning their treatment of the savage people, because they scarcely considered them as distinct from beasts ; and, indeed, the practice of all the European nations, and among others, of the English barbarians that cultivate the southern islands of America, proves, that this opinion, however absurd and foolish, however wicked and injurious, still continues to prevail. Interest and pride harden the heart, and it is in vain to dispute against avarice and power.' (*Introd. to World Displayed, Works*, v. 218.) No miserable sophistry could convince him, with his clear mind and his ardour for liberty, that slavery can be right. ' An individual,' he wrote (*post*, iii. 202), ' may, indeed, forfeit his liberty by a crime ; but he cannot by that crime forfeit the liberty of his children.' How deeply he felt for the wrongs done to helpless races is shown in his dread of discoverers. No man had a more eager curiosity, or more longed that the bounds of knowledge should be enlarged. Yet he wrote, 4 March, 1773 :—' I do not much wish well to discoveries, for I am always afraid they will end in conquest and robbery.' (*Letters*, No. 299.) In his *Life of Savage*, 210, written in 1744, he said :—' Savage has not forgotten . . . to censure those crimes which have been generally committed by the discoverers of new regions, and to expose the enormous wickedness of making war upon barbarous nations because they cannot resist, and of invading countries because they are fruitful. . . . He has asserted the natural equality of mankind, and endeavoured to suppress that pride which inclines men to imagine that right is the consequence of power.' He loved the University of Salamanca, because it gave it as its opinion that the conquest of America by the Spaniards was not lawful (*ante*, i. 455). When, in 1756, the English and French were at war in America, he said that ' such is the contest, that no honest man can heartily wish success to either party. . . . It is only the quarrel of two robbers for the spoils of a passenger ' (*Obs. State of Affairs, Works*, vi. 114–15). When, from political considerations, opposition was raised in 1766 to the scheme of translating the Bible into Erse, he wrote :— ' To omit for a year, or for a day, the most efficacious method of advancing Christianity, in compliance with any purposes that terminate on this side of the grave, is a crime of which I know not that the world has yet had an example, except in the practice of the planters of America, a race of mortals whom, I suppose, no other man wishes to resemble ' (*ante*, ii. 27). Englishmen, as a nation, had no right to reproach their fellow-subjects in America with being drivers of negroes ; for England shared in the guilt and the gain of that infamous traffic. Nay, even as the Virginian delegates to Congress in 1774 complained :—' Our repeated attempts to exclude all further importations of slaves from Africa by prohibition, and by imposing duties which might amount to prohibition, have hitherto been defeated by his Majesty's negative— thus preferring the immediate advantages of a few British corsairs to the lasting interests of the American States, and to the rights of human nature, deeply wounded by this infamous practice.' Bright's *Speeches*, ed. 1869, i. 171. Franklin (*Writings*, 1907, v. 431), writing from London in 1772, speaks of ' the hypocrisy of this country, which encourages such a detestable commerce by laws for promoting the Guinea trade ; while it piqued itself on its virtue, love of liberty, and the equity of its courts, in setting free a single negro.' From the slightest stain of this hypocrisy Johnson was free. He, at all events, had a right to protest against ' the yelps ' of those who, while they solemnly asserted that among the unalienable rights of all men are liberty and the pursuit of happiness, yet themselves were drivers of negroes.

APPENDIX B.

This appendix consists of notes, to the whole of this volume, for which space could not be found on the pages to which they relate : they are, with few exceptions, new ; to these exceptions Dr. Hill's name is appended.

Page 5, lines 12–14. Goldsmith's *Traveller* was published on 19 Dec. 1764 (Iolo A. Williams, *Seven 18th-c. Bibliographies*, 1924, 135). Johnson concludes his notice of it in the *Critical Review* (Dec. 1764, xviii. 462) with the same encomium as that reported by Boswell :

' Such is the poem, on which we now congratulate the public, as on a production to which, since the death of Pope, it will not be easy to find anything equal.'

The second paragraph of the short notice in the *London Chronicle* (18–20 Dec. 1764, 589) runs :

' It were injustice to this ingenious gentleman not to allow him a degree of poetical merit beyond what we have seen for several years, and we must acknowledge him possessed of a strength and connexion of thought which we little expected to see.'

Pages 6, 7. Boswell wrote in his copy of the fifth edition of the *Traveller* (1770) :

' In Spring 1783 Dr. Johnson at my desire marked with a pencil the lines in this admirable Poem, which he furnished viz. l. 18 on p. 23 and from the 3 line on the last page to the end except the last couplet but one. " These (he said) are all of which I can be sure." '

Similarly he noted in his copy of the *Deserted Village* (1770) :

' The four last lines were marked at my desire by Dr. Johnson, Spring 1783 as all that he wrote of this admirable Poem.'

Both these volumes are in Mr. R. B. Adam's collection.

W. Cook, quoting Goldsmith's statement in the Dedication of the *Traveller* to his brother that ' a part of this Poem was formerly written to you from Switzerland ', adds that ' the manuscript lay by the Doctor some years, without any determined idea of publishing, till persuaded to it by his friend Dr. Johnson, who gave him some general hints towards enlarging it ' (*Monthly Mag.* 1793, xxiv. 92).

Page 17, lines 10, 11, and note 5. Johnson showed an active interest in Lye's Dictionary : see *Letters*, Nos. 174 and 174·1. The Club is represented in the List of Subscribers by Goldsmith, Bennet Langton, Percy, Sir Joshua Reynolds, and the ' Rev. Samuel Johnson, LL.D.'

Page 20, line 17. The subject of Boswell's thesis, which was printed, but not offered for sale, was Tit. x. Lib. xxxiii, ' De Supellectile Legata ', of the Pandects. Boswell's copy is at the Birthplace, Lichfield. See Mr. F. A. Pottle's *Lit. Career of James Boswell*, p. 24.

Page 25, lines 14, 15 and note 3. In Boswell's revise the words ' Gwyn's " London and Westminster Improved " ' are substituted for ' Adam's " Treatise on the Globes " ' (*ante*, ii. 44) and the epithet ' noble ' is blotted. As Mr. Chapman points out, Boswell would certainly consider it applicable to the Dedication to the last-mentioned book. See *Johnson and Boswell Revised*, 1928, p. 36.

Page 25, lines 17 ff. In the account of Miss Williams by Lady Knight printed in the *European Mag.* (1799, xxxvi, p. 225) and reprinted by Dr. Hill (*Johnsonian Miscellanies*, ii. 171–6) Johnson is unfairly charged with dilatoriness in promoting the publication of the *Miscellanies in Prose and Verse*. 'As to her poems, she many years attempted to publish them,' writes Lady Knight ; ' the half-crowns she had got towards the publication, she confessed to me, went for necessaries, and that the greatest pain she ever felt was from the appearance of defrauding her subscribers ; " but what can I do ? the Doctor always puts me off with, Well, we'll think about it, and Goldsmith says, Leave it to me." ' No cognizance is taken of the fact that Johnson wrote the Proposals for the collection as early as 1750 (*Gent. Mag.* Sept., p. 423 : Johnson's *Works*, v. 354), soon after his acquaintance with Miss Williams had begun (see *ante*, i. 232, note 1 and Nichols, *Lit. Anecd.* ii. 180, note). According to Lady Knight ' Miss Williams ultimately got a hundred and fifty pounds by her poems ' (*Europ. Mag.* xxxvi, p. 226).

Page 26, lines 2, 3. Miss Williams's ' Verses to Mr. Richardson, on his Sir Charles Grandison ' were printed in the *Gent. Mag.* 1754, p. 40. They were also separately printed, but not published, in 1753 in a handsome quarto to which no printer's or publisher's name is attached. There is a copy of this pamphlet in the Forster Collection, South Kensington Museum, which contains two corrected lines in Johnson's handwriting. For

' The Firm and Kind, the Daring and Polite ' (l. 37)

Johnson suggested or substituted

' Firm, Kind, and Good, Intrepid and Polite ',

and the penultimate line

' Thy Dust shall emblematic Shades embow'r '

he improved into

' Shades emblematic shall thy Dust embow'r '.

Johnson's readings were not adopted, either for the *Gent. Mag.* (1754) or *Miscellanies* (1766). There can be little doubt that Richardson himself printed the panegyric.

Page 26, line 5 and note 2. For an account by W. P. Courtney of Stephen Grey, or Gray, F.R.S., who ' established a new era in the history of electricity ', see *Notes and Queries*, 10 S. vi, 1906, pp. 161 ff., 354. He died in the Charterhouse, 15 Feb. 1735/6.

Page 30, lines 30 ff. Johnson, in a letter to Miss Porter, 7 June 1768, writes : ' Mr. Heely, whom you may perhaps remember to have married a cousin Betty Ford of mine, is come up to town from Scotland very poor, his wife my cousin died on the road and I procured him money to bury her.' *Letters*, No. 207·1. Mrs. Heely's identity has not been completely established. A. L. Reade's *Gleanings*, iv. 51. Boswell says, *post*, iv. 370, that she died childless.

Page 31, lines 18 ff. The Rev. Thomas Hussey made the following note on Cuthbert Shaw's *The Race* in his copy of the *Life* (now owned by Mr. Nichol Smith) : ' Upon mentioning this Poem to Johnson (I did not know by whom it was written) the Dr. said, " the Author bore me no ill-will, he has paid me a great compliment and I am obliged to him ".'

Page 32, lines 16 ff. Tom Hervey's open letter to Johnson entitled ' *Mr. Hervey's Answer to a Letter He received from Dr Samuel Johnson, Wherein he had endeavoured to dissuade him from parting with his supposed Wife* ', was published in 1772 (British Museum 10825 c. 37). Hervey begins by saying ' Sir, I am persuaded, that you are a very good Man, but you have thought fit to be an Advocate for the most worthless Woman that ever was on Earth '. He then proceeds to accuse his wife, through sixteen pages, of ingratitude, violence of speech and temper, extravagance and lying, and concludes ' when you come duly to consider these Things, I am of Opinion that you will heartily repent of your Intercession. Upon which presumption, I have already forgiven you, and am again your Friend.'

According to a manuscript note in the British Museum copy, Hervey's pamphlet was ' first printed, and written, in 1763 '.

Page 33, line 2 from foot, and note 4. Mr. Barnard, later Sir Frederick Augusta Barnard, F.S.A., F.R.S., is stated to have been a son of Frederick, Prince of Wales. E. Edwards (*Lives of Founders of British Museum*, 1870, p. 468) says that George III ' in the choice of a librarian was not infelicitous, though the selection was in part dictated by a feeling of brotherly kindness. For he chose a very near relative—Mr. afterwards Sir Frederick Barnard '. Mr. O. F. Morshead, the present Librarian, Windsor Castle, tells me that Barnard was born in 1743 and died in 1830. Mr. R. B. Adam reproduces a portrait of him and prints another letter from Johnson to him (4 Sept. 1784) in his new catalogue (*The Adam Collection*, vol. i).

Page 34, note 1. Boswell wrote on his revise as a direction to the printer : ' N.B. The same number of the Conversation as a separate publication with its own title-page, to be thrown off as of the Letter to Lord Chesterfield.'

I am informed that there is no record of the interview in the Royal archives at Windsor.

Page 43, lines 9 ff. Johnson, writing to Dr. Lawrence about Catherine Chambers, 20 June 1767, says ' she had been totally inactive for more than eight months '. *Letters*, No. 189·2. She died 3 Nov. 1767 and was buried in St. Chad's churchyard on the 7th. There is a tablet in the church bearing the inscription :

' In memory of
Catherine Chambers
the faithful servant of
Michael Johnson and his family,
Who died 3rd of November, 1767,
Aged 59 Years.

" My dear old friend Catherine Chambers. She buried my father and my brother and my mother . . . I humbly hope to meet again and to part no more." Samuel Johnson.

Erected 18th of September 1910.'

Her tombstone bore the simpler inscription :

' To the Memory of
Catherine Chambers,
Spinster, who died Nov. 3d.
1767. Aged 59.'

Mr. A. M. Broadley in *The Outlook*, May, 1912, p. 692. This stone and that of Lucy Porter were discovered side by side in the chancel of St. Chad's by Mr. Dennis Wood in 1910. See Lady Charnwood's 'A Habitation's Memories ' (*Cornhill Mag.*, Nov. 1927, p. 546).

Mrs. Piozzi, commenting (in the 1816 edition of the *Life*) on Johnson's account of his parting with his ' old friend ', says :

' Johnson told me this tender Story with many Tears ; and cried Poor Kitty ! Poor dear Kitty ! so often in the Course of the Even^g.—I rejoyced to see new Faces come in, and turn the Course of his Ideas.'

Mr. A. L. Reade, in his account of her, writes ' Catherine Chambers was evidently not a mere servant, and may have been a connexion of Mrs. Johnson '. By her will, dated 28 Nov. 1760, she appointed Lucy Porter her sole executrix and residuary legatee. *Reades of Blackwood Hill*, p. 242.

Page 44, lines 12 ff. The following Dedication, addressed to Edward, Duke of York (*ante*, ii. 2), to William Payne's *Introduction to Geometry*, 1767, may be safely ascribed on internal evidence to Johnson. I owe my knowledge of it to Mr. R. B. Adam.

' Sir,

They who are permitted to prefix the names of Princes to treatises of science, generally enjoy the protection of a patron, without fearing the censure of a judge.

The honour of approaching your Royal Highness, has given me many opportunities of knowing that the work which I now presume to offer, will not partake of the usual security. For as the knowledge which your Royal Highness has already acquired of Geometry extends beyond the limits of an introduction, I expect not to inform you ; I shall be happy if I merit your approbation.

An address to such a patron admits no recommendation of the science. It is superfluous to tell your Royal Highness that Geometry is the primary and fundamental art of life ; that its effects are extended through the principal operations of human skill ; that it conducts the soldier in the field, and the seaman in the ocean ; that it gives strength to the fortress, and elegance to the palace. To your Royal Highness all this is already known ; Geometry is secure of your regard, and your opinion of its usefulness and value has sufficiently appeared, by the condescension in which you have been pleased to honour one who has so little pretension to the notice of Princes, as,

Sir,

Your Royal Highnesses

Most obliged,

Most obedient,

And most humble Servant,

William Payne.'

Page 45, line 19. The version of Johnson's Prologue to Goldsmith's *Good Natured Man* as first printed in the *Public Advertiser* (3 Feb. 1768) differs from that given in the first edition of the play (5 Feb.). See Courtney *Bibliography*, p. 113, and Goldsmith's *Works*, ed. Gibbs, ii. 146–7.

Page 51, note 3. Martin repeats, with variations, the story of St. Kilda's epidemic cold in his *Description of the Western Islands of Scotland*, 1703, p. 284 :

' The Inhabitants . . . are not subject to many Diseases : they contract a Cough, as often as any Strangers land and stay for any time among them, and it continues for some eight or ten days ; they say the very Infants on the Breast are infected by it.'

Page 54, lines 16 ff. Maupertuis's opinion that the scorpion does not commit suicide was communicated to the world in his *Expériences sur les Scorpions* in 1731 (*Hist. de l'Acad. royale des Sciences*, 1733, p. 228). His actual account, which differs from Johnson's summary or Boswell's report of this, is as follows :

' On dit que si on le renferme dans un cercle de charbons, il se picque lui-même & se tuë. Je fis une enceinte de charbons; j'y mis un Scorpion qui, sentant la chaleur, chercha passage de tous côtés ; n'en trouvant point, il prit le parti de traverser les charbons qui le brûlèrent à demi ; je le remis dans l'enceinte ; & n'ayant plus eu la force de tenter le passage, il mourut bien-tôt, mais sans avoir la moindre volonté d'attenter à sa vie. . . . Voici je crois ce qui a pû donner lieu à l'histoire. Dès que le Scorpion se sent inquiété, son état de deffense est de retrousser sa queüe sur son dos, prête à picquer ; il cherche même de tous côtés à enfoncer son aiguillon ; lorsqu'il sent la chaleur des charbons, il prend cette posture, & ceux qui n'y regardent pas d'assés près, croyent qu'il se picque. Mais quand même il le voudroit, il auroit beaucoup de peine à le faire & je ne crois pas qu'il en pût venir à bout ; tout son corps étant cuirassé comme celui des Écrevisses.'

Giovanni Battista Morgagni, 1682–1771, to whose opinion Johnson would have deferred, was Professor of Anatomy at Padua. ' On peut considérer Morgagni comme le fondateur de l'école anatomo-pathologique.' *La Grande Encyclopédie*, t. xxiv. p. 338.

Page 55, lines 18 ff. and note 4. Du Halde published his account of China in 1735, in four folio volumes, under the title : *Description geographique, historique, critique, chronologique, politique, et physique de l'empire de la Chine et de Tartarie chinoise.* Voltaire, who was among those who ' consulted ' his book, writes :

Duhalde (Jean-Baptiste), jésuite, quoiqu'il ne soit point sorti de Paris, et qu'il n'ait point su le chinois, a donné sur les Mémoires de ses confrères la plus ample et la meilleure description de l'empire de la Chine qu'on ait dans le monde.' *Siècle de Louis XIV*, *Œuvres*, 1878, t. xiv. 68.

For Goldsmith's indebtedness to Du Halde, in respect of *The Citizen of the World*, see A. L. Sells, *Les Sources françaises de Goldsmith*, 1924.

There were two English translations : (1) ' The General History of China . . . Printed by and for John Watts ', 1736, 4 volumes, octavo. (A ' third edition ', merely a reprint with a new title-page, bears the date 1741.) This was by R. Brookes.

(2) ' A Description of the Empire of China and Chinese-Tartary, Together with the Kingdoms of Korea, and Tibet : containing the Geography and History of those Countries.' Published by Cave in 1738–41, in two volumes folio, price bound three guineas. Johnson gave extracts from this translation, with brief comments, in *Gent. Mag.* 1742, pp. 320–3, 353–7, 484–6. The *Letter on Du Halde's History of China*, signed ' Eubulus ', originally published in *Gent. Mag.*, 1738, p. 365, and included in Johnson's *Works*, 1788, xiv. 552–6, may have been touched by Johnson, but is not, I think, wholly his.

Page 56, lines 26 ff. The lady whom Boswell greatly admired and desired to marry was Mlle Isabella de Zuylen, the daughter of a Dutch nobleman, Diederik Jacob van Tuyll, seigneur de Zuylen, near Utrecht, of which province he was a governor. She was of the same age as Boswell, who apparently first met her at Utrecht late in 1763. Her life has been written by M. Philippe Godet (*Madame de Charrière et ses amis*, 2 t., Genève, 1906 : abridged edition, 1928) and by Mr. Geoffrey Scott (*A Portrait of Zélide*, 1925) ; M. Godet has also published her letters to Constant d' Hermenches (David Louis, baron de Constant de Rebecque, seigneur d'Hermenches), a friend and correspondent of

Voltaire, under the title *Lettres de Belle de Zuylen à Constant d'Hermenches* (Genève, 1909). These letters contain many references to Boswell. The first occurs in a letter written presumably at the end of February or beginning of March 1764 : Zélide, for that is the name she adopted, writes (*Lettres*, p. 50) :

' Quand je vais à l'assemblée, je cause et je joue avec un jeune Écossais tout plein de sens, d'esprit et de naïveté.'

By May they were on intimate terms. Zélide writing to her confidant of Boswell on the 27th says (*Ib.* 57) :

' Il est fort mon ami, et fort estimé de mon père et de ma mère, de sorte qu'il est toujours bien reçu quand il vient me voir.'

And a week later (*Ib.* 61) :

' Il me dit l'autre jour que quoique je fusse *a charming creature*, il ne serait pas mon mari, eussé-je pour dot les sept provinces unies ; et je trouvai cela fort bon.'

In June Boswell left Utrecht for Berlin, whence he sent, 9 July, the seventeen-page love-letter, which according to the recipient contained ' dix-sept mille pensées ' (*Ib.* 69 : Boswell's *Letters*, No. 25, i. 45 ff.).

It is of interest to note that even at this time Boswell was afraid of Zélide's talents. He writes :

' I am very certain that if we were married together, it would not be long before we should be both very miserable. My wife must be a character directly opposite to my dear Zelide, except in affection, in honesty and in good humour.'

An opinion which was confirmed by Zélide herself (*Lettres*, p. 117) :

' Boswell ne m'épousera jamais ; s'il m'épousait, il en aurait mille repentirs, car il est convaincu que je ne lui conviens pas.'

They never met again and their correspondence was fitful. ' Zelide has been in London this winter. I never hear from her ', writes Boswell (4 Mar. 1767, to Temple [*Letters*, No. 55, i. 104]). In November he says ' Do you know I had a letter from *Zelide* the other day, written in English, and shewing that an old flame is easily rekindled ' (*Ib.* No. 75, p. 136). In March 1768 Boswell sent her his *Corsica*. She writes to Hermenches, 27 March (*Lettres*, p. 326) :

' Mon ami Boswell vient de m'envoyer son livre : *An account of Corsica.* L'héroïsme de ce peuple, les grandes qualités de leur chef, le génie de l'auteur, tout est intéressant et admirable. . . . Je veux essayer de le traduire. Il y a ça et là des singularités qui vous paraîtraient ridicules et que je n'approuve pas trop.'

The ' superiority of talents ' shown by Zélide's criticism ultimately caused the abandonment of the translation and the extinction of the rekindled flame. Writing on 2 June, 1768, with reference to the translation she says (*Lettres*, p. 329) :

' J'étais très avancée, mais je voulais qu'on me permît de changer des choses qui étaient mal, d'en abréger d'autres que l'impatience française aurait trouvées *d'une longueur assommante.* L'auteur, quoiqu'il fût dans ce moment presque décidé à m'épouser, si je le voulais, n'a pas voulu sacrifier à mon goût une syllabe de son livre. Je lui ai écrit que j'étais très décidée à ne jamais l'épouser, et j'ai abandonné la traduction.'

Zélide married in 1771 M. de Charrière, her brother's tutor.

Since writing this note I have seen the second volume of Lieut.-Colonel Isham's *Boswell Papers*, edited by Mr. Geoffrey Scott. This contains, in addition to other hitherto unpublished letters between Boswell and Zélide, two proposals of marriage : the first, dated 16 Jan. 1766, and originally written on twenty-six quarto pages, was addressed by Boswell to Zélide's father; the second, dated 26 Feb. 1768, was made to Zélide herself.

Page 67, note 2. The inscription in the Baskerville Virgil given by Johnson to Trinity College, Oxford, is as follows :

' 1775 Hunc librum D.D. Samuel Johnson, L.L.D., quod hic loci studiis interdum vacaret.'

The date is in a different ink from the rest. The inscription is not in Johnson's hand, but in that of Tom Warton (*ante*, i. 270 note 1).

Page 68, lines 13 ff. Boswell writing to Sir Alexander Dick, 12 Sept. 1769, says :

' I had a good journey to London and then I went to Shakespeare's Jubilee which you might suppose I could not resist. The papers will inform you of our Entertainments. I enclose you some verses which I hope you will think both in character, and applicable to the occasion.' (Sotheby, Wilkinson, & Hodge, *Auction Catalogue*, 16 June 1899, lot 1092.)

Boswell is here referring to the ' Verses in the Character of a Corsican, at Shakespeare's Jubilee at Stratford-on-Avon, Sept. 6 1769 ' which he printed as a broadside at Stratford during the festival. The verses were printed by Boswell in his autobiographical memoir (*Europ. Mag.*, 1791, xix. 405), in *London Chron.*, 1769, xxvi. 256, and other periodicals. The only copy of the broadside which is known to have survived was found ' in a Continental town ' in 1927 (see *The Times*, 10 Oct.). It is now owned by Lieut.-Colonel Isham. Boswell entered in his Journal, also owned by Lieut.-Colonel Isham, under date 7 Sept. : ' He [the printer] brought me a proof to the Masquerade Ball about two in the morning. But could not get my verses thrown off in time, for me to give them about in my Corsican dress.' See F. A. Pottle's *Lit. Career of James Boswell*, pp. xxxviii ff. and 84–5.

Page 76, lines 4 ff. Mr. Seward reports that ' Dr. Johnson used to advise his friends to be upon their guard against romantic virtue, as being founded upon no settled principle ; " a plank," added he, " that is tilted up at one end, must of course fall down on the other ".' *Anecdotes, Suppl. Anecd.*, 1797, v. 149.—HILL.

Page 76, lines 20 ff. Professor C. B. Tinker suggests that the gentleman whom Boswell censured for marrying a second time was his own father. Lord Auchinleck did not marry until 25 Nov. 1769, nearly two months after the date of the conversation, but it is to be presumed that Boswell would know of the approaching match. Boswell's letters tell us that his father's second marriage caused him so much uneasiness that he was unable to refrain from imprudently expressing his extreme aversion to it (*Letters*, Nos. 102, 204, i. 177, ii. 307). See *post*, iii. 241.

Page 82, lines 13 ff. and note 1. Among the Apophthegms, &c. collected by Sir John Hawkins there is the following account :

' When he [Johnson] was first introduced to general Paoli, he was much struck with his reception of him ; he said he had very much the air of a man who had been at the head of a nation : he was particularly pleased with his manner of receiving a stranger at his own house, and said it had dignity and affability joined together.' Johnson's *Works*, 1787, xi. 208 : John. Misc. ii. 16.

Beattie who met Paoli in London in 1773 has left a description of him which corroborates Johnson's :

' Paoli is of a fair and florid complexion with dark and piercing eyes, and about five feet nine inches tall (as I guess) ; strongly made, but not in the least clumsy. He uses many gestures in his conversation as other Italians do, but they are not finical, but there is a freedom and dignity in his whole manner, equally free from assurance on the one hand, and from affected reserve on the other. He looks and speaks like one who has been accustomed to command, yet there is nothing rough or assuming about him, but on the contrary the utmost politeness.' Margaret Forbes, *Beattie and his Friends*, 1904, p. 81.

Mr. V. Rendall reminds me that Paoli is one of the few foreigners of whom there is a bust in Westminster Abbey.

Page 82, lines 14 ff. Mrs. Piozzi records a similar definition by Johnson of good breeding :

Officers (he said) were falsely supposed to have the carriage of gentlemen ; whereas no profession left a stronger brand behind it than that of a soldier ; and it was the essence of a gentleman's character to bear the visible mark of no profession whatever.' *Anecd.* p. 156 : John. Misc. i. 254.

Page 84, lines 5 ff. and note 3. Croker, after remarking that ' Boswell was himself the object of this sarcasm ', quotes a similar story from Northcote's *Reynolds* (ii. 189) :

' Boswell lamented that he had not been so happy as to have lived at that period . . . called the Augustan age of England, when Swift, Addison, Pope, &c., flourished. Sir Joshua . . . thought that Mr. Boswell had no reason to complain, as it was better to be alive than dead. . . . Johnson laughing said, " No, Sir, Boswell is in the right, as perhaps he has lost the opportunity which he might then have had, of having his name immortalized by being put into the Dunciad ! " '

Page 89, line 13. Mrs. Piozzi fills the blank in her copy of the 1816 edition of the *Life* with the name 'Jephson '. Her identification, which at first sight seems improbable, as Jephson's first tragedy was not produced until 1775, is strongly supported by a suppressed passage in Isaac Reed's edition of Baker's *Biographia Dramatica* (1782). The cancelled leaf (vol. ii, sig. D 2), one of several, was preserved by Malone and is now in his copy in the Bodleian. This reads, s.v. *Braganza*, ' When the present tragedy was read to a lady who has defended Shakspeare with much ability and address, she is reported to have said that she trembled for her favourite bard, lest the splendor of his dramatic works should be eclipsed by the superior blaze of Mr. Jephson's production. *Credat Judæus Apella.*' The appositeness of Johnson's severe criticism no doubt induced Boswell to depart from his usual chronological arrangement.

The writer of the passage was, so Malone tells us, George Steevens (see *post*, iii. 281 n. 3) :

' All the satirical articles in this work were written by George Steevens Esq[re] who lived on good terms with Mr. Reed to the last. Mr. Reed and Dr. Farmer, it is believed, were the only friends he ever had, with whom he did not quarrel.'

The article is characteristically spiteful. Steevens writes :

' By confident and continual puffing in a variety of modes till then unthought of, together with the excellent performance of Mrs. Yates, *Braganza* was received with tempestuous applause, and brought no inconsiderable profit to its author. Such turbulence of praise at length subsiding, it was reduced to the rank it now holds in the public esteem. Indeed no man was ever more injured than Mr. Jephson by the absurd admiration of his friends.'

Of *The Law of Lombardy* Steevens wrote :

' This second tragedy, by Mr. Jephson, met with such unfavourable treatment, that his profits were perhaps the most trivial ever received by any author whose performance was not driven from the stage before a third representation. . . . The phraseology, sentiments, and images of it, like those of its predecessor *Braganza*, are collected from all the plays that were ever written. Mr. Jephson should seem to mistake his own ease of adaptation and strength of memory, for copiousness of language and fertility of invention.'

This passage was also suppressed and Malone noted on the cancelled leaf (vol. ii. sig. N 5) : ' All this abuse of the Law of Lombardy was written by Mr. George Steevens for no other reason but because the author Mr. Jephson was my intimate friend.' There can be little doubt that Malone, who supplied him with a good deal of information, induced Reed to cancel these severe criticisms on his friend, and it is not improbable that Boswell's tenderness in suppressing Jephson's name was also due to Malone's influence. The friendship between the two men was certainly great. Malone not only wrote the epilogue to Jephson's *Count of Narbonne* (1781), and the prologue and part of the epilogue to *Julia* (1786), but according to Prior (*Life of Malone*, p. 198), stood in the position of second parent to his tragedies. James Boswell junior, in his *Memoir of Malone* (1814, p. 20), says that ' he [Malone] at all times felt the strongest attachment to Jephson '. See also *D.N.B.* s.v. Malone.

For the other cancelled passages see my note ' George Steevens and Isaac Reed's " *Biographia Dramatica* " ' in *Review of English Studies*, July 1929.

Page 91, line 3. Professor Edward Bensly suggests that the ' wit about town ' who wrote bawdy verses was Benjamin Loveling. He was the son of the Reverend Benjamin Loveling, vicar of Banbury, Oxon., was born in 1711 and matriculated at Oxford, Trinity College, 13 July 1728. Foster, *Alumni Oxon.* See *Notes and Queries*, 12 Ser. xi, 1922, p. 414. He published his *Latin and English Poems* in 1738 and 1741.

Professor Bensly describes the Latin poems as startlingly, not to say disgustingly, frank and fully deserving of Johnson's epithet ; he knows of no published Latin verse by any English writer of the time that comes near Loveling's in sustained indecency.

Page 91, lines 12, 13. The manuscript of Boswell's Dictionary of words peculiar to Scotland was sold at the sale of James Boswell junior's library in 1825. *Bibliotheca Boswelliana*, p. 101.

Page 92, lines 7, 8. Boswell, in the dedication to Garrick of the edition of Shakespeare published by Donaldson in 1771, writes :

' An edition of Shakespear is inscribed to you with such peculiar propriety, that it cannot fail of meeting with universal approbation. You, Sir, by animating his characters on the stage, have shewn the British nation the astonishing treasures of the Father of their Drama : And I even question if ever his genius was sufficiently acknowledged by the general voice till you appeared.'

The dedication is signed ' The Publisher ', but Boswell's authorship is established by his letter, 18 Sept. 1771, to Garrick (Boswell's *Letters*, No. 110, i. 185.). See F. A. Pottle's *Lit. Career of Boswell*, pp. 86–8.

Page 96, lines 8, 9. The elder Scaliger's praise of George Buchanan is conveyed in an iambic poem entitled ' Ad Georgium Buchananum ', beginning ' Felix Georgi lacteae venae pater '; lines 11–16 are :

> ' Te natum ad alta Pegasi cacumina
> Tepente susceptum sinu
> Regina sacri magna Calliope soni
> Liquore non noto imbuit
> Deditque palmam ferre de tot gentibus,
> Latina quot colit cohors.'

(Poemata, 1574, pars i, p. 178.)

Joseph Scaliger praises him in prose : ' Buchananus unus est in tota Europa omnes post se relinquens in Latina Poësi ' (*Scaligerana, Thuana*, etc., 1740, ii. 39) and in verse in the ' Epitaphium Georgii Buchanani ', the last couplet of which runs :

> ' Imperii fuerat Romani Scotia limes :
> Romani eloquii Scotia finis erit.'

(Poemata Omnia, 1864, pp. 104–5.)

Professor E. Bensly has kindly supplied me with these references.

Page 99, lines 1 ff. ' That no man loves labour for itself ' was a favourite assertion of Johnson. See *post*, iii. 19 ; iv. 219 ; *Lives of the Poets*, *Dryden* 201, *Pope* 298 ; and *Letters*, ed. Hill, ii. 439.

Page 99, line 3 from foot. Bartholomew de Dominiceti, an Italian quack who came to England in 1753, and in 1765 settled in Cheyne Walk, Chelsea, where he established ' baths, fumigatory stoves, and sweating chambers '. See R. Blunt *In Cheyne Walk*, 1914, pp. 137 ff.

Page 101, line 5. Johnson enters in his Dictionary '*To Codle*, to parboil ; to soften by the heat of water '. The earliest authority recorded by the Oxford Dictionary for the sense ' to treat as an invalid in need of nourishing food and nursing ; to cocker ' is Jane Austen (*Emma*, 1815). Mr. F. A. Pottle informs me that Frau Liebeskind correctly rendered the passage ' Ich würde das Kind nicht brühen ' in her abridged version of the *Life* (1797). The word is not italicized in Boswell's first edition.

Page 104, line 13. Malone prints, in the fourth edition of the *Life* (ii. 99), the following note on belief in the Thirty-Nine Articles :

' Dr. Simon Patrick . . . thus expresses himself on this subject, in a letter to the learned Dr. John Mapletoft, dated Feb. 8, 1682–3 : " I always took the Articles to be only articles of communion ; and so Bishop Bramhall expressly maintains against the Bishop of Chalcedon ; and I remember well, that Bishop Sanderson, when the King was first restored, received the subscription of an acquaintance of mine, which he declared was not to them as articles of *faith*, but *peace*. I think you need make no scruple of the matter, because all that I know so understand the meaning of subscription, and upon other terms would not subscribe." The above was printed some years ago in the European Magazine, from the original, now in the hands of Mr. Mapletoft . . . grandson to Dr. John Mapletoft.'

Page 106, line 2 and note 1. An early use of *lacerate* by Johnson is provided by *The Vanity of Human Wishes* (line 274) :

' Now Kindred Merit fills the sable Bier,
Now lacerated Friendship claims a Tear.'

He quoted this line in his Dictionary, with the variant of ' Here ' for ' Now '. Mrs. Piozzi suggests (*British Synonymy*, i. 345) that ' its familiarity with the Surgeon's profession may be deemed ' a cause for the rare use of the word *lacerate* in conversation. She adds that ' in serious and steady talk concerning any important event, we yet retain it '.

Page 110, foot. Boswell's ' little epigrammatick song ', *A Matrimonial Thought*, was first printed in the *London Chronicle*, 22 Dec. 1768, where it is addressed to Matthew Henderson : the single variant is ' s—l ' for ' soul '. For Henderson, whose death in 1790 was mourned by Burns, see *Boswelliana*, 1874, p. 253.

Page 114, lines 20 ff. and note 3. Richard Farmer responded to Steevens's appeal for assistance with his catalogue of 'Ancient Translations from Classic Authors '. The Advertisement to the Reader of the Johnson-Steevens edition of Shakespeare, 1773, gives (vol. i, sig. E vi verso) the following acknowledgement :

' The reader may not be displeased to have the Greek and Roman poets, orators, &c., who had been rendered accessible to our author, exposed at one view ; especially as the list has received the advantage of being corrected and amplified by the Reverend Mr. Farmer, the substance of whose very decisive pamphlet is interspersed through the notes which are added in this revisal of Dr. Johnson's Shakespeare.'

Page 115, lines 4 ff. Johnson and Steevens were obliged ' to incommode their readers with a supplement '. At one time, as Johnson's letter of 2 Feb. 1771 to Rivington shows, the intention was to print the additions by themselves ' for the benefit of former purchasers ' (*Letters*, No. 243). This supplement occupies forty-five unpaged leaves at the end of the last volume and consists of an Appendix, or rather three Appendices, to which the following note by Johnson is prefixed :

Some apology perhaps is necessary for the inconvenience of an Appendix, which, however, we can justify by the strongest of all pleas, the plea of necessity. The Notes it contains, whether communicated by correspondents, or collected from published volumes, were not within our reach when the plays were printed, to which they relate. Of that which chance has supplied, we could have no previous knowledge, and he that waited till the river should run dry, did not act with less reason than the Editor would do, who should suspend his publication for possibilities of intelligence, or promises of improvement. Had we foreseen the Oxford edition, the assistance we expected from it might have persuaded us to pause ; but our volumes were completely finished before its publication.'

Then follows the main Appendix which is composed of notes to each of the ten volumes, each note being signed by the contributor. Appendix II consists of notes communicated too late for insertion in their proper places in the foregoing Appendix ; the greater part is formed by notes communicated by Farmer in a letter to Steevens. Appendix III consists of a few notes taken from Tyrwhitt's *Observations and Conjectures upon some Passages of Shakespeare* (Oxford, 1766), which were ' omitted in their proper places '.

Page 116, line 7 from foot. ' Assistant Preacher ' is, as Sir Frank MacKinnon informs me, a popular description of one whose technical title is now and always has been the ' Reader ' of the Temple Church. The office is filled by the Inner Temple and the Middle Temple in turn.

Page 118, line 4 from foot. Although their friendship was intimate, there is not, as Chalmers points out (*British Essayists*, xxiii. p. xiv), a single instance of a meeting between Johnson and Hawkesworth in Boswell's narrative. The paucity of their correspondence is explained by Johnson's letter to Mrs. Desmoulins, *Letters*, No. 430.

Page 127, line 11. Professor Bensly tells me that in the Preface to the 1546 edition of Boethius's *Opera*, published at Basel, occur these words : ' Ego igitur, ut ingenue fatear id quod res est (etsi scio quàm magnam mihi moueam hac opinione inuidiam, & plus quàm Camarinam, dicendum tamen est, quod animo sedet meo) mihi quidem magis Philosophicum opus uidetur, quàm Christianum.' This preface was written by Henricus Loritus Glareanus.

Page 128, lines 16 ff. John Ireland has preserved (*Letters and Poems by the late Mr. John Henderson*, 1786, p. 268), the following humorous representation of Johnson's gloomy views on re-marriage :

'When I once came with him [Henderson] from the late Doctor Johnson's, I remarked that we had forgotten to mention one of his old friends having just married a third wife. I added, " What would the Doctor have said to it ? " " Sir," replied Henderson, " he would have said, man is born to be deceived. We see daily instances when expectation subdues experience. This will be an additional example of the fallacy of hope, and disappointment of expectation. Yet we must allow the man has *courage*, or after the sufferings of two campaigns, he would not voluntarily expose himself on the forlorn hope.—*He will be blown up, Sir !* " '

Page 133, lines 13 ff. and note 1. Johnson had read the original *Retirement*, not the *London Magazine* version. It occurs in Walsh's *Letters and Poems*, 1692, p. 109 :

> ' One who has early known the Pomps of State ;
> (For things Unknown 'tis Ign'rance to condemn)
> And after having viewed the gawdy Bait,
> Can boldly say, The Trifle I contemn.
> In her blest Arms contented cou'd I live
> Contented cou'd I die.'

The *London Mag.*, 1732, p. 200, reads ' pomp ' (l. 1), ' contemn ' (l. 2), and ' coldly ' (l. 4).

Page 133, note 1, lines 20, 21. Croker's conjecture that the celebrated historian, of whom the verses quoted by Johnson were regarded as characteristic, was Gibbon is confirmed by Mrs. Piozzi. In a marginal note to the 1816 edition of the *Life* she writes :

' It was no greater a person than poor H. L. P. who adapted the lines to Gibbon : I wrote them in his first 4to volume. They are translated from some old Latin Verses at the End of Cluverius's Geography.'

This volume of Gibbon containing the verses, with some variant readings, on the fly-leaf was purchased at the sale of the Streatham library in 1816. The purchaser, the great-grandfather of Sir Frank MacKinnon, wrote about them to Mrs. Piozzi, who replied in the sense of the above marginal note, adding that ' Doctor Johnson was . . . pleased with the Adaptation of the Lines to Gibbon, which prompted me to write them '. She thought that the original Latin verses occurred in the 1729 edition of Cluverius. I, and others, have been unable to find them in this or any edition. See Sir Frank MacKinnon's letter 'A note to a footnote' in *Times Lit. Suppl.*, 13 Jan. 1921.

Page 144, lines 11 ff. Johnson's letter to Banks is printed, without the covering letter to Reynolds, in the *European Mag.*, July 1789, p. 5, where it is dated 'March 26, 1772'. This supplies two readings which are obviously superior to Boswell's : ' given her a distich ' and ' may some time have an epic poem from some happier hand than that of '. The distich for the goat's collar is given in a note and not as part of the letter, with the variant 'Perpetui'. Mrs. Piozzi, who says that Johnson gave her this distich, 'in the year 1777 I think', also reads 'Perpetui' (*Anecd.* p. 70 : John. Misc. i. 195), which would, as Prof. Bensly remarks, make excellent sense, meaning that the goat never failed to give milk on shipboard.

Mrs. Piozzi says that the goat had accompanied Sir Joseph Banks on ' two of his adventurous expeditions ', but Banks went round the world once only, with Capt. Cook in the Endeavour.

In the so-called ' Specimens of a diary ' published by Thomas Byerley (' Stephen Collet ') in *Relics of Literature*, 1823, p. 310, it is stated that the goat accompanied Capt. Wallis in the Dolphin (1766–8), and Capt. Cook in the Endeavour (1768–71), and died, at Mile End, 28 April 1772.

Prof. Bensly suggests (*Notes and Queries*, 9 Ser. x. 317) the possible reading ' masters' ' for ' master's ' in the English version of the distich.

Page 154, lines 11 ff. The 'lady of quality . . . who was a wonderful mimick ' was, according to Mrs. Piozzi, Lady Emily Hervey. Mrs. Piozzi adds :

' She was never mad as I know of : seven years after this Date—or more, we met in a Library at Brighton ; "Don't you remember your old acquaintance Dr. Johnson ? " said she. " Ah Lady Emily !—have you left off your old Tricks ? " was the Reply. " *All the bad ones*, I hope," answer'd Lady Emily coldly,—& turned away.' (Marg. note to 1816 edit. of the *Life*.)

Lady Emily (Amelia Caroline Nassau) was the third daughter of Baron Hervey of Ickworth († 1743) and sister of the second, third, and fourth earls of Bristol. Walpole records, 11 June 1753, that she and her sisters were given the rank of an earl's daughter. *Letters*, iii. 164.

Page 159, line 13. Among the subscribers to ' old Mr. Sheridan's ' work on Elocution (1762) are : ' The Hon. Lord Auchinlech, 2 copies ', ' James Boswell, Esq.', ' The Rev. Mr. Dodd ', ' David Garrick, Esq.' The author apologizes for mistakes of spelling, &c., because he took the names at the door of the lecture hall. He adds that a third of the subscribers' names are missing owing to ' the casual loss of some of the lists '. The absence of Johnson's name is probably not due to accident.

Page 163, lines 21 ff. and note 4. The English translation of Drelin-court's treatise *Les consolations de l'âme fidèle contre les frayeurs de la mort*, made by C. D'Assigny and entitled *The Christian's Defence against the Fears of Death*, was first published in 1675, and there were successive editions in 1682, 1692, 1701, 1707, 1709, &c., down to the 24th in 1810 (Forster's statement that there were fifty editions is an exaggeration). Defoe's ghost-story *A true Relation of the Apparition of one Mrs Veal, the next Day after her Death to one Mrs Bargrave at Canterbury, the 8th of September 1705* was first published, by R. Bragg, in November 1706 (*Term Catal.* iii. 525) ; the third edition, of which there is a copy in the Library of Trinity College, Dublin, was prefixed to the fifth edition of Drelincourt, dated 1707 ; from this time onwards Defoe's threepenny pamphlet became an integral part of Drelincourt's long treatise, and, during the eighteenth century, does not appear to have been published apart from it.

Of *A true Relation* Mr. G. A. Aitken states (*Nineteenth Century*, 1895, Jan., p. 97) ' the characters are real persons, and that, in fact, Defoe invented nothing, or next to nothing, but simply told, very skilfully, a ghost story which was attracting notice at the time '. It is of interest in this connexion to find from a certified copy of an entry in the registers of the church of St. Mary the Virgin, Dover, that a Mrs. Veal was buried on 10 Sept. 1705, i. e. on the third day after the date on which Defoe's Mrs. Veal is stated to have died. Although Defoe's narrative is a piece of pure journalism, it does in fact advertise Drelincourt. It is true that other edifying writings are mentioned in the course of the narrative, such as ' Dr. Horneck's Ascetick ' and Mr. Norris's ' fine Copy of Verses, call'd, *Friendship in Perfection* ', but these are not commended so highly as Drelincourt. Defoe writes : ' Then Mrs. Veal reminded Mrs. Bar-grave of the many friendly Offices she did her in former Days, and much of the Conversation they had with each other in the times of their Adversity ; what Books they read, and what Comfort in particular they receiv'd from Drelincourt's *Book of Death*, which was the best, she said, on that Subject, ever wrote. She also mention'd Dr. Sherlock, and two Dutch Books which were translated, wrote upon Death, and several others : But Drelincourt, she said, had the clearest Notions of Death, and of the future State, of any who have handled that Subject ': and later on, without any reference to the context, it is stated that ' Drelin-court's Book of DEATH is, since this happen'd, bought up strangely '. That the publisher had a hand in this advertising is proved by the following 'Advertisement ' printed on the last page of the first edition of *A true Relation* : ' Drelincourt's Book of the Consolations against the Fears of Death, has been four times Printed already in English, of which many Thousands have been Sold, and not without great

Applause : And its bearing so great a Character in this Relation, the Impression is near Sold off.'

The publishers of Drelincourt, Clavell, Robinson, and Churchill, to whom Bragg must have sold his copyright, did not curiously enough mention *A true Relation* on the title-pages of the edition which included it : the Preface, however, of the fifth and successive editions records ' the high Esteem and Commendation that a late Apparition, too well attested to be slighted, hath given of this Book '.

Page 164, line 3. Mason published his edition of Gray in 1775. The title-page runs :

The Poems of Mr. Gray. To which are prefixed Memoirs of His Life and Writings By W. Mason, M.A. York : Printed by A. Ward ; and sold by J. Dodsley, Pall-Mall, London ; and J. Todd, Stonegate, York. MDCCLXXV. Quarto.

The poems occupy about one-fifth of the book. Walpole, writing to him on 3 April 1775, says : ' Well ! your book is walking the town in mid day.' (*Letters*, 1904, ix. 173.) A second edition, also in quarto, was published in the same year.

Page 164, line 5. The edition of Akenside described by Johnson as ' splendid ' was the first collected edition brought out by Akenside's friend and executor, Jeremiah Dyson (Johnson's *Life of Akenside*, 6, 11, and *D.N.B.* s.v. Dyson). It was announced in *The Public Advertiser*, 26 March, ' This Day is published Elegantly printed on Royal Quarto, Price 18*s*. sewed in Boards The Poems of the late Dr. Akenside '. The full title is *The Poems of Mark Akenside, M.D. London, Printed by W. Bowyer and J. Nichols: and sold by J. Dodsley, in Pall Mall. MDCCL-XXII.* There was an octavo edition in the same year.

Page 171, note 2. In a note to the original MS. of Dr. Carlyle's *Autobiography* Colonel Alexander Ferguson, the author of *Henry Erskine and his time*, writes :

' The character of Mr. Elphinstone is to my knowledge most erroneous. He was a worthy and excellent man, an able scholar, and most attentive to his pupils, both as a teacher and as a guardian of their morals. Whatever were his political opinions his only care was to make his pupils good men and good subjects, and it was probably owing to the instruction and sound principles which he then imbibed that Mr. Colt [Dr. Carlyle's friend in question] attained that reputable character for which he is . . . justly praised.' Carlyle's *Autobiography*, new ed., 1910, p. 518.

Johnson put at least one boy to him : writing to Mrs. Thrale, 25 March 1773, he says ' I am going this evening to put young Otway to school with Mr. Elphinston '. *Letters*, No. 304.

Page 173, lines 15 ff. Perhaps it was at this very dinner that Johnson in reply to Erskine, who had ventured to praise *Tom Jones*, said : ' Why, sir, Richardson was worth a whole race of Fieldings, supposing every individual of the race to be a regiment.' S. Rivington's *Publishing Family of Rivington*, 1919, p. 34.

Burney contributed the following note to the third edition :

' Johnson's severity against Fielding did not arise from any viciousness in his style, but from his loose life, and the profligacy of almost all his male characters. Who would venture to read one of his novels aloud to modest women ? His novels are *male* amusements, and very amusing they certainly are.—Fielding's conversation was coarse, and so tinctured with the rank weeds of *the Garden*, that it would now be thought only fit for a brothel.'

Page 174, note 2. Lady Mary Wortley Montagu, a great reader of novels, both English and French, preferred Fielding to Richardson. She described *Tom Jones* as ' agreeable ', and said that Fielding in *Amelia* was ' inferior to himselfe, superior to most others ', while *Clarissa* is denounced as ' miserable stuff ', and in *Sir Charles Grandison* she found ' mean sentiments meanly express'd '. See *Sotheby's Catalogue*, 1 Aug. 1928, pp. 85, 86, 95. Lady Mary was Fielding's cousin.

Page 182, line 7 and note 3. Boswell and Mickle were both contributors to the second volume of *A Collection of Original Poems by Scotch Gentlemen*, published by Donaldson, 1762. They had been in correspondence since 1768, but did not meet till much later. On 5 Aug. 1769 Boswell says :

' I wish you was acquainted with me ; for I may venture to tell you that you would find me possessed of a heart and soul more valuable than any talents ; and what faults I have would not hurt me much with a true poet.' *Universal Mag.*, 1809, Jan. p. 103.

The correspondence was apparently opened by Mickle, who asked Boswell in June 1768 to read his ill-fated tragedy, *The Siege of Marseilles* (*Ibid.* p. 24). Boswell did read it and recommended it to Garrick at least four times, but when he found that Garrick would not produce it, strongly advised Mickle to acquiesce in this decision and to refrain from giving vent to his resentment. (*Ibid.* pp. 103, 224 ff. 301 ff.)

In the first edition of the *Lusiad* (1776, p. 133) Mickle says in a note that Mallet's *Elvira*

' is one of the many neglected unsufferable loads of unanimated dulness, which, though honoured with the approbation of Mr. Garrick, have disgraced the English theatre, and rendered *Modern Tragedy* a name of contempt '.

Page 189, note 3. Mr. Byrne Hackett, of New York, tells me that Johnson's English Bible (the quarto edition of Dr. Blayney's ' standard ' Bible, published by the Clarendon Press in 1769, divided by Johnson into seven volumes) contained a hundred annotations and that many passages were marked with the three successive dates on which he read them. At the sale of Johnson's library it fetched £2 10s. (No. 533, ed. Newton, 1925). It found its way to America via the Protestant College at Malta.

Johnson also less freely annotated his copy of the 1743 edition, published at Oxford, of the Bible and Prayer Book. The first of the two volumes contains the inscription (not in Johnson's hand) : ' Thomas Johnson, Aug. 12, 1773. The Gift of his Cousin Dr. Samuel Johnson.' The volumes were exhibited in London in 1925 and are now (January 1929) owned by Mr. Gabriel Wells of New York. See *The Times*, 30 Nov. 1928. For Thomas Johnson, see *post*, iv. App. F.

Page 194, note 3. I have examined the Matriculation Register of the University and I find under the date 18 June 1723 : ' Gul: Murray 18 David fi: Civ. Bath C. Som.' There is also the following marginal note : ' This is a mistake of sound— It ought to be " Perth in Scotia "; according to information communicated by L^d. Mansfield himself to Dr. Buckler Keeper of the Archives in the year 1778.'

Pages 196–200. *Vicious Intromission.* The original petition, signed by Boswell, ' of James Wilson late of Haghouse, now Heritor in Kilmaurs, unto the Right Honourable, The Lords of Council and Session ' is in the National Library of Scotland (Hermand's Session Papers, vol. ii). Mr. D. Nichol Smith has collated the Johnsonian section, which runs from p. 17 to p. 22. The readings of the original, or words not in the *Life*, are here printed in italics.

P. 196, l. 3 from foot : it is necessary that it be known ; *and that it may be known* it is necessary

P. 197, l. 10 from foot : *fraud*

P. 197, l. 6 from foot : *inclose*

P. 198, l. 9 : necessary *for me* to examine

P. 198, l. 13 : *deceased person*

P. 198, l. 23 : The original has an additional sentence concluding the quotation from Lord Kames.

P. 198, l. 34 : *advantage*

P. 199, l. 9 : *coven*

P. 199, l. 11 : less *ferocious*

P. 199, l. 17 : and two *are* proper

P. 199, l. 32 : temptation to *intromission*

P. 199, l. 36 : is *in itself* a proof

P. 199, l. 39 : If *the* temptation

P. 200, l. 2 : *can* operate

Pages 201 last line, 202 lines 1, 2. Boswell, in a letter written in October 1773 to Beattie, repeated Johnson's encomium on his *Essay*, adding :

'Such a testimony must give you great satisfaction. It is a noble evidence both of the real worth and of the literary merit of your book.' Margaret Forbes, *Beattie and his Friends*, 1904, p. 71.

Evidence of Johnson's approval came also from another source. Beattie entered (1 June 1773) in the diary which he kept during his stay in London :

' Garrick . . . repeated a speech that Johnson once made to him in regard to my book on Truth. Garrick had been praising it highly as a most excellent work, which he always does when he speaks of it. Johnson seconded him warmly. " Why, sir, there is in it a depth of reasoning and a splendour of language which make it one of the first-rate productions of the age." ' *Ib.* p. 79.

On 16 May he wrote :

' Dined with Mr. Strachan (the printer). He says my Essay has knocked up the sale of Mr. David Hume's essays, which he has access to know, being a proprietor of those essays.' (*Ib.* 76.)

Creech's statement (*Ib.* p. 71) that the ' Masters of Arts [at Oxford] must stand an examination upon the *Essay* before they take their degree ' is an exaggeration. It is possible that the book may have been recommended by a tutor as providing material for a disputation or dissertation. See Christopher Wordsworth's *Scholae Academicae*, 1877, pp. 219 ff.

The first edition (1770) consisted of 750 copies, the second (1771) of 1,000 (Forbes, *o. c. s.*, p. 50) ; the third edition was published in 1772, the fourth in 1773, the fifth in 1774 ; of the edition called the sixth there were two issues, one with an Edinburgh imprint (Creech), dated 1777, the other with a London imprint (Dilly), dated 1778. Johnson's copy of the second edition is in the British Museum ; it was a present and bears the inscription in Johnson's hand ' Given me by the Authour, Oct. 4, 1771 '. Another note in the hand of Queeny Thrale, afterwards Viscountess Keith, tells us that it was ' Purchased for H. M. Thrale by Wm. Seward Esqr.'

Page 205, lines 8 ff. and notes 1, 2. There is in the *London Mag.* (1774, xliii. p. 82) an ' Essay on Masquerade ; with an Account of one given at Edinburgh by Lady Macdonald, 15 Jan. 1773 ', which Mr. F. A. Pottle (*Lit. Career of Boswell*, p. 223) attributes on internal evidence to Boswell. The account is much fuller than that given in the *Gent. Mag.* (Jan. 1773, p. 43). The writer says :

' To attempt, for the second time, to introduce the amusement of masquerade into Scotland was reserved for Lady Macdonald, formerly the beautiful Miss Bosville of Yorkshire. Her husband, Sir Alexander, was pleased with the scheme, and they had a select invited party of very genteel company, on the 15th of January, 1773, at Duff-house, which they then possessed. Of the masks, there was a rich and fanciful variety. Lady Macdonald, in the character of Flora, was so charming, that if there were any truth in ancient mythology, Jupiter or Pluto must have undoubtedly made part of the company and carried her off. Sir Alexander appeared first in the character of a showman leading a dancing bear, having a stuffed skin . . ., which he managed with agility and drollery ; and next in the character of a macaroni baker, squeaking and selling minced pies.'

The account concludes with the statement that ' some animadversions were made upon this experiment by some of the more serious people of Edinburgh ', so that perhaps the synod did have something to say, as Johnson anticipated. There is no mention of Boswell's presence.

Page 205, line 14. In *An Account of the Expence of correcting and improving sundry Books*, published by the Booksellers in 1774, it is stated that Johnson was paid £300 for ' Improvements in the third Edition ' of his Dictionary. There are no material alterations or corrections in this edition ; perhaps the fourth edition published in 1773 is meant.

Page 205, last line and note 4. The title *She Stoops to Conquer* was given by Goldsmith to his comedy at the very last moment. He sent it, with the accepted Epilogue, actually the fourth to be written, to the stage manager on the day, Sunday, before the first performance ; the playbills had to be altered on the Monday morning. The title is derived from the opening lines of the accepted Epilogue ' spoken by Mrs. Bulkley, in the character of Miss Hardcastle ' :

> ' Well, having stoop'd to conquer with success,
> And gain'd a husband without aid from dress,
> Still, as a bar-maid, I could wish it too,
> As I have conquer'd him to conquer you.'

In the printed text Goldsmith makes Kate Hardcastle say (Act IV), ' I'll still preserve the character in which I stoop'd to conquer ', but in the licenser's MS. this line runs, ' I'll still preserve the character in which I conquer'd '. See Miss K. C. Balderston, *Collected Letters of Goldsmith*, 1928, p. xlvi, *Mod. Lang. Notes*, xlv. 84, and *Public Advertiser*, 13 and 15 March 1773.

Page 206, line 22. Mrs. Piozzi's comment on Johnson's postscript runs : ' Poor Mrs. Thrale was obliged to say so in order to keep well with Johnson.' Hayward's *Mrs. Piozzi* (ed. 2), ii. p. 124.

Page 206, lines 25 ff. Boswell, in a letter of thanks (11 June 1792) to Abercrombie for the two letters to American gentlemen, says : ' I received them in time to be inserted in the second edition of my *Life* . . ., which is now in the press. . . . A copy from the author shall be sent to you, hoping that you will allow it a place in your library ', adding, it is interesting to note, ' Meantime, Sir, my grateful acknowledgements to you shall be wafted across the Atlantic '. Boswell's *Letters*, No. 310, ii. 442. Boswell was as good as his word and the copy he presented is now in the Adam Collection. It has the inscription ' To James Abercrombie, Esq: of Philadelphia, from his much obliged humble servant The Author.' Abercrombie was a graduate of the University of Pennsylvania. Professor Tinker notes that he was for a time a merchant in Philadelphia, but became a priest and was from 1794 to 1832 Assistant Minister of the United Episcopal Churches of Philadelphia. Boswell's *Letters*, ii. 442 n. 3.

Page 207, line 7, and note 1. ' Mr. B—d ' was, according to the Edinburgh edition of the *Letters of Johnson*, published in 1822, ' Mr. Bond, Consul-General for the Middle and Southern States of America '.

Page 207, line 23 and note 2. Professor Walter Graham, of the University of Illinois, has kindly supplied me with Bishop White's all too brief account of his acquaintance with Johnson. This is printed in Julius Ward's *Bp. W. White*, 1892, pp. 23, 24, and is as follows :

' My introduction to him was a letter from the Rev. Jonathan Odell, formerly missionary at Burlington. The doctor was very civil to me. I visited him occasionally, and I know some who would be tempted to envy me the felicity of having one morning found him in the act of preparing his dictionary for a new edition. His harshness of manners never displayed itself to me, except in one instance, when he told me that, had he been Prime Minister during the then recent controversy concerning the Stamp Act, he would have sent a ship of war and levelled one of our principal cities to the ground. On the other hand, I have heard from him sentiments expressive of a feeling heart, and convincing me that he would not have done as he said. Having dined in company with him in Kensington, at the house of Mr. Elphinstone, well-known to scholars of that day, and returning on the stage-coach with the doctor, I mentioned to him there being a Philadelphia edition of his ' Prince of Abyssinia '. He expressed a wish to see it. I promised to send him a copy on my return to Philadelphia, and did so.'

Page 207, line 3 from foot. The *Rasselas* which Johnson received was a copy of the first American edition, now very rare. It bore the title '*The History of Rasselas, Prince of Abissinia. An Asiatic Tale. . . America: Printed for every purchaser. MDCCLXVIII* '. The printer was Robert Bell, and the place of publication Philadelphia. The phrase ' printed for every purchaser ', not unusual in American books, explains Johnson's comment ' the printer seems to have expected that it would be scattered among the people '. See Prof. C. B. Tinker's *Rasselas in the New World* (New Haven), 1925.

Page 208, line 1. The Italian version of *Rasselas* mentioned by Johnson was made by Cosimo Mei, who published it under the anagram of Mimiso Ceo, at Padua, in 1764. Baretti in a marginal note to the *Piozzi Letters* (i. 203) describes him as ' a foolish fellow, who called himself Cavalier Mei '. He adds : ' I knew him a beggar at Padua. He neither knew English, nor Italian, though a Tuscan by birth.' He characterizes his translation as ' a damned one '—a judgement which is regarded by Prof. L. Piccioni as neither unjust nor exaggerated (*Giorn. stor. della lett. ital.*, 1910, lv. 344).

Courtney records two anonymous Italian translations (1823, Londra, and 1825, Livorno), and Prof. Piccioni (*o. c. s.*) adds three others (Alexander Dodsworth, 1797, Florence ; Guiseppe Arnaud, 1828, Milan, reprinted 1852 ; and Aurelio Gotti, 1883, Milan).

Page 208, line 1 and note 2. Baretti's French translation was completed in 1764 and, although its publication was sanctioned by the ecclesiastical authorities in Venice, it was never printed. The MS., which is in the Biblioteca Nazionale, Turin, has been fully described by Prof. Piccioni, who points out that Baretti submitted his work to the revision of first one person and then of two others, more expert in the language than himself. Johnson's French in the opening paragraph is corrected in three places. *Giorn. stor. della lett. ital.*, 1910, lv. 351. Baretti included chapters x, xviii, xxv–xxix, or parts of these, in his series of parallel translations *An Introduction to the most useful European Languages* (1772).

The first French translation of *Rasselas* was made by Mme Belot in 1760. Voltaire in acknowledging a copy which she sent to him writes, 16 May 1760: ' Il m'a paru d'une philosophie aimable, et très-bien écrit.' *Œuvres*, 1880, xl. 390. In the Preface the translator says : Le succès de Candide semble présager celui de son contemporain Rasselas, Prince d'Abissinie. Ces deux ouvrages renferment trop sensiblement les mêmes vues, pour n'avoir pas droit au même accueil.'

To the numerous French translations specified by Courtney (p. 94) may be added that by M. Duchiron, Vienna, 1798, which appears to be rare (it is certainly very bad). That published at Lyons in 1833 was by Mme de Fresne ; see Bruyère, *Jean Reboul*, 1925, p. 414.

Page 208, line 1. The first German translation of *Rasselas* was published in 1762. According to Meusel's edition of Hamberger's *Das gelehrte Teutschland* (1797, iv. 303) it was made by Elieser Gottlieb Küster (1732–1799). The title-page runs : *Der Prinz von Abyssinien. Eine Geschichte in zwey Theilen. Nach der dritten Auflage aus dem Englischen übersetzt. Frankfurth, Leipzig und Zelle*, 1762. *Bey George Conrad Gsellius*. There is a copy in the Preussische Staatsbibliothek.

Page 208, last line and note 5. The following letter (printed by Mr. R. B. Adam in his *Johnsonian Catalogue*) from Kearsley the bookseller to Goldsmith shows the lengths to which one at least of the author's friends was prepared to go in order to ensure *She Stoops to Conquer* a kind reception :

' If you think two or three printers men disposed of properly in the galleries may be of any service this evening send me an order for their admission. I go with a party of your Globe friends into the pitt. I need not inform you that I wish you great success.'

Robert Day, the Irish judge, told Prior in 1831 that he was one of Goldsmith's friends who ' assembled in great force in the pit ' to protect the play. He adds ' we had no difficulty to encounter ; for it was received throughout with the greatest acclamations '. Prior's *Goldsmith*, ii. 361. For Colman's discomfiture, and specimens of the ridicule cast upon him, see *Ibid.* 402 ff. Miss K. C. Balderston gives (*Collected Letters of Goldsmith*, 1928, p. xlix) Colman's supplicatory letter (23 March 1773) to Goldsmith :

' Let me beseech you to put me out of my pain one way or other. Either take me off the rack of the Newspapers, or give me the *Coup de Grace*. In a word, & without a figure, I beg if you think I was vile enough to *wish* ill to your play (whatever I thought of it) e'en say so in yr. preface to it—but if you acquit me of this in your own mind, absolve me in the face of the World.'

Page 209, line 1. Beattie noted in his diary, 24 May 1773 :

' I sat two hours with Dr. Samuel Johnson, who was in exceedingly good humour and spirit ; showed me some Latin verses he had lately composed, on finishing the last edition of his Dictionary, and allowed me to take a copy.' Margaret Forbes, *Beattie and his Friends*, 1904, p. 78.

The Latin verses are presumably those to which he gave the title Γνῶθι σεαυτόν (*Post Lexicon Anglicanum auctum et emendatum*). See *ante*, i. 298 n. 4. I am informed that the copy made by Beattie is not with the Beattie papers in Aberdeen University Library.

Page 209, lines 19 ff. and note 2. The affray between Goldsmith and Evans took place on Friday, 26 March 1773. Percy noted in his diary on that date : ' I was at the Club : Dr Goldsmith came to us with a bloody Face.'

Page 211, line 13. The saying of Demosthenes is reported in *Decem Oratorum Vitae*, *Demosthenes*, 845 B, formerly ascribed to Plutarch and included in editions of his *Moralia* :

' When he [Demosthenes] was demaunded the question which was the first point of eloquence, he answered, Action ; which the second, he made answer, Action ; and which was the third, he said, Action, still.' (P. Holland's transl. 1603.)

The passage is similarly translated by Bacon (*Essays, Of Boldnesse*, 1625). Cicero tells the anecdote in three places (*De Oratore* iii. 56, § 213 : *Brutus*, 38, 142 : *Orator*, 17, 56), in each of which he uses the word *actio*. Quintilian in giving the same story (xi. 3. § 6) has the word *pronuntiatio*. The Greek word translated *actio* by Cicero and *pronuntiatio* by Quintilian is ὑπόκρισις, which is now generally accepted as meaning, in this context, *delivery* : ' an orator's delivery, including declamation, gesticulation, and all that he borrowed from actors ' (Liddell and Scott). See Archdeacon Hare, *Guesses at Truth*, 1827, i. 257–60, and J. E. Sandys, Cicero's *Orator*, 1885, p. 64.

Pages 211, last line, and 212, lines 1 ff. and note 1. Percy originally undertook to edit the *Spectator*, together with the *Guardian* and the *Tatler*, in 1763–5. Writing to Dr. Birch, 21 April 1763, he says :

' I shall be glad to be favoured with any hints, either for perfecting that work [*Key to Rehearsal*] or the proposed edition of the Spectator, Guardian, and Tatler.' Nichols, *Illustr.* vii. 568.

A year later, 26 April 1764, he writes :

' Mr. Tonson, who is about to print a new edition of the " Spectator ", has applied to me to overlook the impression, and to rectify whatever mistakes are crept into the modern copies, collating them with the old original papers. In this work I have made a considerable progress.' *Ibid.* 573.

On the same day, after reporting to Tonson that he has 'gone through the two first volumes of the Spectator with the most minute attention', he complains that his materials are scanty and suggests that the printing should be deferred 'for a month or two longer' in order that he might do his business effectually. He then submits his plan of the edition, which was adopted by an agreement dated '25 May 1764'. This agreement was for an edition of both the *Spectator* and the *Guardian* 'with explanatory notes', and the Tonsons agreed to pay him £105, 'one half part thereof on putting the said work to the press, and the other half when the whole is finished'. Percy agreed on his part to deliver 'one volume of the Spectator . . . within one month from the date hereof, and the other seven volumes of the Spectator on or before Christmas next'. He received 'in part of payment' one sum of ten guineas on 31 May, and another on 12 June, 1764. (On 16 March 1765 he agreed with Tonson for an edition of the *Tatler* on the same lines for £52 10s.) See Nichols, *Illustr.* vi. 557 ff. Percy's work on the revision apparently ceased soon after this, to be taken over by Dr. John Calder, secretary to the Duke of Northumberland. Calder, who died in 1815, in an undated autobiographical memoir writes :

'On my coming to settle in London, above half a century ago, I was engaged to prepare a new Edition of the Tatler, Spectator, and Guardian. . . . I had begun this work at Alnwick for Dr. Percy, late Bishop of Dromore, who, on my coming to town, entirely relinquished his contract for this purpose to me, on whom it devolved with the consent and at the request of the Booksellers.' *Ibid.* iv. 800.

From a letter of Beattie to Calder, dated 26 Jan. 1772, we learn that he had on that date been at work some time. Beattie writes : 'You say your Tatler is just coming out. I shall be glad to hear the same account of the Spectator.' *Ibid.* p. 820. Calder's work on the essays was interrupted by an attempt to re-edit Chambers's *Cyclopedia*, a task on which he bestowed such 'superfluous diligence' that in 1776 the booksellers broke the contract. *Ibid.* pp. 800 ff. and Johnson's *Letters*, No. 453. John Nichols writing to Percy, 10 April 1784, says :

'By the indefatigable attention of Dr. Calder the *Tatlers* begin to make some progress.' *Illustr.* viii. 71.

He writes again, 22 April 1786 :

'A set of the *Tatlers*, which were published on Wednesday last, awaits your Lordship's order as to the mode of conveyance. And it will give Dr. Calder, as well as myself, much pleasure if the execution meets with your Lordship's approbation. The " Spectator " will follow as soon as the nature of it will allow. We shall hope to be favoured with your Lordship's hints and remarks, and with the communication of some Notes by Swift, which your Lordship formerly mentioned.' *Illustr.* viii. 73.

Boswell in a letter to Percy, dated 12 July 1786, writes : 'I am much pleased with the edition of the *Tatler*, with notes ; but I should have

been better pleased had the notes been all *by one hand* ; your Lordship
will understand me.' To this Percy added the note 'The Bishop of
Dromore had no hand in this edition. T. D.' Boswell's *Letters*,
No. 241, ii. 336 ; Nichols, *Illustr*. vii. 305.

The *Spectator* followed in 1789. It was published by Nichols and
was the first edition to be annotated (Aitken, *Life of Steele*, i. 321). The
Editor's Preface contains the following statement :

'There being an immediate demand for an impression of the Spectator in
this form, and two volumes of it having been printed some years ago with great
accuracy, under the direction of a Writer of distinguished taste and talents ; the
other six volumes have been suitably adapted to them on the same improved
but contracted plan.'

Nichols adds that 'the distinguished person alluded to was the Rev.
Dr. Percy'. *Lit. Anecd*. ix. 56. This edition appears to be rare : I
have failed to find it in any of our public libraries or elsewhere.

Calder's position as Private Literary Secretary to the Duke of
Northumberland, 'with whom he was hospitably domesticated at Alnwick Castle and in the Metropolis' (Nichols, *Lit. Anecd*. ix. 804), would
bring him into touch with Percy. Mr. S. K. Jones, Librarian of Dr.
Williams's Library, tells me that Calder acted as Deputy Librarian from
about March 1773 till Michaelmas 1775.

Among other Johnsoniana, of undoubted authenticity, in the *European
Magazine*, July 1789, p. 5, there is the following 'Advertisement to the
Re-publication of the Spectator, in 1776', the first part of which is
clearly by Johnson.

'To the Public. The Book thus offered to the Public is too well known to
be praised : It comprizes precepts of criticism, sallies of invention, descriptions
of life, and lectures of virtue : It employs wit in the cause of truth, and makes
elegance subservient to piety : It has now for more than half a century supplied
the English nation, in a great measure, with principles of speculation, and rules
of practice ; and given Addison a claim to be numbered among the benefactors
of mankind.

Though the Public have been long supplied with this work at an exceeding
cheap rate, yet as the purchase of the whole together may be inconvenient to
many who might otherwise be glad to be possessed of it ; to render this book
more generally useful, the present Proprietors propose printing an handsome
edition of a convenient size for the pocket, to be published on the following
conditions.'

What the conditions were I cannot say, as I have not succeeded in
discovering where the Advertisement originally appeared. There was
a duodecimo edition of the *Spectator* published in 1776 (Aitken, *Life of
Steele*, ii. 401).

Page 215, line 20. The young woman whom Boswell did not know,
was, according to Mrs. Piozzi (note in the 1816 edit. of the *Life*), Poll,
Miss Carmichael. *Post*, iii. 368.

Page 220, lines 19 ff. Vincenzio Martinelli's *Istoria d'Inghilterra* (1770–73) extends from the Roman occupation to the death of Q. Anne ; he, however, records the raising of Walpole to the peerage and closes his book with a eulogy of Horatio, first Lord Wolterton, whose second son, Thomas (see Collins's *Peerage* 1812, v. 673), bore the cost of publication and to whom the three quarto volumes are dedicated.

Other works by Martinelli are *Istoria critica della vita civile* (London, 1752) ; *Lettere familiari e critiche* (London, 1758) ; *Istoria del governo d'Inghilterra e delle sue colonie in India e nell'America Settentrionale* (Firenze, 1776 : 2nd ed. Pescia, 1777) ; and the edition of the *Decameron* (London, Nourse, 1762 and 1764), subscriptions for which he was collecting when Casanova met him in London (*Mémoires*, 1860, v. p. 379).

Miss Burney has left a not very flattering account of him. According to her he piqued himself upon treating the Great with rudeness : ' He was boasting to this effect in his broken English, and said—" I hear the nobleman talk—I give him great attention—I make him low bow—and I say, My Lord ! you are a very great man,—but for all that,—a blockhead ! " ' *Early Diary*, ed. 1907, i. p. 135.

Page 224, lines 21 ff. The history of John Angell and his son, also named John, has been written by Mr. A. Tremaine Wright in *The Two Angells of Stenography*, 1919. John, the father, was a feltmaker or hatter, who carried on business in Johnson's parish, St. Clement Danes, Westminster. His *Stenography ; or Short-hand Improved* was first published in 1758 (*Critical Rev.* Oct. 1758) ; on the title-page of the first edition, which is undated, Angell states that he had ' practised this Art above 30 Years ', but it does not appear that he ever taught it professionally. He also published *An Essay on Prayer*, 1760, and a *History of Religion* which came out in parts. He died in London in 1764. His son brought out at least three new editions of *Stenography*, numbered the second, fourth, and fifth : the second received the approval of the Dublin Society at a meeting held on 25 Jan. 1770. It was this John Angell who acted as an official shorthand writer in Ireland and taught shorthand in Dublin, where he died in 1827.

Johnson does not definitely say that he wrote the Preface or Dedication to Angell's book, but that Angell asked him to do so. The Preface, which exhibits no trace of Johnson's style, could not have been by him, as it is for the most part a summary, with much direct plagiarism, of Philip Gibbs's *An historical Account of Compendious and Swift Writing*, 1736. Angell does indeed describe some books not seen by Gibbs and he continues the history of the subject beyond him, but to have written this original part of the Preface would have, in the opinion of a competent authority, involved Johnson in a study of the principles of shorthand, for which there is no evidence. The only passage in the Dedication which is at all Johnsonian is the opening paragraph :

' The Improvement of Arts and Sciences has always been esteemed laudable ; and in Proportion to their Utility and Advantage to Mankind, they have generally gained the Patronage of Persons the most distinguished for Birth, Learning and Reputation in the World.'

All that we can say for certain is that ' Mr. Samuel Johnson, A.M. London ' appears in the list of subscribers to the first edition. See also *Notes and Queries*, 4 Ser. v. 108, 352, 476 (where some additional genealogical information concerning the Angells is given).

I have great pleasure in thanking Mr. J. M. Warden of Edinburgh for his courteous assistance in drafting this note.

Page 231, lines 26 ff. *The fable of the little fishes.* Prof. E. Bensly suggests that Goldsmith had in mind Henry Brooke's story of the three silver trouts (*Fool of Quality*, 1766, ch. ii). Only one of the three, it is true, asks for wings. It addresses the Almighty ' There are your favourite little birds, who fly this way and that way, and mount up to the very heavens . . . because you have given them wings. Give me such wings also as you have given to them.' These little fishes certainly do not talk like WHALES.

Page 235, note 2. The original of Johnson's letter to Goldsmith is now the property of the Johnson Club, through the generosity of one of its members, Mr. R. B. Adam.

Page 236, note 2. Dr. Hill in his Addenda (vol. vi) cited Gibbon's testimony ; who, writing of the year 1759, says, ' The old reproach, that no British altars had been raised to the muse of history, was recently disproved by the first performances of Robertson and Hume, the histories of Scotland and of the Stuarts.' *Memoirs*, ed. Hill, p. 122. Dr. Hill added a number of other judgements, chiefly adverse, of English historians in an Appendix to this passage (p. 295).

Page 245, line 19. The second and third editions read erroneously ' it is not '.

Page 253, lines 3 ff. Johnson probably alludes to the following passage from Baxter's *Holy Commonwealth* (Add. to Preface b 2) published in 1659 :

' We grant that the Consciences of men are out of the reach of the Magistrates judgment ; further then they are manifested by their Words or Deeds : And we grant that the Unity and Peace of the Church, must not be laid on lower Controversies, but on the Essentials of Religion, even of Faith and Communion : and that we must tolerate all tolerable differences among honest men : In well doing all men should be encouraged, In ill doing through mistakes, well meaning men must be tolerated as far as Charity to Church and State, and to their own and others souls will bear it.'

Page 258, line 5. Farington reports that Boswell ' would only willingly permit from Dr. Johnson ' the familiar contraction of his name to ' Bozzy ', and that when Metcalfe (*post*, iv. 159) indulged in it, Boswell in return called him ' Mettie '. *Diary*, i. 96.

Page 260, lines 9 ff. There is no doubt of Goldsmith's inability to conceal his envy. Beattie entered in his diary, 14 June 1773 :

> ' Miss Reynolds told me to-day some particulars of Goldsmith. He, it seems, not only is, but even acknowledges himself to be, envious of all contemporary authors whose works are successful, and has several times spoken with some peevishness of the attention that has been shown me in England. " Why should he have a pension ? " he said, one day when I happened to be mentioned. " For writing the ' Minstrel ' ? then surely I have a better claim." One of the company told him that my claim was founded on the "Essay on Truth", a work of public utility and which had been attended with danger or at least inconvenience to the author.' Margaret Forbes, *Beattie and his Friends*, 1904, p. 81.

Fifteen years later Beattie wrote at greater length on the same subject :

> ' What she [Mrs. Piozzi] says of Goldsmith is perfectly true. He was a poor fretful creature, eaten up with affectation and envy. He was the only person I ever knew who acknowledged himself to be envious. In Johnson's presence he was quiet enough ; but in his absence expressed great uneasiness in hearing him praised. He envied even the dead ; he could not bear that Shakespeare should be so much admired as he is. There might, however, be something like magnanimity in envying Shakespeare and Dr. Johnson. . . . But surely Goldsmith had no occasion to envy me ; which, however, he certainly did, for he owned it (though when we met he was always very civil) ; and I received undoubted information, that he seldom missed an opportunity of speaking ill of me behind my back.' Sir W. Forbes, *Life of Beattie*, ii. 233-4.

Murphy speaks of ' the leaven of envy which corroded Goldsmith's mind ' (*Essay on Johnson*, p. 97 : John. Misc. i. 421). See *ante*, ii. 201 n. 3.

Page 263, line 10. Johnson had suffered from inflammation of his sound eye as early as 1756. On 15 Feb. of that year he recorded that light had been restored to his eye (*Prayers and Med.* ¶ 30: John. Misc. i. p. 19), and four days later he wrote : ' The inflammation is come again into my eye, so that I can write very little ' (*Letters*, No. 90). In his letter to Mrs. Thrale, 24 May 1773, he refers to the attack quoted by Boswell : 'My fever . . . has left me a very severe inflammation in the seeing eye ' (*Ib.* No. 311). That the attack was severe is shown by the following letter (printed by Mr. R. B. Adam in his *Catalogue*, 1929, iii. 15) from Baretti to Mrs. Thrale, 5 June 1773:

> ' I went yesterday to dine at the Royal Academy where I met with Mr. Mudges (*ante*, i. 378), who told me that he never said he apprehended of any Gutta Serena in Mr. Johnson's eye but that he thought that eye looked very bad and that unless Mr. Johnson took the greatest care to have the inflammation removed the danger of losing his sight was very great.'

The continuation of the passage cited by Boswell shows that the inflammation was removed ' by two copious bleedings, and the daily use of catharticks for a long time '. Johnson adds (the passage is dated 22 July) ' the effect yet remains '. *Prayers and Med.* ¶ 103 : John. Misc. i. 67.

Page 263, line 16 and note 5. The *Confutatio stultissimae Burdonum Fabulae* was really the work of Joseph Justus Scaliger, and the person on whom he fathered it, under the initials I. R., was Janus Rutgersius, his pupil. See Bernays, *J. J. Scaliger*, 1855, pp. 214, 295. D. Heinsius married Rutgersius's sister. *Allgemeine Deutsche Biographie*, xxx. p. 42.

Page 264, lines 13 ff. Newcastle was Chambers's birthplace, and for the short time that Johnson stayed there he was Chambers's guest. Writing to his mother, 3 Aug. 1773, Chambers says :

' On Friday or Saturday morning I shall set out for Newcastle in Company with my Friend Dr. Johnson. . . . We shall I hope get to Newcastle before dinner, and I must beg that you will endeavour to accomodate my Friend with a bed, during the two or three days that he may probably stay with us.' (*Michelmore's Catalogue*, 1925.)

Page 265, last line. Johnson writing to Beattie on 5 Aug. says :

' I shall set out to-morrow with less cheerfulness, because I shall not find you and Mrs. Beattie at the College, but as my journey is regulated by the vacation of the Courts, I cannot delay it.' *Letters*, No. 316·1 : Margaret Forbes, *Beattie and his Friends*, p. 89.

Page 267, note 1. The time of the year when Johnson's visit was made and the shortness of his stay at the Scottish University towns combined to render the conferment of an honorary degree impracticable, except perhaps at Edinburgh on the return journey. Johnson arrived at Edinburgh in the evening of Saturday 14 Aug. (*post*, v. 21) and left on the following Wednesday, 18 Aug. (*Ib.* p. 51), for St. Andrews, which he reached on the same day (*Ib.* p. 57) : he left there on Friday 20 Aug. about noon (*Ib.* p. 70), arriving at Aberdeen the next day, Saturday 21 Aug., ' at half an hour past eleven ' at night (*Ib.* p. 84), where he stayed till ' about eight in the morning ' of Tuesday 24 Aug. (*Ib.* p. 96). The stay at Glasgow was as brief; it lasted from Thursday 28 till Saturday 30 October (*Ib.* 369–71). At Edinburgh, however, Johnson spent ten full days : he arrived on the night of Tuesday 9 November (*Ib.* p. 385), and left on Saturday 20 (*Ib.* 401). The authorities of the University of Edinburgh have courteously examined the Minutes of the Senatus for 1773. The Senatus met on 27 July, 3 and 13 September, and 12 November. There is no mention of Johnson in the Minutes.

Page 268, line 24. Edmund Allen (see *post*. iii. 141) writing to Percy, 20 Nov. 1773, says : ' Dr. Johnson is not yet returned from his Northern Rambles ; when we heard last from him he was in good Health, and said he had never once wanted for Tea and Whiskey ' (R. B. Adam's *Johnsonian Catalogue*, 1929, iii. 4).

Page 274, line 17. Croker noted that Miss Wilton was the daughter of Joseph Wilton, R.A. (1722–1803), the sculptor. ' After Sir Robert Chambers's death she returned to England, and died at Brighton, in April, 1839, aged 88. Miss Chambers, her daughter, married Colonel Macdonald, the son of Flora [*post*, v. 187].'

Page 279, lines 7 ff. and note 5. The Erse or Gaelic books enumerated by Boswell are : (1) The first translation of the N.T. into Gaelic, made by the Rev. James Stuart, for 53 years minister of Killin, and published at Edinburgh in 1767. See also Johnson's *Journey Western Islands*, 1924, p. 110. (2) The translation of Baxter's *Call to the Unconverted* made by the Rev. Alexander Macfarlane, minister of Melford and Killinvir, published at Glasgow in 1750. (3) *The Confession of Faith, Larger and Shorter Catechisms, Agreed upon by the Assembly of Divines at Westminster. . . . Translated into the Irish Language by the Synod of Argyle*, Edinburgh 1725. There was a second edition in 1727 and a third in 1756 (Glasgow). (4) The Gaelic version of the Rev. John Willison's *The Mother's Catechism for the Young Child,* the first edition of which was published at Glasgow in 1752. (5) Alexander McDonald's *Galick and English Vocabulary*, Edinburgh, 1741. This is of interest as being the first Gaelic dictionary.

Johnson in his letter of 1 Oct. (*ante*, ii. 285) acknowledges the receipt of four books only, and these were no doubt presented by him to Bodley, but we cannot be certain that more than two are now there. These are (1) and (2), each of which contains an inscription in Johnson's hand. The Library possesses a copy of the first edition of (3), and three copies of (5), only one of which could have been given by Johnson ; I find no copy of (4). The ' metrical psalms ', suggested by Johnson in the same letter as a desirable complement, was no doubt Alexander McFarlane's amended version of the Synod of Argyle's *Caogad*, 1753. There is a copy in Bodley, but there is no evidence that it came from Johnson. I have dealt with these books more fully in the *Bodleian Quarterly Record*, December 1928.

Page 285, note 1. Mr. F. A. Pottle points out that the convict on whose behalf Boswell wrote to Johnson, was John Reid, sheep-stealer. Boswell first defended him in 1766 and secured his acquittal in the face of the strongest evidence. (See Boswell's *Letters*, No. 53, i. 96, and *Scots Mag.* Dec. xxviii. 668.) In 1774 Reid was again put on trial for a second lapse and again defended by Boswell, but this time he was convicted and sentenced to death. Boswell's efforts to obtain a reprieve failed and Reid was hanged on 21 Sept. The account of his execution in the *London Chron.* (29 Sept. xxxvi. 311) was from Boswell's pen.

Page 286, lines 23 ff. The Rev. H. F. B. Compston gives in *Notes and Queries* (12 S. iii. 1917, pp. 319 ff.) an account of the Reverend William

Hetherington and his Charity. Hetherington, Fellow of Eton, Rector of Farnham Royal, Governor of Christ's Hospital, was born in December 1698 and died 1 Dec. 1778 : on the death of his brother in 1767 he became lord of the manors of North Cray and Ruxley, Kent, and ' probably the richest Clergyman in England ' (Nichols, *Lit. Anecd.* iv. 294 n.). He founded the Charity in 1774, when by a deed dated 29 March he transferred £20,000 in South Sea Annuities to eight governors of Christ's Hospital, by whom it is still administered. Among these governors was Hetherington's kinsman, Thomas Coventry, Bencher of the Inner Temple and Sub-Governor of the South Sea Company, who is described by Lamb in *The Old Benchers of the Inner Temple* (see Sir F. D. MacKinnon's edition, 1927). To him fell on Hetherington's death the ' agreeable seat at North Cray ', reported to be of the annual value of £1,400. The Clerk of Christ's Hospital courteously informs me that Coventry by an indenture dated 19 July 1782 made over £10,365 in Lincoln Corporation 3% stock to the Charity ; so that Lamb's statement that he ' gave away £30,000 at once in his lifetime to a blind charity ' is an exaggeration.

Miss Williams's application was not successful, and her ' petition ' has not been preserved. There were over 700 applicants and 50 vacancies. Mr. Compston writes that ' at the present day more than eight hundred poor blind folk are in receipt of annual grants of £10'.

Page 289, lines 22 ff. I have failed to trace a copy of ' Charlotte's Proposals '. In the *London Chronicle*, 2–4 March 1775, there is the following Advertisement : ' This Day were published Proposals for printing by Subscription a new and elegant Edition of the Original Works of Mrs. Charlotte Lennox. Dedicated to the Queen. Subscriptions will be taken in, and receipts delivered by, Mr. Dodsley, in Pall Mall.'

Page 290, lines 8, 9. George Robinson the bookseller agreed, 4 Oct. 1774, to pay Baretti £75 for his *Easy Lessons*, £25 upon Baretti's signing the agreement, £25 when the book was printed, and £25 when it was printed a second time. R. B. Adam, *Johnsonian Catalogue*, iii. 15.

Page 290, line 13 and note 2. Johnson sent a copy of *A Journey to the Western Islands* to Mrs. Thrale on 17 Dec. 1774. In a note accompanying the book he wrote : ' Mr. Strahan does not publish till after the Holidays, and insists that only the King and you shall have it sooner ' (*Letters*, No. 365·1). In another letter to Mrs. Thrale, undated, but written about this time, Johnson says : ' The King fell to reading the book as soon as he got it, when anything struck him, he read aloud to the Queen, and the Queen could not stay to get the King's book, but borrowed Dr. Hunter's ' (*Ibid.* No. 369·1). Preliminary warnings that the book was to be published on 18 Jan. appear in the *Public Advertiser* for 12 and 17 Jan., and the number for the 18th contains the Advertisement : ' This Day was published Handsomely printed in one volume octavo, Price 5s. sewed, A Journey to the Western Islands of Scotland.' Copious extracts are given in the newspaper, the *London Chronicle* (*ante*, ii. 103), for 17–19 Jan. The announcement ' This Day is published ' &c., occurs again on 13 Feb. 1775 (*Public Advertiser*). This probably refers to the second impression (see *ante*, ii. 310 and Mr. R. W. Chapman's edition, 1924, p. 480).

Page 291, foot, and note 6. From an examination of Boswell's Fee Book, now in the National Library of Scotland, courteously made for me by Mr. T. B. Simpson, it appears that for the period covered, 1766– 1772, Boswell earned a total sum of 1,134½ guineas, of which 321 were earned before Lord Auchinleck sitting as Lord Ordinary, i. e. alone. Of the remaining fees a large proportion would be earned before the Session, including Lord Auchinleck ; it is therefore safe to say that two in three of Boswell's guineas were made before his father, and that he earned a good deal more before him than before any other judge sitting as Lord Ordinary. See *Juridical Review*, xxxiv, 1922, p. 201. Sir Frank MacKinnon points out that Roger North practised constantly before his brother, and that when the latter was promoted from Chief Justice of Common Pleas to Lord Keeper, he at once transferred himself from Common Law to Chancery. See R. North's *Life of Lord Guildford*, § 103, and *Autobiography*, §§ 120, 208.

Page 293, note 2. Boswell's historical picture of Mary Queen of Scots was painted by William Hamilton, R.A. The engraving from it, by Francis Legat, published by John Boydell, 2 Jan. 1786, is without Johnson's inscriptions. See Boswell's *Letters*, No. 148 a, ii. 520. See also *ante*, ii. 270, 283.

Page 294, line 12. Long extracts from Burke's *Speech on American Taxation* are given in the *London Chronicle*, 14–17, and 17–19 Jan. 1775. The last number contains the Advertisement : ' This Day was published, in 4to, Price 2s. 6d. Speech of Edmund Burke, Esq. ; on American Taxation. April 19, 1774. Printed for J. Dodsley.' Writing to the Marquis of Rockingham, 12 Jan. 1775, to tell him that a copy had been sent to Lady Rockingham, Burke says : 'As far as the speech has circulated, it produces rather a good effect.' Burke's *Corres.*, 1844, ii. 8.

Page 294, lines 21, 22. Boswell alludes to the following notice issued by Becket. It is printed in the *London Chronicle* and the *St. James's Chronicle* 19–21 Jan. 1775.

' To the Public. Doctor Johnson having asserted in his late publication, that the Translator of Ossian's Poems " never could shew the Original, nor can it be shewn by any other ", I hereby declare, that the Originals of Fingal and other

Poems of Ossian, lay in my shop for many months in the year 1762, for the inspection of the curious. The Public were not only apprized of their lying there, for inspection, but even proposals for publishing the Originals of the Poems of Ossian were dispersed through the kingdom, and advertized in the news-papers. Upon finding that a number of Subscribers, sufficient to bear the expences, were not likely to appear, I returned the manuscripts to the Proprietor, in whose hands they still remain.

Adelphi, Jan. 19, 1775. Tho. Becket.'

Blair referring to this Advertisement in 1797 stated that Becket 'found no one person had ever called to look at' the original manuscripts. *Report Highland Soc.*, 1805, App. p. 60.

Page 296, note 1. It is of interest to find that Johnson had presented to Dr. Lawrence's son, Soulden, later Sir Soulden, the seventh edition of *The Rambler*. The first two volumes survive ; both bear the inscription 'From the Author', and in the first is written, in Johnson's hand, 'To Mr. S. Lawrence'. Lawrence was seventeen in 1767.

Page 297, lines 26 ff. It appears from letters published by Sir Leslie Stephen in *The Academy*, 19 Oct. 1878, pp. 383 ff., that some one, probably Strahan, had shown Macpherson, previous to publication, the passage in the *Journey to the Western Islands* in which he is attacked (*ante*, ii. 292 note 1). On Sunday 15 Jan. 1775, Macpherson wrote to Strahan, the publisher of the *Journey*, desiring him to use his influence with Johnson, 'that *impertinent fellow*', to induce him to soften the passage, 'though it should occasion the loss of a few days in the publication'. He enclosed the following 'ostensible letter' for Johnson, which was to be shown to no one else :

'Dear Sir,

A friend of mine has, this moment, put into my hands a sentence from a work entituled *A Journey to the Western Islands of Scotland*, which, I am informed, is written by Dr. Johnson. In expressing his incredulity, with regard to the authenticity of the poems of Ossian, he makes use of the words *insolence*, *audacity*, and *guilt*. To his want of belief on this subject I have not the smallest objection. But I suppose you will agree with me, that such expressions ought not to be used by one gentleman to another ; and that whenever they are used, they cannot be passed over with impunity. To prevent consequences that may be, at once, disagreeable to Dr. Johnson and to myself, I desire the favour that you will wait upon him, and tell him that I *expect* he will cancel from his *Journey* the *injurious expressions* above mentioned. I hope that, upon cool reflection, he will be of opinion, that this expectation of mine is not unreasonable.

I am, Dear Sir, Your most obedient humble servant

James Macpherson.

Manchester Buildings,

Jan. 15th. 1775. William Strahan, Esq.'

Failing to induce Johnson to cancel the passage, Macpherson endeavoured to make him apologize for it publicly. In a letter to Strahan, which is merely dated 'past 4 o'clock', he writes :

'As I expect to have Dr. Johnson's final answer to my, I think, very just demands, at seven o'clock, I beg leave to inclose to you the purport of such an advertisement, as would satisfy me. As I am *very serious* upon this business I insist, that you will keep it to yourself ; for were it not [for] the *present* circumstances of an affair, in which *you* (as well as I) are concerned, I should before this time have *traced out* the author of this journey, in a very *effectual* manner. Unless I have a satisfactory answer, I am determined (indeed it is necessary) to bring that business to a *conclusion* before I *begin* any other.'

The suggested Advertisement was in the following terms :

' The Author of the *Journey to the Western Islands of Scotland* finding, when it was too late to make any alterations, that some expressions in page   and   have given offence to the gentleman alluded to, he takes this method of informing the public, that he meant no personal reflection ; and that, should this work come to a second impression, he will take care to expunge such words as seem, though undesignedly, to convey an affront. This is a piece of justice, which the author owes to himself as well as to that gentleman.'

It is reasonable to suppose that upon Johnson's refusal to sanction the publication of this Advertisement, Macpherson wrote the letter which drew from Johnson his famous answer (20 Jan.). No copy of this letter has been traced, and our knowledge of it is derived from Johnson's reply and the description given, on the authority of an unnamed friend, by John Clark in his *Answer to Mr. Shaw's Inquiry*, 1781, where it is stated (p. 49) that ' Mr. Macpherson had written to him [Johnson] by the hands of a gentleman, that as he had declined to withdraw from his book the injurious expressions reflecting on Mr. Macpherson's *private* character, his age and infirmities, alone, protected him from the treatment due to an infamous liar and traducer '. The Rev. Dr. Thomas Campbell (*ante*, ii. 338 n. 2) records an important variant from Clark's account : on 25 March 1775 he entered in his diary ' Baretti . . . repeated to me upon memory the substance of the letters which passed between Dr. Johnson and Mr. McPherson. The latter tells the Doctor, that neither his age nor infirmity's should protect him if he came in his way ' (*Johnsonian Misc.* ii. 43). One passage in Macpherson's ' ostensible letter ', quoted above, seems to hint at the possibility of a duel, and it may be that his ' foolish and impudent letter ' actually contained a challenge : this conjecture receives some support from the statement of a certain William Duncan, who, writing to Sir John Sinclair, 9 June 1806, says : ' I was the bearer (which perhaps you do not know) of a letter of challenge he [Macpherson] wrote to the late Dr. Samuel Johnson, in consequence of what he published in the year 1775 . . . respecting his belief in the authenticity of the Poems of Ossian ' (*Poems of Ossian*, 1807, i. p. ccxx). This letter is addressed from Brunswick Square, London, and the writer, as Mr. F. Miller of Annan points out to me, must not be confused with the Dumfries minister of the same name who contributed to Sir John Sinclair's *Statistical Account*. Mr. Bailey Saunders (*Life and Letters of James Macpherson*, 1894, pp. 249,

250) thinks that Macpherson wrote two letters to Johnson, and describes that reported by Clark as the first.

The version of Johnson's reply to Macpherson published, during Johnson's lifetime, by the Rev. William Shaw (*An Enquiry into the Authenticity of the Poems ascribed to Ossian*, 1781, p. 11 : see *post*, iv. 252), and subsequently by Hawkins (*Life of Johnson*, 1785, p. 491) and T. Campbell (*Strictures on the History of Ireland*, 1790, p. 173), differs from the original and from Boswell's print, to which latter however it has some striking resemblances. It is as follows :

' Mr. James Macpherson,

I received your foolish and impudent letter.—Any violence that shall be attempted upon me, I will do my best to repel ; and what I cannot do for myself, the law shall do for me : for I will not be hindered from exposing what I think a cheat, by the menaces of a ruffian. What would you have me retract ? I thought your work an imposture [*Hawkins prints* imposition] ; I think so still ; and for my opinion, I have given reasons which I here dare you to refute. —Your abilities, since your Homer, are not so formidable ; and what I hear of your morality, inclines me to credit rather what you shall prove, than what you shall say.

S. Johnson.'

The *St. James's Chronicle* 28–31 Jan. 1775, in a brief account of the dispute says that Macpherson wrote ' a very illiberal letter ' to Johnson, who ' returned a very short Answer to this Purpose : " I shall never be frightened from detecting a Cheat, by the Menaces of a R—ff—n ".' And the *Morning Post*, 1 Feb., provides the variant : ' I am not to be deterred from detecting an impostor, wherever I find him, by the menaces of a ruffian.' See also *Johnsonian Misc.* ii. 43.

There is at least one record of a meeting between Johnson and Macpherson. This is given by Percy in a letter, dated 23 July 1764, to Evan Evans about his book *Some Specimens of the Antient Welsh Bards*. Percy writes :

' I can give you a more valuable testimony of its merit than my own, Mr. Johnson . . . who has been with me on a visit for this month past, has read it over with attention, and is very much pleased with your performance. . . . The only thing he blames in your book is the credit you have given at the beginning of it to the Pretensions of McPherson and his erse Poetry. . . . The very unsatisfactory answers that are given by McPherson himself whenever pressed on this subject, contain a strong presumption that all is not sound. To some he blusters, pretending to esteem their doubts so contemptible as not to deserve an answer. To others he gives bare affirmations, without any proof. He fell in company with Mr. Johnson, who put to him several questions relating to his publications : he answered each of Mr. Johnson's questions with a short round assertion ; but got off from the subject as soon as he could ; & turned the discourse to something else.' (Add. MS. 32,330 ff. 95.)

Percy was evidently repeating to Evans what Johnson had just told him.

Page 298, line 9 and note 1. Hume writes of Macpherson :

' Finding the style of his Ossian admired by some, he attempts a translation of Homer in the very same style. He begins and finishes, in six weeks, a work that was for ever to eclipse the translation of Pope, whom he does not even deign to mention in his preface ; but this joke was still more unsuccessful [than his *History of Britain*].' J. H. Burton's *Hume*, i. 478.

Hume says of him, that he had ' scarce ever known a man more perverse and unamiable '. *Ib.* p. 470.—HILL.

Page 306, lines 4, 5. Boswell elsewhere describes himself as ' a citizen of the world '. See *post*, v. 20.

Page 307, lines 3 ff. Johnson's note, like other manuscripts which Boswell said he had deposited in the British Museum, is not there. See *ante*, ii. 297 note 2.

Page 307, lines 19 ff. and note 3. Lord Camden, when pressed by Dr. Berkeley (the Bishop's son) to appoint a Scotchman to some office, replied : ' I have many years ago sworn that I *never* will introduce a Scotchman into any office ; for if *you* introduce *one*, he will contrive some way or other to introduce *forty* more cousins or friends.' G. M. Berkeley's *Poems*, p. ccclxxi.—HILL.

Page 309, line 4. *One old Erse MS.* Lachlan Mac Vuirich, the hereditary bard of the Clanranald family, testifies in 1800 that ' he remembers that his father had a book which was called the *Red Book* . . . and which, as his father informed him, contained a good deal of the history of the Highland Clans, together with part of the works of Ossian. . . . That he remembers well that Clanronald made his father give up the red book to James Macpherson '. *Report of the Committee of the Highland Soc.*, 1805, App. p. 278. The Red Book referred to is the same as the Book of Clanranald. It is fully described and translated in Alexander Cameron's *Reliquiæ Celticæ*, 1892, ii. 138 ff. Cameron states that ' the only MS. which was recovered after Macpherson's death was the Clanranald MS. got from Neil Mac Vurich '. He adds : ' that it once contained Ossianic poetry is certain, it now contains none.'

Page 309, lines 16 ff. Ranald Macdonald, who was a firm believer in the authenticity of the Ossianic poems, published the first volume of his collection in 1776 at Edinburgh under the title *Comh-Chruinneachidh Orannaigh Gaidhealach*. In the Preface he admitted that ' Most of the pieces in the first volume have been composed within the last two hundred years ' (p. viii), but promised that ' the second volume will consist of poems of a much older date . . ., some being as far back as the third and fourth centuries ' (p. xi). This second volume was never published.

Page 311. Mr. S. M. Radcliffe prints in the *Times Literary Suppl.*, 26 April 1923, a description of Johnson in 1775 by Sir Joshua Reynolds's nephew, Samuel Johnson, a young man of 21. Writing to his sister, 17 March 1775, he says :

' I din'd at my Uncle's with Cousin Jo the day before yesterday (Tuesday). Dr. Johnson din'd there. One gains more of the knowledge of Life from him in an hour than from all the other companies one may fall into in a month. One declaration of his ought to be remember'd. . . . After inveighing against the common practice of people's puffing their own works in the papers and writing encomiums on themselves He declared I will give you his own words " In my whole life I think I never put anything into the papers good or bad about myself ". . . His knowledge is infinite and my Aunt says that She never found him ignorant of one thing but the method of splitting Pease (for his knowledge descends to all mechanical arts even to the making of Custards). . . . I have been told that his grief for the loss of his wife went near to cost him his life that is, his despair drove him to drink which brought on a Fever. . . .

Perhaps Miss Reynolds, the writer's aunt, was responsible for this last statement ; there is no other authority for it. The letter continues :

' He is a constant attendant on the Evening Prayer at St. Clements, and this is a great thing when we find that a certain Person who is reckon'd an amiable man and is perhaps the best of his set has not seen the inside of a Church for years.'

Johnson himself states that he was irregular in his attendance at church : see *ante*, i. 67 n. 2 and *post*, iii. 401. Mr. Radcliffe believes that the ' certain Person ' who stayed away altogether was Sir Joshua.

Page 312, line 5. *Taxation no Tyranny* was published on 8 March, after a preliminary warning, ' To-morrow Noon will be published ' &c., on the preceding day. *Public Advertiser*, March 7 and 8, 1775. A long extract was printed in the *London Chronicle*, March 9–11.

Pages 313, line 7, and 314, lines 10 ff. Johnson wrote to Strahan 1 March 1775 :

' I am sorry to see that all the alterations proposed are evidences of timidity. You may be sure that I do not wish to publish, what those for whom I write do not like to have published. . . . The changes are not for the better, except where facts were mistaken. The last paragraph was indeed rather contemptuous, there was once much more of it which I put out myself.' *Letters*, No. 381.

On the 3rd he wrote again :

' Your pages were sent back the next post, for there was nothing to do. I had no great difficulty in persuading myself to admit the alterations, for why should I in defense of the ministry provoke those, whom in their own defense they dare not provoke.' *Ib*. No. 382.

Page 315, lines 11, 12. No copy of Johnson's *Political Tracts* with the words ' by the Author of the Rambler ' is known. Boswell probably copied them from the advertisement in the *Public Advertiser*, 25 May 1776 : ' This Day is published, Price four Shillings in Boards, POLITICAL TRACTS. By the AUTHOR of the RAMBLER. Now first Collected. Printed for W. Strahan, and T. Cadell, Strand.'

Page 316, lines 32 ff. Temple's Character of Gray was first made public by Boswell (see Boswell's *Letters*, No. 137, i. 217) in the *London Magazine*, xli. 1772, March, p. 140, as ' by a gentleman of Cambridge, of much learning and ingenuity, who knew him well '. Mason reprints it at the end of his *Memoirs of Gray* (1775, i. 402), with the following introduction :

> ' I might here lay down my pen, yet if any reader should still want his Character, I will give him one which was published very soon after Mr. Gray's decease. It appears to be well written ; and, as it comes from an anonymous pen, I chuse the rather to insert it, as it will, on that account, be less suspected of partiality.'

Its authorship is divulged by Boswell in his review of Mason's *Gray* contributed to *London Mag.*, xliv. 1775, May, p. 217 :

> ' Mr. Gray's Character . . . was written by the Reverend Mr. Temple, rector of Mamhead in Devonshire, in a letter to Mr. Boswell, to whom we are indebted for communicating it ; and as Mr. Mason has given it his sanction and enriched it with notes, we shall now again present it to the publick.'

The review ends (*Ib.* p. 219) :

> ' Let it be remembered, that a Character of Mr. Gray in *our* Magazine has been thought worthy of being placed by the hands of Mason as an *apex* upon the top of *the monument of Gray*.'

Mr. Bettany points out that Johnson when he copied the Character in his life of Gray omitted Temple's testimony to his good breeding (cf. Johnson's *Gray* 22). The passage as printed in the *London Magazine* (1772 and 1775) and by Mason reads :

> ' He was also a good man, a well-bred man, a man of virtue and humanity.'

The omission was, I suggest, not intentional but parableptic. Mitford in the first form of his life of Gray instead of correcting Johnson follows him ; see his editions of Gray, 1814 (i. p. lvi), 1816 (i. p. liv), and Aldine Edition, 1836 (i. p. lxxii): in the second form he leaves out the whole passage ; see Gray's *Poet. Works*, ed. Moultrie, 1847, p. xlv. See also Mr. Bettany's *Temple's Diaries*, p. xvii.

Page 322, line 8. I have Sir Charles Firth's authority for saying that Johnson's statement was a conversational exaggeration.

Page 322, lines 10 ff. and note 1. Johnson's father also took the oaths of allegiance, supremacy and abjuration in 1726. The actual document he signed is in the Birthplace, Lichfield. A. L. Reade, *Gleanings*, iv. 201–3. See *ante*, i. 37.

Page 327, lines 6 ff. Mr. Leonard Whibley kindly supplies the following note on Gray's ' dullness ' : ' It is clear from all testimonies that in the society of strangers or of those with whom he was not on easy terms, Gray was shy, reserved and sometimes silent; and that he often appeared fastidious and affected. It is equally clear that with his intimate friends, or when he felt at ease, his conversation was an unreserved expression of his knowledge and his temperament. Mitford in his Life of Gray (Gray's *Works*, Aldine edition, pp. lxiv ff.) collects the evidence. Gray himself, writing at a time of depression, in 1758 after seeing the Garricks at Stoke, says, " I grow so old, that, I own, People in high spirits & gayety overpower me, & entirely take away mine. I can yet be diverted with their sallies, but if they appear to take notice of my dullness, it sinks me to nothing." Gray's *Letters*, ed. Tovey, ii. 47. Walpole in 1760 repeated to George Montagu Lady Ailesbury's story of Gray opening his lips but once, and then only to say " Yes, my Lady, I believe so ". Walpole's *Letters*, iii. 405. Norton Nicholls, whose *Reminiscences* are almost entirely records of Gray's intimate conversation, in commenting on Gray's lack of facility for conversation in general says, " this arose, perhaps, partly from natural reserve, and what is called shyness, and partly from having lived retired in the university during so great a part of his life, where he had lost, as he told me himself,' the versatility of his mind ' ". Gray's *Works*, ed. Mitford, v. p. 48. Beattie also says Gray " was, in general company, much more silent than one could have wished ", but is emphatic in his praise of the conversation he enjoyed with him. Mitford's *Gray*, i. p. lxv. The regard and affection of Gray's friends imply a freedom of conversation which they enjoyed. Letters often reflect a man's colloquial qualities, and we cannot doubt that the irony, wit and humour of Gray's letters were shown also in his conversation, and the letters themselves need no praise. Cowper writes of them : " I have been reading Gray's Works, and think him the only poet since Shakespeare entitled to the character of sublime. . . . I once thought Swift's letters the best that could be written ; but I like Gray's better. His humour or his wit, or whatever it is to be called, is never ill-natured or offensive, and yet I think equally poignant with the Dean's." Cowper's *Letters* (ed. Wright, 1904), i. 141.'

Page 336, lines 15 ff. By ' Lady Miller's collection of verses ' Boswell means *Poetical Amusements at a Villa near Bath*, published anonymously at Bath in January 1775. Among the contributors, whose names are rarely given in full, were, in addition to the Duchess of Northumberland, Henry Temple, Viscount Palmerston, Admiral Keppel, C. W. Bampfylde, the Rev. C. Jenner, ' Hon. Master Fielding, second son to the Earl of Denbigh, eleven years old ', George Ogle, the Rev. Richard Graves, and the ' Hon. Mrs. G—v—l ' (' G—v—lle ' in vol. 3) ; Mr. Miller and Mrs. Miller contributed twelve pieces between them. Other volumes followed in 1776, 1777, and 1781 ; a fifth was in preparation when Lady Miller died in that year. Christopher Anstey, Garrick, W. Hayley, the Rev. R. Potter, Edward Jerningham, Anna Seward, S. J. Pratt, and T. S. Whalley were contributors to these later volumes. See Miss R. A. Hesselgrave's *Lady Miller and the Batheaston literary circle*, 1927.

It is not known that William Seward wrote for the Vase, and there is no evidence that Graves was acquainted with Johnson at this time (1775).

Mr. F. W. Hilles has kindly supplied me with the following extract from a letter written, 26 Dec. 1785, by Graves to Sir Joshua Reynolds, which gives the degree and date of Graves's acquaintance with Johnson : 'Though I never saw, I was not entirely unknown to, Dr. Johnson and by means of a common friend, had an obliging message from him about 2 years since, but he was gone into the country before I got to Town to the royal exhibition.' See *The Letters of Sir Joshua Reynolds*, ed. Hilles, Appendix iii, p. 250. Boswell's journal, so Mr. Pottle tells me, reveals the name of the 'block-head' as Capt. Phipps (see *post*, v. 236).

Page 336, line 18. *Bouts-rimés* were, if not actually invented, rendered popular by a Norman priest named Dulot in the middle of the seventeenth century. Pellisson in an introduction to Sarasin's heroi-comic poem, *Dulot vaincu*, against this type of verse writes (*Œuvres de Sarasin*, 1656, éd. Festiguière, t. i. 460 ff.) :

'Les bouts-rimés n'ont été connus que depuis quelques années. L'extravagance d'un poète ridicule, nommé Dulot, donna lieu à cette invention. Un jour, comme il se plaignait en présence de plusieurs personnes qu'on lui avait dérobé ses papiers, et particulièrement trois cents sonnets qu'il regrettait plus que tout le reste, quelqu'un s'étonnant qu'il en eût fait un si grand nombre, il répliqua que c'étaient des *sonnets en blanc*, c'est-à-dire les bouts-rimés de tous ces sonnets qu'il avait dessein de remplir. Cela sembla plaisant, et depuis on commença à faire par une espèce de jeu dans les compagnies ce que Dulot faisait sérieusement, chacun se piquant à l'envi de remplir heureusement et facilement les rimes bizarres qu'on lui donnait.'

A collection of these sonnets was printed in 1649, under the title *L'Élite des bouts-rimés de ce temps*. After a short period of popularity the conceit lost favour, to be revived in 1653 or 1654 by Fouquet, who mourned the death of Mme du Plessis-Bellière's parrot in ' un sonnet de bouts-rimés '. Pellisson continues :

' Cet exemple réveilla tout ce qu'il y avait de gens en France qui savaient rimer ; on ne vit, durant quelques mois, que des sonnets sur ces mêmes bouts-rimés, et leur sujet ordinaire était le *Perroquet* ou *Sainte-Menehould*. . . . M. Sarasin fit aussi un de ces sonnets sur le perroquet ; mais, s'ennuyant à la fin qu'une poésie comme cella-là ôtât, pour ainsi dire, le cours à toutes les autres, il commença à parler partout contre les bouts-rimés et conçut le dessein de ce poème [i. e. *Dulot vaincu*].'

Tallemant des Réaux devoted No. 406 of his *Historiettes* to Dulot.

Page 338. Dr. T. Campbell mentions the dinner on 5 April :

' Dined with Dilly in the Poultry, as guest to Mr. Boswell, where I met Dr. Johnson, (and a Mr. Miller, who lives near Bath, who is a dilletanti man, keeps a weekly day for the Litterati, and is himself so litterate, that he gathereth all the flowers that ladies write, and bindeth into a garland, but enough of him), with several others, particularly a Mr. Scott, who seems to be a very sensible plain man.' (*Johnsonian Misc.* ii. 47.)

Page 338, line 3 and note 2. Dr. Birkbeck Hill printed extracts from Dr. Thomas Campbell's *Diary* in *John. Misc.*, ii. 39 ff. and Mrs. Napier printed it in its entirety in her collection of *Johnsoniana*, 1884. Mrs. Piozzi in a marginal note to the 1816 edit. of the *Life* says : ' Dr. Campbell was a very tall handsome Man, & speaking of some other *High-bernian*, used this Expression—Indeed now, & upon my Honour Sir ; I am but a *Twitter to him.*' (See *Piozzi Letters*, i. 329, where the phrase is cited as ' Dr. C—l's '.) Annotating ii. 343, lines 9, 10, she writes : ' I dare say he did say so ; he [Campbell] was a fine showy talking Man —Johnson liked him of all Things in a Year or so.'

Page 345, last line. Mr. Hatchett, from the records of the Club, informed Croker that the numerous company on this occasion consisted of Charles Fox (president), Reynolds, Johnson, Percy, Beauclerk, Boswell, Chamier, Gibbon, Langton, and Steevens. ' One of the company ' who suggested the absence of the wolf from the Ossianic poetry as an internal objection to its antiquity was probably Percy, who was engaged in writing the history of the wolf in England (*ante*, ii. 455).

Page 346, lines 9, 10, and note 5. It must not be supposed that Addison was ignorant of Italian. In his *Remarks on Several Parts of Italy* (1705), he discusses the Italian opera (pp. 98, 408), criticizes the Venetian comedies (p. 100), and translates St. Anthony of Padua's famous sermon to the fishes (pp. 62–74).

Page 349, line 12. Mrs. Piozzi in a marginal note to the *Tatler* No. 208 says :

' I never had any flatterer in my life ; I have acted the part myself always . . . *for my own diversion.* I was head flatterer to poor Dr. Johnson for many years and for one year or two to Mrs. Siddons.' (*Dr. Birkbeck Hill's MS. notes.*)

Page 352, foot. Sir Frank MacKinnon suggests that Johnson may have had in mind a rather notable instance of nepotism. Lord North was Prime Minister from 1770 to 1782 : his young brother, Brownlow North, was appointed Bishop of Lichfield in 1771 at the age of 30 ; in 1774 he was translated to Worcester, and in 1781 to Winchester (one of the richest sees in England).

Page 357, line 1. The identity of the two gentlemen who called on Johnson on Good Friday, 1775, is partially revealed by his note on the same day : ' Dilly and Millar called ' *Pr. and Med.* ¶ 109. Dr. Hill, misled by the wrong spelling, identified the latter as Andrew Millar ; he however died in 1768 (Nichols, *Lit. Anecd.* iii. 388), and there can be no doubt that it was the future Sir John Miller, who had dined with Johnson at the Dillys' in the previous week (*ante*, ii. 338). He did not impress Dr. T. Campbell very favourably (see above, note to p. 338).

Page 362, lines 14 ff. and note 2. Mrs. Thrale drew up ' a tabular character sketch of the society of Streatham, based on a system of marks for different qualities, 20 being full marks '. Good humour, by which she meant ' only the Good Humour necessary to conversation ', is one of the qualities, and for this she did not award a single mark to Baretti, Beattie, Burke, Garrick, Langton, Seward, Thrale, and Johnson himself. Boswell and Burney received 19 marks. Beauclerk and Reynolds are not included. See C. Hughes, *Mrs. Piozzi's Thraliana*, 1913, p. 21.

Page 363, lines 14 ff. Sir Walter Scott replied to Johnson's remark on the insufficiency of education in Scotland in his Address at the Opening of the Edinburgh Academy in 1824. He is reported (Lockhart's *Life*, ed. 1837, v. 364) as saying :

' It might be said . . . that it was better education should be divided into mouthfuls, than served up at the banquet of some favoured individuals, while the great mass were left to starve. . . . But sturdy Scotsman as he was, he was not more attached to Scotland than to truth ; and it must be admitted that there was some foundation for the Doctor's remark.'

Page 363, last line. The Preface to Moses Browne's edition of *The Compleat Angler* contains evidence of Johnson's admiration for Walton. Browne, who was Johnson's fellow worker on the *Gentleman's Magazine*, wrote in his first edition, 1750 :

' At the Instigation of an ingenious and learned Friend, whose Judgment of Men and Books is sufficiently established, by his own Writings, in the Opinion of the World, I undertook this Employment.'

He adds in a footnote that this friend was

' Mr. Samuel Johnson, who may probably, on another Occasion, oblige the Publick with the Life of Mr. Walton '.

The second edition, published in 1759, reads ' At the Invitation of a very ingenious and learned Friend ', who is described in the note as ' Mr. Samuel Johnson, Author of the Folio Dictionary of the English Language '. See also *ante*, ii. 279 n. 7.

Walton's ' most honoured friend ', John Offley of Madeley Manor, to whom he dedicated the *Compleat Angler*, was the great-grandfather of Johnson's pupil at Edial, Lawrence Offley (*ante*, i. 97, 531), to whom, by common descent from the said John, the Misses Aston, Johnson's Lichfield friends, and Topham Beauclerk, were cousins. See A. L. Reade, *Gleanings*, v. App. M. pp. 237 ff.

Page 365, line 20. Mrs. Harris of Salisbury has recorded her opinion of her fellow guests. She wrote to her son, afterwards Lord Malmesbury, 20 Apr. 1775 (*Letters of the 1st Earl of Malmesbury*, 1870, i. 302–2) :

' Tuesday Dr. Johnson, his fellow-traveller through the Scotch Western Isles, Mr. Boswell, and Sir Joshua Reynolds dined here. I have long wished to be in company with this said Johnson ; his conversation is the same as his writing, but a dreadful voice and manner. He is certainly amusing as a novelty, but seems not possessed of any benevolence, is beyond all description awkward, and more beastly in his dress and person than anything I ever beheld. He feeds nastily and ferociously, and eats quantities most unthankfully. As to Boswell, he appears a low-bred kind of being.'

Page 369, lines 3 ff. Garrick drew up and signed the following memorandum, dated 17 March 1773 :

' Mr. Sheridan has desir'd me to remember that he will marry Miss Lindley without any other Conditions than giving up 2000 pounds of her Fortune to her Father for the Loss he may sustain by not having the use of her Talents for two years and a half to come, the remaining time of Apprenticeship to him—but he desires me to take Notice That if Mr. Lindley should prove that he and his Wife are sinking into distress by her not Singing with her Father as usual, That he will then agree to make a publick use of her talents as formerly to satisfy ye Father That he means not to distress him but make him as happy as will be in Mr. Sheridan's Power.'

This document formerly belonged to Mr. G. E. Solly, the direct descendant of Mrs. Samuel Solly, only daughter of the Rev. Thomas Rackett, Garrick's friend and Mrs. Garrick's executor. It is here printed from a copy courteously made for me by the present owner, Mr. T. W. Best, of Boston, Mass. See Sotheby & Co.'s sale catalogue, 19 June 1928, lot 246. Farington (*Diary*, i. 133) noted, 12 Jan. 1796, ' In April 1773 He [Sheridan] married Miss Linley. After the marriage she twice sang in publick, but her name was never inserted in the Bills after marriage.' For her father, Thomas Linley the elder, see *D.N.B.* It was reported to Farington that he left a fortune of £25,000.

Page 371, lines 13, 14. Johnson had probably read Gassendi's life of Peiresc, originally published in Latin in 1641. This was translated by W. Rand, under the title *Mirrour of true Nobility and Gentility. Being the Life of the Renowned Nicolaus Claudius Fabricius Lord of Peiresk* in 1657 : on p. 234 we find :

' There was added to the Edition [of Peiresc's Funeral Oration] printed at Rome, . . . a rare fardle of Funeral Elegies, which because they were expressed, in almost all the Languages of the World (for they were near upon forty [quadraginta enim, proximéve sunt *orig.*]) : Therefore they were entituled *Panglossia*, or the Lamentations of Mankind, in all Languages expressed, for the Death of their Darling.'

The edition referred to is entitled ' Monvmentum Romanvm | Nicolao Claudio | Fabricio Perescio | Senatori Aqvensi | Doctrinae Virtutisqve Cavsa | Factvm. | Romæ | Typis Vaticanis CIƆ IƆ CXXX IIX', and on pp. 81–119 will be found the ' rare fardle of funeral elegies ', styled ' ΠΑΓΓΛΩΣΣΙΑ | Sive Generis Hvmani | Lessus | In Fvnere Delicii Svi | Nicolai Clavdii Fabricii | Perescii '. This consists of forty-six poems in about forty different languages or dialects, including Basque, Breton, Georgian, Japanese, and Peruvian. I am obliged to Professor E. Bensly for these references.

Page 383, line 7 from foot. Mrs. Piozzi, in her copy of the 1816 edit. of the *Life*, flatly contradicted Johnson's statement that she had a great regard for Boswell. She wrote : ' Not I—never had : I thought him a clever & a comical Fellow.' Cf. *ante*, ii. 498, note to p. 206, l. 22.

Page 386, line 19. Boswell inserted the following announcement in the *London Mag.*, Oct. 1775, p. 545 :

' Birth. October 9. At Edinburgh, the lady of James Boswell, Esq ; of Auchinleck, of a son and heir.'

Marriages and deaths are normally recorded, but not births : but Boswell was a proprietor (Boswell's *Letters*, Nos. 110 and 137, i. 183, 217).

Page 388, line 5 from foot. Mrs. Adey and Mrs. Cobb were widowed sisters, daughters of Richard Hammond (†1738), a Lichfield apothecary (see *ante*, i. 39). The elder, Felicia, married Joseph Adey (1704–63), Town Clerk of Lichfield ; she died in April, 1778. See *post*, iii. 393 ; *Letters*, Nos. 202, 535, 605 ; and A. L. Reade, *Gleanings*, i. 12 : iv. 145–6. The younger, Mary, was the relict of Thomas Cobb. For many years she lived at The Friary, Lichfield, with her niece, Mary, daughter of Mrs. Adey mentioned above. She died 9 Aug. 1793, aged 76, leaving the bulk of her property to her niece. See *ante*, ii. 466 : *post*, iii. 412 : iv. 142, 143 : *Letters*, Nos. 406, 939 : A. L. Reade, *Gleanings*, i. 12, and *Reades of Blackwood Hill*, p. 229. This niece, the Miss Adey or Adye of the *Life*, married in 1794 (she was born in 1742), as his third wife John Sneyd (1734–1809), High Sheriff of Staffs ; she died in 1830. See *ante*, i. 38 : the references to Mrs. Adey cited above, and *Gleanings*, iv. 137, 145.

Page 389, lines 13 ff. The ' small paper-book ' containing the MS. of Johnson's French journal from 10 Oct. to 5 Nov. 1775 is now in the British Museum (Add. MS. 35299). On the inside of the cover is written : ' Delivered to Mr. Boswell, by the desire of Dr. Scott, July 21st 1787. Edmond Malone.' Boswell says (*ante*, ii. 399 note 2) that he deposited it in the British Museum himself, but the Museum authorities record that it was presented on 12 June 1899 by the daughters of William Sharpe of 1 Highbury Terrace, from the collection of Samuel Rogers, the poet, their great uncle. Dr. Scott was one of the three executors of Johnson's will (*post*, iv. 402 note 2).

Johnson's writing, although not always legible, is very level and the lines are evenly spaced. I have given in the critical notes the principal variants of the MS. from Boswell's print. Boswell corrected obvious blunders, as ' the ' for ' they ' (p. 389, l. 25), ' thence ' (p. 390, l. 4), and ' then ' (p. 396, l. 28), and he occasionally altered Johnson's spelling, e. g. ' gothick ' for ' gothic ' (p. 400, l. 24). The following are representative of Johnson's own revisions and alterations : ' observatory ' for ' infirmary ' (p. 389, l. 27), ' was almost wainscotted ' for ' was glazed ' (p. 391, l. 13), ' Sevre ' for ' Seve ' (p. 395, l. 14) ; and after ' Queen at dinner ' (p. 394, l. 19) there is a determined erasure affecting over two lines.

Page 389, line 21. The *École militaire* was a recent institution in 1775. M. Marcel Poëte writes (*Une vie de Cité. Album*, 1925, p. 229) :

' Un édit de l'année 1751 créa l'École royale militaire à l'usage de cinq cents jeunes gentilshommes n'étant pas riches. L'année suivante, les bâtiments s'élevèrent sur les plans de Gabriel, mais l'École ne fut ouverte qu'en 1760 et ce ne fut qu'en 1769 qu'on posa la première pierre de sa chapelle.'

The institution as then constituted was dissolved 1 Feb. 1776, re-established 17 July 1777, again dissolved 9 Oct. 1787, and definitely ceased to exist 1 Apr. 1788. Farcy, *Monographie de l'École Militaire de Paris*, 1890. For Col. Drumgould or Dromgold, its commandant, see *post*, ii. 526, note to p. 401.

Page 391, lines 23 ff. Johnson appears to have confused Julien Le Roy, who died in 1759, with his more famous son, Pierre (1717-1785). In 1766 the Académie royale des sciences awarded him a prize for the chronometer, which, according to Lieut.-Commander R. T. Gould, ' stamps him as one of the very greatest masters of horology who ever lived '. *Marine Chronometer*, 1923, p. 86. Among other chronometers made by him was ' a small marine watch, called from its shape, " la petite ronde ", whose mechanism was much simpler than that of his larger machines '. *Ibid.* p. 86. It was this perhaps which Johnson saw.

Page 395, line 25, and note 3. Professor D. S. Margoliouth kindly informs me that the word ordinarily used for camel in Egypt is *hagin*, fem. *haginah*, pronounced elsewhere with the *g* soft. Palgrave (*Journey*, i. 325) asserts that the word should be used for 'dromedary', i. e. high-bred camel, not, however, with two humps. Burton (*Pilgrimage*, 1893, i. 418) renders the word ' she-dromedary '. Prof. Margoliouth says that from his own experience in Egypt it there means simply *camel*. Bos-well's spelling *huguin* represents to him the Egyptian pronunciation exactly. Johnson wrote *Higheen*.

Page 397, line 1. In 1721 the Bibliothèque du Roi was moved from the rue Vivienne to the Hôtel de Nevers, rue Richelieu, which the bankruptcy and flight of John Law in the previous year had left free. A. Franklin, *Précis de l'histoire de la Bibl. du Roi*, 1875, p. 217. Mercier, writing soon after Johnson's visit, gives a gloomy account of its administration :

' Ce vaste dépôt n'est ouvert que deux fois la semaine et pendant deux heures et demie. Le bibliothécaire prend des vacances à tout propos. Le public y est mal servi, et d'un air dédaigneux. La magnificence royale devient inutile devant les réglemens des subalternes, paresseux à l'excès.' (*Tableau de Paris*, ch. cxciv, 1782, ii. 312.)

Page 397, lines 2 ff. Of the *Speculum humanæ Salvationis* there are four early editions, two in Latin and two in Dutch: three of these were printed entirely, as far as the text is concerned, from movable metal type, but one of the Latin editions has twenty xylographic pages. It was a copy of this edition which Johnson saw. For an account of the work, see E. Gordon Duff, *Early Printed Books*, 1892, p. 12.

Page 397, lines 4 ff. There are three Bibles older than that printed at Mainz in 1462, viz. (1) the 42-line or Mazarin Bible : (2) the 36-line set up, in part at least, from it (Duff *o. c. s.*, p. 25) : (3) the Bible printed by Mentelin at Strasbourg, *c.* 1460. A copy of the first of these was acquired by the Bibliothèque du Roi in 1739 (*Mém. de l'Acad. des Inscr. & Belles Lettres*, xiv. pp. 238, 251) and it was this copy that Johnson saw. Dr. P. Schwenke, who has subjected this edition to an exhaustive examination, concludes that printing was begun at the earliest towards the end of 1453 and completed about the middle of 1455 (*Festschrift zur Gutenbergfeier*, 1900). It was printed at Mainz by Gutenberg, or by Gutenberg and Fust, from moveable metal type of course. Johnson's doubt that this Bible and the *Durandi Sanctuarium* (which remains unidentified) were printed with wooden types is justified. It has been proved experimentally, so Dr. A. W. Pollard informs me, that it is possible to make and print from wooden types, but the making would be so laborious that it is inconceivable that any book should have been printed from them. See also Johnson's *Letters*, No. 206.

Page 397, line 13. The Sorbonne was suppressed by a decree of 5 April 1792, but the library remained intact till the end of 1795 ; soon after which date the printed books were distributed among various public libraries and the MSS. handed over to the Bibliothèque Nationale. A. Franklin, *La Sorbonne*, 1875, pp. 213–15.

Page 397, line 14. Martène (*Marbone* is a ghost) and Durand were the compilers of two works which form a collection of 14 folios. Ch. V. Langlois writes (*Manuel de bibliographie historique*, 1904, ii. p. 301) :

' Dom Martène [1654–1739] et son acolyte Dom Durand [1682–1773], chargés de visiter les archives et les bibliothèques de France pour y recueillir des matériaux à l'usage des rédacteurs du *Gallia Christiana* [see below], y ramassèrent en même temps de quoi former leur *Thesaurus novus anecdotorum* (Paris, 1717, 5 vol. in-fol.). Chargés plus tard d'explorer les dépôts d'Allemagne et des Pays-Bas pour y recueillir des matériaux à l'usage des rédacteurs du *Recueil des historiens*, ils y ramassèrent en même temps de quoi former leur *Veterum scriptorum et monumentorum historicorum, dogmaticorum, moralium, Amplissima Collectio* (Paris, 1724–33, 9 vol. in-fol.).'

They were also the joint authors of the *Voyage littéraire de deux religieux Bénédictins de la Congrégation de S. Maur* (Paris, 1717).

Page 397, lines 14, 15. *Scriptores de rebus Gallicis* is not the title of any known collection or series.

Page 397, line 15. The *Histoire généalogique* which Johnson saw was the third edition, by the Augustine Fathers Ange de Sainte-Rosalie and Simplicien, of Father Anselme de Sainte-Marie's *Histoire généalogique et chronologique de la maison royale de France, des pairs, des grands officiers de la Couronne et de la Maison du Roy et des anciens barons du royaume, avec les qualités, l'origine, les progrès et les armes de leurs familles* (1726–33). This is in nine volumes, folio. The first edition was published in 1674, and the second in 1712, both in two volumes.

Page 397, line 16. The first edition of *Gallia Christiana* was published at Paris in 1626 'cura Claudii Robertii Longonensis presbyteri', in one volume, quarto. The second edition *Gallia Christiana in provincias ecclesiasticas distributa* was undertaken by the Benedictines of St. Maur (see above). The first volume appeared in 1715, the twelfth—the last which Johnson saw—in 1770, and the thirteenth in 1785. During the Revolution the materials for the provinces not previously dealt with were dispersed. Publication was resumed by M. Hauréau in 1856 and completed with the sixteenth volume in 1865. See Ch. V. Langlois, *Manuel*, 1906, ii. 297–8.

Page 397, line 19. The members of the Sorbonne were divided into two classes, *Hospites* and *Socii*. 'Les *Hospites* trouvaient dans la Maison tous les moyens de s'instruire, mais ne prenaient aucune part à son administration. . . . Les *Socii* s'intitulaient *bacheliers* ou *docteurs de la Maison et Société de Sorbonne.* Tout dans le collége était géré par eux, mais, quels que fussent leur âge ou leur grade universitaire, l'égalité la plus absolue régnait entre eux, " omnes sumus sicut socii et æquales ", disaient les anciens Sorbonistes.' A. Franklin, *La Sorbonne*, 1875, p. 18.

Page 397, lines 24–6. Johnson's MS. reads : ' In the library— Beroald, Cymon, Titus—from Boccace, Oratio Proverbialis—to the Virgin from Petrarch.' Professor E. Bensly tells me that these four pieces occur in the single volume collection, of which there are many editions, entitled : *Orationes, Prelectiones, Præfationes & quædam Mythicæ Historiæ Philippi Beroaldi.* ' Cymon ' (*Historia de Galeso Cymone*) and ' Titus ' (*Historia Gisippi & Titi*) are translations of Novel 1 Day 5 and Novel 8 Day 10 of the *Decameron.* The words ' to the Virgin ' should not be connected, as Boswell connects them, with ' Oratio Proverbialis ' (*Proverbialis Oratio Philippi Beroaldi*) ; they refer to *Pæanes beatæ virginis ex Francisci Petrarchæ pœmate vernaculo in latinum conuersi*, a verse translation by Beroaldo of Petrarch's canzone ' Vergine bella, che di sol vestita '.

Page 397, line 25. ' Falkland to Sandys ' is obscure : it may refer to one of the three refutations of the statement, said to have been made by Falkland and Sir Edward Nicholas, that Sandys repented of his adoption of the Parliamentary cause : one of which is entitled ' The Declaration of Col. Edwyn Sandys, In Vindication of himself from those calumnious Aspersions cast upon him by the Lord Falkland and Secretary Nicholas'. This was printed by order of ' the Commons House of Parliament ',

17 Oct. 1642. For Sandys, see *D.N.B.* under his father, Sir Edwin Sandys.

Page 397, last line. The blank, which is in Johnson's MS., was filled to read 'Strickland's' by Mrs. Piozzi in her copy of the 1816 edition. For Mrs. Strickland see *post*, iii. 118 n. 3.

Page 399, lines 1–8. The books which Johnson saw in the library of St. Germain-des-Prés were :

(1) *Rationale divinorum officiorum*, of Durandus, printed at Mainz by Fust and Schoeffer in 1459. The copy (Coté Vélins 126) now in the Bibliothèque Nationale bears the stamp of St. Germain-des-Prés.

(2) *Psalmorum Codex*, printed by Fust and Schoeffer at Mainz in 1457. See Johnson's *Letters*, No. 206.

(3) J. Meursius's *Opera Omnia*, ed. Lamius, published at Florence, 1741–63, in 12 folio volumes.

(4) Probably the first three volumes, containing the first three books, of the French translation of *Amadis de Gaula* by Nicholas de Herberay, seigneur des Essars : these were first published in folio in 1540 (vol. 1), 1541 (vol. 2), and 1542 (vol. 3).

(5) The *Catholicon* of Joannes Balbus, printed, probably by Gutenberg, in 1460. No copy without a colophon is recorded by the monumental *Gesamtkatalog der Wiegendrucke* which gives a census of all known copies (iii. 279). As the colophon occurs, not at the very end of the book, but before the 'tabula rubricarum', it is possible that Johnson overlooked it.

(6) The only 15th-c. edition of St. Augustine's *De Civitate Dei* 'without name of printer, date, or place of printing' is that printed by Mentelin at Strasbourg. The copy in the John Rylands Library contains the rubricator's note that his work was finished in 1468.

M. Dacier, of the Bibliothèque Nationale, has obligingly examined all the copies in the library of the *Catholicon* of 1460, the *Psalmorum Codex*, and of the St. Augustine which answer to Johnson's description, and found that none of them bear the stamp of St. Germain-des-Prés. A large number of books were burnt in the fire of 19 August 1794. See A. Franklin, *Les Anciennes Bibliothèques de Paris*, i. 123–4, and *Bibliothèque de l'École des Chartes*, 1927, p. 387.

Page 399, line 14. The passage in Maffeus's *Historiarum Indicarum libri xvi* which caught Johnson's eye occurs, in the 1589 edition, on page 4 :

'Ægidius Annius, qui Syrtibus euitatis, & accuratè obseruato maris æstu, recessuque, Ganariam promontorium eximia nauigandi arte ac scientia denique flexit ; & Christiane fidei ad Hesperios Aethiopas aliasque inaccessas antea nationes aditum aperuit.'

Page 401, last line. Jean Drumgould, or Dromgold, (1720–81), was of an Irish family which fled to France with James II. He obtained the professorship of rhetoric at the College of Navarre before reaching the age of 22, and published in 1745 a reply to Voltaire's *Bataille de Fontenoy*, which he thought had not done justice to the Irish. He was aide-de-camp to Louis de Bourbon-Condé, comte de Clermont, and, after the death of this prince, was appointed commandant of the *École Militaire*. See Michaud's *Biogr. Universelle*, t. xi. p. 313.

Page 413, lines 13 ff. In a letter to Mickle (*ante*, ii. 182) dated 5 Aug. 1769 Boswell writes : ' Thomas Boswell, the first of our family, was killed at Flowden Field. I am proud of this ' (*Universal Mag.*, 1809, Jan., p. 103).

Page 424, lines 13 ff. The Preface to the book mentioned by Boswell, *The Life of Edward Earl of Clarendon . . . being a Continuation of the History of the Grand Rebellion from the Restoration to his Banishment in 1667* (Oxford, 1759), may be cited in amplification of his statement :

' The late Lord Hyde . . . left by his Will this, and the other Remains of his Great Grandfather, in the Hands of Trustees, to be printed at our Press, and directed that the Profits arising from the Sale should be employed towards establishing a Riding School in the University. But Lord Hyde dying before his Father, the then Earl of Clarendon, the property of these Papers never became vested in him, and consequently this Bequest was void. However, the noble Heiresses of the Earl of Clarendon, out of their Regard to the Publick, and to this Seat of Learning, have been pleased to fulfil the kind Intentions of Lord Hyde, and adopt a Scheme recommended both by him and his Great Grandfather. To this End They have sent to the University this History, to be printed at our Press on Condition that the Profits arising from the Publication or Sale of this Work be applied, as a Beginning for a Fund for supporting a Manage or Academy for Riding, and other Exercises in Oxford.'

The Advertisement to *Religion and Policy*, the only other unpublished work by Lord Clarendon,—it remained unpublished till 1811,—contains a similar statement, with the additional information that Lord Hyde's bequest was made by a codicil to his will, dated Aug. 10, 1751, and that the Duchess-Dowager of Queensbury gave the MSS., together with ' all the monies which had arisen or might arise from the sale or publication of them ', by deed to three trustees, the Archbishop of York (Dr. R. Drummond), the Earl of Mansfield, and the Bishop of Chester (Dr. W. Markham). See also Johnson's *Letters*, No. 386. The bequest was evidently discussed in the University during the years 1775 and 1776, when there were negotiations with the Clarendon Trustees for the establishment of the riding-school. By March 1776 agreement had been reached, but the profits arising from the sale of the *Life of Clarendon* were considered insufficient. This is shown by Johnson's two letters to Dr. Douglas (*Letters*, Nos. 459 and 461·2), and by Johnson's letter to Dr. Wetherell (*ante*, ii. 425), which Dr. Douglas's reply called forth. There can be little doubt that Dr. Douglas is the ' respectable dignitary of the church ' mentioned by Boswell ; his name is also given in John-son's letter to Wetherell as ' Dr. ******* '. He was at this time Canon of Windsor and subsequently became Bishop of Carlisle (1787–91) and of Salisbury (1791–1807) ; he had edited the *Diary and Letters of Henry, Fourth Earl of Clarendon*, published by the Clarendon Press, in 1763 : I suspect that he was in fact the editor of the *Life of Lord Clarendon* ; his editorship would explain why it was that he had in his hands the accounts between the Trustees and the University relating to this book. Johnson in his second letter (9 March 1776), which is in much the same terms as the first, states that ' the business is at a stand only till the Bishop of Chester can be informed how ⟨much⟩ money the Book has produced ', and asks Douglas to ' lay out his first hours of leisure upon the settlement of the account '. *Letters*, No. 461·2. Douglas's reply gave another direction to Johnson's thoughts, and we henceforth hear no more of the riding-school from him or Boswell.

John Macray, the first Taylorian librarian, raised the question of the Clarendon Bequest in 1854 (*N. & Q.* 1 Ser. x. 185), and from inquiries made by him and others it was found that in 1860 the sum in the hands of the Trustees amounted to £10,000 (*Ibid.* 2 Ser. x. 74). The scheme for a riding-school was dropped and in 1868 the money was applied to the establishment of a laboratory, called the Clarendon Laboratory, attached to the University Museum (see W. D. Macray, *Annals of the Bodleian Library*, 1890, p. 225).

The person recommended to Johnson as fit to superintend the pro-posed riding-school was a protégé of the Thrales, a Mr. Carter, who was according to Baretti ' a poor riding-master in the Borough of South-wark ' (marg. note to *Piozzi Letters*, i. 212). Mrs. Piozzi mentions him as the master of ' Lizard the well-known war-horse who carried Duke William over the plains of Culloden, and is immortalized in Johnson's letters '. See P. Merritt's *The true Story of the so-called Love Letters of Mrs. Piozzi*, 1927, p. 78, and Johnson's *Letters*, No. 419. For John-son's efforts to get him appointed Master of Horsemanship in the University, see his letters to Mr. and Mrs. Thrale from February to August, 1775. *Letters*, Nos. 379, 383, &c., &c.

Page 432, line 6 from foot. Blackfriars was perhaps their original destination, but ' they landed at the Temple-stairs ' (*ante*, ii. 434).

Page 443, lines 2, 3, and note 1. Dr. Hill's conjecture that Gibbon is here attacked is supported by Boswell's description of him as the Infidel. See *post*, iii. 230, n. 5.

Page 444, line 12. Jason Denores, or de Nores, was a native of Cyprus, born about 1530. At an early age he went to Padua, where he studied under Trifone Gabriele, with whom he became very intimate. Gabriele died in 1553, and Denores to solace his grief wrote down and added to

his friend's comments on the *Ars Poetica* : these he published, together
with the text, under the title *In Epistolam Q. Horatii Flacci de Arte
Poetica Iasonis de Nores, Ciprii, ex quotidianis Tryphonis Gabrielii ser-
monibus interpretatio* . . . Venetiis, 1553. There was a Paris edition in
1554, and the commentary was reprinted in the edition of Horace's
works, known as that of the forty commentators, published at Basel in
1555 and 1580. Professor Edward Bensly states that his commentary
is unconventional and finds that some of his innovations have been
adopted by modern critics. Bentley, whose edition of Horace was published in 1711, mentions Denores among the critics who accept in line
59, as against the vulgate reading *producere*, the reading *procudere*, which
he himself champions. Denores fled from Cyprus when the island was
captured by Selim II and took refuge first in Venice, where he was
appointed Reader in Rhetoric, and then in Padua, where he became
Professor of Moral Philosophy. He died in 1590. For an estimate of
him as a literary critic, see Mr. F. E. Budd in *Modern Language Review*,
1927, vol. xxii, pp. 421–34.

Page 444, lines 15 ff. Phil. Jones was a Scholar of Pembroke. He
came into residence 27 Oct. 1727 and continued to reside all through
Johnson's time at College. Mr. A. L. Reade notes that the weekly
charges in the Buttery Books against his name ' do not suggest excessive
indulgence in food or drink', but were regular and normal, being almost
always 8*s.* or thereabouts. *Gleanings*, v. 132. He took his B.A. degree
in 1731 and proceeded M.A. in 1735. Evidence of preferment or even
ordination is lacking, but Mr. Reade has identified him with the ' Philip
Jones, Clerk, A.M.', who died, Aug. 1764, at Overbury, Worcs., leaving
all his effects to the Vicar, Matthew Bloxam (*post*, iii. 304), a college
contemporary of his and Johnson's, to whom he was in all probability
acting as curate. See Reade, *Gleanings*, v. 14–15, 129–35.

Page 444, lines 16 ff. John Fludyer, or, as he himself preferred to
spell it, Fludger, was a Scholar and Fellow of Pembroke. He matriculated 27 Nov. 1728 and was in residence with Johnson. He took his B.A.
in 1732 and his M.A. in 1735. From a brief biography preserved in
Bodley (MS. *Rawl. J. fol. 3* f. 121) we learn that he was ' chosen
lecturer of St. John's Clerkenwell, London, Jan^ry 27, 1737, & Novr 3^d,
1739 was presented by Ld Chancellor Hardwick to the Rectory of St.
Nicholas in Abington Berks. [his native town, of which his father,
John Fludyer, had been mayor], March 25, 1747 appointed curate of
Putney . . ., October 12, 1751 appointed Chaplain to his Grace George
Duke of St. Albans.' In 1754 he was presented to the rectory of St.
Aldate's, Oxford, the advowson of which then belonged to Pembroke
College ; he held this living, together with the curacy of Putney, till his
death in December 1773. He was the editor of a massive *Exposition on*

the Common-Prayer-Book of the Church of England (1739), and author of a sermon, *The Judgment of God Considered* (1755), which exhibits some evidence of Whiggism. See A. L. Reade, *Gleanings*, v. 14–15, 135–9.

Page 445, line 1. Dr. Edward Bentham was Canon of Christ Church from 1754 and Regius Professor of Divinity from 1763 till his death on 1 August, 1776. See *D.N.B.* and Johnson's *Letters*, No. 387·1.

Page 445, lines 7 ff. The connexion of Durham, of which city St. Cuthbert is the patron saint, with University College is through the latter's virtual but unwitting founder, William, archdeacon of Durham (see Rashdall, *Universities of Europe*, 1895, ii. 469 ff. and *D.N.B.* s.v. William of Durham). St. Cuthbert is also the patron saint of the college, and to him the college chapel is dedicated.

Page 445, line 3 from foot. James Boswell, Jun., writes in the sixth edition of the *Life* (1811, ii. 465 n.) :

' The vision which Johnson speaks of, was not in the original publication of Walton's life of Dr. Donne, in 1640. It is not found in the three earliest editions ; but was first introduced into the fourth, in 1675. I have not been able to discover what modern republication is alluded to in which it was omitted. It has very properly been restored by Dr. Zouch.'

The first issue of Thomas Zouch's edition was published in 1796 at York. Major in his edition of 1825, which was printed from a copy of the edition of 1675 ' corrected by Walton's own pen ', has the following note on the Vision (p. 36) :

' The whole of this narrative . . . is wanting in the earlier editions as well as in the collection of 1670 : and it has been supposed that he did not insert it that he might have time to ascertain its truth.'

Page 446, line 13 and note 3. ' Almost nothing ' occurs in the first edition. Similarly Boswell was doubtful about the correctness of ' almost no ' (*post*, iii. 154, note 1 and 283 note 3). The Oxford Dictionary records many instances of this usage, the earliest being from Lord Berners's translation of Froissart (1523). Boswell's ' accurate English friend ' was possibly Malone. Beattie regarded the usage as not English (*Scoticisms*, p. 9).

Page 447, lines 5 ff. Charles Dartiquenave (1664–1737), ' or, as his name is commonly spelled, *Dartineuf*, the convivial friend of Swift, Steele, and Addison, was celebrated as an epicure and a punster ' (N. Drake's *Essays*, 1814, iii. 372). Swift describes him as ' the man that knows every thing, and that every body knows ' (*Journal to Stella*, 22 March, 1711), and Pope alludes to his epicurean tastes :

> ' Each mortal has his pleasure : none deny
> Scarsdale his bottle, Darty his Ham-pie '
> (*Imit. Hor.* Bk. ii. Sat. i. 46).

and

> ' Hard task ! to hit the palate of such guests,
> When Oldfield loves what Dartineuf detests '
>
> (*Ib*. Bk. ii. Ep. ii. 87).

He held several remunerative offices, as Paymaster of the Royal Works, Surveyor-General of the King's Gardens, and Surveyor-General of the Royal Roads. Mr. R. Straus says (*Robert Dodsley*, p. 12), ' there is nothing to fix the dates of Dodsley's entry into, or departure from, Dartineuf's service '.

Page 447, lines 8 ff. Dr. John Campbell's *A Political Survey of Britain*, published in 1774 in two volumes, royal quarto, price two guineas in sheets, went off slowly. It is advertised on 31 May 1776 in the *Public Advertiser* as ' This Day is published '. Campbell died 28 Dec. 1775.

Page 450, note 1. Boswell wrote a song, entitled *Lurgan Clanbrassil*, in Mrs. Rudd's honour. His relations with her are discussed in *Notes and Queries*, cxlix. 4. Hannah More writing in 1776 states (W. Roberts, *Memoirs*, 1836, i. 65) :

' Foote says that the Empress of Russia, the Duchess of Kingston, and Mrs. Rudd, are the three most extraordinary women in Europe ; but the Duchess disdainfully, and I think unjustly, excludes Mrs. Rudd from the honour of deserving to make one in the triple alliance.'

Lady Charnwood, who owns the manuscript, prints Boswell's song, together with the following memorandum, in the *Cornhill Mag.* Dec. 1927, p. 664 :

' The enclosed song was written and composed by James Boswell, the biographer of Johnson, in commemoration of a Tour he made with Mrs. Rudd whilst she was under his protection, for living with whom he displeased his Father so much that he threatened to disinherit him. . . .

' My Father having heard that Boswell used to sing this song on the Home Circuit requested it of him and he wrote it out and gave it him. H. W. B. (Feby. 1828).'

See also Mr. F. A. Pottle, *Lit. Career of Boswell*, p. 270.

Page 452, line 6, and note 1. Gilbert Burnet tells us that Archbishop Leighton

' used often to say that if he were to choose a place to die in, it should be an inn ; it looking like a pilgrim's going home, to whom this world was all as an inn, and who was weary with the noise and confusion in it. He added that the officious tenderness and care of friends was an entanglement to a dying man, and that the unconcerned attendance of such as could be procured in such a place would give less disturbance. And he obtained what he desired, for he died at the Bell inn, in Warwick lane.' *History of his own Times*, ed. Airy, ii. 429.

Page 452, lines 7 ff. and note 2. According to Richard Graves Shenstone wrote the famous stanza quoted by Boswell ' in a summer-house ' at Edgehill and not at Henley-in-Arden. *Recollection of Shenstone*, 1788, p. 152.

Page 452, lines 13 ff. Shenstone's good opinion of Johnson is also expressed in his letters to Percy. Writing on 4 Jan. 1758 he says :

' Do you hear that Mr. Johnson's Shakespear will be published this Winter ? I have a Prejudice (if Prejudice it may be call'd) in favour of all he Undertakes, & wish ye world may recompence him for a Degree of Industry very seldom connected with so much real Genius.' (Hecht's *Percy und Shenstone*, 1909, p. 7.)

On 15 Feb. 1760 he reiterates and amplifies his praise of the *Rambler* :

' As to reading, I have, for the first time, perus'd a vol: or two of ye rambler, & think for Judgment & perspicuity he equals any writer I ever read, & for ye musick of wellturn'd Periods I do not know his equal. For I am hardly satisfy'd with any one in ye eng: Language, beside Him.' (*Ibid.*, p. 32.)

Of *Rasselas* he had not so high an opinion. Writing to Graves, 26 Oct. 1759, he says :

' Rasselas has a few refined sentiments thinly scattered, but is upon the whole below Mr. J——.' (Shenstone's *Works*, iii. 340.)

There is no evidence that Johnson and Shenstone ever met and no letter between them has survived, but it would seem from Percy's letter of 29 July 1760, that he had tried to make them acquainted. Percy writes :

' I not long since wrote to Johnson and took occasion to repeat the Apology you made for not having answered his Letter, viz. that you waited so long in order to pick up something worth communicating to him, that you began to be ashamed to write at all ; I concluded with repeating some of the civil & respectful things I have heard you say of him, and doubt not but he will remain very well satisfied.' (Hecht's *Percy und Shenstone*, p. 38.)

Shenstone replying on 11 August writes :

' I thank you heartily for your Letter to Johnson. I do very unfeignedly respect both the Writer & the Man, and should be sorry to forfeit, by a neglect on my side, any degree of Esteem he discovers for Me.' (*Ibid.*, p. 40.)

In May 1761 Percy was in London making terms with the booksellers for the publication of his *Reliques*. After explaining these to Shenstone he writes :

' Mr. Johnson & I have had a good deal of talk about you : I explained to him the reason, why you did not write to him & I believe he is entirely satisfied on that head. He even talks of taking a Journey down to the Leasows, but this you must not much depend on ; he is no more formed for long Journeys than a Tortoise. 'Tis two years that he has been resolving to come & see me, who consider myself as in the neighbourhood of London.' (*Ibid.*, p. 54.)

For Johnson's brief visit to the Leasowes in 1774 see *post*, v. 457.

Page 453, lines 13 ff. Percy, Shenstone, Lord Kames, and Johnson all saw Grainger's *Sugar Cane*, or parts of it, in manuscript. On 5 June 1762 Grainger wrote to Percy desiring him, when the poem was complete, ' to peruse the MS. with the utmost attention ', and, if he thought it worth publication, ' to polish it with the utmost exactness '; Nichols, *Illustr*. vii. 278. He asked the same favour of Shenstone, to whom the second book was addressed. *Ibid*. 278, 280. Shenstone had seen it by 20 Nov. 1762, for on that date he told Graves that it was ' capable of being rendered a good Poem '. Shenstone's *Works*, iii. 387. Writing to Percy on 18 April 1763 Grainger says : ' I have now completed the Cane Piece, such as I could wish to have it appear.' Later in the year he returned to England bringing his manuscript with him : on 30 November 1763 he tells Percy from London that he has just returned from Scotland where he had shown the manuscript to Lord Kames, who approved of it. Nichols, *Illustr*. vii. 282, 284. On 22 Jan. 1764 he writes : ' Sam Johnson has got the 2nd book. But whether he has yet perused it, I know not. Perhaps it may lie in his desk untouched till I call for it.' R. B. Adam's *Catalogue*, 1929, iii. 112. It was in the press in March, for on the 24th he wrote ' I have had but one proof of the " Sugar Cane " since I came to London.' Nichols, *Illustr*. vii. 286. On the 14th of May he told Percy that ' The Sugar Cane is printed, but when it will be published I know not '. *Ibid*. 288. It was published on the 26th of the month. Straus, *Robert Dodsley*, p. 382.

The reading of the manuscript which caused so much hilarity among the wits assembled at Sir Joshua's took place, therefore, in the winter of 1763-4, whether before Johnson's visit to Langton or after I am unable to say. It is not clear from Boswell's narrative who read the poem. Miss Reynolds says that it was Grainger himself and that ' when he came to the line, " Say, shall I sing of Rats ? " ', Johnson ' cry'd with great vehemency, " No " '. She continues : ' This he [Johnson] related to me himself, laughing heartily at the conceit of Dr. Grainger's refractory Muse ! Where it happen'd I do not know, but I am certain, very certain, that it was not, as Mr. Boswell asserts, at Sir Joshua Reynolds's, for they were not, I believe, even personally known to each other.' *Johnsonian Misc*. ii. 265. That Johnson and Reynolds were well known to each other before the winter of 1763-4 is certain (see *ante*, i. 477, 486, and Leslie and Taylor's *Reynolds*, ii. 454). Mrs. Piozzi on the other hand says that Johnson read the poem at the Club. Her account is given in a marginal note to D'Israeli's *Curiosities of Literature*, ii. 61, now in Pembroke College Library. She says :

' Doctor Johnson expected something beautiful from the Pen of Grainger whom he greatly esteemed—and when the Manuscript called the Sugar Cane was put into his Hands . . . he took it with him to the Literary Club unexamined, & in some Pause of Conversation pulling it out of his Pocket, said if you Please Gentlemen I'll read you a Poem sent from the West Indies.—Begin Sir, said Reynolds, and Johnson set out with these Lines

Where shall the Muse her arduous Task begin ?
Where breathless end ? Say shall we sing of *Rats* ?

No more was listened to, the Laugh was general, & Doctor Johnson protested he was never so ashamed in his Life. " I'll beware Manuscripts in future " said he.'

That Johnson read the manuscript to the Club is possible (see *post*, iv. 10); that he read it aloud unexamined is extremely unlikely; but Mrs. Piozzi's additional lines show independent knowledge.

The couplet quoted by Boswell from *The Sugar Cane* occurs in book ii. lines 62–3. Johnson and Percy are mentioned in book iii. 507 ff. :

> Yet, 'mid this blest ebriety, some tears,
> For friends I left in Albion's distant isle,
> For Johnson, Percy, White, escape mine eyes.

Grainger, writing to Percy in 1765 (the letter was received in Sept.), says :

'I am perfectly satisfied with the reception the " Sugar Cane " has met with, and am greatly obliged to you and Mr. Johnson for the generous care you took of it in my absence.' Nichols, *Illustr.* vii. p. 291.

For Boswell's original version of the passage about Grainger see *post*, iv. App. K.

Page 454, line 13. Grainger's Tibullus (*A Poetical Translation of the Elegies of Tibullus ; and of the Poems of Sulpicia ; with the Original Text, and Notes critical and explanatory*, 2 vols.) was published by Andrew Millar in Dec. 1758. Percy translated the first Elegy and Ovid's elegy on Tibullus, and read the proofs. *Tibullus*, Advt. i. pp. xiii, Nichols, *Illustr.* vii. pp. 240 ff., Hecht, *Percy und Shenstone*, p. 9. Grainger in presenting a copy to his elder brother, William Grainger, made the following acknowledgement of his gratitude :

'To Mr. Grainger of Wariston (to whom the public is chiefly indebted for aught that can be found praiseworthy in the following translation of Tibullus), from his affectionate brother, and humble servant', &c. (Grainger's *Works*, ed. Anderson, 1836, i. p. vi).

Shenstone told his friend Jago, 6 Jan. 1759, that it afforded ' an elegant edition of a good translation and of the text '. Shenstone's *Works*, iii. 328.

Page 455, lines 21 ff. The ' ingenious acquaintance ' was Grainger, the West-India gentleman Mr. Bourryau, the young woman whom Grainger married Miss Burt, and the island upon which he settled St. Christopher's. See *post*, iv. App. K. and Nichols, *Illustr.* vii, 266 ff. In the *Westminster Mag.* Dec. 1773, pp. 685–7, and *Whitehall Evening Post* 4–6 Jan. 1774, Mrs. Grainger's character is defamed : Percy in her defence wrote (*Whitehall Evening Post*, 13 Jan. 1774) :

'In Autumn, 1763, Dr. Grainger was sent for over to Britain by his elder brother, who was in a declining state of health, and required the Doctor's personal attendance to assist him in settling his affairs. Dr. Grainger was so far from forsaking his family with the dejection and disgust represented in the Memoirs, that during his stay of several months in this Island, he enjoyed, in a high degree, his wonted chearfulness and good humour, . . . During the whole time of his absence, the Doctor appeared to correspond in the most affectionate manner with his wife and family; whose absence from him he mentioned, upon all occasions, as the subject of his most tender regret. No man ever felt the benevolent and tender affections with a more generous warmth than Dr. Grainger; and his fondness for his little girl (for at that time he had but one) was even excessive. This account is not given by an accidental collector of hear-say reports, but by a FRIEND of the Doctor's, at whose house he spent more than six weeks of the few months he resided in England.'

Percy described the statement 'that Grainger's peace of mind was destroyed, and his life shortened by any suspicion (much less conviction) of his wife's want of fidelity' as 'utterly false'. The article concludes by saying, 'it would have been a criminal silence, not to have given the earliest refutation of so vile a slander, the moment it was known to A FRIEND OF DR. GRAINGER'S'. This account was inserted at the instance of Edmund Allen (*post*, iii. 141). In a letter, dated 15 Jan. 1774, to Percy thanking him for 'rescuing from the fangs of detraction' the character of so worthy a man, he says, 'as I threatened them [the proprietors of the *Whitehall Evening Post*] with a prosecution for defamation, they readily inserted it without a fee'. Nichols, *Illustr.* vii. 295.

Page 456, lines 18 ff. Mr. Lloyd was Sampson Lloyd the Third (1728–1807), the founder of Lloyds Bank. He married, 11 Nov. 1762, Rachel Barnes. At the time of Johnson's visit they lived in the Square, No. 13. See J. Hill & R. K. Dent, *Mem. of the Old Square*, 1897, pp. 101 ff. and next note.

Page 458. *Johnson's discussion on baptism with Mr. Lloyd.* In *Farm and its Inhabitants, with some Account of the Lloyds of Dolobran*, by Rachel J. Lowe (priv. pr. 1883), a further account is given of the controversy between Johnson and Mr. Lloyd the Quaker, on the subject of Barclay's *Apology*.

'Tradition states that, losing his temper, Dr. Johnson threw the volume on the floor, and put his foot on it, in denunciation of its statements. The identical volume is now in the possession of G. B. Lloyd, of Edgbaston Grove.

'At the dinner table he continued the debate in such angry tones, and struck the table so violently that the children were frightened, and desired to escape.

'The next morning Dr. Johnson went to the bank, and by way of apology called out in his stentorian voice, " I say, Lloyd, I'm the best theologian, but you are the best Christian ".' P. 41.

It could not have been ' the next morning ' that Johnson went to the bank, for he left for Lichfield on the evening of the day of the controversy (*ante*, ii. 461). He must have gone in the afternoon, while Boswell was away seeing Mr. Boulton's great works at Soho (*ib.*, p. 459).

Mr. G. B. Lloyd, the great-grandson of Johnson's host, in a letter written this summer (1886), says : ' Having spent much of my boyhood with my grandfather in the old house, I have heard him tell the story of the stamping on the broad volume.'

Boswell mentions (*ib.* p. 457) that ' Mr. and Mrs. Lloyd, like their Majesties, had been blessed with a numerous family of fine children, their numbers being exactly the same '. The author of *Farm and its Inhabitants* says (p. 46) : ' There is a tradition, that when Sampson Lloyd's wife used to feel depressed by the care of such a large family (they had sixteen children), he would say to her, " Never mind, the twentieth will be the most welcome ".' His fifteenth child Catharine married Dr. George Birkbeck,[1] the founder of the Mechanics' Institutes (*ib.* p. 48).

A story told (p. 50) of one of Mr. Lloyd's sons-in-law, Joseph Biddle, is an instance of that excess of forgetfulness which Johnson called ' morbid oblivion ' (*post*, v. 68). ' He went to pay a call in Leamington. The servant asked him for his name, he could not remember it ; in perplexity he went away, when a friend in the street met him and accosted him, " How do you do, Mr. Biddle ? " " Oh, Biddle, Biddle, Biddle, that's the name ", cried he, and rushed off to pay his call.'

The editor is in error in stating (p. 45, *n.* 1) that a very poor poem entitled *A bone for Friend Mary to pick*, is by Johnson. It may be found in the *Gent. Mag.* for 1791, p. 948.—HILL.

Page 459, line 1. Mr. Pott's sermons were preached in 1788 and 1789, and published in 1790 under the title : *Two Sermons for the Festivals and Fasts of the Church of England. By Joseph Holden Pott, M.A. Prebendary of Lincoln, and Archdeacon of St. Albans.* Boswell became acquainted with him in March 1790, when he preached an ' admirable ' sermon before the Humane Society, of which Boswell was a Steward. Boswell's *Letters*, No. 273, ii. 392.

Page 459, lines 8 ff. Johnson had visited the works of Matthew Boulton on his return from Wales in Sept. 1774 (*post*, v. 458). Mr. H. M. Cashmore, of the Birmingham Public Libraries, tells me that Boulton's house and works were only a few yards apart, the house standing on a little hill overlooking the works. Its setting is described in Bisset's *Poetic Survey round Birmingham* (1800), p. 12 :

> ' On Yonder gentle slope, which shrubs adorn,
> Where grew, of late, " rank weeds ", gorse, ling, and thorn,
> Now pendant woods, and shady groves are seen,
> And nature there assumes a nobler mien.
> There verdant lawns, cool grots, and peaceful bow'rs,
> Luxuriant, now, are strew'd with sweetest flow'rs,

[1] The godfather of Dr. Birkbeck Hill. (*Letters of G. B. Hill*, ed. Lucy Crump, 1906, p. 1.)

> Reflected by the lake, which spreads below,
> All Nature smiles around—there stands Soho ! '

Boulton called his residence ' Soho House ', but the name Soho was applied indiscriminately to the house, the works, and the district. See S. Smiles, *Lives of Boulton and Watt*, 1865, ch. ix.

Page 459, lines 23 ff. The particulars of Johnson's early life which Boswell obtained from Hector he entered in his note-book (see Boswell's *Note Book*, 1925, pp. 4, 9). When Boswell came to write the *Life* he expanded with freedom : e.g. ' That he seemed to learn by intuition the contents of any book ' becomes ' He seemed to learn by intuition ; for though indolence and procrastination were inherent in his constitution, whenever he made an exertion he did more than any one else ' (*ante*, i. 47). One particular which Boswell did not think worthy of admittance into the *Life* was the fact ' That he [Johnson] used to have oatmeal porridge for breakfast '. Boswell evidently tested Hector's information and found that it was sometimes not accurate. In his note-book he recorded : ' Mr. Hector told me that the Master of Pembroke used to see him idling away his time in the quadrangle & that he set him a task to turn Pope's Messiah into Latin ' ; against this Boswell noted ' wrong. He was asked very civilly by Jorden to do it ' (*Note Book*, p. 9).

Page 459, last line. Mrs. Thrale met Hector's sister, Mrs. Careless or Carless, on her return from Wales, 20 Sept. 1774. She writes : ' Mr. Johnson said how much he had been in love with Mr. Hector's sister, the old lady who made breakfast for us in the morning, and when I recollected her figure I thought she had the remains of a beauty.' A. M. Broadley, *Dr. Johnson and Mrs. Thrale*, 1910, p. 214. She is mentioned in one of the last letters Johnson wrote : ' I send my kindest respects to dear Mrs. Careless ' (*post*, iv. 378). She died in 1788. Her husband, the Reverend Walter Carless, was first cousin of Johnson's distant connexion Dorothy Hickman, to whom the sonnet ' Bright Stella, form'd for universal reign ' (*Works*, i. 136) is addressed. He died in 1757. See A. L. Reade's *Reades of Blackwood Hill*, p. 152.

Page 460, lines 11 ff. Charles Congreve's record is given in Foster's *Alumni Oxon*. He was the son of John Congreve, of Stretton, Staffs. ; he matriculated at the age of 18 from Magdalen Hall, 11 March 1726, took his B.A. in 1729 (?) and M.A. in 1734. He obtained ' considerable preferment in Ireland ' as Archdeacon of Armagh, 1738, and Vicar-general, 1746. He died 7 June 1777. The Rev. Thomas Campbell dined with him on 15 March 1775 and on the next day discussed him with Johnson. Campbell reports that Johnson ' talked of him as a man of great coldness of mind, who could be two years in London without letting him know it '. *Johnsonian Misc*. ii. 40, 42. Johnson writing to

Dr. Taylor, 7 March 1776, describes Congreve's unsocial condition and conversational incapacity in much the same terms as those used in the lament reported by Boswell :

' I called the other day upon poor Charles whom I had not seen for many months. He took no notice of my absence, nor appeared either glad or sorry to see me, but answered everything with monosyllables . . . ; at last I enquired the time, which gave him hopes of being delivered from me, and enabled him to bounce up with great alacrity and inspect his watch. He sits in a room about ten feet square, and though he takes the air every day in his chaise, fancies that he should take cold in any other house, and therefore never pays a visit.' *Letters*, No. 461.

This visit was obviously the same as that described to Hector. See also A. L. Reade, *Gleanings*, iii. 126 ff.

Page 461, lines 19 ff. C. P. Moritz, a young Prussian clergyman who published an account of a pedestrian tour that he made in England in the year 1782, thus describes Lichfield as he saw it on a day in June :

' At noon I got to Litchfield : an old fashioned town, with narrow dirty streets, where, for the first time, I saw round panes of glass in the windows. The place, to me, wore an unfriendly appearance ; I therefore made no use of my recommendation, but went straight through, and only bought some bread at a baker's, which I took along with me.' *Travels in England* (ed. Matheson, 1924, p. 168).

The ' recommendation ' was an introduction to an inn given him by the daughter of his landlord at Sutton, who told him that ' the people in Litchfield were, in general, very proud ' (*Ibid*. p. 167). Travelling, as he did, on foot and without luggage, he was looked upon with suspicion at the inns, and often rudely refused lodging.—HILL.

Page 461, line 20. Alderman W. A. Wood, of the Johnson Society, states that the Three Crowns Inn has undergone little change in appearance or arrangement since Johnson's time.

Page 462, line 2 from foot. We learn from *Boswelliana* (1874, p. 220) that the lady who told Boswell the ludicrous story of the German baron was his old flame Mlle de Zuylen. See *ante*, ii. note to p. 56. According to the original version the German baron only succeeded in jumping ' upon the chairs and down again '.

Page 463, line 11. The phrase ' to leave one's can ' did not always connote temperance ; in the song *Old Simon the Kinge* it implies the reverse :

> ' A puritan left his cann,
> & tookee him to his iugge,
> & there he playde the man
> so long as he cold tugg.'
>
> (*Percy's Folio MS., Loose & Humorous Songs*,
> p. 126.)

Page 466, lines 22 ff. The Friary in which Mrs. Cobb lived was the ancient Franciscan convent 'converted into a good house'. Harwood's *Lichfield*, p. 486. The religious house was founded about 1229, but Harwood writing in 1806 says, 'the present structure was erected in 1545'. *Ibid*. p. 481. Alderman W. A. Wood of the Johnson Society, Lichfield, tells me that the house, although very much as it was in Johnson's time, is now (1929) no longer used as a residence, but is incorporated with the buildings of a secondary school for girls, called the Friary School. The house, which formed part of the Friary Estate given by Sir Richard Ashmole Cooper to the city of Lichfield in 1921, was sold by the Corporation to the Staffordshire Education Committee in 1926, with the provision that all the old building should be preserved intact.

Page 467, lines 5 ff. The Reverend Thomas Seward was Canon of Lichfield and Salisbury. He acted as travelling tutor to Lord Charles Fitzroy (third son of the Duke of Grafton), who died at Rome in 1739 when on his travels. According to his brother, William Seward (*Journal from Savannah to Philadelphia*, &c., 1740, p. 82), he was then appointed chaplain to a man-of-war commanded by Lord Augustus Fitzroy, and given a benefice in Derbyshire worth £400 a year by Lord Burlington. From information kindly supplied to me by the Secretary to the Admiralty (Sir Oswyn Murray) it appears that Mr. Seward's career as a Naval Chaplain was short and uneventful. He was appointed Chaplain of H.M.S. 'Eltham' (Captain Lord Augustus Fitzroy) on 29 Dec. 1739, but the 'Eltham' was being stripped preparatory to being paid off and Mr. Seward never made an official appearance on board : on 29 Feb. 1739/40 he was appointed to H.M.S. 'Orford' (Captain Lord Augustus Fitzroy), and he took up duty on 6 March ; but on 27 March following he was discharged at his own request. The Derbyshire living was the rectory of Eyam, to which he was inducted 28 April 1740 (Fletcher's *Eyam*, p. 72). Seward went to live at Lichfield *c.* 1750, when his daughter, Anna, was in her seventh year, and took up residence in the Bishop's Palace in or about 1755. See *Monthly Mirror*, iii. 10. The edition of Beaumont and Fletcher (*The Works of Francis Beaumont and John Fletcher, collated with all the former editions, and corrected. With notes critical and explanatory by Mr. Theobald, Mr. Seward, and Mr. Sympson*), for which he was mainly responsible, was published in 1750 in 10 volumes octavo. It drew from Erasmus Darwin the descriptive line 'by Seward's arm the mangled Beaumont bled' (Krause's *Life of E. Darwin*, 1887, p. 41) and from Coleridge some caustic criticism (*Notes and Lectures upon Shakespeare*, &c., 1849, i. 291, 306, 315). Seward's contributions to Dodsley's *Collection of Poems* appeared first in the second edition, 1748 ; they are : 'The Female Right to Literature ', ' On Shakespeare's Monument at Stratford upon Avon ', 'A Song ' the first line of which is ' When fair Serena first I knew ', ' Chiswick ', and ' The

Indifferent. From the Italian of Metastasio '. They were published anonymously ' by mistake ' (*Monthly Mirror*, 1797, iii, p. 9). Other works published by Seward are *The Conformity between Popery and Paganism*, 1746, two sermons in 1750 and 1756, and a charge to the Lichfield clergy. See *D.N.B.* and W. P. Courtney's *Dodsley's Collection of Poetry*, 1910, pp. 21, 128–9.

Page 470, lines 1 ff. The houses on Stowhill in which the two sisters, Mrs. Aston (her rank was brevet) and Mrs. Gastrell lived were owned by the first-named lady. That in which she lived, known to-day as Stowe Hill, was built by her about 1754 ; on her death in 1785 she left it to her sister Margaret, Mrs. Walmesley (see *ante*, i. 82). Mrs. Gastrell's house, the ' lower house ' as Johnson calls it, now named Stowe House, was built about 1750 ; she inherited it on her sister's death. See A. L. Reade, *Gleanings*, v. 249–51. When staying at Lichfield Johnson never omitted to call upon the ladies, but there is no evidence that he lived in either house, as is implied by the story that ' a great portion of the *Lives of the Poets* was written at Stow Hill '. See *Johnsonian Misc.* ii. 414 where Dr. Hill shows that this statement ' is a great exaggeration '. The frequency of his visits is shown in his letters. On 7 July 1770, lamenting Mrs. Aston's absence, he writes : ' When she is at home, she lives on the top of Stow Hill, and I commonly climb up to see her once a day ' (*Letters*, No. 232) ; nine years later, 29 May 1779, he records six visits in eight days (*Ib.* No. 616) ; on 13 Aug. 1777 he says : ' I have always gone the shortest way to Stowhill, and hardly anywhere else ' (*Ib.* No. 537). See also *Ib.* Nos. 409, 511, 538–9, 557, 613, 643.

Stowe House, now the home of Lady Charnwood, has been described by her in two articles entitled 'A Habitation's Memories ' contributed to the *Cornhill Mag.* Nov. and Dec. 1927. Lady Charnwood states that ' in the manifold alterations and enlargements of close on two hundred years the original structure remains unchanged '.

According to the Rev. S. H. Parker (see A. L. Reade, *Reades of Blackwood Hill*, p. 282), ' Dr. Johnson's friendship for Mrs. Elizabeth Aston commenced at the palace in Lichfield, the residence of Mr. Walmesley (*ante*, i. 81) : with Mrs. Gastrel he became acquainted in London, at the home of her brother-in-law, Mr. Hervey (*Ib.* 83 n. 4) '. *Johnsonian Misc.* ii. 413. Of Mrs. Aston Johnson wrote to Mrs. Thrale in 1781 ' we have known each other long, and, by consequence, are both old ' (*Letters*, No. 741) ; and he inscribed a presentation copy of *The Rambler* (1752 reissue), now owned by Mr. R. B. Adam : ' To Mrs. Gastrel in memory of a long friendship and in acknowledgment of many favours these volumes are presented by Her most obedient and most humble servant The Authour.'

Page 470, lines 17 ff. Mrs. Gastrell lived until 30 Oct. 1791, so that she had time to read Boswell's references to her husband's ' Gothick barbarity ' and her own participation therein. By strange irony Boswell's informant, Malone, was to be in a few years dubbed a ' meddling sacrilegious varlet' for causing the coloured effigy of Shakespeare in Stratford church to be painted white (see Lamb's *Last Essays of Elia, Detached Thoughts*, and M. H. Spielmann in the Shakespeare Head edition of Shakespeare's Works, 1907, x, p. 380).

Lady Charnwood inherited from her grandfather, A. J. Mundella, a tea caddie made from the wood of Shakespeare's mulberry tree, which bears the following inscription :

' In 1756 Shakespeare's mulberry tree was cut down by order of the Rev. Francis Gastrel, Vicar of Frodsham in Cheshire, the then owner. The wood was afterwards purchased by Mr. Thos. Sharp of Stratford, who, well knowing the value the world had set upon it, turned it much to his advantage by converting it into small boxes.'

This box rests to-day in the room that once was Mrs. Gastrell's drawing-room. See Lady Charnwood's 'A Habitation's Memories ' (*Cornhill Mag.* Nov. 1927, p. 540).

Page 471, lines 4, 5. ' Theodosius ', or ' The Force of Love ', a tragedy by N. Lee, was first acted in 1680. ' The Stratford Jubilee ', a two-act comedy by Francis Gentleman (*ante*, i. 384), was first printed in 1769. See *Biographia Dramatica* (ed. Reed, 1782), ii, pp. 356, 368.

Page 471, line 20. Mr. Pearson was the Reverend John Batteridge Pearson, Perpetual Curate of St. Michael's, Lichfield, from 1774 to 1782. Johnson writing to Lucy Porter, 4 March 1779, says : ' I have seen Mr. Pearson, and am pleased to find that he has got a living ' (*Letters*, No. 605). The living was the vicarage of Croxall, Derbyshire. Lucy Porter left him the bulk of her property, and he, ' in gratitude for her liberal acts of friendship conferred on him ', erected a monument to her in St. Chad's, Lichfield. He died, a Prebendary of Lichfield, in 1808. See A. L. Reade, *Gleanings*, i. 14 ff. Johnson told Mrs. Thrale that once when Mr. Pearson contradicted Lucy Porter, in her own house, she, being somewhat offended, uttered the following reproof : ' Why, Mr. Pearson, you are just like Dr. Johnson, I think : I do not mean that you are a man of the greatest capacity in all the world like Dr. Johnson, but that you contradict one every word one speaks, just like him.' *Anecdotes*, p. 223 : John. Misc. i. 298.

Page 472, lines 1–11. It is probable that each of these three remarks was made to Boswell by way of reproof. The first was perhaps caused by Boswell and Dr. Wetherell talking of Johnson ' without reserve in his own presence '. For Johnson's irritation at being questioned by Boswell, see *post*, iii. 57 and 268.

Page 473, lines 18 ff. Mrs. Thrale describes Dr. Taylor's establishment in 1774 :

' Dr. Taylor took possession of us very kindly. . . . We went to the Church, where Dr. Taylor has a magnificent seat ; indeed, everything around him is both elegant and splendid. He has very fine pictures which he does not understand the beauties of, a glorious Harpsichord which he sends for a young man out of the town to play upon, a waterfall murmuring at the foot of his garden, deer in his paddock, pheasants in his menagerie, the finest coach horses in the County, the largest horned cattle, I believe, in England, particularly a Bull of an enormous size, his table liberally spread, his wines all excellent in their kinds.' (A. M. Broadley, *Dr. Johnson and Mrs. Thrale*, 1910, p. 164.)

Dr. Taylor had inherited from his father, who died in 1731, an extensive estate, which included the Mansion at Ashbourne ; this estate was still further increased on the death of his only brother in 1744. He had obtained, by purchase, the living of Market Bosworth in 1740 and became Prebendary of Westminster in 1746 ; he was also Preacher of Broadway Chapel, Westminster (1740), Rector of Lawford, Essex (1751), and Perpetual Curate of St. Botolph's, Aldersgate (1769, resigned in 1776) ; on the death of Dr. T. Wilson in 1784 he became Rector of St. Margaret's, Westminster (Johnson's *Letters*, No. 960). See the Rev. Thomas Taylor's *Life of John Taylor* (undated, but published in 1910). For his failure to obtain other preferment, the Deanery of Rochester in 1779 and the Deanery of Lincoln in 1781, see Johnson's *Letters*, Nos. 635 and 749. Mr. Jourdain, one time Rector of Market Bosworth, estimated his income at £7,000 a year, and Mr. Taylor computed that under his will (proved 13 March 1788) he distributed, exclusive of real estate, legacies amounting to £4,350 and life annuities amounting to £140 (*op. cit. supra* pp. 72, 79).

The two portraits of Dr. Taylor, one by Opie, the other by Wright of Derby, fully bear out Boswell's description of him as 'a hearty English 'Squire, with the parson super-induced '. His biographer has reproduced both.

Page 474, line 9. Mr. Peters, whose Christian name was Richard, was left £100 by his master. T. Taylor's *Life of Dr. Taylor*, p. 77. He died in November 1788, aged 78, some nine months after him. E. A. Sadler in *Derbyshire Archaeol. & Nat. Hist. Soc. Jrnl.* (1926).

Page 477. The late Mrs. Edmund Hobhouse used to recall her grandmother (Mrs. Sarah Williams, daughter of Charles Blackstone, Sir William Blackstone's brother) telling her that she was once at a luncheon party in All Souls with her uncle, at which Johnson was present ; there were some American apples on the table and when one of the ladies took one Johnson said solemnly : ' It is to be hoped, Madam, that these apples will not revolt.' Dr. Edmund Hobhouse, who kindly communicates this pleasant story, informs me that his stepmother, Mrs.

Hobhouse, daughter of Mrs. Williams and the Rev. D. Williams, Warden of New College, died 10 May 1925, aged 101. Mrs. Williams, the original relater of the story, died about 1850–1, in her 91st year. There is no other evidence that Johnson ever lunched at All Souls or that he ever met Blackstone, who however was an old Pembroke man. Johnson was in Oxford twice in 1775, for the first week of March and the first week of June (*Letters*, Nos. 379–84, 399–404), in 1776, for two days in March, when we should certainly have heard about a visit to All Souls if it had been made, as Boswell was with him (*ante*, ii. 438–50), and in 1777, from 28 July to 5 Aug. (*Letters*, Nos. 532–5). Johnson did not visit Oxford again till after Blackstone's death, which occurred in April 1780.

THE END OF THE SECOND VOLUME.